Final Report of the Thirty-sixth Antarctic Treaty Consultative Meeting

ANTARCTIC TREATY
CONSULTATIVE MEETING

Final Report of the Thirty-sixth Antarctic Treaty Consultative Meeting

Brussels, Belgium
20–29 May 2013

Volume II

Secretariat of the Antarctic Treaty
Buenos Aires
2013

Published by:

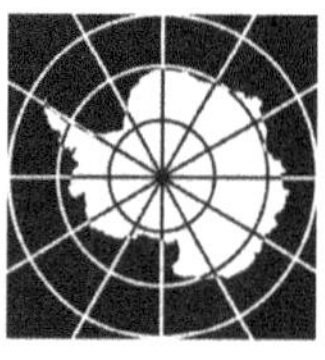

Secretariat of the Antarctic Treaty
Secrétariat du Traité sur l' Antarctique
Секретариат Договора об Антарктике
Secretaría del Tratado Antártico

Maipú 757, Piso 4
C1006ACI Ciudad Autónoma
Buenos Aires - Argentina
Tel: +54 11 4320 4260
Fax: +54 11 4320 4253

This book is also available from: *www.ats.aq* (digital version) and online-purchased copies.

ISSN 2346-9897 ISBN 978-987-1515-58-5

Contents

VOLUME I

Acronyms and Abbreviations

PART I. FINAL REPORT

1. Final Report
2. CEP XVI Report
3. Appendices
ATCM XXXVI Communiqué
Preliminary Agenda for ATCM XXXVII

PART II. MEASURES, DECISIONS AND RESOLUTIONS

1. Measures
Measure 1 (2013) ASPA No 108 (Green Island, Berthelot Islands, Antarctic Peninsula): Revised Management Plan
Measure 2 (2013) ASPA No 117 (Avian Island, Marguerite Bay, Antarctic Peninsula): Revised Management Plan
Measure 3 (2013) ASPA No 123 (Barwick and Balham Valleys, Southern Victoria Land): Revised Management Plan
Measure 4 (2013) ASPA No 132 (Potter Peninsula, King George Island (Isla 25 de Mayo), South Shetland Islands): Revised Management Plan
Measure 5 (2013) ASPA No 134 (Cierva Point and offshore islands, Danco Coast, Antarctic Peninsula): Revised Management Plan
Measure 6 (2013) ASPA No 135 (North-east Bailey Peninsula, Budd Coast, Wilkes Land): Revised Management Plan
Measure 7 (2013) ASPA No 137 (Northwest White Island, McMurdo Sound): Revised Management Plan
Measure 8 (2013) ASPA No 138 (Linnaeus Terrace, Asgard Range, Victoria Land): Revised Management Plan
Measure 9 (2013) ASPA No 143 (Marine Plain, Mule Peninsula, Vestfold Hills, Princess Elizabeth Land): Revised Management Plan
Measure 10 (2013) ASPA No 147 (Ablation Valley and Ganymede Heights, Alexander Island): Revised Management Plan
Measure 11 (2013) ASPA No 151 (Lions Rump, King George Island, South Shetland Islands): Revised Management Plan

Measure 12 (2013) ASPA No 154 (Botany Bay, Cape Geology, Victoria Land): Revised Management Plan
Measure 13 (2013) ASPA No 156 (Lewis Bay, Mount Erebus, Ross Island): Revised Management Plan
Measure 14 (2013) ASPA No 160 (Frazier Islands, Windmill Islands, Wilkes Land, East Antarctica): Revised Management Plan
Measure 15 (2013) ASPA No 161 (Terra Nova Bay, Ross Sea): Revised Management Plan
Measure 16 (2013) ASPA No 170 (Marion Nunataks, Charcot Island, Antarctic Peninsula): Revised Management Plan
Measure 17 (2013) ASPA No 173 (Cape Washington and Silverfish Bay, Terra Nova Bay, Ross Sea): Management Plan
Measure 18 (2013) Antarctic Historic Sites and Monuments: Location of the first permanently occupied German Antarctic research station "Georg Forster" at the Schirmacher Oasis, Dronning Maud Land
Measure 19 (2013) Antarctic Historic Sites and Monuments: Professor Kudryashov's Drilling Complex Building, Vostok Station
Measure 20 (2013) Antarctic Historic Sites and Monuments: Upper "Summit Camp", Mount Erebus
Measure 21 (2013) Antarctic Historic Sites and Monuments: Lower "Camp E", Mount Erebus

2. Decisions

Decision 1 (2013) Recognition of the Czech Republic as a Consultative Party
Decision 2 (2013) Re-appointment of the Executive Secretary
Annex: Letters to Dr Manfred Reinke and Mr Hector Timerman
Decision 3 (2013) Renewal of the Contract of the Secretariat's External Auditor
Annex: Tasks to be carried out by the external auditor
Decision 4 (2013) Secretariat Report, Programme and Budget
Annex 1: Audited Financial Report 2011/12
Annex 2: Provisional Financial Report 2012/13
Annex 3: Secretariat Programme 2013/14
Decision 5 (2013) Multi-Year Strategic Work Plan for the Antarctic Treaty Consultative Meeting
Annex: Multi-Year Strategic Work Plan
Decision 6 (2013) Information Exchange on Tourism and Non-Governmental Activities
Annex: Information Exchange Requirements
Decision 7 (2013) Additional availability of information on lists of Observers of the Consultative Parties through the Secretariat of the Antarctic Treaty

3. Resolutions
Resolution 1 (2013) Air Safety in Antarctica
Resolution 2 (2013) Antarctic Clean-Up Manual
Annex: Antarctic Clean-up Manual
Resolution 3 (2013) Site Guidelines for visitors
Annex: List of Sites subject to Site Guidelines
Resolution 4 (2014) Improved Collaboration on Search and Rescue (SAR) in Antarctica
Resolution 5 (2013) International cooperation in cultural projects about Antarctica
Resolution 6 (2013) Biological Prospecting in Antarctica
Heads of Delegation picture and picture diagram

VOLUME II

PART II. MEASURES, DECISIONS AND RESOLUTIONS (Cont.)

4. Management Plans **11**
ASPA No 108 - Green Island, Berthelot Islands, Antarctic Peninsula 13
ASPA No 117 - Avian Island, Marguerite Bay, Antarctic Peninsula 25
ASPA No 123 - Barwick and Balham Valleys, Southern Victoria Land 41
ASPA No 132 - Potter Peninsula, King George Island (Isla 25 de Mayo), South Shetland Islands 51
ASPA No 134 - Cierva Point and offshore islands, Danco Coast, Antarctic Peninsula 63
ASPA No 135 - North-east Bailey Peninsula, Budd Coast, Wilkes Land 77
ASPA No 137 - Northwest White Island, McMurdo Sound 105
ASPA No 138 - Linnaeus Terrace, Asgard Range, Victoria Land 115
ASPA No 143 - Marine Plain, Mule Peninsula, Vestfold Hills, Princess Elizabeth Land 125
ASPA No 147 - Ablation Valley and Ganymede Heights, Alexander Island 141
ASPA No 151 - Lions Rump, King George Island, South Shetland Islands 163
ASPA No 154 - Botany Bay, Cape Geology, Victoria Land 179
ASPA No 156 - Lewis Bay, Mount Erebus, Ross Island 201
ASPA No 160 - Frazier Islands, Windmill Islands, Wilkes Land, East Antarctica 211
ASPA No 161 - Terra Nova Bay, Ross Sea 231
ASPA No 170 - Marion Nunataks, Charcot Island, Antarctic Peninsula 251
ASPA No 173 - Cape Washington and Silverfish Bay, Terra Nova Bay, Ross Sea 267

PART III. OPENING AND CLOSING ADDRESSES AND REPORTS

1. Reports by Depositaries and Observers **287**
Report of the USA as Depositary Government of the Antarctic Treaty and its Protocol 289
Report of Australia as Depositary Government of CCAMLR 307
Report of the UK as Depositary Government of CCAS 308
Report of Australia as Depositary Government of ACAP 312
Report by the CCAMLR Observer 313
Report of SCAR 319
Report of COMNAP 322

2. Reports by Experts **327**
Report of ASOC 329
Report of IHO 332
Report of IAATO 336

PART IV. ADDITIONAL DOCUMENTS FROM ATCM XXXVI

1. Additional Documents **341**
Abstract of SCAR Lecture 343

2. List of Documents **345**
Working Papers 347
Information Papers 355
Secretariat Papers 365
Background Papers 367

3. List of Participants **369**
Consultative Parties 371
Non-Consultative Parties 376
Observers, Experts and Guests 377
Host Country Secretariat 378
Antarctic Treaty Secretariat 378

Acronyms and Abbreviations

ACAP	Agreement on the Conservation of Albatrosses and Petrels
ASOC	Antarctic and Southern Ocean Coalition
ASMA	Antarctic Specially Managed Area
ASPA	Antarctic Specially Protected Area
ATS	Antarctic Treaty System or Antarctic Treaty Secretariat
ATCM	Antarctic Treaty Consultative Meeting
ATCP	Antarctic Treaty Consultative Party
CAML	Census of Antarctic Marine Life
CCAMLR	Convention on the Conservation of Antarctic Marine Living Resources and/or Commission for the Conservation of Antarctic Marine Living Resourcess
CCAS	Convention for the Conservation of Antarctic Seals
CEE	Comprehensive Environmental Evaluation
CEP	Committee for Environmental Protection
COMNAP	Council of Managers of National Antarctic Programmes
EIA	Environmental Impact Assessment
HCA	Hydrographic Committee on Antarctica
HSM	Historic Site and Monument
IAATO	International Association of Antarctica Tour Operators
ICG	Intersessional Contact Group
ICSU	International Council for Science
IEE	Initial Environmental Evaluation
IHO	International Hydrographic Organization
IMO	International Maritime Organization
IOC	Intergovernmental Oceanographic Commission
IP	Information Paper
IPCC	Intergovernmental Panel on Climate Change
IPY	International Polar Year
IPY-IPO	IPY Programme Office
IUCN	International Union for Conservation of Nature and Natural Resources
RFMO	Regional Fishery Management Organization
SATCM	Special Antarctic Treaty Consultative Meeting
SCAR	Scientific Committee on Antarctic Research

SCALOP	Standing Committee for Antarctic Logistics and Operations
SC-CAMLR	Scientific Committee of CCAMLR
SP	Secretariat Paper
SPA	Specially Protected Area
UNEP	United Nations Environment Programme
UNFCCC	United Nations Framework Convention on Climate Change
WG	Working Group
WMO	World Meteorological Organization
WP	Working Paper
WTO	World Tourism Organization

PART II

Measures, Decisions and Resolutions (Cont.)

4. Management Plans

Management Plan for

Antarctic Specially Protected Area No. 108

GREEN ISLAND, BERTHELOT ISLANDS, ANTARCTIC PENINSULA

Introduction

The primary reason for the designation of Green Island, Berthelot Islands, Antarctic Peninsula (65°19'S, 64°09'W; area 0.2 km^2) as an Antarctic Specially Protected Area (ASPA) is to protect environmental values, and primarily the rich *Chorisodontium-Polytrichum* moss turf present within the Area.

Green Island, was originally designated as a Specially Protected Area (SPA) through Recommendation IV-9 (1966, SPA No. 9) after a proposal by the United Kingdom. It was designated on the grounds that the vegetation "is exceptionally rich, [and] is probably the most luxuriant anywhere on the west side of the Antarctic Peninsula". The Recommendation noted: "in some places the humus is 2 metres thick and that this area, being of outstanding scientific interest, should be protected because it is probably one of the most diverse Antarctic ecosystems". A Management Plan for the site was prepared by the United Kingdom and adopted through Recommendation XVI-6 (1991). The original reasons for designation were extended and elaborated, although following comparisons to other sites in the vicinity, Green Island was no longer considered to be particularly diverse. Nevertheless, the vegetation on the island was described as extensive on the north-facing slopes, with well-developed continuous banks of moss turf formed by *Chorisodontium aciphyllum* and *Polytrichum strictum* that, over much of their extent, overlie peat of more than one metre in depth. Antarctic hair grass (*Deschampsia antarctica*), one of only two native vascular plants that grow within the Antarctic Treaty area, was noted as frequent in small patches near a blue-eyed cormorant (*Phalacrocorax atriceps*) colony. The colony of blue-eyed cormorants, located on the steep, rocky northwestern corner of the island, was noted as being possibly one of the largest along the Antarctic Peninsula. The Management Plan was revised through Measure 1 (2002).

The Area fits into the wider context of the Antarctic Protected Area system by protecting moss turf and peat which are rare in the west Antarctic Peninsula area and, unlike moss banks within more northerly ASPAs, are largely unimpacted by Antarctic fur seal damage (*Arctocephalus gazella*). Resolution 3 (2008) recommended that the Environmental Domains Analysis for the Antarctic Continent, be used as a dynamic model for the identification of Antarctic Specially Protected Areas within the systematic environmental-geographical framework referred to in Article 3(2) of Annex V of the Protocol (see also Morgan et al., 2007). Using this model, ASPA 108 is contained within Environment Domain B (Antarctic Peninsula mid-northern latitudes geologic). Other protected areas containing Domain B include ASPAs 115, 134, 140 and 153 and ASMA 4. ASPA 108 sits within Antarctic Conservation Biogeographic Region (ACBR) 3 Northwest Antarctic Peninsula.

1. Description of values to be protected

Following management visits to the ASPA in February 2011 and January 2013, the values specified in the earlier designation were reaffirmed. These values are set out as follows:

- The primary value worthy of protection is the *Polytrichum strictum* moss banks, with associated *Chorisodontium aciphyllum*, which may be one of the most extensive examples of this vegetation feature in the west Antarctic Peninsula region, occupying an area of over 0.5 ha. Moreover, in recent years many comparable moss banks on more northerly islands have suffered damage as a result of an increase in Antarctic fur seals. The vegetation at Green Island has thus far escaped any significant damage.
- *Chorisodontium aciphyllum* is close to the southern-most limit of its range at the Berthelot Islands.
- The area contains a large number of breeding blue-eyed cormorants (*Phalacrocorax atriceps*), which may represent one of the largest breeding populations known within the Antarctic Peninsula.
- Green Island has been afforded protection throughout most of the period of scientific activity in the region, with entry permits having been issued for only the most compelling scientific reasons. The island has not been

subjected to intensive visitation, research or sampling and is potentially valuable as a baseline site for future studies.

2. Aims and objectives

Management at Green Island aims to:

- avoid degradation of, or substantial risk to, the values of the Area by preventing unnecessary human disturbance to the Area;
- prevent or minimise the introduction to the Area of non-native plants, animals and microbes;
- minimise the possibility of the introduction of pathogens which may cause disease in fauna populations within the Area;
- allow scientific research in the Area provided it is for compelling reasons which cannot be served elsewhere and which will not jeopardize the natural ecological system in that Area; and
- preserve the natural ecosystem of the Area as a reference area for future studies.

3. Management activities

The following management activities shall be undertaken to protect the values of the Area:

- Copies of this Management Plan shall be made available to vessels and aircraft planning to visit the vicinity of the Area.
- Markers, signs or other structures (e.g. cairns) erected within the Area for scientific or management purposes shall be secured and maintained in good condition and removed when no longer required.
- The Management Plan shall be reviewed at least every five years and updated as required.
- A copy of this Management Plan shall be made available at Akademik Vernadsky Station (Ukraine; 65°15'S, 64°16'W).
- All scientific and management activities undertaken within the Area should be subject to an Environmental Impact Assessment, in accordance with the requirements of Annex I of the Protocol on Environmental Protection to the Antarctic Treaty.
- National Antarctic Programmes operating in the Area shall consult together with a view to ensuring the above management activities are implemented.

4. Period of designation

Designated for an indefinite period.

5. Maps and photographs

Map 1. Overview map, showing the location of Green Island on the Antarctic Peninsula. Map specifications: WGS84 Antarctic Polar Stereographic. Central meridian -55°, Standard parallel: -71°.

Map 2. Local area map showing the location of ASPA No. 108 Green Island, Berthelot Island, in relation to stations and other protected Areas in the vicinity. Map specifications: WGS84 Antarctic Polar Stereographic. Central meridian -64°, Standard parallel: -71°.

Map 3. ASPA No. 108 Green Island, Berthelot Islands, Antarctic Peninsula, topographic map. Map derived from ground survey 24 February 2001 and digital orthophotography (source aerial photography taken 14 February 2001 by the British Antarctic Survey). Map specifications – Projection: UTM Zone 20S; Spheroid: WGS84; Datum: mean sea level (EGM96).

6. Description of the Area

6(i) Geographical coordinates, boundary markers and natural features

General description

Green Island (65°19'S, 64°09'W, approximately 0.2 km^2; Map 1) is a small island situated 150 m north of the largest of the Berthelot Islands group, within Grandidier Channel, approximately 3 km off the Graham Coast of the Antarctic Peninsula (Map 2). Green Island is 520 m from north to south and 500 m from east to west, rising to a rounded peak at a height of 83 m. The island rises steeply on all sides, with high precipitous cliffs on the south and east side. The largest extent of low ground occurs above the northern coast, which comprises a gently sloping rock platform. There are several permanent snow patches with the largest occurring around the summit and to the south and east of the summit. There are no permanent freshwater bodies on the island.

Boundaries

The designated Area comprises all of Green Island, with the boundary defined as the low tide level. Offshore islets and rocks are not included within the Area. Boundary markers have not been installed. The coast itself is a clearly defined and visually obvious boundary feature.

Climate

No climate data are available for Green Island, but conditions are expected to be similar to those at Akademik Vernadsky Station (Ukraine) on Galindez Island, Argentine Islands, 8 km to the north. The mean summer temperature at Vernadsky is 0 °C while the extreme maximum summer temperature is 11.7 °C. In winter, the mean temperature is -10 °C and the extreme minimum temperature is -43.3 °C. The mean wind speed is 7.5 knots.

Geology and soils

Green Island, together with the rest of the Berthelot Islands, is composed of gabbro of Lower Jurassic to Lower Tertiary age (British Antarctic Survey, 1981). Excluding the large peat deposits, soil is sparse and seldom exceeds 20 cm in depth, except occasionally in rock depressions and gullies. This is predominantly an ahumic coarse mineral soil derived from weathering of the parent rock. Ledges and gullies close to the blue-eyed cormorant colony contain an organically richer soil derived in part from decayed moss and guano. Over much of the steep northern slopes the mosses *Chorisodontium aciphyllum* and *Polytrichum strictum* have developed a deep turf of living moss overlying at least 1 m of barely altered or decomposed moss peat (Smith, 1979, Fenton and Smith, 1982). The moss peat may of use in determining climatic characteristics over the late Holocene (Royles et al., 2012). The permafrost layer is found 20-30 cm below ground level. Elsewhere on the island, notably the north-eastern side, there are small areas of scree. There are no well-developed periglacial features, although a few small stone circles are evident occasionally.

Vegetation

The most significant feature of the vegetation is the extensive continuous stand of *Polytrichum strictum* on the northern slopes of the island (Map 3). The stand is approximately 140 m wide, extends from an elevation of approximately 25 m up to 70 m, and covers over 0.5 ha (Bonner and Smith, 1985). Growth is lush and the permanently frozen peat in places reaches two metres deep. The surface of the hard compact moss is stepped, which is thought to be a result of slumping of the active layer on the steep slope. Extensive erosion of the moss banks is evident in places, but this appears to be a consequence of the peat bank reaching a maximum sustainable depth on the steep slope and is not due to fur seal damage, as observed in banks in more northerly ASPAs (e.g. ASPA 113). *Chorisodontium aciphyllum* is abundant at the edges of the bank and around the periphery of small gullies in the bank, where there is some shelter and moisture available from drifted snow. Both these tall turf-forming mosses are usually intimately intermixed in such communities further north in the maritime Antarctic; however, in the Grandidier Channel region the more xeric *P. strictum* often occurs alone. *C. aciphyllum* is close to its southernmost limit on Green Island (Smith, 1996). Amongst the *C. aciphyllum*, *Pohlia nutans* is frequent, together with the liverworts *Barbilophozia hatcheri* and *Cephaloziella varians*. Epiphytic lichens are not abundant on the live *Polytrichum* and *Chorisodontium*, but *Sphaerophorus globosus* is frequent in the more exposed north-western area. Several species of *Cladonia* are widespread on the moss banks. The white encrusting epiphyte *Ochrolechia frigida* is present but not abundant here; black crustose species occur on moribund moss.

Wet hollows among rocks and melt runnels support small stands of the mosses *Warnstorfia fontinaliopsis*, *Brachythecium austro-salebrosum* and *Sanionia uncinata*. Elsewhere lichens dominate the vegetation. On rocks and boulders away from the shore and the influence of seabirds, a community dominated by *Usnea antarctica* and species of *Umbilicaria* (*U. antarctica, U. decussate, U. hyperborea* and *U. umbilicarioides*) prevail, with the mosses *Andreaea depressinervis* and *A. regularis* and various crustose lichens associated. Cliffs above the shore possess the most diverse and heterogeneous communities, composed predominantly of lichens. These are a modification of the *Usnea-Umbilicaria* community with various nitrophilous taxa, especially close to seabird nests, including species of *Acarospora, Buellia, Caloplaca, Lecanora, Mastodia, Omphalodina, Physcia* and *Xanthoria*. Plant records from the Area have been used in studies to predict moss and lichen species diversity on the Antarctic Peninsula at both a regional scale and a local scale (Casanovas et al., 2012). The only flowering plant thus far recorded on Green Island is Antarctic hair grass (*Deschampsia antarctica*), which is frequent in small patches above the cormorant colony and on rock ledges on the western side of the island. The green foliose alga *Prasiola crispa* is widespread in wet areas of the island

Breeding birds

A sizeable colony of blue-eyed cormorants (*Phalacrocorax atriceps*) is present on the steep, rocky northwestern flank of the island (65°19'21"S, 64°09'11"W; Map 3). This is one of the largest known blue-eyed cormorant colonies along the Antarctic Peninsula (Bonner and Smith, 1985), although numbers may vary substantially from year to year (Casaux and Barrera-Oro, 2006). Approximately 50 pairs were estimated as present in 1971 (Kinnear, 1971), while 112 birds were recorded in 1973 (Schlatter and Moreno, 1976). During a visit in March 1981, 500-600 individuals (of which 300-400 were immature) were present. Harris (2001) recorded 71 chicks on 24 February 2001, while approximately 100 birds were noted on 15 February 2011 and 200-250 birds on 22 January 2013, of which c. 100 were adults. Brown skuas (*Catharacta loennbergi*) are numerous over much of the island, particularly on the extensive moss banks. South polar skuas (*C. maccormicki*) are also present, along with a few possible hybrids. Over 80 birds were noted in March 1981, but only ten breeding pairs were confirmed, most of which were rearing two chicks. No other breeding birds were noted.

Invertebrates

There is little information on the invertebrate fauna at Green Island, although 15 species were recorded in a study that suggested the invertebrate fauna on Green Island was comparatively diverse for the region (Usher and Edwards, 1986). The most abundant species were *Cryptopygus antarcticus, Belgica antarctica* and *Nanorchestes gressitti*. Larval *B. antarctica* were particularly abundant on Green Island compared to neighbouring Darboux Island. Other species recorded in the Area are *Alaskozetes antarcticus, Ereynetes macquariensis, Eupodes minutus, Eupodes parvus grahamensis, Friesea grisea, Gamasellus racovitzai, Halozetes belgicae, N. berryi, Oppia loxolineata, Parisotoma octo-oculata, Rhagidia gerlachei* and *Stereotydeus villosus*.

Human activities and impacts

There have been few reported visits to Green Island. The first recorded landing on the island was by the Première Expédition Antarctiques Française in 1903-05. The Deuxième Expédition Antarctiques Française visited Green Island several times during the winter in 1909. The British Graham Land Expedition landed on the island on 18 March 1935. Vegetation studies were undertaken on Green Island by Smith in 1981 (Bonner and Smith, 1985) and Komárková in 1982-83 (Komárková, 1983). Numerous 30 cm lengths of 2.5 mm diameter iron wire, marking the corners of 50 m square quadrats of the *Polytrichum strictum* moss turf overlying the peat banks, were recorded (and left *in situ*) by an inspection team in January 1989 (Heap, 1994). It is not known precisely when these markers were installed. The number of markers, their distribution and the nature of any possible contamination these may have had on the moss is unknown. In January 2013, a metal rod, approximately 20 cm long and of unknown origin, was found located on the moss bank at 65°19'23"S, 64°09'02"W.

In recent years a number of important vegetation sites in the Antarctic Peninsula region have been subjected to damage from trampling and nutrient enrichment by increasing numbers of Antarctic fur seals (*Arctocephalus gazella*). No Antarctic fur seals were observed on Green Island during a site visit made on 24 February 2001, although there was some evidence of recent trampling and nutrient enrichment on parts of the lower moss banks. However, damage appeared limited and most of the extensive moss banks remained intact. During site visits in February 2011 and January 2013, no evidence of further seal damage was noted.

6(ii) Access to the Area

- Access to the Area shall be by boat, or over sea ice by vehicle or foot. No special restrictions apply to the routes used to move to and from the Area by boats or over sea ice.

- The recommended landing site for small boats is on the rocky northern coast, with the recommended landing site located in a small cove at 65°19'17.6"S, 64°08'46.0"W (Map 3). Access by small boat at other locations around the coast is allowed, provided this is consistent with the purposes for which a Permit has been granted.
- When access over sea ice is viable, there are no special restrictions on the locations where vehicle or foot access may be made, although vehicles are prohibited from being taken on land.
- Aircraft are prohibited from landing within the Area.
- Boat crew, or other people on boats, are prohibited from moving on foot beyond the immediate vicinity of the landing site unless specifically authorised by Permit.

6(iii) Location of structures within and adjacent to the Area

There are no structures present in the Area. The nearest scientific research station is Akademik Vernadsky (Ukraine) (65°15'S, 64°16'W), approximately 8 km north of the Area on Galindez Island.

6(iv) Location of other protected Areas in the vicinity

Other protected areas in the vicinity include:

- ASPA 113, Lichfield Island, Arthur Harbour, Anvers Island, Palmer Archipelago, 64°46'S, 64°06'W, 62 km to the north.
- ASPA 139, Biscoe Point, Anvers Island, Palmer Archipelago, 64°48'S, 63°46'W, 60 km to the north
- ASPA 146, South Bay, Doumer Island, Palmer Archipelago, 64°51'S, 63°34'W, 60 km to the north west.

ASPAs 113 and 139 lie within Antarctic Specially Managed Area 7 Southwest Anvers Island and Palmer Basin.

6(v) Special zones within the Area

There are no special zones within the Area.

7. Permit conditions

7(i) General permit conditions

Entry into the Area is prohibited except in accordance with a Permit issued by an appropriate national authority. Conditions for issuing a Permit to enter the Area are that:

- it is issued for compelling scientific reasons which cannot be served elsewhere, or for reasons essential to the management of the Area;
- the actions permitted are in accordance with this Management Plan;
- any management activities are in support of the objectives of this Management Plan;
- the actions permitted will not jeopardise the natural ecological system in the Area;
- the activities permitted will give due consideration via the environmental impact assessment process to the continued protection of the environmental or scientific values of the Area;
- the Permit shall be issued for a finite period; and
- the Permit, or an authorised copy, shall be carried when in the Area.

7(ii) Access to, and movement within or over, the Area

- Vehicles are prohibited within the Area and all movement within the Area should be on foot.
- The operation of aircraft over the Areas should be carried out, as a minimum requirement, in compliance with the '*Guidelines for the operations of aircraft near concentrations of birds*' contained in Resolution 2 (2004).
- All movement should be undertaken carefully so as to minimise disturbance to the soil and vegetated surfaces and birds present, walking on snow or rocky terrain if practical.
- Pedestrian traffic should be kept to the minimum necessary to undertake permitted activities and every reasonable effort should be made to minimise trampling effects.

7(iii) Activities which may be conducted within the Area

Activities which may be conducted in the Area include:

- essential management activities, including monitoring;
- compelling scientific research that cannot be undertaken elsewhere and which will not jeopardize the ecosystem of the Area; and
- sampling, which should be the minimum required for approved research programmes.

7(iv) Installation, modification or removal of structures

- Permanent structures or installations are prohibited.
- No structures are to be erected within the Area, or scientific equipment installed, except for compelling scientific or management reasons and for a pre-established period, as specified in a permit.
- All markers, structures or scientific equipment installed in the Area must be clearly identified by country, name of the principal investigator or agency, year of installation and date of expected removal.
- All such items should be free of organisms, propagules (e.g. seeds, eggs, spores) and non-sterile soil (see section *7(vi)*), and be made of materials that can withstand the environmental condition and pose minimal risk of contamination of the Area.
- Removal of specific structures or equipment for which the permit has expired shall be the responsibility of the authority which granted the original permit and shall be a condition of the Permit.

7(v) Location of field camps

When necessary for purposes specified in the Permit, temporary camping is allowed within the Area on the low platform on the northern coast (65°19'18''S, 64°08'55''W; Map 3). Camps should be located on snow surfaces that typically persist at this location or on gravel/rock when snow cover is absent. Camping on vegetated ground is prohibited.

7(vi) Restrictions on materials and organisms which may be brought into the Area

No living animals, plant material or microorganisms shall be deliberately introduced into the Area. To ensure that the floristic and ecological values of the Area are maintained, special precautions shall be taken against accidentally introducing microbes, invertebrates or plants from other Antarctic sites, including stations, or from regions outside Antarctica. All sampling equipment or markers brought into the Area shall be cleaned or sterilized. To the maximum extent practicable, footwear and other equipment used or brought into the Area (including bags or backpacks) shall be thoroughly cleaned before entering the Area. Further guidance can be found in the *CEP non-native species manual* (CEP, 2011) and the *Environmental code of conduct for terrestrial scientific field research in Antarctica* (SCAR, 2009). In view of the presence of breeding bird colonies within the Area, no poultry products, including wastes from such products and products containing uncooked dried eggs, shall be released into the Area or into the adjacent sea.

No herbicides or pesticides shall be brought into the Area. Any other chemicals, including radio-nuclides or stable isotopes, which may be introduced for scientific or management purposes specified in the Permit, shall be removed from the Area at or before the conclusion of the activity for which the Permit was granted. Release of radio-nuclides or stable isotopes directly into the environment in a way that renders them unrecoverable should be avoided. Fuel or other chemicals shall not be stored in the Area unless specifically authorised by Permit condition. They shall be stored and handled in a way that minimises the risk of their accidental introduction into the environment. Materials introduced into the Area shall be for a stated period only and shall be removed by the end of that stated period. If release occurs which is likely to compromise the values of the Area, removal is encouraged only where the impact of removal is not likely to be greater than that of leaving the material in situ. The appropriate authority should be notified of anything released and not removed that was not included in the authorised Permit.

7(vii) Taking of, or harmful interference with, native flora or fauna

Taking of, or harmful interference with, native flora and fauna is prohibited, except in accordance with a permit issued in accordance with Annex II of the Protocol on Environmental Protection to the Antarctic Treaty. Where taking or harmful interference with animals is involved this should, as a minimum standard, be in accordance with the *SCAR code of conduct for the use of animals for scientific purposes in Antarctica* (2011). Any soil or vegetation sampling is to be kept to an absolute minimum required for scientific or management purposes, and carried out using techniques which minimise disturbance to surrounding soil, ice structures and biota.

7(viii) The collection or removal of materials not brought into the Area by the Permit holder

Material may be collected or removed from the Area only in accordance with a permit and should be limited to the minimum necessary to meet scientific or management needs. Material of human origin likely to compromise the values of the Area, and which was not brought into the Area by the Permit holder or otherwise authorised may be removed from the Area unless the environmental impact of the removal is likely to be greater than leaving the material in situ: if this is the case the appropriate national authority must be notified and approval obtained.

7(ix) Disposal of waste

All wastes, including all human wastes, shall be removed from the Area. Human wastes may be disposed of into the sea.

7(x) Measures that may be necessary to continue to met the aims of the Management Plan

- Permits may be granted to enter the Area to carry out scientific research, monitoring and site inspection activities, which may involve the collection of a small number of samples for analysis or to carry out protective measures.
- Any long-term monitoring sites shall be appropriately marked and the markers or signs maintained.
- Scientific activities shall be performed in accordance with the *Environmental code of conduct for terrestrial scientific field research in Antarctica* (SCAR, 2009).

7(xi) Requirements for reports

The principal Permit holder for each visit to the Area shall submit a report to the appropriate national authority as soon as practicable, and no later than six months after the visit has been completed. Such reports should include, as appropriate, the information identified in the *Antarctic Specially Protected Area visit report form* contained in the *Guide to the Preparation of Management Plans for Antarctic Specially Protected Areas* (Appendix 2). The appropriate authority should be notified of any activities/measures undertaken that were not included in the authorised Permit. Wherever possible, the national authority should also forward a copy of the visit report to the Party that proposed the Management Plan, to assist in managing the Area and reviewing the Management Plan. Parties should, wherever possible, deposit originals or copies of such original visit reports in a publicly accessible archive to maintain a record of usage, for the purpose of any review of the Management Plan and in organising the scientific use of the Area.

8. Supporting documentation

Bonner, W. N., and Smith, R. I. L. (Eds.). (1985). *Conservation areas in the Antarctic.* SCAR, Cambridge: 73-84.

Booth, R. G., Edwards, M., and Usher, M. B. (1985). Mites of the genus *Eupodes* (Acari, Prostigmata) from maritime Antarctica: a biometrical and taxonomic study. Journal of Zoology 207: 381-406.

British Antarctic Survey. (1981). Geological Map (Scale 1:500 000). Series BAS 500G Sheet 3, Edition 1. Cambridge: British Antarctic Survey.

Casanovas, P., Lynch, H. L., and Fagan, W. F. (2012). Multi-scale patterns of moss and lichen richness on the Antarctic Peninsula. Ecography 35: 001–011.

Casaux, R., and Barrera-Oro, E. (2006). Review. Shags in Antarctica: their feeding behaviour and ecological role in the marine food web. Antarctic Science 18: 3-14.

Committee for Environmental Protection (CEP). (2011). Non-native species manual – 1st Edition. Manual prepared by Intersessional Contact Group of the CEP and adopted by the Antarctic Treaty Consultative Meeting through Resolution 6 (2011). Buenos Aires, Secretariat of the Antarctic Treaty.

Corner, R. W. M. (1964). Biological report (interim) for Argentine Islands. Unpublished report, British Antarctic Survey Archives Ref AD6/2F/1964/N1.

Fenton, J. H. C, and Smith, R. I. L. (1982). Distribution, composition and general characteristics of the moss banks of the maritime Antarctic. British Antarctic Survey Bulletin 51: 215-236.

Greene, D. M, and Holtom, A. (1971). Studies in *Colobanthus quitensis* (Kunth) Bartl. and *Deschampsia antarctica* Desv.: III. Distribution, habitats and performance in the Antarctic botanical zone. British Antarctic Survey Bulletin 26: 1-29.

Harris, C. M. (2001). *Revision of management plans for Antarctic protected areas originally proposed by the United States of America and the United Kingdom: Field visit report.* Internal report for the National Science

Foundation, US, and the Foreign and Commonwealth Office, UK. *Environmental Research and Assessment*, Cambridge.

Heap, J. (Ed.). (1994). *Handbook of the Antarctic Treaty System.* 8th Edition. U.S. Department of State, Washington.

Kinnear, P. K. (1971). *Phalacrocorax atriceps* population data cited in BAS internal report — original reference unavailable.

Komárková, V. (1983). Plant communities of the Antarctic Peninsula near Palmer Station. Antarctic Journal of the United States 18: 216-218.

Royles, J., Ogée, J., Wingate, L., Hodgson, D. A., Convey, P., and Griffiths, H. (2012). Carbon isotope evidence for recent climate-related enhancement of CO_2 assimilation and peat accumulation rates in Antarctica. Global Change Biology 18: 3112-3124.

SCAR (Scientific Committee on Antarctic Research). (2009). Environmental code of conduct for terrestrial scientific field research in Antarctica. ATCM XXXII IP4.

SCAR (Scientific Committee on Antarctic Research). (2011). SCAR code of conduct for the use of animals for scientific purposes in Antarctica. ATCM XXXIV IP53.

Schlatter, R. P., and Moreno, C. A. (1976). Habitos alimentarios del cormoran Antartico, *Phalacrocorax atriceps bransfieldensis* (Murphy) en Isla Green, Antartica. Serie Cientificia, Instituto Antártico Chileno 4(1): 69-88.

Smith, M. J., and Holroyd, P. C. (1978). 1978 Travel report for Faraday. Unpublished report, British Antarctic Survey Archives Ref AD6/2F/1978/K.

Smith, R. I. L. (1979). Peat forming vegetation in the Antarctic. In: *Proceedings of the International Symposium on Classification of Peat and Peatlands Finland, September 17-21, 1979.* International Peat Society: 58-67

Smith, R. I. L. (1982). Farthest south and highest occurrences of vascular plants in the Antarctic. Polar Record 21:170-173.

Smith, R. I. L. (1996). Terrestrial and freshwater biotic components of the western Antarctic Peninsula. In: Ross, R.M., Hofmann, E.E., and Quetin, L.B. (Eds.) *Foundations for ecological research west of the Antarctic Peninsula.* Antarctic Research Series 70: 15-59.

Smith, R. I. L., and Corner, R.W. M. (1973). Vegetation of Arthur Harbour — Argentine Islands Region. British Antarctic Survey Bulletin 33&34: 89-122.

Stark, P. (1994). Climatic warming in the central Antarctic Peninsula area. Weather 49(6): 215-220.

Usher, M. B., and Edwards, M. (1986). The selection of conservation areas in Antarctica: an example using the arthropod fauna of Antarctic islands. Environmental Conservation 13(2):115-122.

Map 1. Overview map, showing the location of Green Island on the Antarctic Peninsula. Map specifications: WGS84 Antarctic Polar Stereographic. Central meridian -55°, Standard parallel: -71°.

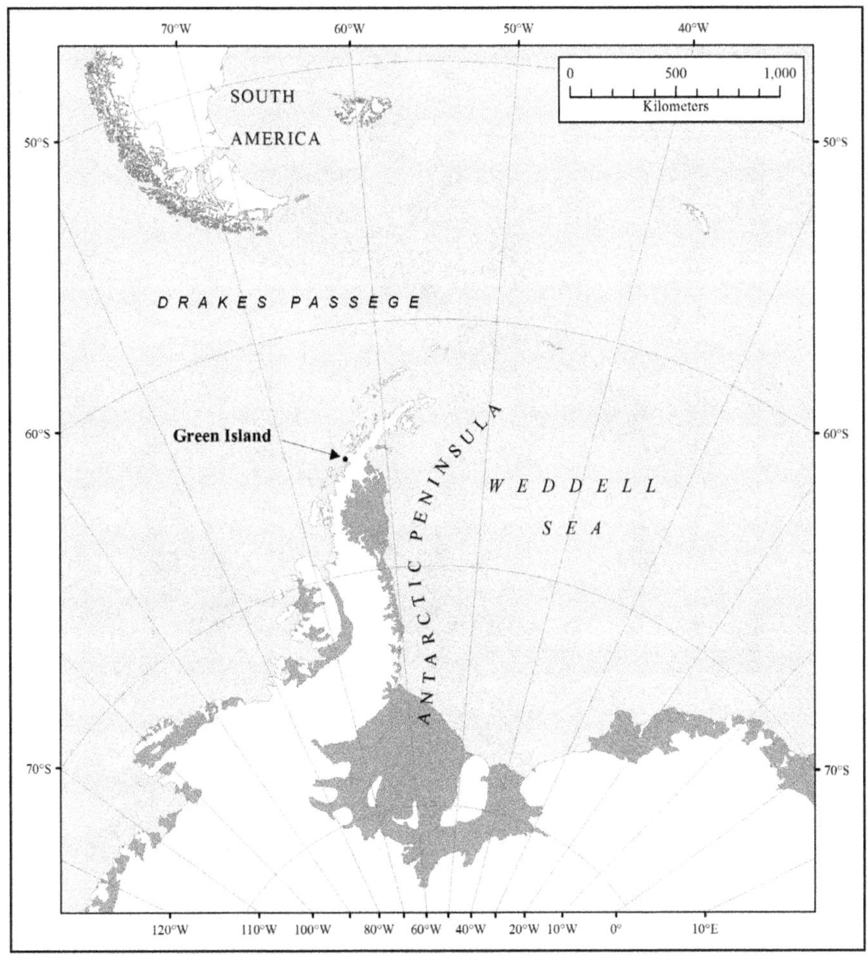

Map 2. Local area map showing the location of ASPA No. 108 Green Island, Berthelot Island, in relation to stations and other protected Areas in the vicinity. Map specifications: WGS84 Antarctic Polar Stereographic. Central meridian - 64°, Standard parallel: -71°.

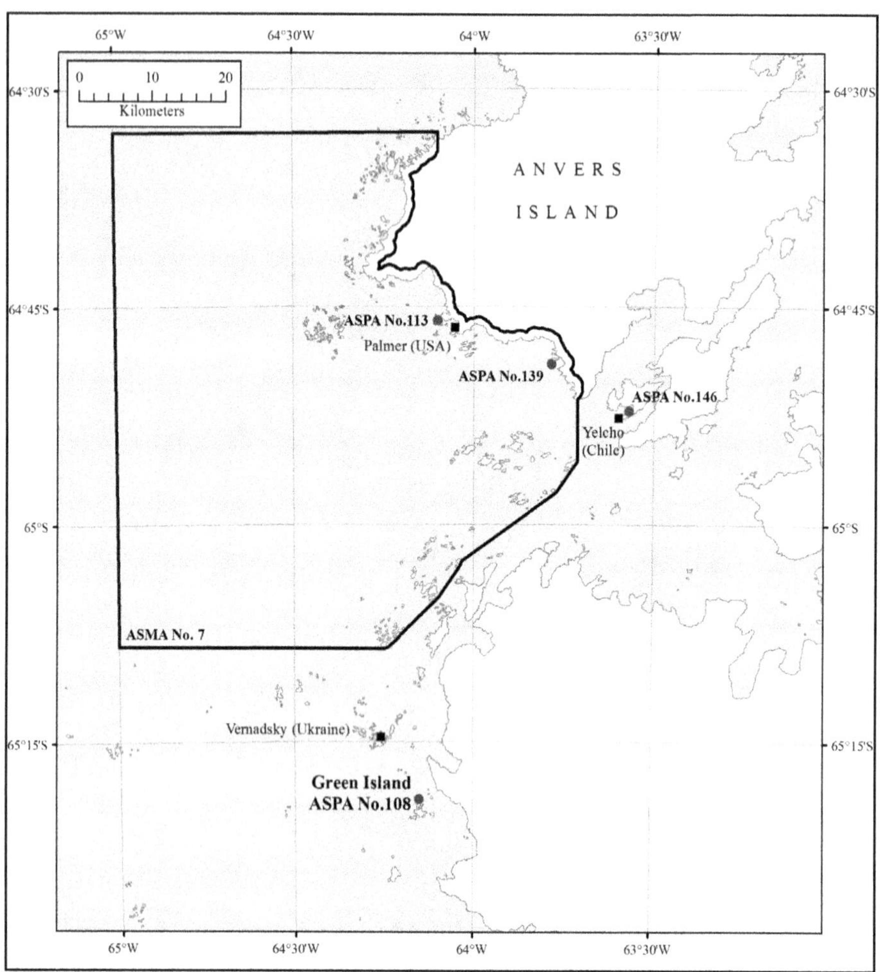

Map 3. ASPA No. 108 Green Island, Berthelot Islands, Antarctic Peninsula, topographic map. Map derived from ground survey 24 February 2001 and digital orthophotography (source aerial photography taken 14 February 2001 by the British Antarctic Survey). Map specifications – Projection: UTM Zone 20S; Spheroid: WGS84; Datum: mean sea level (EGM96).

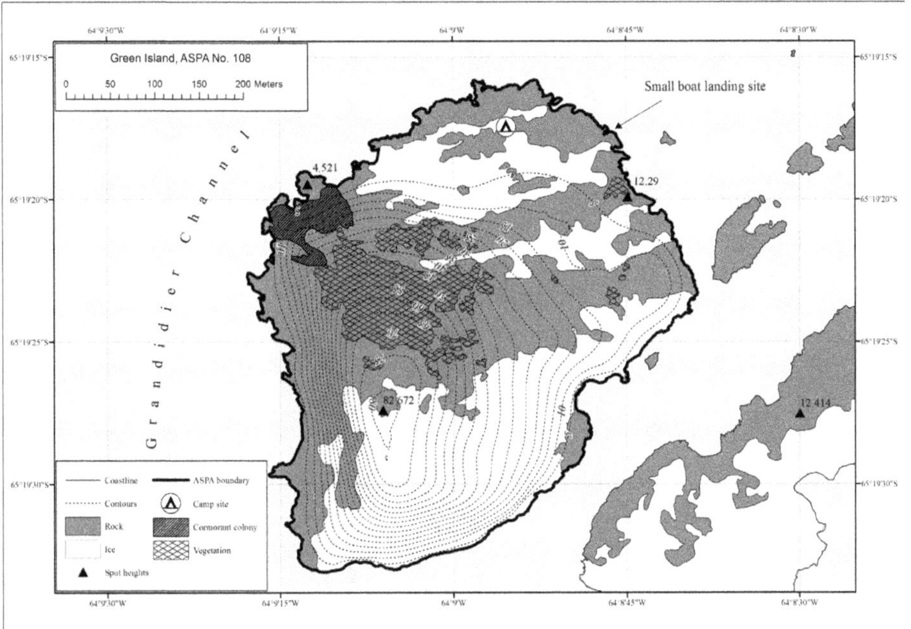

Management Plan for

Antarctic Specially Protected Area No. 117

AVIAN ISLAND, MARGUERITE BAY, ANTARCTIC PENINSULA

Introduction

The primary reason for the designation of Avian Island, Marguerite Bay, Antarctic Peninsula (67°46'S, 68°54'W; 0.49 km^2) as an Antarctic Specially Protected Area (ASPA) is to protect environmental values and primarily the abundance and diversity of breeding seabirds on the island.

Avian Island is situated in northwestern Marguerite Bay, 400 m south of Adelaide Island on the western side of the central Antarctic Peninsula. It was originally designated as Site of Special Scientific Interest (SSSI) No. 30 under Recommendation XV-6 in 1989 after a proposal by the United Kingdom. Included was the island together with its littoral zone, but excluded was a small area near a refuge on the northwestern coast of the island. Values protected under the original designation were described as the abundance and diversity of breeding seabirds present on the island, that the southern giant petrel (*Macronectes giganteus*) colony is one of the most southerly known breeding population of this species, and that the blue-eyed cormorants (*Phalacrocorax atriceps*) are breeding close to the southern limit of their range. The Area was therefore considered of outstanding ornithological importance, meriting protection from unnecessary human disturbance.

Designation as an SSSI was terminated with redesignation of Avian Island as a Specially Protected Area (SPA) through Recommendation XVI-4 (1991, SPA No. 21) after a proposal by the United Kingdom. The boundaries were similar to the original SSSI, but included the entire island and the littoral zone without the exclusion zone near the refuge on the northwestern coast. After re-designation as ASPA 117 through Decision 1 (2002), the ASPA Management Plan was approved through Measure 1 (2002).

The Area fits into the wider context of the Antarctic Protected Area system by protecting the breeding site of seven seabird species, including southern giant petrels which are vulnerable to disturbance. No other ASPA in the region protects such a wide diversity of breeding bird species. Resolution 3 (2008) recommended that the Environmental Domains Analysis for the Antarctic Continent, be used as a dynamic model for the identification of Antarctic Specially Protected Areas within the systematic environmental-geographical framework referred to in Article 3(2) of Annex V of the Protocol (see also Morgan et al., 2007). Using this model, Avian Island is described as Domain E (Antarctic Peninsula and Alexander Island main ice fields), which is also found in ASPAs 113, 114, 126, 128, 129, 133, 134, 139, 147, 149, 152 and ASMAs 1 and 4. However, given that Avian Island is predominantly ice-free this domain may not be fully representative of the environment encompassed within the Area. Although not specifically described as such in Morgan et al., Avian Island may be better represented by Domain B (Antarctic Peninsula mid-northern latitudes geologic). Other protected areas containing Domain B include ASPAs 108, 115, 129, 134, 140 and 153 and ASMA 4. The ASPA sits within Antarctic Conservation Biogeographic Region (ACBR) 3 Northwest Antarctic Peninsula (Terauds et al., 2012).

1. Description of values to be protected

The outstanding environmental value of the Area, which is the primary reason for designation as an ASPA, is based on the following:

- the Adélie penguin (*Pygoscelis adeliae*) colony is one of the largest in Palmer Land, containing around 77,515 breeding pairs;
- the blue-eyed cormorant (*Phalacrocorax atriceps*) colony is one of the largest known breeding sites in the Antarctic and is close to the southern limit of this species' breeding range;
- the outstanding and unique attribute of being the only known site on the Antarctic Peninsula where seven seabird species are breeding in such close proximity to each other within the confined space of a single, small island, with unusually high population densities and virtually the whole island occupied by breeding birds throughout the summer;
- the southern giant petrel (*Macronectes giganteus*) colony is one of the two largest on the Antarctic Peninsula;

- the kelp gull (*Larus dominicanus*) colony is also large and is breeding near the southern extent of its range; and
- the moss *Warnstorfia fontinaliopsis* on Avian Island is near the southern limit of its known range.

2. Aims and objectives

The aims and objectives of this Management Plan are to:

- avoid degradation of, or substantial risk to, the values of the Area by preventing unnecessary human disturbance to the Area;
- prevent or minimise the introduction to the Area of non-native plants, animals and microbes;
- minimise the possibility of the introduction of pathogens which may cause disease in fauna populations within the Area;
- allow scientific research in the Area provided it is for compelling reasons which cannot be served elsewhere and which will not jeopardize the natural ecological system in that Area; and
- preserve the natural ecosystem of the Area as a reference area for future studies.

3. Management activities

The following management activities shall be undertaken to protect the values of the Area:

- A copy of this Management Plan shall be made available at Teniente Luis Carvajal Station (Chile; 67°46'S, 68°55'W), Rothera Research Station (UK; 67°34' S, 68°07'W) and General San Martín Station (Argentina; 68°08' S, 67°06'W).
- The Management Plan shall be reviewed at least every five years and updated as required.
- Visiting field parties shall be briefed fully by the national authority on the values that are to be protected within the Area and the precautions and mitigation measures detailed in this Management Plan.
- All scientific and management activities undertaken within the Area should be subject to an Environmental Impact Assessment, in accordance with the requirements of Annex I of the Protocol on Environmental Protection to the Antarctic Treaty.
- Copies of this Management Plan shall be made available to vessels and aircraft planning to visit the vicinity of the Area.
- All pilots operating in the region shall be informed of the location, boundaries and restrictions applying to entry and over-flight in the Area.
- Markers, signs or other structures erected within the Area for scientific or management purposes shall be secured and maintained in good condition and removed when no longer required.
- In accordance with the requirements of Annex III of the Protocol on Environmental Protection to the Antarctic Treaty, abandoned equipment or materials shall be removed to the maximum extent possible provided doing so does not adversely impact on the environment and the values of the Area.
- National Antarctic Programmes operating in the Area shall consult together with a view to ensuring the above management activities are implemented.

4. Period of designation

Designated for an indefinite period.

5. Maps and photographs

Map 1. Avian Island, ASPA No. 117, in relation to Marguerite Bay, showing the locations of the stations Teniente Luis Carvajal (Chile), Rothera (UK) and General San Martín (Argentina). The location of other protected areas within Marguerite Bay (ASPA No. 107 at Emperor Island (Dion Islands), ASPA No. 115 at Lagotellerie Island, and ASPA No. 129 at Rothera Point) are also shown. Inset: the location of Avian Island on the Antarctic Peninsula.

Map 2. Avian Island, ASPA No. 117, topographic map. Map specifications – projection: Lambert conformal conic; standard parallels: 1st 67° 30' 00"S; 2nd 68° 00' 00"S; central meridian: 68° 55' 00"W; latitude of origin: 68° 00' 00"S; spheroid: WGS84; datum: mean sea level; vertical contour interval 5 m; horizontal accuracy: ±5 m; vertical accuracy ±1.5 m.

Map 3. Avian Island, ASPA No. 117, breeding wildlife sketch map. Positions of nests and colonies are accurate to ±25 m. Information was derived from Poncet (1982). Map specifications – projection: Lambert conformal conic; standard parallels: 1st 67° 30' 00"S; 2nd 68° 00' 00"S; central meridian: 68° 55' 00"W; latitude of origin: 68° 00' 00"S; spheroid: WGS84; datum: mean sea level; vertical contour interval 5 m; horizontal accuracy: ±5 m; vertical accuracy ±1.5 m.

6. Description of the Area

6(i) Geographical coordinates, boundary markers and natural features

General description

Avian Island (67°46'S, 68°54'W, 0.49 km^2), is situated in the northwest of Marguerite Bay, 400 m south of the southwestern extremity of Adelaide Island (Map 1). The island is 1.45 km long by 0.8 km at its widest, and is of roughly triangular shape. It is rocky with a low relief of generally less than 10 m in the north, rising to about 30 m at the centre, and 40 m in the south where several rock and ice slopes of up to 30 m drop steeply to the sea. The coastline is irregular and rocky with numerous offshore islets, although there are several accessible beaches on the northern and eastern coasts. The island is usually ice-free in summer. It contains habitat particularly suitable for a variety of breeding birds: well-drained north-facing slopes suitable for blue-eyed cormorants (*Phalacrocorax atriceps*); broken rock and boulders with crevices suitable for small nesting birds such as Wilson's storm petrels (*Oceanites oceanicus*); elevated rocky heights suitable for southern giant petrels (*Macronectes giganteus*); extensive expanses of snow-free ground for Adélie penguins (*Pygoscelis adeliae*). The presence of the latter attracts skuas (*Catharacta maccormicki* and *C. loennbergi*) and kelp gulls (*Larus dominicanus*).

Boundaries

The designated Area comprises the whole of Avian Island and the littoral zone, offshore islets and rocks, and a buffer zone of the surrounding marine environment (including sea ice when present) within 100 m of the shoreline of the main island (Map 2). Boundary markers have not been installed because the coast forms a visually obvious reference for the marine boundary.

Climate and sea ice

No extended meteorological records are available for Avian Island, but records from 1962-74 for Adelaide Base (formerly UK; now Teniente Luis Carvajal, Chile), 1.2 km distant, show a mean daily maximum temperature of 3 °C in February (extreme maximum 9 °C) and a mean daily minimum of -8 °C in August (extreme minimum -44°C). The same general pattern was observed in year-round observations made on the island in 1978-79 (Poncet and Poncet, 1979). Precipitation on the island in this year was usually as snow, most of which fell between August and October, but with occasional snowfalls and some rain in the summer.

Marguerite Bay may freeze in winter, although the extent and character of sea ice shows considerable inter-seasonal variation. Despite the extent and frequent persistence of regional sea ice, a recurrent polynya has been observed near Avian Island, which can provide ice-free conditions locally from October onward. In addition, strong tidal currents around Avian Island help to keep surrounding waters ice-free for much of the year, which facilitates easy access to feeding grounds for several species. The island is not particularly windy, with an annual average of 10 knots in 1978-79. However, the strong katabatic winds that descend from Adelaide Island, perhaps for 1-3 days a few times every month, reduce snow accumulation on the island and push sea ice away from the coast, helping to form the polynya. The relatively snow-free conditions are important for bird colonisation.

Geology, geomorphology and soils

The bedrock of Avian Island forms part of a down-faulted block at the southwestern end of Adelaide Island and is composed of interbedded lithic-rich and feldspar-rich volcaniclastic sandstones. Bedded tuffaceaous sandstones, pebbly sandstones rich in volcanic lithics, and a volcanic granule breccia also occur. The latter is probably a primary volcanic deposit, while the rest of the sequence is largely composed of reworked volcanic material. The sequence forms part of the Mount Liotard Formation of Adelaide Island and is probably late Cretaceous in age (Griffiths, 1992; Moyes et al., 1994; Riley et al., 2012). Apart from rock outcrop, the surface consists mainly of frost-shattered rock with permafrost. Ornithogenic soils are widespread, particularly in the north; organic peat soil is virtually absent, but where present is not well-developed and is associated with moss growth. Several raised beaches have been noted on Avian Island, but the geomorphology has not otherwise been described.

Streams and lakes

Avian Island has several ephemeral freshwater ponds of up to 10,000 m^2 and of about 40 cm in depth, the largest being on the eastern coast, at about 5 m altitude, and on the north-western coast near sea level. Numerous small pools and meltwater channels develop from seasonal snow melt, and small streams drain valleys in the vicinity of the ponds. Both the ponds and melt-pools freeze solid in winter. Freshwater bodies on the island are organically enriched by guano, a source of nutrients, and in summer a number of the ponds show a rich benthic flora and fauna of algae, Phyllopoda, Copepoda, Nematoda, Protozoa, Rotifera, and Tardigrada. Large numbers of the crustacean *Branchinecta* sp. have been observed (Poncet and Poncet, 1979). The freshwater ecology of the island has not been studied in detail.

Breeding birds

Seven species of birds breed on Avian Island, which is a high number compared to other sites on the Antarctic Peninsula. Several species have unusually high populations, being some of the largest for their species in the Antarctic Peninsula region (Map 3). Detailed year-round data for all species were collected in 1978-79 (Poncet and Poncet, 1979), while data are otherwise sporadic. Descriptions below are thus often based on a single season's observations and it should be emphasised that these data are therefore not necessarily representative of longer term population trends. However, this is the best information that is presently available.

The Avian Island Adélie penguin (*Pygoscelis adeliae*) colony occupies the northern half and central eastern coast of the island (Map 3). The initial management plan referred to the Adélie penguin colony as "the largest on the Antarctic Peninsula [containing] a third of the total population breeding in the region". While this is not substantiated by recent data (e.g. one Antarctic Peninsula colony has over 120,000 pairs (Woehler 1993)), the Avian Island colony still represents one of the largest breeding populations in Palmer Land. Recent research suggests that Adélie penguin numbers are decreasing at almost all locations on the Antarctic Peninsula (Lynch et al., 2012). However, the most recent data available for Adélie penguins on Avian Island indicated a population of 77,515 breeding pairs (± 5%; January 2013) (W. Fraser, pers. comm. 2013; Sailley et al., in press), which compares to only 36,500 breeding pairs recorded on 11 November 1978 (Poncet and Poncet, 1979; Woehler, 1993). An estimate of Adélie penguin numbers, based on aerial photographs taken in December 1998, revealed 87,850 birds (± 0.16 S.D.).

In 1978-79 Adélie penguins were recorded on the island from October until the end of April, with egg laying occurring through October and November, and the first chicks hatching around mid-December. Chick crèches were observed around mid-January, with the first chicks becoming independent near the end of January. Most of the moulting adults and independent chicks had departed the island by the third week of February, although groups returned periodically throughout March and April.

A large colony of blue-eyed cormorants (*Phalacrocorax atriceps*) has been recorded in three groups located on the south-western coastal extremity of the island (Map 3). However, during a visit on 26-27 January 2011, it was noted that the two more northerly colony sites were not occupied and the nesting mounds were in a poor state, suggesting that these sites may have been abandoned for some time. Stonehouse (1949) reported about 300 birds present in October 1948; a similar number of birds was recorded in mid-November 1968, most of which were breeding (Willey 1969). Poncet and Poncet (1979) observed 320 pairs in 1978, and approximately 670 pairs on 17 January 1989 (Poncet, 1990). A count on 23 February 2001 recorded 185 chicks, although it is probable some had departed by the time of the count; approximately 250 nest sites were counted. A count in mid- to late January 2013 recorded 302 breeding pairs (W. Fraser, pers. comm., 2013). In 1968 blue-eyed cormorants were observed to be present on the island from 12 August, with egg laying occurring from November, and chicks hatching in December (Willey 1969). In 1978-79 they were observed from September until June, with egg laying occurring from November through to January, when the first chicks hatched, and chicks started to become independent in the third week of February (Poncet and Poncet, 1979).

Of the southern giant petrel (*Macronectes giganteus*) colonies known south of the South Shetland Islands, Avian Island is one of the two largest, and may comprise a substantial proportion of the breeding population in the southern Antarctic Peninsula region (estimated at 1190 pairs in 1999/2000; Patterson et al., 2008). In 1979 the southern giant petrels occupied principally the elevated rocky outcrops of the central and southern half of the island in four main groups (Map 3). Data on the numbers of birds present on the island are shown in Table 1.

Table 1: Southern giant petrel (*Macronectes giganteus*) numbers at Avian Island.

Year	Number of birds	Number of pairs	Number of chicks	Source
1948	~100	n/a	n/a	Stonehouse, 1949

1968	400	163	n/a	Willey, 1969
1979	n/a	197	n/a	Poncet and Poncet, 1979
1989	n/a	250	n/a	Poncet, 1990
2001	n/a	n/a	237	Harris, 2001
2013	n/a	470	n/a	W. Fraser, pers. comm., 2013

n/a - not available.

In 1978-79 the birds were present on Avian Island from mid-September through to as late as June. In this season, egg laying occurred from late October through to the end of November, with hatching occurring throughout January and chicks generally achieving independence by April. In the 1978-79 austral summer up to 100 non-breeders were observed on the island during the courtship period in October, with these numbers decreasing to a few non-breeders as the season progressed.

Approximately 200 adult kelp gulls (*Larus dominicanus*), of which over 60 pairs were breeding, were recorded on Avian Island in 1978-79. These birds were distributed widely, but principally in the elevated central and southern parts of the island (Poncet and Poncet 1979) (Map 3). In the 1978-79 austral summer the majority of breeders arrived in early October, followed by egg laying around mid-November and hatching a month later. Detailed data are not available because of concern that human disturbance by data collection would seriously impair the breeding performance of this species. However, no more than 12 chicks were observed on the island near the end of January 1979, which would suggest breeding performance in this season was low: the exact cause – whether human disturbance or natural factors – could not be determined. In 1967, 19 pairs and 80-120 birds were recorded (Barlow, 1968).

An estimate of at least several hundred pairs of breeding Wilson's storm petrels (*Oceanites oceanicus*) on the island was made in 1978-79 (Poncet and Poncet, 1979). Wilson's storm petrels were observed on the island from the second week of November, with laying and incubation probably occurring through to mid-December. Departure of adults and independent chicks was largely complete by the end of March. Most of the rocky outcrops on the northern half of the island and all of the stable rocky slopes in the south are ideal habitat for this species.

In 1978-79 about 25-30 pairs of south polar skuas (*Catharacta maccormicki*) were breeding on Avian Island. The skua nests were distributed widely over the island, although the majority were on the central and eastern part of the island, especially on slopes overlooking the Adélie penguin colony (Map 3). Large groups of non-breeders (around 150 birds; Poncet and Poncet 1979) were observed to congregate around the shallow lake on the eastern side of the island. Barlow (1968) reported approximately 200 non-breeding birds in 1968. In 2004, 880 pairs of south polar skuas were recorded (W. Fraser, pers. comm., in Ritz et al., 2006). In the 1978-79 austral summer the south polar skuas took up residence around the end of October, with egg laying in early December and hatching complete by the end of January. Independent chicks and adults generally departed by the end of March, with some late-breeders remaining until mid-April. A breeding success of one chick per nest was reported in the 1978-79 austral summer. Barlow (1968) reported 12 breeding pairs of brown (=subantarctic) skuas (*Catharacta loennbergi*), although this number could include south polar skuas. One breeding pair of brown skuas was recorded on the southwest of the island in the 1978-79 austral summer. This is the southernmost record of this species breeding along the Antarctic Peninsula. Several non-breeding brown skuas were also recorded in the same season.

Several other bird species, known to breed elsewhere in Marguerite Bay, are frequent visitors to Avian Island, notably Antarctic terns (*Sterna vittata*), snow petrels (*Pagodroma nivea*), and southern fulmars (*Fulmarus glacialoides*). These species have not been observed nesting on Avian Island. Small numbers of Antarctic petrels (*Thalassoica antarctica*) have been seen on a few occasions. The cape petrel (*Daption capense*) was observed on Avian Island in October 1948 (Stonehouse, 1949). Solitary individuals of king (*Aptenodytes patagonicus*) and chinstrap (*Pygoscelis antarctica*) penguins were observed in 1975 and 1989, respectively.

Terrestrial biology

Vegetation on Avian Island is generally sparse, and the flora has not been described in detail. Phanerogams are absent from the island and there is a limited range of cryptogams, although there is a rich lichen flora. To date, nine moss and 11 lichen species have been identified within the Area.

Mosses described are *Andreaea depressinervis*, *Brachythecium austro-salebrosum*, *Bryum argenteum*, *B. pseudotriquetrum*, *Ceratodon purpureus*, *Pohlia cruda*, *P. nutans*, *Sanionia georgico-uncinata*, *S. uncinata*, *Syntrichia magellanica* and *Warnstorfia fontinaliopsis*. The latter species is at the southern limit of its known range on Avian Island (Smith, 1996). Moss development is confined to those parts of the island that are unoccupied by breeding Adélie penguins or blue-eyed cormorants, and occurs in moist depressions or by melt pools. Patches of moss of up to 100 m^2 surround the shore of a small pond on the hill in the south of the Area, at ca. 30 m elevation. The green foliose alga *Prasiola crispa* is widespread in wet areas of the island and a liverwort, *Cephaloziella varians,* has also been identified.

Lichens identified on Avian Island are *Acarospora macrocyclos, Cladonia fimbriata, C. gracilis, Dermatocarpon antarcticum, Lecanora dancoensis, Lecidea brabantica, Physcia caesia, Rinodina egentissima, Siphulina orphnina, Thamnolecania brialmontii*, and *Usnea antarctica*. The most extensive communities are on the rocky outcrops in the south of the island.

The microinvertebrate fauna, fungi and bacteria on Avian Island have yet to be investigated in detail. Thus far only one mesostigmatid mite (*Gamasellus racovitzai*) (BAS Invertebrate Database, 1999) has been described, although a Collembollan (springtail) and several species of Acari (mites) have been observed but not identified (Poncet, 1990). A number of nematode species (dominated by *Plectus* sp.) (Spaull, 1973) and one fungus (*Thyronectria hyperantarctica*) (BAS Invertebrate Database, 1999) have been recorded on the island.

Breeding mammals and marine environment

Weddell seals (*Leptonychotes weddellii*) were common on and around Avian Island in 1978-79. During the winter more than a dozen remained, hauled out on coastal ice (Poncet, 1990). Several pups were born on the shores of the island in the last week of September 1978. An elephant seal (*Mirounga leonina*) was reported pupping on the northeastern coast of Avian Island on 10 October 1969 (Bramwell, 1969). Aerial photography taken on 15 December 1998 revealed 182 elephant seals hauled out in groups, mostly close to the ponds. Leopard seals (*Hydrurga leptonyx*) have been observed around the shoreline, and one was observed ashore in winter 1978. A number of non-breeding Antarctic fur seals (*Arctocephalus gazella*) were reported on the island in March 1997 (Gray and Fox, 1997), at the end of January 1999 (Fox, pers. comm., 1999) and January 2011. At least several hundred were present on 23 February 2001 (Harris, 2001), particularly on beaches and low-lying ground in the central and northern parts of the island. Crabeater seals (*Lobodon carcinophagus*) are regularly seen in Marguerite Bay, but have not been reported on Avian Island. The marine environment surrounding Avian Island has not been investigated.

Human activities / impacts

Human activity at Avian Island has been sporadic. The first record of a visit was made in October 1948, when members of the UK Stonington Island expedition discovered the large Adélie penguin colony on Avian Island (then referred to as one of the Henkes Islands). Subsequent visits have comprised a mixture of science, base personnel recreation, tourism and logistic activity (survey, etc.). Refuges were constructed on the island in 1957 and 1962 by Argentina and Chile respectively (see section *6(iii)*).

A geological field party of two camped for about 10 days on the southeast of the island in November 1968 (Elliott, 1969). In the same year, a UK Naval hydrographic survey team camped on the eastern coast of Avian Island over the summer. Permanent chains and rings for mooring lines to the survey vessel were installed in a small bay on the northwestern coast, and were still present in 1989 (Poncet, 1990).

In 1969, a field party camped on the island for a month conducting research on the common cold virus: accompanying dogs were inoculated with a virus and then returned to base (Bramwell, 1969). Dogs often accompanied personnel on the regular visits to Avian Island during the period of operation of the UK base on Adelaide Island, but impacts are unknown.

A two-person party spent a year on the island in 1978-79, based on the yacht *Damien II*, making detailed observations of the avifauna and other aspects of the biology and natural environment of the island (Poncet and Poncet, 1979; Poncet, 1982; Poncet, 1990). The yacht was moored in a small cove on the northwest coast. This yacht party regularly visited the island over the next decade before SPA designation.

Map survey work and aerial photography was conducted on and over the island in 1996-98 (Fox and Gray, 1997, Gray and Fox, 1997), and 1998-99 (Fox, pers. comm., 1999).

The impacts of these activities have not been described and are not known, but are believed to have been relatively minor and limited to transient disturbance to breeding birds, campsites, footprints, occasional litter, human wastes, scientific sampling and markers. Despite the likely transient nature of most disturbance, it has been reported that human visits have caused loss of eggs and chicks, either through nest abandonment or by opportunistic predation. Several species, such as southern giant petrels and kelp gulls are particularly vulnerable to disturbance, and have been observed to abandon nests at particular periods of the nesting cycle, perhaps at the sight of people as much as 100 m distant (Poncet, 1990). Approximately 140 people, including a tour vessel of 100, were reported to have visited Avian Island in the 1989-90 summer. Growing concern over the number and unregulated nature of visits prompted SPA designation.

The most lasting and visually obvious impacts are associated with the two refuges and two beacon structures described in section *6(iii)*, which are situated close to breeding birds. Both refuges were in poor repair in February 2001 and, during an environmental management visit in January 2011, further deterioration was noted in both refuges. Birds and seals were observed among rubbish around the refuges in February 2001 and January 2011. The refuge erected on the eastern coast (67°46'26"S, 68°53'01"W) in 1957 was open to the weather; the door, having come off its hinges, lay on the floor and the base of the southern wall of the refuge contained a large hole (c. 0.25 m^2). Rusting tins and broken glass were found on the floor. Rusting metal work, (including corrugated cladding, stakes and guy lines), decomposing timber fragments and broken glass were found in the immediate area around the refuge. To the south of the hut lay an empty corroding 205 L fuel drum.

The larger refuge erected on the northwestern coast (67°46'08"S, 68°53'29"W) in 1962 was also in a poor state of repair. The refuge showed significant deterioration due to damp, with warping of timbers and extensive areas of mould and algae on the walls and ceiling material. A large portion of the ceiling had collapsed revealing the roof above. The door no longer shut properly and was tied shut. At the time of the visit in January 2011, a large bundle of sawn timber covered in a blue tarpaulin was stored inside the hut, the purpose of which was not known. Some timber and metalwork lay on ground to the eastern side of the hut.

The older of the two beacon structures is disused and its iron structure, while standing, is rusting and deteriorating. The new beacon, erected in February 1998, appeared to be in good repair in January 2011.

6(ii) Access to the Area

- Small boat landings should be made at the designated locations on the central northwestern coast (67°46'08.1"S, 68°53'30.1"W) or on the central eastern coast of the island (67°46'25.5"S, 68°52'57.0"W) (Map 2). If sea or ice conditions render this impractical, small boat landings may be made elsewhere along the coast as conditions allow.
- Access by vehicle to the coast when sea ice is present should also use these access points, and vehicles shall be parked at the shore.
- Travel by small boat or vehicle within the marine part of the Area is not confined to specific routes, but shall be by the shortest route consistent with the objectives and requirements of the permitted activities.
- Vehicle or boat crew, or other people on vehicles or boats, are prohibited from moving on foot beyond the immediate vicinity of the landing site unless specifically authorised by Permit.
- Aircraft should avoid landing within the Area throughout the year
- A Permit may be granted for helicopter use when this is considered necessary for essential purposes and where there is no practical alternative, such as for the installation, maintenance or removal of structures. In such instances the need for helicopter access, including alternatives, and the potential disturbance to breeding birds shall be adequately assessed before a Permit may be granted. Such a Permit shall clearly define the conditions for helicopter access based on the findings of the assessment.

6(iii) Location of structures within and adjacent to the Area

Two small abandoned refuges and two beacon structures are present within the Area. A refuge erected by Chile in 1962 is located on the northwestern coast of the island at 67°46'08"S, 68°53'29"W. A refuge constructed by Argentina in 1957 is 650 m SE of this position, on the eastern coast at 67°46'26"S, 68°53'01"W. Both refuges were in a poor state of repair in January 2011. Further deterioration of the huts has potential to impact on nesting birds.

An old iron frame structure, believed to have been erected by the UK during the operation of Adelaide Base and used as a navigational aid, is located at approximately 38 m near the highest point of the island (67°46'35.5" S, 68°53'25.2" W). The structure remains standing, although is rusting.

A new beacon was constructed by Chile in February 1998 on an adjacent site at a similar elevation (67°46'35.3" S, 68°53'26.0" W). This structure is a solid cylindrical painted iron tower of approximately 2 m diameter and 2.5 m in height, set in a concrete pad of approximately 2.5 x 2.5 m. A lit beacon, protective rails and solar panels are affixed to the top of the structure. No other structures are known to exist on the island.

Four survey control markers were installed on the island on 31 January 1999 (Map 2). The southernmost marker is located adjacent to the navigation beacon and consists of a survey nail in bedrock covered by a cairn. A similar marker is installed on the high point of the low ridge on the northeastern coast of the island, also covered by a cairn. The remaining two markers are survey nails affixed to the roof of each of the refuges.

The nearest scientific research station is 1.2 km northwest at Teniente Luis Carvajal (Chile), on southern Adelaide Island (latitude 67°46'S, longitude 68°55'W). Since 1982 this has been operated as a summer-only facility, open from

October until March. Over this period the station has generally accommodated up to 10 personnel. Formerly, this facility was established and operated continuously by the UK from 1961 until 1977.

6 (iv) Location of other protected Areas in the vicinity

Other protected areas in the vicinity include:

- ASPA 107, Emperor Island, Dion Islands, Marguerite Bay, Antarctic Peninsula, 67°52'S, 68°42'W, 12.5 km south-southeast;
- ASPA 129, Rothera Point, Adelaide Island, 67°34'S, 68°08'W, 40 km to the northeast; and
- ASPA 115, Lagotellerie Island, Marguerite Bay, Graham Land, 67°53'20"S, 67°25'30"W, 65 km east (Map 1)

6(v) Special zones within the Area

None.

7. Permit conditions

7(i) General permit conditions

Entry into the Area is prohibited except in accordance with a Permit issued by an appropriate national authority. Conditions for issuing a Permit to enter the Area are that:

- it is issued for compelling scientific reasons which cannot be served elsewhere, or for reasons essential to the management of the Area;
- the actions permitted are in accordance with this Management Plan;
- any management activities are in support of the objectives of this Management Plan;
- the actions permitted will not jeopardise the natural ecological system in the Area;
- the activities permitted will give due consideration via the environmental impact assessment process to the continued protection of the environmental or scientific values of the Area;
- the Permit shall be issued for a finite period; and
- the Permit, or an authorised copy, shall be carried when in the Area.

7(ii) Access to, and movement within or over, the Area

- Land vehicles (skidoos, quad bikes, etc.) are prohibited on land within the Area.
- All movement on land within the Area shall be on foot. Pedestrian traffic should be kept to the minimum necessary to undertake permitted activities and every reasonable effort should be made to minimise trampling effects.
- Movement within the Area on foot shall be by routes that minimise any disturbance to breeding birds, and to achieve this it may be necessary to take a longer route to the destination than would otherwise be the case.
- Walking routes have been designated with the intention of avoiding the most sensitive bird breeding sites, and should be used when it is essential to traverse across the island (Map 2). Visitors should bear in mind that specific nest sites may vary from year to year, and some variations on the recommended route may be preferable. Routes are provided as a guide, and visitors are expected to exercise good judgement to minimise the effects of their presence. In other areas, and where practical and safe, it is usually preferable to adopt a route that follows the coastline of the Area. Three routes are designated (Map 2): Route 1 crosses the central part of the island, linking the Chilean and Argentine refuges. Route 2 facilitates access to the beacons on the south of the island, and extends from the central eastern coast up the eastern slopes of the hill. However, during a management visit in 2011, this route was found to be colonized by birds. Consequently, Route 3 has also been designated, which runs directly east from the Argentine refuge to a narrow inlet on the western side of the island, and then proceeds southwest up a gully/slope to a flat area above the abandoned (as of January 2011) blue-eyed cormorant colonies. From this point the route proceeds east to the beacons. Care should be taken to avoid trampling moss patches in the vicinity of a melt water pool c. 70 m north of the beacons.
- Access into areas where southern giant petrels are nesting (Map 3) shall only be undertaken for purposes specified in the Permit. When access to the beacon is necessary (e.g. for maintenance), visitors shall follow the most

appropriate designated access route as closely as possible, trying to avoid nesting birds. Much of the area leading up to and surrounding the beacon is occupied by breeding petrels, so great care must be exercised.

- Movements should be slow, noise kept to a minimum, and the maximum distance practicable should be maintained from nesting birds.
- Visitors shall watch carefully for signs of agitation and preferably retreat from approach if significant disturbance is observed.
- The operation of aircraft over the Areas should be carried out, as a minimum requirement, in compliance with the '*Guidelines for the operations of aircraft near concentrations of birds*' contained in Resolution 2 (2004).

7(iii) Activities which may be conducted in the Area

Activities which may be conducted in the Area include:

- essential management activities, including monitoring;
- compelling scientific research that cannot be undertaken elsewhere and which will not jeopardize the ecosystem of the Area; and
- sampling, which should be the minimum required for approved research programmes.

Restrictions on times at which activities may be conducted apply within the Area, and are specified in the relevant sections of this Management Plan.

7(iv) Installation, modification or removal of structures

- Any new or additional permanent structures or installations are prohibited.
- Existing abandoned or dilapidated structures should be removed or renovated.
- Installation, modification, maintenance or removal of structures shall be undertaken in a manner that minimises disturbance to breeding birds. Such activities shall be undertaken between 1 February and 30 September inclusive to avoid the main breeding season.
- No structures are to be erected within the Area, or scientific equipment installed, except for compelling scientific or management reasons and for a pre-established period, as specified in a permit.
- All markers, structures or scientific equipment installed in the Area must be clearly identified by country, name of the principal investigator or agency, year of installation and date of expected removal.
- All such items should be free of organisms, propagules (e.g. seeds, eggs, spores) and non-sterile soil (see section *7(vi)*), and be made of materials that can withstand the environmental condition and pose minimal risk of contamination of the Area.
- Removal of specific structures or equipment for which the permit has expired shall be the responsibility of the authority which granted the original permit and shall be a condition of the Permit.

7(v) Location of field camps

Camping should be avoided within the Area. However, when necessary for purposes specified in the Permit, temporary camping is allowed at two designated campsites: one on the central eastern coast of the island (67°46'25.8"S, 68°53'00.8"W), the other on the central northwestern coast of the Area (67°46'08.2"S, 68°53'29.5"W) (Map 2).

7(vi) Restrictions on materials and organisms that may be brought into the Area

No living animals, plant material or microorganisms shall be deliberately introduced into the Area. To ensure that the floristic and ecological values of the Area are maintained, special precautions shall be taken against accidentally introducing microbes, invertebrates or plants from other Antarctic sites, including stations, or from regions outside Antarctica. All sampling equipment or markers brought into the Area shall be cleaned or sterilized. To the maximum extent practicable, footwear and other equipment used or brought into the Area (including bags or backpacks) shall be thoroughly cleaned before entering the Area. Further guidance can be found in the *CEP non-native species manual* (CEP, 2011) and the *Environmental code of conduct for terrestrial scientific field research in Antarctica* (SCAR, 2009). In view of the presence of breeding bird colonies within the Area, no poultry products, including wastes from such products and products containing uncooked dried eggs, shall be released into the Area, including the marine component of the Area.

No herbicides or pesticides shall be brought into the Area. Any other chemicals, including radio-nuclides or stable isotopes, which may be introduced for scientific or management purposes specified in the Permit, shall be removed from the Area at or before the conclusion of the activity for which the Permit was granted. Release of radio-nuclides or stable isotopes directly into the environment in a way that renders them unrecoverable should be avoided. Fuel or other chemicals shall not be stored in the Area unless specifically authorised by Permit condition. They shall be stored and handled in a way that minimises the risk of their accidental introduction into the environment. Materials introduced into the Area shall be for a stated period only and shall be removed by the end of that stated period. If release occurs which is likely to compromise the values of the Area, removal is encouraged only where the impact of removal is not likely to be greater than that of leaving the material in situ. The appropriate authority should be notified of anything released and not removed that was not included in the authorised Permit.

7(vii) Taking of, or harmful interference with, native flora or fauna

Taking of, or harmful interference with, native flora and fauna is prohibited, except in accordance with a permit issued in accordance with Annex II of the Protocol on Environmental Protection to the Antarctic Treaty. Where taking or harmful interference with animals is involved this should, as a minimum standard, be in accordance with the *SCAR code of conduct for the use of animals for scientific purposes in Antarctica* (2011). Any soil or vegetation sampling is to be kept to an absolute minimum required for scientific or management purposes, and carried out using techniques which minimise disturbance to surrounding soil and biota.

7(viii) The collection or removal of materials not brought into the Area by the permit holder

Material may be collected or removed from the Area only in accordance with a permit and should be limited to the minimum necessary to meet scientific or management needs. Material of human origin likely to compromise the values of the Area, and which was not brought into the Area by the Permit holder or otherwise authorised may be removed from the Area unless the environmental impact of the removal is likely to be greater than leaving the material in situ: if this is the case the appropriate national authority must be notified and approval obtained. Permits shall not be granted if there is a reasonable concern that the sampling proposed would take, remove or damage such quantities of soil, native flora or fauna that their distribution or abundance on Avian Island would be significantly affected. Samples of flora or fauna found dead within the Area may be removed for analysis or audit without prior authorisation by Permit.

7(ix) Disposal of waste

All wastes, except human wastes, shall be removed from the Area. Preferably, all human wastes should be removed from the Area, but if this is not possible, they may be disposed of into the sea.

7(x) Measures that may be necessary to continue to met the aims of the Management Plan

1. Permits may be granted to enter the Area to carry out scientific research, monitoring and site inspection activities, which may involve the collection of a small number of samples for analysis or to carry out protective measures.
2. Any long-term monitoring sites shall be appropriately marked and the markers or signs maintained.
3. Scientific activities shall be performed in accordance with the *Environmental code of conduct for terrestrial scientific field research in Antarctica* (SCAR, 2009).

7(xi) Requirements for reports

The principal Permit holder for each visit to the Area shall submit a report to the appropriate national authority as soon as practicable, and no later than six months after the visit has been completed. Such reports should include, as appropriate, the information identified in the *Antarctic Specially Protected Area visit report form* contained in the *Guide to the preparation of Management Plans for Antarctic Specially Protected Areas* (Appendix 2). The appropriate authority should be notified of any activities/measures undertaken that were not included in the authorised Permit. Wherever possible, the national authority should also forward a copy of the visit report to the Party that proposed the Management Plan, to assist in managing the Area and reviewing the Management Plan. Parties should, wherever possible, deposit originals or copies of such original visit reports in a publicly accessible archive to maintain a record of usage, for the purpose of any review of the Management Plan and in organising the scientific use of the Area.

8. Supporting documentation

Barlow, J. (1968). Biological report. Adelaide Island. 1967/68. Unpublished British Antarctic Survey report, BAS Archives Ref. AD6/2T/1967/N.

Bramwell, M.J. (1969). Report on elephant seal pupping on Avian Island. Unpublished British Antarctic Survey report, BAS Archives Ref. AD6/2T/1969/N.

Bramwell, M.J. (1970). Journey report: Avian Island 7 Oct – 4 Nov 1969. Unpublished British Antarctic Survey report, BAS Archives Ref. AD6/2T/1969/K3.

Committee for Environmental Protection (CEP). (2011). Non-native species manual – 1st Edition. Manual prepared by Intersessional Contact Group of the CEP and adopted by the Antarctic Treaty Consultative Meeting through Resolution 6 (2011). Buenos Aires, Secretariat of the Antarctic Treaty.

Elliott, M.H. (1969). Summer geological camp on Avian Island 26 Nov – 4 Dec 1968. Unpublished British Antarctic Survey report, BAS Archives Ref. AD6/2T/1968/K3.

Fox, A., and Gray, M. (1997). Aerial photography field report 1996-97 Antarctic field season. Unpublished British Antarctic Survey report, BAS Archives Ref. AD6/2R/1996/L2.

Gray, M., and Fox, A. (1997). GPS Survey field report 1996-97 Antarctic field season. Unpublished British Antarctic Survey report, BAS Archives Ref. AD6/2R/1996/L1.

Griffiths, C. (1992). Geological fieldwork on Adelaide Island 1991-92. Unpublished British Antarctic Survey report, BAS Archives Ref. AD6/2R/1991/GL1.

Harris, C.M. (2001). Revision of management plans for Antarctic protected areas originally proposed by the United States of America and the United Kingdom: Field visit report. Internal report for the National Science Foundation, US, and the Foreign and Commonwealth Office, UK. Environmental Research and Assessment, Cambridge.

Lynch, H. J., Naveen, R., Trathan, P. N., and Fagan, W. F. (2012). Spatially integrated assessment reveals widespread changes in penguin populations on the Antarctic Peninsula. Ecology 93:1367–1377.

Moyes, A. B., Willan, C. F. H., Thomson, J. W., et al. (1994). Geological map of Adelaide Island to Foyn Coast, BAS GEOMAP Series, Sheet 3, Scale 1:250,000, with supplementary text. British Antarctic Survey, Cambridge.

Patterson, D. L., Woehler, E. J., Croxall, J. P., Cooper, J., Poncet, S., Peter, H.-U., Hunter, S., and Fraser, W. R. (2008). Breeding distribution and population status of the northern giant petrel *Macronectes halli* and the southern giant petrel *M. giganteus*. Marine Ornithology 36: 115-124.

Poncet, S., and Poncet, J. (1979). Ornithological report, Avian Island, 1978-79. Unpublished British Antarctic Survey report, BAS Archives Ref. AD6/2R/1978/Q.

Poncet, S. (1982). Le grand hiver: Damien II base Antarctique. Les Éditions Arthaud, Paris.

Poncet, S., and Poncet, J. (1987). Censuses of penguin populations of the Antarctic Peninsula, 1983-87. British Antarctic Survey Bulletin 77: 109-129.

Poncet, S. (1990). Avian Island, Marguerite Bay, Antarctic Peninsula, SPA proposal. Unpublished report to the SCAR Group of Specialist on Environmental Affairs and Conservation, 1990.

Riley, T. R., Flowerdew, M. J. and Whitehouse, M. J. (2012). Litho- and chronostratigraphy of a fore- to intra-arc basin: Adelaide Island, Antarctic Peninsula. Geological Magazine 149: 768-782.

Ritz, M. S., Hahn, S., Janicke, T., and Peter, H.-U. (2006). Hybridisation between South Polar Skua (*Catharacta maccormicki*) and Brown Skua *(C. antarctica lonnbergi*) in the Antarctic Peninsula region. Polar Biology 29: 153–159.

Sailley, S. F., Ducklow, H. W., Moeller, H. V., Fraser, W. R., Schofield, O. M., Steinberg, D. K., Price, L. M., and Doney, S. C. (2013). Carbon fluxes and pelagic ecosystem dynamics near two western Antarctic Peninsula Adélie penguin colonies: an inverse model approach. Marine Ecology Progress Series, in press.

SCAR (Scientific Committee on Antarctic Research). (2009). Environmental code of conduct for terrestrial scientific field research in Antarctica. ATCM XXXII IP4.

SCAR (Scientific Committee on Antarctic Research). (2011). SCAR code of conduct for the use of animals for scientific purposes in Antarctica. ATCM XXXIV IP53.

Smith, H. G. 1978. The distribution and ecology of terrestrial protozoa of sub-Antarctic and maritime Antarctic islands. BAS Scientific Report 95, British Antarctic Survey, Cambridge.

Smith, R. I. L. (1996). Terrestrial and freshwater biotic components of the western Antarctic Peninsula. In Ross, R. M., Hofmann, E. E. and Quetin, L. B. *Foundations for ecological research west of the Antarctic Peninsula.* Antarctic Research Series 70: American Geophysical Union, Washington D.C.: 15-59.

Stonehouse, B. (1949). Report on biological activities at Base E 1948-49. Unpublished British Antarctic Survey report, BAS Archives Ref. AD6/2E/1948/N1.

Stonehouse, B. (1950). Preliminary report on biological work Base E 1949-50. Unpublished British Antarctic Survey report, BAS Archives Ref. AD6/2E/1949/N.

Terauds, A., Chown, S. L., Morgan, F., Peat, H. J., Watt, D., Keys, H., Convey, P., and Bergstrom, D. M. (2012). Conservation biogeography of the Antarctic. Diversity and Distributions 18: 726–41.

Willey, I. M. (1969). Adelaide Island bird report 1968. Unpublished British Antarctic Survey report, BAS Archives Ref. AD6/2T/1968/Q.

Woehler, E. J. (ed). (1993). The distribution and abundance of Antarctic and sub-Antarctic penguins. SCAR, Cambridge.

Map 1. Avian Island, ASPA No. 117, in relation to Marguerite Bay, showing the locations of the stations Teniente Luis Carvajal (Chile), Rothera (UK) and General San Martín (Argentina). The location of other protected areas within Marguerite Bay (ASPA No. 107 at Emperor Island (Dion Islands), ASPA No. 115 at Lagotellerie Island, and ASPA No. 129 at Rothera Point) are also shown. Inset: the location of Avian Island on the Antarctic Peninsula.

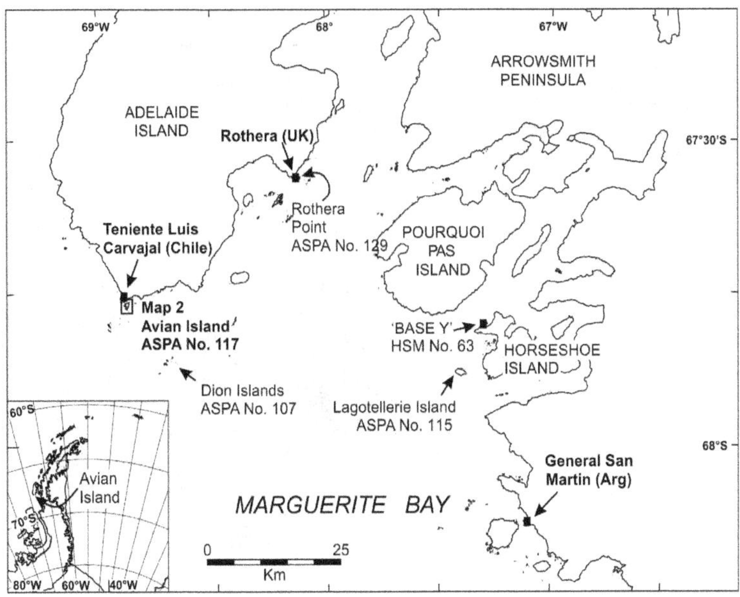

Map 2. Avian Island, ASPA No. 117, topographic map. Map specifications – projection: Lambert conformal conic; standard parallels: 1st 67° 30' 00"S; 2nd 68° 00' 00"S; central meridian: 68° 55' 00"W; latitude of origin: 68° 00' 00"S; spheroid: WGS84; datum: mean sea level; vertical contour interval 5 m; horizontal accuracy: ±5 m; vertical accuracy ±1.5 m.

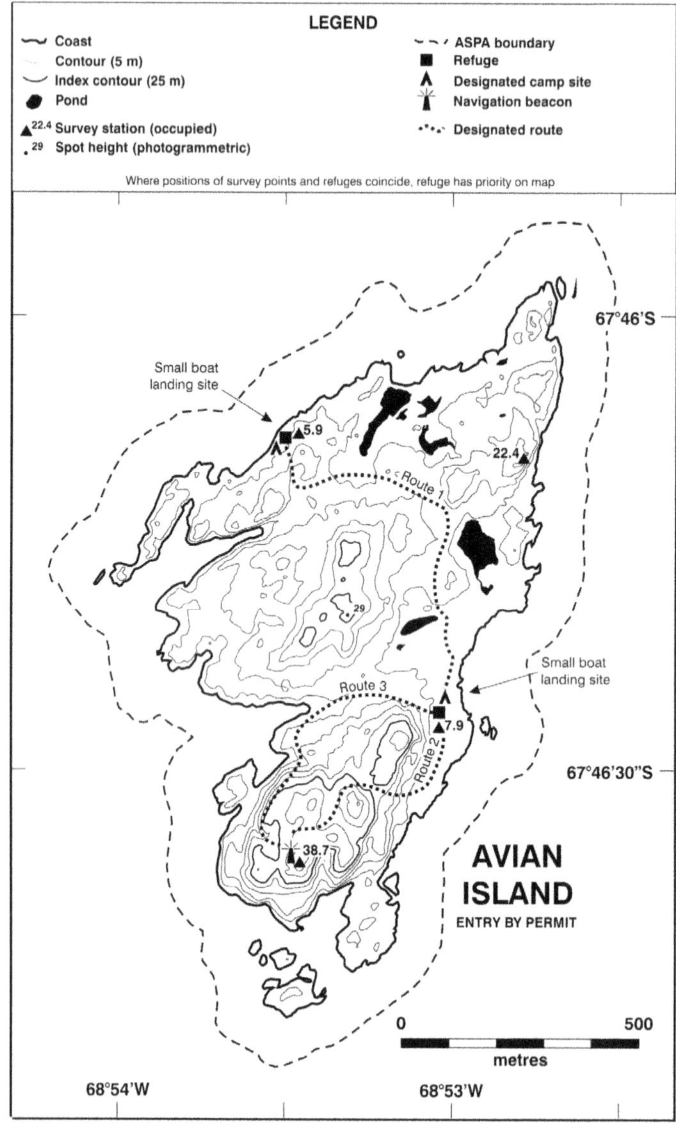

Map 3. Avian Island, ASPA No. 117, breeding wildlife sketch map. Positions of nests and colonies are accurate to ±25 m. Information was derived from Poncet (1982). Map specifications – projection: Lambert conformal conic; standard parallels: 1st 67° 30' 00"S; 2nd 68° 00' 00"S; central meridian: 68° 55' 00"W; latitude of origin: 68° 00' 00"S; spheroid: WGS84; datum: mean sea level; vertical contour interval 5 m; horizontal accuracy: ±5 m; vertical accuracy ±1.5 m.

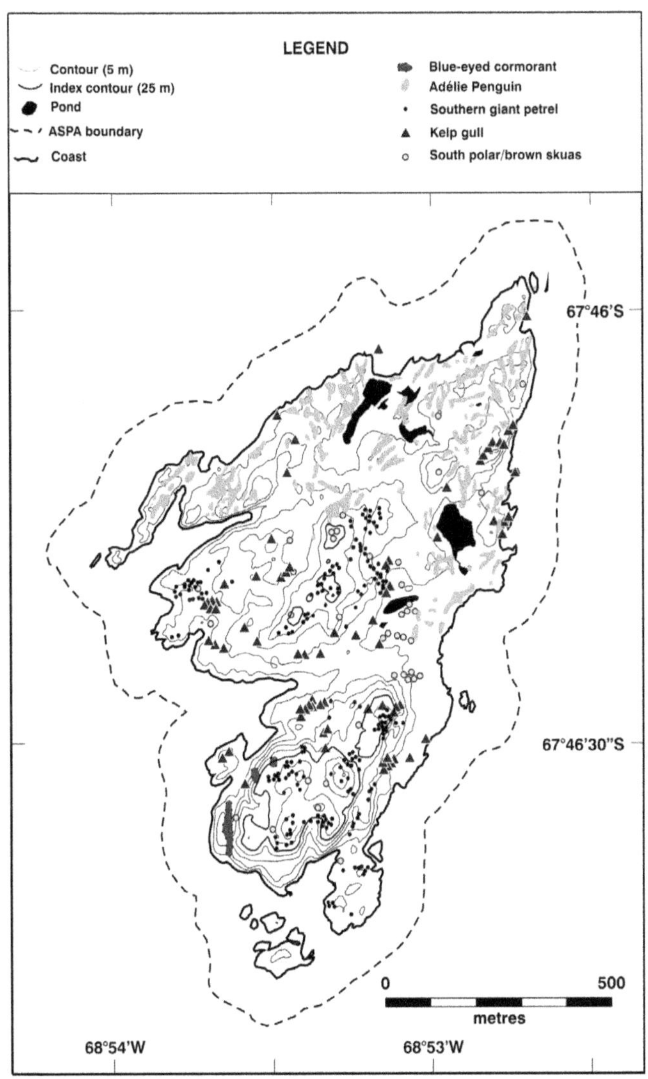

Management Plan for

Antarctic Specially Protected Area (ASPA) No. 123

BARWICK and BALHAM VALLEYS,

SOUTHERN VICTORIA LAND

Introduction

The Barwick and Balham Valleys are located within Antarctic Specially Managed Area (ASMA) No. 2 McMurdo Dry Valleys, Victoria Land, Ross Sea. The Area is centered at 160° 57' E, 77° 21' S and is approximately 423 km^2 in area. The Barwick and Balham Valleys are rarely visited and are an important reference area for comparing changes in other Dry Valley ecosystems which are regularly visited for scientific purposes. The Area contains examples of a wide variety of the environments found in the polar desert ecosystem. Some of the best examples of the physical surface features associated with this unique and extreme environment are found on the valley floors, where there are also fine examples of microbial life, lichens, as well as soil and lake microflora.

Barwick and Balham Valleys were originally designated as Site of Special Scientific Interest (SSSI) No. 3 through Recommendation VIII-4 (1975) after a proposal by the United States of America. A number of Recommendations extended the Management Plan expiry dates (Recommendation X-6 (1979), Recommendation XII-5 (1983), Recommendation XIII-7 (1985), and Resolution 7 (1995)). Measure 2 (2000) advanced the expiry date of the management plan from 31 December 2000 until 31 December 2005. Decision 1 (2002) renamed and renumbered SSSI No. 3 as Antarctic Specially Protected Area No. 123. Measure 1 (2002) designated the Area for an indefinite period, enlarged the original Area to include more of the Balham Valley catchment and rationalized it to exclude the Victoria Upper Glacier catchment. Measure 6 (2008) amended the Management Plan to include additional provisions to reduce the risk of microbial and vegetation introductions from soils at other Antarctic sites or from regions outside Antarctica. The 2013 review updated the literature, confirmed the values remain valid, improved the map of the Area, and made minor adjustments to provisions on aircraft access. Improved mapping enabled refinement of the boundary so that it follows the Barwick / Balham catchments more precisely.

The Area is classified as Environment S – McMurdo - South Victoria Land geologic, based on the Environmental Domains Analysis for Antarctica and is classified as Victoria Land South / Dry Valleys in the Antarctic Conservation Biogeographic Regions (ACBR) system.

1. Description of values to be protected

An area of 325 km^2 at Barwick Valley, including part of adjacent Balham Valley, was originally designated in Recommendation VIII-4 (1975, SSSI No. 3) after a proposal by the United States of America on the grounds that it was "one of the least disturbed and contaminated of the Dry Valleys of Victoria Land" and was important as a reference base against which to measure changes in comparable ecosystems of the other Dry Valleys where scientific investigations were being regularly conducted. The site remains distant from field stations and has not been subjected to intensive visitation or research. The Barwick Valley was first visited in 1958 and several subsequent expeditions were conducted in the 1960s through to 1975, after which time visits have been few because of the designation of the SSSI. Although some human impacts from these early expeditions were visible within the region in 1993-94, Barwick and Balham Valleys are believed to remain one of the least impacted areas in the Victoria Land Dry Valleys region of Antarctica.

The boundaries of the original Area were re-designed in Measure 1 (2002) so they followed the Barwick and Balham catchments more faithfully, resulting in a total area of 418 km^2 (correction from 480 km^2, an error in Measure 1 (2002)), which were again adopted without change in Measure 6 (2008). The current Management

Plan has refined the catchment boundaries further based on improved mapping data, resulting in a slight increase in total area from 418 km^2 to 423 km^2.

The Victoria Land Dry Valleys have a unique and extreme polar desert ecosystem. The Area contains examples of a wide variety of the environments found in this ecosystem, including desert pavements, sand dunes, patterned ground, glacial and moraine features, streams, freshwater and saline lakes, valleys and high-altitude ice-free ground. Some of the best examples of ventifact pavements and weathering-pitted dolerites are found on the valley floors, along with examples of chasmolithic lichens, layered communities of endolithic lichens, fungi, algae and associated bacteria, and populations of soil and lake microflora. Special protection of the Area provides the opportunity to conserve a relatively pristine example of this ecosystem as a baseline for future reference. Protection on a catchment basis serves to provide greater representation of the ecosystem features, and also facilitates management of the Area as a geographically distinct and integrated ecological system. The high ecological values, as well as the scientific, aesthetic and wilderness values derived from the isolation and relatively low level of human impact are important reasons for special protection at Barwick and Balham Valleys.

2. Aims and objectives

Management at Barwick and Balham Valleys aims to:

- avoid degradation of, or substantial risk to, the values of the Area by preventing unnecessary human disturbance to the Area;
- conserve the natural ecosystem as a reference area largely undisturbed by direct human activities;
- allow scientific research on the natural ecosystem and physical environment in the Area provided it is for compelling reasons which cannot be served elsewhere;
- minimize human disturbance to the Area by preventing unnecessary sampling;
- prevent or minimize the introduction to the Area of alien plants, animals and microbes;
- allow visits for management purposes in support of the aims of the management plan.

3. Management activities

The following management activities shall be undertaken to protect the values of the Area:

- Signs showing the location of the Area (stating the special restrictions that apply) shall be displayed prominently, and a copy of this Management Plan shall be kept available, at permanent scientific stations located within the Ross Sea region;
- All pilots operating in the region shall be informed of the location, boundaries and restrictions applying to entry, overflight and landings within the Area;
- National programs shall take steps to ensure the boundaries of the Area and the restrictions that apply within are marked on relevant maps and nautical / aeronautical charts;
- Markers, signs or structures erected within the Area for scientific or management purposes shall be secured and maintained in good condition, and removed when no longer required;
- Any abandoned equipment or materials shall be removed to the maximum extent possible provided doing so does not adversely impact on the environment and the values of the Area;
- Visits shall be made as necessary to assess whether the Area continues to serve the purposes for which it was designated and to ensure management and maintenance measures are adequate;
- National Antarctic Programs operating in the region shall consult together with a view to ensuring the above management activities are implemented.

4. Period of designation

Designated for an indefinite period.

5. Maps

Map 1: ASPA No. 123 Barwick and Balham Valleys – topography and boundary.

Map specifications: Projection: Lambert conformal conic; Standard parallels: 1st 77° 15' S; 2nd 77° 25' S; Central Meridian: 161° 10' E; Latitude of Origin: 78° 00' S; Spheroid and datum: WGS84.

Inset 1: Ross Sea region, showing the location of the McMurdo Dry Valleys and Inset 2.

Inset 2: McMurdo Dry Valleys and Ross Island, showing location of McMurdo Station (US) and Scott Base (NZ), Antarctic Specially Managed Area No. 2 McMurdo Dry Valleys (ASMA No.2).

6. Description of the Area

6(i) Geographical coordinates, boundary markers and natural features

Barwick Valley (161° 57' E, 77° 21' S) is situated about 65 km inland from the Ross Sea coast of southern Victoria Land (Map 1 and Insets). The Area includes Barwick and Balham Valleys and their respective catchments and is bordered on the south, west and north by the McKelvey Valley, the Willet Range and the divide between the Victoria and Barwick Valleys, respectively.

The boundary of the Area extends from its eastern extremity in the lower Barwick Valley (around the confluence of the Barwick, Victoria and McKelvey Valleys) several kilometers south towards the ridge leading SW to the summit of Mount Insel (1345 m, 161 30.74' E, 77 23.50' S), from where the boundary follows the high points of the ridge of the Insel Range over Halzen Mesa for 5.5 km before descending to a low pass between the McKelvey and Balham Valleys at the location of Bullseye Lake (722 m, 161° 14.41' E, 77° 24.78' S). The boundary crosses the lake before ascending the ridge to a further high point on Canfield Mesa on the Insel Range (approximately 1250 m), and continues over Green Mesa to follow Rude Spur to Mount Cassidy (1917 m) and onwards to the upper reaches of the Balham Valley. As the terrain becomes gentler in the upper Balham and approximately 6.5 km southeast of the summit of Shapeless Mountain (2736 m), the boundary extends northward at an elevation of between 1800 – 1900 m towards the Huka Kapo Glacier and Apocalypse Peaks. The boundary extends NW from the Huka Kapo Glacier for approximately 9 km towards a prominent ridge leading to the summit of Mount Bastion (2477 m, 160°29.39' E, 77°19.18' S). This ridge is followed in a northerly direction to the top of McSaveney Spur, thence follows the upper ridgeline of the cirque containing Webb Icefall to the summit of Vishniac Peak (2280 m, 160° 31.82'E, 77° 14.71' S). The boundary thence follows the main ridge northeast for 5 km to the summit of Skew Peak (2537 m, 160° 42.07'E, 77° 13.16' S), located at the head of the Barwick Valley. The boundary then descends along the east ridge of Skew Peak above Webb Cirque, before following the catchment boundary in a more southerly direction to Parker Mesa. From Parker Mesa the boundary descends further to follow the upper ridge of The Fortress and the Cruzon Range, which is the dividing ridge between the catchments of the Victoria Upper Glacier and the Barwick Valley. The boundary extends east along this ridge for ~12 km via Loewenstein Peak (1539 m) and Shulman Peak (1400 m) to Sponsors Peak (1454 m, 161°24.4' E, 77°18.2' S). The boundary descends the SE ridge of Sponsors Peak and Nickell Peak (approximately 1400 m, 161° 28.25' E 77° 19.21' E) to the lower Barwick to the eastern extremity of the Area, which is about 4 km northwest of Lake Vida, Victoria Valley.

An extensive névé south of Skew Peak feeds the Webb Glacier in the upper Barwick Valley. Very little ice from the Polar Plateau flows over the scarp into the Barwick Valley, as flow vectors and debris cover patterns on the Webb Glacier in this location indicate that this part of the glacier is almost stationary. The Barwick and Balham Valleys merge in the southeast of the Area, 9 km from where the Barwick joins the Victoria Valley. A series of lakes occupy the Barwick Valley, the largest being Webb Lake (approximate elevation 658 m) at the snout of Webb Glacier. Lake Vashka (approximate elevation 476 m), partially filling an unusually deep circular depression (Chinn 1993), is the second largest and 5.7 km down-valley from Webb Lake. Hourglass Lake (approximate elevation 617 m), the next largest, is approximately half way between Webb Lake and Lake Vashka. An intermittent stream connecting this series of lakes terminates at Lake Vashka, which has a level well below its overflow threshold. Early observations of the smooth surfaces of Lakes Webb and Vashka suggested that they are 'ice-block' lakes that contain no significant liquid water (Chinn 1993). However, liquid water up to several meters in depth was observed at the perimeter of Lake Vashka in December 1993. Recent studies on the physical features of any of the Barwick Valley lakes have not been made. Lake Balham, a small lake in a depression (671 m elevation) below Apocalypse Peaks, is the only lake in Balham Valley (generally around 800 m in elevation).

Multiple glaciations, mainly between 13 Ma and 3.5 Ma ago, have resulted in a thick ground moraine on both valley floors (Péwé 1960). These deposits are mantled by solifluction sheets at the head of Balham Valley. In addition the valleys bear a small number of fresh and saline lakes on the drift surfaces. In many cases the lakes have evaporated to leave extensive salt deposits. The walls of Barwick and Balham Valleys display remnants of glacial benches at about 800 m and 1,200-1,500 m altitude (Bull *et al.* 1962). The soils near Lake Vashka consist of moraine debris derived largely from dolerite and sandstone, but granites, gneiss and schist make up as much as 35% of boulders locally (Claridge 1965). Weathering is often indicated by deep red staining due to oxidation of iron compounds, usually eroded by wind-driven sand on the boulders' windward side (Claridge & Campbell 1984). The valley floors are extensively covered with patterned ground of sand-wedge polygons, typical of permafrost areas in the Dry Valleys (Campbell & Claridge 1987). The majority is old (high centered), with young (hollow centered) polygons found in recent stream channels, and both typically measure 20 m across.

No invertebrates have been found in the dry soils of the Barwick Valley and there is little obvious vegetation (Freckman & Virginia 1998). Algal crusts and mats fringe the lakes and streams but the flora reported is essentially microbial: chasmolithic lichens are present in jagged screes of the Apocalypse Range and dense layered communities of endolithic lichens, fungi, algae and associated bacteria are occasionally found in boulders of Beacon Sandstone (Edwards *et al.* 1998, 2005). Black lichen growth is reported to be well developed in areas of sandstone on the valley floor of Balham Valley (Russell *et al.* 1998). Significant heterotrophic bacterial populations have been reported in sandy samples from Barwick Valley. The population contained lactose-fermenters, nitrate-reducers, nitrogen-fixers, yeasts and algae but no detectable filamentous fungi or Protozoa (Cowan *et al.* 2002).

While the Barwick and Balham Valleys are one of the most remote areas of the Dry Valleys, south polar skuas (*Catharacta maccormicki*) are known to visit the Area, with about 40 carcasses found at Lake Vashka in 1959-60. The mummified carcasses of two seals have been found near the snout of Webb Glacier, and seven more, mainly crabeaters (*Lobodon carcinophagus*) were found near the Balham / Barwick Valley junction (Dort 1981).

Inspection of the Barwick and Balham Valleys in December 1993 from Bullseye Lake to Lake Vashka revealed evidence of prior human activity, particularly around Lake Vashka where field camps had been in use for scientific research in the 1960s. Impacts observed in the Lake Vashka vicinity included stone circles for tents at old camp sites, soil pits and a trench, remains of a wooden crate, a wooden box containing rocks and a paper poster, and a broken food cache partially submerged in the lake (Harris 1994). Bamboo poles are situated near the snout of Webb Glacier and at Vashka Crag. Dynamite charges have been used in the vicinity of Lake Vashka and at least one other unknown location in the Barwick Valley. Remediation of the site was carried out in 1995/96 by a New Zealand team.

The only visit made to the Area since the last Management Plan review (2008) was by a New Zealand team of two persons between 6-13 January 2012 to map the spatial distribution of soils in Barwick and Balham valleys. The team made small, shallow excavations to determine soil properties, which were carefully remediated and their positions were recorded by GPS (Antarctica NZ 2012). The team camped at a previously established site near Lake Vashka (161° 09.284' E, 77° 20.931' S) (Map 1). Walking routes and sampling sites were kept to the minimum to accomplish objectives and sensitive areas were avoided. Precautions were taken to minimize the risk of introduction of non-native species by cleaning equipment, and all wastes were removed. The team made observations of former soil excavations at three locations (161° 08.822' E, 77° 20.951' S; 161° 09.078' E, 77° 20.989' S; and 161° 09.085' E, 77° 20.989' S). No structures were observed within the Area and the team noted that the sites visited appeared to remain pristine. A poster enclosed in a map roll at Lake Vashka (recording names of visitors to Lake Vashka and observed in December 1993 (Harris 1994)) was removed from the Area because it was deteriorating.

6 (ii) Access to the area

The Area may be accessed by traversing over land or ice, or by air. Particular access routes have not been designated for entering the Area. Access restrictions apply within the Area, the specific conditions for which are set out in Section 7(ii) below.

6(iii) Location of structures within and adjacent to the Area

There are no structures within or near the Area.

6(iv) Location of other protected areas in the vicinity

Barwick and Balham Valleys lie within Antarctic Specially Managed Area (ASMA) No.2, McMurdo Dry Valleys. The nearest protected areas to Barwick and Balham Valleys are Linnaeus Terrace (ASPA No.138) 35 km south in the Wright Valley, and Canada Glacier (ASPA No.131) and Lower Taylor Glacier and Blood Falls (ASPA No. 172), both of which are approximately 45 km southeast in the Taylor Valley (Inset 2, Map 1).

6 (v) Special zones within the Area

There are no special zones within the Area.

7. Terms and conditions for entry permits

7 (i) General permit conditions

Entry into the Area is prohibited except in accordance with a permit issued by an appropriate national authority. Conditions for issuing a permit to enter the Area are that:

- it is issued for compelling scientific reasons that cannot be served elsewhere, or for reasons essential to the management of the Area;
- the actions permitted are in accordance with this Management Plan;
- the activities permitted will give due consideration via the environmental impact assessment process to the continued protection of the environmental, ecological, scientific, aesthetic and wilderness values of the Area, including the pristine value of the Area and its potential as a largely undisturbed reference site;
- the permit shall be issued for a finite period;
- the permit, or a copy, shall be carried when in the Area.

7(ii) Access to, and movement within or over, the Area

Access to and movement within the Area shall be on foot or by aircraft. Vehicles are prohibited within the Area.

Access on foot

- Pedestrians are encouraged to access the Area at a practicable point closest to the site(s) they are visiting to minimize the amount of the Area that is traversed;
- Pedestrian routes should avoid lakes, ponds, stream beds, areas of damp ground and areas of soft sediments or dunes;
- Pedestrian traffic should be kept to the minimum necessary consistent with the objectives of any permitted activities and every reasonable effort should be made to minimize effects.

Access by aircraft

- Aircraft landings within the Area are prohibited unless authorized by permit for purposes allowed for by the Management Plan;
- Aircraft overflight below 2000 feet (~610 m) is prohibited unless authorized by permit for purposes allowed for by the Management Plan.

7(iii) Activities that may be conducted within the Area

- Compelling scientific research that cannot be undertaken elsewhere and will not jeopardize the values of the Area, or its pristine value and potential as a reference site;
- Essential management activities, including monitoring and inspection.

7(iv) Installation, modification or removal of structures / equipment

- No structures are to be erected within the Area except as specified in a permit;
- Permanent structures are prohibited;
- All structures, scientific equipment or markers installed in the Area shall be authorized by permit and clearly identified by country, name of the principal investigator, year of installation and date of expected removal. All such items should be free of organisms, propagules (e.g. seeds, eggs) and non-sterile soil, and be made of materials that can withstand the environmental conditions and pose minimal risk of contamination of the Area;
- Installation (including site selection), maintenance, modification or removal of structures or equipment shall be undertaken in a manner that minimizes disturbance to the values of the Area;
- Removal of specific structures / equipment for which the permit has expired shall be the responsibility of the authority which granted the original permit, and shall be a condition of the permit.

7(v) Location of field camps

Camping should generally be avoided within the Area, and two campsites outside of, but close to, the east and south boundaries are identified for access into the Area. One of these is at the confluence of the lower Barwick and Victoria Valleys (161° 41.25' E, 77° 21.75' S), while the other is close to Bullseye Lake in the McKelvey Valley (161° 13.13' E, 77° 25.67' S) (see Map 1). If deemed to be essential, camping should be at previously impacted sites, preferably on snow or ice-covered ground if available. One such previously established camp site is located on slopes ~150 m above the SW shore of Lake Vashka (161° 09.284' E, 77° 20.931' S) (Map 1), which is marked by a circle of stones, and this site should be used to meet research needs as appropriate. Researchers should consult with the appropriate national authority to obtain up-to-date information on any other sites where camping may be preferred.

7(vi) Restrictions on materials and organisms which may be brought into the Area

In addition to the requirements of the Protocol on Environmental Protection to the Antarctic Treaty, restrictions on materials and organisms which may be brought into the area are:

- Deliberate introduction of animals, plant material, micro-organisms and non-sterile soil into the Area is prohibited. Precautions shall be taken to prevent the accidental introduction of animals, plant material, micro-organisms and non-sterile soil from other biologically distinct regions (within or beyond the Antarctic Treaty area);
- Visitors shall ensure that scientific equipment, particularly for sampling, and markers brought into the Area are clean. To the maximum extent practicable, footwear and other equipment used or brought into the area (including backpacks, carry-bags and tents) shall be thoroughly cleaned before entering the Area. Visitors should also consult and follow as appropriate recommendations contained in the Committee for Environmental Protection Non-native Species Manual (CEP 2011), and in the Environmental Code of Conduct for terrestrial scientific field research in Antarctica (SCAR 2009);
- To reduce the risk of microbial contamination, the exposed surfaces of footwear, sampling equipment and markers should, to the greatest extent practical, be sterilized before use within the Area. Sterilization should be by an acceptable method, such as by washing in 70% ethanol solution in water or in a commercially available solution such as 'Virkon';
- No herbicides or pesticides shall be brought into the Area;
- The use of explosives is prohibited within the Area;
- Fuel, food, chemicals, and other materials shall not be stored in the Area, unless specifically authorized by permit and shall be stored and handled in a way that minimises the risk of their accidental introduction into the environment;
- All materials introduced shall be for a stated period only and shall be removed by the end of that stated period; and
- If release occurs which is likely to compromise the values of the Area, removal is encouraged only where the impact of removal is not likely to be greater than that of leaving the material *in situ*.

7(vii) Taking of, or harmful interference with, native flora or fauna

Taking of, or harmful interference with, native flora and fauna is prohibited, except in accordance with Annex II of the Protocol on Environmental Protection to the Antarctic Treaty.

Where animal taking or harmful interference with animals is involved, this should, as a minimum standard, be in accordance with the SCAR Code of Conduct for the Use of Animals for Scientific Purposes in Antarctica.

7(viii) Collection or removal of anything not brought into the Area by the permit holder

Material may be collected or removed from the Area only in accordance with a permit and should be limited to the minimum necessary to meet scientific or management needs. Material of human origin likely to compromise the values of the Area, which was not brought into the Area by the permit holder or otherwise authorized, may be removed unless the impact of removal is likely to be greater than leaving the material *in situ*. If this is the case the appropriate authority must be notified and approval obtained.

7(ix) Disposal of waste

All wastes, including water used for any human purpose and including all human wastes, shall be removed from the Area.

7(x) Measures that may be necessary to continue to meet the aims of the Management Plan

Permits may be granted to enter the Area to:

- carry out monitoring and Area inspection activities, which may involve the collection of a small number of samples or data for analysis or review;
- install or maintain signposts, markers, structures or scientific equipment;
- carry out protective measures.

7(xi) Requirements for reports

- The principal permit holder for each visit to the Area shall submit a report to the appropriate national authority as soon as practicable, and no later than six months after the visit has been completed.
- Such reports should include, as appropriate, the information identified in the visit report form contained in the Guide to the Preparation of Management Plans for Antarctic Specially Protected Areas. If appropriate, the national authority should also forward a copy of the visit report to the Party that proposed the Management Plan, to assist in managing the Area and reviewing the Management Plan.
- Parties should, wherever possible, deposit originals or copies of such original visit reports in a publicly accessible archive to maintain a record of usage, for the purpose of any review of the Management Plan and in organising the scientific use of the Area.
- The appropriate authority should be notified of any activities/measures undertaken, and / or of any materials released and not removed, that were not included in the authorized Permit.

8. Supporting documentation

Antarctica New Zealand 2012. Antarctic Specially Protected Area Visit Report. Unpublished report by M. McLeod on visit made to Barwick and Balham Valleys in January 2012. Antarctica NZ, Christchurch.

Bull, C., McKelvey, B.C. & Webb, P.N. 1962. Quaternary Glaciations in Southern Victoria Land, Antarctica. *Journal of Glaciology* **4** (31): 63-78.

Campbell, I.B. & Claridge, G.G.C. 1987. *Antarctica: Soils, weathering processes and environment. Developments in Soil Science* **16**. Elsevier Science Publishers, Amsterdam.

Chinn, T.J. 1993. Physical Hydrology of the Dry Valley Lakes. In Green, W.J. & Friedmann, E.I. (eds) Physical and biogeochemical processes in Antarctic Lakes. *Antarctic Research Series* **59**:1-51. American Geophysical Union, Washington, D.C.

Claridge, G.G.C. 1965. The clay mineralogy and chemistry of some soils from the Ross Dependency, Antarctica. *New Zealand Journal of Geology and Geophysics* **8** (2):186-220.

Claridge, G.G.C. & Campbell, I.B. 1984. Mineral transformations during the weathering of dolerite under cold arid conditions. *New Zealand Journal of Geology and Geophysics* **27**: 533-45.

Committee for Environmental Protection (CEP) 2011. *Non-native Species Manual – 1st Edition.* Manual prepared by Intersessional Contact Group of the CEP and adopted by the Antarctic Treaty Consultative Meeting through Resolution 6 (2011). Buenos Aires: Secretariat of the Antarctic Treaty.

Cowan, D.A., Russell, N.J., Mamais, A. & Sheppard, D.M. 2002. Antarctic Dry Valley mineral soils contain unexpectedly high levels of microbial biomass. *Extremophiles* **6** (5): 431-36.

Dort, W., Jr. 1981. The mummified seals of southern Victoria Land, Antarctica. In Parker, B., Ed. Terrestrial Biology III, *Antarctic Research Series* **30**: 123–54. American Geophysical Union, Washington, D.C.

Edwards, H.G.M., Moody, C.D., Jorge Villar, S.E. & Wynn-Williams, D.D. 2005. Raman spectroscopic detection of key biomarkers of cyanobacteria and lichen symbiosis in extreme Antarctic habitats: Evaluation for Mars lander missions. *Icarus* **174**: 560-71.

Edwards, H.G.M., Russell, N.C. & Wynn-Williams, D.D. 1997. Fourier Transform Raman spectroscopic and scanning electron microscopic study of cryptoendolithic lichens from Antarctica. *Journal of Raman Spectroscopy* **28** (9): 685–90.

Freckman, D.W. & Virginia, R.A. 1998. Soil Biodiversity and Community Structure in the McMurdo Dry Valleys, Antarctica. In Priscu, J., Ed.. Ecosystem Dynamics in a Polar Desert, The McMurdo Dry Valleys, Antarctica. *Antarctic Research Series* **72**: 323–35. American Geophysical Union, Washington, D.C.

Harris, C.M. 1994. Ross Sea Protected Areas 1993/94 Visit Report. Unpublished report on inspection visits to protected areas in the Ross Sea. International Centre for Antarctic Information and Research, Christchurch.

Péwé, T.L. 1960. Multiple glaciation in the McMurdo Sound region, Antarctica – A progress report. *Journal of Geology* **68** (5): 498-514.

Russell, N.C., Edwards, H.G.M. and Wynn-Williams, D.D. 1998. FT-Raman spectroscopic analysis of endolithic microbial communities from Beacon sandstone in Victoria Land, Antarctica. *Antarctic Science* **10** (1): 63-74.

SCAR (Scientific Committee on Antarctic Research) 2009. *Environmental Code of Conduct for terrestrial scientific field research in Antarctica.* Cambridge, SCAR.

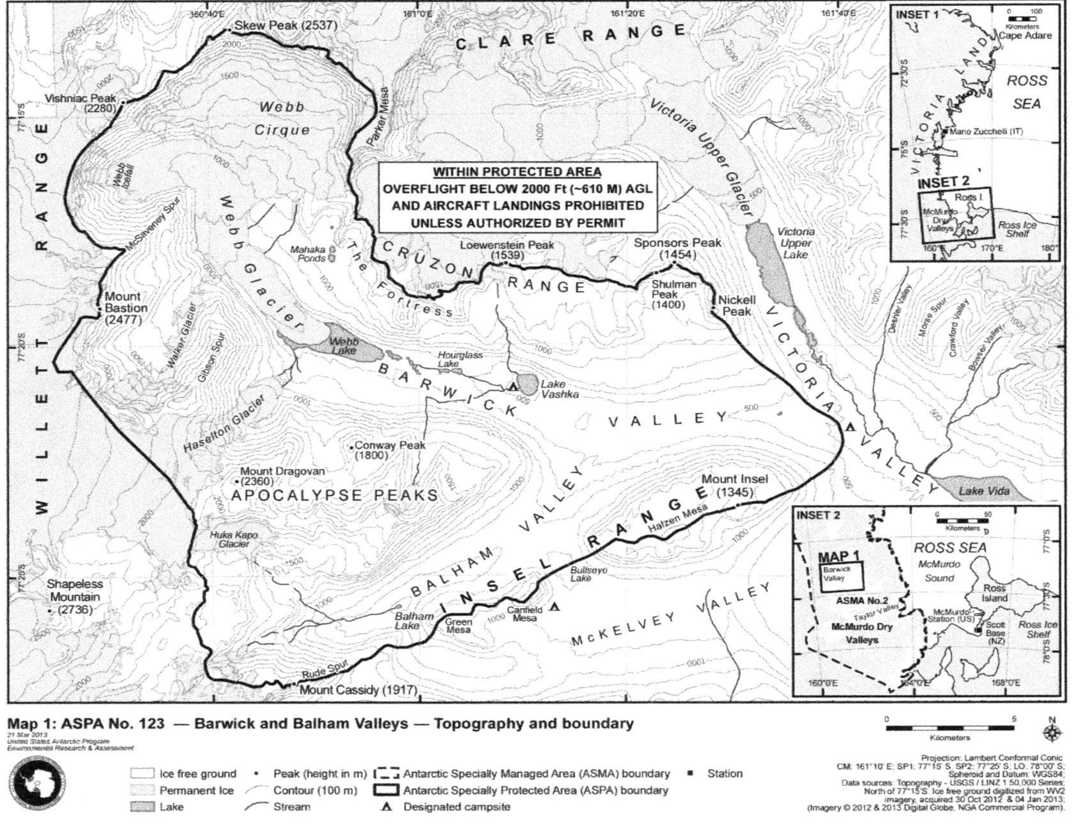

Map 1: ASPA No. 123 — Barwick and Balham Valleys — Topography and boundary

Ice free ground; Permanent Ice; Lake; • Peak (height in m); Contour (100 m); Stream; Antarctic Specially Managed Area (ASMA) boundary; Antarctic Specially Protected Area (ASPA) boundary; Δ Designated campsite; ■ Station

Management Plan for Antarctic Specially Protected Area No. 132

POTTER PENINSULA

Introduction

This area was originally designated as Site of Special Scientific Interest No. 13 in ATCM Recommendation XIII-8, following a proposal by Argentina, given its diverse and extensive vegetation and fauna, which constitutes a representative sample of the Antarctic ecosystem.

In 1997, the Management Plan was adapted to the requirements of Annex V of the Protocol on Environmental Protection to the Antarctic Treaty, and approved through Measure 3 (1997). This version consists of the revision to the Management Plan approved pursuant to Measure 2 (2005), and this is the second revision since entry into force of Annex V.

The original goals for designating this Area are still relevant. Potter Peninsula is designated as an Antarctic Specially Protected Area to protect its outstanding environmental values and to facilitate ongoing and planned scientific research. The anthropic disturbance could jeopardise the long-term studies conducted in the Area, especially during the breeding season.

The main reason for the ASPA designation is that Potter Peninsula constitutes a representative sample of assemblages of species of the Antarctic ecosystem. The coastal areas host important bird colonies, marine mammal breeding areas and diverse vegetal species. It has a great scientific value since several studies about the impacts of the climate change in the biotic and abiotic factors as well as its consequences in the food web can be conducted in the area (e.g. Carlini *et al.* 2009, Carlini *et al.* 2010, Casaux *et al.* 2006, Daneri and Carlini 1999, Rombolá *et al.* 2010, Torres *et al.* 2012). It is crucial to keep these scientific activities, like the monitoring program that is being conducted since 1982, including the CCAMLR Ecosystem Monitoring Programme, as it can produce invaluable scientific data to this purpose.

There are several features that make this area particularly susceptible to human interference, like the configuration of the zone, that is, a relatively narrow coastal area, enclosed between the sea and a cliff, where there is no area for movement that do not interfere with the breeding colonies. The high concentration of activities, scientific stations and the easy land and marine accessibility to the area, even if it is through small vessels, represent a potential threat to the biological values and the research activities.

The environmental situation in the South Shetland Islands, according to recent studies, shows that the portion of the Southern Ocean near Potter Peninsula has been severely altered, first by almost complete extraction of once unimaginably abundant fish- and krill-eating fur seals (*Arctocephalus* spp.) followed by balleen whales. More recently, fur seals have largely recovered and baleen whales are beginning to do so (Ainley *et al.* 2010), but climate change is increasingly altering ecological processes through physical changes in temperature, water circulation and sea ice extension among others . As a result of reduced prey, not only to climate change and recovering competitors, but also others factors currently unknown, penguin populations are decreasing (Ducklow *et al.* 2007, Ainley and Blight 2009, Ainley *et al.* 2010, Trivelpiece *et al.* 2010). In this sense, currently, the ASPA 132 has acquired special relevance, given that the study of Adelie penguin colonies present in the Area offers responses to environmental changes observed in the Antarctic Peninsula, especially the lower frequency of cold years associated to the reduction of sea ice extensions, and its effects in the abundance of krill.

Potter Peninsula also provides exceptional opportunities for other scientific studies of terrestrial and marine biological communities.

Among the researches that are currently being conducted at ASPA 132 are:

- Coastal Biomonitoring: effect of global climate change and xenobiotics on Antarctic food webs key species.
- Persistent organic pollutants and trace elements in biotic and abiotic matrices of the Antarctic environment.
- Energy Acquisition, prey type and potential responses of Pinnepeds to climate anomalies and sea ice extent in the Antarctic Peninsula Region and the Scotia Arc
- Response of Antarctic bird populations to the interannual variability of their prey in areas with obvious global warming effects
- *Deschampsia Antartica* phylogeography based on molecular, morphological and karyological studies
- Distribution and nutritional status of Brown Skuas and South Polar Skuas.

1. Description of values to be protected

The coastal areas host important bird colonies, marine mammal breeding colonies and profuse vegetation (vast moss carpets in coastal areas and lichen forests in rocky areas). Scientific research programmes on the breeding ecology of elephant seals (*Mirounga leonina*), the Adelie penguin (*Pygoscelis adeliae)* and the gentoo *(Pygoscelis papua*), including the CCAMLR Ecosystem Monitoring Programme, among others, have been developed in the area since 1982. The breeding colonies are sited at a particular coastal location. The area mainly comprises raised beaches, largely covered with mid-sized pebbles, basaltic structures and lateral and terminal moraines. The shoreline is very irregular and it has a number of small bays shaped among rocky headlands. The above reasons, gives the area an exceptional scientific and aesthetic value.

According to Morgan *et al.* (2007) ASPA 132 represents “Antarctic Peninsula offshore islands” Environmental Domain. Also, according to Terauds *et al.* (2012), the area represents the region "North-west Antarctic Peninsula" from the "Antarctic Conservation Biogeographic Regions classification.

For more detailed characteristics please see section 6

2. Aims and Objectives

- Preserve the natural ecosystem and prevent unnecessary human disturbance;
- Permit the development of any scientific research provided it does not compromise the values awarding protection to the Area;
- Avoid major changes in the structure and composition of the flora and fauna communities;
- Prevent or minimise the introduction to the Area of alien plants, animals and microbes;
- Minimise the possibility of introduction of pathogens which may bring disease to fauna populations within the Area.

3. Management Activities

- The staff to be posted at Carlini Base (former Jubany Base, Argentine base adjacent to the ASPA), in particular, staff authorised to enter the ASPA, will be specifically trained on the conditions of the Management Plan;
- Copies of this Management Plan shall be available at the Carlini Base.
- Approach distances to fauna should be respected, except when scientific projects may require otherwise, and provided that the relevant permits have been issued.
- Collection of samples will be limited to the minimum required for the development of authorised scientific research plans.
- All markers and structures erected within the ASPA for scientific or management purposes shall be properly secured and maintained in good conditions.
- In accordance with the requirements of Annex III of the Protocol on Environmental Protection to the Antarctic Treaty, abandoned equipment or materials shall be removed to the maximum extent possible provided doing so does not adversely impact on the environment and the values of the Area.
- The Management Plan shall be reviewed no less than once every five years and updated as required.
- All pilots operating in the region shall be informed of the location, boundaries and restrictions applying to entry and over-flight in the Area.

4. Period of designation

Designated for an indefinite period.

5. Maps

Map 1, included at the end of this Management Plan, shows the location of ASPA 132 (in diagonal lines) in relation to the Potter Peninsula (King George Island).

6. Description of the Area

6(i) Geographical coordinates and boundaries and natural features

Geographical coordinates and boundaries

This Area is located on the east coast of Maxwell Bay, southwest of King George Island, between the southern tip of Mirounga Point (Northwest of Potter Peninsula) and the outcrop known as "Spur 7", on the north-eastern border of Stranger Point. The area stretches along the coastal strip up at low tide water levels up to the cliff edge, which reaches heights of 15-50 metres. The front of the cliff edge is included within the ASPA. This coastal strip has a variable width, stretching up to 500 metres from the shore at low tide water levels. The Area mainly comprises raised beaches, largely covered with mid-sized pebbles, basaltic structures and lateral and terminal moraines. The shoreline is very irregular and it has a number of small bays shaped among rocky headlands.

This topography constitutes a natural boundary for the settlement of the breeding colonies of marine mammal and penguin, justifying the ASPA extension.

6(ii) Natural features

The area encompasses important scientific values due to the presence of breeding colonies of elephant seals *(Mirounga leonina)*, and non-breeding groups of Antarctic fur seals *(Arctocephalus gazella)* and occasionally of Weddell seals *(Leptonychotes weddelli)*, crabeater seals *(Lobodon carcinophagus)* and leopard seals *(Hydrurga leptonyx).* The breeding season brings together around 400 elephant seals, and between 200 and 600 during the fledging season. The non-breeding groups of Antarctic fur seals can add up to 300 individuals, although that figure may vary considerably from one year to the next.

Also present are significant colonies of gentoo penguins *(Pygoscelis papua)* and Adelie penguins *(Pygoscelis adeliae),* with 3800 and 3000 pairs, respectively. The population of storm petrels (mostly *Oceanites oceanicus* and, to a much lesser extent, the *Fregetta tropica)* reaches some 200 pairs. Kelp gulls (*Larus dominicanus*), Sheathbills *(Chionis alba),* Antarctic terns *(Sterna vittata),* southern giant petrels *(Macronectes giganteus)* and skuas *(Catharacta sp.)* also breed in the area. Given that some of the nesting sites around Potter Peninsula change their position over time, population figures are estimations.

Adelia and gentoo penguins are distributed around Stranger Point, between the Elefante shelter and Spur 7. Mammal concentrations are distributed along the coastline, between Spur 1 and Spur 7, and giant petrels nesting sites are usually distributed between Spur 7 and Spur 4 (see Map 1). There is an abundant development of plant communities in the Area, dominated by lichens and mosses, on rocky slopes and on the flat surfaces of paleo-beaches, respectively.

Natural features. Flora

The spatial pattern of vegetation is the combination of related variable: substrate type, exposure, slope stability and drainage (water availability). The Potter Peninsula comprises an area of several square kilometres free of permanent snow and ice coverage. Relatively stable substrate is found around the Three Brothers Hills. Moraines near the glacier are only sparsely covered by plants, whilst the vegetation coverage and species richness increase with the distance to the moraines. A plateau located south-west of the Three Brother Hills is covered by an exceptional rich vegetation. It consists in two layers of plants that can reach 100% coverage. Several moss and lichen species found on the Potter Peninsula are restricted to that area. The two native Antarctic vascular plants *Colobanthus quifensis* and *Deschampsia antarctica* are likely to be found near the coast or in places with high nutrient supply.

Pleurocarpous mosses such as *Sanionia uncinata* and *Calliergon sarmentosum* dominate, while rocks are commonly covered by the crustose lichen *Lecidea sciatrapha.* Higher up on the slope, where the ground is better drained and the snow coverage time is shorter, cushion forming mosses like *Andreaea regularis* and *Andreaea gainii* dominate, often together with *Himantormia lugubris.* Associations of Bryophilous lichens such as *Psoroma hypnorum* and a number of acrocarpous mosses are also frequently found. Where snow coverage rarely exceeds 10 cm, even in winter, a two layered canopy build of lichens and mosses is formed.

The upper layer is discontinuous and consists of fruticose lichens such as *Usnea aurantiaco-atra, U. antarctica* and *Pseudephebe pubescens.* The understorey consists in an assemblage of various species of mosses and hepatics. *U. aurantiaco-atra* and *Himantormia lugubris* are often interwoven mats of prostrate form without apothecia. In the apertures the dicranoid moss *Chorisodontium aciphyllum* and cushion forming fruticose lichens such as *Sphaerophorus globosus* are present. The most abundant bryophilous lichen is *Ochrolechia frigida.*(Wiencke *et al.* 1998)

6(iii) Access to the Area

Except for authorised exceptions, access to the Area shall be on foot, from the northern tip, close to the Carlini base helipad (62 ° 14' 17´´. S; 58 ° 40´42´´ W), or from behind the northern slope of the Three Brothers Hill (see Map 1). Access to the Area by sea onto the beaches should be avoided when there is fauna present, especially between October and December because it is concomitant with egg-laying and elephant seals breast feeding peak times.

Complementary information at section 7(ii)

6(iii) *Location of structures within and adjacent to the Area*

Structures within the area

Shelters: The Argentine shelter Elefante is located around 150 m from the coast, 1,000 metres northeast from Point Stranger. From March to October it is used by research groups conducting activities in the ASPA. The shelter can accommodate a maximum of 6 people (see section 7(ix) on Disposal of waste).

Signposts: signposts warning about the entrance to the Protected Area are located at: Mirounga Point (close to the helipad), at the north base of the Three Brothers Hill, and on the beach area close to Spur I. Signposts display information about the existence of the ASPA and the requirement to carry an access Permit.

Structures adjacent to the area

Carlini is a permanent Argentinean station located at 62 ° 14′ Lat. S and 58 ° 39′ Long. W, on Potter Cove, Potter Peninsula, in the SW portion of King George Island. It has several facilities including the Argentine-German *Dallmann* laboratory which is a entrepreneurship between the Alfred Wegener Institute (AWI) and the Argentinean Antarctic Institute (IAA).

Albatros is an Argentinean refuge located at 62°15'09" Lat. S and 58°39'23"Long. W / -62.2525, -58.65639 on Potter Cove, Potter Peninsula.

Other nearby stations are King Sejong, from Korea (62°13′ 394′′ S / 58° 47′190′′W) and Arctowsky from Poland, (62° 9′ 586′′S / 58° 28′ 399′′ W)

6(iv) Location of other Protected Areas within close proximity

- ASPA No. 125, Fildes Peninsula, King George Island (25 de Mayo), South Shetland Islands lies about 20km to the east.
- ASPA No. 128, Western Shore of Admiralty Bay, King George Island (25 de Mayo), South Shetland Islands lies about 10 km northeast.
- ASPA N° 171 Narębski Point (south-eastern coast of the Barton Peninsula, King George Island (25 de Mayo)
- ASPA No. 133, Harmony Point, Nelson Island, lies about 30 km west-southwest.

6(v) Special zones within the Area

No special zones are designated within the Area.

7. *Terms and conditions for entry permits*

7(i) General permit conditions

Access to the Area is prohibited except in accordance with a Permit issued by appropriate national authorities.

Conditions for the issuance of a Permit to access the Area:

- the activity serves a scientific, ASPA management or outreach purpose, consistent with Management Plan objectives, which may not be served anywhere else, and any management activities (inspection, maintenance or review) are in accordance with the Management Plan; the Permit is carried by staff authorised to access the Area
- a post-visit report is supplied to the appropriate national authority mentioned in the Permit upon completion of the activity, within the terms established by national authorities issuing the Permit.

Neither tourism nor any other recreational activities are permitted.

7(ii) Access to and movements within the Area

Where practicable, movements within the Area shall be on foot, along existing tracks known by staff familiar with the Area and regular visitors to it. These are the beach area and the upper boundary of the Area, northeast of the Three Brothers Hill.

Vehicles of any kind are prohibited within the Area, except for those essential for the maintenance of the shelter, which shall only be operated by logistics staff and pursuant to an access Permit. In such a case, access to the ASPA will be through a gentle slope close to the Albatros shelter, and vehicles should be driven avoiding vegetated areas and bird and mammal concentrations (see Map 1).

Operation of aircraft over the ASPA shall follow, as a minimum standard, the provisions contained in Resolution 2 (2004), "Guidelines for the operation of aircrafts over bird colonies". As a general rule, no aircraft is allowed to fly over the ASPA below 610 metres (2000 feet). Maintain a horizontal separation of 460 m (1/4 nautical mile) from the coastline where possible. Aircraft landing operations on the Area are forbidden, except in cases of emergency or air safety.

7(iii) Activities which may be conducted in the Area

- scientific research which cannot be conducted elsewhere and which will not jeopardise the natural ecosystem of the Area;
- Essential management activities, including visits to assess the effectiveness of the Management Plan and management activities;
- Activities for educational and outreach purposes, contributing to raise awareness of scientific activities, under National Antarctic Programs.
- Maintenance of the shelter Elefante, except between October and December. During this period, maintenance of the shelter should be avoided or, if necessary, reduced to the maximum extent practicable, and tasks should always be performed pursuant to a Permit. This period is considered particularly sensitive because it is concomitant with egg-laying and elephant seals breast feeding peak times.

7(iv) Installation, modification or removal of structures

No new structures are to be erected within the Area, or scientific equipment installed, except for compelling scientific or management reasons and subject to the relevant Permit.

Any scientific equipment to be installed in the Area, as well as any research marker, shall be approved by a Permit and be clearly labelled, indicating the country, name of principal investigator and year of installation. All such materials should be of such nature as to pose minimal risks of contamination to the Area, or the risk of interfering with the fauna or damaging the vegetation.

Structures and installations must be removed when they are no longer required, or on the expiry of the permit, which ever is the earlier. No research traces are to remain once the Permit has expired. If a specific project cannot be finished within the timeframe specified in the Permit, such circumstance shall be informed in the post-visit report, and an extension of the validity of the Permit authorising any materials to remain in the Area shall be requested.

Tents will be allowed for the sole purpose of storing scientific instruments or equipment, or to be used as an observation post.

7(v) Location of field camps

To avoid major disturbance to the fauna, and taking into account that there are alternatives places to accommodate, it is not allowed to camp at ASPA 132. Projects authorised to work within the ASPA may request accommodation at the Carlini Base, subject to availability. When necessary for scientific reasons, the Elefante shelter (located inside the Area) or the Albatros shelter (outside the Area, though very close) may be used. The use of the Elefante shelter for scientific purposes, by staff other than Argentine Antarctic Program staff shall be arranged in advance with such Program.

The location of camps on the vicinity of the ASPA, is responsibility of the corresponding National Antarctic Program, but for security reasons, it is recommended to inform the leader of Carlini Station.

7(vi) Restriction on material and organisms which may be brought into the Area

- No living animals or plant material shall be deliberately introduced into the ASPA. All reasonable precautions against the unintentional introduction of alien species to the Area shall be adopted. It should be taken into account than alien species are most frequently and effectively introduced by humans. Clothes (pockets, boots, velcro fasteners on garments) and personal equipment (bags, backpacks, camera bags, tripods), as well as scientific instruments and work tools may carry insect larvae, seeds, propagules, etc. For more information, refer to the "Non-Native Species Manual – CEP 2011"
- No uncooked poultry products shall be introduced into the Area.
- No herbicides or pesticides shall be brought into the Area. Any other chemicals, which shall be introduced with the corresponding Permit, shall be removed from the Area on or before the conclusion of the activity for which the Permit was granted. The purpose and type of chemicals shall be documented in as much detail as possible for other scientists´ information.
- No fuel, food or any other materials are to be stored in the Area, unless required for essential purposes connected with the activity for which the Permit has been granted, provided they are stored inside the Elefante shelter or close to it, for removal upon completion of the activity. Any fuel used at the Elefante shelter shall be handled pursuant to contingency plan established by the Argentine Antarctic Program for Carlini Station.

7(vii) Taking or harmful interference with native flora and fauna

Taking of, or harmful interference with, native flora and fauna is prohibited, except in accordance with a Permit.

Approach distances to fauna should be respected, except when scientific projects may require otherwise, and provided that the relevant permits have been issued.

For penguins the recommended distance is 10 m during reproduction and moult periods and 5 m to juveniles. A 100 m distance is recommended to Giant petrels nests while in the case of Antartic fur seals, Weddell seals, Leopard seals and Crabeater seals a minumim distance of 10 m should be kept. It is important to consider that these distances are aimed to orientate and must vary and become larger if the response to human proximity clearly stress the animal out.

Where an activity involves taking or harmful interference, it should be carried out in accordance with the SCAR Code of Conduct for Use of Animals for Scientific Purposes in Antarctica, as a minimum standard.

Information on taking and harmful interference will be duly exchanged through the Antarctic Treaty Information Exchange system and its record shall, as a minimum standard, be lodged with the Antarctic Master Directory or, in Argentina, with the National Antarctic Data Centre (Centro de Datos Nacionales Antárticos).

Scientists taking samples of any kind will shall refer to the EIES and/or contact the relevant National Antarctic Programmes in order to minimise the risk of a potential duplication.

7(viii) Collection or removal of anything not brought into the ASPA by the permit holder

Material may be collected or removed from the Area only in accordance with a Permit. Removal of dead biological specimens for scientific purposes be analysed case by case in order to not exceed such levels as to entail the deterioration of the nutritional base of local scavengers. It will depend on the species to be collected and, if necessary, advice from specialist should be required prior to the extent of the Permit.

7 (ix) Disposal of waste

All non-physiological waste shall be removed from the Area. Wastewater and liquid domestic waste may be dumped into the sea, in accordance with Article 5 of Annex III to the Madrid Protocol.

Waste from research activities conducted in the Area may be temporarily stored next to the Elefante shelter awaiting removal. Such waste must be disposed of pursuant to Annex III to the Madrid Protocol, labelled as trash and duly sealed to prevent accidental leaks.

7(x) *Measures that may be necessary to continue to meet the aims of the Management Plan*

Access Permits to the Area may be granted in order to conduct biological monitoring and site inspection activities, including the collection of plant material and animal samples for scientific purposes, the erection or maintenance of signposts, and any other management measures.

7(xi) Requirements for reports

The principal Permit holder for each Permit issued shall submit a report of activities conducted in the Area once the activity has been completed. Such report must respect the format provided previously, together with the Permit, and be sent to the authority issuing the Permit.

The information of the reports will be used for the purpose of any review of the Management Plan and in organizing the scientific use of the Area.

The records of ASPA permits and post-visit reports will be exchanged with the other Consultative Parties, as part of the Information Exchange system, as specified in Article 10.1 of Annex V.

Such reports shall be stored and made available for inspection by all interested Parties, SCAR,

CCAMLR and COMNAP, so as to provide the information on human activities within the Area necessary to ensure proper management.

8. Supporting documentation.

Ainley, D.G., Ballard,G.., Blight, L.K., Ackley, S., Emslie, S.D., Lescroël, A., Olmastroni, S., Townsend, S.E., Tynan, C.T., Wilson, P., Woehler, E. 2010. Impacts of cetaceans on the structure of southern ocean food webs. *Mar. Mam. Sci.* **26**: 482-489.

Ainley, D.G., Blight, L.K. 2009. Ecological repercussions of historical fish extraction from the Southern Ocean. *Fish Fisheries* **10**: 13-38.

Atkinson, A., Siegel, V., Pakhomov, E., Rothery, P. 2004. Long-term decline in krill stock and increase in salps within the Southern Ocean. *Nature* **432**:100–103.

Carlini A.R., Coria N.R., Santos M.M., Negrete J., Juares M.A., Daneri G.A. 2009. Responses of *Pygoscelis adeliae* and *P. papua* populations to environmental changes at Isla 25 de Mayo (King George Island). *Polar Biology* **32**:1427–1433.

Carlini A.R., Daneri G.A., Márquez M.E.I., Negrete J., Mennucci J., Juares M. 2010. Food consumption estimates of southern elephant seal females at Isla 25 de Mayo (King George Island), Antarctica. XXXI Scientific Committee on Antarctic Research and Open Science Conference. Buenos Aires, Argentina.

Casaux, R. J., Barrera-Oro, E.R. 2006. Shags in Antarctica: their feeding behaviour and ecological role in the marine food web. *Antarctic Science* **18**: 3-14.

Daneri G.A., Carlini A.R.1999. Spring and summer predation on fish by Antarctic fur seal, *Arctocephalus gazella*, at King George Island, South Shetland Islands. *Canadian J. of Zoology* **77:** 1165-1170.

Ducklow, H. W., Baker, K., Martinson, D.G., Quetin, L.B., Ross, R.M., Smith, R.C., Stammerjohn, S.E., Vernet, M., Fraser. W. 2007. Marine pelagic ecosystems: the west Antarctic Peninsula. Phil. *Trans. Roy. Soc. Lond. Ser. B* **362**: 67–94.

Guidelines for the Operation of Aircrafts. Resolution 2. 2004 – ATCM XXVII - CEP VII, Cape Town (available at *http://www.ats.aq/documents/recatt/Att224_e.pdf*)

Marschoff, E.R., Barrera-Oro, E.R., Alescio, N.S., Ainley, D. G. 2012. Slow recovery of previously depleted demersal fish at the South Shetland Islands, 1983-2010. *Fisheries Research.*, **125–**126, pp:: 206–213.

Montes-Hugo, M., Doney, S.C., Ducklow, H.W., Fraser, W., Martinson, D., Stammerjohn, S.E., Schofield, O. 2009. Recent changes in phytoplankton communities associated with rapid regional climate change along the western Antarctic Peninsula. *Science* **323**: 1470–1473.

Morgan, F., Barker, G., Briggs, C., Price, R. and Keys H. 2007. Environmental Domains of Antarctica version 2.0 Final Report, Manaaki Whenua Landcare Research New Zealand Ltd, pp. 89.

Non-Native Species Manual. Resolution 6 (2011) – ATCM XXXIV - CEP XIV , Buenos Aires (available at *http://www.ats.aq/documents/atcm34/ww/atcm34_ww004_e.pdf*)

Rambolá, E. F., Marschoff, E., Coria, N. 2010. Inter-annual variability in Chinstrap penguin diet at South Shetland and South Orkneys Islands. *Polar biology*. **33** (6), 799-806

Russell, J.L., Dixon, K.W., Gnanadesikan, A., Stouffer, R.J., Toggweiler, D.J.R., 2006. The Southern Hemisphere westerlies in a warming world: propping open the door to the deep ocean. *J. Clim.* **19**: 6382–6390.
Stammerjohn, S.E., Martinson, D.G., Smith, R.C., Yuan, X., Rind, D., 2008. Trends in Antarctic annual sea ice retreat and advance and their relation to El Niño–Southern Oscillation and Southern Annular Mode variability. *J. Geophys. Res.*, **113**:C03S90.

Terauds, A., Chown, S., Morgan, F., Peat, H., Watts, D., Keys, H., Convey, P. and Bergstrom, D. 2012. Conservation biogeography of the Antarctic. *Diversity and Distributions*, 22 May 2012, DOI: 10.1111/j.1472-4642.2012.00925.x

Thompson, D.W.J., Solomon, S., 2008. Interpretation of recent Southern Hemisphere climate change. *Science* **296**: 895-899.

Torre, L., Servetto, N., Eöry, L. M., Momo, F., Abele, D., Sahade, R. 2012.Respiratory responses of three Antarctic ascidians and a sea pen to increased sediment concentrations. *Polar biology* **35**(11): 1743-1748.

Trivelpiece, W.Z., Hinke, J.T. Miller, A.K. Reiss, C.S. Trivelpiece, S.G., Watters, G.M., 2010. Variability in krill biomass links harvesting and climate warming to penguin population changes in Antarctica. *Proc. Natl. Acad. Sci.*, doi/10.1073/pnas.1016560108.

Wiencke, C., Ferreyra, C., Arntz, W. and Rinaldi, C. 1998. The Potter Cove coastal ecosystem, Antarctica. Synopsis of research performed within the frame of the Argentinean - German Cooperation at the Dallmann Laboratory and Jubany Station (King George Island, Antarctica, 1991 -1 997). *Ber. Polarforsch,* **299,** pp: 342.

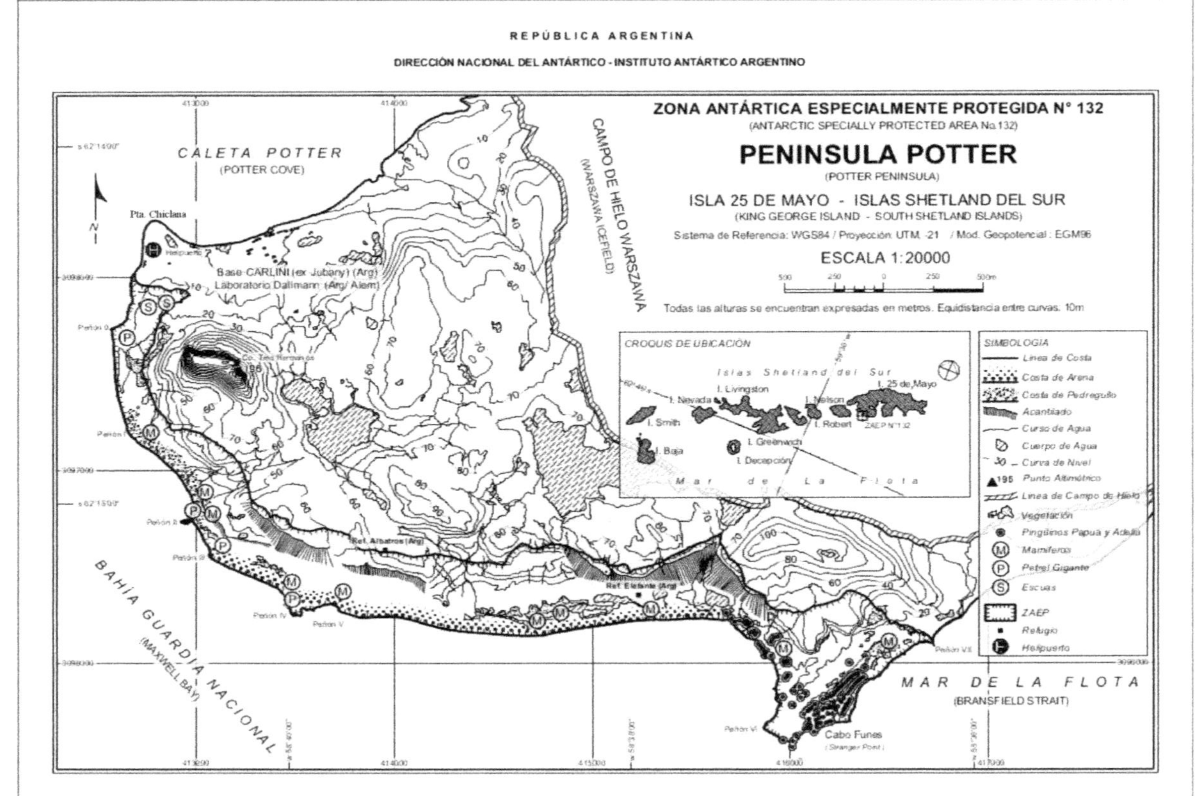

Map 1: Management Plan for Antarctic Specially Protected Area No. 132 in relation to the Potter Peninsula. Permanent water bodies are shown in broken diagonal lines.

Management Plan for Antarctic Specially Protected Area No. 134

CIERVA POINT AND OFFSHORE ISLANDS, DANCO COAST, ANTARCTIC PENINSULA

Introduction

This Area was originally designated as SSSI No. 15 in Recommendation XIII-8 of the ATCM XIII (1985), after a proposal by Argentina, due to its great diversity of vegetation and the fact that it has breeding colonies of at least ten bird species.

During the XXI Antarctic Treaty Consultative Meeting (Christchurch, 1997), the revised Management Plan for the Area was adopted in accordance with the format established by Annex V of the Madrid Protocol and Measure 3 (1997). During the XXV Antarctic Treaty Consultative Meeting (Warsaw, 2002), and once Annex V entered into force, *Site of Special Scientific Interest* No. 15 became, by Decision 1 (2002), *Antarctic Specially Protected Area* No. 134. The Management Plan was subsequently revised and in the XXIX Antarctic Treaty Consultative Meeting, (Edinburgh, 2006), Measure 1 (2006) adopted the new version of the above, now replaced by this Management Plan.

The original reasons for the designation of the Area remain in force and other reasons have been added in recent years, giving the designation of the Area greater relevance.

This Area has great scientific value due to its unusual biodiversity, which includes numerous species of birds, flora, and invertebrates. The unique topography of the Area, together with the abundance and diversity of vegetation, create highly favourable conditions for the formation of numerous microhabitats, which, in turn, support the development of rich biodiversity and give the Area exceptional aesthetic value.

At present, there is a need to increase the volume of studies related to the abundance and reproduction of marine birds and mammals, given that they hold the potential to be used as indicators of ecological processes on a global scale (Croxall *et al*, 1998). In this regard, the geographical location of ASPA 134 is a key to achieving these kinds of studies as well as other comparative observations between its fauna and the fauna inhabiting other areas in Antarctica. Climatic and oceanographic variations have been shown to have an effect on the populations of marine birds, generally with profound implications, such as a reduction of the reproductive success and alterations in the mating cycles of some species (Chambers et al. 2011). The region of the Antarctic Peninsula is one of the areas of the planet where the most extensive effects of global climate change have been observed, directly impacting on the formation and duration of marine ice and, as a result, affecting the entire food chain. Stability in the positive phase of the SAM (Southern Hemisphere Annular Mode) has had an impact on the winds, the circulation of water and the spread of marine ice (Stammerjohn *et al.* 2008; Thompson and Solomon 2002) and has repercussions on Antarctic flora and fauna.

In this context, ASPA 134 has characteristics which allow for comparative studies between populations that inhabit areas with frequent human disturbance (accumulation of refuse, pollution, tourism and fishing) and those which suffer little disturbance (Woehler *et al.* 2001, Patterson *et al.* 2008). In recent years, there has been a trend of increasing abundance in some populations which inhabit the ASPA, as is the case for penguins, contrary to what is observed in other areas, where the frequency of human disturbance is proportionate to the decrease in abundance of some populations (Woehler *et al 2001,* Lynch *et al.* 2008, Gonzalez-Zeballos *et al.* 2013).

Its designation as ASPA guarantees that the current research programmes will not be adversely affected by accidental human interference, destruction of vegetation and soil, pollution of water bodies and disturbance of birds, especially at times that coincide with reproductive periods.

Scientific research currently being conducted in ASPA N° 134 includes:

1) "*Primavera Mammals*" project: Study of the potential effects of climate change on 3 Antarctic pinnipeds with different affinity to marine ice: *Arctocephalus gazella, Leptonychotes weddellii*, and *Hydrurga leptonyx* in relation to the ice cover in the Area and global phenomena such as El Niño Southern Oscillation (ENSO) through an evaluation of the impact of these predators on marine resources, their feeding strategies and their relationship with the availability of prey. Project in cooperation between Argentina and Australia.

2) Project "*Response of Antarctic bird populations to interannual variability of their prey in areas with obvious effects of global warming*", whose goal is the implementation, during incubation periods, of bird census, with the aim of understanding population sizes of their colonies and determining the reproduction chronology as well as the reproductive success of their different sectors. These studies include: (1) Ringing giant petrels and skuas, both adults and chicks nearing independence, in order to continue the marking and monitoring programme for these birds (2) Obtaining in vivo dietary samples (3) Placing equipment to record the time and depth of dives (TDR) and (4) Collecting endoparasites in birds found dead and in faeces as well as ectoparasites in live birds.

3) "Project phylogeography of *Deschampsia antarctica* on the basis of molecular, morphological and cariological studies: a window to the past under scenarios of change" whose purpose is to evaluate the genetic structure and diversity of *Deschampsia antarctica* and other species of vegetation.

Description of the values to be protected

The coastal area is home to a significant quantity of bird colonies, breeding colonies of marine mammals and extensive vegetation. The coverage of lichens, mosses and communities dominated by grasses is very extensive in Cierva Point. The Area's values are linked to its high biological diversity in terms of flora and fauna and its topographic characteristics, further enhanced by a high landscape value.

In addition, its particular geographic location in the northwest of the Antarctic peninsula gives the numerous scientific research programmes that take place in the Area crucial importance in attempting to explain, at least party, alterations in Antarctic ecosystems caused by climate change and human disturbance.

According to Morgan et al. (2007) ASPA 134 contains environment domain "Antarctic peninsula mid-northern latitudes geologic" and according to Terauds *et al.* (2012) the Area is located in the biogeographical region "Northeast of the Antarctic Peninsula".

For more details on the characteristics of the Area refer to point 6 of this document.

2. Aims and objectives

Management of ASPA 134 aims to:

- Protect the biodiversity of the Area, avoiding major changes in the structure and composition of communities of flora an fauna.
- Prevent unnecessary human disturbance.
- Allow the development of scientific research that cannot be conducted elsewhere, and the continuance of long-term biological studies established in the Area, as well as the development of any other type of scientific research that does not compromise the values for which the Areas is protected.
- Avoid or minimize the unintentional introduction of seeds, plants, animals or microbes, as well as pathogens that could potentially be harmful to the flora and fauna.
- Allow the development of studies and monitoring activities to assess the direct and indirect effects of the activities of the neighbouring station (Primavera Base).

3. Management Activities

The following management activities will be undertaken to protect the values of the Area:

- Primavera Base (Argentina) staff will be specifically instructed as to the conditions of the Management Plan.
- Copies of the management plan of this Area will be provided in Primavera Base.

- Movement will be limited to areas free of vegetation, avoiding proximity to fauna, except when otherwise required by scientific projects and the corresponding permits of harmful interference have been obtained.
- Collection of samples will be limited to the minimum required for approved scientific research plans.
- Visits shall be made as necessary, to ensure that management and maintenance measures are adequate.
- All signs, as well as other structures erected in the Area with scientific or management objectives, will be adequately secured and maintained in proper conditions.
- Pedestrian paths to research sites will be marked to limit movement.
- In accordance with requirements of Annex III of the Protocol on Environmental Protection to the Antarctic Treaty, any abandoned or disused equipment or material must be removed on condition that this does not have an adverse impact on the environment.
- The management plan should be reviewed no less than once every five years, and updated if necessary.
- All those responsible for aircraft operating in the Area should be informed of the location, boundaries and restrictions that apply to the entry and overflight of the Area.
- Preventive measures will be implemented to prevent the introduction of non-native species and for the eradication of the recorded introduced species (example of *Poa pratensis*)

4. Period of designation

Designated for an indefinite period.

5. Maps

Map 1 shows the general location of ASPA 134. Map 2 shows the ASPA in relation to Danco Coast. The shaded area indicates the group of areas that make up ASPA 134 (the subtidal marine environment between the continental and insular portions is not included in the ASPA). Map 3 shows the area surrounding Primavera Base in detail, (excluded from ASPA No. 134).

6. Description of the Area

6 (I) Geographical coordinates, limits, and natural features

Geographic coordinates and limits

Cierva Point (Lat. 64 ° 10 ' 1.05 " S, Lon. 60 ° 56 ' 38.06 " W) is located on the south coast of Cierva Cove, to the north of Hughes Bay, between the Danco and Palmer Coasts, in the northwestern portion of the Antarctic Peninsula. The site comprises the ice-free area between the southwest coast of Cierva Cove and the northeast coast of Santucci Cove. Also included are Apéndice (Lat. 64 ° 11 ' 41.99 " S, Long. 61° 1 ' 3.25 " W) and José Hernández islands (Lat. 64 ° 10 ' 10.06 " S, Long. 61° 6 ' 11.34 " W) and Moss (Lat. 64 ° 10 ' 2.22 " S, Long. 61° 1 ' 49.43 " W) and Penguin islets (Lat. 64° 8 ' 35.90 "S, Long. 60 ° 59 ' 11.43 " W), found to the west/southwest of Cierva Point. Although the intertidal zone of each of these areas is included in the Area, the subtidal marine environment is not.

Primavera Base (Argentina) and its associated installations, as well as the beach area utilized for access to the base, are excluded from the Area.

Natural Characteristics

The Area is rich is species of both animals and vegetation, and in some cases, the abundance of some species is exceptional.

Also, the Area has great aesthetic value thanks to the great diversity in relief and coastal forms, the presence of different lithologies and a pronounced system of fractures. In addition to this, an extensive and varied vegetation cover provides unusual scenic diversity for the Antarctic environment.

Cierva point displays a relatively simple structural design. It is dominated by three summits: The Mojón, Escombrera and Chato hills, aligned in an East-West direction, with steep South facing hillside slopes, permanently covered by snow, and the other hillside a moderate to gente North facing slope, free of snow during the summer. On the latter slopes we observe a very developed vegetation, with areas of a continuous cover by bryophyte grasses and associated lichens, as well as numerous species of birds, including the settlement of a colony of Gentoo Penguins (P. papua) (Novatti 1978, Agraz et al, 1994). These characteristics give the Area an exceptional scientific and aesthetic value.

In previous studies, Agraz *et al.* (1994) divided Cierva Point into two environmental zones according to the type of substrate and vegetation cover, (1) rocky wall (or coastal zone) and (2) exposed slope. The rocky wall is a strip of coastline with abrupt slopes, a rocky surface with scree of different sized pieces. In some sectors this substrate is unstable and is crossed by numerous canyons. Most of it is free from snow during the austral summer. The vegetation is very scant, with lichens and grasses. There are many natural cavities between the rocks. This first area is the nesting site of five bird species. The second site, the exposed side, comprises a large variety of environments and of exposures, extending from the coast up to the peaks. The slopes are moderate to abrupt, the rocks of variable sizes, consolidated or not, and the surface is free of ice during the austral summer. The highest areas have glaciers which, in summer, give rise to numerous little water streams. These feed the lowest areas, where the vegetation is most developed.

There are 10 species of nesting birds in the Area: Chinstrap Penguin (*Pygoscelis antarctica*), Gentoo Penguin (*P. papua*), Southern Giant Petrel (*Macronectes giganteus*), Cape Petrel (*Daption capense*), Wilson's Storm Petrel (*Oceanites oceanicus*), Antarctic Shag (*P. bransfieldensis*), Pale-faced Sheathbill (*Chionis alba*), Skuas (predominant species *Catharacta maccormickii*), Kelp Gull (*Larus dominicanus*) and Antarctic Tern (*Sterna vittata*).

The most numerous colonies are those of the Chinstrap Penguin (*Pygoscelis antarctica*), Gentoo Penguin (*P. papua*), Wilson's Storm Petrel (*Oceanites oceanicus*), South Polar skua (*Catharacta maccormickii*) and Kelp Gull (*Larus dominicanus*).

Summary of the estimated number of nesting pairs by species and nesting site is shown in tables 1, 2 and 3.

Table 1. Number of reproductive pairs by location for *Pygoscelis papua*. The year in which the estimation was made is indicated in brackets. (data from Gonzalez-Zeballos *et al.* 2013)

Localidad	Novatti (1978)	Poncet & Poncet (1987)	Quintana et al. (1998)	Favero et al. (2000)	**Gonzalez-Zeballos et al. (2013)**
Punta Cierva	559-614 (1954-58)	600 (1984)	800-1041 (1991-96)	593 (1998)	2680
Isla Apéndice		450 (1987)		905 (1998)	2795

Table 2. Number of reproductive pairs by location for *Pygoscelis antarctica*. The year in which the estimation was made is indicated in brackets. (data from Gonzalez-Zeballos *et al.* 2013)

Localidad	Muller-Schwarze (1975)	Poncet & Poncet (1987)	Woehler (1993)	Favero et al. (2000)	**Gonzalez-Zeballos et al. (2013)**
Ite. Pingüino o Mar		500 (1984)		1553 (1998)	2763
I. José Hernández	2060 (1971)	200 (1987)		546 (1998)	180
I. Apéndice		1100 (1987)		152 (1998)	33

Table 3. Number of reproductive pairs by species and location. PB: Phalacrocorax bransfieldensis, **MG**: Macronectes giganteus, DP: Daption capense, **CA**: Chionis alba, **SM**: Stercorarius maccormicki, **LD**: Larus dominicanus, **SV**: Sterna vittata **The year in which the estimation was made is indicated in brackets**. (data from Gonzalez-Zeballos et al. 2013)

Localidad	PB			MG			DP			CA			SM			LD			SV		
	$N_{S}1$	$N_{S}2$	λ	$N_{S}1$	$N_{S}2$	λ	$N_{S}1$	$N_{S}2$	λ	$N_{S}1$	$N_{S}2$	λ	$N_{S}1$	$N_{S}2$	λ	$N_{S}1$	$N_{S}2$	λ	$N_{S}1$	$N_{S}2$	λ
Punta Cierva	0	0	-	0	0	-	7	3	0.94	2	1	0.95	145	166	1.01	158	73	0.94	45	57	1.02
Ite. Pingüino o Mar	9	0	0	0	0	-	1	0	0	3	1	0.92	3	3	1	8	10	1.02	0	3	-
Ite. Musgo	0	0	-	35	42	1.01	28	17	0.96	3	4	1.02	10	26	1.08	120	70	0.96	15	19	1.02
José Hernández	21	21	1	0	7[b]	-	0	0	-	1	1	1	3	17	1.14	15	9	0.96	35	11[b]	0.91
I. Apéndice	0	0	-	5[b]	41	1.17	23	11	0.94	1[b]	2	1.05	2[b]	12	1.15	68	12	0.87	15	12	0.98

The flora is very abundant and is located in both wet and dry areas. In wet areas mosses dominate, in the form of carpet cover (*Drepanocladus uncinatus*) and turf (*Polytrychum alpestre*). In dry places, on rocks, lichen of genus *Usnea* and *Xanthoría* are dominant. *Deschampsia antarctica* grass is also abundant.

The cover of mosses, lichens, and grasses is very extensive. The most conspicuous vegetation communities are associations of dominant lichens, moss turf dominated by *Polytrichum alpestre* and *Chorisodontium aciphillum* as well as *Deschampsia-Colobanthus* subformation. The moss turf covers areas of more than one hundred square metres, with an average depth of about 80 cm. The flora that is present includes the two Antarctic flowering plant species, 18 moss species, 70 lichen species, two hepatic, as well as 20 species of fungi. The non-marine microalgae, especially on Moss and Penguin Islets, are very abundant with unusual records. Terrestrial arthropods are also very numerous and are occasionally associated with tidal pools in the littoral zone of the Area.

Relevant data is the record of a non-native grass, *Poa pratensis*. The grass was introduced to Ciera Point inadvertently during experiments which involved transplanting *Nothofagus antarctica* and *N. ward* between 1954 and 1955 (Ross *et al* 1996, Court 1961, Smith 1996). From 1995, a rise in the spread of this species was recorded. It is likely that its recent expansion is related to environmental changes recorded in the Area, increasing scientific interest in this species. Consequently, studies of *Poa pratensis* have resumed, also extending to the communities to which this grass is associated, in order to define the eradication strategy with minimal impact on the ecosystem (see Information Document 13, presented to ATCM XXXV). Also, there is a unique record of an alien arthropod found in the Area.(Convey y Quintana 1997)

6 (II) Access to the Area.

Only in the case of authorised exceptions, the Area must only be accessed on foot from Primavera base.

The adjacent islands will be accessed by small boats. This sea access is permitted to any point of the islands included in the Area.

Access to the Area via the beaches should always be avoided if animal fauna is present, especially during breeding season.

For further information see section *7 (II)*.

6 (III) Structures located within the Area and in its vicinity.

Location of structures within the Area

There are no structures within the Area.

Structures adjacent to the Area

Adjacent to the ASPA, but beyond the limits of the Area, is Primavera Base (Argentina. 64 ° 09' S; 60 ° 58 ' W), located to the northwest of Cierva Point and adjacent to the Area. Primavera Base is only open during the summer months. It consists of eight buildings and a designated helicopter landing area. The buildings are interconnected by walkways to prevent damage to vegetation.

6. (IV) Location of other nearby Protected Areas

- *ASPA No. 152 , western portion of the Bransfield Strait (Mar de la Flota), off the coast of Low Island, South Shetland Islands, about 90 kilometres to the northwest of ASPA 134. It is located off the west and south coast of Low Island, between 63 ° 15' S and 63 ° 30' S and between 62 ° 00' W and 62 ° 45 ' W.*
- *ASPA 153, eastern portion of the Dallmann Bay, off the western coast of Brabant Island, Palmer Archipelago, about 90 kilometres west of ASPA 134. It is located between latitudes 64 ° 00' S and 64 ° 20' S and from 62 ° 50 ' W eastward to the western coast of Brabant Island, (approximately 520 km2)*

6 (V)Special areas within the Area.

There are no special areas within the Area.

7. Terms and conditions of entry Permit

7 (I) General permit conditions

Entry into the Area is prohibited, except with a permit issued by appropriate national authorities.

Conditions for issuing a permit to enter the Area are that:

- *It is issued for a scientific purpose, in accordance with the objectives of the Management Plan, and that cannot be conducted elsewhere.*
- *The actions permitted will not harm the natural ecological system of the Area.*
- *It is issued for any management activities (inspection, maintenance, or revision) in support of the objectives of the Management Plan.*
- *The actions permitted are in accordance with this Management Plan.*
- *The Permit, or an authorised copy, is carried by the principal investigator authorized to enter the Area.*
- *A post-visit report is given to the competent National Authority mentioned in the Permit.*
- *Tourism and any other recreational activity is not permitted.*

7 (II). Access to and movements within the Area

Any access to the Area will be by permit issued by a competent authority, and will only be issued for activities which are in accordance with this Management Plan.

The only access for helicopters is outside the boundaries of the Area, in the area adjacent to Primavera Base. Helicopters may only land in the specified area to the east-southeast of the Base. The flight route to be used is limited to a north approach and departure. The operation of aircrafts over the Area will be carried out, as a minimum requirement, in compliance with that established in Resolution 2 (2004), "Guidelines for the Operation of Aircraft near Concentrations of Birds" As a general rule, no aircraft should fly over the ASPA at less than 610 metres (2000 feet), except in cases of emergency or air security.

Movements within the Area will be carried out avoiding disturbance to the flora and fauna, especially during the breeding season

Vehicle traffic of any type is not permitted.

7 (III) Activities which are or may be conducted within the Area

- *Scientific research activities that cannot be conducted elsewhere and that do not harm the ecosystem of the Area.*
- *Essential management activities, including monitoring.*
- *If it is considered necessary for scientific or conservation reasons, access to determined bird nesting sites and mammal colonies may include greater restrictions between the end of October and the beginning of December. This period is considered especially sensitive because it coincides with peaks in egg-laying for nesting birds in the Area.*

7 (IV). Installation, modification or removal of structures

No additional structures will be built or equipment installed within the Area, except for essential scientific or management activities with an appropriate permit.

Any scientific equipment installed in the Area, as well as any research signage, should be approved by permit and clearly labelled, indicating the country, the name of the principal investigator, and the year of installation. All the installed materials should be of such nature that they pose a minimum of contamination risk to the Area or the minimum risk of causing disturbance to the vegetation or to the fauna.

Research signage should not remain after the permit expires. If any specific project cannot be finished within the permitted time period, an extension should be requested which authorizes any object to remain in the Area.

7 (V) Location of field camps

The Parties that utilise the Area will normally have access to Primavera Base for lodging, subject to prior coordination with the Argentine Antarctic Programme. Only the installation of tents with the purpose of housing scientific material or instruments, or to be used as an observation base, shall be permitted.

7 (VI) Restrictions on materials and organisms which may be brought into the Area

- No living animals or plant material shall be deliberately introduced into the Area. All necessary recommendations must be adopted in preventing all intentional introduction of non-native species to the Area. In this regard, it should be noted that these species are often introduced by humans. Clothing as well as personal equipment or scientific instruments and work tools can introduce insect larvae, seeds, propagules, etc. For further information see the Manual for non-native species - CEP 2011.
- No uncooked farm products shall be introduced.
- No herbicides or pesticides shall be introduced into the Area. Any other chemical product, which should be introduced with the corresponding permit, shall be removed from the Area upon conclusion of the activity for which the permit was granted. The use and type of chemical products should be documented, as clearly as possible, for other researchers to be made aware of.
- Fuel, food, and other materials are not to be stored in the Area, unless required for essential purposes by the activity authorized in the corresponding permit.

7 (VII). Taking or causing harmful interference to flora and fauna

Any taking or causing harmful interference, except in accordance with a permit, is prohibited. When an activity involves taking or causing harmful interference, these should, as a minimum requirement, be consistent with the SCAR Code of Conduct for the Use of Animals for Scientific Purposes in Antarctica.

Information on taking or causing harmful interference will be duly exchanged through the System of Information Exchange of the Antarctic Treaty, and its record should be incorporated, at the least, in the *Antarctic Master Directory* or, in Argentina, in the *National Antarctic Data Centre*.

Scientists who collect samples of any kind must refer to the electronic information exchange system of the Antarctic Treaty (EIES) and/or communicate with the corresponding national Antarctic programmes that might be involved in sampling in the Area, in order to minimise the risk of a possible duplication.

7 (VIII). Collection or removal of any item not brought into the Area by the permit holder

Any material from the Area may only be collected and removed from the Area with an appropriate Permit. Collection of dead biological specimens for scientific purposes should not exceed such a level that the collection degrades the nutritional base of local scavenger species. This will depend on the species in question and on the need to seek the advice of an expert prior to the extension of the permit.

7 (IX). Waste Disposal

Any non-physiological waste shall be removed from the Area.

In the case of residual waters and domestic residual liquids, sanitation facilities are available in Primavera Base (Argentina), provided they are open. In the case of research carried out on adjacent islands, residual waters can be discharged into the ocean, in accordance with Article 5 of Annex III of the Madrid Protocol.

Waste resulting from research activities in the Area can be temporarily stored at Primavera Base, pending removal. Said storage should be carried out in compliance with Annex III to the Madrid Protocol, marked as waste, and appropriately closed to avoid accidental escape.

7 (X). Measures that may be necessary to ensure that the aims and objectives of the Management Plan remain in force

Permits to enter the Area may be granted to conduct biological monitoring and inspection activities, which may include the collection of samples of plants and animals for research purposes, the erection and maintenance of signs, or other management measures. All the structures and signage installed in the Area for scientific purposes, including signs, should be approved in the Permit and clearly identified by country, indicating the name of the principal investigator and the year of installation.

7 (XI). Requirements for reports on visits to the Area

For each permit and once the activity has finished, the main permit holder shall submit a report of the activities conducted in the Area, using the format provided beforehand along with the Permit. The report should be sent to the permit issuing authority.

Records of permits and post-visit reports relating to the ASPA will be exchanged with the other Consultative Parties as part of the System of Information Exchange according to Art. 10.1 of Annex V.

The permits and reports should be stored and made accessible to any interested Party, SCAR, CCAMLR and COMNAP, so as to provide necessary information on human activities in the Area to ensure adequate management.

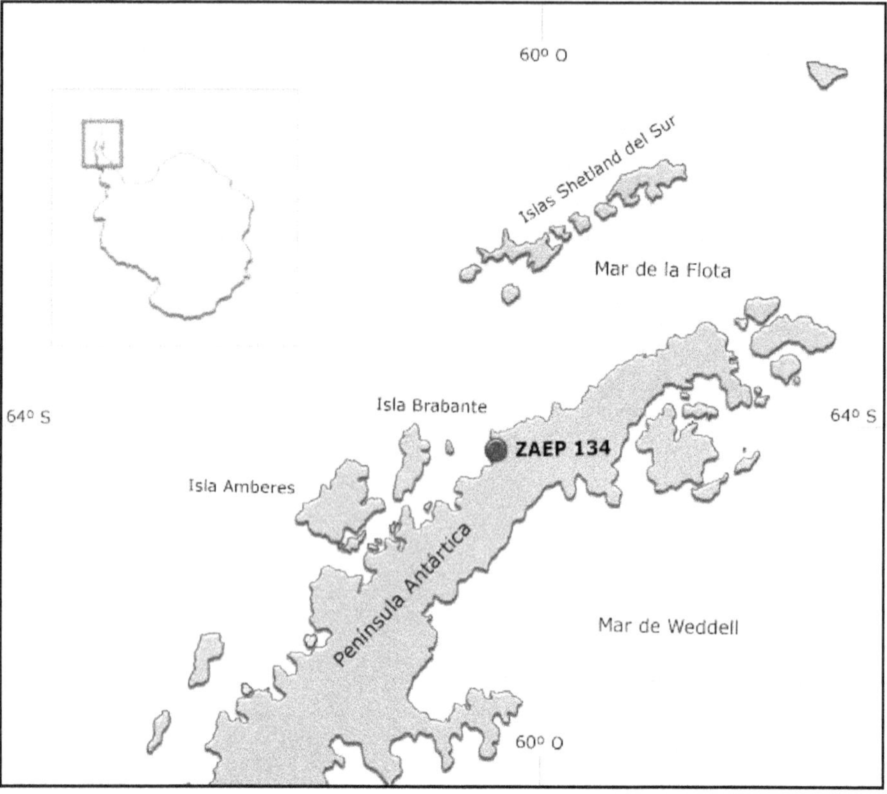

Figure 1: General location of Antarctic Specially Protected Area No. 134, Cierva Point and offshore islands, Danco Coast, Antarctic Peninsula.

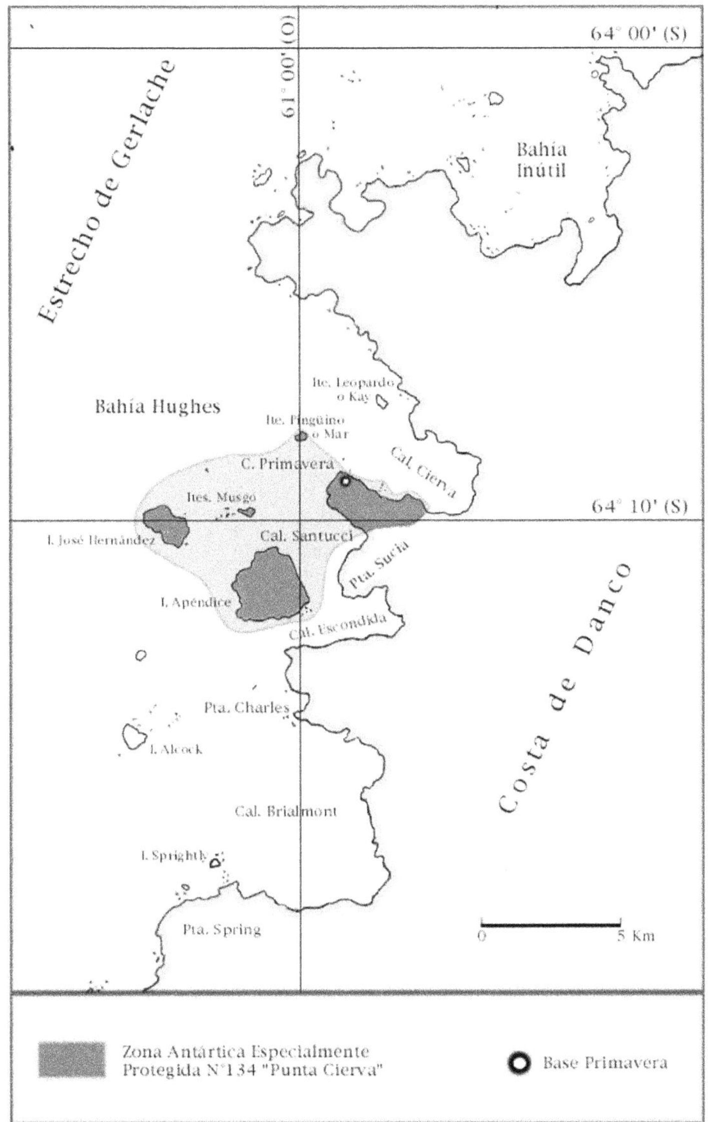

Figure 2: Antarctic Specially Protected Area No. 134, Cierva Point and offshore islands, Danco Coast, Antarctic Peninsula. The shaded area indicates the group of areas that make up ASPA 134 (the subtidal marine environment between the continental and insular portions is not included in the ASPA).

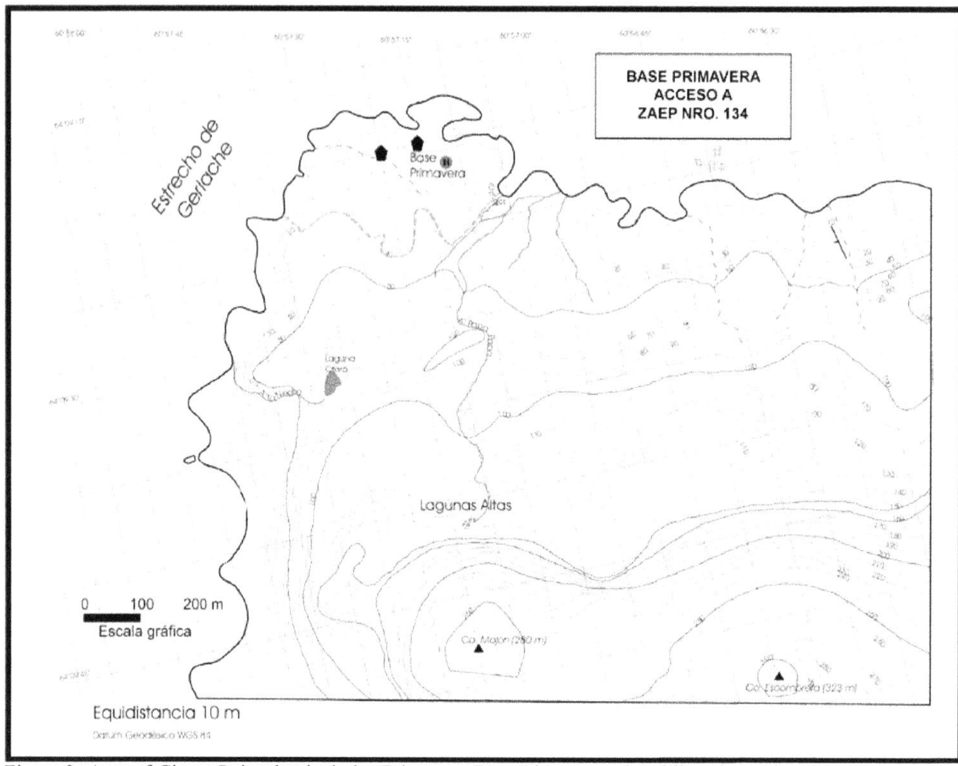

Figure 3: Area of Cierva Point that includes Primavera Base (the grey pointed line above the 40 m contour line indicates the base area, excluded from ASPA 134).

8. Bibliography

Agraz, J. L., Quintana, R.D. y Acero, J. M. 1994. Ecología de los ambientes terrestres en Punta Cierva (Costa de Danco, Península Antártica). *Contrib. Inst. Ant. Arg.*, **439**, 1-32.

ATCM XXXV IP 13. Colonisation status of the non-native grass Poa pratensis at Cierva Point, Danco Coast, Antarctic Peninsula.

Chambers L.E., Devney C.A., Congdon B.C., Dunlop N., Woehler E.J. & Dann P. 2011. Observed and predicted effects of climate on Australian seabirds. *Emu* **111**: 235-251.

Convey P. y Quintana. R.D.1997. The terrestrial arthropod fauna of Cierva Point SSSI, Danco Coast, northern Antartic Peninsula. *European Journal of Soil Ecology*, 33 (1): 19-29.

Corte, A . 1961. La primera fanerogama adventicia hallada en el continente Antartico. *Contribucion del Instituto Antártico Argentino* 62, 1–14.

Croxall, J.P., Prince, P.A. Rothery, P. & Wood, A.G. 1998. Population changes in albatrosses at South Georgia. In: Robertson, G. & Gales, R. (Eds). Albatross biology and conservation. Chipping Norton: Surrey Beatty. pp. 69–83.

Favero M., Coria N.R. & Beron M.P. 2000. The status of breeding birds at Cierva Point and surroundings, Danco Coast, Antarctic Peninsula. *Polish Polar Research* **21**, 181_187.

González-Zevallos, D., Santos, M., Rombola, E. F. Juáres, M., Coria, N. 2013. Abundance and breeding distribution of seabirds in the northern part of the Danco Coast, Antarctic Peninsula. Polar Research, 32, 11133, http://dx.doi.org/10.3402/polar.v32i0.11133

Guidelines for the Operation of Aircrafts. Resolution 2. 2004 – ATCM XXVII - CEP VII, Cape Town (available at http://www.ats.aq/documents/recatt/Att224_e.pdf)

Lynch H.J., Naveen R. & Fagan W.F. 2008. Censuses of penguin, blue-eyed shag *Phalacrocorax atriceps* and southern giant petrel *Macronectes giganteus* populations on the Antarctic Peninsula, 2001_2007. *Marine Ornithology* **36:** 83-97.

Morgan, F., Barker, G., Briggs, C., Price, R. and Keys H. 2007. Environmental Domains of Antarctica version 2.0 Final Report, Manaaki Whenua Landcare Research New Zealand Ltd, pp. 89.

Muller-Schwarze C. & Muller-Schwarze D. 1975. A survey of twenty-four rookeries of pygoscelid penguins in the Antarctic Peninsula region. In B. Stonehouse (ed.): The biology of penguins. Pp. 309_320. London: Macmillan.

Novatti R. 1978. Notas ecológicas y etológicas sobre las aves de Cabo Primavera, Costa de Danco, Península Antártica. (Ecological and ethological notes on birds in Spring Point, Danco Coast, Antarctic Peninsula.) Contribución Instituto Antártico Argentino 237. Buenos Aires: Argentine Antarctic Institute.

Patterson D.L., Woehler E.J., Croxall J.P., Cooper J., Poncet S., Peter H.-U., Hunter S. & Fraser W.R. 2008. Breeding distribution and population status of the northern giant petrel *Macronectes halli* and the southern giant petrel *M. Giganteus*. *Marine Ornithology* **36:** 115-124.

Poncet S. & Poncet J. 1987. Censuses of penguin populations of the Antarctic Peninsula, 1983_87. *British Antarctic Survey Bulletin* 77, 109_129.

Quintana R.D., Cirelli V. & Orgeira J.L. 1998. Abundance and spatial distribution of bird populations at Cierva Point, Antarctic Peninsula. Marine Ornithology 28, 21_27.

Rogers, T., Ciaglia, M., O'Connell, T., Slip, D., Meade, J., Carlini, A., Márquez, M.2012. WAP Antarctic top predator behaves differently: whiskers reveals WAP leopard seals are krill-feeding specialist. XXXII SCAR Open Science Conference and XXIV COMNAP AGM, Portland, Oregon.

Ross M.R., Hofmann E.E., Quetin L. B. 1996. Foundations for Ecological Research West of the Antartic Peninsula. *American geophysical union.* 448 pp.

SCAR's Code of Conduct for the Use of Animals for Scientific Purposes (available at http://www.scar.org/treaty/atcmxxxiv/ATCM34_ip053_e.pdf).

Smith, R. I. L. 1996. Introduced plants in Antarctica: potential impacts and conservations issues. *Biological Conservation*, 76, 135–146.

Stammerjohn, S.E., Martinson, D.G., Smith, R.C., Yuan, X., Rind, D., 2008. Trends in Antarctic annual sea ice retreat and advance and their relation to El Niño–Southern Oscillation and Southern Annular Mode variability. *J. Geophys. Res.*, **113**:C03S90.

Terauds, A., Chown, S., Morgan, F., Peat, H., Watts, D., Keys, H., Convey, P. and Bergstrom, D. 2012. Conservation biogeography of the Antarctic. *Diversity and Distributions*, 22 May 2012, DOI: 10.1111/j.1472-4642.2012.00925.x

Trivelpiece, W.Z., Hinke, J.T. Miller, A.K. Reiss, C.S. Trivelpiece, S.G., Watters, G.M., 2010. Variability in krill biomass links harvesting and climate warming to penguin population changes in Antarctica. *Proc. Natl. Acad. Sci.*, doi/10.1073/pnas.1016560108.

Thompson, D. W. J. y Solomon, S. 2002. Interpretation of recent Southern Hemisphere climate change. *Science* **296:**895–899.

Woehler E.J. 1993. The distribution and abundance of Antarctic and Subantarctic penguins. Cambridge: Scientific Committee on Antarctic Research.

Woehler E.J., Cooper J., Croxall J.P., Fraser W.R., Kooyman G.L., Millar G.D., Nel D.C., Patterson D.L., Peter H.-U., Ribic C.A., Salwicka K., Trivelpiece W.Z. &Weimerskirch H. 2001. A statistical assessment of the status and trends of Antarctic and Subantarctic seabirds. Cambridge: Scientific Committee on Antarctic Research.

Management Plan for Antarctic Specially Protected Area No 135

NORTH-EAST BAILEY PENINSULA, BUDD COAST, WILKES LAND

Introduction

North-East Bailey Peninsula (66°16'59.9"S, 110°31'59.9"E) is located approximately 200m east of Australia's Casey station, in the Windmill Islands region of the Budd Coast, Wilkes Land, East Antarctica. It was designated as Site of Special Scientific Interest (SSSI) No 16 under Recommendation XIII-8 (1985), after a proposal by Australia. In accordance with Decision 1 (2002) the site was redesignated and renumbered as Antarctic Specially Protected Area (ASPA) No 135. Revised management plans for the Area were adopted under Measure 2 (2003) and Measure 8 (2008). The ASPA is designated primarily as a scientific reference site which, since the early 1980s, has supported a range of studies into the diverse assemblage of vegetation found in the area. The close proximity of the Area to Casey station allows ease of access for field research but also creates the potential for disturbance of study areas.

1. Description of values to be protected

The North-east Bailey Peninsula Antarctic Specially Protected Area (the Area) is representative of a diverse assemblage of the Windmill Islands region flora. As such, the Area has intrinsic ecological value and scientific importance, particularly to botanists, microbiologists, soil scientists and glacial geomorphologists.

The Area contains three extensive and contrasting moss fields that have been the subject of taxonomic, ecological and physiological studies since the summer of 1982/83. Additional studies have included population ecology of invertebrates associated with the vegetation, and soil/water chemistry. Permanent lichen growth monitoring sites are established, as are sites monitoring annual growth increments in mosses (see Map E). Other floral studies have concentrated on the determination of biodiversity, physiological and biochemical attributes, component interactions, impact of anthropogenic pollutants, and potential effects of global climate change.

Global change studies have included a multi-year investigation into the impact of water and nutrients on various components of the vegetation, associated studies into the tolerance of mosses to both submergence and desiccation, and examination of the tolerance of three moss species to increased UV-B as a result of ozone depletion. Fine-scale analysis of genetic diversity of one cosmopolitan moss species *Ceratodon purpureus* has been compared for this location and others in the region. Dating of long cores of mosses has been achieved using ^{14}C and stable carbon isotopes of moss shoots, which provide a signature for changes in site water availability.

The Area is included within the geographic coverage of an Australian Antarctic program State of the Environment Indicator 72 "Windmill Islands terrestrial vegetation dynamics", which involves quantitative analysis of a series of permanent transects across selected vegetation, with the aim of monitoring the effects of climate change on Antarctic cryptogamic communities. This indicator was updated in 2008 and 2012.

Moss and lichen communities are used as indicators of environmental impacts of Casey station. The Area provides baseline data with which to compare changes in similar plant communities in the immediate surroundings of Casey station. The Area also serves as a valuable comparative site for similar plant communities in ASPA 136 Clark Peninsula, which are subject to less environmental stress and disturbance, due to lower human proximity.

2. Aims and objectives

Management of the Area aims to:

- avoid degradation of, or substantial risk to, the values of the Area by preventing unnecessary human disturbance and sampling in the Area;
- preserve a part of the natural ecosystem as a reference Area for the purpose of future comparative studies and to assess direct and indirect effects of Casey station;
- provide for compelling scientific research which cannot be served elsewhere;
- minimize, to the maximum extent practicable, the introduction of non-native plants, animals and microbes to the Area; and
- allow for the continued maintenance and operation of essential communications infrastructure including the transmitter building, towers, antennas, feed lines, storage rack and associated facilities without degradation of the Area's values.

3. Management activities

The following management activities shall be undertaken to protect the values of the Area:

- place signs illustrating the location and boundaries, with clear statements of entry restrictions at appropriate locations at the boundaries of the Area to help avoid inadvertent entry;
- display prominently information on the location of the Area (stating special restrictions that apply) and a copy of this Management Plan at Casey station and make copies of this information available to ships visiting the vicinity;
- secure and maintain in good condition markers, signs and structures erected within the Area for scientific or management purposes and remove them when no longer required;
- remove abandoned equipment or materials to the maximum extent possible provided this does not adversely impact on the values of the Area.
- detailed mapping of ongoing scientific experimental sites to ensure they are not disturbed;
- visit the Area as necessary (no less than once every five years) to assess whether the Area continues to serve the purposes for which it was designated and to ensure that management activities are adequate; and
- review the Management Plan at least every five years and update as required.

4. Period of designation

Designated for an indefinite period.

5. Maps

- Map A: Antarctic Specially Protected Areas, Windmill Islands, East Antarctica
- Map B: Antarctic Specially Protected Areas No 135, North-east Bailey Peninsula: Topography and Bird Distribution
- Map C: Antarctic Specially Protected Areas No 135, North-east Bailey Peninsula: Vegetation
- Map D: Antarctic Specially Protected Areas No 135, North-east Bailey Peninsula: Geology

- Map E: Antarctic Specially Protected Areas No 135, North-east Bailey Peninsula: Long term scientific monitoring sites

  Map specifications:

  Projection: Lambert Conformal Conic (Map A)

  Projection: UTM Zone 49 (Maps B, C D and E)

  Horizontal Datum: WGS84 (All maps)

6. Description of the Area

6(i) Geographical co-ordinates, boundary markers and natural features

General description

The Area is located on Bailey Peninsula in the Windmill Islands region of Budd Coast, Wilkes Land, East Antarctica (Map A). Bailey Peninsula is an area of rock exposures and permanent snow and ice fields lying between Newcomb Bay and O'Brien Bay, two kilometres south of Clark Peninsula.

The Area is located in the north-east of Bailey Peninsula, approximately 200m east of Casey station (66°16'59.9"S, 110°31'59.9"E), and covers an area of approximately 0.28km^2. The boundary is irregular, extending in the north to within approximately 70m south of Brown Bay. Boundary coordinates for the Area are shown in Appendix 1.

Topographically, Bailey Peninsula comprises low lying, rounded ice-free rocky outcrops (maximum altitude approximately 40 m), which rise from the coast to the Løken Moraines (altitude approximately 130 m). Intervening valleys are filled with permanent snow or ice, or glacial moraine and exfoliated debris, and contain water catchment areas. The topography of Bailey Peninsula is shown at Map B.

Climate

The climate of the Windmill Islands region is frigid-Antarctic. Climate records from nearby Casey station (altitude 32 m) show mean temperatures for the warmest and coldest months of 2.2 and -11.4°C respectively, extreme temperatures ranging from 9.2 to -34°C, and mean annual maximum and minimum temperatures of –5.9°C and –12.5°C respectively. The climate is dry with a mean annual snowfall of 219 mm year (rainfall equivalent), precipitation as rain has been recorded in the summer and recently in July 2008 and July 2009.

There is an annual average wind speed of 25km per hour. Gale winds are predominantly from the east, off the polar ice cap. Blizzards may occur very suddenly and are a frequent occurrence especially during winter. Snowfall is common during the winter, but the extremely strong winds scour the snow off exposed areas of the Peninsula. On most hill crests on Bailey Peninsula snow gathers in the lee of rock outcrops and in depressions in the substratum. Further down the slopes snow forms deeper drifts.

Environmental domains analysis

Based on the Environmental Domains Analysis for Antarctica (Resolution 3 (2008)) North-east Bailey Peninsula is located within Environment D *East Antarctic coastal geologic.*

Antarctic Conservation Biogeographic Regions

Based on the Antarctic Conservation Biogeographic Regions (Resolution 6 (2012)) North-east Bailey Peninsula is located within Biogeographic Region 7 *East Antarctica.*

Geology and soils

WINDMILL ISLANDS REGION

The Windmill Islands region represents one of the eastern-most outcrops of a Mesoproterozoic low-pressure granulite facies terrain that extends west to the Bunger Hills and further to the Archaean complexes in Princess Elizabeth Land, to minor exposures in the east in the Dumont d'Urville area and in Commonwealth Bay. The total outcrop areas do not exceed more than a few square kilometres. The Mesoproterozoic outcrop of the Windmill Islands and the Archaean complexes of Princess Elizabeth Land are two of the few major areas in East Antarctica that can be directly correlated with an Australian equivalent in a Gondwana reconstruction. The Mesoproterozoic facies terrain comprises a series of migmatitic metapelites and metapsammites interlayered with mafic to ultramafic and felsic sequences with rare calc-silicates, large partial melt bodies (Windmill Island supacrustals), undeformed granite, charnockite, gabbro, pegmatite, aplites and cut by easterly-trending late dolerite dykes.

BAILEY PENINSULA

Bailey Peninsula is part of the northern gradation of a metamorphic grade transition which separates the northern part of the Windmill Islands region from the southern part. The metamorphic grade ranges from amphibolite facies, sillimanite-biotite-orthoclase in the north at Clark Peninsula, through biotite-cordierite-almandine granulite, to hornblende-orthopyroxene granulite at Browning Peninsula in the south. The Ardery Charnockite of the south is prone to deep weathering and crumbles readily because of its mineral assemblage, whereas the metamorphic sequences of the northerly parts of the region have a much more stable mineral assemblage and crystalline structure. This difference has a significant influence on the distribution of vegetation in the Windmill Islands region with the northern rock types providing a more suitable substrate for slow growing lichens.

The leucocratic granite gneiss, which constitutes the main outcrop on Bailey Peninsula, may be subdivided into leucogneiss and two different types of garnet-bearing gneiss. The outcrop on Bailey Peninsula is characterised as a garnet-bearing gneiss type 1 which is white, medium grained and foliated. The foliation is defined by the alignment of an early biotite generation that is tight to openly folded, with a garnet and a later biotite generation that overgrows the fabric. Unmetamorphosed and undeformed dolerite dykes occur over Bailey Peninsula such as at "Penguin Pass" (66°17'18"S, 110°33'16"E), to the south of the Area. Small outcrops of metapelite, metapsammite and leuco- gneisses occur on the Peninsula. Recent geochronology of the rocks of the Windmill Islands region suggest two major phases of metamorphism, the first at c. 1400-1310 Ma, an upper amphibolite facies event, followed by a granulite facies overprint c. 1210-1180 Ma. The geology of Bailey Peninsula is shown at Map D.

GLACIATION

The Windmill Islands region was glaciated during the Late Pleistocene. The southern region of the Windmill Islands was deglaciated by 8000 corr. yr B.P., and the northern region, including Bailey Peninsula deglaciated by 5500 corr. yr B.P. Isostatic uplift has occurred at a rate of between 0.5 and 0.6 m/100 yr, with the upper mean marine limit, featured as ice-pushed ridges, being observed on Bailey Peninsula at approximately 30m where they extend in continuous rows from the present sea- level.

SOILS

Soils on Bailey Peninsula are derived from weathered gneiss, moraine deposits and outwash gravels stemming from glacial episodes. Seabirds have a large impact on soil formation in the entire landscape. Soils are frozen much of the year during summer, the upper 30-60 cm thaws with the few top centimetres, refreezing at night. Soils are mainly formed by cryoturbation and cryoclastic weathering. In the vicinity of Casey station most soils are classified by Blume, Kuhn and Bölter (2002) as cryosols with lithic, leptic, skeletal, turbic and stagnic subunits. Other soils in the Area are gelic subunits of histosols, podzols, and regosols, boulder and rock outcrops with ecto- and endolithic flora are classified as Lithosols. ASPA 135 was the site of an abandoned penguin colony, isolated due to isostatic uplift between 3-8000 years ago, that provides a rich ancient guano nutrient source for the current vegetation.

Lakes

Cold monomictic lakes and ponds occur throughout the Windmill Islands region in bedrock depressions and are usually ice-free during January and February. Nutrient rich lakes are found near the coast, in close proximity to penguin colonies or abandoned colonies, sterile lakes are located further inland and are fed by meltwater and local precipitation. A number of these lakes and ponds occur across Bailey Peninsula with two large lakes located 500m to the west of the Area. Two ponds occur within the protected Area, the largest being approximately 75m by 50m and the smaller soak approximately 25m diameter. The distribution of lakes and ponds on Bailey Peninsula is shown at Map B.

Vegetation and microbial communities

WINDMILL ISLANDS REGION

The Windmill Islands region supports some of the most extensive and best-developed plant communities in eastern Antarctica. The region is floristically diverse with rich associations of macrolichens and bryophytes that occupy very specific ecological niches. The flora of the Windmill Islands region comprises at least 36 species of lichen, 4 bryophytes (3 mosses and 1 liverwort), 150 non-marine algae and at least 120 fungal taxa. An ascomycete mycorrhizal fungus has been shown in the liverwort *Cephaloziella varians*.

Lichens constitute the largest part of the Windmill Islands region flora, with bryophytes being dominant in moister areas. At least 11 cryptogamic community types have been identified. These vegetation groupings exist within a continuum of ecological variation along environmental gradients influenced by soil moisture, soil chemistry, and microclimate. On the peninsulas in the region, the major community types are distinguished by the dominance of three bipolar lichens, *Usnea sphacelata, Pseudephebe minuscula* and *Umbilicaria decussata*. Vegetation communities on the islands are dominated by algal species such as *Prasiola crispa*, with bryophyte and lichen being considerably poorer developed than on the peninsulas. Mosses and lichens are all but absent in eutrophic sites near bird colonies with a prevalence of *Prasiola crispa, Prasiococcus calcareus* and *Desmococcus olivaceus* chlorophyte algae occurring.

The vegetation of Bailey Peninsula is exceptionally well developed and diverse and the Area represents one of the most important botanical sites on continental Antarctica. Within the relatively complex plant communities and contrasting habitats found on Bailey Peninsula, are found at least 23 lichens, three mosses, and a liverwort. There are expansive dense stands of macrolichens and in the more moist and sheltered areas bryophytes form closed stands of 25-50 m^2 with turf up to 30 cm in depth. Together with the lichens *Umbilicaria decussata, Pseudephebe minuscula* and *Usnea sphacelata* mixed bryophytes dominate the vegetation cover of most of the ice-free areas. This is particularly so on the north-east and centre of the Peninsula where there are dense communities similar to those found on Clark Peninsula. The most complex bryophyte communities are restricted to small locally moist hollows adjacent to melt pools and streams in the central north-east and central parts of the Peninsula. Vegetation is absent or poorly developed on the ice-free areas of the Peninsula's southern coast. Appendix 2 provides a list of bryophytes and lichens identified in the Area. In many areas mosses appear to be becoming increasingly moribund and are being out-competed or overgrown by lichens. Stable isotopes analysis of moss shoots has shown that growth rates have slowed since the 1980s associated with drying of the moss beds.

Two principal cryptogamic subformations are recognised; a lichen-dominated association occupying a variety of windswept substrata ranging from bedrock to gravel, and, a short cushion and turf moss subformation comprising four moss dominated groupings. The vegetation of Bailey Peninsula is shown at Maps C and E.

At least 150 taxa of non-marine algae and cyanobacteria have been isolated; these include 50 cyanobacteria, 70 chlorophytes and 23 chromophytes. The taxa have been found in snow and ice, soil, rocks, ephemeral ponds, tarns and lakes; 24 cyanobacterial and algal species occur in the snow. Snow algae are abundant and widespread in the icy corridors between the rocky outcrops and in semi-permanent snow drifts. A list of cyanobacterial and algal species from the Area, Bailey Peninsula, and the Windmill Islands region is shown in Appendix 3.

The vegetated soils of Bailey Peninsula contain fungal hyphae, yeasts, fungal propagules, an assortment of algae, cyanobacteria, protozoa, and provide a significant habitat for soil microfauna such as nematodes, mites, rotifers and tardigrades. There is relatively low fungal diversity in the Windmill Islands region, with 35 taxa representing 22 genera of fungi being isolated from soils, mosses, algae and lichens. Thirty fungal taxa have been detected in soils in the vicinity of Casey station with 12 of these taxa restricted to anthropogenically influenced soils around the station suggesting that there may be a non-native element in this flora, *Penicillium* species dominate in these sites. Within the Windmill Islands region, 21 fungal taxa have been isolated the mosses, with 12 taxa isolated from algae and 6 from lichens. A number of fungi have also been found associated with animals of the region. Appendix 4 provides detail of the taxa and their source.

Genomic analysis of soil microbial flora is currently under investigation. There have been some genomic analyses of mosses, especially *C. purpureus*.

Birds

Four species of birds are known to nest in the vicinity of Bailey Peninsula. These include Adélie penguin *Pygoscelis adeliae*, the most abundant bird species in the Area. The nearest breeding colony is on Shirley Island about 1.5km west of Casey station. Snow petrels *Pagodroma nivea* are seen all year round and breed throughout the Windmill Islands region including Reeve Hill about 750m west of the Area and Budnick Hill, 600m to the north-west. Wilson's storm petrels *Oceanites oceanicus* breed throughout the Windmill Islands region and nest in the Area. The Antarctic skua *Catharacta maccormicki* breeds throughout the Windmill Islands region at widely dispersed nests, mostly near Adélie penguin colonies. Skuas use the lake in the ASPA for bathing.

Other birds that breed in the Windmill Islands region but not in the immediate vicinity of Bailey Peninsula include southern giant petrel *Macronectes giganteus*, cape petrel *Daption capense*, southern fulmar *Fulmarus glacialoides* and Antarctic petrel *Thalassoica antarctica*. The emperor penguin *Aptenodytes forsteri* is a common visitor to the Windmill Islands region and a breeding colony of approximately 2000 pairs is established in the area of Peterson Bank, 65km north-west of Casey station.

Terrestrial invertebrates and microbial communities

The Antarctic flea *Glaciopsyllus antarcticus* has been found in the nests of southern fulmars. The anopluran louse *Antarctophthirus ogmorhini* is found on the Weddell seal *Leptonychotes weddellii*. A number of species of mallophagan lice have also been found on birds.

The free-living mite *Nanorchestes antarcticus* has been found on Bailey Peninsula at sites characterised as having sandy or gravelly soils, free of extensive moss or lichen cover, and moist but not water- logged.

Five species of tardigrades have been collected on Bailey Peninsula: *Pseudechiniscus suillus, Macrobiotus* sp., *Hypsibius antarcticus, Ramajendas frigidus* and *Diphascon chilenense*. Significant positive associations between bryophytes and the most common species of tardigrades *P. suillus, H. antarcticus* and *D. chilenense*, have been found, and strong negative associations between those species and algae and lichens have been established. No systematic or ecological accounts of nematodes have yet been published for the Windmill Islands region.

Protozoa have been studied at a number of sites on Bailey Peninsula and in the Area ciliates and testate amoebae are active. Twenty seven ciliate species and six testacean species have been found (see Appendix 5).

6(ii) Access to the Area

The north-west boundary of the Area is located approximately 200m east of Casey station, and the Area is easily accessible by foot. Vehicle access to and within the Area is covered under section 7(ii) of this plan.

6(iii) Location of structures within and adjacent to the Area

Casey station (Australia) is located approximately 200m west of the Area. Prior to the designation of the Area in 1986 an array of radio transmitters had been progressively established at the site since 1964. During the 2001/2002 and 2007/2008 summers redundant aerials and some other infrastructure were removed. A number of structures remain within the Area, including a small storage rack holding antenna spares in the north-west, the transmitter building (which can also be used as an emergency refuge), a 45m high tandem delta antenna mast and a non-directional beacon antenna located in the south-east (Map E). Another 35m high mast is located approximately 100m south of the Area. These form the basis of the Casey High Frequency (HF) Transmit installation.

6(iv) Location of other Protected Areas in the vicinity

Other protected areas in the vicinity include (see Map A):

- ASPA No 136, Clark Peninsula, is located 2.5km to the north-east, across Newcomb Bay.
- ASPA No 103, Ardery and Odbert Islands, is located approximately 11km to the south, west of Robinson Ridge.
- ASPA No 160, Frazier Islands, is located in the eastern part of Vincennes Bay approximately 16km to the west-north-west.

6(v) Special zones within the Area

There are no special zones within the Area.

7. Terms and conditions for entry permits

7(i) General permit conditions

Entry to the Area is prohibited except in accordance with a Permit issued by an appropriate national authority. Conditions for issuing a Permit to enter the Area are that:

- it is issued for compelling scientific research, maintenance of the communications installation and associated facilities, removal of obsolete structures/materials, or for essential management purposes consistent with the Management Plan's objectives and provisions;
- the actions permitted are in accordance with this Management Plan;
- the activities permitted will give due consideration via the environmental impact assessment process to the continued protection of the ecological or scientific values of the Area or interfere with existing scientific studies;
- the Permit shall be issued for a finite period; and
- the Permit shall be carried when in the Area.

Additional conditions, consistent with the Management Plan's objectives and provisions, may be included by the issuing authority.

7(ii) Access to, and movement within or over, the Area

Helicopters are prohibited from landing within the Area.

Vehicles are prohibited from entering the Area, except for the purpose of conducting ongoing maintenance of the transmitter building, associated buildings and antennas, or for the removal of structures/materials. Access to the transmitter building near the south-east end of the Area should be via the over-snow access route to Law Dome, several kilometres to the south. Within the Area, vehicles should follow the most direct practicable route between the Area boundary and the communications facilities, avoiding vegetation and cables. Vehicle use in the Area shall be kept to a minimum and only use the route specified in the permit.

The north-west boundary of the Area is located approximately 200m east of Casey station, and the Area is easily accessible by foot. Visitors should avoid walking on visible vegetation. Care should be exercised when walking in areas of moist ground, where foot traffic can easily damage sensitive soils, plant or algae communities, and degrade water quality. Pedestrian traffic should be kept to the minimum necessary to undertake permitted activities and every reasonable effort should be made to walk around such areas, keeping to ice-covered areas or bare rock where it is practicable and safe to do so.

7(iii) Activities which may be conducted in the Area

Activities which may be conducted within the Area include:

- Compelling scientific research which cannot be undertaken elsewhere and which will not jeopardise the ecosystem of the Area.
- Essential management activities, including monitoring, erection of signs and removal of structures/materials.
- Sampling, but this should be the minimum required for the approved research programs.
- Operation, maintenance and other essential activities associated with the communications installation including the transmitter building, towers, antennas, feed lines, storage rack and associated facilities.

7(iv) Installation, modification or removal of structures

- Any structures erected or installed within the Area are to be specified in a Permit. Scientific markers and equipment must be secured and maintained in good condition, clearly identifying the permitting country, name of principal investigator and year of installation. All such items should be made of materials that pose minimum risk of contamination of the Area. Markers or equipment should not be made of material that may impact on the surrounding environment.
- Installation (including site selection), maintenance, modification or removal of structures and equipment shall be undertaken in a manner that minimises disturbance to the values of the Area.
- Equipment associated with scientific research, shall be removed before the Permit (or authorisation) for that research expires, as a condition of the Permit (or authorisation). Details of markers and equipment left in situ should be reported to the permitting Authority. Such details should include a description, expected "use by date", and accurate GPS location with longitude and latitude in decimal degrees to 6 decimal places (where practicable, details should also be given regarding the horizontal datum used, model of GPS, base station details, and horizontal and vertical accuracies).
- Removal of specific structures or equipment shall be a condition of the Permit for when the Permit expires.
- Permanent structures or installations are prohibited with the exception of permanent survey markers.

- All such items should be free of organisms, propagules (e.g. seeds, eggs) and non-sterile soil, and be made of materials that can withstand the environmental conditions and pose minimal risk of contamination of the Area.
- All temporary structures and installations must be removed when they are no longer required, or on the expiry of the permit, whichever is the earlier, to the extent that this does not cause more damage than benefit to the vegetation/values of the area.

7(v) Location of field camps

Camping is prohibited within the Area.

7(vi) Restrictions on materials and organisms which may be brought into the Area

- No living animals, plant material or microorganisms shall be deliberately introduced into the Area. To help maintain the ecological and scientific values of the plant communities found in the Area, persons entering the Area shall take special precautions against unintentional introductions. Of particular concern are microbial or vegetation introductions sourced from soils at other Antarctic sites, including stations, or from regions outside Antarctica. To minimise the risk of introductions footwear and any equipment – including carry cases, sampling equipment and markers – to be used in the Area shall be thoroughly cleaned before entering the Area.
- No herbicides or pesticides shall be brought into the Area unless assessed necessary to control or eradicate an alien species. Chemicals may be introduced for scientific or management purposes specified in a Permit and shall be removed from the Area at or before the conclusion of the permitted activity.
- Permanent fuel depots are prohibited. Fuel may be temporarily stored in the Area for essential purposes connected with an activity for which a Permit has been granted. Such fuel shall be stored in sealed and bunded containers.
- Any materials introduced for a stated period shall be removed at or before the conclusion of the stated period, and shall be stored and handled so that the risk of dispersal into the environment is minimised.

7(vii) Taking of, or harmful interference with native flora and fauna

Taking of or harmful interference with native flora and fauna is prohibited, except in accordance with a Permit. Where taking of or harmful interference with animals is involved this should, as a minimum standard, be in accordance with the *SCAR Code of Conduct for the Use of Animals for Scientific Purposes in Antarctica.*

7(viii) The collection or removal of material not brought into the Area by the permit holder

Material may only be collected or removed from the Area in accordance with a Permit and should be limited to the minimum necessary to meet scientific or management needs.

Material of human origin likely to compromise the values of the Area, and which was not brought into the Area by the Permit Holder or otherwise authorised, may be removed unless the impact of the removal is likely to be greater than leaving the material *in situ*. In such cases the appropriate national authority must be notified and approval obtained.

7(ix) Disposal of waste

All wastes, including all human wastes, shall be removed from the Area.

7(x) Measures that may be necessary to continue to meet the aims of the Management Plan

Permits may be granted to enter the Area to carry out the following measures, provided they do not adversely impact on the values of the Area:

- biological monitoring and Area inspection and management activities, which may involve the collection of small samples for analysis or review;
- erect or maintain signposts;
- maintenance or removal of the storage rack, buildings, antenna masts and associated supplies located in the north-west of the Area; and
- other protective measures as required.

7(xi) Requirements for reports

The principal Permit Holder for each Permit issued shall submit to the appropriate national authority a report describing the activities undertaken. Such reports should include, as appropriate, the information identified in the Visit Report form contained in the *Guide to the Preparation of Management Plans for Antarctic Specially Protected Areas*. Parties should maintain a record of such activities and, in the Annual Exchange of Information, should provide summary descriptions of activities conducted by persons subject to their jurisdiction, which should be in sufficient detail to allow evaluation of the effectiveness of the Management Plan. Parties should, wherever possible, deposit originals or copies of such original reports in a publicly accessible archive to maintain a record of usage; to be used both in any review of the Management Plan and in organising the scientific use of the Area.

8. Supporting documentation

Adamson, E., and Seppelt, R. D. (1990) A comparison of airborne alkaline pollution damage in selected lichens and mosses at Casey Station, Wilkes Land, Antarctica. In: Kerry, K. R. and Hempel, G. (eds.) *Antarctic Ecosystems: Ecological Change and Conservation* Springer- Verlag, Berlin, pp. 347-353.

Azmi, O. R., and Seppelt, R. D. (1997) Fungi in the Windmill Islands, continental Antarctica. Effect of temperature, pH and culture media on the growth of selected microfungi. *Polar Biology* **18**: 128-134.

Azmi, O. R., and Seppelt, R. D. (1998) The broad scale distribution of microfungi in the Windmill Islands region, continental Antarctica. *Polar Biology* **19**: 92-100.

Bednarek-Ochyra, H., Váòa, J., Ochyra, R., Lewis Smith, R. I. (2000) *The Liverwort Flora of Antarctica*. Polish Academy of Sciences, Institute of Botany, Cracow.

Bergstrom D. and Robinson, S (2010) Casey: the Daintree of Antarctica. http://www.antarctica.gov.au/about-antarctica/fact-files/plants/casey-the-daintree-of-antarctica

Beyer, L., (2002) Properties, Formation and Geography of Soils in a Coastal Terrestrial Ecosystem of East Antarctica (Casey Station, Wilkes Land) [cited 26 November 2012]. Available from internet: http://books.google.com.au/books?hl=en&lr=&id=m-MB7TZrwg0C&oi=fnd&pg=PA3&dq=Beyer,+L.,+(2002)+Properties,+Formation+and+Geography+of+Soils+in+a+Coastal+Terrestrial+Ecosystem+of+East+Antarctica&ots=snaw67pzBU&sig=xU4CR0XzXafitWuROLhm1nR1FT0#v=onepage&q&f=false

Beyer, L., Pingpank, K., Bölter, M. and Seppelt, R. D. (1998) Small-distance variation of carbon and nitrogen storage in mineral Antarctic cryosols near Casey Station (Wilkes Land). *Zeitschrift fur Pflanzenahrung Bodendunde* **161**: 211-220.

Beyer, Lothar, Kristina Pingpank, Manfred Bölter and Rod D. Seppelt (2002): Soil organic matter storage on soil profile and on landscape level in permafrost affected soils in the coastal region of East Antarctica (Casey Station, Wilkes Land). In: Tarnocai et al. (Eds.). *Cryosols - Permafrost-Affected Soils*. Lewis Publishers, Boca Raton (in press).

Blight, D. F. (1975) The Metamorphic Geology of the Windmill Islands Antarctica, Volume 1 and 2, PhD thesis, University of Adelaide.

Blight, D. F. and Oliver, R. L. (1982) Aspects of the Geological history of the Windmill Islands, Antarctica. In: Craddock, C. (Ed.) *Antarctic Geoscience*, University of Wisconsin Press, Madison, WI, pp. 445-454.

Blight, D. F. and Oliver, R. L. (1997) The metamorphic geology of the Windmill Islands Antarctica: a preliminary account. *Journal of the Geological Society of Australia.* **24** (5): 239-262.

Block, W. (1992) *An Annotated Bibliography of Antarctic Invertebrates (Terrestrial and Freshwater)*.British Antarctic Survey, Natural Environmental Research Council, Cambridge.

Block, W. (2002) A dataset of Antarctic and sub-Antarctic invertebrates. [www site], [cited 26 November 2012]. Available from internet: http://gcmd.nasa.gov/KeywordSearch/Metadata.do?Portal=amd_au&KeywordPath=Parameters%7C%28%5BFreetext%3D%27invertebrates%27%5D+AND+%5BFreetext%3D%27sub-antarctic%27%5D%29&OrigMetadataNode=AADC&EntryId=block_invertebrates&MetadataView=Full&MetadataType=0&lbnode=mdlb5

Blume, H-P., Kuhn, D. and Bölter, M. (2002) Soils and landscapes. In: Beyer, L. and Bölter, M. (eds.) *Geoecology of Antarctic Ice-Free Coastal Landscapes.* Springer-Verlag, Berlin, pp. 94-98, 105-108.

Bramley-Alves, J. *King, DH, Miller, RE & Robinson SA. (2013) Dominating the Antarctic Environment: bryophytes in a time of change. In Photosynthesis of Bryophytes and Seedless Vascular Plants. Eds Hanson DT & Rice SK. Volume in series Advances in Photosynthesis and Respiration. Springer (in press).

Bureau of Meteorology (2004) Climate and History, Climate of Casey [www site], [cited 22 June 2004] Available from internet: *http://www.bom.gov.au/weather/ant/casey/climate.shtml*

Clarke, L.J., Robinson, S.A., Ayre, D.J. (2008) Somatic mutation and the Antarctic ozone hole Journal of Ecology 96 378-385. Editor's choice article for March 2008.

Clarke, L.J., Robinson, S.A. Cell wall-bound UV-screening pigments explain the high UV tolerance of the Antarctic moss, Ceratodon purpureus (revised submission to New Phytologist Feb 2008)

Clarke, L.J., Robinson, S.A., Ayre, D.J. Genetic structure of Antarctic populations of the moss Ceratodon purpureus. Antarctic Science 21 51-58

Clarke, L.J., Robinson, S.A., Hua, Q., Ayre D.J. & Fink, D. (2012) Radiocarbon bomb spike reveals biological effects of Antarctic climate change. Global Change Biology, **18** 301-310 plus front cover.

Cowan, A. N. (1979) Giant petrels at Casey, Antarctica. *Australian Bird Watcher.* **8** (2): 66-67. Cowan, A. N. (1981). Size variation in the Snow petrel (Pagodroma nivea). *Notornis* **28**: 169-188. Dunn, J. (2000) Seasonal variation in the pigment content of three species of Antarctic bryophytes Honours thesis University of Wollongong .; [Ref:10167]; AAS Projects 941, 1310

Dunn, J.L., Robinson, S.A. (2006) Ultraviolet B screening potential is higher in two cosmopolitan moss species than in a co-occurring Antarctic endemic moss: implications of continuing ozone depletion. Global Change Biology 12. 2282-2296; [Ref:12830]; AAS Projects 1310, 2542

Dunn, J.L., Robinson, S.A. (2006) UV-B screening potential is higher in two cosmopolitan moss species than in a co-occurring Antarctic endemic moss - implications of continuing ozone depletion Global Change Biology 12 (12). 42pp; [Ref:12867]; AAS Projects 1310, 2542

Dunn, JL, *Turnbull, JD & Robinson, SA (2004) Comparison of solvent regimes for the extraction of photosynthetic pigments from leaves of higher plants. Functional Plant Biology 31: 195-202.

Giese, M. (1998) Guidelines for people approaching breeding groups of Adélie penguins (Pygoscelis adeliae). *Polar Record.* **34** (191): 287-292.

Goodwin, I. D. (1993) Holocene deglaciation, sea-level change, and the emergence of the Windmill Islands, Budd Coast, Antarctica. *Quaternary Research.* **40**: 70-80.

Hallingbäck, Tomas and Hodgetts, Nick. (Compilers) (2000) *Mosses, Liverworts, and Hornworts: Status Survey and Conservation Action Plan for Bryophytes.* IUCN/SSC Bryophyte Specialist Group.

Heatwole, H., Saenger, P., Spain, A., Kerry, E. and Donelan, J. (1989) Biotic and chemical characteristics of some soils from Wilkes Land Antarctica. *Antarctic Science.* **1**(3): 225-234.

Hogg ID, Stevens MI (2002) Soil Fauna of Antarctic Coastal Landscapes. In: Beyer L and Bölter M (eds). Geoecology of Antarctic Ice-Free Coastal Landscapes. Ecological Studies Volume 154, pp 265-282. Springer-Verlag, Berlin

Hovenden, M. J. and Seppelt, R. D. (1995) Exposure and nutrients as delimiters of lichen communities in continental Antarctica. *Lichenologist* **27**(6): 505-516.

Leslie, S. (2003) The Combined Effects of Desiccation and UV-B Radiation on the Accumulation of DNA Damage, Pigment Composition and Photosynthetic Efficiency in three species of Antarctic moss. Thesis. Bachelor of Biotechnology (Honours) Degree, University of Wollongong. 1-87; [Ref:11456]; AAS Project 1310

Ling, H. U. (1996) Snow algae of the Windmill Islands region, Antarctica. *Hydrobiologia* 336: 99-106. Ling, H. U. (2001) Snow Algae of the Windmill Islands, Continental Antarctica: *Desmotetraaureospora*, sp. nov. and D. antarctica, comb. nov. (Chlorophyta). *Journal of Phycology* **37**: 160-174.

Ling, H. U. and Seppelt, R.D. (1990) Snow algae of the Windmill Islands, continental Antarctica. esotaenium berggrenii (Zygnematales, Chlorophyta) the alga of grey snow. *Antarctic Science* 2(2): 143-148

Ling, H. U. and Seppelt, R.D. (1993) Snow algae of the Windmill Islands, continental Antarctica. 2. Chloromonas rubroleosa sp. nov. (Volvocales, Chlorophyta), an alga of red snow. *European Journal of Phycology* : 77-84.

Ling, H. U. and Seppelt, R.D. (1998) Non-marine algae and cyanobacteria of the Windmill Islands region, Antarctica, with descriptions of two new species. *Archiv für Hydrobiologie Supplement 124, Algological Studies* 89: 49-62.

Ling, H. U. and Seppelt, R.D. (1998) Snow Algae of the Windmill Islands, continental Antarctica 3. Chloromonas polyptera (Volvocales, Chlorophyta) *Polar Biology* 20: 320-324.

Ling, H. U. and Seppelt, R.D. (2000) Snow Algae of the Windmill Islands Region, Adaptations to the Antarctic Environment. Davison, W., Howard-Williams, C., Broady, P. (eds.) *Antarctic Ecosystems: Models for Wider Ecological Understanding.* pp. 171-174.

Longton, R. E. (1988) *Biology of polar bryophytes and lichens.* Cambridge University Press, Cambridge. 307-309.

Lovelock, C.E., Robinson, S.A. (2002) Surface reflectance properties of Antarctic moss and their relationship to plant species, pigment composition and photosynthetic function. Plant, Cell and Environment. 25. 1239-1250; [Ref:10869]; AAS Projects 941, 1310

Lucieer, A, Robinson, S and Bergstrom D. (2010) Aerial 'OktoKopter' to map Antarctic moss *Australian Antarctic Magazine*, Issue 19. pp. 1-3 http://www.antarctica.gov.au/about-antarctica/australian-antarctic-magazine/issue-19-2010/aerial-oktokopter-to-map-antarctic-moss.

Melick, D. R., Hovenden, M. J., and Seppelt, R. D. (1994) Phytogeography of bryophyte and lichen vegetation in the Windmill Islands, Wilkes land, Continental Antarctica. *Vegetatio* 111: 71-87.

Melick, D. R., and Seppelt, R. D. (1990) Vegetation patterns in Relation to climatic and endogenous changes in Wilkes Land, continental Antarctica. *Journal of Ecology* 85: 43-56.

Miller, W. R., Miller, J. D. and Heatwole, H. (1996) Tardigrades of the Australian Antarctic Territories: the Windmill Islands, East Antarctica. *Zoological Journal of the Linnean Society* 116: 175-184.

Murray, M. D., and Luders, D. J. (1990) Faunistic studies at the Windmill Islands, Wilkes Land, East Antarctica, 1959-80. *ANARE Research Notes* **73**, Antarctic Division, Kingston.

Orton, M. N. (1963) A Brief Survey of the fauna of the Windmill Islands, Wilkes Land, Antarctica. *The Emu* **63** (1): 14-22.

Øvstedal, D. O. and Lewis Smith, R. I. (2001) Lichens of Antarctica and South Georgia: A Guide to their Identification and Ecology. Cambridge University Press, Cambridge.

Paul, E., Stüwe, K., Teasdale, J. and Worley, B. (1995) Structural and metamorpohic geology of the Windmill Islands, East Antarctica: field evidence for repeated tectonothermal activity. *Australian Journal of Earth Sciences* **42**: 453-469.

Petz, P. (1997) Ecology of the active microfauna (Protozoa, Metazoa) of Wilkes Land, East Antarctica. *Polar Biology* 18: 33-44.

Petz, P. and Foissner, W. (1997) Morphology and infraciliature of some ciliates (Protozoa, Ciliophora) from continental Antarctica, with notes on the morphogenesis of *Sterkiella histriomuscorum*. *Polar Record* **33**(187): 307-326.

Robinson, S.A., Wasley, J., Popp, M., Lovelock, C.E. (2000) Desiccation tolerance of three moss species from continental Antarctica. Australian Journal of Plant Physiology 27. 379-388; [Ref:9083]; AAS Projects 941, 1087, 1313

Robinson, S.A., Dunn, J., Turnbull, D., Clarke, L. (2006) UV-B screening potential is higher in two cosmopolitan moss species than in a co-occurring Antarctic endemic ? implications of continuing ozone depletion. Abstracts of the Combio 2006 Conference, Brisbane Sept 24-28th 2006. p. 101; [Ref:12837]; AAS Projects 1310, 2542

Robinson, SA, *Turnbull, JD & Lovelock, C.E. (2005) Impact of changes in natural UV radiation on pigment composition, surface reflectance and photosynthetic function of the Antarctic moss, *Grimmia antarctici*. Global Change Biology **11:** 476-489.

Robinson SA. & *Waterman M. (2013) Sunsafe bryophytes: photoprotection from excess and damaging solar radiation. In Photosynthesis of Bryophytes and Seedless Vascular Plants. Eds Hanson DT & Rice SK. Volume X in series Advances in Photosynthesis and Respiration. Springer (in press).

Robinson, SA, *Wasley, J & Tobin, AK (2003) Living on the edge-plants and global change in continental and maritime Antarctica. Global Change Biology **9** 1681-1717. *Invited review.*

Roser, D. J., Melick, D. R., Ling, H. U. and Seppelt, R. D. (1992) Polyol and sugar content of terrestrial plants from continental Antarctica. *Antarctic Science* **4** (4): 413-420.

Roser, D. J., Melick, D. R. and Seppelt, R. D. (1992) Reductions in the polyhydric alcohol content of lichens as an indicator of environmental pollution. *Antarctic Science* **4** (4): 185-189.

Roser, D. J., Seppelt, R. D. and Nordstrom (1994) Soluble carbohydrate and organic content of soils and associated microbiota from the Windmill Islands, Budd Coast, Antarctica. *Antarctic Science* **6**(1): 53-59.

Selkirk, P. M.and Skotnicki, M. L (2007) *Measurement of moss growth in continental Antarctica*, Polar Biology 30(4): pp. 407-413; Springer-Verlag, Berlin, illus. incl. 2 tables; 21 refs.

Seppelt, R. D. (2002) Plant Communities at Wilkes Land. In: Beyer, L. and Bölter, M. (eds.) *Geoecology of Antarctic Ice-Free Coastal Landscapes* Springer-Verlag, Berlin, 233-242.

Seppelt, R. D. (2002) Wilkes Land (Casey Station). In: Beyer, L. and Bölter, M. (eds.) *Geoecology of Antarctic Ice-Free Coastal Landscapes.* Springer-Verlag, Berlin, pp. 41-46.

Seppelt, R. D. (2008) Dr R. Seppelt, Senior Research Scientist, Australian Antarctic Division. Personal communication.

Smith, R. I. L. (1980) *Plant community dynamics in Wilkes Land, Antarctica,* Proceedings NIPR Symposium of polar biology **3**: 229-224.

Smith, R. I. L. (1986) Plant ecological studies in the fellfield ecosystem near Casey Station, Australian Antarctic Territory, 1985-86. *British Antarctic Survey Bulletin.* **72**: 81-91.

Terauds A., Chown, S.L., Morgan, F., Peat, H.J., Watts, D., Keys, H., Convey, P. and Bergstrom, D.M. (2012) Conservation biogeography of the Antarctic. Diversity and Distributions, 18, 726–741

Turnbull, JD, Leslie, SJ & Robinson, SA (2009) Desiccation protects two Antarctic mosses from ultraviolet–B induced DNA damage. Functional Plant Biology **36** 214-221.

Turnbull, J.D., Robinson, S.A. Susceptibility to Ultraviolet Radiation Induced DNA Damage In Three Antarctic Mosses (submitted to Global Change Biology)

Turnbull, JD & Robinson, SA (2009) Accumulation of DNA damage in Antarctic mosses: correlations with ultraviolet-B radiation, temperature and turf water content vary among species. Global Change Biology **15** 319-329.

Turnbull, J.D., Robinson, S.A., Leslie, S.J., Nikaido, O. (2008) Desiccation confers protection from UV – B radiation but an endemic Antarctic moss is more susceptible to DNA damage than co- occurring cosmopolitan species. (in prep)

Turner, D., Lucieer, A. and Watson, C. (2012) An Automated Technique for Generating Georectified Mosaics from Ultra-High Resolution Unmanned Aerial Vehicle (UAV) Imagery, Based on Structure from Motion (SfM) Point Clouds. Remote Sens. 4, 1392-1410

Wasley, J., Robinson, S.A., Lovelock, C.E., Popp, M. (2006) Climate change manipulations show Antarctic flora is more strongly affected by elevated nutrients than water. Global Change Biology 12. 1800-1812; [Ref:12682]; AAS Project 1087

Wasley, J., Robinson, S.A., Lovelock, C.E., Popp, M. (2006) Some like it wet — biological characteristics underpinning tolerance of extreme water stress events in Antarctic bryophytes. Functional Plant Biology 33. 443-455; [Ref:12318]; AAS Project 1087

Wasley, J., Robinson, S.A., *Turnbull, J.D., *King D.H., Wanek, W. Popp, M. (2012) Bryophyte species composition over moisture gradients in the Windmill Islands, East Antarctica: development of a baseline for monitoring climate change impacts. Biodiversity DOI:10.1080/14888386.2012.712636.

Woehler, E. J., Penney, S. M., Creet, S. M. and Burton, H. R. (1994) Impacts of human visitors on breeding success and long-term population trends in Adélie penguins at Casey, Antarctica. *Polar Biology* **14**: 269-274.

Woehler, E. J., Slip, D. J., Robertson, L. M., Fullagar, P. J. and Burton, H. R. (1991) The distribution, abundance and status of Adélie penguins *Pygoscelis adeliae* at the Windmill Islands, Wilkes Land, Antarctica. *Marine Ornithology* **19**(1): 1-18.

Appendix 1: North-east Bailey Peninsula, Antarctic Specially Protected Area

No 135, boundary coordinates

Boundary	Longitude	Latitude	**Boundary**	Longitude	Latitude
1	110°32’56”	66°17’11”	**15**	110°32’16”	66°16’52”
2	110°32’50”	66°17’11”	**16**	110°32’19”	66°16’53”
3	110°32’41”	66°17’10”	**17**	110°32’19”	66°16’55”
4	110°32’22”	66°17’7”	**18**	110°32’24”	66°16’55”
5	110°32’20”	66°17’6”	**19**	110°32’25”	66°16’53”
6	110°32’18”	66°17’2”	**20**	110°32’29”	66°16’53”
7	110°32’18”	66°17’0”	**21**	110°32’44”	66°16’54”
8	110°32’14”	66°17’0”	**22**	110°33’9”	66°17’5”
9	110°32’9”	66°16’56”	**23**	110°33’11”	66°17’6”
10	110°32’8”	66°16’54”	**24**	110°33’10”	66°17’9”
11	110°32’5”	66°16’54”	**25**	110°33’2”	66°17’11”
12	110°32’7”	66°16’52”			
13	110°32’7”	66°16’52”			
14	110°32’12”	66°16’51”			

Appendix 2: Mosses, liverworts and lichens identified from North-east Bailey Peninsula Antarctic Specially Protected Area No 135, (from Melick 1994, Seppelt pers. comm.)

Mosses
Bryum pseudotriquetrun (Hedw.) Gaertn., Meyer et Scherb.
Ceratodon purpureus (Hedw.) Brid.
Schistidium antarctici Card.
Liverworts
Cephaloziella varians Steph.
Lichens
Acarospora gwynii Dodge & Rudolph
Amandinea petermannii (Hue) Matzer, H. Mayrhofer & Scheid.
Buellia cf. cladocarpiza Lamb?
Buellia frigida Darb.
Buellia grimmiae Filson
Buellia cf. lignoides Filson
Buellia papillata Tuck.
Buellia pycnogonoides Darb.
Buellia soredians Filson
Caloplaca athallina Darb.
Caloplaca citrina (Hoffm.) Th. Fr.
Candelariella flava (C.W. Dodge & Baker) Castello & Nimis
Lecanora expectans Darb.
Lecidea spp.
Lecidea cancriformis Dodge & Baker (=*Lecidea phillipsiana* Filson)
Lecidea andersonii Filson
Lepraria sp.
Pleopsidium chlorophanum (Wahlenb.) Zopf
Rhizocarpon geographicum
Rhizoplaca melanophthalma (Ram.) Leuck. & Poelt
Rinodina olivaceobrunnea Dodge & Baker
Physcia caesia (Hoffm.) Hampe
Umbilicaria aprina Nyl.
Umbilicaria decussata (Vill.) Zahlbr.
Umbilicaria cf. propagulifera (Vainio) Llano
Xanthoria elegans (Link) Th. Fr.
Xanthoria mawsonii Dodge.
Pseudephebe minuscula (Nyl ex Arnold) Brodo & Hawksw.
Usnea antarctica Du Rietz
Usnea sphacelata R. Br.

Appendix 3: Fungi isolated from soils, mosses, lichens and algae from ASPA No 135 and from species of wider distribution in the Windmill Islands region (from Azmi 1998 and Seppelt pers. comm. 2008)

Note: This is only a partial list of the taxa isolated from the Windmill Islands

	ASPA No 135	Bailey Peninsula	Bryum pseudotri-quetrum	Ceratodon purpureu	Grimmia antarctici	Algae	Lichens*
Acremonium sp.					9		
Acremonium crotociningenum (Schol-Schwarz) W. Gams		9					9
Alternaria alternata (Fr.) Keissl.		9					
Arthrobotrys			9	9			
Aspergillus nidulans (Eidam) G. Winter		9					
Aspergillus sp.						9	
Botrytis cinerea Pers.		9					
Chrysosporium sp	9		9	9	9		
Chrysosporium pannorum (Link.) S. Hughes	9	9	9	9	9	9	9
Cladosporium sp.		9					
Diplodia sp.		9					
Fusarium oxysporum E.F. Sm., & Swingle		9					
Geomyces sp.		9	9	9		9	9
Geotrichum sp.							
Mortierella sp.		9	9		9	9	9
Mortierella gamsii Milko		9	9				
Mucor pyriformis Scop.		9	9		9		
Mycelia sterilia 1**	9		9	9	9	9	9
Mycelia sterilia 2**	9		9	9	9	9	
Mycelia sterilia 3**	9		9	9	9		
Mycelia sterilia 4**		9					
Nectria peziza Berk.		9	9		9		
Penicillium chrysogenum Thom	9		9		9	9	
P. commune Thom		9					
P. corylophilum Dierckx		9					
P. expansum Link		9	9	9		9	
P. hirsutum Dierckx		9					
P. palitans Westling		9	9	9	9		
P. roqueforti Thom		9					
Penicillium sp.			9	9	9	9	
Penicillium sp. 1							
Penicillium sp. 2							

	ASPA No 135	Bailey Peninsula	Bryum pseudotri-quetrum	Ceratodon purpureu	Grimmia antarctici	Algae	Lichens*
Phialophora malorum (Kidd & Beaumont) McColloch		9	9	9	9	9	
Phoma herbarum Westend		9	9	9	9		
Phoma sp.	9						
Phoma sp. 1			9	9	9		
Phoma sp. 2				9	9		
Rhizopus stolonifer (Ehrenb.) Vuill.		9				9	
Sclerotinia sclerotiorum (Lib.) de Bary		9					
Thelebolus microsporus (Berk. & Broome) Kimbr.	9	9	9	9	9	9	9
Trichoderma harzianum Rifai		9					
T. pseudokoningi Rifai		9					

*Lichens are *Xanthoria mawsonni, Umbilicaria decussata and Usnea sphacelata.*

** Mycelia sterilia is a general term for sterile mycelia. Approximately 45% of all the isolates obtained from the Windmill Islands have not been identified because they remained sterile in culture.

Appendix 4: Cyanobacterial and algal species identified from the Windmill Islands region

The taxa are listed in alphabetical order under each phylum together with their habitats and whether they are maintained in culture. A = Aquatic, T = Terrestrial (from soil),

S = Snow or ice and C = Culture. (from Ling 1998 and Seppelt pers. comm. 2008).

Cyanobacteria	
Aphanothece castagnei (Breb.) Rabenh.	A
Aphanocapsa elachista var. irregularis Boye-Pet.	A
Aphanocapsa muscicola (Menegh.) Wille	A
Aphanothece saxicola Nageli	A
Aphanothece sp.	A
Calothrix parietina Thur.	A
Chamaesiphon subglobosus ((Ros-Taf) Lemmerm.	A
Chroococcus dispersus (Keissl.) Lemmerm.	A
Chroococcus minutus (Kutz.) Nageli	A
Chroococcus turgidus (Kutz.) Nageli	A
Dactylococcopsis antarctica F E. Fritsch	A
Dactylococcopsis smithii R. et E.Chodat (= *Rhabdogloea smithii* (R. et E.Chodat)	A
Eucapsis sp.	T
Gloeocapsa dermochroa Nageli	A
G. kuetzingiana Nageli	A
Hammatoidea sp.	A
Homoeothrix sp.	A
Isocystis pallida Woron.	AT
Katagnymene accurata Geitler	AT
Lyngbya attenuata Fritsch	A
Lyngbya martensiana Menegh.	A
Merismopedia tenuissima Lemmerm.	AT
Myxosarcina concinna Printz	A
Nodularia harveyana var. *sphaerocarpa* (Born. et Flah.) Elenkin	A
Nostoc commune Vaucher	ATC
Nostoc sp.	T
Oscillatoria annae Van Gook	A
Oscillatoria fracta Carlson	A
Oscillatoria irrigua Kutz	A
Oscillatoria lemmermannii Wolosz.	A
Oscillatoria proteus Skuja	A
Oscillatoria sp. (Broady 1979a, *Oscillatoria* cf. *limosa* Agardh)	A
Oscillatoria sp. (BROADY 1979a, *Oscillatoria* sp. C)	T
Phormidium autumnale(Agardh) Gomont	T
Phormidium foveolarum Gomont	A
Phormidium frigidum F.E. Fritsch	A
Phormidium subproboscideum (W et G. S. West) Anagnost et Komarek	A
Phormidium sp.	A
Plectonema battersii Gomont	A
Plectonema nostocorum Bornet	A
Pseudanabaena mucicola (Hub.-Pest. et Naum.) Bour.	A
Schizothrix antarctica F E. Fritsch	A
Stigonema mesentericum Geitler f.	T
Stigonema minutum (AGARDH) Hassall	T
Stigonema sp.	T
Synechococcus aeruginosus Nageli	T
Synechococcus maior Schroeter	AT
Tolypothrix byssoidea (Berk.) Kirchner f	A
Tolypothrix distorta var. *penicillata* (Agardh)Lemmerm.(= Tolypothrix penicillata Thuret)	A
Chlorophyta	
Actinotaenium cucurbita (Breb.) Teiling	AC
Apodochloris irregularis Ling et Seppelt	AC
Asterococcus superbus (Cienk.) Scherff.	AC
Binuclearia tatrana Wittr.	AC
Binuclearia tectorum (KÜTZ.) Beger	AC
Chlamydomonas pseudopulsatilla Gerloff	S
Chlamydomonas sphagnicola (F.E. Fritsch) F.E. Fritsch et Takeda	TC
Chlamydomonas subcaudata Wille	A
Chlamydomonas sp. 1	A

Chlamydomonas sp. 2	A
Chlorella vulgaris Beij.	AT
Chloromonas brevispina Hoham, Roemer et Mullet	S
Chloromonas polyptera (F.E. Fritsch) Hoham, Mullet et Roemer	SC
Chloromonas rubroleosa Ling et Seppelt	SC
Chloromonas sp. 1	SC
Chloromonas sp. 2	A
Coenochloris sp.	T
Desmococcus olivaceus (Pers. ex Ach.) Laundon	ATC
Desmotetra sp. 1	SC
Desmotetra sp. 2	SC
Dictyosphaerium dichotomum Ling et Seppelt	T
Fernandinella alpina Chodat	AC
Geminella terricola Boye-Pet.	T
Gloeocystis polydermatica (Kutz.) Hindak	T
Gloeocystis vesiculosa Nageli	T
Gongrosira terricola Bristol	AC
Gonium sociale (Dujard.) Warm.	AC
Hormotila sp.	SC
Kentrosphaera bristolae G.M.Smith	A
Klebsormidium dissectum var. 1(Broady 1979a, *Chlorhormidium dissectum* var. A)	T
Klebsormidium subtilissimum (Rabenh.) Silva, Mattox et Blackwell	A
Klebsormidium sp. (BROADY 1981, *Klebsormidium* sp. A)	SC
Lobococcus sp.?	T
Lobosphaera tirolensis Reisigl	TC
Macrochloris multinucleate (Reisigl) Ettl et Gartner	ATC
Mesotaenium berggrenii (Wittr.) Lagerh. f.	S
Monoraphidium contortum (Thur.) Komark.-Legn.	A
Monoraphidium sp.	S
Myrmecia bisecta Reisigl	T
Palmella sp. 1	TC
Palmella sp. 2	A
Palmellopsis sp.	SC
Prasiococcus calcarius (Boye-Pet.) Vischer	ATSC
Prasiola calophylla (Carmich.) Menegh.	TC
Prasiola crispa (Lightf.) Menegh.	ATSC
Prasiola sp.?	A
Pseudochlorella subsphaerica Reisigl	T
Pseudococcomyxa simplex (Mainx) Fott	T
Pyramimonas gelidfcola McFadden, Moestrup et Wetherbee	A
Pyramimonas sp.	A
Raphidonema helvetica Kol	S
Raphidonema nivale Lagerh.	S
Raphidonema sempervirens Chodat	TC
Raphidonema tatrae Kol	S
Schizogonium murale Kutz.	ATC
Schizogonium sp.	AT
Staurastrum sp.	A
Stichococcus bacillaris Nageli	TSC
Stichococcus fragilis (A. Braun) Gay	A
Stichococcus minutus Grintzesco et Peterfi	S
Tetracystis sp. 1	TC
Tetracystis sp. 2	TC
Trebouxia sp.	TC
Trichosarcina mucosa (B Broady) Chappell et O'Kelly	TC
Trochiscia sp. (Broady 1979x,	A
Trochiscia sp. A)	
Ulothrix implexa (Kutz.) Kutz. A	
Ulothrix zonata (Weber et Mohr) Kutz	
Ulothrix sp. 1	A
Ulothrix sp. 2	S
Uronema sp.	S
Xanthophyta	
Botrydiopsis sp.	TC
Bumilleriopsis sp.	TC
Ellipsoidion sp.?	S
Fremya sp.	ATC
Gloeobotrys sp.	A
Heterococcus filiformis Pitschm.	TC
Heterococcus sp.	TC
Heterothrix debilis Vischer	TC
Tribonema microchloron Ettl	A

Chrysophyta	
Chrysococcus sp.	S
Chroomonas lacustris Pascher et Ruttner	A
Dinophyta	
Gymnodinium sp.	A
Bacillariophyta	
**Achnanthes coarctata* var. *elliptica* Krasske	S
Amphora veneta Kutz.	A
**Cocconeis imperatrix* A. Schmidt	S
**Diploneis subcincta* (A. Schmidt) Cleve	S
**Eucampia balaustium* Castray	S
Fragilaria sp.	A
Fragilariopsis antarctica (Castray) Hust.	A
Hantzschia amphioxys (Ehrenb.) Grun.	A
Navicula atomus (Nag.) Grun.	A
Navicula murrayi W. et G. S. West	A
Navicula muticopsis Van Heurck	AT
Navicula sp.	A
Nitzschia palea (Kutz.) W. S M.	AT
Pinnularia borealis Ehrenb.	AT
Torpedoes laevissima W et G. S. West	A

*Believed to be marine diatoms from wind-borne sea spray.

Appendix 5: Ciliates and testate amoebae active in the vicinity of Casey

Station on Bailey Peninsula

(Modified from Petz and Foissner 1997)

Ciliates
Bryometopus sp
Bryophyllum cf. loxophylliforme
Colpoda cucullus (Mueller, 1773)
Colpoda inflata (Stokes, 1884)
Colpoda maupasi Enriques, 1908
Cyclidium muscicola Kahl, 1931
Cyrtolophosis elongata (Schewiakoff, 1892)
Euplotes sp.
Fuscheria terricola Berger and others, 1983
Gastronauta derouxi Blatterer and Foissner, 1992
Halteria grandinella (Mueller, 1773)
Holosticha sigmoidea Foissner, 1982
Leptopharynx costatus Mermod, 1914
Odontochlamys wisconsinensis (Kahl, 1931)
Oxytricha opisthomuscorum Foissner and others, 1991
Parafurgasonia sp.
Paraholosticha muscicola (Kahl, 1932)
Platyophrya vorax Kahl, 1926
Pseudocohnilembus sp.
Pseudoplatyophrya nana (Kahl, 1926)
Pseudoplatyophrya cf. saltans
Sathrophilus muscorum (Kahl, 1931)
Sterkiella histriomuscorum (Foissner and others, 1991)
Sterkiella thompsoni Foissner, 1996
Trithigmostoma sp.
Vorticella astyliformis Foissner, 1981
Vorticella infusionum Dujardin, 1 841
Testate amoebae
Assulina muscorum Greeff, 1888
Corythion dubium Taranek, 1881
Euglypha rotunda Wailes and Penard, 1911
Pseudodifflugia gracilis var. *terricola* Bonnet and Thomas, 1960
Schoenbornia viscicula Schoenborn, 1964
Trachelocorythion pulchellum (Penard, 1890)

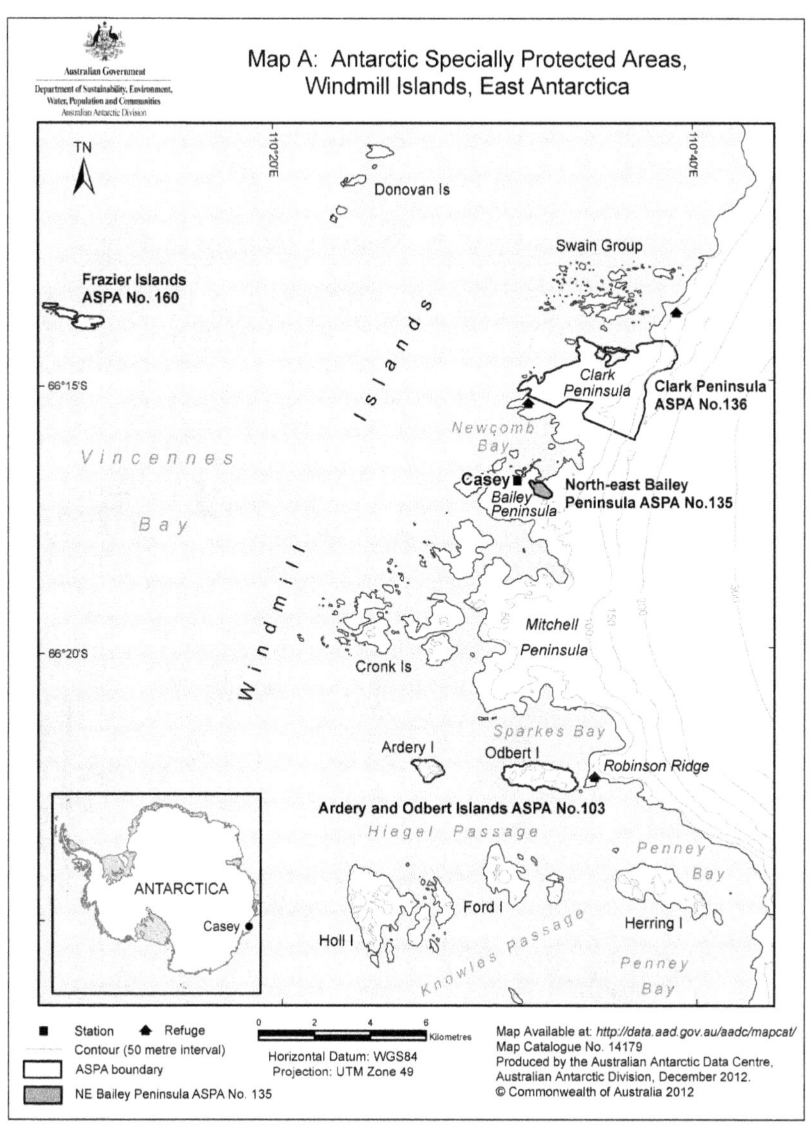
Australian Government
Department of Sustainability, Environment, Water, Population and Communities
Australian Antarctic Division
Map A: Antarctic Specially Protected Areas, Windmill Islands, East Antarctica
TN
110°20'E
110°40'E
Donovan Is
Swain Group
Frazier Islands ASPA No. 160
66°15'S
Clark Peninsula
Clark Peninsula ASPA No.136
Newcomb Bay
Vincennes Bay
Windmill Islands
Casey
Bailey Peninsula
North-east Bailey Peninsula ASPA No.135
Mitchell Peninsula
66°20'S
Cronk Is
Sparkes Bay
Ardery I
Odbert I
Robinson Ridge
Ardery and Odbert Islands ASPA No.103
Hiegel Passage
Penney Bay
ANTARCTICA
Casey
Ford I
Herring I
Holl I
Knowles Passage
Penney Bay
Station
Refuge
Contour (50 metre interval)
ASPA boundary
NE Bailey Peninsula ASPA No. 135
0 2 4 6 Kilometres
Horizontal Datum: WGS84
Projection: UTM Zone 49
Map Available at: http://data.aad.gov.au/aadc/mapcat/
Map Catalogue No. 14179
Produced by the Australian Antarctic Data Centre, Australian Antarctic Division, December 2012.
© Commonwealth of Australia 2012

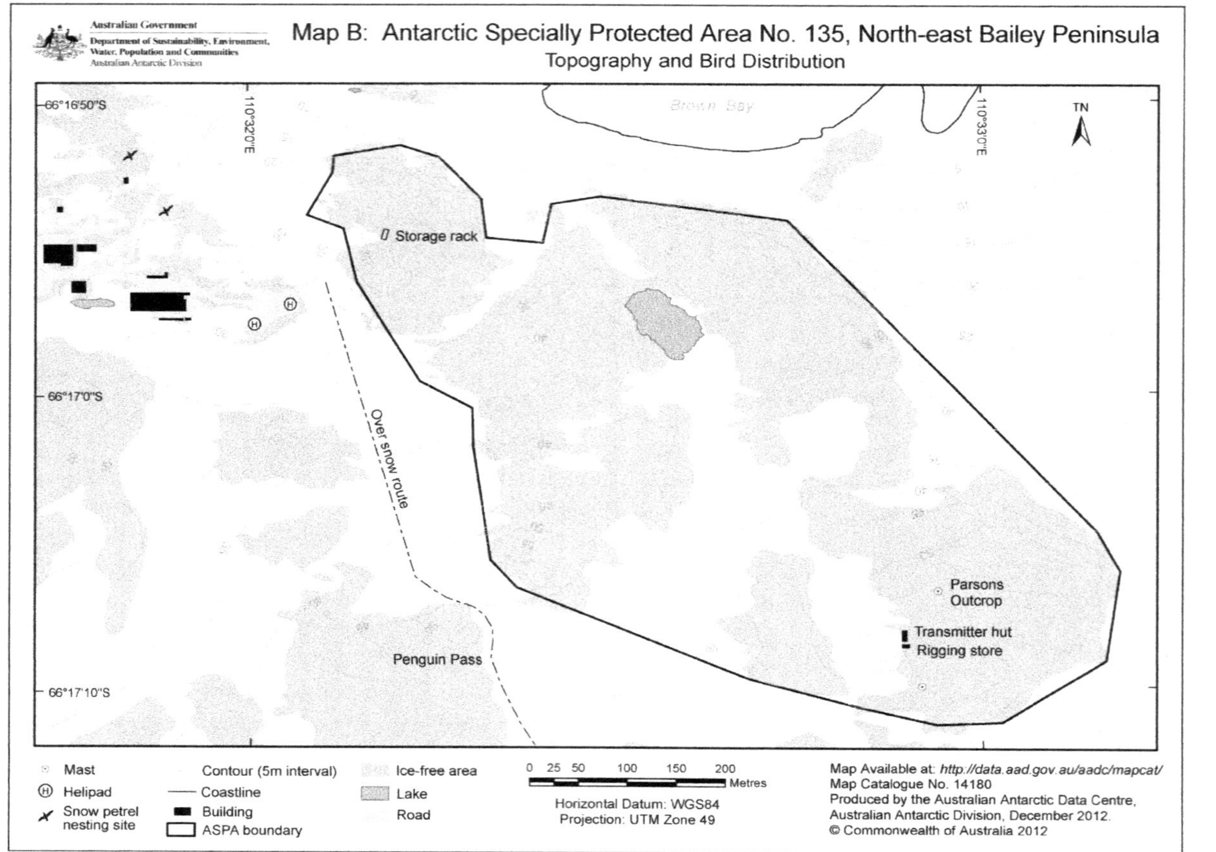
Australian Government
Department of Sustainability, Environment, Water, Population and Communities
Australian Antarctic Division
Map B: Antarctic Specially Protected Area No. 135, North-east Bailey Peninsula
Topography and Bird Distribution
66°16'50"S
66°17'0"S
66°17'10"S
110°32'0"E
110°33'0"E
TN
Brown Bay
Storage rack
Over snow route
Penguin Pass
Parsons Outcrop
Transmitter hut
Rigging store
Mast
Helipad
Snow petrel nesting site
Contour (5m interval)
Coastline
Building
ASPA boundary
Ice-free area
Lake
Road
0 25 50 100 150 200 Metres
Horizontal Datum: WGS84
Projection: UTM Zone 49
Map Available at: http://data.aad.gov.au/aadc/mapcat/
Map Catalogue No. 14180
Produced by the Australian Antarctic Data Centre, Australian Antarctic Division, December 2012.
© Commonwealth of Australia 2012

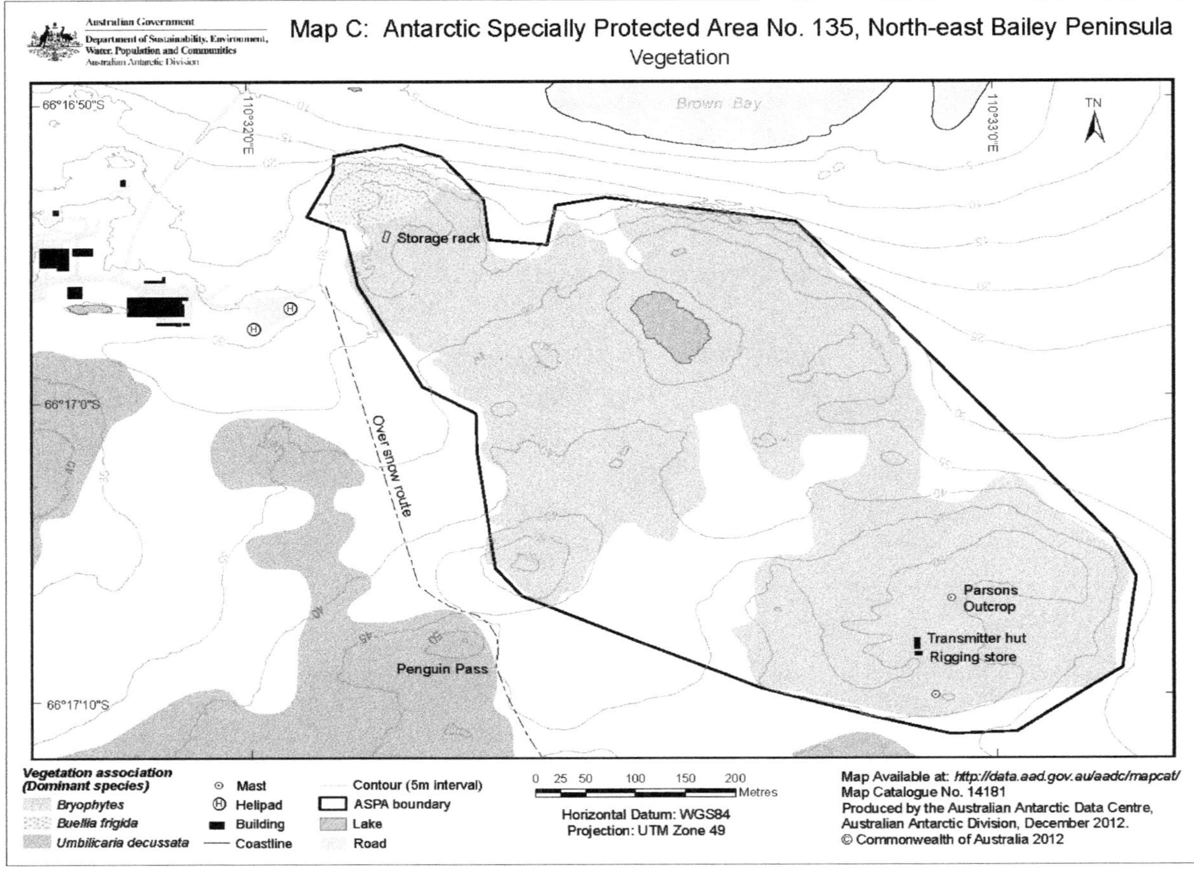

Australian Government
Department of Sustainability, Environment, Water, Population and Communities
Australian Antarctic Division
Map C: Antarctic Specially Protected Area No. 135, North-east Bailey Peninsula
Vegetation
66°16'50"S
66°17'0"S
66°17'10"S
110°32'0"E
110°33'0"E
TN
Brown Bay
Storage rack
Over snow route
Penguin Pass
Parsons Outcrop
Transmitter hut
Rigging store
Vegetation association (Dominant species)
Bryophytes
Buellia frigida
Umbilicaria decussata
Mast
Helipad
Building
Coastline
Contour (5m interval)
ASPA boundary
Lake
Road
0 25 50 100 150 200 Metres
Horizontal Datum: WGS84
Projection: UTM Zone 49
Map Available at: http://data.aad.gov.au/aadc/mapcat/
Map Catalogue No. 14181
Produced by the Australian Antarctic Data Centre, Australian Antarctic Division, December 2012.
© Commonwealth of Australia 2012

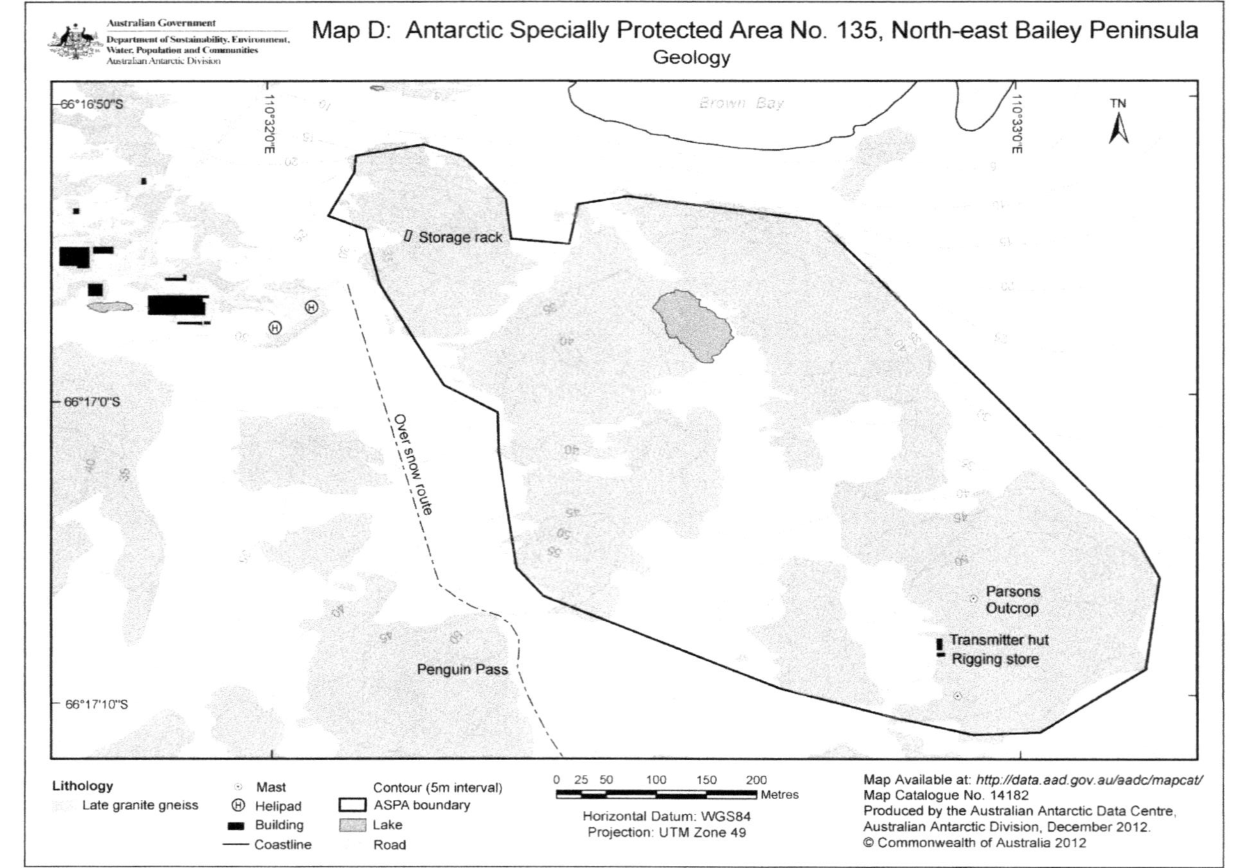
Australian Government
Department of Sustainability, Environment, Water, Population and Communities
Australian Antarctic Division
Map D: Antarctic Specially Protected Area No. 135, North-east Bailey Peninsula
Geology
66°16'50"S
66°17'0"S
66°17'10"S
110°32'0"E
110°33'0"E
Brown Bay
TN
Storage rack
Over snow route
Penguin Pass
Parsons Outcrop
Transmitter hut
Rigging store
Lithology
Late granite gneiss
Mast
Helipad
Building
Coastline
Contour (5m interval)
ASPA boundary
Lake
Road
0 25 50 100 150 200 Metres
Horizontal Datum: WGS84
Projection: UTM Zone 49
Map Available at: http://data.aad.gov.au/aadc/mapcat/
Map Catalogue No. 14182
Produced by the Australian Antarctic Data Centre, Australian Antarctic Division, December 2012.
© Commonwealth of Australia 2012

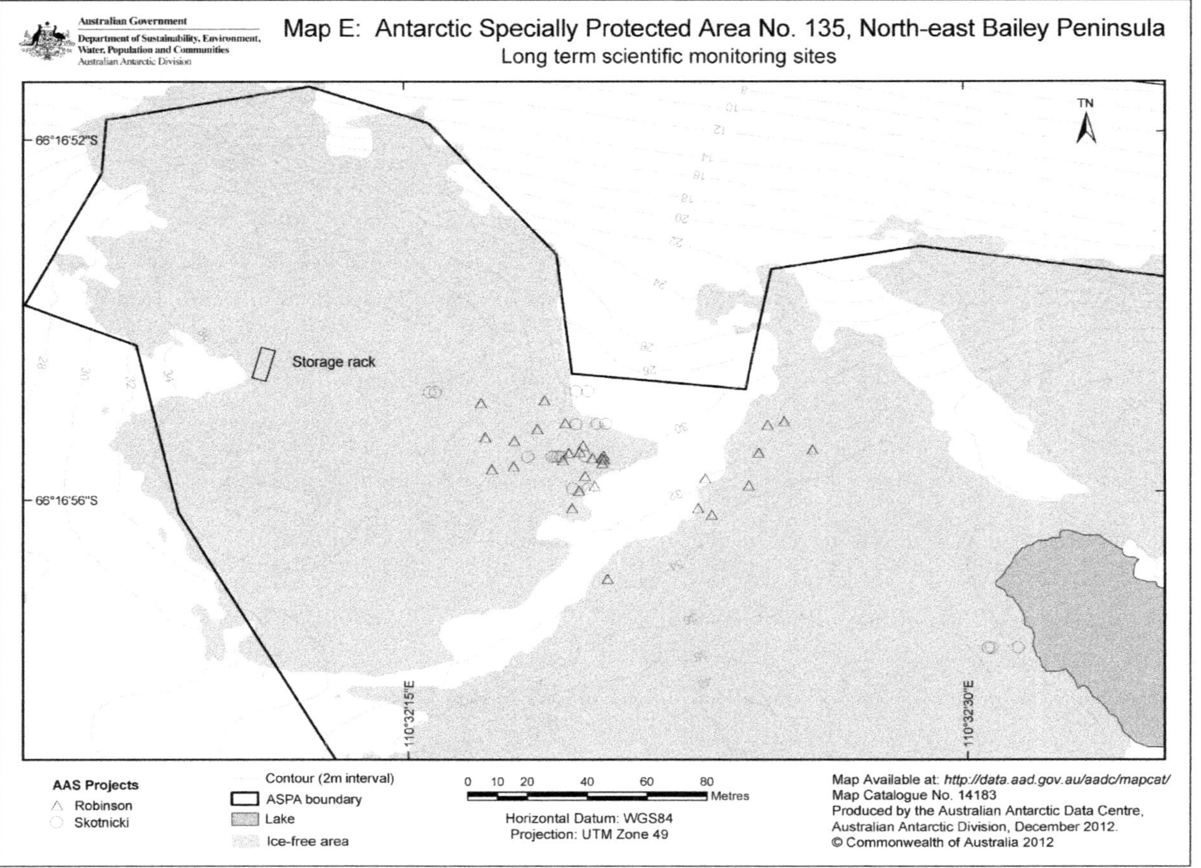
Australian Government
Department of Sustainability, Environment, Water, Population and Communities
Australian Antarctic Division
Map E: Antarctic Specially Protected Area No. 135, North-east Bailey Peninsula
Long term scientific monitoring sites
TN
66°16'52"S
66°16'56"S
110°32'15"E
110°32'30"E
Storage rack
AAS Projects
Robinson
Skotnicki
Contour (2m interval)
ASPA boundary
Lake
Ice-free area
0 10 20 40 60 80
Metres
Horizontal Datum: WGS84
Projection: UTM Zone 49
Map Available at: http://data.aad.gov.au/aadc/mapcat/
Map Catalogue No. 14183
Produced by the Australian Antarctic Data Centre,
Australian Antarctic Division, December 2012.
© Commonwealth of Australia 2012

Management Plan for

Antarctic Specially Protected Area (ASPA) No. 137

Northwest White Island, McMurdo Sound

Introduction

White Island is located approximately 25 km SE of McMurdo Station (United States) and Scott Base (New Zealand), Hut Point, Ross Island. The Area comprises a strip of five kilometers wide extending around the north-western and northern coastline of White Island, centered at 167° 18.3' E, 78° 02.5' S, and is approximately 141.6 km^2 in area. The primary reason for designation of the Area is to protect the most southerly known pinniped population; a small, completely enclosed, naturally-occurring colony of Weddell seals (*Leptonychotes weddellii*) that is of high scientific importance. The seal colony was established around the mid-1940s to mid-1950s by a few individuals from Erebus Bay before an advancing McMurdo Ice Shelf cut off the newly-founded colony from access to open water in McMurdo Sound. Cracks exist in the ice shelf where it abuts the coastline of White Island, which allow the seals access to forage in the water underneath. The seal population has remained small, around 30 individuals, and the pup survival rate is low. The pups are sensitive to disturbance arising from multiple visits over short time intervals. Scientific work is usually conducted during the breeding season. On-going research aims to understand the impact of isolation on the genetics of the White Island seal colony. The colony offers unique opportunities for scientific insights into the effects of in-breeding on small isolated populations, as well as valuable control information for larger scale studies of population dynamics and environmental variability of Weddell seals. It is essential that this natural 'experiment' is not disrupted, accidentally or intentionally, by human activities.

The Area was originally designated as Site of Special Scientific Interest (SSSI) No. 18, following a proposal by the United States of America, which was adopted through Recommendation XIII-8 (1985). Recommendation XVI-7 (1991) extended the expiry date of SSSI 18 until 31 December 2001. Measure 3 (2001) extended the expiry date further until 31 December 2005. Measure 1 (2002) revised the original boundaries of the ASPA based on new data on the spatial distribution of the seals on the ice shelves. Decision 1 (2002) renamed and renumbered SSSI 18 as Antarctic Specially Protected Area No. 137. Measure 9 (2008) updated the Management Plan to include recent census data on the seal colony, which led to a further revision of the boundary to include part of the Ross Ice Shelf in the north-east where seals were observed. Additional guidance on aircraft overflight and access was also included. The 2013 review updated the literature, confirmed the values remain valid, improved the map of White Island, and made minor adjustments to provisions on aircraft access.

The Area lies within Environment P – Ross and Ronne-Filchner ice shelves, based on the Environmental Domains Analysis for Antarctica and lies outside of the areas covered under the Antarctic Conservation Biogeographic Regions classification.

1. Description of values to be protected

An area of 150 km^2 of coastal shelf ice on the northwestern coast of White Island was originally designated following a proposal by the United States on the grounds that this locality contains an unusual breeding population of Weddell seals (*Leptonychotes weddellii*) which is the most southerly known, and which has been physically isolated from other populations by advance of the McMurdo Ice Shelf and Ross Ice Shelf (Map 1). The original boundaries were adjusted in 2002 (Measure 1) and again in 2008 (Measure 9) in light of new data recording the spatial distribution of the seals on the ice shelves. In the south, the boundary of the Area was shifted north and east to exclude the region north of White Strait where no observations of the seals have been recorded. In the north, the Area was extended to encompass an additional part of the Ross Ice Shelf in order to ensure inclusion of more of the region within which the seals may be found. The Area is now approximately 141.6 km^2.

The Weddell seal colony appears unable to relocate to another area because of its distance from the open ocean of McMurdo Sound, and as such it is highly vulnerable to any human impacts that might occur in the vicinity. There is no evidence that the colony was present in the early 1900s, as there is no mention of seals by naturalists who visited White Island many times during Scott's 1902, 1903 and 1910 expeditions. An ice breakout occurred in the region between 1947 and 1956, and the first two seals were observed near the northeastern end of the island in 1958 (R. Garrott, pers. comm. 2007). Year-round studies have detected no evidence of immigration or emigration of seals from the population, which appears to have grown to around 25 to 30 animals from a population of around 11 in the 1960s. The seals do not have the breathing capacity needed to dive the 20 km required to reach the open ocean, and there is only one record of a seal from the colony making the journey over the ice shelf surface.

The seals gain access to the sea below the ice shelf through pressure cracks, which are formed by tidal motion and movement of the McMurdo and Ross ice shelves. The series of cracks and ridging area is convoluted and dynamic, and while most seals are found along the coastal tide crack, it is likely they utilize the ridge crack leads extending off the coast and may move through there throughout the year.

The Weddell seals at White Island are on average greater in size and weight than their McMurdo Sound counterparts and have been shown to make more shallow dives. NW White Island is one of very few sites where Weddell seals are known to feed under shelf ice. The population has exceptional scientific value because of its period of physical isolation from interaction with other seals, thought to be around 60-70 years, and investigations of the extent to which the group may be considered a genetically distinct population are currently underway. Genetic techniques have been used to construct a complete pedigree for the NW White Island population. The results of these studies support the conclusion that the year in which the colony was founded is likely to have been around 60 years ago, which agrees with historical sightings. The colony offers unique opportunities for scientific insights into the effects of in-breeding on small isolated populations, as well as valuable control information for larger scale studies of population dynamics and environmental variability of Weddell seals. It is essential that this natural 'experiment' is not disrupted, accidentally or intentionally, by human activities.

NW White Island is relatively accessible by shelf ice from the nearby United States and New Zealand research stations at Hut Point, Ross Island. In addition, a flagged access route between these stations and Black Island traverses within approximately 2 km of the Area (Map 1).

The Area requires long-term special protection because of the exceptional importance of the Weddell seal colony, outstanding scientific values and opportunities for research, and the potential vulnerability of the Area to disturbance from scientific and logistic activities in the region.

2. Aims and objectives

Management at NW White Island aims to:

- avoid degradation of, or substantial risk to, the values of the Area by preventing unnecessary human disturbance to the Area;
- allow scientific research on the ecosystem, in particular on the Weddell seals, while ensuring protection from excessive disturbance, oversampling or other possible scientific impacts;
- allow other scientific research provided it is for compelling reasons that cannot be served elsewhere and that will not jeopardize the natural ecological system in the Area;
- prevent or minimize the introduction to the Area of non-native plants, animals and microbes;
- minimise the possibility of the introduction of pathogens that may cause disease in faunal populations within the Area;
- allow visits for management purposes in support of the aims of the Management Plan.

3. Management activities

The following management activities shall be undertaken to protect the values of the Area:

- Signs showing the location of the Area (stating the special restrictions that apply) shall be displayed prominently, and a copy of this Management Plan shall be kept available in appropriate places, in particular at McMurdo Station, Scott Base and at the Black Island facilities;
- All pilots operating in the region, all personnel travelling overland to Black Island on the marked route across McMurdo Ice Shelf, and any other personnel travelling overland within 2 km of the boundary of the Area, shall be informed of the location, boundaries and restrictions applying to entry, overflight and landings within the Area;
- National programs shall take steps to ensure the boundaries of the Area and the restrictions that apply within are marked on relevant maps and aeronautical charts;
- Markers, signs or structures erected within the Area for scientific or management purposes shall be secured and maintained in good condition, and removed when no longer required;
- Any abandoned equipment or materials shall be removed to the maximum extent possible provided doing so does not adversely impact on the environment and the values of the Area;
- Visits shall be made as necessary (no less than once every five years) to assess whether the Area continues to serve the purposes for which it was designated and to ensure management and maintenance measures are adequate;
- National Antarctic Programs operating in the region shall consult together with a view to ensuring the above management activities are implemented.

4. Period of designation

Designated for an indefinite period.

5. Maps and photographs

Map 1: ASPA No.137 – NW White Island – Topographic map.

Map specifications: Projection: Lambert Conformal Conic; Standard parallels: 1st 78° 00' S; 2nd 78° 12' S; Central Meridian: 167° 05' E; Latitude of Origin: 77° 30' S; Spheroid and datum: WGS84.

Inset 1: Ross Sea region.

Inset 2: Ross Island region, key features and nearby stations.

Map notes: Map 1 coastlines and ice shelf positions are derived from the Antarctic Digital Database (Version 5.0, SCAR, 2007). This framework is positionally inaccurate in the Ross Island / White Island region. Accurate ground control available for Hut Point Peninsula was used to adjust the geographical position of the framework by approximately +240 m (x direction) and +100 m (y direction). This shift improves the accuracy of Map 1, but the result is only an approximation. Topographic contours on White Island were derived by Environmental Research & Assessment (2013) from a 4 m LiDAR DEM (estimated accuracy of ~10 m horizontally and ~1 m vertically) produced by OSU/NASA/USGS (Schenk et al. 2004). Survey marker positions are from LINZ (2000) and Denys & Pearson (2000). Observations of seal positions provided by R. Garrott (pers. comm. 2008) were made using handheld GPS and are considered accurate to approximately 200 m of their true positions. Observations of seal positions provided by M. La Rue (pers. comm. 2012) are considered accurate to approximately 50 m of their true positions.

6. Description of the Area

6(i) Geographical coordinates, boundary markers and natural features

General description

White Island, part of the McMurdo volcanic complex, is situated approximately 20 km SE of the edge of the McMurdo Ice Shelf and 25 km SE of Hut Point, the location of McMurdo Station (United States) and Scott Base (New Zealand) on Ross Island (Inset 2, Map 1). The roughly triangular island is approximately 30 km long and 15 km wide at its maximum, and rises to a maximum elevation of 762 m in several locations (Map

1). The northern and western shores of White Island descend steeply, with water depths of 600 m occurring within 5 km of the island. The island is predominantly ice-covered with most of the rock outcrops being in the north. It is surrounded by the permanent shelf ice of the McMurdo Ice Shelf and Ross Ice Shelf, which is between 10 m and 100 m in thickness in this area. Black Island is situated 2.5 km west of White Island, separated by the shelf ice of White Strait. The GPS entry and exit points for the access route to Black Island from McMurdo through White Strait are 166° 50.0'E , 78° 12.0' S, and 166° 45.5' E, 78° 14.283' S respectively.

The westward movement of the McMurdo Ice Shelf is greatest at the northern end of White Island and movement of ice away from the NW coast ensures open water in cracks in the shelf at this locality is present year-round. The Weddell seal population uses the cracks for access to seawater and feeding grounds under the shelf ice, and inhabits and breeds in the region within approximately 5 km of their positions. The cracks occur parallel to and within a few hundred meters of the coast of White Island, and intermittently extend along the coast from the northern extremity of the island up to 15 km to the south.

Boundaries and coordinates

The Area includes 141.6 km^2 of the shelf ice and open-water cracks of both the Ross Ice Shelf and McMurdo Ice Shelf up to 5 km offshore northeast, north and west from the White Island coast. The northeastern boundary extends from the northeastern coast of Cape Spencer-Smith (167° 32.7' E, 78° 0.717' S) 5 km due east to 167° 46.617' E, 78° 0.717' S. The boundary then extends northwest, and follows a line parallel to and 5 km from the coast, around Cape Spencer Smith and then heading southwest to 167° 00' E, 78° 05.0' S. The boundary then extends due south for 7.8 km to 167° 0.0' E, 78° 09.2' S, and thence 1.5 km east to the southern-most significant outcrop of rock on the western coast of White Island (167° 05.0' E, 78° 09.2' S). The boundary then extends northwards, following the coastline around Cape Spencer Smith to the northeastern limit of the Area. The White Island coast is distinguished by a change in surface slope where the transition between the floating ice-shelf and land occurs: the transition is in some places gradual and indistinct, and the exact position of the coast is not precisely known. For this reason the coastal (generally east) boundary of the Area is considered to follow the line of the coast as evidenced by a surface elevation rise towards the land of two meters above the average elevation of the adjacent McMurdo Ice Shelf.

Weddell seal colony

It was estimated there were 25-30 resident seals in 1981 (Castellini *et al.* 1984). A similar estimate of between 25 to 30 animals was made in 1991 (Gelatt *et al.* 2010). In 1991, An estimated 26 seals were greater than one year of age, 25 of which were of breeding age (>4) (Gelatt *et al.* 2010). Since 1991, 17 different females have produced pups at White Island (R. Garrott pers. comm. 2008). Between 2003 and 2007, 11 females were sighted at White Island, but only six of these individuals have produced pups (R. Garrott pers. comm. 2008). Between two and four live pups were recorded from 1963 to1968 (Heine 1960; Caughley 1959), in 1981, and in 1991. Annual censuses since 1991 recorded between four and ten pups from 1991 to 2000, but lower numbers (between two and four pups each year) from 2000 to 2007. Pup mortality is high, possibly due to inbreeding, and pup production is low in comparison to the population in Erebus Bay (R.Garrott pers. comm 2008).

The seals are physically isolated by the barrier of the shelf ice, and are unable to swim the 20 km distance under the ice to reach the seasonally open waters of McMurdo Sound: Weddell seals have been estimated to be capable of swimming a distance of around 4.6 km (2.5 nautical miles) on a single breath. The apparent isolation of the colony is substantiated by tag observation data on Weddell seals in McMurdo Sound, where in more than 100,000 tag observations over a 20-year period no tagged seals from White Island have been observed in McMurdo Sound (Stirling 1967, 1971; Ward, Testa & Scotton 1999). These data suggest that the White Island seals do not generally traverse the 20 km distance to the open ocean over the surface of the shelf ice. However, there is at least one record of a yearling from the White Island colony found to have made the journey across to the Williams airfield close to McMurdo station (G. Kooyman pers. comm. 2007).

Adult female seals begin to appear on the shelf ice in early November, one month later than other pupping areas in the southern Ross Sea. They pup at the NW extremity of the island during which time sub-adults and non-breeding adults can be found up to 15 km to the SW near open cracks on the west side of the island (Gelatt *et al.* 2010). Adult male seals are not observed on the sea-ice during this time, remaining in the water to establish and defend territories. The females remain on the ice until pups are weaned at about 6-8 weeks of age. After December, adults and sub-adults mix in the pupping area and along the cracks formed at the northwestern corner of the island.

The harsh surface conditions probably confine the seals to the water during the winter months. Winter surface temperatures reach as low as -60°C and it is thought that the seals expend considerable time maintaining open air holes in the cracks. This is considered to be a key factor limiting the population size (Yochem *et al.* 2009), with pups and sub-adults possibly excluded from use of the limited breathing holes by more dominant and aggressive adults. Some pups may be unable to maintain their own breathing holes and may become trapped on the ice surface if dominant seals do not allow them entry into the water (Castellini *et al.* 1992; Harcourt *et al.* 1998).

Studies have suggested that the Weddell seals at White Island have a diet similar to their counterparts at McMurdo Sound (Castellini *et al.* 1992). Studies of fish otoliths recovered from Weddell seal fecal samples have revealed a diet comprised primarily of the nototheniid fish *Pleuragramma antarcticum*, also with fish from the genus *Trematomus* (Burns *et al.* 1998). Invertebrates are thought to comprise the remainder of the diet, along with a cephalopod belonging to the family Mastogoteuthidae (Burns *et al.* 1998). Consumption of the latter was found to be considerably greater amongst White Island seals than those at McMurdo Sound (Castellini *et al.* 1992).

Other aspects of the physiology and behavior of seals at White Island appear to differ from nearby populations at McMurdo Sound and at Terra Nova Bay: the seals at White Island appear to be significantly fatter (Stirling 1972; Castellini *et al.* 1984), with recorded weights of up to 686 kg (1500 lb.) at White Island compared to no more than 500 kg at McMurdo Sound or Terra Nova Bay (Proffitt *et al.* 2008) . On average adult female seals are considerably longer than those in McMurdo Sound, and young seals at White Island have been observed to exhibit faster growth rates than their McMurdo counterparts. Average diving depths at White Island are shallower than at McMurdo Sound (Castellini *et al.* 1992).

Observations of seal positions provided by M. La Rue (PGC, pers. comm. 2012) were made by visual inspection of six high resolution satellite images (Quickbird, WorldView 1 & 2, and GeoEye: imagery © 2010, 2011 Digital Globe; courtesy of NGA Commercial Imagery Program) acquired in November of 2010 and 2011. Weddell seals tend to exhibit more stable haul-out behavior at this time of year. The satellite images were acquired between 0900-1100 hours local time, which corresponds with the period of lowest seal haul-out activity. Images were searched over a broad area extending up to approximately 10 km beyond the ASPA boundary. A combined total of nine seals were observed in three of the six images studied (Map 1). No seals were observed outside of the ASPA boundaries. No seals were detected in imagery acquired in early November, with all detections made in mid- and late-November imagery. It was not possible to determine whether an individual was counted more than once, or to distinguish adults from pups, in the analysis. The observations confirm, however, the continued presence of the colony.

6 (ii) Access to the area

Pedestrian and vehicular access to the Area is from the Hut Point – Black Island marked route that passes approximately two kilometers from the boundary at its nearest point. Access to the Area from the marked route is across the ice shelf. Aircraft access to the Area is prohibited unless in accordance with a permit, and all aircraft operating within or over the Area must follow the restrictions on overflight and landing set out in detail in Section 7(ii).

6(iii) Location of structures within and adjacent to the Area

There are no structures within the Area. Several small survey markers (LINZ 2000; Denys & Pearson 2000) are installed on White Island in close proximity to the Area (Map 1). Transantarctic Mountains Deformation Network (TAMDEF) WTE0 is installed at 167° 29.755' E, 78° 11.385' S at an elevation of 453.5 m. The marker comprises a threaded stainless steel rod embedded into a boulder and is identified by a yellow plastic disc. A Land Information New Zealand (LINZ) Antarctic Datum Unification Network Survey Mark named 'HEIN', comprising a brass pin grouted into rock, is located on Mount Heine at 167° 27.042' E, 78° 04.561' S at an elevation of 737.7 m.

6(iv) Location of other protected areas in the vicinity

The nearest protected areas to NW White Island are on Ross Island: Arrival Heights (ASPA No.122) adjacent to McMurdo Station and Discovery Hut (ASPA No.158) on the Hut Point Peninsula are the closest at 20 km to the northwest; Cape Evans (ASPA No.155) and Cape Royds (ASPA No.121) are 47 km and 55 km northwest respectively; and Tramway Ridge (ASPA No.130) near the summit of Mt. Erebus is 60 km to the north.

6(v) Special zones within the Area

There are no special zones within the Area.

7. Terms and conditions for entry permits

7(i) General permit conditions

Entry into the Area is prohibited except in accordance with a permit issued by an appropriate national authority. Conditions for issuing a permit to enter the Area are that:

- it is issued for scientific study of the Weddell seal ecosystem, or for compelling scientific reasons which cannot be served elsewhere, or for reasons essential to the management of the Area;
- the actions permitted are in accordance with this Management Plan;
- the activities permitted will give due consideration via the environmental impact assessment process to the continued protection of the environmental, ecological and scientific values of the Area;
- the permit shall be issued for a finite period;
- the permit, or a copy, shall be carried when in the Area;

7(ii) Access to, and movement within, or over the Area

Access into the Area is permitted on foot, by vehicle, or by aircraft.

Access on foot or by vehicle

No special access routes are designated for access to the Area on foot or by vehicle over the shelf ice. Vehicles are permitted on the ice shelf but are strongly discouraged from approaching closer than 50 m from seals, and closer approaches should be on foot. Vehicle and pedestrian traffic should be kept to the minimum necessary consistent with the objectives of any permitted activities and every reasonable effort should be made to minimize disturbance.

Access by aircraft

- Aircraft landings within the Area are prohibited unless authorized by permit for purposes allowed for by the Management Plan;
- Aircraft overflight below 2000 feet (~610 m) is prohibited, unless authorized by permit for purposes allowed for by the Management Plan;
- Aircraft approach and departure shall avoid overflight of the White Island coastline and tide-cracks within the Area, where the seals are most commonly found.
- Aircraft landings within ½ nautical mile (~930 m) of Weddell seals are prohibited. Pilots should make a reconnaissance of suitable landing sites from above 2000 feet (~610 m) before descending to land. When seals are not visible, aircraft landings shall be made at least ½ nautical mile (~930 m) from the coastline of White Island and the tide-crack.

7(iii) Activities that may be conducted within the Area

- Scientific research that will not jeopardize the values of the Area;
- Essential management activities, including monitoring and inspection.

7(iv) Installation, modification or removal of structures / equipment

- No structures are to be erected within the Area except as specified in a permit; and, with the exception of permanent signs, permanent structures or installations are prohibited;
- All structures, scientific equipment or markers installed in the Area shall be authorized by permit and clearly identified by country, name of the principal investigator, year of installation and date of expected

removal. All such items should be free of organisms, propagules (e.g. seeds, eggs) and non-sterile soil, and be made of materials that can withstand the environmental conditions and pose minimal risk of contamination of the Area;

- Installation (including site selection), maintenance, modification or removal of structures or equipment shall be undertaken in a manner that minimizes disturbance to the values of the Area;
- Removal of specific structures / equipment for which the permit has expired shall be the responsibility of the authority which granted the original permit, and shall be a condition of the permit.

7(v) Location of field camps

Permanent field camps are prohibited within the Area. Temporary camp sites are permitted within the Area. There are no specific restrictions to a precise locality for temporary camp sites within the Area, although sites selected shall be more than 200 m from the ice-shelf cracks inhabited by the seals, unless authorized by permit when deemed necessary to the accomplishment of specific research goals.

7(vi) Restrictions on materials and organisms which may be brought into the Area

In addition to the requirements of the Protocol on Environmental Protection to the Antarctic Treaty, restrictions on materials and organisms which may be brought into the area are:

- The deliberate introduction of animals (including Weddell seals from outside of this colony), plant material, micro-organisms and non-sterile soil into the Area is prohibited. Precautions shall be taken to prevent the accidental introduction of animals, plant material, micro-organisms and non-sterile soil from other biologically distinct regions (within or beyond the Antarctic Treaty area).
- Of particular concern are microbial and viral introductions from other seal populations. Visitors shall ensure that sampling equipment, measuring devices and markers brought into the Area are clean. To the maximum extent practicable, footwear and other equipment used or brought into the area (including backpacks, carry-bags and tents) shall be thoroughly cleaned before entering the Area. Visitors should also consult and follow as appropriate recommendations contained in the Committee for Environmental Protection *Non-native Species Manual* (CEP 2011), and in the *Environmental Code of Conduct for terrestrial scientific field research in Antarctica* (SCAR 2009);
- No herbicides or pesticides shall be brought into the Area;
- The use of explosives is prohibited within the Area;
- Fuel, food, chemicals, and other materials shall not be stored in the Area, unless specifically authorized by permit and shall be stored and handled in a way that minimises the risk of their accidental introduction into the environment;
- All materials introduced shall be for a stated period only and shall be removed by the end of that stated period; and
- If a release occurs which is likely to compromise the values of the Area, removal is encouraged only where the impact of removal is not likely to be greater than that of leaving the material in situ.

7(vii) Taking of, or harmful interference with, native flora or fauna

Taking of, or harmful interference with, native flora and fauna is prohibited, except in accordance with Annex II of the Protocol on Environmental Protection to the Antarctic Treaty.

Any proposed taking of, or harmful interference with, Weddell seals within the Area that are for purposes that could be achieved just as effectively on Weddell seals from populations outside of the Area should not be permitted.

Where animal taking or harmful interference is involved, this should, as a minimum standard, be in accordance with the SCAR Code of Conduct for the Use of Animals for Scientific Purposes in Antarctica and, where applicable, follow stricter animal care or research standards or guidelines in accordance with national procedures.

7(viii) Collection or removal of anything not brought into the Area by the permit holder

- Material may be collected or removed from the Area only in accordance with a permit and should be limited to the minimum necessary to meet scientific or management needs.
- Material of human origin likely to compromise the values of the Area, which was not brought into the Area by the permit holder or otherwise authorized, may be removed unless the impact of removal is likely to be greater than leaving the material *in situ*: if this is the case the appropriate authority must be notified and approval obtained.

7(ix) Disposal of waste

All wastes, including all human wastes, shall be removed from the Area.

7(x) Measures that may be necessary to continue to meet the aims of the Management Plan

Permits may be granted to enter the Area to:

- carry out monitoring and Area inspection activities, which may involve the collection of a small number of samples or data for analysis or review;
- install or maintain signposts, markers, structures or scientific equipment;
- carry out protective measures.

7(xi) Requirements for reports

- The principal permit holder for each visit to the Area shall submit a report to the appropriate national authority as soon as practicable, and no later than six months after the visit has been completed;
- Such reports should include, as appropriate, the information identified in the visit report form contained in the Guide to the Preparation of Management Plans for Antarctic Specially Protected Areas. If appropriate, the national authority should also forward a copy of the visit report to the Party that proposed the Management Plan, to assist in managing the Area and reviewing the Management Plan;
- Parties should, wherever possible, deposit originals or copies of such original reports in a publicly accessible archive to maintain a record of usage, to be used both in any review of the Management Plan and in organizing the scientific use of the Area;
- The appropriate authority should be notified of any activities / measures undertaken, and / or of any materials released and not removed, that were not included in the authorized permit.

8. Supporting documentation

Burns, J.M., Trumble, S.J., Castellini, M.A. & Testa, J.W. 1998. The diet of Weddell seals in McMurdo Sound, Antarctica as determined from scat collections and stable isotope analysis. *Polar Biology* **19**: 272-82.

Castellini, M.A., Davis, R.W., Davis, M. & Horning, M. 1984. Antarctic marine life under the McMurdo ice shelf at White Island: a link between nutrient influx and seal population. *Polar Biology* **2** (4):229-231.

Castellini, M.A., Davis, R.W. & Kooyman, G.L. 1992. Annual cycles of diving behaviour and ecology of the Weddell seal. *Bulletin of the Scripps Institution of Oceanography* **28**:1-54.

Caughley, G. 1959. Observations on the seals of Ross Island during the 1958–1959 summer. Dominion Museum, Wellington.

Committee for Environmental Protection (CEP) 2011. *Non-native Species Manual – 1st Edition.* Manual prepared by Intersessional Contact Group of the CEP and adopted by the Antarctic Treaty Consultative Meeting through Resolution 6 (2011). Buenos Aires: Secretariat of the Antarctic Treaty.

Denys, P. & Pearson, C. 2000. *The Realisation of Zero, First and Second-Order Stations for the Ross Sea Region Geodetic Datum 2000.* Report Number 2000/0728 - v 2.2. Land Information New Zealand, Wellington.

Gelatt, T.S., Davis, C.S., Stirling, I., Siniff, D.B., Strobeck, C. & Delisle, I. 2010. History and fate of a small isolated population of Weddell seals at White Island, Antarctica. *Conservation Genetics* **11**: 721-35.

Harcourt, R.G., Hindell, M.A. & Waas, J.R. 1998. Under-ice movements and territory use in free-ranging Weddell seals during the breeding season. *New Zealand Natural Sciences* **23**: 72-73.

Heine, A.J. 1960. Seals at White Island, Antarctica. *Antarctic* **2**:272–73.

Kooyman, G.L. 1965. Techniques used in measuring diving capacities of Weddell seals. *Polar Record* **12** (79): 391–94.

Kooyman, G.L. 1968. An analysis of some behavioral and physiological characteristics related to diving in the Weddell seal. In Schmitt, W.L. and Llano, G.A. (Eds.) *Biology of the Antarctic Seas III. Antarctic Research Series* **11**: 227–61. American Geophysical Union, Washington DC.

LINZ (Land Information New Zealand) 2000. *Realisation of Ross Sea Region Geodetic Datum 2000*. LINZ OSG Report 15. Wellington.

Proffitt, K.M., Carrott, R.A. & Rotella, J.J. 2008. Long term evaluation of body mass at weaning and postweaning survival rates of Weddell seals in Erebus Bay, Antarctica. *Marine Mammal Science* 24 (3): 677-89.

SCAR (Scientific Committee on Antarctic Research) 2009. *Environmental Code of Conduct for terrestrial scientific field research in Antarctica.* Cambridge, SCAR.

Schenk, T., Csathó, B., Ahn, Y., Yoon, T., Shin, S.W. & Huh, K.I. 2004. DEM Generation from the Antarctic LIDAR Data: Site Report (unpublished). Ohio State University, Colombus, Ohio.

Stirling, I. 1967. Population studies on the Weddell seal. *Tuatara* **15** (3): 133-41.

Stirling, I. 1971. Population aspects of Weddell seal harvesting at McMurdo Sound, Antarctica. *Polar Record* **15** (98): 653-67.

Stirling, I. 1972. Regulation of numbers of an apparently isolated population of Weddell seals (*Leptonychotes weddelli*). *Journal of Mammalogy* **53**:107–115.

Testa, W. & Scotton, B.D. 1999. Dynamics of an isolated population of Weddell seals (*Leptonychotes weddellii*) at White Island, Antarctica. *Journal of Mammology* **80** (1): 82-90.

Testa, W. & Siniff, D.B. 1987. Population Dynamics of Weddell seals (*Leptonychotes weddellii*) in McMurdo Sound, Antarctica. *Ecological Monographs* **57** (2):149-65.

Yochem, P.K., Stewart, B.S., Gelatt, T.S. & Siniff, D.B. 2009. *Health Assessment of Weddell Seals, Leptonychotes weddellii, in McMurdo Sound, Antarctica.* Publications, Agencies and Staff of the U.S. Department of Commerce, Paper 203. Washington DC.

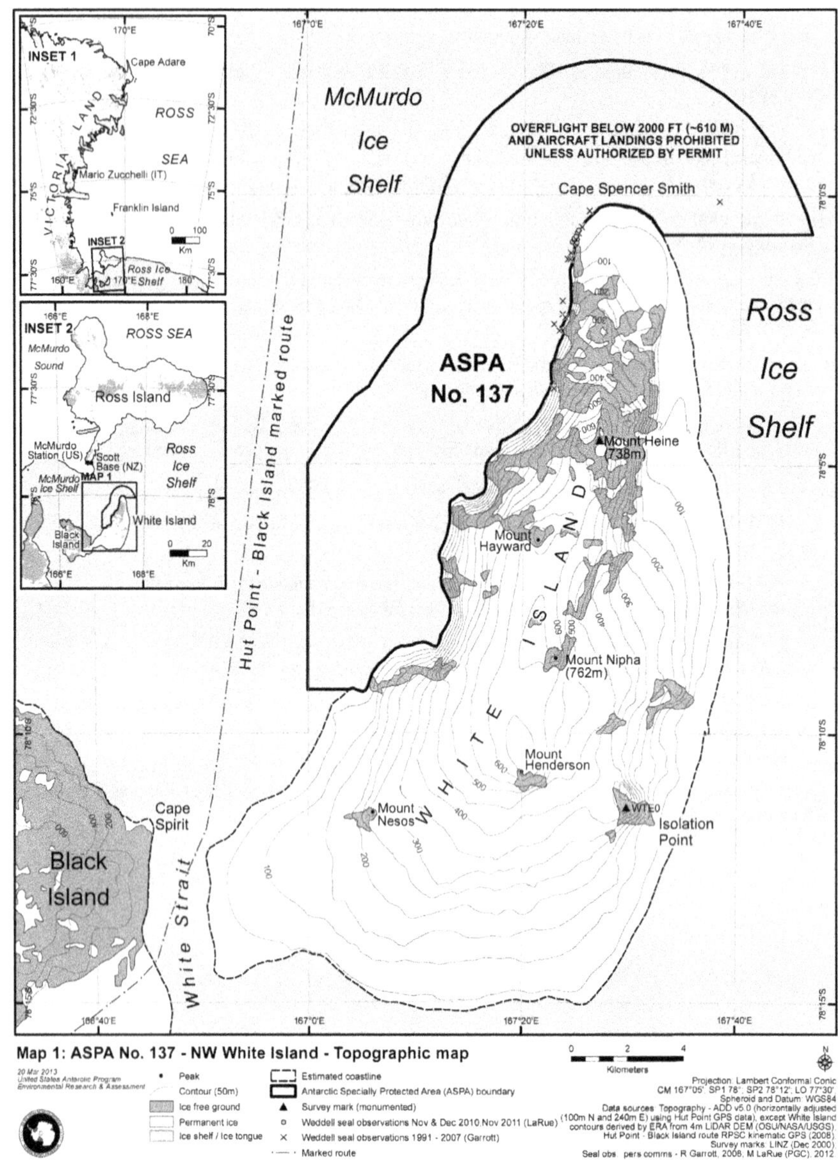

Map 1: ASPA No. 137 - NW White Island - Topographic map

Management Plan for

Antarctic Specially Protected Area (ASPA) No.138

Linnaeus Terrace, Asgard Range, Victoria Land

Introduction

Linnaeus Terrace is an elevated bench of weathered Beacon Sandstone located at the western end of the Asgard Range, 1.5km north of Oliver Peak, at 161° 05.0' E 77° 35.8' S,. The terrace is ~ 1.5 km in length by ~1 km in width at an elevation of about 1600m. Linnaeus Terrace is one of the richest known localities for the cryptoendolithic communities that colonize the Beacon Sandstone. The sandstones also exhibit rare physical and biological weathering structures, as well as trace fossils. The excellent examples of cryptoendolithic communities are of outstanding scientific value, and are the subject of some of the most detailed Antarctic cryptoendolithic descriptions. The site is vulnerable to disturbance by trampling and sampling, and is sensitive to the importation of non-native plant, animal or microbial species and requires long-term special protection.

Linnaeus Terrace was originally designated as Site of Special Scientific Interest (SSSI) No. 19 through Recommendation XIII-8 (1985) after a proposal by the United States of America. The SSSI expiry date was extended by Resolution 7 (1995), and the Management Plan was adopted in Annex V format through Measure 1 (1996). The site was renamed and renumbered as ASPA No 138 by Decision 1 (2002). The Management Plan was updated through Measure 10 (2008) to include additional provisions to reduce the risk of non-native species introductions into the Area.

The Area is situated in Environment S – McMurdo – South Victoria Land Geologic based on the Environmental Domains Analysis for Antarctica and in Region 9 – South Victoria Land based on the Antarctic Conservation Biogeographic Regions. Linnaeus Terrace lies within Antarctic Specially Managed Area (ASMA) No.2, McMurdo Dry Valleys.

1. Description of values to be protected

Linnaeus Terrace was originally designated in Recommendation XIII-8 (1985, SSSI No. 19) after a proposal by the United States of America on the grounds that the Area is one of the richest known localities for the cryptoendolithic communities that colonize the Beacon Sandstone. Exposed surfaces of the Beacon Sandstone are the habitat of cryptoendolithic microorganisms, which may colonize a zone of up to 10 millimeters deep below the surface of the rocks. The sandstones exhibit a range of biological and physical weathering forms, as well as trace fossils, and many of the formations are fragile and vulnerable to disturbance and destruction by trampling and sampling.

Cryptoendolithic communities are known to develop over time periods in the order of tens of thousands of years, and damaged rock surfaces would be slow to recolonize. The excellent examples of these communities found at the site are the subject of the original detailed Antarctic cryptoendolithic descriptions. As such, Linnaeus Terrace is considered a type locality with outstanding scientific values related to this ecosystem. These values, as well as the vulnerability of the site to disturbance and destruction, require that it receives long-term special protection.

The Management Plan has been updated to include new provisions agreed within the Guide to the Preparation of ASPA Management Plans (2011), revisions to Antarctic Specially Managed Area No. 2 McMurdo Dry Valleys, observations made during a field inspection of the Area made in January 2012, and the latest measures related to managing the risk of non-native species introductions agreed by the Antarctic Treaty Parties.

2. Aims and objectives

Management at Linnaeus Terrace aims to:

- avoid degradation of, or substantial risk to, the values of the Area by preventing unnecessary human disturbance to the Area;
- allow scientific research on the ecosystem, in particular on the cryptoendolithic communities, while ensuring protection from excessive disturbance, oversampling, damage to fragile rock formations, or other possible scientific impacts;
- allow other scientific research provided it is for compelling reasons that cannot be served elsewhere and that will not jeopardize the natural ecological system in the Area;
- prevent or minimize the introduction to the Area of alien plants, animals and microbes;
- allow visits for management purposes in support of the aims of the management plan.

3. Management activities

The following management activities shall be undertaken to protect the values of the Area:

- Signs showing the location of the Area (stating the special restrictions that apply) shall be displayed prominently, and a copy of this Management Plan shall be kept available, at permanent scientific stations located within 150 km of the Area;
- All pilots operating in the region shall be informed of the location, boundaries and restrictions applying to entry and landings within the Area;
- National programs shall take steps to ensure the boundaries of the Area and the restrictions that apply within are marked on relevant maps and nautical / aeronautical charts;
- Durable wind direction indicators should be erected close to the designated helicopter landing site whenever it is anticipated there will be a number of landings at the Area in a given season. These should be replaced as needed and removed when no longer required;
- Brightly colored markers, which should be clearly visible from the air and pose no significant threat to the environment, should be placed to mark the designated helicopter landing site;
- Markers, signs or structures erected within the Area for scientific or management purposes shall be secured and maintained in good condition, and removed when no longer required;
- Visits shall be made as necessary (preferably no less than once every five years) to assess whether the Area continues to serve the purposes for which it was designated and to ensure management and maintenance measures are adequate;
- National Antarctic Programs operating in the region shall consult together with a view to ensuring the above management activities are implemented.

4. Period of designation

Designated for an indefinite period.

5. Maps and photographs

Map 1: ASPA No. 138: Linnaeus Terrace, Wright Valley.

Projection: Lambert conformal conic; Standard parallels: 1st 77° 30' S; 2nd 77° 40' S; Central Meridian: 161° 53' E; Latitude of Origin: 78° 00' S; Spheroid and datum: WGS84;
Data sources: USGS 1:50,000 Series (1970); Contour interval 250 m; ASMA No.2 McMurdo Dry Valleys management plan.

Map 2: ASPA No. 138 Linnaeus Terrace, topography and boundary.

Projection: Lambert conformal conic; Standard parallels: 1st 77° 35' S; 2nd 77° 36' S; Central Meridian: 161° 05' E; Latitude of Origin: 78° 00' S; Spheroid and datum: WGS84;

Data sources Topography & boundary Gateway Antarctica,
derived from an orthophotograph with an estimated positional accuracy of 0.5m, contour interval 5 m; instruments, cairns, former facilities sites: ERA field survey (Jan 2012).

Figure 1: Photograph illustrating some of the fragile rock formations and trace fossils found on Linnaeus Terrace.

6. Description of the Area

6(i) Geographical coordinates, boundary markers and natural features

Linnaeus Terrace (161° 05.0' E, 77° 35.8' S) is a bench of weathered Beacon Sandstone approximately 1.5 km in length and 1 km in width at an elevation of about 1600 m (Map 1). It is located at the western end of the Asgard Range, 1.5 km north of Oliver Peak (161° 02.5' E, 77° 36.7' S, 2410 m). The Area overlooks the South Fork of the Wright Valley, is approximately 4.5 km from Don Juan Pond and ~10 km from the terminus of the Wright Upper Glacier (Map 1).

The lower (northern) boundary of the Area is characterized by the presence of a predominantly sandstone outcrop of approximately 3 m in height which extends for much of the length of the terrace (Map 2). The lower boundary of the Area is defined as the upper edge of this outcrop, and as straight lines adjoining the visible edges where the outcrop is covered by surface talus. The upper (southwestern) boundary of the Area is characterized by a line of sandstone outcrop of about 2-5 m in height, occurring between the elevations of 1660 - 1700 m about 70 m above the general elevation of the terrace. The upper boundary of the Area is defined as the uppermost edge of this outcrop, and shall be considered a straight line between the visible edges where the outcrop is covered by surface talus. The western end of the Area is defined as where the terrace narrows and merges with a dolerite talus slope on the flank of the NW ridge of Oliver Peak. The boundary at the west dips steeply from where the upper outcrop disappears, following the border of the dolerite talus with the terrace sandstone down to the westernmost corner. The east boundary is defined as the 1615 m contour, which follows closely the edge of an outcrop which extends much of the width of the terrace (Map 2). At the southernmost corner of the Area the terrace merges with the slopes into the valley to the east: from this point the boundary extends upward to the 1700 m contour, from where it follows the line of outcrop defining the southwestern boundary.

Winter air temperature at Linnaeus Terrace ranges between -20°C and -45°C, while in January the daily mean is approximately -5°C (Friedmann *et al.* 1993). However, there is extreme daily variation in air temperature at the rock surface, due to alternating wind speeds and solar irradiation patterns. Therefore, cryptoendolithic microorganisms inhabit the more stable temperature zone which begins about 1-2 mm under the rock surface (McKay & Friedmann 1985). Cryptoendolithic microorganisms typically colonize porous Beacon sandstones with a 0.2 - 0.5 mm grain size, with an apparent preference for rocks stained tan or brown by $Fe3+$ -containing oxyhydroxides. A silicified crust of about 1 mm thickness on many of the rocks probably facilitates colonization by stabilizing the surface and reducing wind erosion (Campbell & Claridge 1987). Five cryptoendolithic microbial communities have been described by Friedmann *et al.* (1988), two of which can be found on Linnaeus Terrace: the Lichen Dominated and Red-Gloeocapsa Communities (Friedmann *et al.* 1988). Linnaeus Terrace is the type locality of the endemic green algal genus *Hemichloris* and of the endemic Xanthophycean algal species *Heterococcus endolithicus*. The Area is unusual in that so many different living and fossil endolithic communities are present within a small area. The main physical and biological features of these communities and their habitat are described by Friedmann (1993) and Siebert *et al.* (1996). More recently, non-invasive techniques, such as *in-situ* micro-spectrometry, have been used to detect the organic chemical footprint of the microbial communities from scans of the rock surface (Hand *et al.* 2005).

Fragile weathered rock formations, such as trace fossils in eroded sandstone and brittle overhanging low rock ledges (ranging from approximately 10 cm up to 1 m in height), are present throughout the Area (Figure 1).

A small area (Map 2) has been contaminated by release of the ^{14}C radioactive isotope. While the contamination poses no significant human or environmental threat, any samples gathered within this area are considered unsuitable for scientific work using ^{14}C techniques.

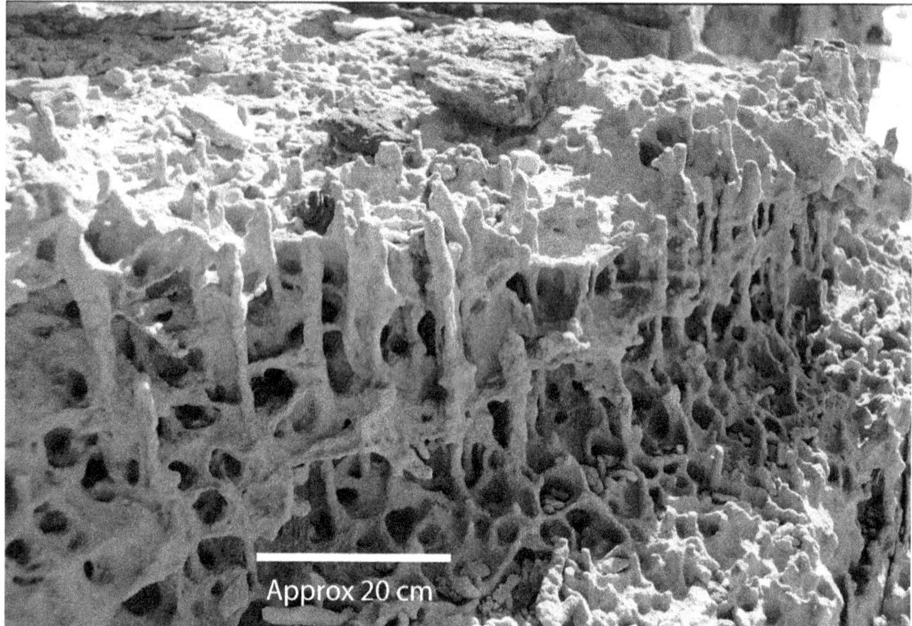

Figure 1: Photograph of the fragile rocks that are common throughout the Area (photo Colin Harris, ERA).

6(ii) Access to the area

The Area may be accessed by helicopter or on foot. Access by air is usually from either the Wright or the Taylor valleys. Access over land is difficult but possible on foot from the South Fork of the Wright Valley, although is generally impractical from other directions. Particular access routes have not been designated for entering the Area, although elevated terrain south of the Area means that helicopter access will usually be made from the other directions, particularly from the north over the Wright Valley. Access restrictions apply within the Area, the specific conditions for which are set out in Section 7(ii) below.

6(iii) Location of structures within and adjacent to the Area

A joint US / NZ inspection visit made 17 January 2012 identified evidence of past activities within the Area (Harris 2013). At least four markers (wooden stakes) exist at former experimental sites within the Area (Map 2). These markers could be useful so future researchers can identify and revisit these sites. While weathered, these markers do not appear to represent a significant threat to the values of the Area, and should be left *in situ* and their continued presence kept under review.

A rock cairn has been constructed close to where several small instruments have been installed into rocks (Map 2). A large, torn and faded cloth is stored within the cairn, weighed down by rocks. Future researchers may find the cairn useful to relocate these experimental sites, and it should be left *in situ*. The cloth appears to serve no useful purpose, and should be removed on a future visit.

Three sites with several small instruments embedded into rocks were identified within the Area in January 2012 (Map 2). The instruments at Marker #2 consist of a line of 'screws' embedded in the rock. At the other sites, one rock contains three instruments of about 10 mm across, which are fully and securely embedded into drill holes in the rock. Another rock contains two similar instruments, one of which protrudes above the rock surface by about 10 mm. The instruments are assumed to be old temperature or moisture probes, or similar. The instruments do not represent a significant threat to the values of the Area, and should be left *in situ* and their continued presence kept under review.

Two former helicopter landing sites and campsites in the north-eastern and eastern part of the Area are evident by remnant stone circles (Map 2). These stone circles should be left *in situ* in order to identify sites within the Area that have previously been disturbed.

6 (iv) Location of other protected areas in the vicinity

Linnaeus Terrace lies within Antarctic Specially Managed Area (ASMA) No.2, McMurdo Dry Valleys. The nearest protected areas to Linnaeus Terrace are Barwick and Balham Valleys (ASPA No.123), 35 km to the north, Lower Taylor Valley and Blood Falls (ASPA No.172), ~9 km to the south, and Canada Glacier (ASPA No.131), ~48 km to the southeast (Map 1). The nearest Restricted Zone designated under ASMA No.2 is Don Juan Pond, ~4.5 km northeast in the South Fork of the Wright Valley.

6(v) Special zones within the Area

There are no special zones within the Area.

7. Terms and conditions for entry permits

7(i) General permit conditions

Entry into the Area is prohibited except in accordance with a permit issued by an appropriate national authority. Conditions for issuing a Permit to enter the Area are that:

- it is issued only for scientific study of the cryptoendolithic ecosystem, or for compelling scientific reasons that cannot be served elsewhere, or for reasons essential to the management of the Area;
- the actions permitted are in accordance with this Management Plan;
- the activities permitted will give due consideration via the environmental impact assessment process to the continued protection of the environmental, ecological, and scientific values of the Area;
- the permit shall be issued for a finite period.
- the permit, or a copy, shall be carried when in the Area;

7(ii) Access to and movement within the Area

Access to and movement within the Area shall be on foot or by helicopter. Vehicles are prohibited within the Area. No special restrictions apply to the routes used to move to and from the Area.

Access on foot

- Movement within the Area should generally be on foot;
- Pedestrians should avoid damage to fragile rock formations: care should be exercised to avoid walking on trace fossils (Figure 1) and brittle overhanging low rock ledges which are easily broken;
- Pedestrian traffic should be kept to the minimum necessary consistent with the objectives of any permitted activities and every reasonable effort should be made to minimize effects.

Access by aircraft

- Aircraft landings within the Area are prohibited unless authorized by permit for purposes allowed for by the Management Plan;
- Helicopters shall land only at the designated site at the west end of the terrace (161° 04.483' E, 77° 35.833' S, elevation 1610 m: Map 2), except when specifically authorized by Permit otherwise for a compelling scientific or management purpose.
- When transporting permitted visitors, pilots, air crew, or passengers en route elsewhere on helicopters are prohibited from moving on foot beyond the immediate vicinity of the designated landing and camping sites unless specifically authorized by a Permit.

7(iii) Activities that are or may be conducted in the Area, including restrictions on time or place

- Scientific research that will not jeopardize the values of the Area;

- Essential management activities, including monitoring and inspection.

7(iv) Installation, modification or removal of structures / equipment

- No structures are to be erected within the Area except as specified in a permit;
- Permanent structures are prohibited;
- All structures, scientific equipment or markers installed in the Area shall be authorized by permit and clearly identified by country, name of the principal investigator, year of installation and date of expected removal. All such items should be free of organisms, propagules (e.g. seeds, eggs) and non-sterile soil, and be made of materials that can withstand the environmental conditions and pose minimal risk of contamination of the Area;
- Installation (including site selection), maintenance, modification or removal of structures or equipment shall be undertaken in a manner that minimizes disturbance to the values of the Area;
- Existing scientific equipment or markers shall not be removed except in accordance with a permit.
- The small instruments observed within the Area (Map 2) in January 2012 are assumed to be no longer in use, although they do not appear to pose any significant threat to the values of the Area. They could be useful to future researchers as markers of former experimental sites. As such, these instruments should be left *in situ* until the next management plan review, at which time further consideration should be given to whether or not they should be removed;
- Removal of specific structures / equipment for which the permit has expired shall be the responsibility of the authority which granted the original permit, and shall be a condition of the permit.

7(v) Location of field camps

Permanent field camps are prohibited within the Area. Temporary field camps are permitted within the Area only at the designated site in the immediate vicinity of the helicopter landing site (Map 2).

7(vi) Restrictions on materials and organisms which may be brought into the Area

In addition to the requirements of the Protocol on Environmental Protection to the Antarctic Treaty, restrictions on materials and organisms which may be brought into the area are:

- deliberate introduction of animals, plant material, micro-organisms and non-sterile soil into the Area is prohibited. Precautions shall be taken to prevent the accidental introduction of animals, plant material, micro-organisms and non-sterile soil from other biologically distinct regions (within or beyond the Antarctic Treaty area);
- Visitors shall ensure that scientific equipment, particularly for sampling, and markers brought into the Area are clean. To the maximum extent practicable, footwear and other equipment used or brought into the area (including backpacks, carry-bags and tents) shall be thoroughly cleaned before entering the Area. Visitors should also consult and follow as appropriate recommendations contained in the Committee for Environmental Protection *Non-native Species Manual* (CEP 2011), and in the *Environmental Code of Conduct for terrestrial scientific field research in Antarctica* (SCAR 2009);
- No herbicides or pesticides shall be brought into the Area;
- The use of explosives is prohibited within the Area;
- Fuel, food, chemicals, and other materials shall not be stored in the Area, unless specifically authorized by permit and shall be stored and handled in a way that minimises the risk of their accidental introduction into the environment;
- All materials introduced shall be for a stated period only and shall be removed by the end; and
- If release occurs which is likely to compromise the values of the Area, removal is encouraged only where the impact of removal is not likely to be greater than that of leaving the material *in situ*.

7(vii) Taking of, or harmful interference with, native flora or fauna

Taking or harmful interference with native flora or fauna is prohibited, except in accordance with Annex II of the Protocol on Environmental Protection to the Antarctic Treaty.

Where animal taking or harmful interference is involved, this should, as a minimum standard, be in accordance with the SCAR Code of Conduct for the Use of Animals for Scientific Purposes in Antarctica.

7(viii) Collection or removal of anything not brought into the Area by the permit holder

- Material may be collected or removed from the Area only in accordance with a permit and should be limited to the minimum necessary to meet scientific or management needs;
- Material of human origin likely to compromise the values of the Area, and which was not brought into the Area by the permit holder or otherwise authorized, may be removed unless the impact of removal is likely to be greater than leaving the material *in situ*: if this is the case the appropriate authority should be notified and approval obtained. At least four markers (wooden stakes) exist at former experimental sites within the Area (Map 2). These markers do not appear to represent a significant threat to the values of the Area and could be useful for future research projects. Therefore, they should be left *in situ* and their continued presence kept under review

7(ix) Disposal of waste

All wastes, including all human wastes, shall be removed from the Area.

7(x) Measures that may be necessary to continue to meet the aims and objectives of the Management Plan

Permits may be granted to enter the Area to:

- carry out monitoring and Area inspection activities, which may involve the collection of a small number of samples or data for analysis or review;
- install or maintain signposts, markers, structures or scientific equipment;
- carry out protective measures.

7(x) Requirements for reports

- The principal permit holder for each visit to the Area shall submit a report to the appropriate national authority as soon as practicable, and no later than six months after the visit has been completed;
- Such reports should include, as appropriate, the information identified in the visit report form contained in the Guide to the Preparation of Management Plans for Antarctic Specially Protected Areas. If appropriate, the national authority should also forward a copy of the visit report to the Party that proposed the Management Plan, to assist in managing the Area and reviewing the Management Plan;
- Parties should, wherever possible, deposit originals or copies of such original reports in a publicly accessible archive to maintain a record of usage, to be used both in any review of the Management Plan and in organizing the scientific use of the Area;
- The appropriate authority should be notified of any activities / measures undertaken, and / or of any materials released and not removed, that were not included in the authorized permit.

8. Supporting documentation

Campbell, I.B. & Claridge, C.G.C., 1987. *Antarctica: soils, weathering processes and environment. Developments in Soil Science* **16**. Elsevier Science Publishers, Amsterdam.

Committee for Environmental Protection (CEP) 2011. *Non-native Species Manual – 1st Edition.* Manual prepared by Intersessional Contact Group of the CEP and adopted by the Antarctic Treaty Consultative Meeting through Resolution 6 (2011). Buenos Aires: Secretariat of the Antarctic Treaty.

Darling, R.B., Friedmann, E.I. & Broady, PA. 1987. *Heterococcus endolithicus* sp. nov. (Xanthophyceae) and other terrestrial *Heterococcus* species from Antarctica: morphological changes during life history and response to temperature. *Journal of Phycology* **23**:598-607.

Friedmann, E.I. & Ocampo, R. 1976. Endolithic blue-green algae in the Dry Valleys: primary producers and the Antarctic desert ecosystem. *Science* **193**: 1247–9.

Friedmann, E.I., McKay, C.P. & Nienow, J.A. 1987. The cryptoendolithic microbial environment in the Ross Desert of Antarctica: satellite-transmitted continuous nanoclimate data, 1984 to 1986. *Polar Biology* **7**: 273-87.

Friedmann, E.I., Hua, M. & Ocampo-Friedmann, R. 1988. Cryptoendolithic lichen and cyanobacterial communities of the Ross Desert, Antarctica. *Polarforschung* **58** (2/3): 251-59.

Friedmann, E.I. (ed) 1993. *Antarctic microbiology*. Wiley-Liss, New York.

Harris, C.M. 1994. Ross Sea Protected Areas 1993/94 Visit Report. Unpublished report on inspection visits to protected areas in the Ross Sea. International Centre for Antarctic Information and Research, Christchurch.

Harris, C.M. 2013. Antarctic Specially Protected Area No. 138 Linnaeus Terrace: Site Visit Report for Management Plan review on a joint US/ NZ inspection visit on 17 Jan 2012. Unpublished report for the US Antarctic Program and Antarctica New Zealand. Cambridge, Environmental Research & Assessment Ltd.

Hand, K.P., Carlson, R.W., Sun, H., Anderson, M., Wadsworth,W. & Levy, R. 2005. Utilizing active mid-infrared microspectrometry for in situ analysis of cryptoendolithic microbial communities of Battleship Promontory, Dry Valleys, Antarctica. *Proc. SPIE* 5906, *Astrobiology and Planetary Missions*, 590610.

McKay, C.P. & Friedmann, E.I. 1985. The cryptoendolithic microbial environment in the Antarctic cold desert: temperature variations in nature. *Polar Biology* **4**: 19-25.

SCAR (Scientific Committee on Antarctic Research) 2009. *Environmental Code of Conduct for terrestrial scientific field research in Antarctica*. Cambridge, SCAR.

Siebert, J., Hirsch, P., Hoffman, B., Gliesche, C.G., Peissl, K. & Jendrach, M. 1996. Cryptoendolithic microorganisms from Antarctic sandstone of Linnaeus Terrace (Asgard Range): diversity, properties and interactions. *Biodiversity & Conservation* **5** (11): 1337-63.

Tschermak-Woess, E. & Friedmann, E.I. 1984. *Hemichloris antarctica*, gen. et sp. nov. (chlorococcales, chlorophyta), a cryptoendolithic alga from Antarctica. *Phycologia* **23** (4): 443-54.

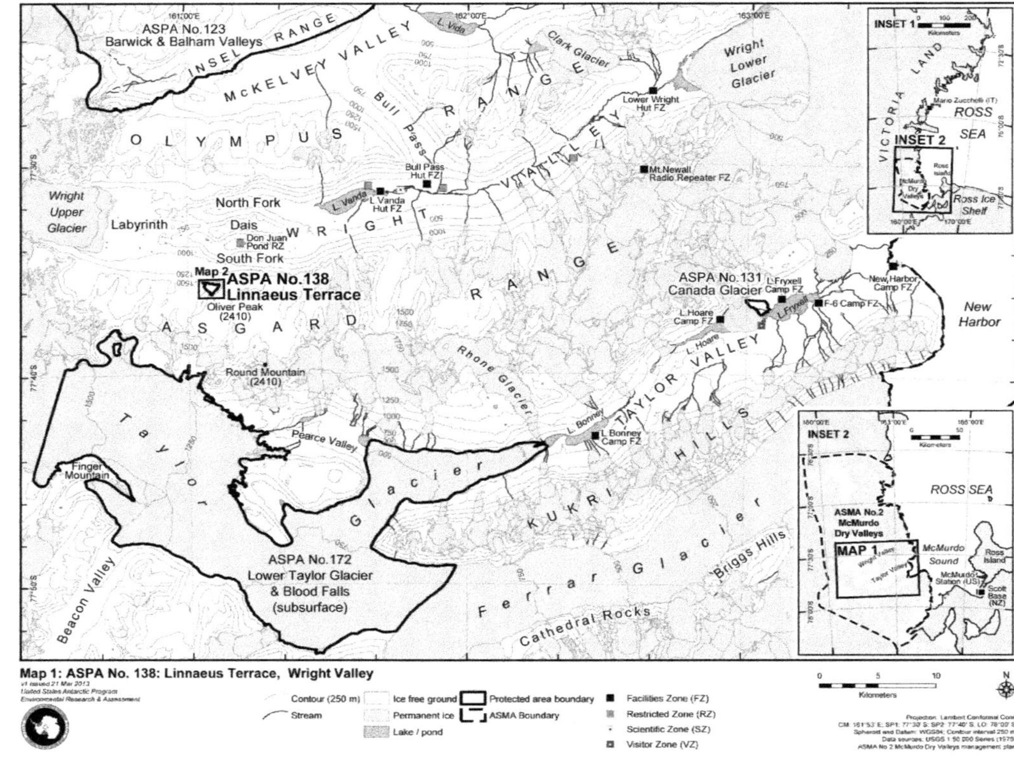
ASPA No.123
Barwick & Balham Valleys
INSEL RANGE
McKELVEY VALLEY
O L Y M P U S R A N G E
Bull Pass
Bull Pass Hut FZ
L. Vida
Clark Glacier
Wright Lower Glacier
Lower Wright Hut FZ
Mt.Newall Radio Repeater FZ
WRIGHT VALLEY
Wright Upper Glacier
Labyrinth
North Fork
Dais
South Fork
Don Juan Pond RZ
L. Vanda
L. Vanda Hut FZ
Map 2
ASPA No.138
Linnaeus Terrace
Oliver Peak (2410)
A S G A R D R A N G E
Round Mountain (2410)
ASPA No.131
Canada Glacier
L.Fryxell Camp FZ
L.Fryxell
L.Hoare Camp FZ
L.Hoare
F-6 Camp FZ
New Harbor Camp FZ
New Harbor
Rhone Glacier
TAYLOR VALLEY
L.Bonney
L.Bonney Camp FZ
Pearce Valley
Taylor Glacier
Finger Mountain
ASPA No.172
Lower Taylor Glacier & Blood Falls (subsurface)
KUKRI HILLS
Ferrar Glacier
Briggs Hills
Cathedral Rocks
Beacon Valley
INSET 1
VICTORIA LAND
Mario Zucchelli (IT)
ROSS SEA
INSET 2
Ross Ice Shelf
ROSS SEA
ASMA No.2 McMurdo Dry Valleys
MAP 1
McMurdo Sound
Ross Island
McMurdo Station (US)
Scott Base (NZ)
Map 1: ASPA No. 138: Linnaeus Terrace, Wright Valley
Contour (250 m)
Stream
Ice free ground
Permanent ice
Lake / pond
Protected area boundary
ASMA Boundary
Facilities Zone (FZ)
Restricted Zone (RZ)
Scientific Zone (SZ)
Visitor Zone (VZ)
Kilometers

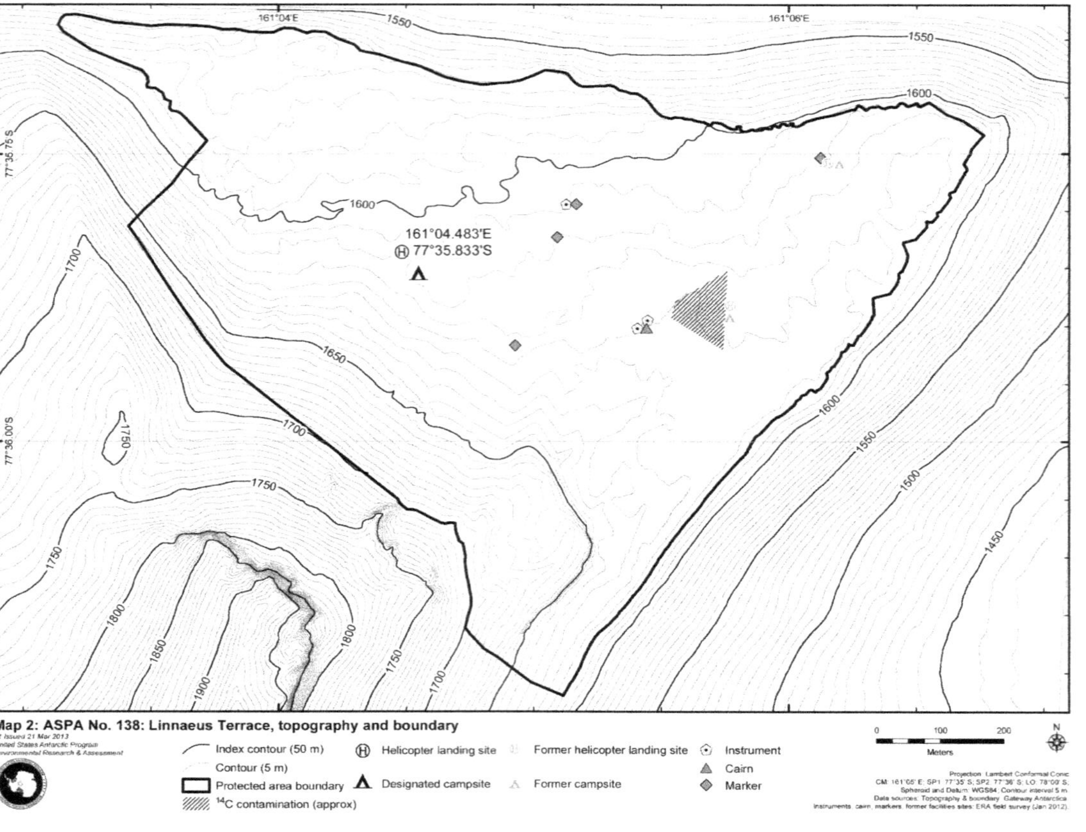

Map 2: ASPA No. 138: Linnaeus Terrace, topography and boundary
v1 Issued 21 Mar 2013
United States Antarctic Program
Environmental Research & Assessment

Management Plan for Antarctic Specially Protected Area No. 143

MARINE PLAIN, MULE PENINSULA, VESTFOLD HILLS, PRINCESS ELIZABETH LAND

Introduction

Marine Plain is located approximately 10 km south-east of Davis station in the Vestfold Hills (68°37'50.2" S, 78°07'55.2" E). The Marine Plain Antarctic Specially Protected Area (the Area) covers an area of 23.4 km^2 and opens into an arm of Crooked Fjord on the southern side of Mule Peninsula, the southernmost of the three major peninsulas that comprise the Vestfold Hills.

The Area is representative of a major Antarctic terrestrial ice-free ecosystem and is primarily designated to protect outstanding fossil fauna and rare geological features. It is of exceptional scientific interest because of its relevance to the palaeoecological and palaeoclimatic record of Antarctica.

The Area was originally designated as Site of Special Scientific Interest No. 25 Recommendation XIV-5 (1987) after a proposal by Australia. In accordance with Decision 2 (2002) the site was redesignated and renumbered as ASPA No. 143. A revised management plan for the area was adopted under Measure 2 (2003).

1. Description of values to be protected

The Area is representative of a major Antarctic terrestrial ice-free ecosystem with outstanding fossil fauna and rare geological features. It is of exceptional and ongoing scientific interest because of its relevance to the palaeoecological and palaeoclimatic record of Antarctica. It has been subject to several detailed geological, palaeontological, geomorphological and glaciological studies.

The Area has yielded outstanding vertebrate fossil fauna including *Australodelphis mirus*, the first higher vertebrate named from the Oligocene-Pleistocene interval on land in Antarctica, and the first cetacean fossil from the polar margin of circum-Antarctic Southern Ocean that postdates the break-up of Gondwana. It has also revealed four other species of cetaceans; a species of fish; and a diverse invertebrate fauna comprising molluscs, gastropods, marine diatoms and the first Pliocene decapod crustacean from Antarctica.

The Area contains a roughly horizontal section of ca 8 m thick Pliocene marine sediments known as the Sørsdal Formation (Map C), which is in some areas exposed, but elsewhere underlies Holocene sediments up to 1 m thick. A diatom biostratigraphy placed the Sørsdal Formation in the *Fragilariopsis barronii* Zone, Early Pliocene (ca 4.5-4.1 Ma). The early Pliocene deposits are crucial as a source of information on the environment at this stage of Antarctic history.

The fossil fauna provides insight into the early Pliocene Antarctic environments, including high-latitude climate and oceanography. By examining the diatom microfossils, it is possible to reconstruct the probable palaeoenvironmental conditions relating to the Sørsdal Formation and test hypothetical models of ice sheet behaviour against the geological record. This will also provide insight into the Antarctic ice sheet's response to climate change.

The Vestfold Hills cover an ice-free area of approximately 413 km^2. The hills are typically less than 180m in elevation. They have been subject to intermittent glaciations and exposed rocks are characterised by polishing, striation and fracturing. The glacial striae show the direction of past ice movements. These features, together with other periglacial and glacial features, have been extensively studied to investigate the region's geomorphological and glacial history.

In addition, the Area possesses the largest periglacial thermokarst in East Antarctica. Sediments are normally cemented by permafrost (in addition to any cement formed during diagenesis), however thawing can lead to undercutting and collapse. The thermokarst landforms have been produced by thermal back wearing of low scarps and include thaw pits, thaw lakes, ground ice sumps, linear depressions and very small scale beaded drainage features. Human impact may accelerate the permafrost thawing which may disturb important geomorphological values and threaten fossils contained in the diatomite.

The Area is intrinsically linked to Burton Lake. Located west of Marine Plain, Burton Lake is a hypersaline lagoon with a seasonal connection with the marine environment. This lagoon represents a stage in the biological and physio-chemical evolution of a terrestrial water body (i.e. the geological creation of a lake).

The meromictic and saline Burton Lake, together with several smaller lakes and ponds around the Area, provide important examples in the spectrum of hypersaline to fresh water lake types in the Vestfold Hills and present opportunities for important geochemical and limnological research. The interrelationships between environment and biological communities in such lakes provide considerable insight into the evolution of lake environments and more broadly Antarctic environmental development. Burton Lake is currently the only meromictic lagoon that has been protected within East Antarctica.

Given its proximity to Australia's Davis station, there is a risk that the scientific values of the Area may be compromised or damaged by accidental interference. The Area lies on the pedestrian route (Map B) to the Mule Peninsula lakes (Clear, Laternula, and McCallum) from Ellis Rapids and is easily accessible.

The Area merits protection given there is a demonstrable risk of interference which may jeopardise scientific investigation. Accordingly it is critical that the Area's fossil fauna is protected from unrecorded sampling, collection or interference.

2. Aims and objectives

Management for the Marine Plain ASPA aims to:

- avoid degradation of, or substantial risk to, the values of Marine Plain by preventing unnecessary human disturbance in the ASPA;
- allow scientific research for geological, palaeoclimatic, palaeontological, geomorphological and limnological purposes, while ensuring protection from over-sampling;
- allow other scientific research provided it is for compelling reasons that cannot be served elsewhere;
- minimise damage to landforms, particularly Marine Plain; the plain south of Poseidon Lake and east of Pickard Ridge (68°37'22.8"S, 78°07 9.9"E); glacial and periglacial features; and potential fossil sites; and
- allow visits for management purposes in support of the aims of this management plan.

3. Management activities

The following management activities will be undertaken to protect the values of the Area:

- information on the location of the Area (stating special restrictions that apply) shall be displayed prominently and a copy of this management plan kept available:

  - at the adjacent Davis station;
  - at the Marine Plain Refuge; and
  - on ships visiting the vicinity;
- installation of boundary markers to identify boundary turning points;
- signs that illustrate the location and boundaries, with clear statements of entry restrictions, shall be placed at appropriate locations at the boundaries of the Area to prevent inadvertent entry;
- markers, signs or structures erected within the Area for scientific or management purposes shall be secured and maintained in good condition and removed when no longer required;
- abandoned equipment or materials shall be removed to the maximum extent possible provided doing so does not adversely impact on the values of the Area;
- the Area will be visited no less than once every five years to facilitate an assessment as to whether the Area continues to serve the purposes for which it was designated and to ensure that management activities are adequate; and
- review of the management plan at least every five years and update as required.

4. Period of designation

Designated for an indefinite period.

5. Maps

Map A: Vestfold Hills, East Antarctica, showing the locations of Marine Plain ASPA; Davis station and surrounding refuges. Inset: The location of the Vestfold Hills in Antarctica. Map Specifications: Projection: UTM Zone 44 Horizontal Datum: WGS84.

Map B: The region immediately surrounding Marine Plain ASPA including topography and fauna distribution. Map Specifications: Projection: UTM Zone 44 Horizontal Datum: WGS84 Contour Interval: 20m.

Map C: Geological map of Marine Plain ASPA including the Sørsdal Formation. Map Specifications: Projection: UTM Zone 44 Horizontal Datum: WGS84.

6. Description of the Area

6(i) Geographical co-ordinates, Boundary Markers and Natural Features

General description

The Area is located approximately 10 km southeast of Davis station in the Vestfold Hills (68°37'50.2" S, 78°07'55.2" E). It covers an area of 23.4 km^2 and opens into an arm of Crooked Fjord on the southern side of Mule Peninsula, the southernmost of the three major peninsulas that comprise the Vestfold Hills.

The Vestfold Hills are a largely ice-free oasis of approximately 512 km^2 of bedrock, glacial debris, lakes and ponds on the eastern side of Prydz Bay, Princess Elizabeth Land.

The Area includes Marine Plain (approximately 3 km^2) which occupies the centre of the Area in a north-south orientation. Pickard Ridge (maximum elevation of 70 m) separates this site from Poseidon Basin in the northeast.

Both locations are low-lying areas with elevations less than 20 m. Sections elsewhere above 20m are mostly low rugged hills of Precambrian rock which are characterised by a marked change in slope at their base which may represent a Holocene shoreline. The surface of the lower area below 20 m is marked by a series of concave-to-the-south recessional moraine ridges. A series of south westerly facing sand slopes occupy Marine Plain east of Burton Lake.

Starting at the most northerly point of the Area, the boundary description is as follows:

> Commencing at 68°36'34"S, 78°09'28"E, then south-easterly to 68°36'45"S, 78°10'30"E; then south-easterly to 68°37'30"S, 78°12'30"E, then south along meridian of longitude 78°12'30"E to its intersection with the northern shore of Pineapple Lake; then west along that shore to the edge of the Sørsdal Glacier; then westerly along the northern edge of the Sørsdal Glacier to its intersection with the low water mark of the north eastern shore of Crooked Fjord; then westerly along the low water mark of the northern shore of Crooked Fjord (cutting across the outlet of Burton Lake into Crooked Fjord) to its intersection with the meridian of longitude 78°03'0"E; then north along meridian of longitude 78°03'0"E to its intersection with the parallel of latitude 68°37'30"S, then north-easterly to 68°36'56"S, 78°05'39"E, then north-easterly to the point of commencement.

Geology and palaeontology

The three major lithologies forming the Vestfold Hills (Map C) are (in order of age) Chelnock Paragneiss, Mossel Gneiss and Crooked Lake Gneiss. This is repeated in units from east-northeast to west-southwest. Intruded into these are groups of mafic dykes in a rough north-south orientation (Map C). These dykes are a major feature of the Vestfold Hills.

The Precambrian rock is overlain in low-lying areas (approximately 10–17 m above sea level) by ca 8 m of early Pliocene (ca 4.5-3.5 Ma) diatomite with limestone lenses in the upper half. The limestone contains molluscs, especially bivalves including *Chlamys tuftsensis*. Holocene (ca 6.49 ka) glacial debris disconformably covers the marine deposit (0.5-1 m), extending over an area of 8-10 km^2. A layer of lenticular sandstone separates the Pliocene and Holocene units.

Low scarps in the Pliocene marine sediments have yielded a diverse array of fossil marine vertebrates and invertebrates. The cetacean specimens occur as large assemblages of vertebral columns, skulls and complete specimens approximately 2m or more in length in the upper 2m of the Marine Plain section. The main occurrences are along the margins of the "Big Ditch" near Burton Lake and in the scarp on the eastern side of Marine Plain. One notable cetacean fossil is *Australodelphis mirus* which illustrates a remarkable convergence between living dolphins (Family Delphinidae) and the living beaked whale genus *Mesoplodon*.

Marine Plain has also yielded the first Pliocene decapod crustacean from Antarctica. The specimen is incomplete, making it difficult to identify precisely, although it probably belongs with the Palinuridae. Other species include a beaked whale and baleen whale (and others not yet studied), possibly penguins, fish, bivalves, gastropods, serpulid worms, bryozoans, asteroids, ophiuroids, echinoids and abundant leiospheres that are probably planktonic in origin.

Marine Plain has been subject to significant fluvial activity since the mid-Holocene resulting in small patches of lake sediment on its eastern side. Stream valleys and source lakes (now virtually empty) have been identified.

The Pliocene diatomite at Marine Plain appears to be the only such deposit in the Vestfold Hills. In some areas the Holocene till and glacials are very thin and consequently are easily disturbed. A thin crust over the loose powdery surface is easily crushed by footfall, releasing a plume of diatom and sand rich dust which leaves a sharply defined colour-contrasting footprint.

Permafrost occurs below ca 1m depth and the local landforms have evolved due to very slow progressive melting of ground ice. Terrain produced by this process is known as periglacial thermokarst because the resulting depressions give the topography an appearance similar to that of conventional limestone karst.

The Sørsdal Glacier (near the edge of the Antarctic ice sheet) is the southern boundary for the ice-free Vestfold Hills. A 1 km length of the northern edge of Sørsdal Glacier has retreated c.

800 m away from the southern edge of Marine Plain in the 40 years from 1947. This retreat is due to movement through the deep channel that the glacier fills and the formation of ice ridges in the glacier which subsequently collapse into Crooked Fjord.

Lakes

Burton Lake is a major feature of the western side of the Area. There are several unnamed ponds and small lakes within the Area. Burton Lake is a seasonally isolated marine lagoon with a maximum depth of 18m. It is meromictic and hypersaline. Burton Lake is ice-covered for 10-11 months of the year and is seasonally connected to Crooked Fjord by a tidal channel approximately 20 m wide and up to 2 m deep. The lake is isolated from Crooked Fjord for about 6-7 months of the year by ice.

The lake contains a range of photosynthetic bacteria. The dominant species are *Chlorobium vibriofome* and *C. limiola* while minor species are *Thiocapsa roseopersicina* and *Rhodopseudomonas palustris.* The lake also harbours psychrophilic bacteria which are relatively uncommon in Antarctic coastal ice zones. These thrive on the increased availability of nutrients from continental inputs, pelagic algal blooms and the breakout of pelagic algae into the water column from melting ice. One novel species of bacterium is *Psychroserpens burtonensis* which has not been cultured from or recorded in any other environment.

Marine algae are abundant in Burton Lake. A diatom floristic study of the lagoon revealed 41 diatom species.

The ultrastructure of *Postgaardi mariagerensis* was reported for the first time from research in Burton Lake. This very unusual organism is not a euglenid but rather a member of the clade *Euglenozoa – Euglenozoa incertae sedis.* Additionally, Burton Lake is one of two Antarctic lakes from which the first account of choanoflagellate (including *Diaphanoeca grandis, Diaphanoeca sphaerica* and *Saepicula leadbeateri*) were reported. It is also type location for *Spiraloecion didymocostatum* gen. et sp. nov.

Four metazoan species have been regularly recorded in the zooplankton of Burton Lake: *Drepanopus bispinosus* and *Paralabidocera antarctica* (Copepoda), *Rathkea lizzioides* (Anthomedusae) and an un-named cydippid ctenophore. Many holotrichia, at least two species of nematode and a large marine amphipod have been recorded in the benthic community. Tardigrades are also present.

One species of fish, *Pagothenia borchgrevinki,* has been observed in the lake on one occasion. This species is common in coastal areas and fjords of the Vestfold Hills, however it does not appear to inhabit the lake continuously. Due to the seasonal marine connection it remains probable that additional algae, zooplankton and fish enter the lake but do not survive the winter.

Vegetation

Mosses and lichens occur in the vicinity of small ephemeral watercourses that drain radially down the 'talus skirt' fringing the Precambrian hills. Numerous small crevices and cracks in the knoll jutting into the northern end of Burton Lake provide a rich lichen site, while the northern end of Poseidon Lake is rich in mosses. The moss and lichen flora of the Area has not been documented, however the Vestfold Hills supports at least six moss species and at least 23 lichens.

Vertebrates

Several vertebrates occur sporadically within the Area between November and February. Wilson's storm petrels (*Oceanites oceanicus*) and Snow petrels (*Pagodroma nivea*) nest in the higher Precambrian rocks. South polar skuas (*Catharacta maccormicki*) nest on Marine Plain and occasionally around the water's edge. Weddell seals *(Leptonychotes weddellii*), Southern Elephant seals (*Mirounga leonina*), Adélie penguins (*Pygoscelis adeliae*) and Emperor penguins

(*Aptenodytes forsteri*) also occur in small groups in the Area but have not been specifically studied here.

Climate

Meteorological data for the Area are confined almost entirely to observations at Davis station, 10 km northwest of Marine Plain. The Vestfold Hills area has a polar maritime climate that is cold, dry and windy. Summer days are typically sunny with a midday temperature from -1C to +3C and a summer maximum of +5C. For most of the year temperatures are below 0C. During winter the temperature may fall as low as –40.7C. The maximum temperature recorded at Davis station from 1957 to 2001 was +13°C. The record illustrates the seasonal climate expected for high latitudes but on average Davis station is warmer than other Antarctic stations at similar latitudes. This has been attributed to the "rocky oasis" which results from the lower albedo of rock surfaces compared to ice (whereby solar energy is absorbed and re-radiated as heat).

Environmental domains analysis

Based on the Environmental Domains Analysis for Antarctica (Resolution 3 (2008)) Marine Plain is located within Environment D *East Antarctic coastal geologic.*

Antarctic Conservation Biogeographic Regions

Based on the Antarctic Conservation Biogeographic Regions (Resolution 6 (2012)) Marine Plain is located within Biogeographic Region 7 *East Antarctica.*

6(ii) Access to the Area

The vicinity of the Area can be accessed on foot, by small boat or by Helicopter, in accordance with requirements outlined in section 7(ii) of this plan.

6(iii) Location of structures within and adjacent to the Area

There are no refuges within the Area however two refuges are located nearby. Marine Plain Refuge (68°36'54"S, 78°65'30"E) is approximately 150 m north of the northern boundary of the Area. A helicopter landing site is immediately adjacent to this refuge. Watts Hut (68°35'54"S, 78°13'48"E) is located at the eastern end of Ellis Fjord, approximately 5 km east-northeast of the Marine Plain Refuge and 2.9 km east-northeast of the northern-most point of the Area.

Evidence of past research activity remains at Marine Plain. Two parallel lines of small boulders mark out a helicopter landing site 30 m north of a fossil site (68°37'37"S, 78°08'11"E). Here a black sheet of polythene (3 m x 1.7 m) held down by rocks is currently covering an excavation site. At the north western side of the embayment there are approximately 10 wooden stakes 1m high in a rough line, north to south. In the next embayment to the north three red painted rock cairns form a triangle area (approximately 50 m in side length).

Within Marine Plain there also remains plastered hessian covering fossil bones; five shallow unfilled pits; a large unfilled pit (near Burton Lake); a major unfilled excavation occurring on one high flank of a natural trough (the trough locally known as "Big Ditch") and some old filled trench sites. On the north western side of Burton Lake lies a pipe and rope (possibly for lake monitoring).

Boundary markers are to be installed at boundary turning points.

6(iv) Location of other protected areas in the vicinity

Hawker Island Antarctic Specially Protected Area No. 167 (68°38'S, 77°51'E) is located approximately 8km east of Marine Plain.

Two Historic Sites and Monuments are located in the Vestfold Hills at least 25 km north of Marine Plain:

1) on the largest of the Tryne Islands (68° 18'29"S, 78° 23'44"E) in Tryne Bay (29 km north-east of Davis), HSM No. 72 is a cairn and wooden mast erected in 1935 by Captain Klarius Mikkelsen marking the first landing in the Vestfold Hills area.

2) Walkabout Rocks Cairn HSM No. 6 (68°22'14"S, 78°32'19"E) 40 km north-east of Davis is a rock cairn erected in 1939 by Sir Hubert Wilkins. The cairn contains a canister containing a record of his visit.

6(v) Special zones within the Area

There are no special zones within the area.

7. Terms and conditions for entry Permits

7(i) General permit conditions

Entry into the Area is prohibited except in accordance with a permit issued by an appropriate national authority. Conditions for issuing a permit to enter the Area are that:

- it is issued only for scientific (palaeontological, palaeoclimatic, geological, geomorphological, glaciological, biological and limnological) research, or for compelling scientific, educational or cultural reasons, or for essential management purposes consistent with the management plan;
- the actions permitted will not jeopardise the values of the Area or other permitted activities;
- the actions permitted are in accordance with this management plan;
- the permit, or an authorised copy, shall be carried within the Area;
- a visit report will be supplied to the authority that approved the permit as soon as practicable after the visit to the ASPA has been completed but no later than six months after the visit has occurred;
- permits will be issued for a finite period;
- permit holders shall notify the appropriate authority of any activities or measures undertaken that were not authorised permit; and
- permits shall be issued for a stated period.

7(ii) Access to, and movement within or over, the Area

- Movement within the Area should be kept to a minimum with every reasonable effort made to minimise impact. The brittle surface crust is easily crushed under foot, risking damage to fossil material and long-term evidence of human impact. Where possible, movement on Precambrian (bedrock) areas is preferred, while movement on the scarps is to be avoided. All movement should be undertaken carefully so as to minimise disturbance to the soil, vegetation, diatomite, thermokarst, sediment outcrops and other geofeatures that provide scientific and environmental value to the site. The landing of aircraft, the use of vehicles and camping is prohibited on the Sørsdal Formation.

- Normally the helicopter landing site immediately adjacent to the Marine Plain refuge should be used. In order to minimise foot traffic within Marine Plain, a helicopter landing site within the Area may be authorised for a particular visit. The landing site shall be:
    - measured against overall usage in keeping with protected area status;
    - on a debris free bedrock surface where minimal disturbance would be caused by the aircraft to water bodies, vegetation or sediment deposits; and

- at a location that will minimise the impact of passage to the intended research site.

- Motorised vessels are not to be used on Burton Lake.
- Over-flights of lakes should be kept to the minimum necessary to achieve specific research or management requirements.
- Movement within the Area by vehicle is prohibited.

7(iii) Activities which may be conducted in the Area

The following activities may be conducted within the Area provided access requirements can be met:

- compelling scientific research which cannot be undertaken elsewhere and that will not jeopardise the values of the Area;
- geological sampling, which should be the minimum required for the approved research programs;
- hydrological sampling, ensuring equipment is washed prior to entry into the Area to prevent contamination from other lakes; and
- essential management activities, including monitoring.

7(iv) Installation, modification, or removal of structures

Permanent structures and installations are prohibited in the Area.

Temporary structures, installations, markers and equipment may only be established in the Area for compelling scientific or management purposes as specified in a permit.

Any temporary structures, installations, markers and equipment established in the Area must be:

- clearly identified by country, name of the principal agency, date of installation and date of expected removal;
- free of organisms, propagules (e.g. seeds, eggs) and non-sterile soil;
- made of materials that can withstand Antarctic conditions;
- made of materials that pose a minimal risk of contamination to the Area; and
- removed when they are no longer required, or upon the expiry of the permit, whichever is earlier.

Descriptions and location coordinates of temporary structures, installations, markers and equipment shall be submitted to the permitting authority.

7(v) Location of field camps

Camping is prohibited on the Sørsdal Formation.

Camping is only permissible elsewhere in the Area if the use of the Marine Plain Refuge (68°36'54"S, 78°6'30"E; see 6(iii)) would pose greater risks to the Area's values.

7(vi) Restrictions on materials and organisms which may be brought into the Area

The following restrictions apply:

- no living animals, plant material or microorganisms shall be deliberately introduced into the Area and precautions shall be taken against accidental introductions;
- no herbicides or pesticides shall be brought into the Area. Any other chemicals, including radio-nuclides or stable isotopes authorised for scientific or management purposes, must be removed from the Area upon or before the conclusion of the activity for which the Permit was granted;

- organic materials (wood, cotton, hessian, etc.) are not to be used for scientific markers or other research unless absolutely necessary. Inorganic materials (stainless steel, polythene, etc.) are to be used;
- fuel is not to be stored in the Area unless required for essential purposes connected with the activity for which the Permit has been granted. Fuel must be removed from the ASPA upon or before completion of the associated activity. Permanent fuel depots are not permitted in the Area; and
- all material introduced to the Area shall be for a stated time period only. All material introduced will be removed upon or before the conclusion of that stated time period, and will be stored and handled in a manner that will minimise the risk of environmental impacts.

7(vii) Taking of, or harmful interference with, native flora and fauna

Taking of or harmful interference with native flora and fauna is prohibited except in accordance with a Permit. Where taking or harmful interference with animals is involved this should, as a minimum standard, be in accordance with the SCAR Code of Conduct for the Use of Animals for Scientific Purposes in Antarctica.

7(viii) Collection or removal of materials not brought into the Area by the permit holder

- Sample material may only be collected or removed from the Area in accordance with a Permit and should be limited to the minimum necessary to meet scientific or management needs.
- Permits shall not be granted if there is a reasonable concern that the sampling proposed would take, displace, remove or damage such quantities of rock, soil, water or native flora or fauna that their distribution or abundance at Marine Plain would be significantly affected. Excavation of fossils is exempted from this requirement.
- Material of human origin likely to compromise the values of the Area, which was not brought into the Area by the Permit holder or otherwise authorised, may be removed unless the impact of the removal is likely to be greater than leaving the material *in situ*. In this event, the appropriate national authority should be notified.

7(ix) Disposal of waste

All wastes, including all human wastes, shall be removed from the Area.

7(x) Measures that may be necessary to ensure that the aims and objectives of the Management Plan can continue to be met

- Permits may be granted to enter the Area to carry out monitoring, site inspections (which may involve the small-scale collection of samples for analysis or review) or protective measures.
- Any specific sites of long-term monitoring shall be appropriately marked and a GPS position obtained for lodgment with the Antarctic Data Directory System through the appropriate national authority.
- To help maintain the geological, palaeontologic, geomorphological, biological, limnological, and scientific values of Marine Plain, persons shall take special care walking or skiing over slopes, moraines, rock exposures and diatomite soil. To minimise the risk of damage to these values, foot traffic to and from Marine Plain and the plain south of Poseidon Basin and east of Pickard Ridge shall be restricted wherever possible.
- To help maintain the ecological and scientific values derived from the relatively low level of human impact within the Area, special precautions shall be taken against introductions. To minimise the risk of introductions, footwear and any equipment to be used in the Area shall be thoroughly cleaned prior to entry into the Area.

- The stratigraphic integrity and endolithic communities of the Area shall be preserved through the closure and securing of excavation sites. Recommended measures include:
    - the placement of excavated soil onto a polythene sheet of adequate thickness;
    - the replacement of soil and sediment in layers in the order in which they were removed;
    - the replacement of larger clasts by correct orientation;
    - the removal of unnatural surface irregularities; and
    - the reorientation of rock and till during closure.
- Abandoned scientific equipment shall be removed and excavations rehabilitated to the maximum extent possible.

7(xi) Requirements for reports

The principal permit holder for each visit to the Area shall submit a report to the appropriate national authority as soon as practicable, and no later than six months after the visit has been completed.

Such visit reports should include, as applicable, the information identified in the recommended visit report form contained in Appendix 4 of the Guide to the Preparation of Management Plans for Antarctic Specially Protected Areas.

If appropriate, the national authority should also forward a copy of the visit report to the Party that proposed the Management Plan, to assist in managing the Area and reviewing the Management Plan.

Parties should, wherever possible, deposit originals or copies of such original visit reports in a publicly accessible archive to maintain a record of usage, for the purpose of any review of the Management Plan and in organising the scientific use of the Area.

8. Supporting Documentation

Adamson, D.A. & Pickard. J. (1983) Late Quaternary Ice Movement across the Vestfold Hills, East Antarctica. In: Oliver, R.L., James, P.R. & Jago, J.B. (eds.) *Antarctic Earth Science: Proceedings of the Fourth International Symposium on Antarctic Earth Sciences, University of Adelaide, South Australia, 16-18 August 1982*, Australian Academy of Science, Canberra, pp. 465-469.

Adamson, D.A. & Pickard. J. (1986a) Cainozoic history of the Vestfold Hills. In: Pickard, J. (ed.) *Antarctic oasis: Terrestrial environments and history of the Vestfold Hills.* Academic Press Australia, Sydney, pp. 63-98.

Adamson, D.A. & Pickard. J. (1986b) Physiography and geomorphology of the Vestfold Hills. In: Pickard, J. (ed.) *Antarctic oasis: Terrestrial environments and history of the Vestfold Hills.* Academic Press Australia, Sydney, pp. 99-139

Bayly, I.A.E. (1986) Ecology of the zooplankton of a meromictic Antarctic lagoon with special reference to *Drepanopus bispinosus* (Copepoda: Calanoida). *Hydrobiologia* 140:199-231.

Bowman, J.P., McCammon, S.A., Brown, J.L., Nichols, P.D. & McKeekin, T.A. (1997) *Psychroserpens burtonensis* gen. nov., sp. nov., and *Gelidibacter algens* gen. nov., sp. nov., psychrophilic bacteria isolated from Antarctic lacustrine and sea ice habitats. *International Journal of Systematic Bacteriology* **47**: 670-677.

Burke, C.M. & Burton, H.R. (1988) The ecology of photosynthetic bacteria in Burton Lake, Vestfold Hills, Antarctica. In: Ferris J.M., Burton H.R., Johnstone G.W. & Bayly I.A.E. (eds.) *Biology of the Vestfold Hills, Antarctica.* Kluwer Academic Publishers, Dordrecht, The Netherlands, pp. 1-12.

Collerson, K. D. & Sheraton, J.W. (1986) Bedrock geology and crustal evolution of the Vestfold Hills. In: Pickard J. (ed.) *Antarctic oasis: Terrestrial environments and history of the Vestfold Hills.* Academic Press Australia, Sydney, pp. 21-62.

Dartnall, H. (2000) A limnological reconnaissance of the Vestfold Hills. *ANARE Reports* **141**: 57 pp.

Daniels, J. (1996) Systematics of Pliocene Dolphins (*Odontoceti: Delphinidae*) from Marine Plain, Antarctica. M.Sc. Thesis University of Otago, Dunedin, New Zealand.

Feldmann, R.M. & Quilty, P.G. (1997) First Pliocene decapod crustacean (Malacostraca: Palinuridae) from the Antarctic. *Antarctic Science* **9** (1): 56-60.

Fordyce, R.E., Quilty, P.G. & Daniels, J. (2002) *Australodelphos mirus*, a bizarre new toothless ziphiid-like fossil dolphin (Cetacea: Delphinidae) from the Pliocene of Vestfold Hills, East Antarctica. *Antarctic Science* **14**: (1) 37-54.

Gibson, J.A.E. (1999) The meromictic lakes and stratified marine basins of the Vestfold Hills, East Antarctica. *Antarctic Science* **11**: 175-192.

Gibson, J.A.E. (2001) Personal Communication. 10 December 2001.

Gore, D.B. (1993) Changes in the ice boundary around the Vestfold Hills, East Antarctica, 1947 – 1990. *Australian Geographical Studies* **31** (1): 49-61.

Harwood, D.M., McMinn, A. & Quilty, P.G. (2002) Diatom biostratigraphy and age of the Pliocene Sørsdal Formation, Vestfold Hills, East Antarctica. *Antarctic Science* **12**: 443-462.

Kiernan, K. & McConnell, A. (2001a) Impacts of geoscience research on the physical environment of the Vestfold Hill, Antarctica. *Australian Journal of Earth Sciences* **48**: 767-776.

Kiernan, K. & McConnell, A. (2001b) Land surface rehabilitation and research in Antarctica. *Proceedings of the Linnean Society of NSW* **123**: 101-118.

Kiernan, K., McConnell, A. & Colhoun, E. (1999) Thermokarst landforms and processes at Marine Plain, Princess Elizabeth Land, East Antarctica. *INQUA XV International Congress, 3-11 August 1999, Durban, South Africa. Book of Abstracts 1998.*

Marchant, H.J. & Perrin, R.A. (1986) Planktonic Choanoflagellates from two Antarctic lakes including the description of *Spiraloecion Didymocostatum* Gen. Et Sp. Nov. *Polar Biology* **5**: 207-210.

Miller, J.D., Horne, P., Heatwole, H., Miller, W.R. & Bridges L. (1988) A survey of terrestrial tardigrada of the Vestfold Hills, Antarctica. In: Ferris, J.M., Burton, H.R., Johnstone, G.W. & Bayly, I.A.E. (eds.) *Biology of the Vestfold Hills, Antarctica.* Kluwer Academic Publishers, Dordrecht, The Netherlands, pp. 197-208.

Pickard, J. (1985) The Holocene fossil marine macrofauna of the Vestfold Hills, East Antarctica. *Boreas* **14**: 189-202.

Pickard, J. (1986) Antarctic oases, Davis station and the Vestfold Hills. In: Pickard, J. (ed.) *Antarctic oasis: Terrestrial environments and history of the Vestfold Hills.* Academic Press Australia, Sydney, pp. 1-19.

Pickard, J., Adamson, D.A., Harwood, D.M., Miller, G.H., Quilty, P.G. & Dell, R.K. (1988) Early Pliocene marine sediments, coastline, and climate of East Antarctica. *Geology* **16**: 158-161.

Quilty, P.G. (1989) Landslides: Extent and economic significance in Antarctica and the subantarctic. In: Brabb, E.E. & Harrod, B.L. (eds.) *Landslides: Extent and Economic Significance.* Balkema, Rotterdam, pp. 127-132.

Quilty, P.G. (1991) The geology of Marine Plain, Vestfold Hills, East Antarctica. In: Thomson, M.R.A., Crame, J.A. & Thomson, J.W. (eds.) *Geological Evolution of Antarctic.* Cambridge University Press, Great Britain.

Quilty, P.G. (1992) Late Neogene sediments of coastal East Antarctica – An Overview. In: Yoshida, Y., Kaminuma, K. & Shiraishi (eds.) *Recent Progress in Antarctic Earth Science*, Terra Scientific Publishing Company, Tokyo, pp. 699-705.

Quilty, P.G. (1996) The Pliocene environment of Antarctica. *Papers and Proceedings of the Royal Society of Tasmania* **130**(2): 1-8.

Quilty, P.G. (2001) Personal Communication. 9 May 2002.

Quilty, P.G., Lirio, J.M. & Jillett, D. (2000) Stratigraphy of the Pliocene Formation, Marine Plain, Vestfold Hills, Antarctica. *Antarctic Science* **12** (2): 205-216.

Roberts, D. & McMinn, A. (1999) Diatoms of the saline lakes of the Vestfold Hills, Antarctica. *Bibliotheca Diatomologica*, Band 44, pp. 1-83.

Roberts, D. & McMinn, A. (1996) Relationships between surface sediment diatom assemblages and water chemistry gradients in saline lakes of the Vestfold Hills, Antarctica. *Antarctic Science* **8:** 331-34.

Seppelt, R. A., Broady, P.A., Pickard, J. & Adamson, D.A. (1988) Plants and landscape in the Vestfold Hills, Antarctica. In: Ferris J.M., Burton H.R., Johnstone G.W. & Bayly I.A.E. (eds.) *Biology of the Vestfold Hills, Antarctica.* Kluwer Academic Publishers, Dordrecht, The Netherlands, pp. 185-196.

Simpson, R.G.B., Van Den Hoff, J., Bernard, C., Burton, H.R. & Patterson, D.J. (1996) The ultrastructure and systematic position of the euglenozoon *Postgaardi Mariagerensis*, Fenchel Et Al. *Archiv fur Protisten Kunde*, 147.

Streten, N.A. (1986) Climate of the Vestfold Hills. In: Pickard, J. (ed.) *Antarctic oasis: Terrestrial environments and history of the Vestfold Hills.* Academic Press, Sydney pp. 141-164.

Whitehead, J.M., Quilty, P.G., Harwood, D.M. & McMinn, A. (2001) Early Pliocene palaeoenvironment of the Sørsdal Formation, Vestfold Hills, based on diatom data. *Marine Micropaleontology* **41**: 125-152.

Williams, R. (1998) The inshore marine fishes of the Vestfold Hills region, Antarctica. In: Ferris J.M., Burton H.R., Johnstone G.W. & Bayly I.A.E. (eds.) *Biology of the Vestfold Hills, Antarctica.* Kluwer Academic Publishers, Dordrecht, The Netherlands, pp. 161-167.

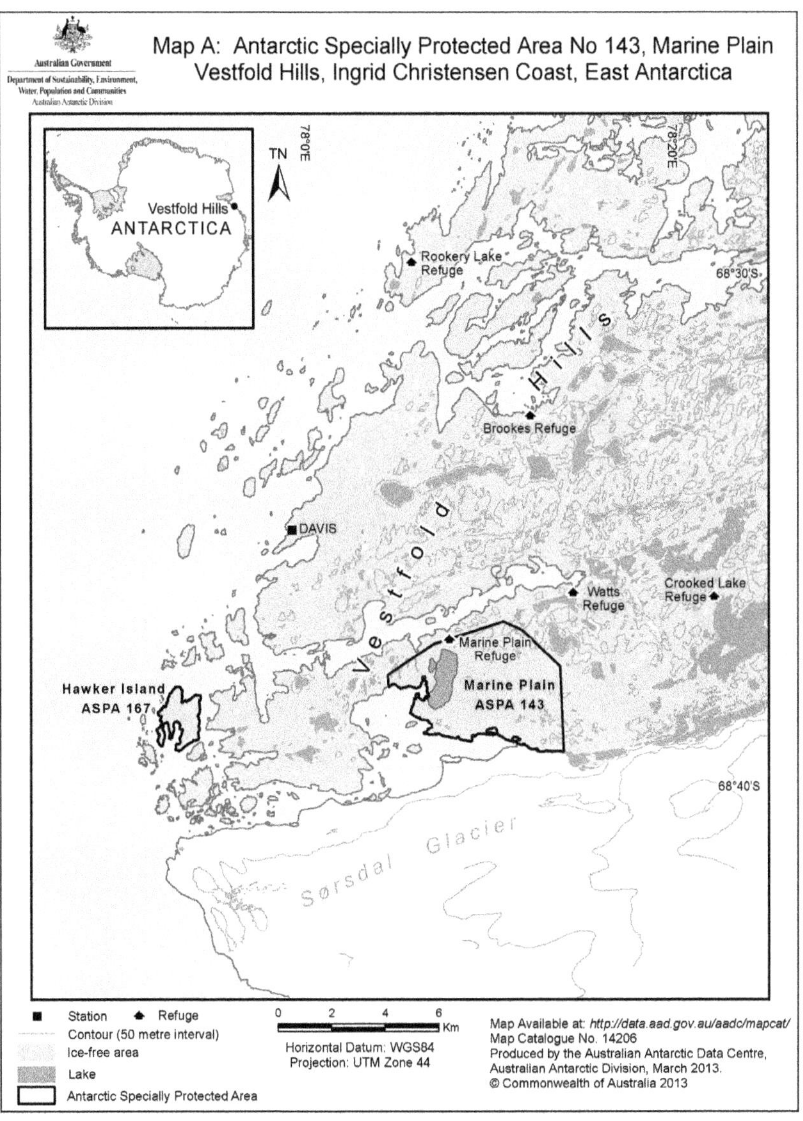
Australian Government
Department of Sustainability, Environment, Water, Population and Communities
Australian Antarctic Division
Map A: Antarctic Specially Protected Area No 143, Marine Plain
Vestfold Hills, Ingrid Christensen Coast, East Antarctica
Vestfold Hills
ANTARCTICA
TN
78°0'E
78°20'E
Rookery Lake Refuge
68°30'S
Vestfold Hills
Brookes Refuge
DAVIS
Watts Refuge
Crooked Lake Refuge
Marine Plain Refuge
Marine Plain ASPA 143
Hawker Island ASPA 167
68°40'S
Sørsdal Glacier
Station
Refuge
Contour (50 metre interval)
Ice-free area
Lake
Antarctic Specially Protected Area
0 2 4 6 Km
Horizontal Datum: WGS84
Projection: UTM Zone 44
Map Available at: http://data.aad.gov.au/aadc/mapcat/
Map Catalogue No. 14206
Produced by the Australian Antarctic Data Centre, Australian Antarctic Division, March 2013.
© Commonwealth of Australia 2013

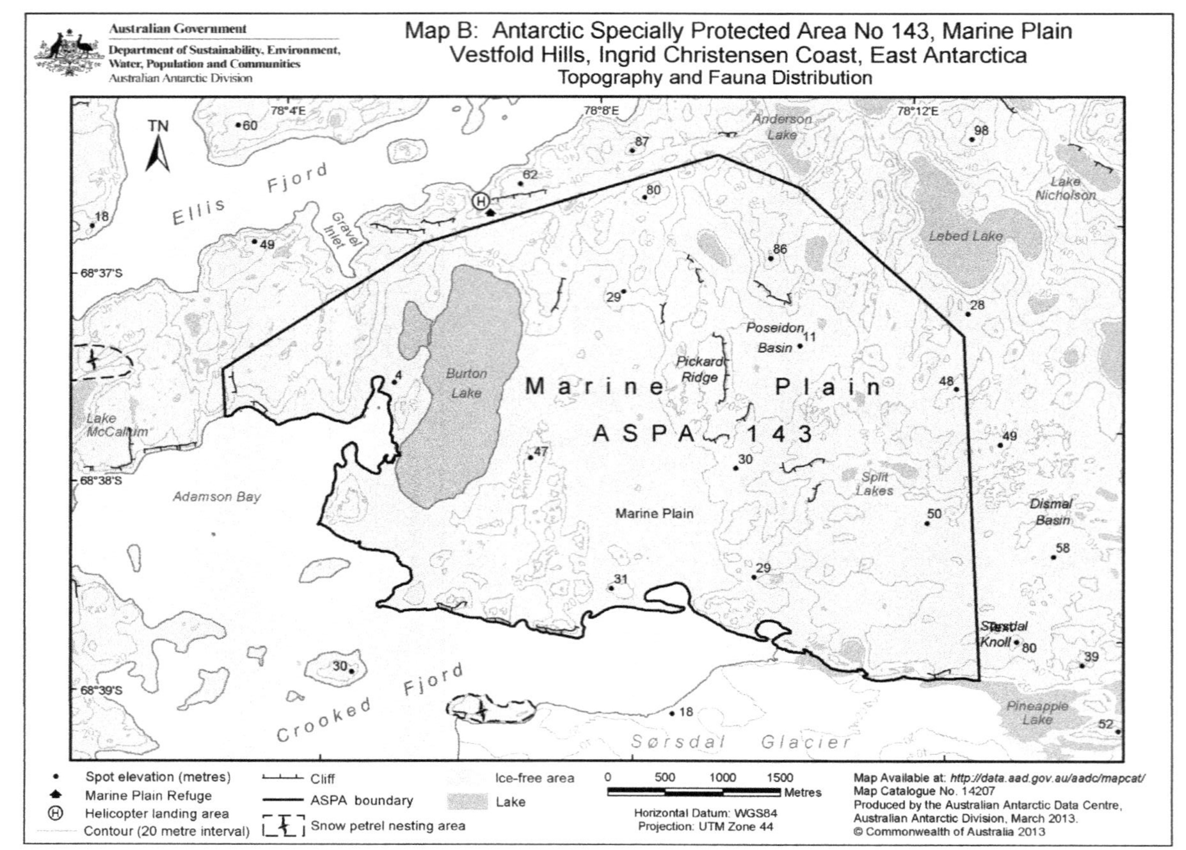
Australian Government
Department of Sustainability, Environment, Water, Population and Communities
Australian Antarctic Division
Map B: Antarctic Specially Protected Area No 143, Marine Plain
Vestfold Hills, Ingrid Christensen Coast, East Antarctica
Topography and Fauna Distribution
TN
78°4'E
78°8'E
78°12'E
68°37'S
68°38'S
68°39'S
Ellis Fjord
Gravel Inlet
Anderson Lake
Lebed Lake
Lake Nicholson
Poseidon Basin
Pickard Ridge
Burton Lake
Marine Plain
ASPA 143
Lake McCallum
Adamson Bay
Split Lakes
Dismal Basin
Knoll
Pineapple Lake
Crooked Fjord
Sørsdal Glacier
Spot elevation (metres)
Marine Plain Refuge
Helicopter landing area
Contour (20 metre interval)
Cliff
ASPA boundary
Snow petrel nesting area
Ice-free area
Lake
0 500 1000 1500 Metres
Horizontal Datum: WGS84
Projection: UTM Zone 44
Map Available at: http://data.aad.gov.au/aadc/mapcat/
Map Catalogue No. 14207
Produced by the Australian Antarctic Data Centre, Australian Antarctic Division, March 2013.
© Commonwealth of Australia 2013

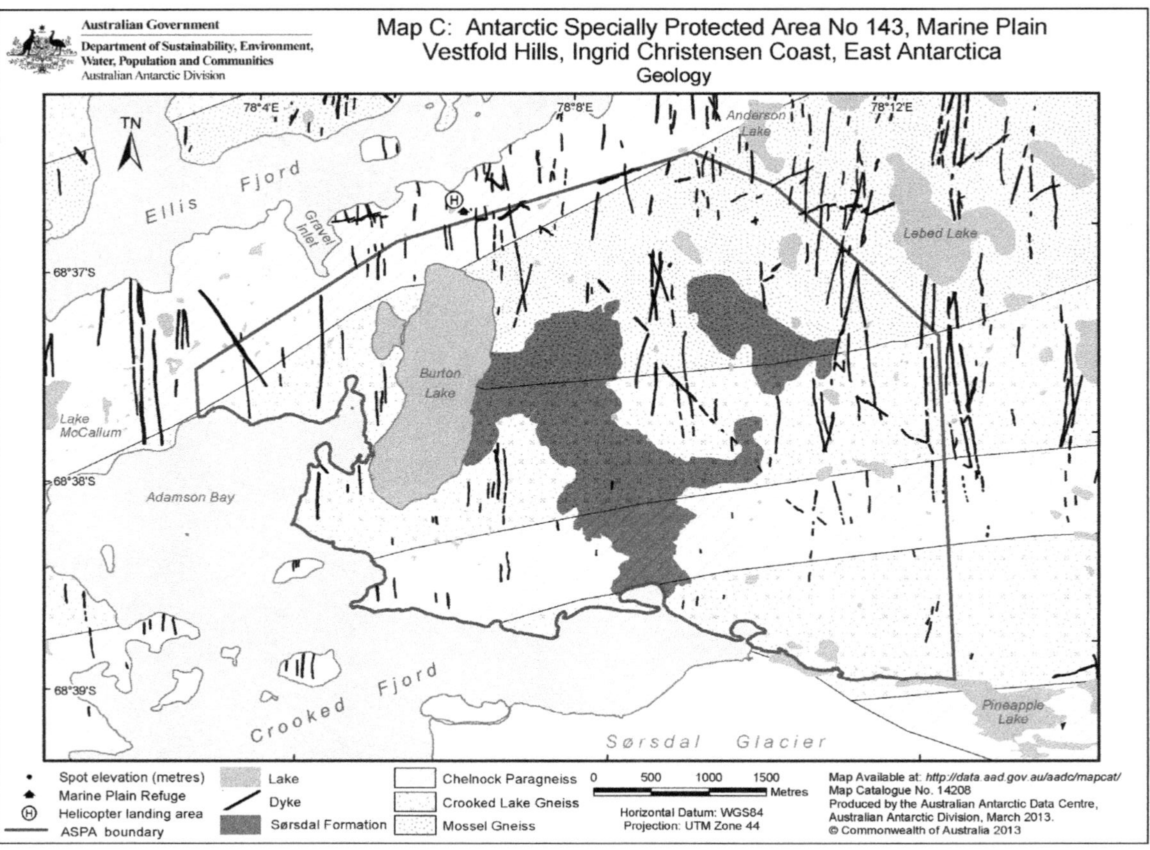

Australian Government
Department of Sustainability, Environment, Water, Population and Communities
Australian Antarctic Division
Map C: Antarctic Specially Protected Area No 143, Marine Plain
Vestfold Hills, Ingrid Christensen Coast, East Antarctica
Geology
TN
78°4'E
78°8'E
78°12'E
68°37'S
68°38'S
68°39'S
Ellis Fjord
Gravel Inlet
Anderson Lake
Lebed Lake
Burton Lake
Lake McCallum
Adamson Bay
Crooked Fjord
Sørsdal Glacier
Pineapple Lake
Spot elevation (metres)
Marine Plain Refuge
Helicopter landing area
ASPA boundary
Lake
Dyke
Sørsdal Formation
Chelnock Paragneiss
Crooked Lake Gneiss
Mossel Gneiss
0 500 1000 1500 Metres
Horizontal Datum: WGS84
Projection: UTM Zone 44
Map Available at: http://data.aad.gov.au/aadc/mapcat/
Map Catalogue No. 14208
Produced by the Australian Antarctic Data Centre, Australian Antarctic Division, March 2013.
© Commonwealth of Australia 2013

Management Plan for Antarctic Specially Protected Area No. 147

ABLATION VALLEY AND GANYMEDE HEIGHTS, ALEXANDER ISLAND

Introduction

The primary reason for the designation of Ablation Valley and Ganymede Heights, Alexander Island (70°48'S, 68°30'W, approximately 180 km^2) as an Antarctic Specially Protected Area (ASPA) is to protect scientific values, relating particularly to the geology, geomorphology, glaciology, limnology and ecology of this extensive ablation area.

Ablation Valley and Ganymede Heights, Alexander Island, was designated originally in 1989 as Site of Special Scientific Interest (SSSI) No. 29 Ablation Point – Ganymede Heights, Alexander Island, through Recommendation XV-6, after a proposal by the United Kingdom. Included was a largely ice-free region between latitudes 70°45'S and 70°55'S and from longitude 68°40'W to the George VI Sound coastline. The Area comprised several valley systems separated by ridges and plateau of about 650-760 m high. The original management plan (Recommendation XV-6) described the Area as "one of the largest ablation areas in West Antarctica…[with]…a complex geology, the main rock types being conglomerates, arkosic sandstones and shales with subordinate pebbly mudstones and sedimentary breccias. The base of the succession is formed of a spectacular mélange, including large blocks of lava and agglomerate. This outcrops on the valley floors and at the base of several cliffs. [The Area] possesses a wide range of geomorphological features including raised beaches, moraine systems and patterned ground. There are several permanently frozen freshwater lakes and many ice-free ponds supporting a diverse flora (including aquatic bryophytes) and fauna. The vegetation is generally sparse, with the unique moss and liverwort-dominated community type being restricted to 'oases' where water issues from otherwise dry barren hillsides. The terrestrial and freshwater ecosystems are vulnerable to human impact and therefore merit protection from uncontrolled human presence". In summary, the principal values of the Area were considered to be the geological, geomorphological, glaciological, limnological, and ecological features, and the associated outstanding scientific interest of one of the largest ice-free ablation area in West Antarctica. The Area was renumbered as ASPA 147 through Decision 1 (2002) and a revised Management Plan was adopted through Measure 1 (2002).

ASPA 147 Ablation Valley and Ganymede Heights, Alexander Island, fits into the wider context of the Antarctic Protected Area system by protecting one of the largest ablation areas in West Antarctica. Equivalent environmental and scientific values are not protected in other ASPAs within the Antarctic Peninsula area. Resolution 3 (2008) recommended that the Environmental Domains Analysis for the Antarctic Continent, be used as a dynamic model for the identification of Antarctic Specially Protected Areas within the systematic environmental-geographical framework referred to in Article 3(2) of Annex V of the Protocol (see also Morgan et al., 2007). Using this model, small parts of ASPA 147 are contained within Environment Domain E Antarctic Peninsula and Alexander Island main ice fields); however, although not stated specifically in Morgan et al., the Area may also include Domain C (Antarctic Peninsula southern geologic). Other protected areas containing Domain E include ASPAs 113, 114, 117, 126, 128, 129, 133, 134, 139, 149, 152, 170 and ASMAs 1 and 4. Other protected areas containing Domain C include ASPA 170 (although not stated specifically in Morgan et al.,

2007). The ASPA sits within Antarctic Conservation Biogeographic Region (ACBR) 4 Central South Antarctic Peninsula, and is one of only two ASPAs in ACBR 4, the other being ASPA 170 (Terauds et al., 2012).

1. Description of values to be protected

The values noted in the original designation are reaffirmed in the present Management Plan. Further values evident from scientific descriptions of Ablation Valley and Ganymede Heights are also considered important as reasons for special protection of the Area. These values are:

- The presence of exposures of the Fossil Bluff Formation, which is of prime geological importance because it is the only known area of unbroken exposure of rocks spanning the Jurassic – Cretaceous boundary in the Antarctic, which makes this a critical locality for understanding the change in flora and fauna at this temporal boundary.
- The presence of an exceptional and unique contiguous geomorphological record of glacier and ice-shelf fluctuations extending over several thousand years, together with an outstanding assemblage of other geomorphological features derived from glacial, periglacial, lacustrine, aeolian, alluvial and slope processes.
- Two perennially frozen freshwater lakes (Ablation and Moutonnée lakes) which have the unusual property of contact with the saline waters of George VI Sound.
- The presence of marine biota, including the fish *Trematomus bernacchii*, in Ablation Lake, where several seals have also been observed, despite the fact that it is almost 100 km from open sea.
- The Area has the greatest bryophyte diversity of any site at this latitude in Antarctica (at least 21 species); it also has a diverse lichen (>35 taxa), algal and cyanobacterial biota. Many of the bryophytes and lichens are at the southern limit of their know distributions. There are several species which are very rare in the Antarctic.
- Several mosses occur in lakes and ponds to depths of 9 m. Although these are all terrestrial species, they tolerate inundation for several months each year when their habitat floods. One species, *Campylium polygamum*, has adapted to an aquatic existence, and some permanently submerged colonies reach large dimensions, with shoots in excess of 30 cm length. These are the best examples of aquatic vegetation in the Antarctic Peninsula region.
- Several bryophyte species within the Area are fertile (producing sporophytes), and some of these are not known or are very rare in this condition elsewhere in the Antarctic (e.g. the liverwort *Cephaloziella varians*, and mosses *Bryoerythrophyllum recurvirostrum*, *Distichium capillaceum*, *Schistidium* spp.).
- The Area has one of the most extensive stands of vegetation on Alexander Island. Many of these occur on seepage areas where the bryophyte and lichen communities cover up to 100 m^2 or more. In the sheltered seepage areas, assemblages of terricolous species develop communities not known elsewhere in Antarctica, while exposed rock ridges and stable boulder fields support a community of locally abundant lichens, usually dominated by *Usnea sphacelata*.
- The Area is comparatively rich in the number and abundance of microarthropod species for its locality this far south, with representation of the springtail *Friesia topo* which is thought to be endemic to Alexander Island. Ablation Valley is also the only site on Alexander Island where the predatory mite *Rhagidia gerlachei* has been described, making the food web more complex than other sites at this latitude.

2. Aims and objectives

The aims and objectives of this Management Plan are to:

- avoid degradation of, or substantial risk to, the values of the Area by preventing unnecessary human disturbance to the Area;
- prevent or minimise the introduction to the Area of non-native plants, animals and microbes;
- allow scientific research in the Area provided it is for compelling reasons which cannot be served elsewhere and which will not jeopardize the natural ecological system in that Area; and
- preserve the natural ecosystem of the Area as a reference area for future studies.

3. Management activities

The following management activities shall be undertaken to protect the values of the Area:

- Markers, signs or other structures (e.g. cairns) erected within the Area for scientific or management purposes shall be secured and maintained in good condition and removed when no longer required.
- Copies of this Management Plan shall be made available to aircraft planning to visit the vicinity of the Area.
- The Management Plan shall be reviewed at least every five years and updated as required.
- A copy of this Management Plan shall be made available at Rothera Research Station (UK; 67°34'S, 68°07'W) and General San Martín Station (Argentina; 68°08'S, 67°06'W).
- All scientific and management activities undertaken within the Area should be subject to an Environmental Impact Assessment, in accordance with the requirements of Annex I of the Protocol on Environmental Protection to the Antarctic Treaty.
- National Antarctic Programmes operating in the Area shall consult together with a view to ensuring the above management activities are implemented.

4. Period of designation

Designated for an indefinite period.

5. Maps and photographs

Map 1. Location of Ablation Valley and Ganymede Heights on the Antarctic Peninsula. Map specifications: WGS84 Antarctic Polar Stereographic. Central Meridian -55°, Standard Parallel: -71°.

Map 2. ASPA No. 147 Ablation Valley and Ganymede Heights, location map. Map specifications: WGS 1984 Antarctic Polar Stereographic. Central Meridian: -71°, Standard Parallel: -71°.

Map 3. ASPA No. 147 Ablation Valley and Ganymede Heights, topographic sketch map. Map specifications: WGS 1984 Antarctic Polar Stereographic. Central Meridian: -68.4°, Standard Parallel: -71.0°.

6. Description of the Area

6(i) Geographical coordinates, boundary markers and natural features

General description

Ablation Valley and Ganymede Heights (between latitudes 70°45'S and 70°55'S and longitudes 68°21'W and 68°40'W, approximately 180 km^2) is situated on the east side of Alexander Island, the largest island off the western coast of Palmer Land, Antarctic Peninsula (Maps 1 and 2). The Area has a central west–east extent of about 10 km and a north–south extent of about 18 km, flanked to the west by the upper part of Jupiter Glacier, to the east by the permanent ice shelf in George VI Sound, to the north by Grotto Glacier and to the south by the lower reaches of Jupiter Glacier. Ablation Valley and Ganymede Heights contain the largest contiguous ice-free area in the Antarctic Peninsula sector of Antarctica, with the smaller permanent ice fields and valley glaciers within the massif representing only about 17% of the Area. The topography of the region is mountainous, comprising steep-sided valleys separated by gently undulating plateau-like ridge crests lying generally between 650-750 m, rising to a maximum altitude of 1070 m (Clapperton and Sugden, 1983). The region has been heavily glaciated, although the relatively flat-lying attitude of the sedimentary rocks and rapid weathering have contributed to a generally rounded form of topography, coupled with sheer cliff 'steps' of thickly-bedded sandstones and conglomerates (Taylor et al., 1979).

The Area includes four principal ice-free valleys (Ablation, Moutonnée, Flatiron and Striation), the first three of which contain large ice-covered freshwater lakes (Heywood, 1977, Convey and Smith, 1997). The largest of these is the proglacial Ablation Lake (approximately 7 km^2), which has been impounded by shelf ice penetrating up-valley under pressure from the westward movement of the 100-500 m thick George VI Ice Shelf, the surface of which lies 30 m above sea level (Heywood, 1977; Clapperton and Sugden, 1982). Biologically, the terrestrial ecosystem is intermediate between the relatively mild maritime Antarctic farther north and the colder, drier continental Antarctic to the south. As a "dry valley" area it is extremely rich in biota and serves as a valuable contrast to the more extreme and biologically impoverished ablation areas on the Antarctic continent (Smith, 1988).

Boundaries

The designated Area comprises the entire Ablation Valley – Ganymede Heights massif, bounded in the west by the principal ridge dividing Jupiter Glacier from the main Ablation – Moutonnée – Flatiron valleys (Map 3). In the east, the boundary is defined by the western margin of George VI Ice Shelf. The northern boundary of the Area is defined as the principal ridge dividing Grotto Glacier from Erratic Valley and other tributary valleys feeding into Ablation Valley, immediately to the south. In the northwest of the Area, the boundary extends across the mostly-glaciated col separating upper Jupiter Glacier from Ablation Valley. The southern boundary of the Area, from east of the principal ridge on the west side of Flatiron Valley to where Jupiter Glacier joins George VI Ice Shelf, is defined as the northern lateral margin of Jupiter Glacier. As the margin between Ablation Lake and George VI Ice Shelf is in places indistinct, the eastern boundary of the Area at Ablation Valley is defined as a straight line extending due south from the eastern extremity of Ablation Point to where the ice shelf abuts land, and from where the eastern boundary follows the land/ice shelf margin. The physiography is similar further south at Moutonnée Lake, and the eastern boundary in this locality is defined as a straight line extending from the eastern extremity of the point on the northern side of (and partially enclosing) Moutonnée Lake to the locality of a prominent meltwater pool where the ice shelf abuts land, and from where the boundary follows the land/ice shelf margin south to where Jupiter Glacier and George VI Ice Shelf adjoin. The Area thus includes the entirety of Ablation and Moutonnée lakes and those parts of the ice shelf behind which they are impounded. The boundary co-ordinates are given in Annex 1.

Climate

No extended meteorological records are available for the Ablation Valley – Ganymede Heights area, but the climate has been described as dominated by the dual influences of easterly-moving cyclonic depressions of the Southern Ocean, against the more continental, north to northwesterly, flow of cold anticyclonic air from the West Antarctic Ice Sheet (Clapperton and Sugden, 1983). The former bring relatively mild weather, strong northerly winds and a heavy cloud cover to the region, whereas the latter induces clear, cold and stable conditions with temperatures below 0° C, and relatively light winds from the south. Based on data recorded nearby (25 km) in the early 1970s, the mean summer temperature was estimated as just below freezing point, with mean annual temperature estimated at about -9 °C (Heywood, 1977); precipitation was estimated at <200 mm of water equivalent per year, with little snow falling in summer. A thin snow cover is common after winter, but the region is generally snow-free by the end of the summer, apart from isolated snow patches that may persist in places.

Geology

The geology of Ablation Valley – Ganymede Heights is complex, but is dominated by well-stratified sedimentary rocks. The most prominent structural feature of the massif is a large asymmetrical anticline with a northwest–southeast orientation, extending from Grotto Glacier to Jupiter Glacier (Bell, 1975, Crame and Howlett, 1988). Thrust faults in the central part of the massif suggest vertical displacements of strata of up to 800 m (Crame and Howlett, 1988). The main lithologies are conglomerates, arkosic sandstones and fossiliferous shales, with subordinate pebbly mudstones and sedimentary breccias (Elliot, 1974; Taylor et al., 1979; Thomson 1979). A range of fossils have been found in the strata, which are of Upper Jurassic–Lower Cretaceous age, including bivalves, brachiopods, belemnites, ammonites, shark teeth and plants (Taylor et al., 1979; Thomson, 1979; Crame and Howlett, 1988; Howlett, 1989). Several interstratified lavas have been observed in the lowest exposures at Ablation Point (Bell, 1975). The base of the succession is formed of a spectacular mélange, including large blocks of lava and agglomerate which crop out on the valley floors and at the base of several cliffs (see Bell, 1975; Taylor et al., 1979). The presence of exposures of the Fossil Bluff Formation is of prime geological importance because it is the only known area of unbroken exposure of rocks spanning the Jurassic – Cretaceous boundary in the Antarctic, which makes this a critical locality for understanding the change in floras and faunas at this temporal boundary.

Geomorphology and soils

The entire area was at one time over-run by glacier ice from the interior of Alexander Island. Thus, landforms of both glacial erosion and deposition are widespread throughout the Area, providing evidence of a former general eastward flow of ice into George VI Sound (Clapperton and Sugden 1983). Misfit glaciers, striated bedrock and erratics indicate considerable deglaciation since the Pleistocene glacial maximum (Taylor et al., 1979; Roberts et al., 2009). Numerous terminal moraines fronting present remnant glaciers, several unexpectedly talus-free sites, and polished and striated roches moutonnées indicate that glacial retreat may have been rapid (Taylor et al., 1979). There is evidence that George VI Ice Shelf was absent between c. 9600 and 7730 calendar years BP, which suggests that the Ablation Valley – Ganymede Heights massif is likely to have been largely free of permanent ice around that time, although there have been a number of subsequent glacier fluctuations in the region (Clapperton and Sugden, 1982; Bentley et al., 2005; Smith et al., 2007a,b; Roberts et al., 2008; Bentley et al., 2009). The absence of the ice shelf suggests that early Holocene ocean-atmosphere variability in the Antarctic Peninsula was greater than that measured in recent decades (Bentley et al., 2005). Roberts et al. (2009) examined deltas adjacent to Ablation and Moutonnée Lakes that were formed higher than the present day lake level and concluded that sea level had fallen by c. 14.4 m since the mid-Holocene in this part of Alexander Island.

The landforms within the Area have been modified by periglacial, gravitational and fluvial processes. Bedrock on the upper plateau surfaces (where it has been largely scraped free of till overburden) has been shattered by frost action into platy or blocky fragments (Clapperton and Sugden, 1983). On valley slopes gelifluction lobes and stone stripes and circles are common, while on valley floors stone circles and polygonal patterned ground are frequently found in glacial till and in fluvioglacial sediments subjected to frost action. Valley walls are also dominated by landforms derived from frost action, rock/ice-fall activity, and seasonal meltwater flows, which have led to ubiquitous talus slopes and, commonly, boulder fans below incised gullies. Mass wasting of fissile sedimentary rocks has also led to the development of steep (about 50°) horizontally rectilinear bedrock slopes thinly veneered with debris. Occasional aeolian landforms have been observed, with dunes of up to 1 m in height and 8 m in length as, for example, in Erratic Valley (Clapperton and Sugden, 1983). Thin layers of peat of up to 10-15 cm in depth are occasionally associated with vegetated areas, and these are the most substantial developments of soil within the Area.

Freshwater ecology

Ablation Valley – Ganymede Heights is an exceptional limnological site that contains a number of lakes, ponds and streams and a generally rich benthic flora. From late December until February running water develops from three main sources: precipitation, glaciers and from melting on George VI Ice Shelf, with run-off generally converging toward the coast (Clapperton and Sugden, 1983). Most of the streams, which are up to several kilometres in length, drain glaciers or permanent snowfields. The principal streams drain into Ablation Lake and Moutonnée Lake, both dammed by the ice shelf. Surveys in the early 1970s recorded these lakes as frozen to 2.0–4.5 m depth year-round, with maximum water depths of around 117 m and 50 m respectively (Heywood, 1977). A stable upper layer of fresh water, down to approximately 60 m and 30 m respectively, overlies increasingly saline waters influenced by interconnection with the ocean beneath the ice shelf and which subjects the lakes to tidal influence (Heywood, 1977). Surface meltwater pools, which in summer form particularly in hollows between lake-ice pressure ridges, flood to higher levels daily and encroach up alluvial fans in the lower valleys (Clapperton and Sugden, 1983).

Some recent observations suggested a decrease in the permanent ice cover of the lakes, for example with about 25% of Moutonnée Lake being free of ice cover in the 1994–95 and 1997–98 summers (Convey and Smith 1997, Convey pers. comm., 1999). However, all three of the main lakes in the Area showed almost complete ice cover in early February 2001 (Harris 2001). Numerous ephemeral, commonly elongated, pools and ponds form laterally along the land/ice shelf margin, varying in length from 10 to 1500 m and up to 200 m wide, with depths ranging from 1 to 6 m (Heywood, 1977; Clapperton and Sugden, 1983). These pools/ponds often rise in level over the melt period, yet on occasion may drain suddenly via sub-ice fissures opening into the ice shelf, leaving former lake shorelines evident in surrounding moraines. The pools/ponds vary widely in their turbidity depending on the presence of suspended glacial sediment. The pools are typically ice-free in summer, while the larger ponds often retain a partial ice cover, and all but the deeper ponds probably freeze solid in winter (Heywood, 1977). Numerous ponds of up to 1 ha and 15 m in depth are present within the valleys, some with moss growth covering extensive areas down to 9 m in depth (Light and Heywood, 1975). The dominant species described were *Campylium polygamum* and *Dicranella*, stems of which reached 30 cm in length. *Bryum pseudotriquetrum* (and possibly a second *Bryum* species), *Distichium capillaceum*, and an unidentified species of *Dicranella* all grew on the benthic substratum at or below 1 m in depth (Smith, 1988). Moss cover was 40-80% in the 0.5-5.0 m depth zone (Light and Heywood, 1975). Much of the remaining area was covered by dense cyanobacterial felts (11 taxa) up to 10 cm thick, dominated by species of *Calothrix*, *Nostoc* and *Phormidium* together with 36 taxa of associated microalgae (Smith, 1988). The extensive growths of moss suggest that these ponds are probably relatively permanent, although their levels may fluctuate from year to year. The water temperature reaches up to c. 7 °C in the deeper ponds and c. 15 °C in the shallower pools in summer, offering a relatively favourable and stable environment for bryophytes. The shallower pools, in which several mosses have been found, may normally be occupied by terrestrial vegetation and flooded for short periods during summer (Smith, 1988). Algae are abundant in slow-moving streams and ephemeral melt runnels, although they do not colonise the unstable beds of fast-flowing streams. For example, large wet areas of level ground in Moutonnée Valley have a particularly rich flora, in places forming over 90% cover, with five species of desmid (which are rare in Antarctica) and the filamentous green *Zygnema* being abundant, and *Nostoc* spp. and *Phormidium* spp. colonising drier, less stable and silted areas (Heywood, 1977).

Protozoa, Rotifera, Tardigrada and Nematoda form a benthic fauna in the pools, ponds and streams (Heywood, 1977). Densities are generally highest in the slow-moving streams. The copepod *Boeckella poppei* was abundant in lakes, ponds and pools, but absent from streams. The marine fish *Trematomus bernacchii* was captured in traps laid in Ablation Lake at a depth of 70 m, within the saline water layer (Heywood and Light, 1975, Heywood, 1977). A seal (species unidentified, but probably crabeater (*Lobodon carcinophagus*) or Weddell (*Leptonychotes weddellii*)) was reported at the edge of Ablation Lake in mid-December 1996 (Rossaak, 1997), and isolated sightings of solitary seals have also been reported in earlier seasons (Clapperton and Sugden, 1982).

Vegetation

Much of the Ablation Valley – Ganymede Heights area is arid, and overall vegetation abundance is low with a discontinuous distribution. However, complex plant communities exist in seepage areas and along stream margins, which are of particular interest because:

they occur in an otherwise almost barren landscape;

the mixed bryophyte and lichen communities are the best-developed and most diverse of any south of 70°S (Smith, 1988; Convey and Smith, 1997);

some bryophyte taxa are profusely fertile and fruiting at their southern limit – an unusual phenomenon in most Antarctic bryophytes, especially so far south (Smith and Convey, 2002);

the region represents the southernmost known locality for many taxa; and

although some of these communities also occur at other sites on southeastern Alexander Island, the Area contains the best and most extensive examples known at this latitude.

The diversity of mosses is particularly high for this latitude, with at least 21 species recorded within the Area, which represents 73% of those known to occur on Alexander Island (Smith, 1997). The lichen flora is also diverse with more than 35 taxa known. Of the macrolichen flora, 12 of the 15 species known to occur on Alexander Island are represented within the Area (Smith, 1997). Ablation, Moutonnée and Striation valleys, and the SE coastal area, contain the most extensive stands of both terrestrial and freshwater vegetation (Smith, 1998; Harris, 2001). Smith (1988, 1997) reported the bryophyte vegetation is generally found in patches of about 10 to 50 m^2, with some stands up to 625 m^2, occurring from around 5 m to 40 m altitude on the north and east-facing gentle slopes of the main valleys. Harris (2001) recorded large stands of near-continuous bryophyte vegetation of up to approximately 8000 m^2 on gentle southeast-facing slopes on the south-eastern coast of the Area, at an elevation of approximately 10 m, close to where the Jupiter Glacier joins George VI Ice Shelf. A continuous stand of approximately 1600 m^2 was recorded on moist slopes in lower Striation Valley. Several large patches of continuous moss (of up to 1000 m^2) were observed on SW/NW-facing eastern slopes of Flatiron Valley, at elevations of 300-400 m. Small discontinuous patches of moss were recorded in this vicinity up to an elevation of 540 m. Mosses were observed on peaks above Ablation Valley at elevations of up to approximately 700 m.

The dominant bryophyte in the wettest areas is frequently the liverwort *Cephaloziella varians*, which forms a blackish mat of densely interwoven shoots. Although the most southerly record of *C. varians* has been reported at 77°S from Botany Bay, Cape Geology (ASPA No. 154) in Victoria Land, the extensive mats it forms in the Ablation Valley – Ganymede Heights massif represent the most substantial stands of this species this far south and in the maritime Antarctic. Cyanobacteria, notably *Nostoc* and *Phormidium* spp., are usually associated either on the surface of the liverwort or soil, or with moss shoots. Beyond the wettest areas, undulating carpets of pleurocarpous mosses dominated by *Campylium polygamum* forms the greenest stands of vegetation, with associated *Hypnum revolutum*. These carpets overlie up to 10-15 cm of peat composed of largely undecomposed moribund moss shoots. Intermixed with these mosses, but often predominating on the drier margins, *Bryum pseudotriquetrum* grows as isolated cushions that may coalesce to develop a convoluted turf. In these drier, peripheral areas, several other turf-forming bryophytes are often associated with *Bryum*. Besides the more hydric species already cited, these include the calcicolous taxa *Bryoerythrophyllum recurvirostrum, Didymodon brachyphyllus, Distichium capillaceum, Encalypta rhaptocarpa, E. procera, Pohlia cruda, Schistidium antarctici, Tortella fragilis, Syntrichia magellanica, Tortella alpicola,* and several unidentified species of *Bryum* and *Schistidium.*

A significant characteristic of the vegetation in the Ablation Valley – Ganymede Heights massif is the unusual occurrence of a number of fertile bryophytes. Antarctic bryophytes seldom produce sporophytes, yet *Bryum pseudotriquetrum, Distichium capillaceum, Encalypta rhaptocarpa, E. procera* and *Schistidium* spp. have all been recorded in the Area as frequently fertile. Most unusually, small quantities of the moss *Bryoerythrophyllum recurvirostre* and the liverwort *Cephaloziella varians* have been observed fruiting in Ablation Valley, which was the first time this had been recorded anywhere in Antarctica (Smith pers comm., cited in Convey, 1995; Smith, 1997; Smith and Convey, 2002); in addition, *D. capillaceum* has never before been recorded with sporophytes throughout the maritime Antarctic (Smith, 1988). *E. procera* has only been reported as fertile in one other Antarctic location (on Signy Island, South Orkney Islands; Smith, 1988). Beyond the permanent seepage areas, bryophyte vegetation is extremely sparse and restricted to habitats where there is free water for at least a few weeks during the summer. Such sites occur sporadically on the valley floors, stone stripes on slopes, and also in crevices in north-facing rock faces. Most of the species occurring in the bryophyte patches have also been observed in these habitats, including lichens, most frequently in the shelter of, or even in crevices beneath, larger stones – especially at the margins of patterned ground features. At elevations of over 100 m aridity increases, and at higher altitudes only *Schistidium antarctici* (at 500 m in Moutonnée Valley) and *Tortella fragilis* (near the summit of the highest peak south-west of Ablation Valley (775 m) have been recorded. In these drier habitats lichens tend to become more frequent, especially where the substratum is stable. Lichens are widespread and locally abundant on the more stable screes, ridges, and plateaux above the valleys, the most predominant species being *Usnea sphacelata*, giving rock surfaces a black hue. This species is often associated with *Pseudephebe minuscula*, several crustose lichen species and, rarely, *Umbilicaria decussata* reaching the highest part of the massif; all but the latter species are also common in Moutonnée Valley. Epiphytic and terricolous lichens, predominantly the white encrusting species *Leproloma cacuminum*, are often frequent where the marginal bryophyte surface is driest. Other taxa such as *Cladonia galindezii, C. pocillum* and several crustose lichens are also sometimes present. Various lichens colonise the dry soil and pebbles in these localities, occasionally spreading onto cushions of moss. These include *Candelariella vitellina, Physcia caesia, Physconia muscigena,* occasional *Rhizoplaca melanophthalma, Usnea antarctica, Xanthoria elegans*, and several unidentified crustose taxa (especially species of *Buellia* and *Lecidea*). An abundance of *Physcia* and *Xanthoria* in isolated places suggests nitrogen enrichment deriving from south polar skuas (*Catharacta maccormicki*) which nest in the Area (Bentley, 2004). A few ornithocoprophilous lichens occur on occasional boulders used as bird perches. Many of the bryophytes and lichens are at the southern limit of their known distributions and several species are very rare in the Antarctic. Rare moss species within the Area include *Bryoerythrophyllum recurvirostrum*, *Campylium polygamum*, *Encalypta rhaptocarpa*, *Tortella alpicola*, and *Tortella fragilis*. Several *Bryum* species, *Encalypta rhaptocarpa*, *Schistidium occultum* and *Schistidium chrysoneurum* are all at the southern limit recorded for these species. Of the lichen flora, Ablation Valley is the only known site where *Eiglera flavida* has been observed in the S. Hemisphere, and *Mycobilimbia lobulata* and *Stereocaulon antarcticum* are also rare. Lichen species with furthest-south records are *Cladonia galindezii*, *Cladonia pocillum*, *Ochrolechia frigida*, *Phaeorrhiza nimbosa*, *Physconia muscigena*, and *Stereocaulon antarcticum*.

Invertebrates, fungi, bacteria

The microinvertebrate fauna thus far described is based on ten samples from Ablation Valley, and comprises seven confirmed taxa (Convey and Smith, 1997): two Collembola (*Cryptopygus badasa*, *Friesea topo*); one cryptostigmatid mite (*Magellozetes antarcticus*); and four prostigmatid mites (*Eupodes parvus*, *Nanorchestes nivalis* (= *N. gressitti*), *Rhagidia gerlachei* and *Stereotydeus villosus*). A number of specimens collected were earlier reported as *Friesea grisea*, a widespread maritime Antarctic species. However, specimens of *Friesia* collected subsequently from Alexander Island (i.e. from 1994 onwards) have been described as a distinct new species, *F. topo* (Greenslade, 1995), which is itself currently thought to be endemic to Alexander Island. The earlier specimens from Ablation Valley have been re-examined, with all those that remain identifiable being reassigned as *F. topo*. While the same number of species has been described at one other site on Alexander Island, the samples from Ablation Valley exhibited a mean total microarthropod population density about seven times greater than other sites in the region. Diversity at Ablation Valley was also greater than at several other documented sites on Alexander Island. Both diversity and abundance are considerably less than has been described at sites in Marguerite Bay and further north (Starý and Block, 1998; Convey et al., 1996; Convey and Smith, 1997; Smith, 1996). The most populous species recorded in Ablation Valley was *Cryptopygus badasa* (96.6% of all arthropods extracted), which was particularly common in moss habitats. *Friesea topo* was found on stones at low population densities and was virtually absent from the moss habitat, showing these species to have distinct habitat preferences. Ablation Valley is the only site on Alexander Island where the predatory mite *R. gerlachei* has been described. Very little research has been conducted on fungi in the Area; however, one study reported an unidentified nematode-trapping fungus present in a pond in Ablation Valley (Maslen, 1982). While further sampling is required to describe the terrestrial microfauna more fully, available data support the biological importance of the Area.

Breeding birds

The avifauna of Ablation Valley – Ganymede Heights has not been described in detail. A few pairs of south polar skuas (*Catharacta maccormicki*) have been reported as nesting close to some of the moist vegetated sites (Smith, 1988). Snow petrels have been noted as "probably breeding" in the vicinity of Ablation Point (Croxall et al., 1995, referring to Fuchs and Adie, 1949). Bentley (2004) reported direct aerial predation by south polar skuas on snow petrels within the Area. No other bird species has been recorded in the Ablation Valley – Ganymede Heights massif.

Human activities/impacts

Human activity at Ablation Valley – Ganymede Heights has been exclusively related to science. The first visit to the Ablation Valley area was by members of the British Graham Land Expedition in 1936, who collected about 100 fossil specimens from near Ablation Point (Howlett, 1988). The next visits were about a decade later, when basic geological descriptions and further fossil collections were undertaken. More intensive palaeontological investigations were made by British geologists in the 1960s through to the 1980s, with detailed studies of the geomorphology (Clapperton and Sugden, 1983). Limnological investigations were undertaken in the 1970s, with a number of expeditions examining the terrestrial biology being initiated in the 1980s and 1990s. Scientific activities since the millennium have focussed on palaeoclimatological research. All known expeditions into the Area have been by British scientists. The impacts of these activities have not been fully described, but are believed to be minor and limited to footprints, aircraft tracks at the Moutonnée Valley terrestrial airstrip (see Section *6(ii)*), removal of small quantities of geological and biological samples, markers, abandoned items such as supplies and scientific equipment, and the remains of human wastes.

An abandoned depot, consisting of two oil drums (one empty, one full), three 5 l cans of skidoo oil, one food box and ten glacier poles, was located on the moraine bench adjacent to George VI Ice Shelf, approximately 500 m north of Moutonnée Lake (70°51'19"S; 68°19'05"W). The depot was partially removed in November 2012 with only the full fuel drum left in situ. Various expeditions in the 1970s-80s placed empty fuel drums as route markers through pressure ice from George VI Sound into Ablation Valley, and a large onshore rock is painted yellow SE of Ablation Lake (McAra, 1984; Hodgson, 2001). Nearby is a large cross made from red painted rocks and cairns, with a wooden marker board in the centre. Evidence of campsites close to the shore of Ablation Lake remained in 2012. One site is on the SW shore near a rich area of vegetation, and another is approximately four kilometres east on the SE shore. At both sites circles of stones mark old tent sites, and circular structures have been built with low (0.8 m) stone walls. At the former site a number pieces of wood (including old markers), an old food box, string and human wastes were observed (Harris, 2001; Hodgson, 2001). Several red-painted rocks were found around the southern and western shores of Ablation Lake in February 2001, and paint fragments were sometimes observed in sediments. In 2000-01 some of the abandoned materials in Ablation Valley were removed: three fuel drums on lake ice, an old food box and some wood and string on the SW shore, and numerous fragments from broken perspex acryllic cloches on the SW shore (nine were deployed in January 1993 – Wynn-Williams, 1993; Rossaak, 1997 – all were destroyed by wind) (Harris, 2001; Hodgson, 2001). In November 2012, metal and rubbish near and old camp with a low stone wall (located at 70°49'58"S; 68°22'16"W) was removed. The painted rocks remain. Snowmobiles have been used on lake and glacier ice, and modified snowmobiles with front wheels were used over gravel terrain in a limited vicinity of the SW shore of Ablation Lake in 1983–84 (McAra, 1984). Some evidence of erosional paths forming on steep scree slopes, presumably a result of field work, was recorded in Moutonnée Valley (Howlett, 1988). Cairns have been built on a number of mountain summits and to mark a number of survey sites throughout the Area.

6(ii) Access to the Area

- Access to the Area shall be by aircraft, vehicle or on foot.
- There are no special restrictions on the points of access to the Area, nor on the overland or air routes used to move to and from the Area. Access overland from George VI Ice Shelf may be difficult because of pressure ice, but is considered to be the most reliable and safe access route for visitors arriving in the vicinity of the Area by fixed-wing aircraft, particularly as some routes into the Area from the glaciers to the west are steep, crevassed and arduous.
- Landing of fixed-wing aircraft within the Area is discouraged. If landings are essential for scientific or management objectives, they are restricted to the ice-covered lakes or to a single terrestrial site immediately west of Moutonnée Lake, provided landings are feasible. Pressure deformation of the ice surface of lakes, meltwater and thinning ice-cover may make landing on lake ice impractical later in the summer. Landings at Ablation Lake and the terrestrial site west of Moutonnée Lake were carried out in November 2000. The terrestrial landing site (Map 3) is oriented E–W and consists of approximately 350 m of

gently sloping coarse gravel on ground raised approximately 2 m above the surrounding valley. Some red-painted stones mark the western (upper) end in the form of an arrow. Tyre-impressions are evident in the gravel. Due to the poor state of the surface and a risk of damage to the aircraft, use of the terrestrial site west of Moutonnée Lake is not recommended.

- Should helicopter access prove feasible, specific landing sites have not been designated but landings are prohibited within 200 m of lake shores, or within 100 m of any vegetated or moist ground, or in stream beds.
- Access is also possible by aircraft to upper Jupiter Glacier (550 m), immediately west of Ablation Valley and outside of the Area, from where access may be made into the Area overland on foot.
- Pilots, air crew, or other people arriving by aircraft, are prohibited from moving on foot beyond the immediate vicinity of any landing site within the Area unless specifically authorised by Permit.

6(iii) Location of structures within and adjacent to the Area

There are no structures known to be present in the Area. A number of cairns have been installed as survey markers throughout the Area (Perkins, 1995; Harris, 2001) and some low walls have been erected at campsites. Nine plastic bright red reflector markers (30 cm high, held down by rocks) were put in place to mark the airstrip in Moutonnée Valley, but these were removed in November 2012. The nearest structure to the Area appears to be an abandoned caboose at Spartan Cwm, approximately 20 km south of the Area. A summer-only scientific camp facility exists at Fossil Bluff (UK), approximately 60 km to the south on the eastern coast of Alexander Island. The nearest permanently occupied scientific research stations are in Marguerite Bay (General San Martín (Argentina) and Rothera Research Station (UK)), approximately 350 km to the north (Map 2).

6(iv) Location of other protected Areas in the vicinity

There are no other protected areas in the immediate vicinity of the Area. The nearest protected area to Ablation Valley – Ganymede Heights is ASPA 170 Marion Nunataks, Charcot Island, Antarctic Peninsula, approximately 270 km to the east of Alexander Island (Map 2).

6(v) Special zones within the Area

There are no special zones within the Area.

7. Permit conditions

7(i) General permit conditions

Entry into the Area is prohibited except in accordance with a Permit issued by an appropriate national authority. Conditions for issuing a Permit to enter the Area are that:

- it is issued for compelling scientific reasons which cannot be served elsewhere, or for reasons essential to the management of the Area;
- the actions permitted are in accordance with this Management Plan;
- any management activities are in support of the objectives of this Management Plan;

- the actions permitted will not jeopardise the natural ecological system in the Area;
- the activities permitted will give due consideration via the environmental impact assessment process to the continued protection of the environmental or scientific values of the Area;
- the Permit shall be issued for a finite period;
- the Permit, or an authorised copy, shall be carried when in the Area.

7(ii) Access to, and movement within or over, the Area

- Movement by vehicle within the Area shall be restricted to snow or ice surfaces.
- Movement over land within the Area shall be on foot.
- All movement should be undertaken carefully so as to minimise disturbance to the soil, vegetated surfaces and sensitive geomorphological features such as dunes, walking on snow or rocky terrain if practical. If practical, visitors should avoid walking in stream or dry lake beds, or on moist ground, to avoid disturbance to the hydrology and/or damage to sensitive plant communities. Care should be taken even when moisture is not obviously present, as inconspicuous plants may still colonise the ground.
- Pedestrian traffic should be kept to the minimum necessary to undertake permitted activities and every reasonable effort should be made to minimise trampling effects.
- The operation of aircraft over the Areas should be carried out, as a minimum requirement, in compliance with the '*Guidelines for the operations of aircraft near concentrations of birds*' contained in Resolution 2 (2004).

7(iii) Activities which may be conducted within the Area,

Activities which may be conducted in the Area include:

- essential management activities, including monitoring;
- compelling scientific research that cannot be undertaken elsewhere and which will not jeopardize the ecosystem of the Area; and
- sampling, which should be the minimum required for approved research programmes.

Diving in lakes within the Area is normally prohibited unless it is necessary for compelling scientific purposes. If diving is undertaken, great care should be taken to avoid disturbance of the water column and of sensitive sediments and biological communities. The sensitivity of the water column, sediments and biological communities to disruption by diving activities shall be taken into account before Permits are granted for these purposes.

7(iv) Installation, modification or removal of structures

- Permanent structures or installations are prohibited.
- No structures are to be erected within the Area, or scientific equipment installed, except for compelling scientific or management reasons and for a pre-established period, as specified in a permit.
- All markers, structures or scientific equipment installed in the Area must be clearly identified by country, name of the principal investigator or agency, year of installation and date of expected removal.
- All such items should be free of organisms, propagules (e.g. seeds, eggs, spores) and non-sterile soil (see section *7(vi)*), and be made of materials that can withstand the environmental condition and pose minimal risk of contamination of the Area.

- Removal of specific structures or equipment for which the permit has expired shall be the responsibility of the authority which granted the original permit and shall be a condition of the Permit.

7(v) Location of field camps

When necessary for purposes specified in the Permit, temporary camping is allowed within the Area. One camp site has been designated within the Area: it is located on the north-western (upper) end of the airstrip in Moutonnée Valley (70°51'48"S, 68°21'39"W) (Map 3). The site is not marked, although tents should be erected as close as practicable to the marker on the north-western end of the airstrip. This site should be used by preference when working in this vicinity. Other specific camp site locations have not, as yet, been designated, although camping is prohibited on sites where significant vegetation is present. Camps should be located as far as practicable (preferably at least 200 m) from lakeshores, and avoid dry lake or stream beds (which may host an inconspicuous biota). By preference and where practical, camps should be located on snow or ice surfaces. Previously existing campsites should be re-used where possible, except where the above guidelines suggest these were inappropriately located.

7(vi) Restrictions on materials and organisms which may be brought into the Area

No living animals, plant material or microorganisms shall be deliberately introduced into the Area. To ensure that ecological values of the Area are maintained, special precautions shall be taken against accidentally introducing microbes, invertebrates or plants from other Antarctic sites, including stations, or from regions outside Antarctica. All sampling equipment or markers brought into the Area shall be cleaned or sterilized. To the maximum extent practicable, footwear and other equipment used or brought into the Area (including bags or backpacks) shall be thoroughly cleaned before entering the Area. Further guidance can be found in the *CEP Non-native species manual* (CEP, 2011) and the *Environmental code of conduct for terrestrial scientific field research in Antarctica* (SCAR, 2009). In view of the possible presence of breeding bird colonies within the Area, no poultry products, including wastes from such products and products containing uncooked dried eggs, shall be released into the Area.

No herbicides or pesticides shall be brought into the Area. Any other chemicals, including radio-nuclides or stable isotopes, which may be introduced for scientific or management purposes specified in the Permit, shall be removed from the Area at or before the conclusion of the activity for which the Permit was granted. Release of radio-nuclides or stable isotopes directly into the environment in a way that renders them unrecoverable should be avoided. Fuel or other chemicals shall not be stored in the Area unless specifically authorised by Permit condition. They shall be stored and handled in a way that minimises the risk of their accidental introduction into the environment. Materials introduced into the Area shall be for a stated period only and shall be removed by the end of that stated period. If release occurs which is likely to compromise the values of the Area, removal is encouraged only where the impact of removal is not likely to be greater than that of leaving the material in situ. The appropriate authority should be notified of anything released and not removed that was not included in the authorised Permit.

7(vii) Taking of, or harmful interference with, native flora or fauna

Taking of, or harmful interference with, native flora and fauna is prohibited, except in accordance with a permit issued in accordance with Annex II of the Protocol on Environmental Protection to the Antarctic Treaty. Where taking or harmful interference with animals is involved this should, as a minimum standard, be in accordance with the *SCAR code of conduct for the use of animals for scientific purposes in Antarctica* (2011). Any soil or vegetation sampling is to be kept to an absolute minimum required for scientific or management purposes, and carried out using techniques which minimise disturbance to surrounding soil, ice structures and biota.

7(viii) The collection or removal of materials not brought into the Area by the Permit holder

Material may be collected or removed from the Area only in accordance with a permit and should be limited to the minimum necessary to meet scientific or management needs. Material of human origin likely to compromise the values of the Area, and which was not brought into the Area by the Permit holder or otherwise authorised may be removed from the Area unless the environmental impact of the removal is likely to be greater than leaving the material in situ: if this is the case the appropriate national authority must be notified and approval obtained.

7(ix) Disposal of waste

All wastes, except human liquid and domestic liquid wastes, shall be removed from the Area. Human liquid and domestic liquid wastes may be disposed of within the Area down ice cracks along the margin of George VI Ice Shelf or Jupiter Glacier, or by burying in moraine along the ice margin in these localities as close as practical to the ice. Disposal of human liquid and domestic liquid wastes in this manner shall be more than 200 m from, and avoiding the catchments of, the main lakes in Ablation, Moutonnée or Flatiron valleys, or shall otherwise be removed from the Area. Human solid waste shall be removed from the Area.

7(x) Measures that may be necessary to continue to met the aims of the Management Plan

- Permits may be granted to enter the Area to carry out scientific research, monitoring and site inspection activities, which may involve the collection of a small number of samples for analysis or to carry out protective measures.
- Any long-term monitoring sites shall be appropriately marked and the markers or signs maintained.
- Scientific activities shall be performed in accordance with the *Environmental code of conduct for terrestrial scientific field research in Antarctica* (SCAR, 2009).

7(xi) Requirements for reports

The principal Permit holder for each visit to the Area shall submit a report to the appropriate national authority as soon as practicable, and no later than six months after the visit has been completed. Such reports should include, as appropriate, the information identified in the *Antarctic Specially Protected Area visit report form* contained in the *Guide to the Preparation of Management Plans for Antarctic Specially Protected Areas* (Appendix 2). Wherever possible, the national authority should also forward a copy of the visit report to the Party that proposed the Management Plan, to assist in managing the Area and reviewing the Management Plan. Parties should, wherever possible, deposit originals or copies of such original visit reports in a publicly accessible archive to maintain a record of usage, for the purpose of any review of the Management Plan and in organising the scientific use of the Area.

8. Supporting documentation

Bell, C. M. (1975). Structural geology of parts of Alexander Island. *British Antarctic Survey Bulletin* 41 and 42: 43-58.

Bentley, M. J. (2004). Aerial predation by a south polar skua *Catharacta maccormicki* on a snow petrel *Pagodroma nivea* in Antarctica. *Marine Ornithology* 32: 115-116.

Bentley, M. J., Hodgson, D. A., Sugden, D. E., Roberts, S. J., Smith, J. A., Leng, M. J., Bryant, C. (2005). **Early Holocene retreat of George VI Ice Shelf, Antarctic Peninsula**. *Geology* 33: 173-176.

Bentley, M. J., Hodgson, D. A., Smith, J. A., Cofaigh, C. O., Domack, E. W., Larter, R. D., Roberts, S. J., Brachfeld, S., Leventer, A., Hjort, C., Hillenbrand, C. D., and Evans, J.

(2009). Mechanisms of Holocene palaeoenvironmental change in the Antarctic Peninsula region. *The Holocene* 19: 51-69.

Butterworth, P. J. (1985). Sedimentology of Ablation Valley, Alexander Island: report on Antarctic field work. *British Antarctic Survey Bulletin* 66: 73-82.

Butterworth, P. J., Crame, J. A., Howlett, P. J., and Macdonald, D. I. M. (1988). Lithostratigraphy of Upper Jurassic – Lower Cretaceous strata of eastern Alexander Island, Antarctica. *Cretaceous Research* 9: 249-64.

Clapperton, C. M., and Sugden, D. E. (1982). Late Quaternary glacial history of George VI Sound area, West Antarctica. *Quaternary Research* 18: 243-67.

Clapperton, C. M., and Sugden, D. E. (1983). Geomorphology of the Ablation Point massif, Alexander Island, Antarctica. *Boreas* 12: 125-35.

Committee for Environmental Protection (CEP). (2011). Non-native species manual – 1st Edition. Manual prepared by Intersessional Contact Group of the CEP and adopted by the Antarctic Treaty Consultative Meeting through Resolution 6 (2011). Buenos Aires, Secretariat of the Antarctic Treaty.

Convey, P., Greenslade, P., Richard, K. J., and Block W. (1996). The terrestrial arthropod fauna of the Byers Peninsula, Livingston Island, South Shetland Islands - Collembola. *Polar Biology* 16: 257-59.

Convey, P., and Smith, R. I. L. (1997). The terrestrial arthropod fauna and its habitats in northern Marguerite Bay and Alexander Island, maritime Antarctic. *Antarctic Science* 9: 12-26.

Crame, J. A. (1981). The occurrence of *Anopaea* (Bivalvia: Inoceramidae) in the Antarctic Peninsula. *Journal of Molluscan Studies* 47: 206-219.

Crame, J. A. (1985). New Late Jurassic Oxytomid bivalves from the Antarctic Peninsula region. *British Antarctic Survey Bulletin* 69: 35-55.

Crame, J. A., and Howlett, P. J. (1988). Late Jurassic and Early Cretaceous biostratigraphy of the Fossil Bluff Formation, Alexander Island. *British Antarctic Survey Bulletin* 78: 1-35.

Croxall, J. P., Steele, W. K., McInnes, S. J., and Prince, P. A. (1995). Breeding distribution of the Snow Petrel *Pagodroma nivea*. *Marine Ornithology* 23: 69-99.

Elliott, M. R. (1974). Stratigraphy and sedimentary petrology of the Ablation Point area, Alexander Island. *British Antarctic Survey Bulletin* 39: 87-113.

Greenslade, P. (1995). Collembola from the Scotia Arc and Antarctic Peninsula including descriptions of two new species and notes on biogeography. *Polskie Pismo Entomologiczne* 64: 305-19.

Harris, C. M. (2001). Revision of management plans for Antarctic protected areas originally proposed by the United States of America and the United Kingdom: Field visit report. Internal report for the National Science Foundation, US, and the Foreign and Commonwealth Office, UK. Environmental Research and Assessment, Cambridge.

Heywood, R. B. (1977). A limnological survey of the Ablation Point area, Alexander Island, Antarctica. *Philosophical Transactions of the Royal Society* B, 279: 39-54.

Heywood, R. B., and Light, J. J. (1975). First direct evidence of life under Antarctic shelf ice. *Nature* 254: 591-92.

Hodgson, D. 2001. Millennial-scale history of the George VI Sound ice shelf and palaeoenvironmental history of Alexander Island. BAS Scientific Report - Sledge Charlie 2000-2001. Ref. R/2000/NT5.

Howlett, P. J. (1986). *Olcostephanus* (Ammonitina) from the Fossil Bluff Formation, Alexander Island, and its stratigraphical significance. *British Antarctic Survey Bulletin* 70: 71-77.

Howlett, P. J. (1988). Latest Jurassic and Early Cretaceous cephalopod faunas of eastern Alexander

Island, Antarctica. Unpublished Ph.D. thesis, University College, London.

Light, J. J., and Heywood, R. B. (1975). Is the vegetation of continental Antarctica predominantly aquatic? *Nature* 256: 199-200.

Lipps, J. H., Krebs, W. N., and Temnikow, N. K. (1977). Microbiota under Antarctic ice shelves. *Nature* 265: 232-33.

Maslen, N. R. (1982). An unidentified nematode-trapping fungus from a pond on Alexander Island. *British Antarctic Survey Bulletin* 51: 285-87.

Morgan, F., Barker, G., Briggs, C., Price, R., and Keys, H. (2007). Environmental Domains of Antarctica Version 2.0 Final Report. Landcare Research Contract Report LC0708/055.

Roberts, S. J., Hodgson, D. A., Bentley, M. J., Smith, J. A., Millar, I. L., Olive, V., and Sugden, D. E. (2008). The Holocene history of George VI Ice Shelf, Antarctic Peninsula from clast-provenance analysis of epishelf lake sediments. *Palaeogeography, Palaeoclimatology, Palaeoecology* 259: 258-283.

Roberts, S. J., Hodgson, D. A., Bentley, M. J., Sanderson, D. C. W., Milne, G., Smith, J. A., Verleyen, E., and Balbo, A. (2009). Holocene relative sea-level change and deglaciation on Alexander Island, Antarctic Peninsula, from elevated lake deltas. ***Geomorphology*** 112: 122-134.

Rowley P. D., and Smellie, J. L. (1990). Southeastern Alexander Island. In: LeMasurier, W. E., and Thomson, J. W., eds. *Volcanoes of the Antarctic plate and southern oceans.* Antarctic Research Series 48. Washington D.C., American Geophysical Union: 277-279.

SCAR (Scientific Committee on Antarctic Research) (2009). Environmental code of conduct for terrestrial scientific field research in Antarctica. ATCM XXXII IP4.

SCAR (Scientific Committee on Antarctic Research) (2011). SCAR code of conduct for the use of animals for scientific purposes in Antarctica. ATCM XXXIV IP53.

Smith, J. A., Bentley, M. J., Hodgson, D. A., Roberts, S. J., Leng, M. J., Lloyd, J. M., Barrett, M. S., Bryant, C., and Sugden, D. E. (2007a). Oceanic and atmospheric forcing of early Holocene ice shelf retreat, George VI Ice Shelf, Antarctica Peninsula. *Quaternary Science Reviews* 26: 500-516.

Smith, J. A., Bentley, M. J., Hodgson, D. A., and Cook, A. J. (2007b) George VI Ice Shelf: past history, present behaviour and potential mechanisms for future collapse. ***Antarctic Science*** 19: 131-142.

Smith, R. I. L. (1988). Bryophyte oases in ablation valleys on Alexander Island, Antarctica. *The Bryologist* 91: 45-50.

Smith, R. I. L. (1996). Terrestrial and freshwater biotic components of the western Antarctic Peninsula. In: Ross, R. M., Hofmann, E. E. and Quetin, L. B. *Foundations for ecological research west of the Antarctic Peninsula.* Antarctic Research Series 70: American Geophysical Union, Washington D.C.: 15-59.

Smith, R. I. L. (1997). Oases as centres of high plant diversity and dispersal in Antarctica. In: Lyons, W.B., Howard-Williams, C. and Hawes, I. *Ecosystem processes in Antarctic icefree landscapes.* A.A. Balkema, Rotterdam: 119-28.

Smith, R. I. L., and Convey, P. (2002). Enhanced sexual reproduction in bryophytes at high latitudes in the maritime Antarctic. *Journal of Bryology* 24: 107-117.

Starý, J., and Block, W. (1998). Distribution and biogeography of oribatid mites (Acari: Oribatida) in Antarctica, the sub-Antarctic and nearby land areas. *Journal of Natural History* 32: 861- 94.

Sugden, D. E., and Clapperton, C. N. (1980). West Antarctic ice sheet fluctuations in the Antarctic Peninsula area. *Nature* 286: 378-81.

Sugden, D. E., and Clapperton, C. M. (1981). An ice-shelf moraine, George VI Sound, Antarctica. *Annals of Glaciology* 2: 135-41.

Taylor, B. J., Thomson, M. R. A., and Willey, L. E. (1979). The geology of the Ablation Point – Keystone Cliffs area, Alexander Island. *British Antarctic Survey Scientific Reports* 82.

Thomson, M. R. A. (1972). Ammonite faunas of south-eastern Alexander Island and their stratigraphical significance. In: Adie, R.J. (ed) *Antarctic Geology and Geophysics,* Universitetsforlaget, Oslo.

Thomson, M. R. A. (1979). Upper Jurassic and Lower Cretaceous Ammonite faunas of the Ablation Point area, Alexander Island. *British Antarctic Survey Scientific Reports* 97.

Thomson, M. R. A., and Willey, L. E. (1972). Upper Jurassic and Lower Cretaceous Inoceramus (Bivalvia) from south-east Alexander Island. *British Antarctic Survey Bulletin* 29: 1-19.

Willey, L. E. (1973). Belemnites from south-eastern Alexander Island: II. The occurrence of the family Belemnopseidae in the Upper Jurassic and Lower Cretaceous. *British Antarctic Survey Bulletin* 36: 33-59.

Willey, L. E. (1975). Upper Jurassic and Lower Cretaceous Pinnidae (Bivalvia) from southern Alexander Island. *British Antarctic Survey Bulletin* 41 and 42: 121-31.

Map 1. Location of Ablation Valley and Ganymede Heights on the Antarctic Peninsula. Map specifications: WGS84 Antarctic Polar Stereographic. Central Meridian -55°, Standard Parallel: -71°.

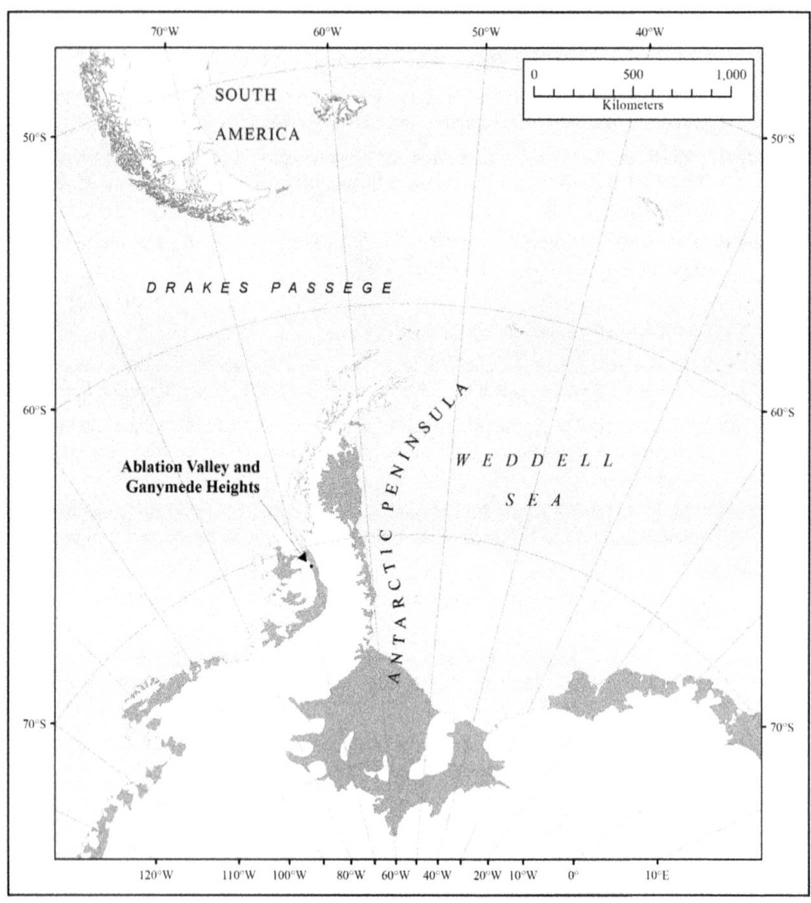

Map 2. ASPA No. 147 Ablation Valley and Ganymede Heights, location map. Map specifications: WGS 1984 Antarctic Polar Stereographic. Central Meridian: -71°, Standard Parallel: -71°.

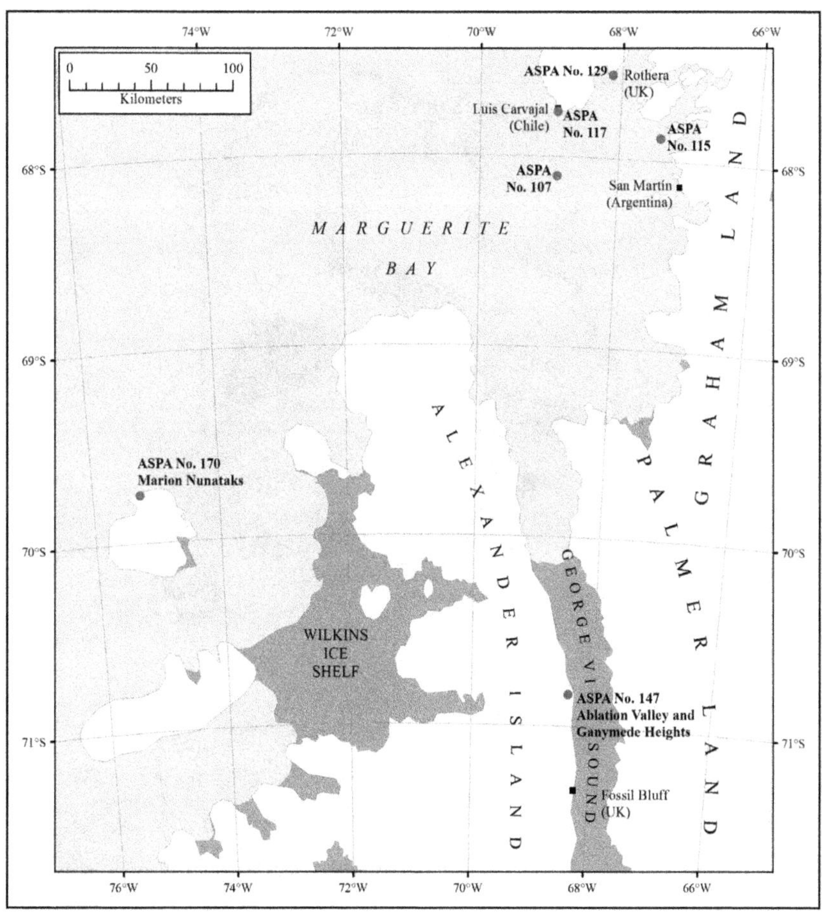

Map 3. ASPA No. 147 Ablation Valley and Ganymede Heights, topographic sketch map. Map specifications: WGS 1984 Antarctic Polar Stereographic. Central Meridian: -68.4°, Standard Parallel: -71.0°.

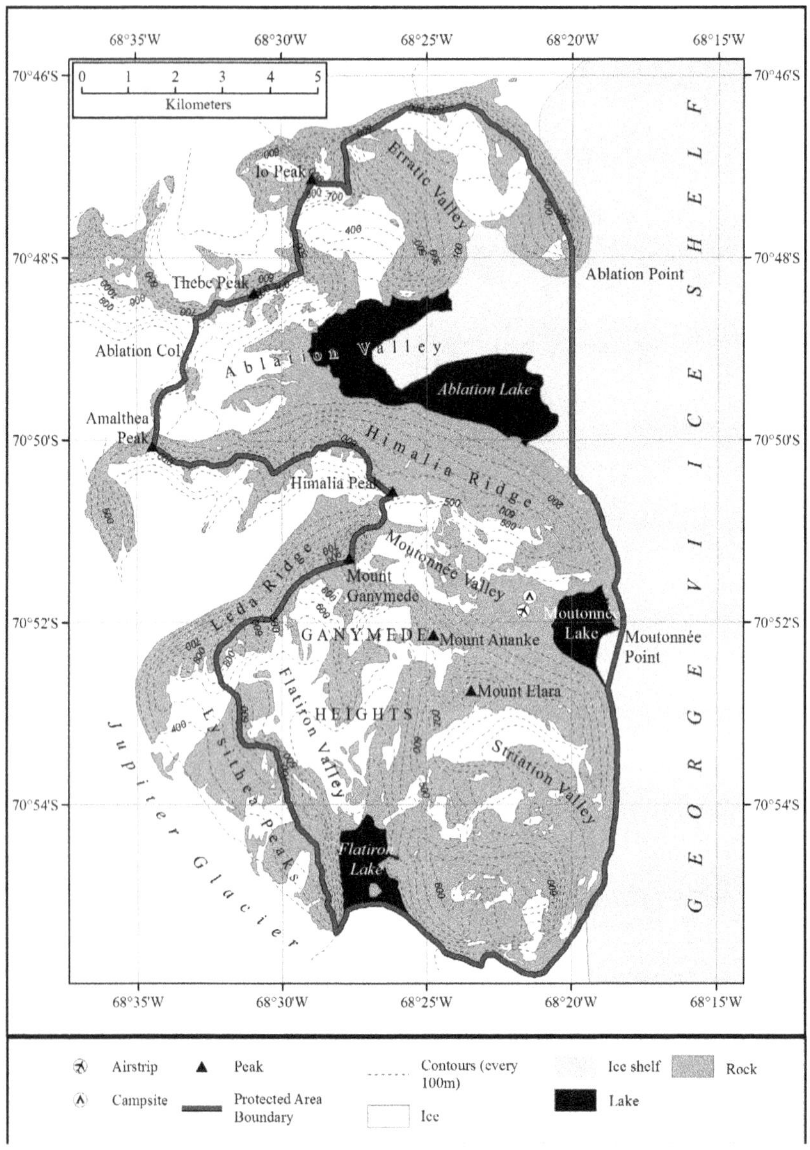

Annex 1

Boundary coordinates for ASPA 147 Ablation Valley and Ganymede Heights, Alexander Island. In large part, the boundary follows natural features and a detailed description is found in Section *6(i)*. In the table below, the boundary coordinates are numbered, with number 1 the most northerly co-ordinate and further coordinates numbered sequentially in a clockwise direction around the Area boundary.

Number	Latitude	Longitude
1	70°46'26"S	68°24'01"W
2	70°46'28"S	68°25'48"W
3	70°46'55"S	68°28'27"W
4	70°47'13"S	68°28'15"W
5	70°47'12"S	68°29'33"W
6	70°48'02"S	68°29'58"W
7	70°48'23"S	68°32'55"W
8	70°49'44"S	68°34'38"W
9	70°50'06"S	68°31'13"W
10	70°49'56"S	68°28'52"W
11	70°50'19"S	68°26'51"W
12	70°51'17"S	68°28'19"W
13	70°52'09"S	68°31'59"W
14	70°53'02"S	68°31'06"W
15	70°53'03"S	68°29'59"W
16	70°55'03"S	68°27'58"W
17	70°54'53"S	68°27'40"W
18	70°55'36"S	68°23'26"W
19	70°55'41"S	68°21'30"W
20	70°54'43"S	68°19'11"W
21	70°52'44"S	68°19'03"W
22	70°52'04"S	68°18'25"W
23	70°51'17"S	68°18'41"W
24	70°50'18"S	68°20'27"W
25	70°48'08"S	68°20'44"W
26	70°47'38"S	68°21'23"W
27	70°46'55"S	68°22'16"W

Management Plan for Antarctic Specially Protected Area No. 151

LIONS RUMP, KING GEORGE ISLAND (ISLA 25 DE MAYO), SOUTH SHETLAND ISLANDS

Introduction

Lions Rump (62°08'S; 58°07'W) is located on the southwestern coast of King George Island (isla 25 de Mayo), South Shetland Islands, covering approximately 1.32 km^2 in area.

The Area takes its name from the distinctive rocky hill lying between the southern extremity of King George Bay and Lions Cove.

The Area was originally designated as Site of Special Scientific Interest No. 34 through Recommendation XVI-2 (1991, SSSI No. 34) after a proposal by Poland on the grounds that it contains diverse biota and geological features and is a representative example of the terrestrial, limnological, and littoral habitats of the maritime Antarctic. In accordance with Decision 1 (2002), the Area was redesignated as Antarctic Specially Protected Area (ASPA 151). A revised Management Plan was adopted through Measure 1 (2000). The Area was designated primarily to protect the site's ecological values. The Area is also valuable as a reference site with diverse avian and mammalian Antarctic fauna, against which disturbance at sites situated near sites of human activity can be measured.

Based on the Environmental Domains Analysis for Antarctica (Resolution 3 (2008)) ASPA No 151 lies within Environment A (Antarctic Peninsula northern geologic), which is a small, terrestrial environment around the northern Antarctic Peninsula consisting entirely of ice-free land cover and sedimentary geology (Morgan et al. 2007). Other protected areas containing Domain A include ASPA No 111, ASPA No 128 and ASMA No 1.

There are four other ASPAs on King George Island (isla 25 de Mayo) and seven more on other islands of the South Shetland Archipelago, but only one of them (ASPA No 128 Western Shore of Admiralty Bay) represents both the same Environmental Domain A, and the same primary reason of designation (area with important or unusual assemblages of species, including major colonies of breeding native birds or mammals). Lions Rump, in contrast to ASPA No 128, is located ca 30 km from the nearest station and has been subjected to minimal disturbance by human activity. Therefore, ASPA No 151 complements ASPA No 128 by protecting a site against which human impact can be measured.

The Area is considered to be sufficiently large to provide adequate protection to the values described below. The biological, geological and scientific values of Lions Rump are vulnerable to human disturbance (e.g trampling, oversampling, disturbance of wildlife). Therefore, it is important that human activities in the Area are managed to minimize the risk of impacts.

The earliest information about penguin populations at Lions Rump was given by Stephens in 1958 (Croxall and Kirkwood 1979). Later studies come from works by Jabłoński (1984), Trivelpiece *et al.* (1987), Ciaputa and Sierakowski (1999) and Korczak-Abshire et al. (2013). Since 2007 a monitoring programme of birds and pinnipeds is carried out in the Area according to CCAMLR standard methods (pinniped census every 10 days, penguins' and other birds' nests census once during breeding season, fledglings weighting once during the season, recording of vagrant birds).

In 1989/90 and 2004 botanical studies were conducted in the Area, and vegetation maps of the Area were done, showing changes in lichen spatial distribution caused by climatic changes (Olech 1993, 1994, pers. comm.). An attempt to estimate ages of lichen colonization on the oldest maraines of the White Eagle Glacier was done (Angiel, Dąbski 2012).

Ornithogenic soils in the area of penguin rookery at Lions Rump were described by Tatur (1989), and than included into regional pedological synthesis (Tatur 2002). Surface loamy weathering cover of the Area was not described in soils categories yet. Large south part of the Area was covered by glacier 30 years ago during investigations preceding establishment of ASPA No 151. Due to retreat of glaciers in the result of regional warming, a new fresh, ice-free, postglacial landscape has appeared (Angiel, Dąbski 2012).

Paleogene and Neogene rocks from the Area and its close surroundings provide data important for world glacial history. The sequence consists of sedimentary and volcanic rocks from preglacial Eocene terrestrial and fresh water sediments to onlapping sequence of Early Oligocene diamictict and Miocene pillow lavas. Eocene sedimentary, pyroclastic and andesite rocks covering a main part of Area belong to "Lions Cove Formation". This unit was introduced by Birkenmajer (1980, 1981) and described in more detail in later papers (Birkenmajer et al. 1991, 1994, Birkenmajer 2001). "Lions Cove Formation" was excluded from "Lions Rump Group" of Barton (1961, 1965). Eocene age for "Lions Cove Formation" was proposed by Smellie et al. (1984) on the base of single K-Ar dating and was confirmed by many K-Ar determinations performed during ACE IPY project (Pańczyk i Nawrocki 2011,Tatur et al. 2009, Krajewski et al. 2009, Krajewski et al. 2010, Tatur et al. 2010., Krajewski et al. 2011). Oligocene tillites and glaciomarine sediments of "Polonez Cove Formation" (see Birkenmajer 2001) border the Area forming steep rocky walls from the west, south and east sides. Central part of the area is covered by the youngest Miocene andesite lavas an pillow-lavas forming hummocks along cliff (K-Ar datings from Ace Group, pers. comm.).

1. Description of values to be protected

Lions Rump was first designated a protected area as a representative of the terrestrial, limnological and littoral ecosystems of King George Island (isla 25 de Mayo), possessing diverse biota and rock formations (volcanic and sedimentary rocks important for world geological history). In the Antarctic Protected Areas Database it is included as an area with important or unusual assemblages of species, including major colonies of breeding native birds or mammals.

The original goals for designating the Area are still relevant.

The breeding avifauna of the Area is diverse and numerous, including three pygoscelid penguin species (Adélie penguin *Pygoscelis adeliae*, Gentoo penguin *Pygoscelis papua* and Chinstrap penguin *Pygoscelis antarctica*), as well as eight other bird species such as Cape pigeon *Daption capense*, Wilson's storm petrel *Oceanites oceanicus*, black-bellied storm petrel *Fregatta tropica*, snowy sheathbill *Chionis alba*, McCormick's skua *Catharacta maccormicki*, Antarctic skua *Catharacta antarctica*, Dominican gull *Larus dominicanus*, and Antarctic tern *Sterna vittata*.

Furthermore, Elephant seals (*Mirounga leonina*), Weddell seals (*Leptonychotes weddellii*), Leopard seals (*Hydrurga leptonyx*), Crabeater seals (*Lobodon carcinophagus*), and Fur seals (*Arctocephalus gazella*) rest and/or breed on the beaches.

ASPA No 151 includes the unique pre-glacial Eocene and partially glacial Oligocene sequences. Continental glacial sequence of "Polonez Formation" (tillites and glacial diamicts bearing erratic clasts) provides the oldest known hard evidence of the coming Cenozoic glaciation (28-32 SIS dating). Outcrops providing hard data of this event should be protected, therefore collecting petrified wood, rare leaves, layers of coal representing lustros (vitrinite) brown-coal methaphase and volcanic bombs from tuff deposits in the Area without Permit is prohibited. Eocene flora (Mozer, in press) is identical with flora cropping from the other side of White

Eagle Glacier (Zastawniak 1981, 1990), and consistent with regional floristic pattern (Pool et al 2001).

Lions Rump contains rich lichen flora, and numerous stands of two native vascular plants, *Colobanthus quitensis* and *Deschampsia antarctica.* The lichen biota of the Area consists of 148 taxa, making it one of the most diverse sites in the Antarctic.

The original values of the Area associated with the marine bottom fauna cannot be confirmed as one of the primary reasons for special protection of the Area because there is a lack of new data available describing the communities. However, future research may reaffirm them. Therefore, marine boundary of the Area has not been redefined.

The Area has not been subjected to frequent visits, scientific research and sampling. Human presence in the Area is currently estimated as two persons carrying out monitoring research between 1st November and 30th March. Therefore, the Area may be regarded as a reference site for future comparative studies.

Since 2007 a monitoring programme of birds and pinnipeds is carried out in the Area, in accordance with standard CCAMLR methods (pinniped census every 10 days, penguins' and other birds' nests census once during breeding season, fledglings weighting once during the season, recording of vagrant birds). Data serve as a basis for the conservation of Antarctic marine living resources, to detect and record significant changes in critical components of the ecological system, and to compare population trends with other areas (such as ASPA No 128 Western Shore of Admiralty Bay) that experience the greater level of human activities..

2. Aims and objectives

Management of the Area aims to:

- avoid degradation of, or substantial risk to, the the values of the Area by preventing unnecessary human disturbance to the Area
- allow scientific research in the Area provided it is for compelling reason which cannot be served elsewhere and which will not jeopardize the natural ecological system in the Area. Invasive practices used during biological research are excluded in this area.
- prevent or minimize the introduction and dispersal of non-native species (plants, animals and microbes)
- preserve the Area as a reference site for future comparative studies

3. Management activities

The following management activities shall be undertaken to protect the values of the Area:

- Visits shall be made as necessary to assess whether the ASPA continues to serve the purposes for which it was designated and to ensure management and maintenance measures are adequate
- The Management Plan shall be reviewed at least every five years and updated as required
- A copy of this Management Plan shall be made available at Arctowski Station (Poland: 62°09'34"S, 058°28'15"W), Comandante Ferraz Station (Brazil: 62°05'07"S, 58°23'32"W), Machu Picchu Station (Perú: 62°05'30"S, 58°28'30"W), Copacabana Field Station (USA: 62°10'45" S, 58°26'49" W), Hennequin Point Refuge (Equador: 62°07'16"S, 58°23'42"W) and in the refuge proximate to the Area (62°07'54"S, 58°09'20"W)

- The staff authorized to access the Area shall be specifically instructed on the conditions of this Management Plan
- Markers, signs and other structures erected within the Area for scientific or management purposes shall be secured and maintained in good condition and removed when no longer required
- Approach distances to fauna must be respected, except when the scientific projects may require otherwise and this is specified in the relevant permits.
- All scientific and management activities within the Area should be subject to an Environmental Impact Assessement (Annex I of the Protocol on Environmental Protection to the Antarctic Treaty)
- Where appropriate, National Antarctic Programmes are encouraged to coordinate activities to prevent excessive sampling of biological and geological material within the Area, to prevent or minimize the danger of introduction and dispersal of non-native species, and to keep environmental impacts, including cumulative impacts, to an absolute minimum.

4. Period of designation

The Area is designated for an indefinite period.

5. Maps

Map 1. The location of Lions Rump in relation to King George Island (isla 25 de Mayo).

Map 2. Lions Rump in greater detail.

Map 3. Vegetation map of Lions Rump.

Map 4. Geological map of Lions Rump.

6. Description of the area

6(i) Geographical co-ordinates, boundary markers and natural features

The Area is located on the southern coast of King George Bay, King George Island (isla 25 de Mayo), in the South Shetlands Islands (Map 1, 2). It is described as all the land and sea falling within the area bounded by the following co-ordinates:

62°07'48"S, 58°09'17"W;

62°07'49"S, 58°07'14"W;

62°08'19"S, 58°07'19"W;

62°08'16"S, 58°09'15"W;

62°08'16"S, 58°09'15"W.

The Area includes the littoral and sublittoral zones extending from the eastern end of Lajkonik Rock to the most northerly point of Twin Pinnacles. From this point the boundary extends to the easternmost end of the columnar plug of Lions Head to the east of White Eagle Glacier. On land, the Area includes the coast with raised beaches, freshwater pools and streams on the south side of King George Bay, around Lions Cove, and the moraines and slopes which lead to the lower ice tongue of White Eagle Glacier, then westward to a small moraine which protrudes through the ice cap south-east of Sukiennice Hills.

The ice-free area of ASPA No 151 exhibits a range of geomorphological features, including beaches of various width and length, moraines, hills and inland rocks (Map 4). The highest point rises to the altitude of c. 190m. Geologically, Lions Rump area is made up mainly of tuff, fuffite, lahar bearing wood and andesite basalt lava layer interbedding, deposited inside tectonic paleovalley. In the upper part of this sequence andesite lava flow (42-45 Ma K/Ar dating) preceded by lahars occur.. These terrestrial pyroclastics were exposed to alluvial erosion and valleys were ultimately filled with massive conglomerate (Conglomorate Bluff). All that complex of rocks belonging to Eocene "Lions Cove Formation" was cut by younger andesite dykes (Lions Rump). "Lions Cove Formation" is topped by glaciomarine clastic sediments of "Oligocene Polonez Cove Formation" (Krakowiak and Low Head Members). Oligocene rocks form steep walls surrounding the Area. Area is largely covered by glacial moraines and slope loamy deposits. The front of White Eagle Glacier is marked by large, dome-shaped moraine ridges belonging to several Holocene stages of glacier advance and retreat. Eocene sediments were affected by complex alteration related to post magmatic changes, weathering processes and low grade metamorphism. Chloritization, palagonization and zeolitization is observed along all the sediments. Terrestial Eocene and glaciomarine Oligocene are covered by Miocene andesite lavas and pillow lavas flows (c. 20 Ma, ACE group pers. com.). That volcanic rock occupy central part of ASPA No 151 territory, and most of them form Sukiennice Hills.

Large numbers of penguins breed throughout the Area. In 2010/11 there were 3,751 occupied nests of Adèlie penguins, 3004 occupied nests of gentoo penguins, and 32 occupied nests of Chinstrap penguins. Since 1995/96 a significant decrease in Adèlie penguin breeding population and a significant increase in gentoo penguin breeding population were observed. Chinstrap population is not numerous enough to detect any statistically significant changes.

There are 8 other bird species breeding in the Area (Cape Pigeon *Daption capense*, Wilson's storm petrel *Oceanites oceanicus*, Black-bellied storm petrel *Fregatea tropica,* sheathbill *Chionis alba*, McCormick's skua *Catharacta maccormicki*, Antarctic Skua *Catharacta antarctica,* Dominican Gull *Larus dominicanus*, and Antarctic Tern *Sterna vittata*). In 2010/11 the most numerous were: Antarctic Tern (57 nests), Cape pigeon (55 nests) and Dominican gull (26 nests).

Elephant seals (*Mirounga leonina*), Weddell seals (*Leptonychotes weddellii*), Leopard seals (*Hydrurga leptonyx*), Crabeater seals (*Lobodon carcinophagus*), and Fur seals (*Arctocephalus gazella*) rest and/or breed on the beaches. In 2010/11 four harems and 71 pups of Elephant seals were observed in the Area. The maximum numbers of Fur seals exceeded 1500 individuals.

Approximately 13 taxa of macroalgae were found in the littoral zone of the Area. The most common among them were: green algae (*Monostroma hariotti*), red algae (*Georgiella confluens, Iridaea cordata* and *Leptosarca simplex*), and brown algae (*Adenocystis utricularis* and *Ascoseira mirabilis*). There is rich and abundant bottom fauna in the marine part of the Area, with Bivalve as the dominant group. Both Amphipoda and Polychaeta also contribute significantly to benthic fauna abundance. Species composition and proportion of endemics indicate that King George Bay is transitional between Antarctic and Subantarctic (unpublished data). Marine part of the Area is shallow, with a lot of skerries and rocks, and is not accessible to ships.

The lichen (lichenized fungi) biota of the Area consist of 148 taxa (Map 3). Moreover 11 lichenicolous fungi species were recorded. The most diverse genera are Caloplaca (19 species) and Buellia (9 species), Lecanora (8 species). The highest species richness was found in places with diversified habitats, eg, with rocks, near penguin colonies or in places of bird perching. The lowest species richness was found in recently deglaciated terraine (young moraines) or in snowbeds. Since 1988/90 changes in lichen spatial distribution were observed, caused by glacial retreat and resulting water deficit. Liverworts have little importance in local plant communities. They occur mostly in moss banks. Fungi are rare or uncommon. Knowledge of the Area freshwater algae is poor.

6 (ii) Access to the Area

Access shall be by small boats landing outside the Area. Accessible beach is situated outside the western boundary of the Area, in front of the refuge (62°07'54"S, 58°09'20"W).

Access to the Area from the recommended landing site shall be on foot.

Helicopters may land in the Area only in case of emergency. Suggested landing site is situated on flat area 50-100 m eastward from refuge, on both sides of the Area boundary. Changeable distribution of marine mammals, snow patches and stream tributories should be taken into account during landing. Landing on vegetation or near the wildlife should be avoided to the maximum extent possible. To avoid overflying breeding sites, approach should be preferably be from the north, or west.

6 (iii) Location of structures within the Area

A sign-board is located on a marine terrace outside the western border of the Area.

A four-berth wooden refuge (62°07'54"S, 58°09'20"W) constructed by Poland is located on a flat marine gravel terrace about 50m outside the western boundary of the Area.

The nearest scientific research stations are located 30 km west (Arctowski Station – Poland, 62°09'34"S, 058°28'15"W) and north-west (Comandante Ferraz – Brazil, 62°05'07"S, 58°23'32"W) from the Area.

6 (iv) Location of other Protected Areas within close proximity

ASPA No 125, Fildes Peninsula, King George Island (25 de Mayo), and ASPA No 150, Ardley Island, Maxwell Bay, King George Island (25 de Mayo), lie about 50 km west of Lions Rump. ASPA No 132, Potter Peninsula, King George Island (25 de Mayo), South Shetland Islands, lies about 35 km to the west. ASMA No 1, Admiralty Bay, King George Island (isla 25 de Mayo) and ASPA No 128, Western shore of Admiralty Bay, King George Island (isla 25 de Mayo), South Shetland Islands, lie about 20 km to the west.

6(v) Special zones within the Area

None

7. Permit conditions

7 (i)General permit conditions

Permits may be issued only by appropriate national authorities as designated under Annex V Article 7 of the Protocol on Environmental Protection to the Antarctic Treaty.

Conditions for issuing a permit for the Area are that:

- it is issued only for a compelling scientific purpose which cannot be served elsewhere, or
- it is issued for essential management purposes such as inspection, maintenance or review
- the actions permitted will not jeopardize the natural ecological system or scientific values of the Area,
- any management activities are in support of the objectives of the Management Plan,
- the actions permitted are in accordance with this Management Plan,
- the permit, or an authorized copy, must be carried within the Area,
- a permit is issued for a stated period only,

- a report is supplied to the authority named in the Permit,
- the appropriate authority should be notified of any activities/measures undertaken that were not included in the Permit.

7 (ii) Access to and movement within the Area

Access to, and movement within the Area shall be on foot from the direction of the recommended landing site on the beach near the refuge.

Access shall be limited in order to avoid disturbance to birds, and damage to vegetation and geological features.

Land vehicles are prohibited in the Area. Helicopters may land only in case of emergency (see *6(ii)*).

Overflight operations by fixed-wing aircraft and helicopters shall be carried out, as a minimum requirement, in accordance with the "Guidelines for the Operation of Aircraft near Concentrations of Birds" contained in Resolution 2 (2004).

No pedestrian routes are designated within the Area, but persons on foot should at all times avoid disturbance to birds and mammals, and damage to vegetation and paleontological (marine fauna in Polonez Cove Formation, wood and rare leaves in lahars) and geological (erratics) evidences.

7 (iii) Activities which are or may be conducted within the Area, including restrictions on time and place

- Compelling scientific research which cannot be conducted outside the Area, and which will not damage or interfere with any aspect of the Area's biological, geological, or aesthetic values.
- Essential management activities, including monitoring.

7 (iv) Installation, modification or removal of structures

No additional structures are to be erected in the Area, or scientific equipment installed, except for compelling scientific or management reasons and for a pre-established period, as specified in a Permit. Installation (including site selection), maintenance, modification or removal of structures and equipment shall be undertaken in a manner that minimises disturbance to the Area. All structures or scientific equipment installed in the Area shall be clearly identified by country, name of the principal investigator and year of installation.

All such items should be free of organisms, propagules (e.g. seeds, eggs) and non-sterile soil, and be made of materials that can withstand the environmental conditions and pose minimal risk of contamination of the Area. Removal of specific structures or equipment for which the Permit has expired shall be a condition of the Permit. Permanent structures or installations are prohibited.

7 (v) Location of the field camps

Camping is prohibited in the Area except in an emergency. A four-berth wooden refuge constructed by Poland is located on a flat marine gravel terrace ca 50 m outside the western boundary of the Area (62°07'54"S, 58°09'20"W). The refuge is used mostly by Polish researchers monitoring birds and pinnipeds in the Area. Additional camping outside the Area is possible on non-vegetated sites near the refuge. Care should be taken to minimise disturbance to wildlife.

7 (vi) Restrictions on materials and organisms which may be brought into the Area

No living animals, plant material or microorganisms shall be deliberately introduced into the Area. To ensure that the floristic and ecological values of the Area are maintained, special precautions shall be taken against accidentally introducing microbes, invertebrates or plants from other Antarctic sites, including stations, or from regions outside Antarctica. Special care must be extended to ensure that non-native grass *Poa annua* that is present in the vicinity of Arctowski Station will not be inadvertently introduced to the Area. All sampling equipment or markers brought into the Area shall be cleaned or sterilized. Introduction of non-sterile soil is prohibited.

To the maximum extent practicable, footwear, outer clothing, backpacks and other equipment used or brought into the Area shall be thoroughly cleaned before entering the Area. *CEP Non-native Species Manual* and *COMNAP/SCAR Checklists for supply chain managers of National Antarctic Programmes for the reduction in risk of transfer of non-native species* shall be used for further guidance. Potential non-native species spotted in the Area should be reported to the appropriate authorities.

In view of the presence of breeding bird colonies within the Area no poultry products, including food products containing uncooked dried eggs, shall be released into the Area or into adjacent sea.

No herbicides or pesticides shall be brought into the Area. Any other chemicals, including radio-nuclides or stable isotopes, which may be introduced for scientific or management purposes specified in the Permit, shall be removed from the Area at or before the conclusion of the activity for which the Permit was granted. Release of radio-nuclides or stable isotopes directly into the environment in a way that renders them unrecoverable should be avoided.

Fuel or other chemicals shall not be stored in the Area unless specifically authorised by Permit condition. They shall be stored and handled in a way that minimises the risk of their accidental spill into the environment, and their quantity shall be kept to the minimum needed for scientific or management purposes specified in the Permit.

Materials introduced into the Area shall be for a stated period only and shall be removed by the end of that stated period.

If release occurs which is likely to compromise the values of the Area, removal is encouraged only where the impact of removal is not likely to be greater than that of leaving the material in situ. The appropriate authority should be notified of anything released and not removed that was not included in the authorised Permit.

7 (vii) Taking or harmful interference with native flora and fauna

Taking or harmful interference with native flora and fauna is prohibited, except by Permit issued in accordance with Annex II to the Protocol on Environmental Protection to the Antarctic Treaty. Where taking of or harmful interference with animals is involved, the *SCAR Code of Conduct for Use of Animals for Scientific Purposes in Antarctica* should be used as a minimum standard.

Information on taking and harmful interference will be duly exchanged through the Antarctic Treaty Information Exchange system.

To prevent human disturbance of the breeding penguin colony, visitors shall not approach within 10 m of the colony during breeding season, unless authorised by Permit for specific scientific or management purposes.

7 (viii) Collection and removal of anything not brought into the Area by the Permit holder

Collection or removal of anything not brought into the Area by the permit holder shall only be in accordance with a Permit and should be limited to the minimum necessary to meet scientific or management needs.

Permits shall not be granted if there is reasonable concern that the sampling proposed would take, remove or damage such quantities of soil, sediment, flora or fauna that their distribution or abundance within the Area would be significantly affected.

Other material of human origin likely to compromise the values of the Area (e.g. plastic debris) which was not brought into the Area by the permit holder or otherwise authorised, may be removed from the Area unless the environmental impact of the removal is likely to be greater than leaving the material in situ; if this is the case the appropriate Authority must be notified and approval obtained.

7 (ix) Disposal of waste

All wastes, including solid human wastes, shall be removed from the Area in accordance with Annex III (Waste disposal nad waste management) of the Protocol on Environmental Protection to the Antarctic Treaty. Liquid human waste may be disposed of into the sea off the Area, at the end of the season.

7 (x) Measures that may be necessary to ensure that the aims and objectives of the Management Plan continue to be met

Permits may be granted to enter the Area to carry out biological monitoring and site inspection activities, which may involve the collection of small samples for analysis or audit, or to erect and maintain signpost, or protective measures. Scientific activities shall be performed in accordance with *SCAR's environmental code of conduct for terrestrial scientific field research in Antarctica.*

Any specific sites of long-term monitoring that are vulnerable to accidental disturbance should be appropriately marked and the information passed to other Parties through appropriate channels.

Interference and overlapping with long-term research and monitoring programmes should be avoided through consultations and an exchange of information in advance of the proposed activities.

7 (xi) Requirements for reports

The principal permit holder for each visit to the Area shall submit a report to the appropriate national authority as soon as practicable, and no later than six months after the visit has been completed..

The reports must include the information outlined in the Visit Report form, in accordance with Resolution 2 (2011). If appropriate, the national authority should also forward a copy of the visit report to the Party that proposed the Management Plan, to assist in managing the Area and reviewing the Management Plan.

Parties should, wherever possible, deposit originals or copies of such original visit reports in a publicly accessible archive to maintain a record of usage, for the purpose of any review of the Management Plan and in organising the scientific use of the Area.

The relevant authority shall be informed of any activity undertaken, any measure taken or material released and not removed which are not covered by a permit.

8. Supporting documentation

Non-Native Species Manual. Resolution 6 (2011) – ATCM XXXIV – CEP XIV, Buenos Aires (available at *http://www.ats.aq/documents/atcm34/ww/atcm34_ww004_e.pdf*)

Guidelines for the Operation of Aircrafts near Concentrations of Birds in Antarctica. Resolution 2 (2004) – ATCM XXVII - CEP VII, Cape Town (available at *http://www.ats.aq/documents/recatt/Att224_e.pdf*)

COMNAP/SCAR Checklists for supply chain managers of National Antarctic Programmes for the reduction in risk of transfer of non-native species – ATCM XXXIV/CEP XIV, Buenos Aires (avaible at https://www.comnap.aq/Shared%20Documents/checklistsbrochure.pdf)

SCAR Code of Conduct for the Use of Animals for Scientific Purposes (available at *http://www.scar.org/treaty/atcmxxxiv/ATCM34_ip053_e.pdf*)

SCAR's Environmental Code Of Conduct For Terrestrial Scientific Field Research In Antarctica (avaible at *http://www.scar.org/researchgroups/lifescience/Code_of_Conduct_Jan09.pdf*

Angiel P.J., Korczak M. 2008. Comparison of population size of penguins concerning present and archive data from ASPA 128 and ASPA 151 (King George Island). Arctic and Antarctic Perspectives in the International Polar Year. SCAR/IASC IPY. Open Science Conference. St. Petersburg, Russia. July 8th - 11th 2008. Abstract volume: 241.

Angiel P.J., Dąbski M. 2012. Lichenometric ages of the Little Ice Age moraines of King George Island and of the last volcanic activity on Penguin Island (West Antarctica). Geografiska Annaler: Series A, Physical Geography, 94, 395–412

Angiel P.J., Korczak-Abshire M. 2011. Recent Climate Change Effect on Penguins and Pinnipeds, King George Island, Antarctica. Newsletter for the Canadian Antarctic Research Network, 30, 10-14

Barton C.M. 1961. The geology of King George Island. Preliminary Report, Falkland Islands Dependencies Survey 12: 1-18

Barton C.M. 1965. The geology of South Shetland Islands. III. The stratigraphy of King George Island. Sci. Rep. of BAS 44, 1-33

Birkenmajer K 1994. Geology of Tertiary glacigenic deposits and volcanics (Polonia Glacier Group and Chopin Ridge Group) at Lions Rump (SSSI No. 34), King George Island, West Antarctica. Bulletin of the Polish Academy of Sciences, Earth Sciences, 42, 165-180

Birkenmajer K. 1980. Report on geological investigations of King George Island, South Shetlands (West Antarctica), in 1978/79. Studia Geologica Polonica, 64, 89-105

Birkenmajer K. 1981. Geological relations at Lions Rump, King George Island. Studia Geologica Polonica, 72, 75-87

Birkenmajer K. 1989. A guide to Tertiary geochronology of King George Island, West Antarctica. Polish Polar Research, 10, 555-579

Birkenmajer K. 2001., Mesozoic and Cenozoic stratigraphic units in parts of the South Shetland Islands and Northern Antarctic Peninsula (as used by the Polish Antarctic Programmes). Studia Geologica Polonica, 118, 5-188

Birkenmajer K., Frankiewicz J.K., Wagner M. 1991. Tertiary coal from the Lions Cove Formation, King George Island, West Antarctica. Polish Polar Research, 12, 221-249

Birkenmajer K., Gaździcki A., Gradziński R., Kreuzer H., Porębski S.J., Tokarski A.K. 1991. Origin and age of pectinid-bearing conglomerate (Tertiary) on King Island, West Antarctica. Geological Evolution of Antarctica, edited by M.R.A. Thomson, J.A. Crame, and J.W. Thomson, pp. 663-665, Cambridge University Press

Ciaputa P., Sierakowski K. 1999. Long-term population changes of Adelie, chinstrap, and gentoo penguins in the regions of SSSI No. 8 and SSSI No. 34, King George Island, Antarctica. Polish Polar Research, 20, 355-365

Croxall J.P., Kirkwood E.D. 1979. The distribution of penguins on the Antarctic Peninsula and islands of the Scotia Sea. Life Science Division, British Antarctic Survey, Cambridge: 186 pp.

Jabłoński B. 1984. Distribution and numbers of penguins in the region of King George Island (South Shetland Islands) in the breeding season 1980/1981). Polish Polar Research, 5, 17-30

Korczak-Abshire M., Angiel P.J., Wierzbicki G. 2011. Records of white-rumped sandpiper (Calidris fuscicollis) on the South Shetland Islands. Polar Record, 47 (242), 262–267

Korczak-Abshire M., Węgrzyn M., Angiel P., Lisowska M. 2012 An analysis of the distribution and population size of penguin species on Lions Rump based on the GIS system. XXIV Sympozjum Polarne, 14-16 czerwca 2012, Sosnowiec, Poland. Streszczenia referatów i posterów str. 91

Korczak-Abshire M., Węgrzyn M., Angiel P.J., Lisowska M. (2013). Pygoscelid penguin breeding distribution and population trends at Lions Rump rookery (South Shetland Islands). Polish Polar Research

Krajewski K., Sidorczyk M., Tatur A., Zieliński G. 2009. Lithostratigraphy and depositional history of the earliest Miocene glaco-marine sequences at Cape Melville Formation, King George Island, West Antarctica (poster). The First ACE IPY Conference in Granada, Spain, September 2009

Krajewski K.P., Tatur A., Molnar F., Mozer A., Pecskay Z., Sidorczuk M., Zieliński G., Kusiak M., Keewook Y.I., Namhoon Kim. 2011. Paleoclimatic Stages in the Eocene-Miocene succession on King George Islans: new chronology data and relevance for glaciation of Antarctica. ACE Symposium Edinburgh

Krajewski K.P., Tatur A., Mozer A., Pecskay Z., Zieliski G. 2010. Cenozoic climate evolution in the northern Antarctic Peninsula region: geochronological paleoenvironments on King George Island. Presentation No PS2-C.40. International Polar Year Conference – Oslo Science Conference. 8-12 June 2010

Morgan, F., Barker, G., Briggs, C., Price, R. and Keys, H. 2007. Environmental Domains of Antarctica Version 2.0 Final Report, Manaaki Whenua Landcare Research New Zealand Ltd. 89 pp.

Mozer A. (in press). Eocene sedimentary facies in volcanogenic succession on King George Island, South Shetland Islands: a record of pre-ice sheet terrestrial environments in West Antarctica. Geological Quaterly

Olech M. 1993. Flora porostów i szata roślinna Południowych Szetlandów (Antarktyka). Wiadomości Geobotaniczne 37, 209-211

Olech M. 1994. Lichenological assessment of the Cape Lions Rump, King George Island, South Shetland Islands; a baseline for monitoring biological changes. Polish Polar Research, 15, 111-130

Olech, M. 2001. Annotated checklist of Antarctic lichens and lichenicolous fungi. Institute of Botany of the Jagiellonian University, Kraków

Olech M., Czarnota P. 2009. Two new *Bacidia* (Ramalinaceae, lichenized Ascomycota) from Antarctica. Polish Polar Research, 30, 339-340

Pańczyk M., Nawrocki J. 2011. Geochronology of selected andesitic lavas from the King George Bay area (SE King George Island). Geological Quarterly, 55, 323–334

Poole D., Hunt R.J., Cantrill D.J. 2001. A Fossil Wood Flora from King George Island: Ecological Implications for a AntarcticEocene Vegetation. Annals of Botany, 88, 33-54

Smellie J.L., Pankhurest R.J., Thompson M.R.A., Davies R.E.S. 1984. The geology of South Shetland Islands. VI. Stratigraphy, geochemistry and evolution. Scientific Reports, British Antarctic Survey, 87: 1-85

Tatur A. 1989. Ornithogenic Soils of the maritime Antarctic. Pol. Polar Res. 10, 4; 481 - 532.

Tatur A. 2002. Ornithogenic Ecosystems in the maritime Antarctic - formation, development and disintegration. In: Beyer L. and Bölter M. (eds). Geoecology of Terrestrial Antarctic Ice-Free Coastal Landscapes, Ecological Studies 154, Springer Verlag 161-184

Tatur A. Krajewski K.P., Pecskay Z., Zieliński G., del Valle R.A., Mozer A. 2010. Suplementary evidence of Paleogene environment changes in West Antarctica. SCAR Conference. Buenos Aires, July 2010

Tatur A., Krajewski K.P., Angiel P., Bylina P., Delura K., Nawrocki J., Pańczyk M., Peckay Z., Zieliński G., Mozer A. 2009. Lithostratigraphy, dating, and correlation of cenozoic glacial and interglacial sequences on King George Island, West Antarctica (poster). The First ACE IPY Conference in Granada, Spain, September 2009.

Trivelpiece W.Z., Trivelpiece S.G., Volkman N. 1987. Ecological segregation of Adélie, gentoo, and chinstrap penguins at King George Island, Antarctica. Ecology 68: 351-361

Zastawniak E. 1981. Tertiary leaf flora from the Point Hennequin Group of King George Island (South Shetland Islands, Antarctica). Preliminary report. Studia Geologica Polonica 72, 97–108, 4 pls

Zastawniak E. 1990. Late Cretaceous leaf flora of King George Island, West Antarctica. In Proceedings of the symposium: Paleofloristic and paleoclimatic changes in the Cretaceous and Tertiary (eds Knobloch, E. & Kvacek, Z.), pp. 81–85 (Geological Survey,Prague)

Maps of Lions Rump:

Battke Z., Cisak J. 1988. Cape Lions Rump, King George Bay, 1:5000. Printed by E. Romer State Cartographic Publishing House, Warsaw

Angiel P.J., Gasek A. Lions Rump and Polonia Glacier, King George Island. Map prepared during the 33rd Polish Antarctic Expedition to Arctowski Station. Glacier front mapped in January 2009. Detailed hydrography only for ASPA 151, generalized in the Polonia Glacier forefront

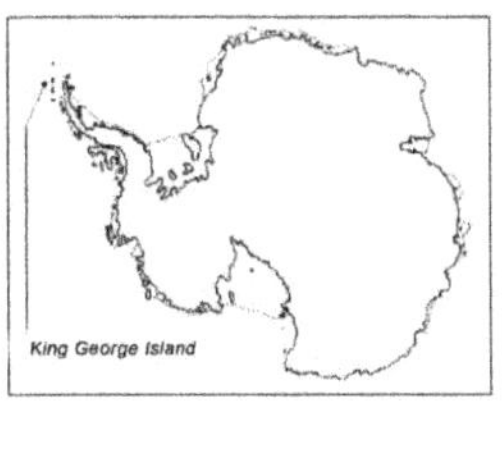

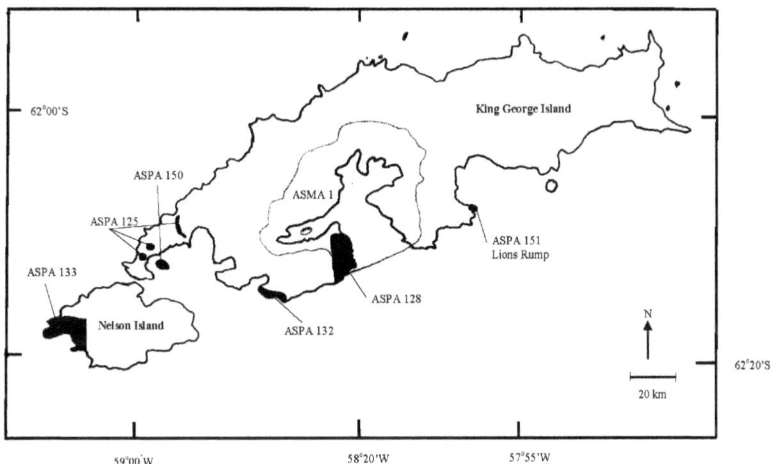

Map. 1. The location of ASPA 151 Lions Rump in relation to King George Island

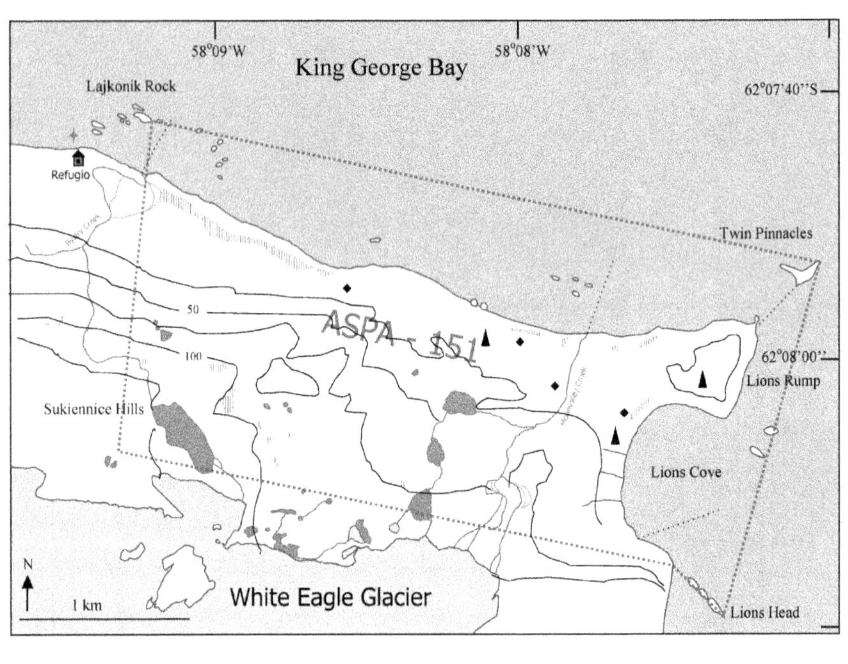

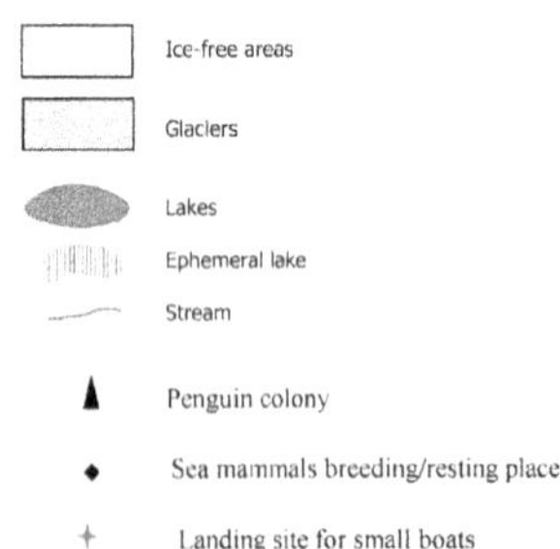

Map 2. Lions Rump in greater detail.

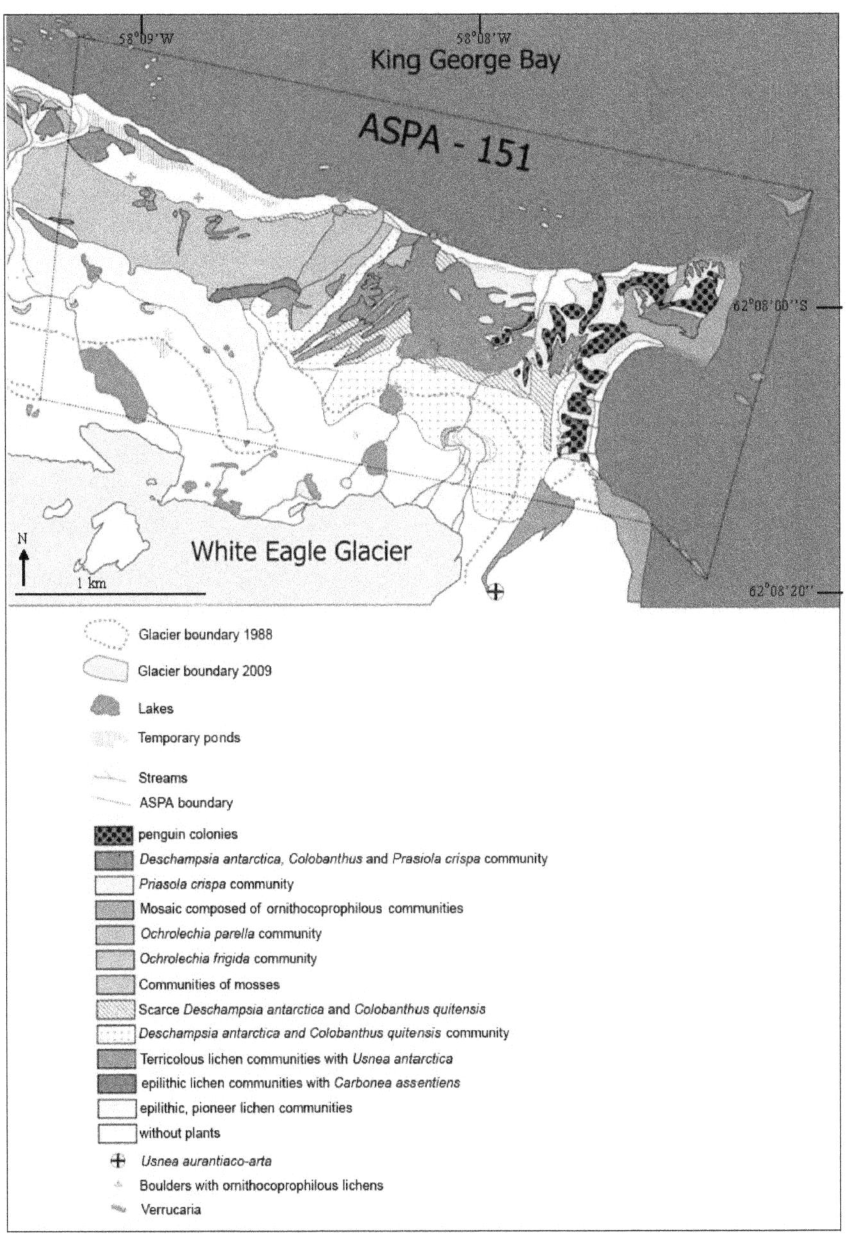

Map 3. Vegetation map of Lions Rump

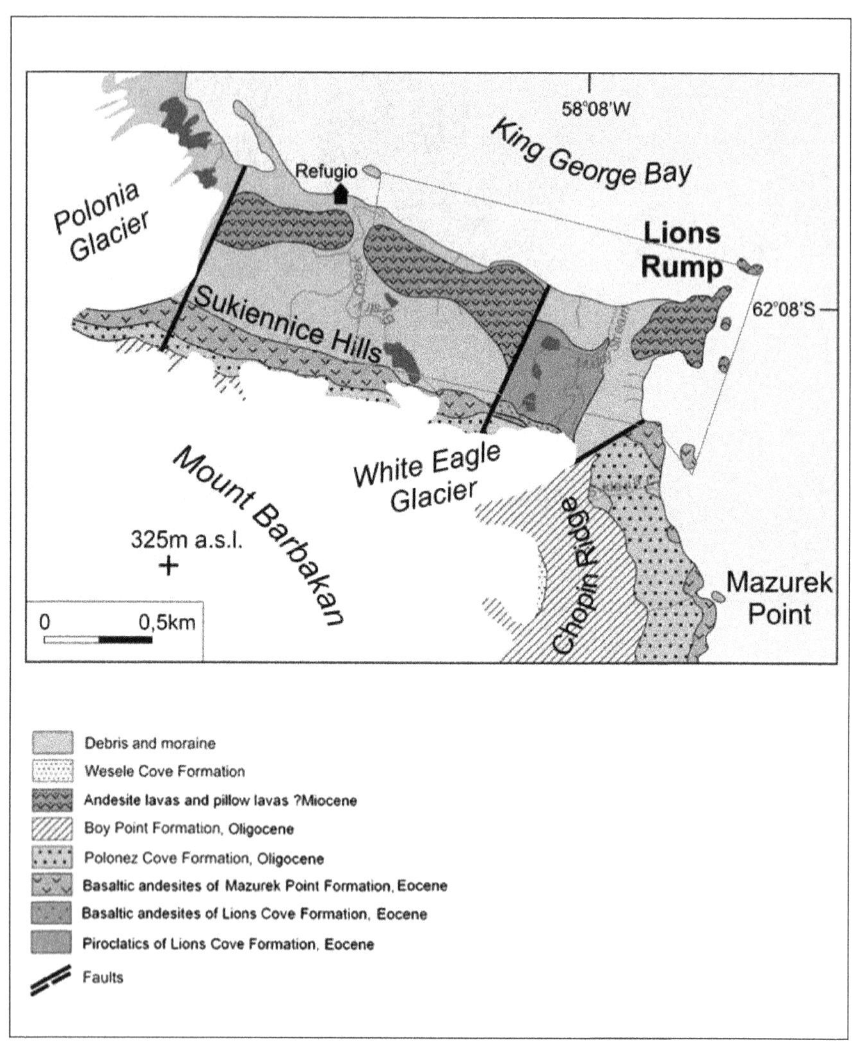

Map 4. Geological map of Lions Rump

Management Plan For
Antarctic Specially Protected Area No. 154
BOTANY BAY, CAPE GEOLOGY, VICTORIA LAND

Introduction

Botany Bay, Cape Geology is situated in the south western corner of Granite Harbour, southern Victoria Land (77°00'14"S, 162°32'52"E; Map A Inset 1and 2). The Area is extremely rich botanically for such a high-latitude location and is one of the richest sites in the whole of continental Antarctica. There is a high diversity and abundance of lichens (at least 30 species) and mosses (9 species) with abundant growths of algae (at least 85 taxa). The Area also has a diverse community of invertebrates (collembola, mites, nematodes, rotifers) and a colony (in excess of 40 pairs) of South polar skua (*Catharacta maccormicki*). The Area is the type locality for the collembolan *Gomphiocephalus hodgsoni* Carpenter and the lichen *Caloplaca coeruleofrigida* Sochting and Seppelt.

In addition to the biological values described, the Area contains within it the remains of a rock shelter and associated artefacts of historical importance (from the British Antarctic Expedition 1910-1913), known as Granite House, designated as Historic Site and Monument (HSM) No. 67 in Measure 4 (1995).

Botany Bay, Cape Geology was originally designated in Measure 3 (1997) as Site of Special Scientific Interest (SSSI) No. 37, after a proposal by New Zealand, on the grounds that the Area is an extremely rich botanical refuge for such a high latitude location, with a lichen and moss species diversity and abundance that is unique for southern Victoria Land. The site was re-designated Antarctic Specially Protected Area (ASPA) No. 154 in Decision 1 (2002). The Management Plan was revised and adopted in Measure 2 (2003) and Measure 11 (2008).

The primary reason for the designation of Botany Bay, Cape Geology as an Antarctic Specially Protected Area is to protect the Area's unusual ecological features and its exceptional scientific and historic values.

1. Description of values to be protected

In the Ross Sea region, areas of abundant mosses and lichens have been identified at Cape Bird, Ross Island (ASPA 116), Beaufort Island (ASPA 105), Canada Glacier in the Taylor Valley (ASPA 131), Kar Plateau in Granite Harbour, Edmonson Point (ASPA 165) and Cape Hallett (ASPA 106). While these sites have a high vegetation ground cover and biomass, the diversity of species present is considerably lower than that found at Botany Bay.

Botany Bay is extremely rich botanically and is also one of the richest sites in the whole of continental Antarctica. The terrestrial lichen and moss flora of Botany Bay comprises one liverwort, nine mosses and at least 30 lichens (Annex 1). There are abundant growths of algae (at least 85 taxa), although the algal flora is not considered particularly unusual for the locality. The Area also has a large population of invertebrates (collembola, mites, nematodes, rotifers) and a colony (in excess of 40 pairs) of South polar skua (*Catharacta maccormicki*). No other birds are known to breed in the Area. The Area is the type locality for the collembolan *Gomphiocephalus hodgsoni* Carpenter and the lichen *Caloplaca coeruleofrigida* Sochting and Seppelt.

The structure and development of the moss and lichen communities at Botany Bay is similar to that found more than 10° of latitude further north. The Area contains by far the most southerly record of the liverwort *Cephaloziella varians*, the lichen *Turgidosculum complicatulum* and the mosses *Bryoerythrophyllum recurvirostrum* and possible *Ceratodon purpureus*. Most are about three degrees of latitude further south than the nearest record to the north in the Terra Nova Bay region.

The boulder beach has rich populations of both epilithic and endolithic lichens. Of great significance is the size (up to 15 cm diameter) of some lichen thalli. At high latitudes, macrolichens are rare and scattered. Botany Bay is exceptional as there is an abundance of several macrolichens including *Umbilicaria aprina, Xanthoria elegans, Physcia caesia* and several forms of microlichens.

The rich flora is the result of a comparatively warm microclimate produced by the unusual sheltered nature of the Area being protected from the southerly and easterly polar winds but fully open to the brightest sun to the north. Different species assemblages or associations within the Area are determined by nutrient input from the skua colony, the occurrence of the source of water, whether solely from snowmelt from the ice field or snowfall, or from some form of melt stream, and by the regularity and speed of water flow and the type of substrate, especially whether it is loose gravel or solid rock.

Under the influence of a changing climate (both global and local), increases in volume and shifts in location of water flow through or over the vegetation would inevitably lead to change in the vegetation distribution, diversity and abundance. The Area would be ideal for assessing the impacts of climate change on continental Antarctic terrestrial ecosystems dominated by moss and lichen vegetation.

In addition to the biological values described, the Area contains within it the remains of a rock shelter and associated artefacts of historical importance, known as Granite House. The shelter was constructed using a natural hollow in the rocks, with walls built up from granite boulders and a roof of seal skins in 1911 for use as a field kitchen by Griffith Taylor's western geological party during the British Antarctic Expedition of 1910-1913. It was enclosed on three sides with granite boulder walls and used a sledge to support a seal-skin roof. The stone walls of the shelter have since partially collapsed and numerous artefacts have disappeared. In January 2012 parts of the walls remained, but the roof had collapsed and the seal skins had blown some way down the beach. The shelter still contains corroded remnants of tins, a seal skin and some fabrics.

The shelter and associated artefacts are vulnerable to disturbance and therefore access is managed with an Access Zone within the Area, which is subject to access restrictions. A tent site used by the Western Geological Party under Griffith Taylor, is identifiable as a flat gravel area with a number of stones that were used to weigh down the tent valance. This area is outside the Access Zone and is subject to access restrictions.

The primary reason for the designation of Botany Bay, Cape Geology as an Antarctic Specially Protected Area is to protect the limited geographical extent of the ecosystem, the unusual ecological features, and the exceptional scientific and historic values of the Area. The vulnerability of the Area to disturbance through trampling, sampling, pollution or alien introductions, are such that the Area requires long-term special protection.

2. Aims and objectives

Management at Botany Bay aims to:

- avoid degradation of, or substantial risk to, the values of the Area by preventing unnecessary human disturbance to the Area;
- allow scientific research on the ecosystem and elements of the ecosystem in particular on lichen and moss species, algae, invertebrates and skuas while ensuring protection from over-sampling;
- allow other scientific research in the Area provided it is for compelling reasons which cannot be served elsewhere and which will not jeopardize the natural ecological system in the Area;
- preserve a part of the natural ecosystem of the Area as a reference area for future comparative studies;
- prevent or minimise the introduction to the Area of alien plants, animals and microbes;
- allow visits to the historic site Granite House, but under strict control by Permit;
- allow conservation visits to other historic sites, but under strict control by Permit;
- allow visits for management purposes in support of the aims of the Management Plan.

3. Management activities

The following management activities shall be undertaken to protect the values of the Area:

- Information on the location of the Area, stating special restrictions that apply, shall be displayed prominently, and a copy of this Management Plan shall be made available, at National Antarctic Programme stations that operate in the vicinity of the Area.
- Signs illustrating the location and boundaries, with clear statements of entry restrictions, shall be placed at appropriate locations on the boundary of the Area to help avoid inadvertent entry.
- Markers, signs or other structures (e.g. cairns) erected within the Area for scientific or management purposes shall be secured and maintained in good condition and removed when no longer required.

- The Area shall be visited as necessary, and no less than once every five years, to assess whether it continues to serve the purposes for which it was designated and to ensure that management and maintenance activities are adequate.
- National Antarctic Programmes operating in the Area shall consult together with a view to ensuring the above management activities are implemented.

4. Period of designation

Designated for an indefinite period.

5. Maps

Map A - Botany Bay, Antarctic Specially Protected Area No. 154: Topographic map. Map specifications: Projection - Lambert conformal conic. Standard parallels - 1st 79° 20' 00" S; 2nd 76° 40' 00"S. Central Meridian - 162° 30' 00" E. Latitude of Origin - 78° 01' 16.211" S. Spheroid: WGS84.

Map B - Botany Bay, Antarctic Specially Protected Area No. 154: Access Zone (with Granite House and viewing area).
Map specifications are the same as those in Map A.

Map C - Botany Bay, Antarctic Specially Protected Area No. 154: Vegetation density. showing the distribution density of moss, lichen and algae within ASPA 154.
Map specifications are the same as those in Map A.

6. Description of the Area

6(i) Geographical coordinates, boundary markers and natural features
Cape Geology is situated in the south-western corner of Granite Harbour, southern Victoria Land, at 77°00'14"S, 162°32'52"E approximately 100 km north-west of Ross Island (Map A, Insets). The Area consists of raised boulder beach terraces, weathered rocky steppes and irregular rock platforms around Cape Geology, rising rapidly to the south to include a well-defined elevated cirque containing a small ice field. The ice field provides a regular supply of meltwater over the Area. The Area faces north and is well protected from strong winds. The intensity of the solar radiation is increased by reflection from the sea ice that normally remains in Granite Harbour until the end of January. Consequently, the site has warmer than expected air temperatures sometimes reaching almost 10°C in January. The most extensive vegetation occurs on the sheltered raised beach terrace known as Botany Bay.

The bedrock geology at Cape Geology has been described as a porphyritic grey biotite-granite, with phenocrysts of orthoclase of reddish colour, casting the weathered rock with a reddish tinge.

The boundaries of the Area include the water catchment and encompass the elevated cirque from the small ice field down to the coastline (Map A). The northwest boundary of the Area is marked by a brass plaque in a boulder along the shoreline (M1,

77°00'19'S, 162°31'53"E) 400 m southwest of Cape Geology. The west boundary is defined by a line extending first 260 m south southeast from M1 to a large boulder (marked by a cairn) with terrier bolt (M2, 77°00'27" S 162°33'08" E) at an elevation of 118 m on the ridge above the campsite; thence the boundary extends 250 m up this ridge to a point at 162 m elevation marked by an iron tube with bamboo pole. The west boundary extends a further 300 m up this ridge to a large pointed rock at 255 m elevation (77°00'40"S, 162°31'46"E) near the edge of the permanent ice field. The boundary then extends 150 m south across the ice field to the west edge of a prominent line of exposed rock and moraine in the southwest corner of the Area at 325 m elevation. The south boundary follows this line of rock east until the exposure is buried by the ice-field, thence southeast across the ice field for 500 m to the edge of a second and more prominent exposure at an elevation of just over 400 m (M3, 77°00'59"S, 162°33'22"E). The boundary follows the upper edge of this exposure and then crosses the ice field southeast to an elevation of approximately 325 m where the ice-free eastern boundary ridge and the ice field converge, (77°01'16"S, 162°34'15"E). The east boundary follows the ridge crest for 1,550 m in a northeast direction to a low point on the ridge approximately 392 m (M4, 77°00'13"S, 162°36'10"E) where the east boundary turns to descend due north to the coast at the eastern extremity of the boulder beach of Botany Bay (M5, 77°00'12" S, 162°36'12" E). The mean high water mark of the coastline forms the northern boundary of the Area between M1 and M5.

The Area also supports an Access Zone and Restricted Zone (Map A and B). The Access Zone has been designated to allow access to Granite House while the Restricted Zone has been designated to protect the most extensive area of vegetation in the Area at Botany Bay. The density of moss, lichen and algae is highest in the Restricted Zone of Botany Bay (Map C) and has been protected to preserve part of the Area as a reference site for future comparative studies.

Under the Environmental Domains Analysis (Resolution 3, 2008) the Area is Environment S – McMurdo – South Victoria Land geologic. Environment Domain S includes known areas of abundant mosses and lichens at Cape Bird, Ross Island (ASPA 116), Beaufort Island (ASPA 105) and Canada Glacier in the Taylor Valley (ASPA 131).

6(ii) Access to the Area

Access to the Area is generally via helicopter with a designated helicopter landing site 60 m outside (77° 00' 20.8"S, 162° 31' 47.7"E; Map A-C) of the northwest boundary corner adjacent to the designated camp site. Access to the helicopter landing site should be from the open water/sea ice to the north of the Area (Map A and B). Overflight of the Area lower than 300 m (~1000 ft) above ground level is normally prohibited. When required for essential scientific or management purposes, transient overflight or landing may be allowed by Permit only. Overflight of the Restricted Zone lower than 300 m (~1000 ft) above ground level is prohibited.

Vehicles are prohibited within the Area and access shall be by foot. Access should preferably be from the designated camp site following the preferred corridor of the Access Zone, 10–20 m from the coast, which is relatively devoid of vegetation. Visitors shall not venture south of Granite House to the Restricted Zone, unless specifically authorised by Permit.

6(iii) Location of structures within and adjacent to the Area
The only structures known to exist in the Area are Granite House and the associated artefacts, the boundary survey mark at M1 and other boundary markers (i.e. cairns, iron tube markers). At the designated camp site, there is a large wooden platform with materials stored beneath and an automatic weather station is installed further down the beach.

6(iv) Location of other protected areas in the vicinity
Botany Bay lies within Antarctic Specially Managed Area (ASMA No. 2), McMurdo Dry Valleys. The nearest protected area to Botany Bay is ASPA 123 Barwick and Balham Valleys, 50km away in a southwest direction.

6(ii) Special zones within the Area
Restricted Zone
The most extensive area of vegetation occurs on the sheltered raised beach terrace known as Botany Bay. This embayment and a portion of the Area directly above Botany Bay is designated as a Restricted Zone in order to preserve part of the Area as a reference site for future comparative studies. The remainder of the Area, which is similar in biology, features and character, is more generally available for research programmes and sample collection.

The western boundary of the Restricted Zone is defined by a line from a marker (iron tube in rock, 20 metres from mean high water mark, elevation 8 m) at the west side of Botany Bay (Map A), extending southwest for 170 m up to a second iron tube marker on the crest of the adjacent ridge (87 m). This boundary extends 100 m to a third iron tube and a cairn (98 m), thence 50 m to a large flat rock in the centre of the main flush (marked '1' on Map A). The southern boundary of the Restricted Zone extends from the flat rock in the flush in a straight line 820 m to the first of two prominent boulders closely adjacent to each other, approximately in the middle of the ice-free slopes above Botany Bay (marked '2' on Map A at 165 m). The eastern boundary extends 300 m from there to a large rock at 135 m elevation (marked '3' on Map A), thence northeast down slope to the northeast boundary point (M5, 5 m). The northern boundary of the Restricted Zone is the mean high water mark of Botany Bay and is coincident with the northern boundary of the Area.

Access to the Restricted Zone is allowed only for compelling scientific or management (such as inspection or review) purposes, which cannot be served elsewhere in the Area.

Access Zone
In order to allow access to the rock shelter known as Granite House (HSM No. 67), an Access Zone has been designated to protect historic artefacts and plant communities within the vicinity, while also allowing access to the rock shelter.

The Access Zone is an area of 470 m by 20 m along the coast and by 80 m at the point that surrounds a rock ridge leading from the coast at Cape Geology to the rock shelter. The boundaries are marked on Map B. The shelter was constructed by members of the 1910-1913 British Antarctic Expedition, and used between December 1911 and January 1912 while the party carried out geological and biological exploration in the vicinity.

Access to the Access Zone may be allowed by Permit, subject to the conditions of this Management Plan.

7. Permit conditions

7(i) General permit conditions

Entry into the Area is prohibited except in accordance with a Permit issued by an appropriate national authority. Conditions for issuing a Permit to enter the Area are that:

- outside of the Restricted and Access Zones, access may be permitted only for scientific study of the ecosystem, or for compelling scientific reasons that cannot be served elsewhere, or for conservation at historic sites, or for essential management purposes consistent with plan objectives such as inspection or review;
- access to the Restricted Zone may be permitted only for compelling scientific or management reasons that cannot be served elsewhere in the Area;
- access to the Access Zone may be permitted for scientific, management, historical, educational or recreational purposes;
- the actions permitted will not jeopardise the ecological, scientific or historic values of the Area;
- any management activities are in support of the objectives of the Management Plan;
- the actions permitted are in accordance with the Management Plan;
- the Permit, or an authorized copy, shall be carried within the Area;
- a visit report shall be supplied to the authority named in the Permit;
- permits shall be issued for a stated period.

7(ii) Access to, and movement within or over, the Area

Vehicles are prohibited within the Area and all movement within the Area should be on foot. Helicopters are normally prohibited from landing within the Area. There is a designated helicopter landing site 60 m outside of the Area (77° 00' 20.8"S, 162° 31' 47.7"E Map A-C). Access to the landing site should be from the open water / sea ice to the north of the Area (Map B). Overflight of the Area lower than 300 m (~1000 ft) above ground level is normally prohibited. When required for essential scientific or management purposes, transient overflight or landing may be allowed. Conduct of such anticipated overflights or landings must be specifically authorised by Permit. Use of helicopter smoke grenades within the Area is prohibited unless necessary for safety, and all grenades should be retrieved. All helicopter landing or overflight lower than 300 m (~1000 ft) above ground level is prohibited within the Restricted Zone.

Access into the Area should preferably be from the designated camp site following the preferred corridor of the Access Zone, 10–20 m from the coast, which is relatively devoid of vegetation. Visitors should avoid walking on visible vegetation, or unnecessary disturbance to bird populations. Care should be exercised walking in areas of moist ground, where foot traffic can easily damage sensitive soils, plant and algal communities, and degrade water quality. Visitors should walk around such areas, on ice or rocky ground. Pedestrian traffic should be kept to the minimum necessary consistent with the objectives of any permitted activities and every reasonable effort should be made to minimise effects.

Access to the Access Zone should preferably be from the coast, following the ridge leading up to Granite House (Map B). An alternative route may be used from the designated camp site and helicopter landing site, along a preferred walking route 10-20 m from the coast, if sea-ice travel is unsafe (Map B). Unless specifically authorised by Permit, visitors are prohibited from entering the historic shelter, and are limited to access and viewing from the rock ridge designated for access from the coast in order to prevent damage to the rich vegetation within the Access Zone. Visitors shall not venture south of Granite House, unless specifically authorised by Permit. A maximum of 10 people is permitted to enter the Access Zone at any one time, and a maximum of 5 people is allowed in the viewing area overlooking Granite House at any one time (Map B).

7(iii) Activities which may be conducted within the Area

Activities which may be conducted within the Area include:

- compelling scientific research which cannot be undertaken elsewhere and which will not jeopardise the ecosystem of the Area;
- essential management activities, including monitoring;
- limited visits to the Access Zone for reasons other than science or management subject to the conditions described in this plan;
- activities with the aim of preserving or protecting the historic artefacts within the Area.

7(iv) Installation, modification, or removal of structures

No new structures are to be erected within the Area, or scientific equipment installed, except for compelling scientific or management reasons, and for a pre-established period, as specified in a Permit. All markers, structures or scientific equipment installed in the Area must be clearly identified by country, name of the principal investigator or agency, year of installation and date of expected removal. All such items should be free of organisms, propagules (e.g. seeds, eggs of invertebrates) and non-sterile soil, and be made of materials that can withstand the environmental conditions and pose minimal risk of contamination of the Area. Removal of specific structures or equipment for which the Permit has expired shall be a condition of the Permit.

7(v) Location of field camps

Camping within the Area is prohibited and should be at a site outside of the Area, 100 m from the northwest corner (Map A) and adjacent to the designated helicopter landing site. This camp site has been disturbed by previous activities and visitors should reoccupy these disturbed positions for tents and other facilities.

7(vi) Restrictions on materials and organisms which may be brought into the Area

In addition to the requirements of the Protocol on Environmental Protection to the Antarctic Treaty, restrictions on materials and organisms which may be brought into the Area are:

- No animals, plant material, microorganisms or non-sterile soil shall be deliberately introduced into the Area and precautions shall be taken to prevent against accidental introductions.
- No herbicides or pesticides shall be brought into the Area.
- Any other chemicals, including radio-nuclides or stable isotopes, which may be introduced for scientific or management purposes specified in the Permit, shall

be removed from the Area at or before the conclusion of the activity for which the Permit was granted.
- Fuel is not to be stored in the Area, unless required for essential purposes connected with the activity for which the Permit has been granted.
- All materials introduced into the Area shall be for a stated period only and shall be removed by the end of that stated period, and shall be stored and handled so that risk of their introduction into the environment is minimised.

7(vii) Taking of, or harmful interference, with native flora or fauna
Taking of, or harmful interference with, native flora and fauna is prohibited, except in accordance with a Permit issued in accordance with Annex II of the Protocol on Environmental Protection to the Antarctic Treaty. Where taking or harmful interference with animals is involved this should, as a minimum standard, be in accordance with the SCAR Code of Conduct for the Use of Animals for Scientific Purposes in Antarctica.

7(viii) The collection or removal of materials not brought into the Area by the permit holder
Material may be collected or removed from the Area only in accordance with a Permit and should be limited to the minimum necessary to meet scientific or management needs. Material of human origin likely to compromise the values of the Area, and which was not brought into the Area by the Permit Holder or otherwise authorised, may be removed from the Area unless the environmental impact of the removal is likely to be greater than leaving the material in situ: if this is the case the appropriate authority must be notified and approval obtained.

Unless specifically authorised by Permit, visitors to the Area are prohibited from interfering with or from handling, taking, damaging or attempting restoration of Granite House or any artefacts found within the Access Zone. Evidence of recent changes, damage or new artefacts observed should be notified to the appropriate national authority. Relocation or removal of artefacts for the purposes of preservation, protection or to re-establish historical accuracy is allowable by Permit.

7(ix) Disposal of waste
All wastes, including all human wastes, shall be removed from the Area.

7(x) Measures that may be necessary to continue to meet theaims of the Management Plan
Permits may be granted to enter the Area to:
- carry out monitoring and Area inspection activities, which may involve the collection of small samples or data for analysis or review;
- erect or maintain signposts, structures or scientific equipment;
- carry out management and conservation activities, especially those associated with the Historic Sites.

Any specific sites of long-term monitoring shall be appropriately marked on site and on maps of the Area. A GPS position should be obtained for lodgement with the Antarctic Data Directory System through the appropriate national authority.

To help maintain the ecological and scientific values of the isolation and relatively low level of human impact at the Area visitors shall take special precautions against introductions. Of particular concern are microbial, animal or vegetation introductions sourced from soils from other Antarctic sites, including stations, or from regions outside Antarctica. To the maximum extent possible, visitors shall ensure that footwear, clothing and any equipment – particularly camping and sampling equipment – is thoroughly clean before entering the Area.

7(xi) Requirements for reports

The principal permit holder for each visit to the Area shall submit a report to the appropriate national authority as soon as practicable, and no later than six months after the visit has been completed.

Such visit reports should include, as applicable, the information identified in the recommended visit report form contained in Appendix 4 of the Guide to the Preparation of Management Plans for Antarctic Specially Protected Areas appended to Resolution 2 (1998).

If appropriate, the national authority should also forward a copy of the visit report to the Party that proposed the Management Plan, to assist in managing the Area and reviewing the Management Plan.

Parties should, wherever possible, deposit originals or copies of such original visit reports in a publicly accessible archive to maintain a record of usage, for the purpose of any review of the Management Plan and in organising the scientific use of the Area.

8. Supporting documentation

Broady, P.A. 2005. The distribution of terrestrial and hydro-terrestrial algal associations at three contrasting locations in southern Victoria Land, Antarctica. Algological Studies 118: 95-112.

Davidson, M.M. and Broady, P.A. 1996. Analysis of gut contents of *Gomphiocephalus hodgsoni* Carpenter (Collembola: Hypogastruridae) at Cape Geology, Antarctica. Polar Biology 16 (7): 463-467.

De los Rios, A., Sancho, L.G., Grube, M., Wierzchos, J. And Ascaso, C. 2005. Endolithic growth of two Lecidea lichens in granite from continental Antarctica detected by molecular and microscopy techniques. New Phytologist 165: 181-190.

Green, T.G.A., Kulle, D., Pannewitz, S., Sancho, L.G. and Schroeter, B. 2005. UV-A protection in mosses growing in continental Antarctica. Polar biology 28(11): 822-827.

Green, T.G.A., Schroeter, B. and Sancho, L.G. 2007. Plant life in Antarctica. In: Pugnaire, F.I. and Valladares, F. (Eds.). Handbook of functional plant ecology. Marcel Dekker Inc., New York, pp 389-433.

Green, T.G.A., Schroeter, B. and Seppelt, R.D. 2000. Effect of temperature, light and ambient UV on the photosynthesis of the moss *Bryum argenteum* Hedw. Pages165-170 in Davison, W., Howard-Williams, C. and Broady, P. (Eds). Antarctic Ecosystems: models for wider ecological understanding. Christchurch, New Zealand: New Zealand Natural Sciences. ISBN 047306877X.

Kappen, L. and Schroeter, B. 1997. Activity of lichens under the influence of snow and ice. Proceedings of the NIPR Symposium on Antarctic Geosciences 10: 163-168.

Kappen, L., Schroeter, B., Green, T.G.A. and Seppelt, R.D. 1998. Chlorophyll a fluorescence and CO_2 exchange of *Umbilicaria aprina* under extreme light stress in the cold. Oecologia 113(3): 325-331.

Kappen, L., Schroeter, B., Green, T.G. A. and Seppelt, R.D. 1998. Microclimate conditions, meltwater moistening, and the distributional pattern of *Buellia frigida* on rock in a southern continental Antarctic habitat. Polar biology 19 (2): 101-106.

Montes, M.J., Andrés, C., Ferrer, S. and Guinea, J. 1997. Cryptococcus: A new Antarctic yeast isolated from Botany Bay, Tierra Victoria. Real Sociedad Española de Historia Natural. Boletín. Sección Biológica. 93 (1-4): 45-50.

Montes, M.J., Belloch, C., Galiana, M., Garcia, M.D., Andres, C., Ferrer, S., Torres-Rodriguez, J.M. and Guinea, J. 1999. Polyphasic taxonomy of a novel yeast isolated from Antarctic environment; description of Cryptococcus victoriae sp. Nov. Systmatics and Applied Microbiology 22(1): 97-105.

Pannewitz, S., Schlensog, M., Green, T.G.A., Sancho, L.G., and Schroeter, B. 2003. Are lichens active under snow in continental Antarctica? Oecologia 135: 30-38.

Pannewitz, S., Green, T.G.A., Maysek, K., Schlensog, M., Seppelt, R.D., Sancho, L.G., Türk, R. and Schroeter, B. 2005. Photosynthetic responses of three common mosses from continental Antarctica. Antarctic science 17(3): 341-352.

Rees, P.M. and Cleal, C.J. 2004. Lower Jurassic floras from Hope Bay and Botany Bay, Antarctica. Special Papers in Palaeontology, Vol. 72, 90p. Palaeontology Association, London, United Kingdom.

Ruprecht, U., Lumbsch, H.T., Brunauer, G., Green, T.G.A. and Turk, R. 2010. Diversity of Lecidea (Lecideaceae, Ascomycota) species revealed by molecular data and morphological characters. Antarctic Science 22: 727-741.

Sancho, L.G., Pintado, A., Green, T.G.A., Pannewitz, S. and Schroeter, B. 2003. Photosynthetic and morphological variation within and among populations of the Antarctic lichen *Umbilicaria aprina*: implications of the thallus size. Bibliotheca lichenologica 86: 299-311.

Schlensog, M., Pannewitz, S., Green, T.G.A. and Schroeter, B. 2004. Metabolic recovery of continental Antarctic cryptogams after winter. Polar biology 27(7): 399-408.

Schroeter, B., Green, T.G.A. and Seppelt, R.D. 1993. History of Granite House and the western geological party of Scott's Terra Nova expedition. Polar Record 29 (170): 219-224.

Schroeter, B., Green, T.G.A., Kappen, L. and Seppelt, R.D. 1994. Carbon dioxide exchange at subzero temperatures. Field measurements on *Umbilicaria aprina* in Antarctica. Cryptogamic Botany 4(2): 233-241.

Schroeter, B., Green, T.G.A., Pannewitz, S., Schlensog, M. And Sancho, L.G. 2010. Fourteen degrees of latitude and a continent apart: comparison of lichen activitiy over two years at continental and maritime Antarctic sites. Antarctic Science 22: 681-690.

Schroeter, B., Green, T.G.A., Seppelt, R.D. and Kappen, L. 1992. Monitoring photosynthetic activity of crustose lichens using a PAM-2000 fluorescence system. Oecologia 92: 457-462.

Schroeter, B., Kappen, L., Green, T.G.A. and Seppelt, R.D. 1997. Lichens and the Antarctic environment: effects of temperature and water availability on photosynthesis. Pages 103-117 in Lyons W.B., Howard-Williams, C. and Hawes, I. (Eds.). Ecosystem processes in Antarctic ice-free landscapes: proceedings of an International Workshop on Polar Desert Ecosystems, Christchurch, New Zealand, 1-4 July 1996. The Netherlands: Balkema Press. ISBN 9054109254.

Schroeter, B. and Scheiddegger, C. 1995. Water relations in lichens at subzero temperatures: structural changes and carbon dioxide exchange in the lichen *Umbilicaria aprina* from continental Antarctica. New Phytologist 131(2): 273-285.

Seppelt, R.D. and Green, T.G.A. 1998. A bryophyte flora for southern Victoria Land, Antarctica. New Zealand Journal of Botany 36 (4): 617-635.

Seppelt, R., Turk, R., Green, T.G.A., Moser, G., Pannewitz, S., Sancho, L.G. and Schroeter, B. 2010. Lichen and moss communities of Botany Bay, Granite Harbour, Ross Sea, Antarctica. Antarctic Science 22: 691-702.

Annex 1: Bryophytes and lichens of the Botany Bay-Cape Geology region, Granite Harbour, Victoria Land, Antarctica (from Seppelt et al., 2010).

HEPATICAE (Liverwort)
[1]*Cephaloziella varians**

MUSCI (Moss)
*Bryoerythrophyllum recurvirostrum**
[2]*Bryum argenteum var. muticum*
Bryum pseudo triquetrum
*Ceratodon purpureus**
[3]*Didymodon brachyphyllus*
Grimmia plagiopodia
Hennediella heimii
Schistidium antarctici
[4]*Syntrichia sarconeurum*

LICHEN
Acarospora gwynnii
Amandinea petermannii
Buellia frigida
[5]*Buellia* cf. *papillata*
[6]*Buellia subfrigida*
Caloplaca athallina
Caloplaca citrina
Caloplaca coeruleofrigida
Caloplaca cf. *schofieldii*
Caloplaca saxicola
Candelariella flava
[7]*Carbonea vorticosa*
Lecanora expectans
Lecanor mons-nivis
Lecidea andersonii
Lecidea cancriformis
Lecidella siplei
[8]*Leproloma cacuminum*
Physcia caesia
Physcia dubia
Rhizocarpon geminatum
Rhizocarpon geographicum
Rhizoplaca melanophthalma
Rhizoplaca cf. *priestleyi*
Sarcogyne privigna
*Turgidosculum complicatulum**
Umbilicaria aprina
[9]*Xanthomendoza borealis*
Xanthoria elegans

---

[1] *Cephaloziella varians* has previously been referred to as *C. exiliflora* (Bednarek-Ochyra et al., 2000).
[2] *Bryum argenteum var. muticum* has previously been referred to as *Bryum subrotundifolium* (Ochyra et al., 2008).
[3] *Didymodon brachyphyllus* has previously been referred to as *Didymodon gelidus* (Ochyra et al., 2008).
[4] *Syntrichia sarconeurum* has previously been referred to as *Sarconeurum glaciale* (Ochyra et al., 2008).
[5] *Buellia* cf. *papillata* has previously been referred to as *Buellia grimmiae.*
[6] *Buellia subfrigida* has previously been referred to as *Aspicilia glacialis* (Seppelt et al., 1995) and *Hymenelia glacialis* (Ovstedal and Lewis Smith, 2001).
[7] *Carbonea vorticosa* has previously been referred to as *Lecidea blackburnii* (Seppelt et al., 1995).
[8] *Leproloma cacuminum* has previously been referred to as *Lepraria* sp.
[9] *Xanthomendoza borealis* has previously been referred to as *Xanthoria mawsonii* (Lindblom and Sochting, 2008).
* *The most southerly record of these species.*

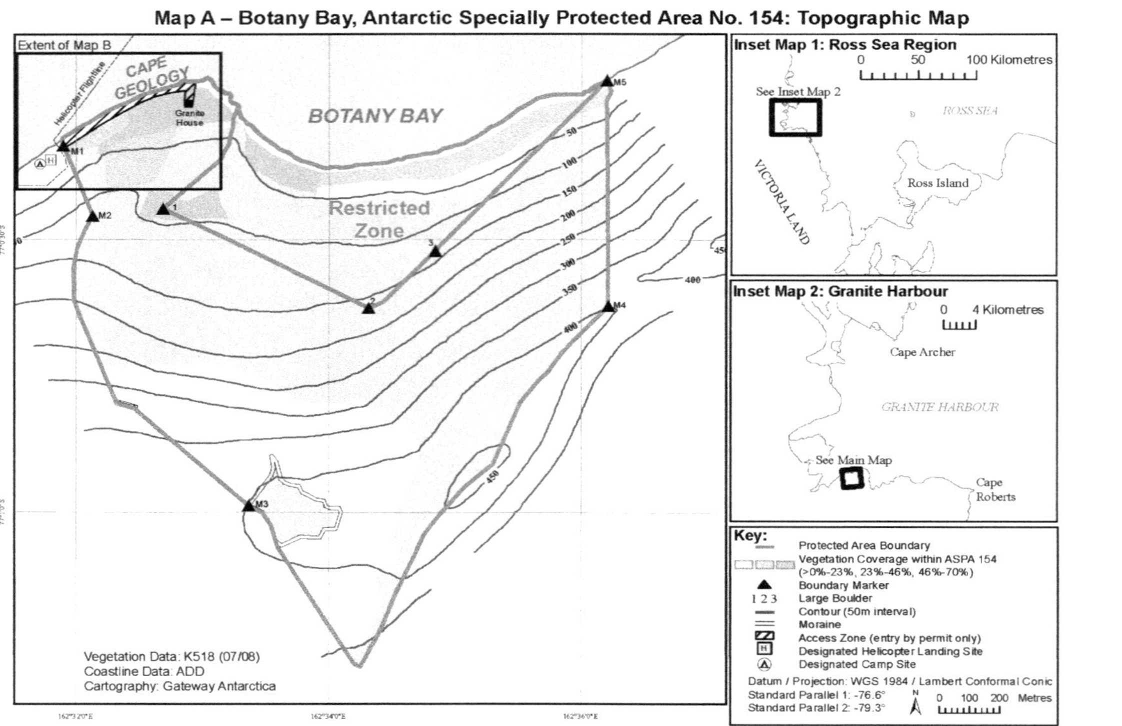
Map A – Botany Bay, Antarctic Specially Protected Area No. 154: Topographic Map
Extent of Map B
CAPE GEOLOGY
Granite House
Helicopter Flightline
BOTANY BAY
Restricted Zone
M1
M2
M3
M4
M5
Vegetation Data: K518 (07/08)
Coastline Data: ADD
Cartography: Gateway Antarctica
Inset Map 1: Ross Sea Region
0 50 100 Kilometres
See Inset Map 2
ROSS SEA
Ross Island
VICTORIA LAND
Inset Map 2: Granite Harbour
0 4 Kilometres
Cape Archer
GRANITE HARBOUR
See Main Map
Cape Roberts
Key:
Protected Area Boundary
Vegetation Coverage within ASPA 154 (>0%-23%, 23%-46%, 46%-70%)
Boundary Marker
Large Boulder
Contour (50m interval)
Moraine
Access Zone (entry by permit only)
Designated Helicopter Landing Site
Designated Camp Site
Datum / Projection: WGS 1984 / Lambert Conformal Conic
Standard Parallel 1: -76.6°
Standard Parallel 2: -79.3°
0 100 200 Metres

Map B – Botany Bay, Antarctic Specially Protected Area No. 154: Access Zone

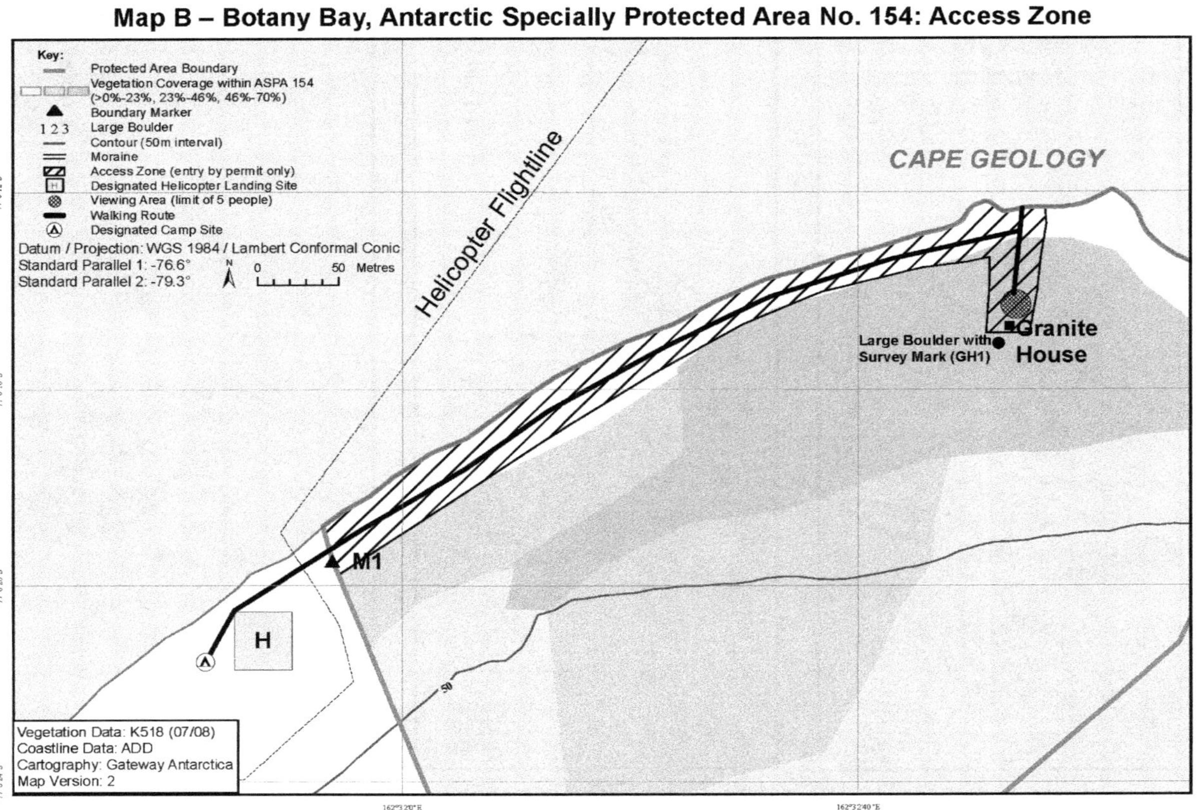

Map C – Botany Bay, Antarctic Specially Protected Area No. 154: Vegetation Density

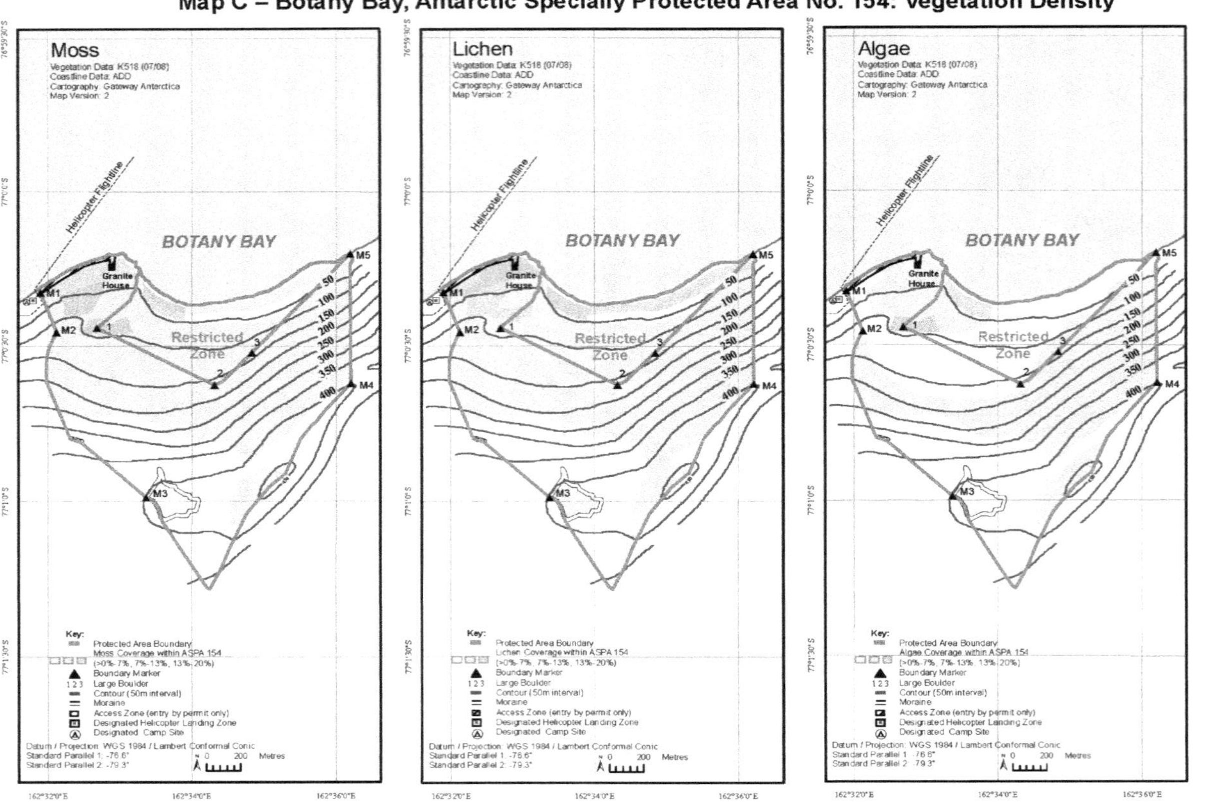

ASPA 154 Botany Bay, Cape Geology, Victoria Land

List of Labels Map A

Map A – Botany Bay, Antarctic Specially Protected Area No. 154: Topographic Map
Extent of Map B
Cape Geology
Helicopter Flightline
Granite House
Botany Bay
Restricted Zone

Vegetation Data: K518 (07/08)
Coastline Data: ADD
Cartography: Gateway Antarctica
Inset Map 1: Ross Sea region
See Inset Map 2
Ross Sea
Victoria Land
Ross Island
Inset Map 2: Granite Harbour
Cape Archer
Granite Harbour
See Main Map
Cape Roberts

Key
Protected Area Boundary
Vegetation Coverage within ASPA 154
Boundary Marker
Large Boulder
Contour (50m intervals)
Moraine
Access Zone (entry by permit only)
Designated Helicopter Landing Site
Designated Camp Site
Datum/Projection: WGS 1984/Lambert Conformal Conic
Standard Parallel 1: -76/6°
Standard Parallel 2:-79.3°

ASPA 154 Botany Bay, Cape Geology, Victoria Land

List of Labels Map B

Map B – Botany Bay, Antarctic Specially Protected Area No. 154: Access Zone
Key
Protected Area Boundary
Vegetation Coverage within ASPA 154
Boundary Marker
Large Boulder
Contour (50m intervals)
Moraine
Access Zone (entry by permit only)
Designated Helicopter Landing Site
Viewing Area (limit of 5 people)
Walking Route
Designated Camp Site
Datum/Projection: WGS 1984/Lambert Conformal Conic
Standard Parallel 1: -76/6°
Standard Parallel 2:-79.3°

Helicopter Flightline
Vegetation Data: K518 (07/08)
Coastline Data: ADD
Cartography: Gateway Antarctica
Map Version: 2

Cape Geology
Granite House
Large Boulder with Survey Mark (GH1)

ASPA 154 Botany Bay, Cape Geology, Victoria Land

List of Labels Map C

Map C – Botany Bay, Antarctic Specially Protected Area No. 154: Vegetation Density

Moss
Vegetation Data: K518 (07/08)
Coastline Data: ADD
Cartography: Gateway Antarctica
Map Version: 2
Helicopter Flightline
Granite House
Botany Bay
Restricted Zone

Key
Protected Area Boundary
Moss Coverage within ASPA 154
Boundary Marker
Large Boulder
Contour (50m intervals)
Moraine
Access Zone (entry by permit only)
Designated Helicopter Landing Site
Designated Camp Site
Datum/Projection: WGS 1984/Lambert Conformal Conic
Standard Parallel 1: -76/6°
Standard Parallel 2:-79.3°

Lichen
Vegetation Data: K518 (07/08)
Coastline Data: ADD
Cartography: Gateway Antarctica
Map Version: 2
Helicopter Flightline
Granite House
Botany Bay
Restricted Zone

Key
Protected Area Boundary
Lichen Coverage within ASPA 154
Boundary Marker
Large Boulder
Contour (50m intervals)
Moraine
Access Zone (entry by permit only)
Designated Helicopter Landing Site

Designated Camp Site
Datum/Projection: WGS 1984/Lambert Conformal Conic
Standard Parallel 1: -76/6°
Standard Parallel 2:-79.3°

Algae
Vegetation Data: K518 (07/08)
Coastline Data: ADD
Cartography: Gateway Antarctica
Map Version: 2
Helicopter Flightline
Granite House
Botany Bay
Restricted Zone

Key
Protected Area Boundary
Algae Coverage within ASPA 154
Boundary Marker
Large Boulder
Contour (50m intervals)
Moraine
Access Zone (entry by permit only)
Designated Helicopter Landing Site
Designated Camp Site
Datum/Projection: WGS 1984/Lambert Conformal Conic
Standard Parallel 1: -76/6°
Standard Parallel 2:-79.3°

Management Plan For Antarctic Specially Protected Area No. 156
LEWIS BAY, MOUNT EREBUS, ROSS ISLAND

Introduction:

An area on the lower slopes of Mount Erebus, above Lewis Bay on the north side of Ross Island, was originally declared a tomb in Recommendation XI-3 (1981) after notification by New Zealand that 257 people of several nationalities lost their lives when the DC-10 aircraft in which they were travelling crashed at this site on 28 November, 1979.

In spite of the determined and courageous actions of the New Zealand and United States Antarctic expeditions the bodies of some of those who died could not be recovered. Expressing deep sympathy with the relatives of those who died and with the Government and people of New Zealand, the tomb was declared in order to ensure that the area be left in peace. Because the site is a tomb, its values are enduring.

The Area was designated as a Specially Protected Area No. 26 by Measure 2 (1997) primarily to ensure the Area is kept inviolate as a mark of respect in remembrance and in order to protect the site's emotional values. The site was re-designated as Antarctic Specially Protected Area No. 156 by Decision 1 (2002) and a revised management plan was adopted by Measure 2 (2003). The management plan was reviewed and continued without changes at CEP XI (2008).

1. Description of values to be protected

The designated Area is the crash site of Air New Zealand flight TE-901, on the slopes of the north side of Mount Erebus, Ross Island. The Area encompasses the crash site and the surrounding glacial ice, 2 km to either side of this site down to the sea, and includes the airspace above this region to an altitude of 1000 m (3280 ft) with the exception of a 200 m wide air access 'corridor' along the coastline. The remains of the aircraft and the bodies of some of those who died that could not be recovered remain in the Area now designated as a tomb.

In late 1979 a six-foot Oregon timber cross was erected close to the crash site as a memorial to those who lost their lives. After damage by wind this cross was replaced on 30 January 1987 with a cross of stainless steel, located on a rocky promontory overlooking and approximately 3 km from the crash site (Figure 1). This site is not part of the protected area, but was designated as Historic Site and Monument (HSM) No. 73 in recognition of the commemorative and symbolic values of the cross. In November 2009, a stainless steel koru time capsule was installed next to the cross containing messages from the victim's families.

Based on the Environmental Domains Analysis for Antarctica (Resolution 3 (2008)) Lewis Bay is located within Environment O *West Antarctic Ice Sheet* (also includes inland Coats Land, Taylor Dome, Ross Island ice cap).

2. Aims and objectives

Management at Lewis Bay aims to:

- avoid degradation of, or substantial risk to, the values of the Area by preventing unnecessary human disturbance to the Area;
- ensure the crash site is kept inviolate and prevent unnecessary human disturbance to the Area;
- allow visits to the nearby site of the memorial cross for the purposes of commemoration or to pay respects;
- allow visits for purposes in support of the aims of the management plan.

3. Management activities

The following management activities are to be undertaken to protect the values of the Area:

- All pilots operating in the region shall be informed of the location, boundaries and restrictions applying to entry and over-flight of the Area;
- The Area shall be visited as necessary to assess whether it continues to serve the purposes for which it was designated and to ensure the management activities are adequate;
- National Antarctic Programmes operating in the region shall consult together with a view to ensuring the above management activities are implemented.

4. Period of designation

Designated for an indefinite period.

5. Maps

Map A: Lewis Bay protected area topographic map. Note: Map A is derived from the Antarctic Digital Database (ADD) Version 1.0, 1993, which was prepared to a base scale of 1:250,000 under the auspices of SCAR. Positional corrections have been applied to the ADD source data using 1993 and 1995 Global Positioning System (GPS) data and 1993 aerial photography. Accuracy of the map remains approximate pending publication of new and accurate Ross Island maps at 1:50,000 scale. The geographical coordinates of the crash site and other features are considered accurate to within approximately 100–200 m horizontally. Elevation data are considered accurate to approximately 100 m vertically.
Specification: Projection: Lambert conformal conic; Standard parallels: 1st 79° 18' 00" S; 2nd 76° 42' 00"S; Central Meridian: 167° 30' 00" E; Latitude of Origin: 78° 01' 16.211" S; Spheroid: GRS80.

6. Description of the Area

6(i) Geographical coordinates, boundary markers and natural features
The designated Area on the slopes of Mount Erebus (Map A) encompasses the crash site, centred on 77° 25' 29"S, 167° 28' 30"E, at an elevation of 520 m (1,720 ft). The Area includes the surrounding glacial ice 2 km to either side of the crash site. The Area extends as a 4 km wide 'rectangle' down to the sea, and includes the airspace above this region to an altitude of 1,000 m (3,280 ft), with the exception of a 200 m wide air access 'corridor' along the coastline.

The west boundary of the Area is the 167° 23' 33" E meridian; the east boundary of the Area is the 167° 33' 27" E meridian. The south boundary is the 77° 26' 33" S parallel, while the north boundary is defined by the coastline (Map A).

The aircraft's primary impact occurred at an elevation of 446.7 m. Debris from the wreckage was spread up-slope 570 m from that point, over an area 120 m wide to an elevation of 580 m (1,900 ft). Much of the aircraft wreckage is now buried in ice and is slowly moving down-slope with the glacier to the sea. The bodies of some of those who died could not be recovered and remain in the Area.

Boundary markers have not been placed to mark the Area for two reasons: their presence is considered detrimental to the inviolate values of the site, and their maintenance would be impractical on the moving glacier.

6(ii) Access to the area
Land vehicles are prohibited within the Area and access shall be by foot or by helicopter. Overflight of the Area is prohibited below 1,000 m (3,280 ft) above sea level with the exception of a 200 m wide air access 'corridor' along the coastline which allows transit of aircraft through the Area at times when visibility or conditions make avoidance of the Area otherwise impractical. No special restrictions apply to the air routes or landing sites used to move to and from the Area by helicopter when access is permitted.

6(iii) Location of structures within and adjacent the Area
The stainless steel memorial cross (HSM No. 73) is located on a rock outcrop (77° 26' 38"S, 167° 33' 43"E, at an elevation of 810 m (2,660 ft)) approximately 3 km southeast of the crash site, and is a symbol of the special significance of the Area. A stainless steel koru time capsule was installed next to the cross containing messages from the victim's families in November 2009. No other structures exist within or near the Area. Debris from the aircraft remains *in situ*.

6(iv) Location of other protected areas in the vicinity
The nearest protected areas to Lewis Bay are:

- ASPA 130 Tramway Ridge, Mount Erebus, 15 km south near the summit of Mount Erebus;

- ASPA 116 Caughley Beach, New College Valley, Cape Bird approximately 35 km northwest on Ross Island;
- ASPA 121 Cape Royds and ASPA 157 Backdoor Bay, approximately 35 km west on Ross Island; and
- ASPA 124 Cape Crozier, 40 km to the east on Ross Island.

6(v) Special zones within the Area
There are no special zones within the Area.

7. Terms and conditions for entry permits

7(i) General permit conditions
Entry into the Area is prohibited except in accordance with a Permit issued by an appropriate national authority. Conditions for issuing a Permit to enter the Area are that:

- it is issued only for compelling reasons that are in support of the aims of the Management Plan;
- the actions permitted are in accordance with the Management Plan;
- the actions permitted will not compromise the values of the Area;
- the Permit shall be issued for a finite period;
- the Permit, or an authorized copy, shall be carried when in the Area; and
- a visit report shall be supplied to the authority named in the Permit.

7(ii) Access to, and movement within or over, the Area
Land vehicles are prohibited within the Area and access shall be by foot or by helicopter. Overflight of the Area is prohibited below 1,000 m (3,280 ft) above sea level, except for essential access related to the values for which this site is protected, or for inspection and monitoring of the site. No special restrictions apply to the air routes used to move to and from the Area by helicopter when access is permitted. At all other times, a 200 m wide air access 'corridor' is located along the coastline which allows transit of aircraft through the Area at times when visibility or conditions make avoidance of the Area otherwise impractical (Map A). Use of helicopter smoke grenades within the Area is prohibited unless absolutely necessary for safety, and then these should be retrieved.

7(iii) Activities which may be conducted within the Area
All visits to the Area for any purpose shall be made recognising the principal values to be protected in the Area, and as far as possible the Area should be left in peace.

Visits may be made for essential management activities including inspection to ensure the values of the Area are being maintained and to determine if materials at the site present a problem by emergence from the ice and then possible wind dispersal, or for securing or removal of such items. Visits may also be made for removal of materials introduced into the Area subsequent to its designation, if appropriate.

7(iv) Installation, modification or removal of structures
No new structures are to be erected within the Area, except as specified in a Permit. It is prohibited to modify or remove any structure that was present within the Area at the time of special protection designation.

7(v) Location of field camps
Camping is prohibited within the Area, unless under exceptional circumstances for management. Where camping is required for such activities, the site selected shall be no closer than 200 m from the location of the wreckage at the time of the visit (77° 25' 29"S, 167° 28' 30"E).

7(vi) Restrictions on materials and organisms which may be brought into the Area
It is prohibited to introduce any materials into the Area. Smoke grenades used when absolutely necessary for safety of air operations should be retrieved.

7(vii) Taking of, or harmful interference with, native flora or fauna
Taking of, or harmful interference with, native flora or fauna is prohibited except in accordance with a permit issued in accordance with Annex II of the Protocol on Environmental Protection to the Antarctic Treaty.

Where taking or harmful interference with animals is involved this should, as a minimum standard, be in accordance with the SCAR Code of Conduct for the Use of Animals for Scientific Purposes in Antarctica.

7(viii) The collection or removal of materials not brought into the Area by the Permit holder
Unless specifically authorized by permit, visitors to the Area are prohibited from interfering with or from handling, taking or damaging anything not brought into the Area by the Permit holder. If it has been determined that materials at the site are emerging from the ice and dispersal by wind presents a management problem, such materials should be appropriately disposed of with due regard to the families of victims and according to national procedures. Materials introduced into the Area subsequent to designation may be removed unless the impact of removal is likely to be greater than leaving the material *in situ.* If this is the case the appropriate authority should be notified.

7(ix) Disposal of waste
All wastes, including all human wastes, shall be removed from the Area.

7(x) Measures that may be necessary to continue to meet the aims of the Management Plan
Permits may be granted to enter the Area for compelling reasons that are in support of the aims of the Management Plan. To help maintain the site's emotional value, visits to the Area should be minimised as far as practicable.

7(xi) Requirements for reports
The principal permit holder for each visit to the Area shall submit a report to the appropriate national authority as soon as practicable, and no later than six months after the visit has been completed. Such visit reports should include, as applicable, the information identified in the recommended visit report form [contained in Appendix 4 of the Guide to the Preparation of Management Plans for Antarctic Specially Protected Areas appended to Resolution 2 (1998)].

If appropriate, the national authority should also forward a copy of the visit report to the Party that proposed the Management Plan, to assist in managing the Area and reviewing the Management Plan.

Parties should, wherever possible, deposit originals or copies of such original visit reports in a publicly accessible archive to maintain a record of usage, for the purpose of any review of the Management Plan and in organising the use of the Area.

Figure 1: Memorial cross for the 1979 Mount Erebus crash victims (HSM No.73) and koru time capsule (installed in November 2009), overlooking the crash site (© Antarctica New Zealand Pictorial Collection: K322 09/10).

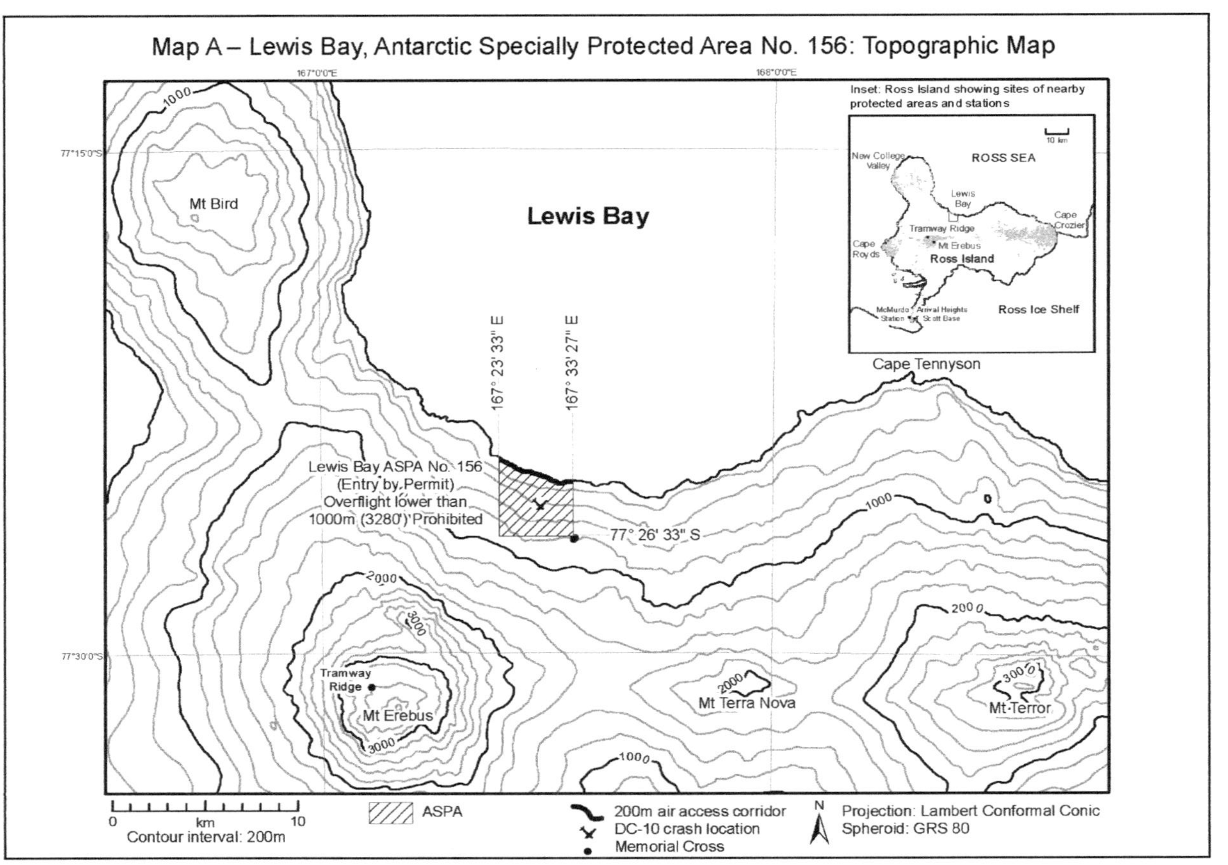
Map A – Lewis Bay, Antarctic Specially Protected Area No. 156: Topographic Map
167°0'0"E
168°0'0"E
77°15'0"S
77°30'0"S
Mt Bird
Lewis Bay
Inset: Ross Island showing sites of nearby protected areas and stations
10 km
New College Valley
ROSS SEA
Lewis Bay
Cape Crozier
Tramway Ridge
Mt Erebus
Cape Royds
Ross Island
McMurdo Station
Arrival Heights
Scott Base
Ross Ice Shelf
Cape Tennyson
167° 23' 33" E
167° 33' 27" E
Lewis Bay ASPA No. 156
(Entry by Permit)
Overflight lower than
1000m (3280') Prohibited
77° 26' 33" S
1000
2000
3000
Tramway Ridge
Mt Erebus
Mt Terra Nova
Mt Terror
0
km
10
Contour interval: 200m
ASPA
200m air access corridor
DC-10 crash location
Memorial Cross
N
Projection: Lambert Conformal Conic
Spheroid: GRS 80

ASPA 156 Lewis Bay, Mount Erebus, Ross Island

List of Labels Map A

Map A – Lewis Bay, Antarctic Specially Protected Area No. 156: Topographic Map
Lewis Bay
Lewis Bay ASPA No. 156
Entry by Permit
Overflight lower than 1000m (3280') Prohibited
Tramway Ridge
Mount Erebus
Mt Terra Nova
Mt Terror
Cape Tennyson

Inset: Ross Island showing sites of nearby protected areas and stations
Ross Sea
New College Valley
Lewis Bay
Tramway Ridge
Mt Erebus
Ross Island
Cape Royds
McMurdo Station
Arrival Heights
Scott Base
Ross Ice Shelf
Cape Crozier

Contour interval: 200m
ASPA
200m air access corridor
DC-10 crash location
Memorial Cross
Projection: Lambert Conformal Conic
Spheroid: GRS 80

Management Plan for Antarctic Specially Protected Area No 160

FRAZIER ISLANDS, WINDMILL ISLANDS, WILKES LAND, EAST ANTARCTICA

Introduction

The Frazier Islands consists of a group of three islands located approximately 16 km offshore from Australia's Casey station, in East Antarctica (see Map A). The islands support the largest of only four known breeding colonies of southern giant petrels *Macronectes giganteus* on continental Antarctica, and were designated as an Antarctic Specially Protected Area under Measure 2 (2003) for the sanctuary of the birds. The management plan for the Area was revised under Measure 13 (2008).

Following their discovery in 1955, the southern giant petrel colonies at the Frazier Islands were visited intermittently during the period mid-January to late March. The aim of these visits was usually the banding of southern giant petrel chicks. Weather permitting, counts of the chicks present were made but were often restricted to Nelly Island. Thus, the early data available do not offer the information needed for an analysis of possible changes in the status of the total population. In more recent years, occupied nests were counted in December, usually covering all three islands. The indication is that the breeding population, especially at Dewart Island, may be increasing.

Apart from visits for seabird observations, the Frazier Islands have been visited very infrequently. On average a visit for seabird observations have occurred every two years since the late 1950s (see Appendix 1). In the mid-1980s, a formal management strategy was implemented to minimise human disturbance to breeding colonies of southern giant petrels in the vicinity of Australia's Antarctic stations. The Australian Antarctic Division restricted access by Australian Antarctic program participants so that census visits occurred once in every three- to five-year period and implemented tight administrative controls over visits for other purposes. The census interval was considered an appropriate compromise between the risk of disturbance to breeding birds from monitoring activities and the need to obtain population data. Current thinking suggests it is desirable to provide for more frequent censuses, if conducted in an appropriate manner, to allow more detailed understanding of population status and trends.

A more recent ostensible increase in the breeding population of southern giant petrels at the Frazier Islands, combined with the apparent positive effects of the existing protective measures, suggests that continued and formalised protection of southern giant petrel breeding colonies is warranted. Long-term protection and monitoring of southern giant petrels at the Frazier Islands will contribute to the development of appropriate regional and global conservation strategies for the species and will provide information for comparisons with populations elsewhere.

This revised management plan reaffirms the values of the original designation and accords with Annex V of the Protocol on Environmental Protection.

1. Description of values to be protected

The Area is primarily designated to protect the breeding colony of southern giant petrels, which is the largest known in the continental Antarctic.

In the late 1980s, the world breeding population of southern giant petrels was estimated at 38,000 pairs. Recent analysis of trend data for the global population over the past three generations (64 years) gives a best case estimate of a 17 % increase and a worst case scenario of a 7.2 % decline; declines consequently do not approach the threshold for classification as Vulnerable on the IUCN Red List of Threatened Species and the species has been down-listed from Near Threatened to Least Concern (BirdLife International, 2012).

The southern giant petrel is listed in Annex 1 of the Agreement on the Conservation of Albatrosses and Petrels (ACAP), a multilateral agreement which seeks to conserve albatrosses and petrels by coordinating international activity to mitigate known threats to their populations, and in Appendix II of the Convention on the Conservation of Migratory Species of Wild Animals.

In East Antarctica, southern giant petrels are uncommon as they are at the southern limit of their distribution range. The most recent estimate of the total population at the Frazier Islands was 237 breeding pairs in 2011. Colonies are found on all three of the islands in the group (Nelly, Dewart and Charlton Islands), the largest being located on Dewart Island. In 2011, automatic cameras were temporarily installed on Nelly Island to establish the breeding chronology and success of the southern giant petrels (Map B).

The Frazier Islands are one of only four known breeding localities of southern giant petrels around the coastline of continental Antarctica and are the only known site in nearly 3000 km of coastline between Davis station and Dumont d'Urville. The other three continental breeding colonies are located near the Australian stations of Mawson (Giganteus Island, Rookery Islands, ASPA 102) and Davis (Hawker Island, ASPA 167), and near the French station Dumont d'Urville (Pointe-Géologie Archipelago, ASPA 120). The southern giant petrels on the Antarctic continent comprise less than 1% of the global breeding population. The current population for continental Antarctica is estimated at approximately 300 pairs, comprised of 2-4 pairs on Giganteus Island (2007), approximately 45 pairs on Hawker Island (2010), 8-9 pairs at Pointe Géologie archipelago (Terre Adélie) (2005) and 237 pairs on the Frazier Islands (2011). However, incidental observations at the coast near Mawson station indicate there may be additional colonies that have not been discovered yet.

The Area also supports breeding colonies of Adélie penguins and several other species of flying birds.

2. Aims and objectives

Management of the Frazier Islands aims to:

- minimise human disturbance to the breeding colonies of southern giant petrels to assist further the protection of the population in the wild;
- conserve the Frazier Islands as a reference area for future comparative studies with other breeding populations of southern giant petrels; and
- minimise the possibility of the introduction of alien plants, animals and microbes to the Frazier Islands.

3. Management activities

The following management activities shall be undertaken to protect the values of the Area:

- research visits to assess population levels and trends of the southern giant petrel colony and/or other wildlife shall be permitted. Wherever feasible, preference shall be given to activities and methodologies which minimise disturbance to the breeding colony (e.g. use of automated cameras);
- where practicable the Area shall be visited outside the breeding season of southern giant petrels (i.e. during the period mid-April to mid-September) as necessary, to assess whether

it continues to serve the purposes for which it was designated and to ensure that management activities are adequate;

- information about the location of the Area and the restrictions that apply shall be produced and prominently displayed at Casey station. Copies of this management plan shall be available at the station. Informative material and the management plan shall be provided to ships visiting the vicinity;
- the management plan shall be reviewed at least every five years and updated/modified as required.

4. Period of designation

Designated for an indefinite period

5. Maps

- Map A: Antarctic Specially Protected Areas, Windmill Islands, East Antarctica.
- Map B: Antarctic Specially Protected Area No. 160 Frazier Islands – Topography and Bird Distribution.

Map Specifications:

Projection: UTM Zone 49

Horizontal Datum: WGS84

6. Description of the Area

6(i) Geographical co-ordinates, boundary markers and natural features

General description

The Frazier Islands are located at latitude 66°14'S, longitude 110°10'E (Map A). The three islands (Nelly, Dewart and Charlton) lie in the eastern part of Vincennes Bay approximately 16km to the west north west of Casey station. Nelly Island is the largest of the three islands (approximately 0.35km^2 in area), and was named for the presence of several colonies of southern giant petrels or "Nellies". The Area comprises the entire terrestrial area of the three islands, with the seaward boundary at the low water mark (Map B). The total area of the Antarctic Specially Protected Area is approximately 0.6km^2. There are no boundary markers.

Southern Giant Petrels

The breeding season for southern giant petrels at the Frazier Islands usually commences in late October to mid November, and extends through to April when the birds depart northward for the winter. Banded chicks from the Frazier Islands dispersed throughout the Southern Hemisphere and have previously been recovered in New Zealand, South America, Easter Island, and South Africa within nine months of departure.

In the mid 1980s, a management strategy was implemented for all three southern giant petrels breeding localities in the vicinity of the Australian stations, to minimise human disturbance. Previously the Australian Antarctic Division restricted census visits to one in every three to five year period and implemented tight administrative controls over all other visits. At this time, this level of visitation was considered an appropriate compromise between the risk of disturbing the birds and the need to obtain meaningful population data. However, this management regime impacted on the level of visitation needed to assess population levels (and trends) and did not appear to significantly benefit the breeding success of the southern giant petrels. With the development of new technology (such as automated cameras), detailed information can now be obtained with little or no human presence during the breeding period.

In December 2011, 80 breeding pairs were observed on Nelly Island including two banded birds, 130 breeding pairs on Dewart Island and 27 breeding pairs on Charlton Island. The four automatic cameras temporarily installed on Nelly Island will assist with establishing/understanding key breeding parameters (Map B).

Other birds

Nelly Island supports the largest and most varied avian community of the three islands, with records indicating that snow petrels (*Pagodroma nivea*), cape petrels (*Daption capense*), Antarctic petrels (*Thalassoica antarctica*), Wilson's storm-petrels (*Oceanites oceanicus*), southern fulmars (*Fulmarus glacialoides*), and South Polar skuas (*Catharacta maccormicki*) all nest on the island. South Polar skua nests have also been observed on Dewart Island (Appendix 2, Map B).

In 1961/62, 100 Adélie penguin (*Pygoscelis adeliae*) nests were reported in one colony on Nelly Island. During the 1989/90 season, three colonies were recorded on the north-west ridge of Nelly Island with a total of 554 nests. The increase corresponds with those recorded for most other Adélie penguin populations in the Windmill Islands region during the period from 1959/60 to 1989/90. In the 2001/02 season, approximately 1,000 pairs were estimated to be nesting on Nelly Island. A brief inspection of the Adélie penguin colonies in 2005/06 suggested that the breeding population continues to increase.

Marine mammals

Recorded sightings of marine mammals at the Frazier Islands are scarce. In 1968 three Weddell seals (*Leptonychotes weddellii*) were observed on an ice floe located between Nelly and Dewart Islands. Orcas (killer whale: *Orcinus orca*) have been also sighted offshore from the islands, including a large pod in late 2011. A few leopard seals (*Hydrurga leptonyx*) were sighted on sea ice near Nelly Island and a small number of Weddell seals were recorded on the sea ice near the Frazier Islands in the 2001/02 season (Appendix 2).

Vegetation

Vegetation recorded at Nelly Island comprises at least 11 species, including lichens *Buellia frigida*, *Usnea antarctica*, *Rhizoplaca melanophthalma*, *Candelariella flava*, a terrestrial alga *Prasiola crispa*, an indeterminate green crust which is thought to be 'a mixture of fungal hyphae and green alga *Desmococcus olivaceus*', and several species of snow algae including *Chlorococcum* sp., *Chloromonas polyptera*, *Chlorosarcina antarctica*, *Prasiococcus calcarius* (Appendix 2). There are no published records of terrestrial invertebrates on the Frazier Islands; however, no surveys have been undertaken.

Geology and geography

The topography of the Frazier Islands is characterised by steep cliffs rising from the sea. The highest peak on Nelly Island is approximately 65 metres. There is a broad 'U' shaped ice-filled valley on both Nelly and Dewart Islands.

The geology of the Frazier Islands is typical of the Windmill Islands group and is characterised by the layered schists and finely crenulated gneisses of the Windmill metamorphics. The geological character of the Frazier Islands developed as a result of two phases of metamorphosis at 1400-1310 Ma and about 1200 Ma of pre-existing volcanics, greywacke and shale. On Nelly Island there are steep cliffs of biotite and gneiss. A red sandstone erratic is located in the 'U' shaped valley on Nelly Island below the 30m contour. Highly polished glacial striae in the gneisses provide evidence of recent glaciation and indicate the former direction of ice flow of 265° and 280° T. Surface sediments consist of fine gravelly sand located in bedrock depressions.

Climate

The climate at the Frazier Islands is characteristic of that experienced at the Windmill Islands and other Antarctic coastal locations in the region. At Casey station, located 16 kilometres to the east south east of the Frazier Islands group, mean temperatures are 0.3°C for the warmest month and -14.9°C for the coldest month. Precipitation is low and the high albedo of the exposed rock surfaces results in persistent ice-free areas that provide attractive nesting sites for the avifauna.

Environmental domains analysis

The Frazier Islands are not classified in accordance with the Environmental Domains Analysis for Antarctica (Resolution 3 (2008)).

Antarctic Conservation Biogeographic Regions

Based on the Antarctic Conservation Biogeographic Regions (Resolution 6 (2012)) the Frazier Islands are located within Biogeographic Region 7 *East Antarctica.*

6(ii) Access to the Area

Depending on sea ice conditions, access to the vicinity of the Frazier Islands can be gained by small boat, in accordance with section 7(ii) of this plan. Sea ice conditions are usually too unstable for over sea-ice access by vehicles.

6(iii) Location of structures within and adjacent to the Area

There are no permanent structures within or adjacent to the Area and none are to be erected. At the time of writing four automatic cameras were temporarily located in proximity to the southern giant petrel colony, for the purposes of ongoing population monitoring (Map B).

6(iv) Location of other protected areas in the vicinity

The following Protected Areas are located on the Budd Coast near the Frazier Islands (see Map A):

- ASPA No 135, North-east Bailey Peninsula (66°17'S, 110°32'E), approximately 16km to the east-south-east.
- ASPA No 136, Clark Peninsula (66°15'S, 110°36'E), approximately 15km to the east-south-east; and
- ASPA No 103, Ardery Island and Odbert Island (66°22'S, 110°30'E), approximately 20km to the south-east.

6(v) Special zones within the Area

There are no special zones within the Area.

7. Terms and conditions for entry permits

7(i) General permit conditions

Entry to the Area is prohibited except in accordance with a Permit issued by an appropriate national authority. Conditions for issuing a Permit to enter the Area are that:

- it is issued for compelling scientific reasons which cannot be served elsewhere, or for reasons essential to the management of the Area;
- the actions permitted are in accordance with this management plan;
- the activities permitted will give due consideration via the environmental impact assessment process to the continued protection of the environmental values of the Area;
- the Permit shall be issued for a finite period; and
- the Permit shall be carried when in the Area.

Additional conditions, consistent with the objectives and provisions of the management plan, may be included by the issuing authority. The principal Permit Holder for each Permit issued should be required to submit to the Permit issuing authority a visit report detailing all activities undertaken within the Area, and include all census data obtained during the visit.

7(ii) Access to, and movement within, or over the Area

- Vehicles are prohibited within the Area and all movement within the Area should be on foot.
- The only permitted access to the Frazier Islands is by watercraft. Boats used to visit the islands must be left at the shoreline and movement within the Area is by foot only. Only personnel who are required to carry out scientific/management work in the Area should leave the landing site;
- Any movement within the Area is to be consistent with the minimum approach distances to nesting birds specified in Appendix 3. Persons shall not approach closer than is necessary to obtain census data or biological data from any nesting southern giant petrels, and in no case closer than 20m;
- To reduce disturbance to wildlife, noise levels including verbal communication are to be kept to a minimum. The use of motor-driven tools and any other activity likely to generate noise and thereby cause disturbance to nesting birds is prohibited within the Area during the breeding period for southern giant petrels (1 October to 30 April);
- Landing of aircraft in the Area is prohibited at any time; and
- Sea-ice conditions are usually too unstable to permit aircraft landings, however permission to land a single-engined helicopter adjacent to the Area may be granted for essential scientific or management purposes when sea-ice conditions are suitable and only if it can be demonstrated that disturbance will be minimal, at a distance of no less than 930m from any breeding colony of bird or seal (emergencies exempted). Only personnel who are required to carry out work in the Area should leave the helicopter;
- Overflights of the islands during the breeding season is prohibited, except where essential for scientific or management purposes. Such overflights are to be at an altitude of no less than 930 m (3050 ft) for single-engined helicopters and fixed-wing aircraft, and no less than 1500 m (5000 ft) for twin-engined helicopters;
- Clothing (particularly all footwear) and field equipment shall be thoroughly cleaned before entering the Area.

7(iii) Activities which may be conducted within the Area

Permits to enter the Area during the non-breeding period for southern giant petrels (1 May to 30 September) may be issued for compelling scientific research that cannot be undertaken elsewhere, or for essential management purposes consistent with the objectives and provisions of this management plan. Permits are only to be issued for activities that will not jeopardise the ecological or scientific values of the Area, or interfere with existing scientific studies.

Permits to enter the Area during the breeding period for southern giant petrels (1 October to 30 April) may be issued for the purpose of conducting censuses. The Permit issuing authority is to refer to the provision under the first dot point of section 3 of this management plan when issuing Permits. Wherever practicable, censuses are to be conducted from outside the giant petrel colonies. In most cases there are vantage points from where the nesting giant petrels may be counted. Access to the Area should be limited to the minimum amount of time and personnel reasonably required to undertake the census. Boat operators and other support personnel should remain at the landing site for safety reasons.

7(iv) Installation, modification, or removal of structures

- No new structures are to be erected within the Area, or scientific equipment installed, except for compelling scientific or management reasons and for a pre-established period, as specified in a permit.
- Permanent structures or installations are prohibited with the exception of permanent survey markers.
- All markers, structures or scientific equipment installed in the Area must be clearly identified by country, name of the principal investigator or agency, year of installation and date of expected removal.
- All such items should be free of organisms, propagules (e.g. seeds, eggs) and non-sterile soil, and be made of materials that can withstand the environmental conditions and pose minimal risk of contamination of the Area.
- Installation (including site selection), maintenance, modification or removal of structures and equipment shall be undertaken in a manner that minimises disturbance to the values of the Area.
- All temporary structures and installations must be removed when they are no longer required, or on the expiry of the permit, whichever is the earlier.
- Removal of specific structures or equipment for which the permit has expired shall be the responsibility of the authority which granted the original permit and shall be a condition of the Permit.

7(v) Location of field camps

Camping is prohibited in the Area except in an emergency.

7(vi) Restrictions on materials and organisms which may be brought into the Area

In addition to the requirements of the Protocol on Environmental Protection to the Antarctic Treaty, restrictions on materials and organisms which may be brought into the area are:

- the deliberate introduction of animals, plant material, micro-organisms and non-sterile soil into the Area shall not be permitted. Precautions shall be taken to prevent the accidental introduction of animals, plant material, micro-organisms and non-sterile soil from other biologically distinct regions (within or beyond the Antarctic Treaty area).
- no poultry products, including dried food containing egg powder, are to be taken into the Area.
- fuel or other chemicals shall not be stored in the Area. Boat refuelling is permitted at shoreline landing sites. A small amount of fuel is permitted for an emergency stove and must be handled in a way that minimises the risk of their accidental introduction into the environment. Any chemical which may be introduced for compelling scientific purposes as authorised in a Permit shall be removed from the Area, at or before the conclusion of the activity for which the Permit was granted. The use of radio-nuclides or stable isotopes is prohibited:

- materials introduced into the Area shall be for a stated period only and shall be removed by the end of that stated period:
- no herbicides or pesticides are to be brought into the Area.

7(vii) Taking of, or harmful interference with, native flora and fauna

Taking of, or harmful interference with, native flora and fauna, is prohibited unless specifically authorised by permit issued in accordance with Article 3 of Annex II to the Protocol on Environmental Protection to the Antarctic Treaty.

Disturbance of southern giant petrels should be avoided at all times. Visitors should be alert to changes in wildlife behaviour, especially changes in posture or vocalisation. If birds are showing signs of wanting to leave the nest, all persons shall retreat immediately.

7(viii) The collection or removal of material not brought into the Area by the permit holder

Material may only be collected or removed from the Area as authorised in a Permit and should be limited to the minimum necessary to meet scientific or management needs.

Material of human origin likely to compromise the values of the Area, which was not brought into the Area by the Permit Holder or otherwise authorised, may be removed unless the impact of the removal is likely to be greater than leaving the material *in situ*. If such material is found, the appropriate national authority must be notified. Where possible, photographic documentation should be obtained and included with site visit report.

7(ix) Disposal of waste

No wastes, including human wastes, are to be deposited or left in the Area.

7(x) Measures that may be necessary to continue to meet the aims of the management plan

A census of southern giant petrels should be conducted at least once in each 5 year period. Censuses of other species may be undertaken during these visits provided no additional disturbance is caused to the southern giant petrels.

All GPS data obtained for specific sites of long-term monitoring shall be registered in the Antarctic Master Directory, through the appropriate national authority.

7(xi) Requirements for reports

Parties should ensure that the principal Permit Holder for each permit issued submits to the appropriate national authority a report on activities undertaken. Such reports should include, as appropriate, the information identified in the Visit Report form contained the *Guide to the Preparation of Management Plans for Antarctic Specially Protected Areas.* Parties should maintain a record of such activities and, in the Annual Exchange of Information, should provide summary descriptions of activities conducted by persons subject to their jurisdiction in sufficient detail to allow evaluation of the effectiveness of the Plan of Management. Parties should, wherever possible, deposit originals or copies of such original reports in a publicly accessible archive to maintain a record of usage, for the purpose of any review of the management plan and in organising the scientific use of the Area. A copy of the report should be forwarded to the Party responsible for development of the management plan to assist in management of the Area, and monitoring of bird populations. Additionally, visit reports should provide detailed information on census data, locations of any new colonies or nests not previously recorded, a brief summary of research findings and copies of photographs taken of the Area.

8. Supporting documentation

Agreement on the Conservation of Albatrosses and Petrels. 2012. ACAP Species assessment: Southern Giant Petrel *Macronectes giganteus*. Downloaded from http://www.acap.aq on 25 September 2012.

ANARE (1968) Unpublished data. Birdlife International (2000) *Threatened birds of the world.* Barcelona and Cambridge U. K: Lynx Edicions and Birdlife International.

BirdLife International (2012) *Macronectes giganteus*. In: IUCN 2012. IUCN Red List of Threatened Species. Version 2012.2. Downloaded from www.iucnredlist.org on 21/11/2012.

BirdLife International (2012) Species factsheet: *Macronectes giganteus*. Downloaded from http://www.birdlife.org on 26/09/2012.

Blight, D.F., Oliver, R. L. Aspects of the Geologic History of the Windmill Islands, Antarctica in Craddock C. (ed.) (1982) *Antarctic Geoscience*. University of Wisconsin Press, Madison: 445-454.

Cooper, J., Woehler, E.J., Belbin, L. (2000) Guest editorial. Selecting Antarctic Specially Protected Areas: Important Bird Areas can help. *Antarctic Science* 12: 129.

Cowan, A.N. (1981) Size variation in the snow petrel. *Notornis* 28: 169-188. Cowan, A.N. (1979) giant petrels at Casey. *Australian Bird Watcher* 8: 66-67.

Creuwels, J.C.S., Stark, J.S., Woehler, E.J., Van Franeker, J.A., Ribic, C.A. (2005) Monitoring of a Southern giant petrel Macronectes giganteus population on the Frazier Islands, Wilkes Land, Antarctica. *Polar Biology* 28:483–493

Croxall, J.P., Steele, W.K., McInnes, S.J., Prince, P.A. (1995) Breeding Distribution of the snow petrel *Pagodroma nivea*. *Marine Ornithology* 23: 69-99.

Environment Australia (2001) *Recovery Plan for Albatrosses and Giant Petrels.* Prepared by Wildlife Scientific Advice, Natural Heritage Division in consultation with the Albatross and Giant Petrel Recovery Team, Canberra.

Environmental Code of Conduct for Australian Field Activities, Australian Antarctic Division.

Garnett, S.T., Crowley, G.M. (2000) *The Action Plan for Australian Birds 2000*. Commonwealth of Australia, Environment Australia, Canberra

Goodwin, I.D. (1993) Holocene Deglaciation, Sea-Level Change, and the Emergence of the Windmill Islands, Budd Coast, Antarctica. *Quaternary Research* 40: 70-80.

Ingham, S.E. (1959) Banding of Giant Petrels by the Australian National Antarctic Research Expeditions, 1955-58. *Emu* 59: 189-200.

IUCN (2001) *IUCN Red List Categories: Version 3.1.* Prepared by the IUCN Species Survival Commission. IUCN, Gland, Switzerland and Cambridge, UK.

Jouventin, P., Weimerskirch, H. (1991) Changes in the population size and demography of southern seabirds: management implications. In: Perrins, C.M., Lebreton, J.-D. and Hirons, G.J.M. *Bird population studies: Relevance to conservation and management.* Oxford University Press: 297-314.

Law, P. (1958) Australian Coastal Exploration in Antarctica. *The Geographical Journal* CXXIV: 151-162.

Mackinlay, S.J. (1997) *A Management Zoning System for Casey Station and the Windmill Islands, East Antarctica.* Project report for the MAppSc degree in Environmental Management, School of Geography, University of New South Wales.

Melick, D.R., Hovenden. M.J., Seppelt, R.D. (1994) Phytogeography of bryophyte and lichen vegetation in the Windmill Islands, Wilkes Land, Continental Antarctica. *Vegetatio* 111: 71-87.

Micol, T., Jouventin, P. (2001) Long-term population trends in seven Antarctic seabirds at Point Géologie (Terre Adélie): Human impact compared with environmental change. *Polar Biology* 24: 175-185.

Murray, M.D. (1972) Banding Giant Petrels on Frazier Islands, Antarctica. *The Australian Bird Bander* 10(3): 57-58.

Murray M.D., Luders D.J. (1990) Faunistic studies at the Windmill Islands, Wilkes Land, East Antarctica, 1959-80. *ANARE Research Notes* 73: 1-45.

Orton, M.N. (1963) A Brief Survey of the Fauna of the Windmill Islands, Wilkes Land, Antarctica. *Emu* 63: 14-22.

Orton, M.N. (1963) Movements of young giant petrels bred in Antarctica. *Emu* 63: 260.

Patterson D.L., Woehler, E.J., Croxall, J.P., Cooper, J., Poncet, S., Fraser, W.R. (2008) Breeding distribution and population status of the northern giant petrel *Macronectes halli* and the southern giant petrel *M. giganteus*. *Marine Ornithology*.

Paul, E., Stüwe, K., Teasdale, J., Worley, B. (1995) Structural and metamorphic geology of the Windmill Islands, east Antarctica: field evidence for repeated tectonothermal activity. *Australian Journal of Earth Sciences* 42: 453-469.

Robertson, R. (1961) Geology of the Windmill Islands, Antarctica. *IGY Bulletin* 43: 5-8.

van den Hoff, J. (2011) Recoveries of juvenile giant petrels in regions of ocean productivity: Potential implications for population change. *Ecosphere* No 2(7).

van Franeker, J.A., Gavrilo, M., Mehlum, F., Veit, R.R., Woehler E.J. (1999) Distribution and Abundance of the Antarctic Petrel. *Waterbirds: The International Journal of Waterbird Biology*, Vol. 22, No 1: 14-28.

Wienecki, B., Leaper, R., Hay, I., van den Hoff, J. (2009) Retrofitting historical data in population studies: southern giant petrels in the Australian Antarctic Territory. Endangered Species Research Vol. 8: 157-164.

Woehler, E.J. (1990) Status of southern giant petrels at Casey. *ANARE News* 61: 18.

Woehler, E.J. (1991) Status and Conservation of the Seabirds of Heard and the McDonald Islands. In: Croxall, J.P. (ed.) Seabird Status and Conservation: A Supplement. *ICBP Technical Publication* No 11: 263-277.

Woehler E.J., Croxall J.P. (1997) The status and trends of Antarctic and subantarctic seabirds. *Marine Ornithology* 25: 43-66.

Woehler, E.J., Johnstone, G.W. (1991) Status and Conservation of the Seabirds of the Australian Antarctic Territory. In Croxall, J.P. (ed.) Seabird Status and Conservation: A Supplement. *ICBP Technical Publication* No 11: 279-308.

Woehler, E.J., Martin, M.R., Johnstone, G.W. (1990) The Status of Southern Giant Petrels *Macronectes giganteus* at the Frazier Islands, Wilkes Land, East Antarctica. *Corella* 14: 101-106.

Woehler, E.J. (2005) Southern giant petrels critically endangered in the Antarctic. World Birdwatch 27(3), 9.

Woehler, E.J. (2006) Status and conservation of the seabirds of Heard Island and the McDonald Islands. In: Green K & Woehler EJ (eds) *Heard Island, Southern Ocean Sentinel*. Surrey Beatty & Sons, Chipping Norton, pp 128-165.

Woehler, E.J., Riddle MJ & Ribic CA (2003) Long-term population trends in southern giant petrels in East Antarctica. In: Huiskes AHL, Gieskes WWC, Rozema J, Schorno RML, van der Vies SM & Wolff W (eds) Antarctic Biology in a global context. Backhuys Publishers, Leiden, pp 290-295.

Woehler, E.J., Cooper, J., Croxall, J.P., Fraser, W.R., Kooyman, G.L., Miller, G.D., Nel, D.C., Patterson, D.L., Peter, H-U, Ribic, C.A., Salwicka, K., Trivelpiece, W.Z., Weimerskirch, H. (2001) *A Statistical Assessment of the Status and Trends of Antarctic and Subantarctic Seabirds*. SCAR/CCAMLR/NSF, 43 pp.; Patterson *et al.* Breeding distribution and population status of the giant petrel; Woehler *et al.* "*Long-term population trends in southern giant petrels*".

Woehler, E.J., Riddle, M.J. (2003) *Long-term population trends in southern giant petrels in the Southern Indian Ocean*. Poster presented at 8th SCAR Biology Symposium 2001, Amsterdam.

Woehler, E.J., Slip, D.J., Robertson, L.M., Fullagar, P.J., Burton, H.R. (1991) The distribution, abundance and status of Adélie penguins *Pygoscelis adeliae* at the Windmill Islands, Wilkes Land, Antarctica. *Marine Ornithology* 19(1): 1-17.

Woehler, E.J., Cooper, J., Croxall, J.P., Fraser, W.R., Kooyman, G.L., Miller, G.D., Nel, D.C., Patterson, D.L., Peter, H-U, Ribic, C.A., Salwicka, K., Trivelpiece, W.Z., Wiemerskirch, H. (2001) *A Statistical Assessment of the Status and Trends of Antarctic and Subantarctic Seabirds*. SCAR/CCAMLR/NSF, 43 pp.

Appendix 1: Southern giant petrel populations at the Frazier Islands, Antarctica

Note: To the extent possible, each observation below has been validated by a review of the primary data records. The comments indicate where variations from published literature were identified. Further consideration of each observation would be required before using and of these data in analyses.

Date	Nelly Island	Dewart Island	Charlton Island	Source	Comment
21, 22 Jan. 1956	250 N	not visited	not visited	Unpublished data: J Bunt 2008 pers. comm.; Law (1958)	Counted at four separate rookeries on higher parts of Nelly Island. Notes say that most nests contained chicks. Many of these nests could be old nests.
24-5 Jan. 1959	25 N	not visited	not visited	Unpublished data: Bird log Magga Dan-Wilkes & Oates Land Voyage (Jan-Mar 1959); Unpublished data: Biology report for Wilkes, (1959/60- 1960-61), R Penny.	It is not clear whether these observations are all chicks, but Penny comments that some of them were chicks.
15 Dec. 1959	60 A	not visited	not visited	Unpublished data: Biology report for Wilkes, Appendix F (1961) M. Orton; Creuwels *et al.* (2005)	20 other birds were associated with nests.
12 Feb. 1960	46 C	not visited	not visited	Unpublished data: Biology report for Wilkes, (1959/60- 1960-61), R Penny; Unpublished data: Biology report for Wilkes, Appendix F (1961) M. Orton.	Orton reports that there were 47 chicks on Nelly Island when in fact it was 46 (Penny 1960).
15 Dec. 1960	not visited	60 N	not visited	Unpublished data: Biology report for Wilkes, Appendix F (1961) M. Orton; Woehler *et al.* (1990); Creuwels *et al.* (2005)	20 other birds were associated with nests. Woehler *et al.* (1990) and Creuwels *et al.* (2005) have both quoted directly from R. Penny's unpublished report.
22 Mar. 1961	34 C	10 C	no data	Unpublished data: Biology report for Wilkes, Appendix F (1961) M. Orton; Unpublished data: Biology: Giant petrel Wilkes report (1961); Creuwels *et al.* (2005)	All chicks observed on Nelly Island were banded. Only a subset of the chicks observed at Dewart Island were banded.
23 Nov. 1962	11 eggs	not visited	not visited	Unpublished data: Davis and Mawson station biology log records (1962)	This count appears to have been a subset of the population only.
21 Jan. 1964	10 C	not visited	not visited	Unpublished data: Wilkes station report, biology log records (1964), L.G. Murray	Birds were observed on the north-east ridge, with about 20 occupied nests in this area, and more on the lower area on the southern side of the ridge. There were many old and uninhabited nests.

Date	Nelly Island	Dewart Island	Charlton Island	Source	Comment
7 Mar. 1968	72	no data	not visited	Unpublished data: Bird Log Nella Dan (1967-8) Vol. 1; Shaughessey (1971); Murray & Luders (1990)	This count is the total for all four rookeries found on Nelly Island. There is a map of their location in the field notes.
20, 21 Jan. 1972	52 C	53 C	10-20 N (aerial survey only)	Murray (1972)	Land survey primarily for banding. 49 of 52 chicks seen were banded on Nelly Island. 51 of 53 chicks seen were banded on Dewart Island. Please note counts quoted in Murray & Luders (1990) are incorrect.
31 Jan. 1974	27 BC	no data	no data	Unpublished data: Biology report for Casey (1974) A. Jones; Murray & Luders (1990); Woehler *et al.* (1990); Creuwels *et al.* (2005)	All peer-reviewed papers appear to have reported an incorrect count of a total of 76, however only 27 chicks were banded in this season.
13-17 Feb. 1977	27 C	43 C	no data	Cowan (1979); Murray & Luders (1990); Woehler et al. (1990); Creuwels et al. (2005)	All peer-reviewed papers appear to have reported the wrong count. Cowan is the original reference, where data has gone straight to peer- reviewed publication.
25 Jan. 1978	48 C	48 C	6 C	Cowan (1979); Murray & Luders (1990); Woehler *et al.* (1990); Creuwels *et al.* (2005)	
30 Jan., 2 Feb. 1979	35 (method unknown)	46 (method unknown)	5 (method unknown)	Murray & Luders (1990); Woehler *et al.* (1990); Creuwels *et al.* (2005)	The earliest reference to this work is Murray & Luders (1990), but they did not do the original counts. For Nelly, Woehler *et al.* (1990) and Creuwels *et al.* (2005) further report the chick count as 37 and not 35 as reported in Murray & Luders (1990). Further work is required to know which figure reflects the correct count. K. de Jong's original data is unable to be located.

Date	Nelly Island	Dewart Island	Charlton Island	Source	Comment
18 Jan. 1980	43 C	10 (method unknown)	no data	Murray & Luders (1990); Woehler *et al.* (1990); Creuwels *et al.* (2005)	Original data not located. Creuwels *et al.* (2005) note that the census data from Dewart Island and Charlton Island are confused with banding data.
28 & 29 Nov. 1983	63 AON	68 AON	9 AON	Unpublished data: Casey station report (1983); Woehler *et al.* (1990); Creuwels *et al.* (2005)	Woehler *et al.* (1990) conducted the survey.
25 & 26 Jan 1984	52 (method unknown)	not visited	not visited	Woehler *et al.* (1990); Creuwels *et al.* (2005)	Original data not located.
3, 6 Mar. 1985	64 C	69 C	no data	Woehler *et al.* (1990); Crewels *et al.* (2005)	Original data not located.
14 Feb. 1986	59	50	9	Woehler *et al.* (1990); Creuwels *et al.* (2005)	Census type cannot be attributed to any island. Original data not located.
23 Dec. 1989	73 AON	106 AON	14 AON	Woehler *et al.* (1990); Creuwels *et al.* (2005)	Apparently occupied nests (AON) may contain a proportion of failed or non- breeding nest sites (Creuwels *et al.* 2005).
18 Feb. 1996	11 C	not visited	not visited	Creuwels *et al.* (2005)	
23 Dec. 1997	96 AON	104 AON	21 AON	Creuwels *et al.* (2005)	Apparently occupied nests (AON) may contain a proportion of failed or non- breeding nest sites (Creuwels *et al.* 2005).
26 Dec. 1998	95 AON	103 AON	17 AON	Creuwels *et al.* (2005)	
14 Mar. 1999	66 C	82 C	11 C	Creuwels *et al.* (2005)	
26 Dec. 2001	93 AON	135 AON	20 AON	Creuwels *et al.* (2005)	
14 Dec. 2005	100 ON	149 ON	25 ON	Unpublished data: E.J. Woehler	
12-13 Dec 2011	80 ON	130 ON	27 ON	Unpublished data: John Van den Hoff	Four automatic cameras installed on Nelly Island

'A' = count of adults, 'AON' = apparently occupied nests, 'BC' = banded chicks, 'C' = count of chicks, 'N' = count of nests,

'ON' = occupied nests

Appendix 2: Biota recorded at the Frazier Islands

	Nelly Island	Dewart Island	Charlton Island
Seabirds			
Adélie penguins (*Pygoscelis adeliae*)	c.>1400 (2005)		
Antarctic petrel (*Thalassoica antarctica*)	P		
Cape petrel (*Daption capense*)	P	P (2001)	P (2001)
Snow petrel (*Pagodroma nivea*)	P	P	
Southern giant petrel (*Macronectes giganteus*)	100N (2005)	149N (2005)	25N (2005)
Wilson's storm petrels (*Oceanites oceanicus*)	P		
South Polar skua (*Catharacta maccormicki*)	1N (2005)	1N (2005)	
Southern fulmar (*Fulmarus glacialoides*)	P	P	
Mammals			
Leopard seal (*Hydrurga leptonyx*)	X (2001)		
Weddell seal (*Leptonychotes weddellii*)	X (2001)		
Orca (killer whale: *Orcinus orca*)	Small pod observed close to island (2005)		
Lichens			
Buellia frigida	R		
Usnea antarctica	R		
Rhizoplaca melanophthalma	R		
Candelariella flava	R	R	
Moss			
Bryum pseudotriquetrum	R		
Algae			
Indeterminate green crust	F		
Prasiola crispa	F		
Chlorococcum sp.	F		
Chloromonas polyptera	F		
Chlorosarcina antarctica	R		
Prasiococcus calcarius	F		

Census data for breeding seabirds provided where available, 'P' indicates recorded breeding seabirds but no census data available, 2001 indicates observations in December 2001 visit, 2005 indicates observations from December 2005 visit, 'X' indicates recorded on or near the island, 'N' a count of nests, 'R' rare, and 'F' frequent. Data compiled from records held by the Australian Antarctic Data Centre, ANARE records 1968, Appendix 1, Melick *et al.* 1994, Seppelt, R. pers. comm., Ling, H. pers. comm., Woehler, E.J. pers. comm., and Woehler, E.J. and Olivier, F. unpublished data (December 2001), Woehler, E.J. unpublished data (December 2005).

Appendix 3: Minimum wildlife approach distances

The minimum (closest) approach distances as set out below are to be maintained when approaching any wildlife on, or in the vicinity of the Frazier Islands unless a closer approach distance is authorised in a Permit. These distances are a guide and should an activity disturb wildlife, a greater distance is to be maintained.

Species	**Approach distance (on foot)**
Giant petrels	100m
Other penguins in colonies Moulting penguins Seals with pups Seal pups on their own Prions and petrels on nest South polar skua on nest	30m
Penguins on sea ice Non breeding adult seals	5m

Notes:

1. Includes cape petrels, Antarctic petrels, Wilson's storm petrels, snow petrels and southern fulmars.

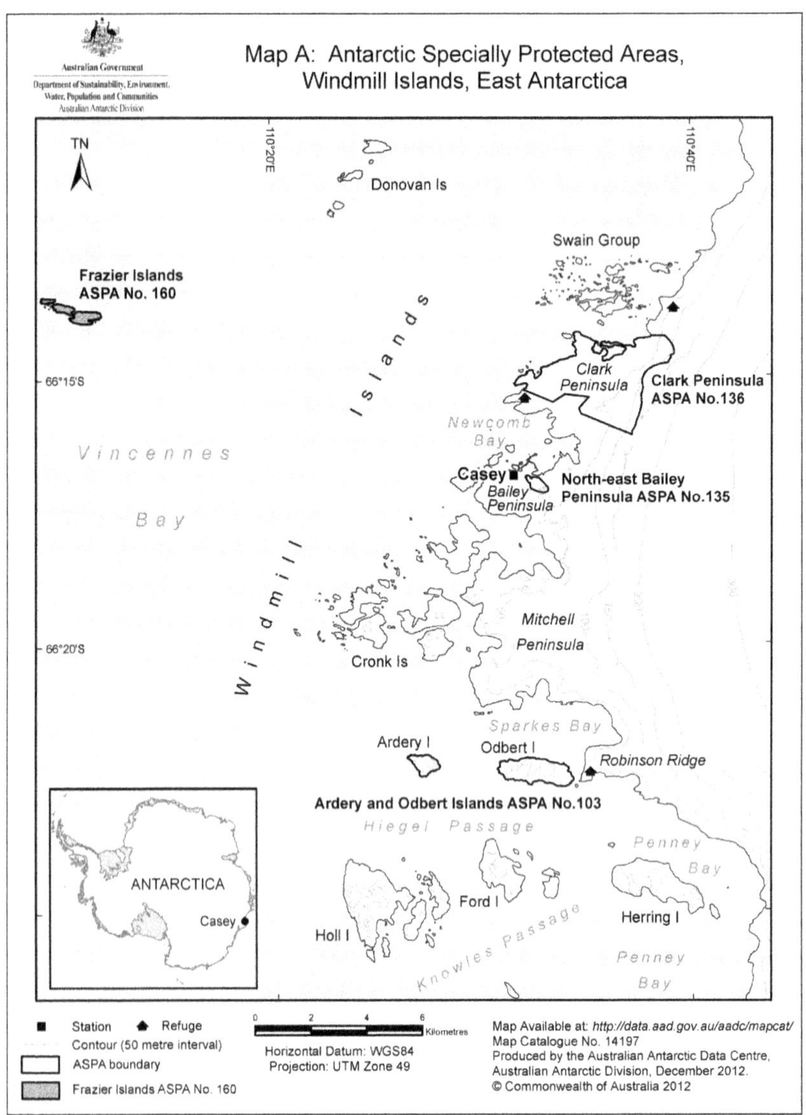
Australian Government
Department of Sustainability, Environment, Water, Population and Communities
Australian Antarctic Division
Map A: Antarctic Specially Protected Areas,
Windmill Islands, East Antarctica
TN
110°20'E
110°40'E
Donovan Is
Swain Group
Frazier Islands
ASPA No. 160
Windmill Islands
66°15'S
Clark Peninsula
Clark Peninsula
ASPA No.136
Newcomb Bay
Vincennes Bay
Casey
Bailey Peninsula
North-east Bailey
Peninsula ASPA No.135
Mitchell Peninsula
66°20'S
Cronk Is
Sparkes Bay
Ardery I
Odbert I
Robinson Ridge
Ardery and Odbert Islands ASPA No.103
Hiegel Passage
Penney Bay
ANTARCTICA
Casey
Ford I
Herring I
Holl I
Knowles Passage
Penney Bay
Station
Refuge
Contour (50 metre interval)
ASPA boundary
Frazier Islands ASPA No. 160
0 2 4 6 Kilometres
Horizontal Datum: WGS84
Projection: UTM Zone 49
Map Available at: http://data.aad.gov.au/aadc/mapcat/
Map Catalogue No. 14197
Produced by the Australian Antarctic Data Centre,
Australian Antarctic Division, December 2012.
© Commonwealth of Australia 2012

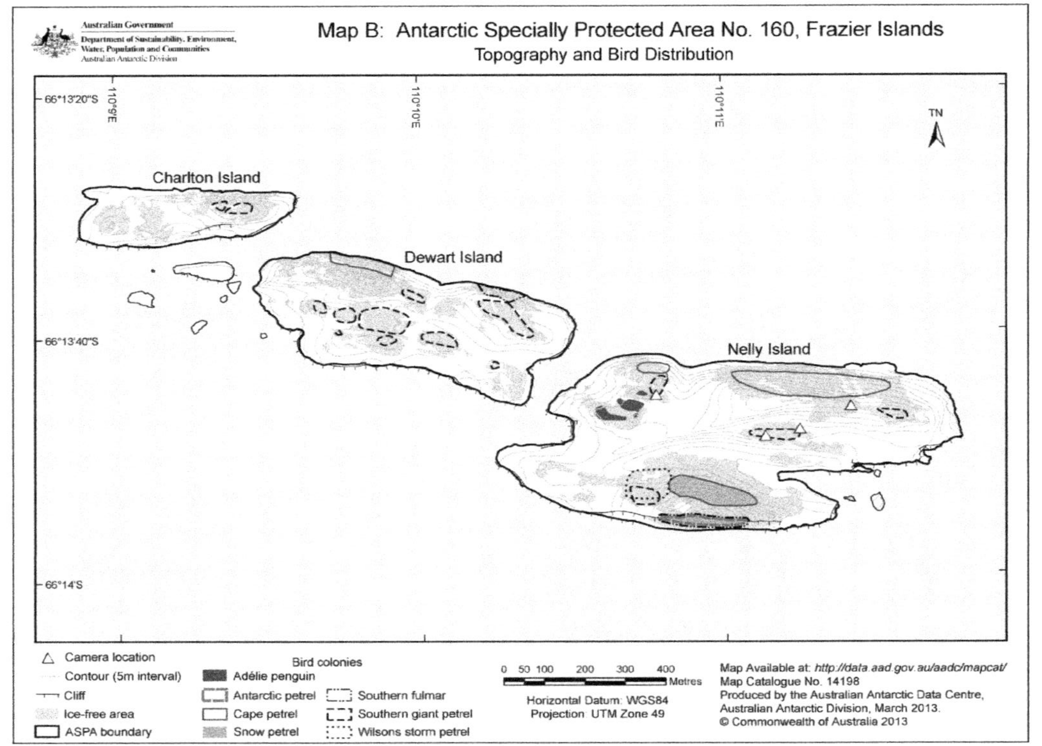
Australian Government
Department of Sustainability, Environment, Water, Population and Communities
Australian Antarctic Division
Map B: Antarctic Specially Protected Area No. 160, Frazier Islands
Topography and Bird Distribution
66°13'20"S
66°13'40"S
66°14'S
110°9'E
110°10'E
110°11'E
TN
Charlton Island
Dewart Island
Nelly Island
Camera location
Contour (5m interval)
Cliff
Ice-free area
ASPA boundary
Bird colonies
Adélie penguin
Antarctic petrel
Cape petrel
Snow petrel
Southern fulmar
Southern giant petrel
Wilsons storm petrel
0 50 100 200 300 400
Metres
Horizontal Datum: WGS84
Projection: UTM Zone 49
Map Available at: http://data.aad.gov.au/aadc/mapcat/
Map Catalogue No. 14198
Produced by the Australian Antarctic Data Centre, Australian Antarctic Division, March 2013.
© Commonwealth of Australia 2013

Antarctic Specially Protected Area (ASPA) No. 161

TERRA NOVA BAY, ROSS SEA

1. Description values to be protected

A coastal marine area encompassing 29.4 km^2 between Adélie Cove and Tethys Bay, Terra Nova Bay, is proposed as an Antarctic Specially Protected Area (ASPA) by Italy on the grounds that it is an important littoral area for well-established and long-term scientific investigations. The Area is confined to a narrow strip of waters extending approximately 9.4 km in length immediately to the south of the Mario Zucchelli Station (MZS) and up to a maximum of 7 km from the shore. No marine resource harvesting has been, is currently, or is planned to be, conducted within the Area, nor in the immediate surrounding vicinity. The site typically remains ice-free in summer, which is rare for coastal areas in the Ross Sea region, making it an ideal and accessible site for research into the near-shore benthic communities of the region. Extensive marine ecological research has been carried out at Terra Nova Bay since 1986/87, contributing substantially to our understanding of these communities which had not previously been well-described.

High diversity at both species and community levels make this Area of high ecological and scientific value. Studies have revealed a complex array of species assemblages, often co-existing in mosaics (Cattaneo-Vietti, 1991; Sarà *et al.*, 1992; Cattaneo-Vietti *et al.*, 1997; 2000b; 2000c; Gambi *et al.*, 1997; Cantone *et al.*, 2000). There exist assemblages with high species richness and complex functioning, such as the sponge and anthozoan communities, alongside loosely structured, low diversity assemblages. Moreover, the sponge and anthozoan communities at Terra Nova Bay show an unique structure and long-term transects have been established to monitor changes in coastal benthic communities, both natural and human-induced. The presence of a population of Adélie penguins (*Pygoscelis adeliae*) at Adélie Cove allows assessment of the effects of this colony on the adjacent marine environment (Povero *et al.*, 2001).

It is important to protect the Area as far as possible from direct human impacts in order that it can be used to monitor potential impacts arising from activities at the nearby permanent scientific station of MZS at Terra Nova Bay (Mauri *et al.*, 1990; Berkman & Nigro, 1992; Focardi *et al.*, 1993; Minganti *et al.*, 1995; Bruni *et al.*, 1997; Nonnis Marzano *et al.*, 2000). The high ecological and scientific values derived from the diverse range of species and assemblages, in particular through the collection of extensive data on these features, together with the vulnerability of the Area to disturbance by pollution, over-sampling and alien introductions, are such that the Area requires long-term special protection.

2. Aims and objectives

Management at Terra Nova Bay aims to:

- avoid degradation of, or substantial risk to, the values of the Area by preventing unnecessary human disturbance to the Area;

- allow scientific research on the ecosystem, in particular on the marine species assemblages, while ensuring it is protected from oversampling or other possible scientific impacts;
- allow other scientific research and support activities provided they are for compelling reasons which cannot be served elsewhere;
- maintain long-term monitoring sites to evaluate natural changes in marine communities;
- monitor the effects of the research station and its associated activities on the marine ecosystem;
- minimise the possibility of introduction of alien plants, animals and microbes to the Area;
- allow visits for management purposes in support of the aims of the management plan.

3. Management activities

The following management activities are to be undertaken to protect the values of the Area:

- A map showing the location of the Area (stating the special restrictions that apply) shall be displayed prominently, and a copy of this Management Plan shall be kept available, at MZS (Italy);
- A sign illustrating the location and boundaries with clear statements of entry restrictions shall be installed at MZS at a prominent location;
- Buoys, or other markers or structures erected for scientific or management purposes shall be secured and maintained in good condition, and removed when no longer necessary;
- Visits shall be made as necessary to assess whether the Area continues to serve the purposes for which it was designated and whether management and maintenance measures are adequate.

4. Period of designation

Designated for an indefinite period.

5. Maps and photographs

Map 1: Terra Nova Bay, Antarctic Specially Protected Area No. 161, bathymetric map.

Map specifications: Projection: UTM Zone 58S; Spheroid: WGS84. Bathymetric contour interval 50 m. Land contours and coast derived from 1:50,000 Northern Foothills Satellite Image Map (Frezzotti *et. al.* 2001). Bathymetry within ASPA derived from high resolution sidescan sonar data surveyed by Kvitek, 2002. Bathymetry outside of ASPA supplied by Italian Hydrographic Office 2000. Marine data collected under Terra Nova Bay marine protected area Project (PNRA 1999-2001). Inset 1: The location of Terra Nova Bay in Antarctica. Inset 2: Terra Nova Bay location map, showing the region covered by Map 1, stations, and sites of nearby protected areas.

6. Description of the Area

6(i) Geographical co-ordinates, boundary markers and natural features

The designated Area is situated in Terra Nova Bay, between the Campbell Glacier Tongue and Drygalski Ice Tongue, Victoria Land. The Area is confined to a narrow strip of coastal waters to the south of MZS (Italy), extending approximately 9.4 km in length and generally within 1.5 – 7 km of the shore, comprising an area of 29.4 km^2 (Map 1). No marine resource harvesting has been, is currently, or is planned to be, conducted within the Area, nor in the immediate surrounding vicinity.

The western boundary of the Area is defined as the mean high water mark along the coastline extending between 74°42'57"S in the north (2.3 km south of MZS) and 74°48'00"S in the south (the southern shore of Adélie Cove), and includes the intertidal zone (Map 1). The northern boundary of the Area is defined as the 74°42'57"S line of latitude, extending from the coast 1.55 km eastward to the 164°10'00"E line of longitude. The boundary position may be recognised near the shore by the presence of a large and distinctive offshore rock in the northernmost cove on the coast south of MZS, which is an unique feature on this stretch of coast. The southern boundary is defined as the 74°48'00"S line of latitude, extending from the coast 3.63 km eastward to the 164°10'00"E line of longitude. The boundary position may be recognised visually as being at the southern shore of the mouth of Adélie Cove, immediately south of a distinctive rocky outcrop at the base of the coastal cliffs. The eastern boundary of the Area is defined as the 164°10'00"E line of longitude extending between 74°42'57"S in the north and 74°48'00"S in the south.

The coastline of Terra Nova Bay is characterised predominantly by rocky cliffs, with large boulders forming occasional 'beaches' (Simeoni *et al.*, 1989). In the sheltered areas, the soft bottom begins at a depth of 20–30 m. The tidal range is 1.5–2 m and pack ice approximately 2–2.5 m thick covers the sea surface for 9–10 months of the year (Stocchino & Lusetti, 1988; 1990). Data available for the summer period suggest that ocean currents in the Area are likely to be slow and to flow generally in a north-south direction. Along the coastline of the Area there are two main coves; the larger Adélie Cove in the south and a smaller cove around 3 km to its north. The sea floor substrate of the smaller consists of pebbles of various sizes, while Adélie Cove is characterised by fine-grained, muddy sediments. An Adélie penguin (*Pygoscelis adeliae*) colony is situated at Adélie Cove, with a 1991 population of 7899 breeding pairs. Outside of the coves, the sea floor characteristics and benthic species assemblages are relatively homogenous along the coastal length of the Area, and are observed to vary more particularly with the vertical gradient.

An aerial survey on cetacean species, conducted in the coastal area surrounding the Italian Station Mario Zucchelli in summer 2004, showed the presence of Killer Whale (*Orcinus orca* (L.)), types B and C and Minke Whale (*Balaenoptera bonaerensis* Burmeister). (Lauriano et al., 2007a; 2007b; Lauriano pers.com.)

The seafloor within the Area is primarily granitic rock, with softer substrates composed of coarse sands or gravels. In the supralittoral zone, only cyanobacteria and diatoms colonise the hard substrates, while the intertidal zone (1.5–2.0 m wide) has, in the most sheltered areas, a high coverage of the green alga *Urospora penicilliformis* and *Prasiola crispa* (Cormaci *et al.*, 1992b). Below the tidal zone, down to 2–3 m depth, the community is very poor, due to the persistent presence and scouring action of pack ice, and is mainly composed of epilithic diatoms and the crustacean amphipod *Paramoera walkeri*. Immediately deeper, rocks can be fully colonised by the red alga *Iridaea cordata* (Cormaci *et al.*, 1996), frequently found with *Plocamium cartilagineum*, to a depth of 12 m (Gambi *et al.*, 1994; 2000a). At this level large sessile animals such as *Alcyonium antarcticum* and *Urticinopsis antarctica* can be occasionally observed, while frequent are the asteroid *Odontaster validus* and the echinoid *Sterechinus neumayeri. Phyllophora antarctica* is another red alga forming expanded mats from 12 to 25 m depth, often fully colonised by sessile organisms, mainly hydroids (Cerrano *et al.*, 2000c, Puce *et al.*, 2002), serpulids and bryozoans (*Celleporella antarctica* and *Harpecia spinosissima*). The upper algal belts represent shelter and a food source for diversified and abundant communities of mobile fauna. Numerous invertebrates, such as the polychaete *Harmothoe brevipalpa*, the mollusc *Laevilittorina antarctica*, the crustacean amphipod *Paramoera walkeri* and the isopod *Nototanais dimorphus* feed on these algal species and can be very abundant. On rocky bottoms in deeper layers, the algal colonisation is replaced by a calcareous crustose coralline alga (*Clathromorphum lemoineanum*) on which sea-urchins feed.

The soft bottoms from 20–40 m depth are coarse sands and gravels, where the community is characterised by the mollusc bivalve *Laternula elliptica* and the polychaete *Aglaophamus ornatus* (Nephtiidae). The bivalve *Yoldia eightsi* is abundant in fine-sand sediments.

Between 30–70 m, the substrate becomes finer and is completely colonised by the bivalve *Adamussium colbecki*, the shells of which are colonised by a micro-community comprising mainly forams, bryozoans (*Aimulosia antarctica, Arachnopusia decipiens, Ellisina antarctica, Micropora brevissima*) and the spirorbid *Paralaeospira levinsenii* (Albertelli *et al.*, 1998; Ansell *et al.*, 1998; Chiantore *et al.*, 1998; 2000; 2001; 2002; Vacchi *et al.*, 2000a; Cerrano *et al.*, 2001a; 2001b). In this region, large predators such as the gastropod *Neobuccinum eatoni* and the nemertean *Parborlasia corrugatus* are frequent. The echinoid *Sterechinus neumayeri* and the starfish *Odontaster validus* are still very frequent at all depths on both hard and mobile substrates (Chiantore *et al.*, 2002; Cerrano *et al.*, 2000b).

Below 70–75 m down to 120–130 m depth, heterogeneous substrates allow hard- and soft-bottom communities to coexist. On the sparse rocky outcrops the encrusting algae disappear and the benthic communities are dominated by the sessile zoobenthos. This diversified filter feeding assemblage is mainly characterised by sponges and anthozoans, while in soft sediments detritus-feeder polychaetes and bivalves dominate. Among sponges, which can reach very high biomass values, *Axociella nidificata, Calyx arcuarius, Gellius rudis, Phorbas glaberrima, Tedania charcoti,* are very abundant (Sarà *et al.*, 1992; 2002; Gaino *et al.*, 1992; Cattaneo-Vietti *et al.*, 1996; 2000c; Bavestrello *et al.*, 2000; Cerrano *et al.*, 2000a). Numerous invertebrates constitute an important component of this assemblage which develops down to 120-140 m depth. These include the epibiont polychaete *Barrukia cristata* on Thouarellid gorgonians, crustacean peracarids, pycnogonids, mollusc opisthobranchs (*Austrodoris kerguelenensis, Tritoniella belli*) (Cattaneo-Vietti, 1991; Gavagnin *et al.*, 1995) and bivalves, ophiuroids and holothuroids, bryozoans, and the endobionts. The conspicuous sponge spicule mats found at these depths underline the important role of sponges in this area, besides the one played by diatoms, in determining the sediment texture and silica content. A peculiar community, dominated by polychaetes and by the bivalve *Limatula hodgsoni*, can be associated with these mats.

Below 130 m the hard substrates become very sparse and are mainly colonised by the polychaete *Serpula narconensis* (Schiaparelli *et al.*, 2000) and several bryozoans (*Arachnopusia decipiens, Ellisina antarctica, Flustra angusta, F. vulgaris* and *Isoschizoporella similis*). The dominant muddy bottoms are instead characterised by tubicolous polychaetes (Gambi *et al.*, 2000b), mainly *Spiophanes*. Much deeper, at about 150-200 m depth, brachiopods and various species of bivalves characterise the environment on small gravels as well as on the soft bottom (Cattaneo-Vietti *et al.*, 2000b). The great heterogeneity of these substrates contributes to the creation of communities with considerable species richness, diversity and biomass.

Finally, the faunal assemblage of the Area includes notothenioid fishes, represented especially by species of the *Trematomus* group, including *T. bernacchi*, *T. pennelli*, *T. hansoni* and *T. loennbergii*. These exert an important role in benthic food webs as consumers of many invertebrate species, mainly crustaceans and polychaetes (Vacchi *et al.*, 1991; 1992; 1994a; 1994b; 1995; 1997; 2000b; La Mesa *et al.*, 1996; 1997; 2000; Guglielmo *et al.*, 1998).

The platelet ice occurring at Terra Nova Bay in early spring has been shown to house an important nursery for the Antarctic silverfish, *Pleuragramma antarcticum,* a key organism in the ecology of Antarctic food webs (La Mesa et al., 2004; Vacchi et al., 2004). The platelet ice environment has strong prooxidant characteristics at the beginning of austral spring, and the marked responsiveness of antioxidant defences represents a fundamental strategy for *P. antarcticum* (Regoli et al., 2005b). The elevated prooxidant challenge, to which these organisms are naturally adapted, also influences the susceptibility of *P. antarcticum* toward prooxidant chemicals of anthropogenic origin (Regoli et al., 2005b).

Oxyradical metabolism and antioxidant defenses have a fundamental role in several marine invertebrates, fish and penguins from Terra Nova Bay, representing important counteractive strategies toward, i.e. extreme environmental conditions, marked seasonal fluctuations of biotic and abiotic factors, symbiotic relationships, specific physiological features, long-term protection of biological macromolecules and aging (Regoli et al., 1997a,b; 2000a,b, 2002, 2004; Corsolini et al., 2001; Cerrano et al., 2004).

Susceptibility to oxidative stress is of particular value also for monitoring the impact of human activities and cellular responses to pollutants were characterized in key Antarctic organisms developing a wide array of biomarkers sensitive to biological disturbance (Focardi et al., 1995; Regoli et al., 1998; Jimenez et al., 1999; Regoli et al., 2005a; Benedetti et al., 2005, 2007; Canapa et al., 2007; Di Bello et al., 2007). At the moment, there is no evidence of polluted areas in Terra Nova Bay, but organisms are exposed to a naturally elevated bioavailability of cadmium causing tissue concentrations generally 10-50 folds higher than those typical of temperate species (Mauri et al., 1990; Nigro et al., 1992, 1997; Canapa et al., 2007). Despite elevated levels of this element do not cause direct adverse effects to the organisms, nonetheless the environmental characteristics of Terra Nova Bay influence the responsiveness of organisms to other chemicals with important implications for monitoring the impact of anthropogenic pressure or accidental spills (Regoli et al., 2005a); in particular, elevated level of cadmium at Terra Nova Bay modulates bioaccumulation and metabolism of polycyclic aromatic hydrocarbons and of organochlorine xenobiotics in local marine organisms suggesting also endocrine effects from the chronic exposure to this element (Regoli et al., 2005a; Benedetti et al., 2007; Canapa et al., 2007).

Human impacts within the Area are believed to be minimal and confined to those arising from the nearby Terra Nova Bay Station and scientific work conducted within the Area. The station can accommodate approximately 80 people, has facilities for helicopter operations and a jetty for the docking of small boats. Fuel used at the station is a light petroleum diesel, stored in three double-walled steel tanks with a total capacity of 1.8 million litres. Fuel is transferred to the station annually from resupply ship either via hoses routed across sea ice or via barge when sea ice is not present. Station waste water, purified by a biological plant, is discharged into the sea adjacent to the station on the eastern side of the peninsula on which the station is located, 2.3 km from the northern boundary of the Area. Combustible rubbish generated at the Station is incinerated and the smoke washed and filtered with water. This water is discharged into the waste water treatment plant at time intervals which intovary with incinerator usage. An atmospheric monitoring facility (locally referred to as 'Campo Icaro') is situated approximately 650 m north of the northern boundary of the Area and 150 m from the shore: no wastes are discharged from this facility. A support ship regularly visits Mario Zucchelli Station during the summer, and there are occasional visits by tourist ships. These usually stop offshore several kilometres to the north of the Area.

6(ii) Restricted zones within the Area

None.

6(iii) Structures within and near the Area

There are no structures within the Area. The nearest structure is the atmospheric monitoring facility (locally referred to as 'Campo Icaro') 650 m north of the northern boundary of the Area, while Mario Zucchelli Station (74°41'42"S, 164°07'23"E) is situated on a small peninsula on the coast adjacent to Tethys Bay, a further 1.65 km to the north.

6(iv) Location of other protected areas within close proximity of the Area

ASPA No. 118, summit of Mount Melbourne, is a terrestrial site situated 45 km to the NE, which is the only other protected area within close proximity.

7. Permit conditions

Entry into the Area is prohibited except in accordance with a Permit issued by the appropriate national authority. Conditions for issuing a Permit are that:

- it is issued for scientific study of the marine environment in the Area, or for other scientific purposes which cannot be served elsewhere; and/or
- it is issued for essential management purposes consistent with plan objectives such as inspection, maintenance or review;
- the actions permitted will not jeopardise the values of the Area;
- any management activities are in support of the objectives of the Management Plan;
- the actions permitted are in accordance with the Management Plan;
- The Permit, or an authorised copy, shall be carried by the holderwithin the Area;
- a visit report shall be supplied to the authority named in the Permit;
- permits shall be issued for a stated period.

7(i) Access to and movement within the Area

Access into the Area shall be by sea, land, over sea ice or by air. There are no specific restrictions on routes of access to and movement within the Area, although movements should be kept to the minimum necessary consistent with the objectives of any permitted activities and every reasonable effort should be made to minimise disturbance. Anchoring is prohibited within the Area. There are no overflight restrictions within the Area and aircraft may land by Permit when sea ice conditions allow. Ship or small boat crew, or other people on small boats or ships, are prohibited from moving beyond the immediate vicinity of their vessel unless specifically authorized by Permit.

7(ii) Activities that are or may be conducted within the Area, including restrictions on time or place

- Scientific research or essential operational activities that will not jeopardise the values of the Area;
- Essential management activities, including monitoring;
- Activities that involve trawling, dragging, grabbing, dredging, or deployment of nets within the Area should be undertaken with great care because of the sensitivity of the rich bottom communities to disturbance: before Permits are granted for such activities careful consideration should be given to the impact of such activities on the ecosystem under special protection versus the expected scientific or management benefits, with consideration given to alternative, more selective and less-invasive, sampling methods;
- The appropriate authority should be notified of any activities/measures undertaken that were not included in the authorized Permit.

7(iii) Installation, modification or removal of structures

Structures or scientific equipment shall not be installed within the Area except as specified in a Permit. All markers, structures or scientific equipment installed in the Area shall be clearly identified by country, name of the principal investigator and year of installation. All such items should be made of materials that pose minimal risk of contamination of the Area. Removal of specific equipment for which the Permit has expired shall be a condition of the Permit. Permanent installations are prohibited.

7(iv) Location of field camps

None within the Area. An occasional field camp has been positioned on the beach at Adélie Cove.

7(v) Restrictions on materials and organisms which can be brought into the Area

No living animals, plant material, pathogens or microorganisms shall be deliberately introduced into the Area. Poultry products, including food products containing uncooked dried eggs, shall not be released into the Area. No herbicides or pesticides shall be introduced into the Area. Any other chemicals, including radio-nuclides or stable isotopes, which may be introduced for scientific or management purposes specified in the Permit, shall be used in the minimum quantities necessary to achieve the purpose of the activity for which the Permit was granted. Such chemicals shall be used with due regard for the values of the Area. All materials shall be stored and handled so that risk of their accidental introduction into the environment is minimized. Where practical, materials introduced shall remain for a stated period only and shall be removed at or before the conclusion of that stated period. If release occurs which is likely to compromise the values of the Area, removal is encouraged only where the impact of removal is not likely to be greater than that of leaving the material *in situ*. The appropriate authority should be notified of any materials released that were not included in the authorized Permit.

7(vi) Taking or harmful interference with native flora or fauna

Taking or harmful interference with native flora or fauna is prohibited, except by Permit issued in accordance with Annex II to the Protocol on Environmental Protection to the Antarctic Treaty. Where taking or harmful interference with animals is involved, the *SCAR Code of Conduct for the Use of Animals for Scientific Purposes in Antarctica* should be used as a minimum standard.

7(vii) Collection and removal of anything not brought into the Area by the Permit holder

Material may be collected or removed from the Area only in accordance with a Permit and should be limited to the minimum necessary to meet scientific or management needs. Permits shall not be granted if there is a reasonable concern that the sampling proposed would take, remove or damage such quantities of substrate, native flora or fauna that their distribution or abundance within the Area would be significantly affected. All samples collected shall be described in terms of their type, quantity and the location from which they were taken. This information shall held in an archive accessible at MZS in order to maintain a record of usage that will assist assessment of the impacts of sampling activities and in the planning of future sampling. Material of human origin likely to compromise the values of the Area, which was not brought into the Area by the Permit Holder or otherwise authorized, may be removed unless the impact of removal is likely to be greater than leaving the material *in situ*: if this is the case the appropriate authority should be notified.

7(viii) Disposal of waste

All wastes, including all human wastes, shall be removed from the Area.

7(ix) Measures that are necessary to ensure that the aims and objectives of the Management Plan can continue to be met

1. Permits may be granted to enter the Area to carry out biological monitoring and site inspection activities, which may involve the collection of limited samples for analysis or review, or for protective measures.
2. Any specific sites of long-term monitoring that are vulnerable to inadvertent disturbance should be appropriately marked on site where practical and, as appropriate, on maps of the Area.
3. To help maintain the ecological and scientific values of the marine communities found within the Area, visitors shall take special precautions against marine pollution. Of concern are the release or spillage of hydrocarbons from ships, and biological introductions. To minimize the risk of such pollution, visitors shall ensure that sampling equipment or markers brought into the Area are clean. Vessels that are found to show fuel leakage, or a significant risk of such leakage, are prohibited from entering the Area. If a fuel leak from a vessel is discovered while within the Area, the vessel shall leave the Area unless the leak can be promptly stopped. Handling of fuels and oil within the Area shall be the minimum necessary consistent with meeting the objectives of the permitted activities.

7(x) Requirements for reports

Antarctic Treaty Parties should ensure that the principal holder for each Permit issued submits to the appropriate authority a report describing the activities undertaken. Such reports should include, as appropriate, the information identified in the Visit Report form suggested by SCAR. Parties should maintain a record of such activities and, in the Annual Exchange of Information, should provide summary descriptions of activities conducted by persons subject to their jurisdiction, which should be in sufficient detail to allow evaluation of the effectiveness of the Management Plan. Parties should, wherever possible, deposit originals or copies of such original reports in a publicly accessible archive to maintain a record of usage, to be used both in any review of the management plan and in organizing the scientific use of the Area.

8. References

Albertelli G., Cattaneo-Vietti R., Chiantore M., Pusceddu A., Fabiano M., 1998. Food availability to an *Adamussium* bed during the austral Summer 1993/94 (Terra Nova Bay, Ross Sea). *Journal of Marine Systems* **17**: 425-34.

Ansell A.D., Cattaneo-Vietti R., Chiantore M., 1998. Swimming in the Antarctic scallop *Adamussium colbecki*: analysis of *in situ* video recordings. *Antarctic Science* **10** (4): 369-75.

Bavestrello G., Arillo A., Calcinai B., Cattaneo-Vietti R., Cerrano C., Gaino E., Penna A., Sara' M., 2000. Parasitic diatoms inside Antarctic sponges. *Biol. Bull.* **198**: 29-33.

Benedetti M., Gorbi S., Bocchetti R., Fattorini D., Notti A., Martuccio G., Nigro M., Regoli F. (2005). Characterization of cytochrome P450 in the Antarctic key sentinel species Trematomus bernacchii. Pharmacologyonline 3: 1-8 ISSN-1827-8620

Benedetti M., Martuccio G., Fattorini D., Canapa A., Barucca M., Nigro M., Regoli F. (2007). Oxidative and modulatory effects of trace metals on metabolism of polycyclic aromatic hydrocarbons in the Antarctic fish Trematomus bernacchii. Aquat. Toxicol. 85: 167-175

Berkman P.A., Nigro M., 1992. Trace metal concentrations in scallops around Antarctica: Extending the Mussel Watch Programme to the Southern Ocean. *Marine Pollution Bulletin* **24** (124): 322-23.

Bruni V., Maugeri M.L., Monticelli L.S., 1997. Faecal pollution indicators in the Terra Nova Bay (Ross Sea, Antarctica). *Marine Pollution Bulletin* **34** (11): 908-12.

Canapa A, Barucca M, Gorbi S, Benedetti M, Zucchi S, Biscotti MA, Olmo E, Nigro M, Regoli F 2007 Vitellogenin gene expression in males of the Antarctic fish *Trematomus bernacchii* from Terra Nova Bay (Ross Sea): A role for environmental cadmium? *Chemosphere, 66:1270-1277.*

Cantone G., Castelli A., Gambi M.C., 2000. The Polychaete fauna off Terra Nova Bay and Ross Sea: biogeography, structural aspects and ecological role. In: *Ross Sea Ecology*, F. Faranda, L. Guglielmo and A. Ianora Eds., Springer Verlag, Berlin Heidelberg: 551-61.

Cattaneo-Vietti R., 1991. Nudibranch Molluscs from the Ross Sea, Antarctica. *J. Moll. Stud.* **57**: 223-28.

Cattaneo-Vietti R., Bavestrello G., Cerrano C., Sara' M., Benatti U., Giovine M., Gaino E., 1996. Optical fibres in an Antarctic sponge. *Nature* **383**: 397-98.

Cattaneo-Vietti R., Chiantore M., Albertelli G., 1997. The population structure and ecology of the Antarctic Scallop, *Adamussium colbecki* in Terra Nova Bay (Ross Sea, Antarctica). *Scientia Marina* **61** (Suppl. 2): 15-24.

Cattaneo-Vietti R., Chiantore M., Misic C., Povero P., Fabiano M., 1999. The role of pelagic-benthic coupling in structuring littoral benthic communities at Terra Nova Bay (Ross Sea) and inside the Strait of Magellan. *Scientia Marina* **63** (Supl. 1): 113-21.

Cattaneo-Vietti R., Chiantore M., Gambi M.C., Albertelli G., Cormaci M., Di Geronimo I., 2000a. Spatial and vertical distribution of benthic littoral communities in Terra Nova Bay. In: *Ross Sea Ecology*, F. Faranda, L. Guglielmo and A. Ianora Eds., Springer Verlag, Berlin Heidelberg: 503-14.

Cattaneo-Vietti R., Chiantore M., Schiaparelli S., Albertelli G., 2000b. Shallow and deep-water mollusc distribution at Terra Nova Bay (Ross Sea, Antarctica). *Polar Biology* **23**: 173-82.

Cattaneo-Vietti R., Bavestrello G., Cerrano C., Gaino E., Mazzella L., Pansini M., Sarà M., 2000c. The role of sponges of Terra Nova Bay ecosystem. In: *Ross Sea Ecology*, F. Faranda, L. Guglielmo and A. Ianora Eds., Springer Verlag, Berlin Heidelberg: 539-49.

Cerrano C., Arillo A., Bavestrello G., Calcinai B., Cattaneo-Vietti R., Penna A., Sarà M., Totti C., 2000a. Diatom invasion in the Antarctic hexactinellid sponge *Scolymastra joubini*. *Polar Biology* **23**: 441-44.

Cerrano C., Bavestrello G., Calcinai B., Cattaneo-Vietti R., Sarà A., 2000b. Asteroids eating sponges from Tethys Bay, East Antarctica. *Antarctic Science* **12**(4): 431-32.

Cerrano C., Puce S., Chiantore M., Bavestrello G., 2000c. Unusual trophic strategies of *Hydractinia angusta* (Cnidaria, Hydrozoa) from Terra Nova Bay, Antarctica. *Polar Biology* **23**(7): 488-94.

Cerrano C., G. Bavestrello, B. Calcinai, R. Cattaneo-Vietti, M. Chiantore, M. Guidetti, A. Sarà, 2001a. Bioerosive processes in Antarctic seas. *Polar Biology* **24**: 790-92.

Cerrano C., S. Puce, M. Chiantore, G. Bavestrello, R. Cattaneo-Vietti, 2001b. The influence of the epizooic hydroid *Hydractinia angusta* on the recruitment of the Antarctic scallop *Adamussium colbecki*. *Polar Biology* **24**: 577-81.

Cerrano C, Calcinai B, Cucchiari E, Di Camillo C, Nigro M, Regoli F, Sarà A, Schiapparelli S, Totti C, Bavestrello G 2004 Are diatoms a food source for Antarctic sponges?. *Chemistry and Ecology, vol. 20: 57-64.*

Chiantore M., Cattaneo-Vietti R., Albertelli G., Misic M., Fabiano M., 1998. Role of filtering and biodeposition by *Adamussium colbecki* in circulation of organic matter in Terra Nova Bay (Ross Sea, Antarctica). *Journal of Marine Systems* **17**: 411-24.

Chiantore M., Cattaneo-Vietti R., Povero P., Albertelli G., 2000. The population structure and ecology of the antarctic scallop *Adamussium colbecki* in Terra Nova Bay. In: *Ross Sea Ecology*, F. Faranda, L. Guglielmo and A. Ianora Eds., Springer Verlag, Berlin Heidelberg: 563-73.

Chiantore M., Cattaneo-Vietti R., Berkman P.A., Nigro M., Vacchi M., Schiaparelli S., Albertelli G., 2001. Antarctic scallop (*Adamussium colbecki*) spatial population variability along the Victoria Land Coast, Antarctica. *Polar Biology* **24**: 139-43.

Chiantore M., R. Cattaneo-Vietti, L. Elia, M. Guidetti, M. Antonini, 2002. Reproduction and condition of the scallop *Adamussium colbecki* (Smith 1902), the sea-urchin *Sterechinus neumayeri* (Meissner, 1900) and the sea-star *Odontaster validus* Koehler, 1911 at Terra Nova Bay (Ross Sea): different strategies related to inter-annual variations in food availability. *Polar Biology* **22**: 251-55.

Cormaci M., Furnari G., Scammacca B., Casazza G., 1992a. Il fitobenthos di Baia Terra Nova (Mare di Ross, Antartide): osservazioni sulla flora e sulla zonazione dei popolamenti. In: Gallardo VA, Ferretti O, Moyano HI (eds) *Actas del Semin. Int. Oceanografia in Antartide*. Centro EULA, Universitad de Concepción, Chile. ENEA: 395-408.

Cormaci M., Furnari G., Scammacca B., 1992b. The benthic algal flora of Terra Nova Bay (Ross Sea, Antarctica). *Botanica Marina* **35**(6): 541-52

Cormaci M., Furnari G., Scammacca B., 1992c. Carta della vegetazione marina di Baia Terra Nova (Mare di Ross, Antartide). *Biologia Marina* **1**: 313-14.

Cormaci M., Furnari G., Scammacca B., Alongi G., 1996. Summer biomass of a population of *Iridaea cordata* (Gigartinaceae, Rhodophyta) from Antarctica. In: Lindstrom SC, Chapman DJ (Eds) Proceedings of the XV Seeweeds Symposium. *Hydrobiologia* **326/327**: 267-72.

Corsolini S, Nigro M, Olmastroni S, Focardi S, Regoli F 2001 Susceptibility to oxidative stress in Adelie and Emperor penguin, *Polar Biology, vol. 24: 365-368.*

Di Bello D., Vaccaio E., Longo V., Regoli F., Nigro M., Benedetti M., Gervasi PG, Pretti C. (2007). Presence and inducibility by β-Naphtoflavone of CYP 1A1, CYP 1B1, UDP-GT, GST and DT-Diaphorase enzymes in Trematomus bernacchii, an Antarctic fish. Aquatic Toxicol. 84: 19-26

Fabiano M., Danovaro R., Crisafi E., La Ferla R., Povero P., Acosta Pomar L., 1995. Particulate matter composition and bacterial distribution in Terra Nova Bay (Antarctica) during summer 1989-90. *Polar Biology* **15**: 393-400.

Fabiano M., Povero P., Danovaro R., 1996. Particulate organic matter composition in Terra Nova Bay (Ross Sea, Antarctica) during summer 1990. *Antarctic Science* **8**(1): 7-13.

Fabiano M., Chiantore M., Povero P., Cattaneo-Vietti R., Pusceddu A., Misic C., Albertelli G., 1997. Short-term variations in particulate matter flux in Terra Nova Bay, Ross Sea. *Antarctic Science* **9**(2): 143-149.

Focardi S., Bargagli R., Corsolini S., 1993. Organochlorines in marine Antarctic food chain at Terra Nova Bay (Ross Sea). *Korean Journal of Polar Research* **4**: 73-77.

Focardi S, Fossi MC, Lari L, Casini S, Leonzio C, Meidel SK, Nigro M. 1995 Induction of MFO Activity in the Antarctic fish *Pagothenia bernacchii*: Preliminary results. *Marine Environmental Research., 39: 97-100.*

Gaino E., Bavestrello G., Cattaneo-Vietti R., Sara' M., 1994. Scanning electron microscope evidence for diatom uptake by two Antarctic sponges. *Polar Biology* **14**: 55-58.

Gambi M.C., Lorenti M., Russo G.F., Scipione M.B., 1994. Benthic associations of the shallow hard bottoms off Terra Nova Bay (Ross Sea, Antarctica): zonation, biomass and population structure. *Antarctic Science* **6**(4): 449-62.

Gambi M.C., Castelli A., Guizzardi M., 1997. Polychaete populations of the shallow soft bottoms off Terra Nova Bay (Ross Sea, Antarctica): distribution, diversity and biomass. *Polar Biology* **17**: 199-210.

Gambi M.C., Buia M.C., Mazzella L., Lorenti M., Scipione M.B., 2000a. Spatio-temporal variability in the structure of benthic populations in a physically controlled system off Terra Nova Bay: the shallow hard bottoms. In: *Ross Sea Ecology*, F. Faranda, L. Guglielmo and A. Ianora Eds., Springer Verlag, Berlin Heidelberg: 527-538.

Gambi M.C., Giangrande A., Patti F.P., 2000b. Comparative observations on reproductive biology of four species of *Perkinsiana* (Polychaeta, Sabellidae). *Bulletin of Marine Science* **67**(1): 299-309.

Gavagnin M., Trivellone E., Castelluccio F., Cimino G., Cattaneo-Vietti R., 1995. Glyceryl ester of a new halimane diterpenoic acid from the skin of the antarctic nudibranch *Austrodoris kerguelenensis*. *Tetrahedron Letters* **36**: 7319-22.

Guglielmo L., Granata A., Greco S., 1998. Distribution and abundance of postlarval and juvenile *Pleuragramma antarticum* (Pisces, Nototheniidae)of Terra Nova Bay (Ross Sea, Antartica). *Polar Biology* **19**: 37-51.

Guglielmo L., Carrada G.C., Catalano G., Dell'Anno A., Fabiano M., Lazzara L., Mangoni O., Pusceddu A., Saggiomo V., 2000. Structural and functional properties of sympagic communities in the annual sea ice at Terra Nova Bay (Ross Sea, Antarctica). *Polar Biology* **23**(2): 137-46.

Jimenez B, Fossi MC, Nigro M, Focardi S. 1999 Biomarker approach to evaluating the impact of scientific stations on the Antarctic environment using *trematomus bernacchii* as a bioindicator organism. *Chemosphere*, 39: 2073-2078.

La Mesa M., Arneri E., Giannetti G., Greco S., Vacchi M., 1996. Age and growth of the nototheniid fish *Trematomus bernacchii* Boulenger from Terra Nova Bay, Antartica. *Polar Biology***16**: 139-45.

La Mesa M., Vacchi M., Castelli A., Diviacco G., 1997. Feeding ecology of two nototheniid fishes *Trematomus hansoni* and *Trematomus loennbergi* from Terra Nova Bay, Ross Sea. *Polar Biology* **17**: 62-68.

La Mesa M., Vacchi M., T. Zunini Sertorio, 2000. Feeding plasticity of *Trematomus newnesi* (Pisces, Nototheniidae) in Terra Nova Bay, Ross Sea, in relation to environmental conditions. *Polar Biology* **23**(1): 38-45.

La Mesa M., J.T. Eastman, M. Vacchi, 2004. The role of notothenioid fish in the food web of the Ross Sea shelf waters: a review. *Polar Biol.*, 27: 321-338.

Lauriano G., Fortuna C.M., Vacchi M., 2007a. Observation of killer whale (*Orcinus orca*)

possibly eating penguins in Terra Nova Bay, Antarctica. *Antarctic Science*, 19(1): 95-96.

Lauriano G., Vacchi M., Ainley D., Ballard G., 2007b. Observations of top predators foraging on fish in the pack ice of the southern Ross Sea. *Antarctic Science*, 19(4): 439-440.

Mauri M., Orlando E., Nigro M., Regoli F., 1990. Heavy metals in the Antarctic scallop *Adamussium colbecki* (Smith). *Mar. Ecol. Progr. Ser.* **67**: 27-33.

Mauri M, Orlando E, Nigro M, Regoli F. 1990 Heavy metals in the Antarctic scallop *Adamussium colbecki* (Smith). *Marine Ecology Progress Series, 67: 27-33.* **I.f. 2.286**

Minganti V., Capelli R., Fiorentino F., De Pellegrini R., Vacchi M., 1995. Variations of mercury and selenium concentrations in *Adamussium colbecki* and *Pagothenia bernacchii* from Terra Nova Bay (Antarctica) during a five year period. *Int. J. Environ. Anal. Chem.* **61**: 239-48.

Nonnis Marzano F., Fiori F., Jia G., Chiantore M., 2000. Anthropogenic radionuclides bioaccumulation in Antarctic marine fauna and its ecological relevance. *Polar Biology* **23**: 753-58.

Nigro M, Orlando E, Regoli F. 1992 Ultrastructural localisation of metal binding sites in the kidney of the Antarctic scallop *Adamussium colbecki. Marine Biology, 113: 637-643.*

Nigro M., Regoli F., Rocchi R., Orlando E. (1997). Heavy metals in Antarctic Molluscs. In "Antarctic Communities" (B. Battaglia, J. Valencia and D.W.H Walton Eds.), Cambridge University Press, 409-412

Povero P., Chiantore M., Misic C., Budillon G., Cattaneo-Vietti R., 2001. Pelagic-benthic coupling in Adélie Cove (Terra Nova Bay, Antarctica): a strongly land forcing controlled system? *Polar Biology* **24**: 875-882.

Puce S., Cerrano C., Bavestrello G., 2002. *Eudendrium* (Cnidaria, Anthomedusae) from the Antarctic Ocean with a description of new species. *Polar Biology* **25**: 366-73.

Pusceddu A., Cattaneo-Vietti R., Albertelli G., Fabiano M., 1999. Origin, biochemical composition and vertical flux of particulate organic matter under the pack ice in Terra Nova Bay (Ross Sea, Antarctica) during late summer 1995. *Polar Biology* **22**: 124-32.

Regoli F, Principato GB, Bertoli E, Nigro M, Orlando E. 1997a Biochemical characterisation of the antioxidant system in the scallop *Adamussium colbecki*, a sentinel organism for monitoring the Antarctic environment. *Polar Biology, 17: 251-25.*

Regoli F, Nigro M, Bertoli E, Principato GB, Orlando E. 1997b Defences against oxidative stress in the Antarctic scallop *Adamussium colbecki* and effects of acute exposure to metals. *Hydrobiologia, 355: 139-144.*

Regoli F, Nigro M, Orlando E. 1998 Lysosomal and antioxidant defences to metals in the Antarctic scallop *Adamussium colbecki. Aquatic Toxicology*, 40: 375-392.

Regoli F, Nigro M, Bompadre S, Wiston G. 2000a Total oxidant scavenging capacity (TOSC) of microsomal and cytosolic fractions from Antarctic Arctic and Mediterranean Scallops: differentiation between three different potent oxidants. *Aquatic Toxicology, 49: 13-25.*

Regoli F, Nigro M, Chiantore MC, Gorbi S, Wiston G 2000b Total oxidant scavenging capacity of Antarctic, Arctic and Mediterranean scallops. *Italian Journal of Zoology, vol. 67: 5-94.*

Regoli F., M. Nigro, M. Chiantore, G.W. Winston, 2002. Seasonal variations of susceptibility to oxidative stress in *Adamussium colbecki*, a key bioindicator species for the Antarctic marine environment. *The Science of the Total Environment*, **289:** 205-211.

Regoli F, Nigro M, Chierici E, Cerrano C, Schiapparelli S, Totti C, Bavestrello G 2004 Variations of antioxidant efficiency and presence of endosymbiontic diatoms in the Antarctic porifera Haliclona dancoi, Marine Environmental Research, vol. 58: 637-640.

Regoli F, Nigro M, Benedetti M, Gorbi S, Pretti C, Gervasi PG, Fattorini D 2005a Interactions between metabolism of trace metals and xenobiotics agonist of the aryl hydrocarbon receptor in the Antarctic fish *Trematomus bernacchii*: environmental perspectives. *Environmental Toxicology and Chemistry, vol.* 24(6): 201-208

Regoli F, Nigro M, Benedetti M, Fattorini D, Gorbi S 2005b Antioxidant efficiency in early life stages of the Antarctic silverfish *Pleuragramma antarcticum*: Responsiveness to pro- oxidant conditions of platelet ice and chemical exposure. *Aquatic Toxicology, vol. 75: 43- 52.*

Sarà A., Cerrano C., Sarà M., 2002. Viviparous development in the Antarctic sponge *Stylocordyla borealis* Loven, 1868. *Polar Biology* **25**: 425-31.

Sarà M., Balduzzi A., Barbieri M., Bavestrello G., Burlando B., 1992. Biogeographic traits and checklist of Antarctic demosponges. *Polar Biology* **12**: 559-85.

Schiaparelli S., Cattaneo-Vietti R., Chiantore M., 2000. Adaptive morphology of *Capulus subcompressus* Pelseneer, 1903 (Gastropoda: Capulidae) from Terra Nova Bay, Ross Sea (Antarctica). *Polar Biology* **23**: 11-16.

Simeoni U., Baroni C., Meccheri M., Taviani M., Zanon G., 1989. Coastal studies in Northern Victoria Land (Antarctica): Holocene beaches of Inexpressible island, Tethys Bay and Edmonson Point. *Boll. Ocean. Teor. Appl.* 7(1-2): 5-16.

Stocchino C., Lusetti C., 1988. Le costanti armoniche di marea di Baia Terra Nova (Mare di Ross, Antartide). F.C. 1128 *Istituto Idrografico della Marina*, Genova.

Stocchino C., Lusetti C., 1990. Prime osservazioni sulle caratteristiche idrologiche e dinamiche di Baia Terra Nova (Mare di Ross, Antartide). F.C. 1132 *Istituto Idrografico della Marina*, Genova.

Vacchi M., Greco S., La Mesa M., 1991. Ichthyological survey by fixed gears in Terra Nova Bay (Antarctica). Fish list and first results. *Memorie di Biologia Marina e di Oceanografia* **19**: 197-202.

Vacchi M., Romanelli M., La Mesa M., 1992. Age structure of *Chionodraco hamatus* (Teleostei, Channichthyidae) samples caught in Terra Nova Bay, East Antarctica. *Polar Biology* **12**: 735-38.

Vacchi M., Greco S., 1994a. Capture of the giant Nototheniid fish *Dissostichus mawsoni* in Terra Nova Bay (Antarctica): Notes on the fishing equipment and the specimens caught. *Cybium* **18**(2): 199-203.

Vacchi M., La Mesa M., Castelli A., 1994b. Diet of two coastal nototheniid fish from Terra Nova Bay, Ross Sea. *Antarctic Science* **6**(1): 61-65.

Vacchi M., La Mesa M., 1995. The diet of Antarctic fish *Trematomus newnesi* Boulenger, 1902 (Notothenidae) from Terra Nova Bay, Ross Sea. *Antarctic Science* 7(1): 37-38.

Vacchi M., La Mesa M., 1997. Morphometry of *Cryodraco* specimens of Terra Nova Bay. *Cybium* 21(4): 363-68.

Vacchi M., Cattaneo-Vietti R., Chiantore M., Dalù M., 2000a. Predator-prey relationship between nototheniid fish *Trematomus bernacchii* and Antarctic scallop *Adamussium colbecki* at Terra Nova Bay (Ross Sea). *Antarctic Science* 12(1): 64-68.

Vacchi M., La Mesa M., Greco S., 2000b. The coastal fish fauna of Terra Nova Bay, Ross Sea (Antarctica). In: *Ross Sea Ecology*, F. Faranda, L. Guglielmo and A. Ianora Eds., Springer Verlag, Berlin Heidelberg: 457-68.

Vacchi M., M. La Mesa, M. Dalù, J. MacDonald, 2004. Early life stages in the life cycle of Antarctic silverfish,*Pleuragramma antarcticum* in Terra Nova Bay, Ross Sea. *Antarctic Science*

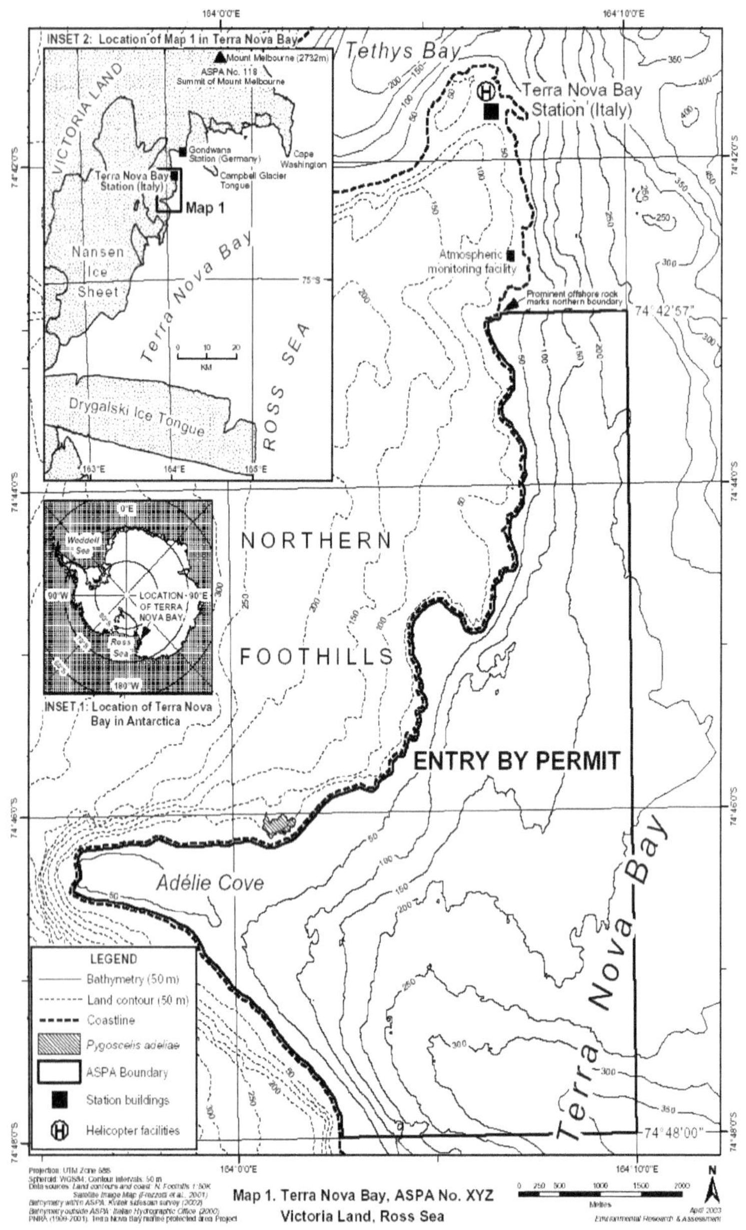

Map 1 Terra Nova Bay ASPA N° 161, Victoria Land, Ross Sea.

Appendix 1

Recent bibliography and other publications of interest for the research activities in the Terra Nova Bay.

Accornero A., Manno C., Arrigo K.R., Martini Atucci S., “The vertical flux of particulate matter in the polynya of Terra Nova Bay. Part I. Chemical constituents” Antarctic Science 15 (1), 119-132, (2003)

Alvaro M.C, Blazewicz-Paszkowycz M., Davey N., Schiaparelli S., 2011. Skin-digging tanaidaceans: the unusual parasitic behaviour of Exspina typica (Lang, 1968) in Antarctic waters and worldwide deep basins. Antarct Sci, vol. 23 (4); p. 343-348, ISSN: 0954-1020, doi: 10.1017/S0954102011000186

Budillon g. & Spezie G., “Thermoaline structure and variability in the Terra Nova Bay polynya (Ross Sea) between 1995-98”. Antarctic science 12, 243-254, (2000)

Ballerini T., Tavecchia G., Olmastroni S., Pezzo F., Focardi S., 2009. Nonlinear effects of winter sea ice on the survival probabilities of Adélie penguins. Oecologia 161:253–265.

Bargagli R.,2005. Antarctic Ecosystems. Environmental Contamination, Climate Change, and Human Impact. Ecological Studies ,vol. 175; Springer-Verlag, Heidelberg, 395 pp.

Bargagli R.,2008. Environmental contamination in Antarctic ecosystems. Sci. Total Environ. 400: 212-226.

Borghesi N., Corsolini S., Focardi S., 2008. Levels of polybrominated diphenyl ethers (PBDEs) and organochlorine pollutants in two species of Antarctic fish (*Chionodraco hamatus* and *Trematomus bernacchii*). Chemosphere, 73, 155–160.

Corsolini S., Kannan K., Imagawa T., Focardi S., Giesy J.P., 2002. Polychloronaphthalenes and other dioxin-like compounds in Arctic and Antarctic marine food webs. Environmental Science and Technology, 36: 3490-3496.

Corsolini S., 2009. Industrial contaminants in Antarctic biota. Journal of Chromatography A, 1216, 598–612.

Corsolini S. Borghesi N., Ademolo N., Focardi S., 2011. Chlorinated biphenyls and pesticides in migrating and resident seabirds from East and West Antarctica. Environment International 37(8): 1329-1335.

Corsolini S., 2011. Antarctic: Persistent Organic Pollutants and Environmental Health in the Region. In: Nriagu JO (ed.) Encyclopedia of Environmental Health, volume 1, pp. 83–96 Burlington: Elsevier,NVRN/978-0-444-52273-3

Castellano M “Aspetti trofo-funzionali dell'ecosistema marino costiero antartico: sostanza organica particellata e disciolta”, Univeristà degli Studi di Genova, PhD Thesys, (2006)

Chiantore M.C., Cattaneo-Vietti R., ELIA L., Guidetti M., Antonini M., "Reproduction and condition of the scallop Adamussium colbecki (Smith, 1902), the sea-urchin Strerechinus neumayeri (Meissner, 1900) and the sea-star Odontaster validus (Koehelr, 1911) at Terra nova Bay (Ross Sea): different related to interannual variations in food availability" Polar Biology 25, 251-255, (2002)

Guglielmo G., Zagami G., Saggiorno V., Catalano G., Granata A., "Copepods in spring annual sea ice at Terra Nova Bay (Ross Sea, Antarctica)" Polar Biology 30, 747-758, (2007)

Mangoni O., Modigh M., Conversano F., Carrada G.C., Saggiorno V., "Effects of summer ice coverege on phytoplankton assemblages in the Ross Sea, Antarctica" Deep-Sea Research I, 51, 1601-1617, (2004)

Massolo S., Messa R., Rivaro P., Leardi R., "Annual and spatial variations of chemical and physical properties in the Ross Sea surface waters (Antarctica)" Continental Shel Research 29, 2333-2344, (2009)

Pane L., Feletti m., Francomacaro B., Mariottini G.L., "Summer coastal zooplankton biomass and copepod community structure near the Italian Terra Nova Base (Terra Nova Bay, Ross Sea, Antarctica)" Journal of Plankton Research, vol 26, issue 12, 1479-1488, (2004)

Povero P., Chiantore M., Misic M.C., Budillon G., Cattaneo-Vietti R.,., "Land forcing controls pelagic-benthic coupling in Adelie Cove (Terra Nova Bay, Ross Sea)" Polar Biology 24, 875-882 (2000)

Povero P., Chiantore M., Misic M.C., Budillon G., Cattaneo-Vietti R.,., "Land forcing controls pelagic-benthic coupling in Adeliè Cove (Terra Nova Bay, Ross Sea)" Polar Biology 24, 875-882, (2001)

Povero P., Castellano M., Ruggieri N., Monticelli L.S., Saggiomo V., Chiantore M.C., Guidetti M., Cattaneo-Vietti R., "Water column features and their relationship with sediments and benthic communities along the Victoria Land coast, Ross Sea, Antarctica, summer 2004" Antarctic Science 18 (4), 603-613, (2006)

Swadling K.M., Penot F., Vallet C., Rouyer A., Gasparini S., Mousseau L., Smith M., Goffart A., Koubbi P., "Interannual variability of zooplancton in the Dumont d'Urville sea (39°E-146°E), east Antarctica, 2004-2008" Polar Science 5, 118-133, (2011)

Tagliabue A. & Arrigo K.R., "Anomalously low zooplankton abundane in the Ross Sea: An alternative explanation" Limnol. Oceanogr. 48, 686-699, (2003)

Van dijken G.L., Arrigo K.R., " Annual cycles of sea ice and phytoplankton in three Ross Sea polynyas" Poster at 3rd International Conference on the Oceanography of the Ross Sea Antarctica. Venezia, Italy, 10-14 Oct., (2005)

Vacchi M., La Mese M., Eastman J.T., "The role of notothenioid fish in the food web of the Ross Sea shelf waters: a review" Polar Biology 27(6), 321-338, (2004)

Appendix 2

During 2010-2012 Italian Antarctic Campaigns, few permits for activities and sampling into the Terra Nova Bay ASPA 161 have been issued:

Antarctic Campaign 2010-11

Activity site	Terra Nova Bay ASPA N° 161
N° of authorized entries	5
Lenght of each entry	4 h
Involved living organisms	teleostei fish, n° 150 Generic zooplancton, 120 samples adamussium colbacki n° 100

Antarctic Campaign 2011-12

Activity site	Terra Nova Bay ASPA N° 161
N° of authorized entries	8
Lenght of each entry	4 h
Involved living organisms	generic zooplancton 150 samples Invertebrate 200 samples Sponges 10 samples Adamussium colbacki n° 30

Sampling and studies activities into the ASPA area have been carried out in 13 different times for a total of 52 hours of work.

Besides, the following fish species and quantities, caught by barracude nets according to CCAMLR rules, have been collected inside the Terra Nova Bay marine ASPA N° 16 during 2011-2012 Italian Antarctic Campaign:

N°	Species	Total weight [kg]
29	Ch. hamatus	13.850
13	T. bernacchii	1.800
1	T. hansoni	0.150
2	Cr. antarcticus	0.300

Management Plan for Antarctic Specially Protected Area No. 170

MARION NUNATAKS, CHARCOT ISLAND, ANTARCTIC PENINSULA

Introduction

The primary reason for the designation of Marion Nunataks, Charcot Island, Antarctic Peninsula (69°45'S, 75°15'W) as an Antarctic Specially Protected Area (ASPA) is to protect primarily environmental values, and in particular the terrestrial flora and fauna within the Area.

Marion Nunataks lie on the northern edge of Charcot Island, a remote ice-covered island to the west of Alexander Island, Antarctic Peninsula, in the eastern Bellingshausen Sea. Marion Nunataks form a 12 km chain of rock outcrops on the mid-north coast of the island and stretch from Mount Monique on the western end to Mount Martine on the eastern end. The Area is 106.5 km^2 (maximum dimensions are 9.2 km north-south and 17.0 km east-west) and includes most, if not all, of the ice-free land on Charcot Island.

Past visits to the Area have been few, rarely more than a few days in duration and focussed initially on geological research. However, during visits between 1997 and 2000, British Antarctic Survey (BAS) scientists discovered a rich biological site, located on the Rils Nunatak at 69°44'56"S, 75°15'12"W.

Rils Nunatak has several unique characteristics including two lichens species that have not been recorded elsewhere in Antarctica, mosses that are rarely found at such southerly latitudes and, perhaps most significantly of all, a complete lack of predatory arthropods and Collembola, which are common at all other equivalent sites within the biogeographical zone. The nunataks are extremely vulnerable to introduction of locally and globally non-indigenous species that could be carried unintentionally to the site by visitors.

ASPA 170 Marion Nunataks was originally designated as an ASPA through Measure 4 (2008) after a proposal by the United Kingdom.

The Area fits into the wider context of the Antarctic Protected Area system by protecting the unique species assemblage found on Marion Nunataks and being the first to protect a substantial area of ground that is representative of the permanent ice-cap and nunataks that exist commonly in the southern Antarctic Peninsula. Resolution 3 (2008) recommended that the Environmental Domains Analysis for the Antarctic Continent, be used as a dynamic model for the identification of Antarctic Specially Protected Areas within the systematic environmental-geographical framework referred to in Article 3(2) of Annex V of the Protocol (see also Morgan et al., 2007). Using this model, ASPA 170 is contained within Environment Domain C (Antarctic Peninsula southern geologic) and Domain E (Antarctic Peninsula and Alexander Island main ice fields). Other protected areas containing Domain C include ASPA 147 (although not specifically stated in Morgan et al., 2007). Other protected areas containing Domain E include ASPAs 113, 114, 117, 126, 128, 129, 133, 134, 139, 147, 149, 152, and ASMAs 1 and 4. The ASPA sits within Antarctic Conservation Biogeographic Region (ACBR) 4 Central South Antarctic Peninsula, and is one of only two ASPAs in ACBR 4, the other being ASPA 147 (Terauds et al., 2012).

1. Description of values to be protected

The outstanding environmental value of the Area, which is the primary reason for designation as an ASPA, is based on the following unique species assemblage found in the terrestrial environment:

- The terrestrial fauna is unique for the maritime Antarctic in that it appears to contain neither predatory arthropods nor Collembola (springtails), which are otherwise ubiquitous and important members of the terrestrial fauna of the zone. As such, the site provides unique opportunities for the scientific study of terrestrial biological communities from the maritime Antarctic where key ecological components are absent.
- The Marion Nunataks flora includes an exceptional development of three mosses that are encountered only rarely at latitudes south of 65°S (*Brachythecium austrosalebrosum*, *Dicranoweisia crispula* and *Polytrichum piliferum*).
- The Area includes two lichen species that are previously unrecorded from Antarctica (*Psilolechia lucida* and *Umbilicaria* aff. *thamnodes*) and represents the furthest south known occurrence for several lichen species (including *Frutidella caesioatra*, *Massalongia* spp., *Ochrolechia frigida*, *Usnea aurantiaco-atra* and *Usnea trachycarpa*).

The values are vulnerable to human impacts including damage to habitat by, for example, trampling, or the introduction of non-indigenous species that may disrupt ecosystem structure and function.

2. Aims and Objectives

The aims and objectives of this Management Plan are to:

- avoid degradation of, or substantial risk to, the values of the Area by preventing unnecessary human disturbance to the Area;
- prevent or minimise the introduction to the Area of non-native plants, animals and microbes;
- minimise the possibility of the introduction of pathogens which may cause disease in fauna populations within the Area;
- allow scientific research in the Area provided it is for compelling reasons which cannot be served elsewhere and which will not jeopardize the natural ecological system in that Area; and
- preserve the natural ecosystem of the Area as a reference area for future studies.

3. Management Activities

Management activities that involve visits to the Area and erection of permanent structures may themselves significantly increase the risk of irreversible human impact, through introductions of locally non-native species. Therefore, the emphasis for management of the site should be to avoid unnecessary visits and importation of materials into the Area. The following management activities are to be undertaken to protect the values of the Area:

- Due to the sensitive nature of the Area and the severity of the consequences should non-native species be introduced, management visits shall be kept to an absolute minimum and erection of permanent structures, including notice boards and signs, on ice-free ground shall be avoided.
- Visiting field parties shall be briefed fully by the national authority on the values that are to be protected within the Area and the precautions and mitigation measures detailed in this Management Plan.
- Copies of this Management Plan shall be made available to vessels and aircraft planning to visit the vicinity of the Area.
- The Management Plan shall be reviewed at least every five years and updated as required.
- A copy of this Management Plan shall be made available at Rothera Research Station (UK; 67°34'S, 68°07'W) and General San Martín Station (Argentina; 68°08'S, 67°06'W).

- All scientific and management activities undertaken within the Area should be subject to an Environmental Impact Assessment, in accordance with the requirements of Annex I of the Protocol on Environmental Protection to the Antarctic Treaty.
- National Antarctic Programmes operating in the Area shall consult together with a view to ensuring the above management activities are implemented.

4. Period of Designation

Designated for an indefinite period.

5. Maps

Map 1. Charcot Island in relation to Alexander Island and the Antarctic Peninsula. Map specifications: WGS84 Antarctic Polar Stereographic. Central meridian -55°, Standard parallel: -71°.

Map 2. Charcot Island, including ASPA 170 Marion Nunataks situated in the northwest of the island. Map specifications: WGS 1984 Antarctic Polar Stereographic. Central Meridian: -75°, Standard Parallel: -71.0°.

Map 3. ASPA 170 Marion Nunataks, Charcot Island, Antarctic Peninsula. Map specifications: WGS 1984 Antarctic Polar Stereographic. Central Meridian: -75°, Standard Parallel: -71.0°. Developed from USGS Landsat Image Mosaic of Antarctica, Scene ID: x-2250000y+0450000. Metadata available at http://lima.usgs.gov/.

6. Description of the Area

6 (i) Geographical coordinates, boundary markers and natural features

Charcot Island is roughly circular in shape, approximately 50 km across and is separated from northwest Alexander Island (~100 km away) by Wilkins Sound to the east and Attenborough Strait to the south (Maps 1 and 2). Until recently, Charcot Island was connected to Alexander Island by the Wilkins Ice Shelf, but substantial collapse occurred in 2008 and the ice bridge gave way in April 2009 (Vaughan et al., 1993; Braun et al., 2009). Charcot Island is ice-covered with the exception of Marion Nunataks (69°45'S, 75°15'W), which form a 12 km chain of rock outcrops that overlook the mid-north coast of Charcot Island, and consist predominantly of steep north–facing cliffs (Map 3). Mount Monique lies towards the western end of the Marion Nunataks chain and Mount Martine to the eastern end. The summits of both peaks are between 750 and 1000 metres above sea level.

The Area boundary is defined as follows:

The point on the northern coast of Charcot Island at 69°43'07"S, 75°00'00"W represents the most north-easterly point of the Area. From here, the Area boundary follows the coastline westwards to the point on the coast at 69°48'00"S, 75°19'19"W. The boundary then extends eastward inland to a point on the Charcot Island ice-cap at 69°48'00"S, 75°00'00"W. From there the boundary extends northwards to the coast at 69°43'07"S, 75°00'00"W. The Area also includes Cheeseman Island (located at 69°43'24"S, 75°11'00"W).

There are no boundary markers delimiting the Area. The maximum dimensions of the Area are 9.2 km north-south and 17.0 km east-west (106.5 km^2). The Area includes ice cap that extends at least 4 km to the south and east of Marion Nunataks, which is intended to act as a buffer zone to prevent accidental importation of species not native to the Area (see Map 3). The steep ice cliffs on the north coast of Charcot Island, make access from the sea difficult.

Climatic conditions

No climatic data are available, but Charcot Island lies in the track of depressions approaching the Antarctic Peninsula from the west. Satellite imagery indicates that the island is predominantly covered by cloud, and may not become free of winter pack ice until late summer, if at all.

Biogeography

Research by Smith (1984) and Peat et al. (2007) describes the recognised biogeographical regions present within the Antarctic Peninsula. Antarctica can be divided into three major biological provinces: northern maritime, southern maritime and continental. Charcot Island lies within the southern maritime zone (Smith, 1984), approximately 600 km north of the major biogeographic discontinuity that separates the Antarctic Peninsula and continental Antarctica known at the Gressitt Line (Chown and Convey, 2007). It also lies within ACBR 4, Central South Antarctic Peninsula (Terauds et al., 2012)

Geology

The rocks of Marion Nunataks are turbiditic sandstones and mudstones, similar in appearance to those found on nearby Alexander Island. However, geochronology and isotopic analyses from detrital minerals (grains that survive erosion, transport and deposition and so preserve information on the source rock) suggest that Charcot Island rocks are different to those on Alexander Island, and possibly the whole of the Antarctic Peninsula (Michael Flowerdew, pers. comm.). Alexander Island rocks are thought to have formed from sediments eroded off rocks from the Antarctic Peninsula. However, Charcot Island sediments were originally deposited within a deep marine trench that formed as a result of the destruction of the Pacific plate beneath the edge of the ancient continent of Gondwana. The sedimentary rocks were scraped off the Pacific plate as it was destroyed and accreted to the Gondwana continent, causing them to be folded and methamorphosed under high pressure. Charcot Island sedimentary rocks are thought to be Cretaceous (deposited around 120 million years ago), and may have been transported over long distances in a relatively short time interval before becoming juxtaposed to Alexander Island around 107 million years ago.

Biology

The known terrestrial biological site (located on the Rils Nunatak at 69°44'56"S, 75°15'12"W) extends approximately 200 m east-west, by a maximum of 50 m north-south and harbours an extensive biota (Convey et al., 2000). This vegetated bluff consists of rock gently sloping to the north-west, which rapidly steepens to broken cliffs that drop to the sea. Water has been observed to be freely available at the site during all summer visits between December 1997 and January 2000.

Biota in the known terrestrial biological site include:

- Bryophytes: 16 mosses (including Andreaea spp., Bartramia patens, Bryum pseudotriquetrum, Brachythecium austrosalebrosum, Ceratodon purpureus, Dicranoweisia crispula, Grimmia reflexidens, Hennediella heimii, Hypnum revolutum, Pohlia spp., Polytrichum piliferum, Schistidium antarctici, Syntrichia princeps) and one liverwort (Cephaloziella varians). The dominant species are Andreaea spp., Dicranoweisia crispula and Polytrichum piliferum, which are usually only common in the sub-Antarctic. The abundance of B. austrosalebrosum is remarkable as it is a hydric species requiring a continuous supply of water. The mosses generally occur on wet rock slabs irrigated by trickling melt water from late snow patches which has allowed the formation of cushions c. 15 cm deep. (Smith, 1998; Convey et al., 2000).
- Foliose alga: Prasiola crispa (Smith, 1998; Convey et al., 2000).
- Lichens: 34 species, plus two identified to genus level. The dominant lichen species are Pseudophebe minuscule, Umbilicaria decussata, Usnea sphacelata and various crustose taxa (Smith, 1998; Convey et al., 2000). Lichen communities occupy much of the dry, windswept stony ground and ridges. Melt channels on sloping rock slabs are lined with large thalli (up to ~15 cm across) of Umbilicaria antarctica. The Area includes two lichen species that are previously unrecorded from Antarctica (Psilolechia lucida and Umbilicaria

aff. thamnodes) and represents the furthest south known occurrence for several lichen species (including Frutidella caesioatra, Massalongia spp., Ochrolechia frigida, Usnea aurantiaco-atra and Usnea trachycarpa). Unusually, the widespread Usnea antarctica was not recorded from the site.

- Invertebrates: Seven species of Acari, seven Nematoda and four Tardigrada were present in collections from Marion Nunataks. Uniquely, neither acarine predators nor Collembola were recorded (Convey, 1999; Convey et al., 2000).
- Vertebrates: A small colony of 60 Adelie penguins (Pygoscelis adeliae) containing many chicks was reported from the small islands just to the northwest of Mount Monique (Henderson, 1976; Croxall and Kirkwood, 1979). The colony was still present at the location in January 2011 with 70 breeding pairs and numerous chicks recorded. This is thought to be the most southerly colony of Adélie penguins on the Antarctic Peninsula. Other than the penguin colony, the Area has little vertebrate influence. South polar skuas (Catharacta maccormicki) are observed in the Area and a single nest was found on moss turf. Other birds observed and considered likely to breed in the area were small numbers of Antarctic terns (Sterna vittata), snow petrels (Pagodroma nivea), Antarctic petrels (Thalassoica antarctica) and Wilson's storm petrels (Oceanites oceanicus Kühl) (Henderson, 1976; Smith, 1998; Convey et al., 2000).

Although all elements of the biota recorded are typical of the maritime Antarctic biogeographical zone (Smith, 1984), community composition differs strikingly in detail from that found at other sites in the biome. The apparent absence of Collembola, recorded at all other known maritime Antarctic sites, contrasts directly with their importance elsewhere. Numbers of other animal species recovered from Marion Nunataks, suggest population densities comparable with those found in many other coastal maritime Antarctic sites and at least an order of magnitude greater than those usually found in Continental Antarctic sites, or on south-east Alexander Island at the southern limit of the maritime Antarctic. The numerical contribution made by springtails to faunas elsewhere in the maritime Antarctic appears to be replaced by several smaller prostigmatid mites (*Nanorchestes nivalis* and *Eupodes minutes*) on Charcot Island. The absence of predatory taxa is also an exceptional element of the Charcot Island arthropod community, particularly given the arthropod population densities.

The terrestrial biological communities on Charcot Island are extremely vulnerable to accidental human-mediated introduction of both native Antarctic and non-native biota. Convey et al. (2000) write:

> *'As visitors to this island will inevitably arrive from other locations within the [Antarctic] Maritime zone, the potential for accidental transfer in soil or vegetation adhering to boots or clothing, rucksacks, etc. is great. Extreme caution is therefore required to avoid the transfer of native species between isolated populations within the Maritime Antarctic, highlighting an urgent need for strict control measures to be applied to all visitors to the site and others like it to conserve them for the future.'*

Past human activity

The Area is extremely isolated and difficult to access, other than by air, and as a result has been visited by only a small number of people, and these visits have been generally brief. Charcot Island was discovered on 11 January 1910 by Dr Jean Baptiste Charcot of the French Antarctic Expedition. The first landing on the island was made on 21 November 1947 by the Ronne Antarctic Research Expedition (RARE) when parts of the island were photographed from the air (Searle, 1963).

A temporary hut (30 m^2) and airstrip were established by the Chilean Antarctic Expedition and Chilean Air Force (FACH) in November 1982. The camp was situated on ice a few kilometres east of Mount Martine (69°43'S, 75°00'W), on what is now the eastern boundary of the Area. The hut was buried by snow during the winter of 1983 and no evidence of the station remains on the surface (Comite Nacional de Investigaciones Antarcticas, 1983; Veronica Vallejos, pers comm.).

British Antarctic Survey (BAS) geologists and cartographers made brief visits to Marion Nunataks in January 1975, 9-13 February 1976 and 17 January 1995. BAS biologists made day trips to Rils Nunatak on 22 December 1997, 20-21 January 1999, 5 February 1999 and 16 January 2000. Reports suggest that there have been less than 10 field party visits to Marion Nunataks since their first visit in 1975. Visits have generally been limited to a few days or hours. Importantly, no further visits have been made to Marion Nunataks, inland from the coast, since the discovery of its unique ecosystems (Convey et al., 2000). As a result, it is probable that the ecosystem still exists in it original pristine state and no introduction of macrobiota has occurred.

Brief boat landings were made at the Adélie penguin colony on the coast northwest of Mount Monique by scientists from the United States in early 2010 and 2011.

6 (ii) Access to the Area

No access points are specified, but landings are usually most safely made by aircraft on areas of permanent ice, as accessing inland locations from the sea is made difficult due to step ice cliffs around much of the coastline. Aircraft landing within the Area must comply with the condition described in section *7(ii)*. In early 2010 and 2011, brief landings were made from the sea by scientist from the United States to visit the Adélie penguin colony situated on ice-free ground to the northwest of Mt. Monique (approximate location 69°45'40" S, 75°25'00" W). The landings were made despite difficult sea ice conditions, which are common in this area. Furthermore, sea ice conditions prevented further landings in 2012. Consequently, this route is not recommended for general access to the Area.

6 (iii) Location of structures within and adjacent to the Area

No installations or caches are known to exist in the Area. One cairn was constructed on the highest point (~126 m above sea level) of the small nunatak at 69°44'55" S, 75°15'00" W during the 1975-76 United States Geological Survey (USGS)-British Antarctic Survey Doppler Satellite Programme (Schoonmaker and Gatson, 1976). The 0.6 m high cairn marks the site of Station Jon and contains a standard USGS brass Antarctica tablet stamped 'Jon 1975-1976' set loosely in faulted rock. A metal tent pole (2.4 m) was erected in the cairn; however, there was no record of it in visit reports from 1995 onwards (Anonymous, 1977; Morgan, 1995).

6 (iv) Location of other protected Areas in the vicinity

There are no other ASPAs or ASMAs in the vicinity, with the nearest protected area being ASPA No. 147 Ablation Valley and Ganymede Heights, which is situated 270 km away on the eastern coast of Alexander Island.

6 (v) Special zones within the Area

There are no special zones in the Area.

7. Terms and conditions for entry permits

7(i) General permit conditions

Entry into the Area is prohibited except in accordance with a permit issued by an appropriate national authority under Article 3, paragraph 4, and Article 7 of Annex V to the Protocol on Environmental Protection to the Antarctic Treaty.

Conditions for issuing a Permit to enter the Area are that:

- it is issued for a compelling scientific reason, which cannot be served elsewhere, or for reasons essential to the management of the Area;

- the activities permitted will give due consideration via the environmental impact assessment process to the continued protection of the environmental and scientific values of the Area;
- the activities permitted are in accordance with this Management Plan;
- the Permit, or an authorised copy, shall be carried when in the Area;
- the Permit shall be issued for a finite period;
- a report is supplied to the authority or authorities named in the Permit; and
- the appropriate authority should be notified of any activities/measures undertaken that were not included in the authorised Permit.

7(ii) Access to, and movement within or over, the Area

Where possible, day visits to the Area are strongly recommended in order to remove the requirement for camping equipment, and therefore reduce the risk of transferring locally non-native species into the Area. If management or scientific requirements cannot be met within the time scale of a single day visit, then longer visits requiring camping within the Area are permitted, but only after all other options have been full explored and rejected.

Entry of personnel or equipment arriving directly from other terrestrial biological field sites to the Area is prohibited. It is a condition of entry into the Area that all visitors and equipment must travel via an Antarctic station or ship where thorough cleaning of clothing and equipment has been performed, as detailed in this Management Plan (section *7(x)*).

To protect the values of the Area and minimise the risk of introduction of locally non-native species, the following restrictions apply within the Area:

(a) <u>Aircraft</u>

Aircraft are only permitted to land in the Area if they have performed the measures as detailed in this Management Plan (section *7(x)*). Otherwise aircraft must land outside the Area. Within the Area, fixed and rotory wing aircraft are prohibited from landing within 100 m of ice-free ground and the associated flora and fauna. The remaining 100 m of the approach to the ice-free ground must be made on foot.

An Adélie penguin colony is present within the Area on coastal ground to the northwest of Mount Monique (approximate location 69°44'40" S, 75°25'00" W). The operation of aircraft over the Area should be carried out, as a minimum requirement, in compliance with the *Guidelines for the Operation of Aircraft near Concentrations of Birds* contained in Resolution 2 (2004).

(b) <u>Ships and small boats</u>

Little information is available on locations appropriate for ship and small boat landings (see section *6(ii)*). Given the unpredictable nature of sea ice conditions in the region, landings by boat are not recommended for general access to the Area. However, boat lands may be appropriate for visiting coastal locations, such as the Adélie penguin colony northwest of Mt. Monique (approximate location 69°45'40" S, 75°25'00" W).

(c) <u>Land vehicles and sledges</u>

Land vehicles shall not be taken into the Area unless essential for scientific, management or safety reasons. Land vehicles and sledges are only permitted within the Area if they are compliant with the measures as detailed in this Management Plan (section *7(x)*). Once inside the Area, skidoos, sledges and other land vehicles are prohibited within 100 m of all ice-free ground and associated flora and fauna. The remaining 100 m of the approach to the ice-free ground must be made on foot.

(d) Human movement

Pedestrian traffic shall be keep to an absolute minimum necessary to be consistent with the objectives of any permitted activities. Where no routes are identified, pedestrian traffic should be kept to the minimum necessary to undertake permitted activities and every reasonable effort should be made to minimise trampling effects. Visitors should avoid areas of visible vegetation and care should be exercised walking in areas of moist ground, particularly the stream course beds, where foot traffic can easily damage sensitive soils, plant and algal communities, and degrade water quality.

Strict personal quarantine precautions shall be undertaken as described in section *7(x)* of this Management Plan.

7(iii) Activities which may be conducted in the Area

Activities which may be conducted in the Area include:

- compelling scientific research that cannot be undertaken elsewhere and which will not jeopardize the ecosystem of the Area;
- sampling, which should be the minimum required for approved research programmes; and
- essential management activities, including monitoring.

7(iv) Installation, modification or removal of structures

- No structures are to be erected within the Area, or scientific equipment installed, except for compelling scientific or management reasons and for a pre-established period, as specified in a permit.
- Permanent structures or installations are prohibited.
- All markers, structures or scientific equipment installed in the Area must be clearly identified by country, name of the principal investigator or agency, year of installation and date of expected removal.
- All such items should be free of organisms, propagules (e.g. seeds, eggs, spores) and non-sterile soil (see section *7(x)*), and be made of materials that can withstand the environmental condition and pose minimal risk of contamination of the Area.
- Removal of specific structures or equipment for which the permit has expired shall be the responsibility of the authority which granted the original permit and shall be a condition of the Permit.
- Existing structures must not be removed, except in accordance with a permit.

7(v) Location of field camps

Camping within the Area is only permitted if scientific and management objectives cannot be achieved during a day trip to the Area. Camping may also occur within the Area during an emergency. Unless unavoidable for safety reason, tents should be erected on permanent snow or ice, at least 500 m from the nearest ice-free area. Field camp equipment must be cleaned and transported as described in section *7(x)* of this Management Plan.

7(vi) Restrictions on materials and organisms which may be brought into the Area

In addition to the requirements of the Protocol on Environmental Protection to the Antarctic Treaty, restrictions on materials and organisms which may be brought into the area are as follows:

- The deliberate introduction of animals, plant material, microorganisms and non-sterile soil into the Area shall not be permitted.
- Precautions shall be taken to prevent the unintentional introduction of animals, plant material, microorganisms and non-sterile soil from other biologically distinct regions

(within or beyond the Antarctic Treaty area). Visitors should also consult and follow, as appropriate, recommendations contained in the *CEP non-native species manual* (CEP, 2011), and in the *Environmental code of conduct for terrestrial scientific field research in Antarctica* (SCAR, 2009). Additional site-specific biosecurity measures are listed in section *7(x)*.

- No poultry products, including food products containing uncooked dried eggs, shall be taken into the Area.
- No herbicides or pesticides shall be brought into the Area. Any other chemicals, including radio-nuclides or stable isotopes, which may be introduced for a compelling scientific purpose specified in the Permit, shall be removed from the Area at or before the conclusion of the activity for which the Permit was granted. Release of radio-nuclides or stable isotopes directly into the environment in a way that renders them unrecoverable should be avoided.
- Fuel, food and other materials are not to be deposited in the Area, unless required for essential purposes connected with the activity for which the Permit has been granted. They shall be stored and handled in a way that minimises the risk of their accidental introduction into the environment. Fuel, food and other materials must only be stored on snow or ice that is at least 500 m from the nearest ice-free ground. Permanent depots are not permitted.
- Materials introduced into the Area shall be for a stated period only and shall be removed by the end of that stated period.

7(vii) Taking of, or harmful interference with, native flora and fauna

Taking of, or harmful interference with, native flora and fauna is prohibited, except in accordance with a permit issued in accordance with Annex II of the Protocol on Environmental Protection to the Antarctic Treaty. Where taking or harmful interference with animals is involved this should, as a minimum standard, be in accordance with the *SCAR code of conduct for the use of animals for scientific purposes in Antarctica* (2011). Any soil or vegetation sampling is to be kept to an absolute minimum required for scientific or management purposes, and carried out using techniques which minimise disturbance to surrounding soil, ice structures and biota.

7(viii) The collection or removal of materials not brought into the Area by the permit holder

Material may be collected or removed from the Area only in accordance with a permit and should be limited to the minimum necessary to meet scientific or management needs. Material of human origin likely to compromise the values of the Area, and which was not brought into the Area by the Permit Holder or otherwise authorised may be removed from the Area unless the environmental impact of the removal is likely to be greater than leaving the material in situ: if this is the case the appropriate national authority must be notified and approval obtained.

7(ix) Disposal of waste

All wastes, including all human waste, shall be removed from the Area.

7(x) Measures that may be necessary to continue to meet the aims of the Management Plan

To help protect the ecological and scientific values derived from the isolation and low level of human impact at the Areas, visitors shall take special precautions against the introduction of non-native species. Of particular concern are animal or plant introductions sourced from:

- soils from any other Antarctic sites, including those near stations
- soils from regions outside Antarctica

It is a condition of entry to the Area that visitors shall minimize the risk of introductions in accordance with the following measures:

(a) <u>Aircraft</u>

The interior and exterior of aircraft shall have been carefully inspected and cleaned as near as possible to the time of departure of the aircraft from the originating Antarctic station or ship. It is recommended that this include thorough sweeping and vacuuming of the inside of the aircraft and steam-cleaning or brushing of the exterior of the aircraft.

Any aircraft that has landed at other rock airstrips or near biologically rich sites since being cleaned at the Antarctic station or ship is not permitted to enter the Area.

Fixed-wing aircraft that departed from a gravel runway must have landed, or trailed their skis, on clean snow outside the Area in an attempt to dislodge any soil from the skis, before landing within the Area.

(b) Small boats

Small boats used to transport visitors from a support vessel to the Area boundary shall be cleaned (with particular attention paid to the inside of the boats) to ensure they are free of soil, dirt and propagules.

(c) Land vehicles and sledges

Before land vehicles and sledges enter the Area, all mud, soil, vegetation and excessive dirt and grease must be removed. Ideally, this should have been completed on the originating Antarctic station or ship before transfer of the vehicles into the field. Land vehicles shall not enter the Area if after cleaning they have been driven over areas of rock or soil outside the Area.

(d) Field camp equipment

All camping equipment, including emergency camping equipment, shall be cleaned thoroughly (i.e. free of soil and propagules and, if practicable, sealed in plastic bags or sheeting) before being taken into the Area. This includes emergency camping equipment carried aboard any aircraft landing in the Area.

(e) Sampling equipment, scientific apparatus and field-site markers

To the greatest extent possible, all sampling equipment, scientific apparatus and markers brought into the Area shall have been sterilized, and maintained in a sterile condition, before being used within the Area. Sterilization should be by an accepted method, including UV radiation, autoclaving or by surface sterilisation using 70% ethanol or a commercially available biocide (e.g. Virkon®) (see the *Environmental code of conduct for terrestrial scientific field research in Antarctica* (SCAR, 2009)).

(f) General field equipment

General equipment includes harnesses, crampons, climbing equipment, ice axes, walking poles, ski equipment, temporary route markers, pulks, sledges, camera and video equipment, rucksacks, sledge boxes and all other personal equipment.

All equipment used inside the Area should be free of biological propagules such as seeds, eggs, insects, fragments of vegetation and soil. To the maximum extent practicable, all equipment used, or brought into the Area, shall have been thoroughly cleaned at the originating Antarctic station or ship. Equipment shall have been maintained in this condition before entering the Area, preferably by sealing in plastic bags or other clean containers.

(g) Outer clothing

Outer clothing includes hats, gloves, fleeces or jumpers, jackets, fabric or fleece trousers, waterproof trousers or salopettes, socks, boots and any other clothing likely to be worn as a surface layer. Outer clothing worn inside the Area should be free of biological propagules such as seeds, eggs, insects, fragments of vegetation and soil. To the maximum extent practicable, footwear and outer clothing used, or brought into the Area, shall have been thoroughly laundered and cleaned since used previously. Particular attention should be given to removing seeds and propagules from Velcro®. New clothing, taken straight out of the manufacturer's packaging just before entering the Area, need not undergo cleaning.

Further procedures for ensuring non-native species are not transferred into the Area on footwear and clothing depend upon whether the visit is via (i) a direct aircraft landing in the Area, (ii) overland movement into the Area from outside its boundaries or (iii) movement to the Area boundary by small boat:

i. Direct aircraft landing in the Area. Sterile protective over-clothing shall be worn. The protective clothing shall be put on immediately prior to leaving the aircraft. Spare boots, previously cleaned using a biocide then sealed in plastic bags, shall be unwrapped and put on just before entering the Area.

ii. Overland movement into the Area from outside its boundaries. Sterile protective over-clothing is not recommended as, once within the Area, significant amounts of travel over crevassed ground may be required and use of sterile protective over-clothing may interfere with safety equipment such as ropes and harnesses. For overland movement into the Area, alternative measures must be used. Each visitor is required to bring at least two sets of outer clothing. The first set shall be worn for the journey to the Area boundary. The second set of outer clothing, which has previously been cleaned and sealed in plastic bags, shall only be worn inside the Area. Immediately before entering the Area, visitors shall change into their clean set of outer clothing. Spare boots, previously cleaned using a biocide then sealed in plastic bags, shall be unwrapped and put on just before entering the Area. The removed unclean outer clothing shall be stored in sealed, labelled plastic bags, preferably outside the Area. On leaving the Area by overland travel, the clothing worn in the Area should be removed and stored in a clean, labelled plastic bag until needed for any further trips into the Area, or returned to the originating Antarctic station or ship for cleaning.

iii. Movement to the Area boundary by small boat. When aboard the support vessel, and immediately prior to entering the small boat to travel to the Area, each visitor, including the boat crew, shall put on clean clothing (including boating suits, life jackets and footwear) which is free of soil, seeds and other propagules. Alternatively, on arrival at the Area boundary, and before exiting the small boat, visitors shall cover all clothing in clean protective oversuits. Additional clothing or footwear required by visitors when within the Area, shall be cleaned before leaving the support vessel, and stored in a sealed container (e.g. plastic bag) until needed.

7(xi) Requirements for reports

The principal permit holder for each visit to the Area shall submit a report to the appropriate national authority as soon as practicable, and no later than six months after the visit has been completed. Such reports should include, as appropriate, the information identified in the *Antarctic Specially Protected Area visit report form* contained in the *Guide to the Preparation of Management Plans for Antarctic Specially Protected Areas* (Appendix 2). In this report, particular note should be made of the specific ice-free locations visited within the Area (including, if possible, GPS coordinates), the length of time spent at each location and the activities undertaken. Wherever possible, the national authority should also forward a copy of the visit report to the Party that proposed the Management Plan, to assist in managing the Area and reviewing the Management Plan. Parties should, wherever possible, deposit originals or copies of such original visit reports in a publicly accessible archive to maintain a record of usage, for the purpose of any review of the Management Plan and in organising the scientific use of the Area.

8. Supporting documentation

Anonymous. (1977). British Antarctic Survey Archives Service, Arc. Ref. ES2/EW360.1/SR17-18/7,8.

Antarctic Treaty Consultative Meeting. (2004). Guidelines for the operation of aircraft near concentrations of birds in Antarctica. ATCM Resolution 2 (2004).

Braun, M., Humbert, A., and Moll, A. (2009). Changes of Wilkins Ice Shelf over the past 15 years and inferences on its stability. The Cryosphere 3: 41-56.

Comite Nacional de Investigaciones Antarcticas. (1983). Informe de las actividades Antarcticas de Chile al SCAR. Santiago, Instituto Antarctico Chileno.

Committee for Environmental Protection (CEP). (2011). Non-native species manual – 1st Edition. Manual prepared by Intersessional Contact Group of the CEP and adopted by the Antarctic Treaty Consultative Meeting through Resolution 6 (2011). Buenos Aires, Secretariat of the Antarctic Treaty.

Chown, S. L., and Convey, P. (2007). Spatial and temporal variability across life's hierarchies in the terrestrial Antarctic. Philosophical Transactions of the Royal Society B - Biological Sciences 362 (1488): 2307-2R31.

Convey, P. (1999). Terrestrial invertebrate ecology. Unpublished British Antarctic Survey internal report Ref. R/1998/NT5.

Convey, P., Smith, R. I. L., Peat, H. J. and Pugh, P. J. A. (2000). The terrestrial biota of Charcot Island, eastern Bellingshausen Sea, Antarctica: an example of extreme isolation. Antarctic Science 12: 406-413.

Croxall, J. P., and Kirkwood, E. D. (1979). The distribution of penguins on the Antarctic Peninsula and islands of the Scotia Sea. British Antarctic Survey, Cambridge.

Henderson, I. (1976). Summer log of travel and work of sledge kilo in northern Alexander Island and Charcot Island, 1975/1976. Unpublished British Antarctic Survey internal report Ref. T/1975/K11.

Morgan, F., Barker, G., Briggs, C., Price, R., and Keys, H. (2007). Environmental Domains of Antarctica Version 2.0 Final Report. Landcare Research Contract Report LC0708/055.

Morgan, T. (1995). Sledge echo travel report, 1994/5 season – geology in central Alexander Island. Unpublished British Antarctic Survey internal report Ref. R/1994/K7.

Peat, H. J., Clarke, A., and Convey, P. (2007). Diversity and biogeography of the Antarctic flora. Journal of Biogeography 34: 132-146.

Schoonmaker, J. W., and Gatson, K. W. (1976). U. S. Geological Survey/British Antarctic Survey Landsat Georeceiver Project. British Antarctic Survey Archives Service, Arc. Ref. ES2/EW360/56.

SCAR (Scientific Committee on Antarctic Research) (2009). Environmental code of conduct for terrestrial scientific field research in Antarctica. ATCM XXXII IP4.

SCAR (Scientific Committee on Antarctic Research) (2011). SCAR code of conduct for the use of animals for scientific purposes in Antarctica. ATCM XXXIV IP53.

Searle, D. J. H. (1963). The evolution of the map of Alexander and Charcot Islands, Antarctica. The Geographical Journal 129: 156-166.

Smith, R. I. L. (1984). Terrestrial plant biology of the sub-Antarctic and Antarctic. In: Antarctic Ecology, Vol. 1. Editor: R. M. Laws. London, Academic Press.

Smith, R. I. L. (1998). Field report: sledge delta, November 1997 - January 1998. Unpublished British Antarctic Survey internal report Ref. R/1997/NT3.

Terauds, A., Chown, S. L., Morgan, F., Peat, H. J., Watt, D., Keys, H., Convey, P., and Bergstrom, D. M. (2012). Conservation biogeography of the Antarctic. Diversity and Distributions 18: 726–41.

Vaughan, D. G., Mantripp, D. R., Sievers, J., and Doake C. S. M. (1993). A synthesis of remote sensing data on Wilkins Ice Shelf, Antarctica. Annals of Glaciology: 17: 211-218.

Map 1. Charcot Island in relation to Alexander Island and the Antarctic Peninsula. Map specifications: WGS84 Antarctic Polar Stereographic. Central meridian -55°, Standard parallel: -71°.

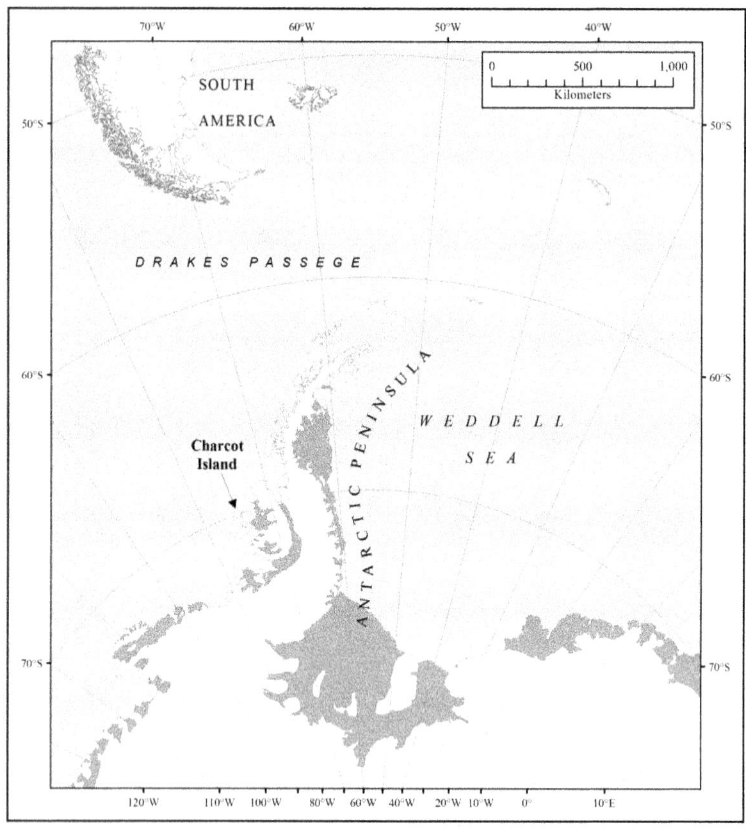

Map 2. Charcot Island, including ASPA 170 Marion Nunataks situated in the northwest of the island. Map specifications: WGS 1984 Antarctic Polar Stereographic. Central Meridian: -75°, Standard Parallel 1: -71.0°.

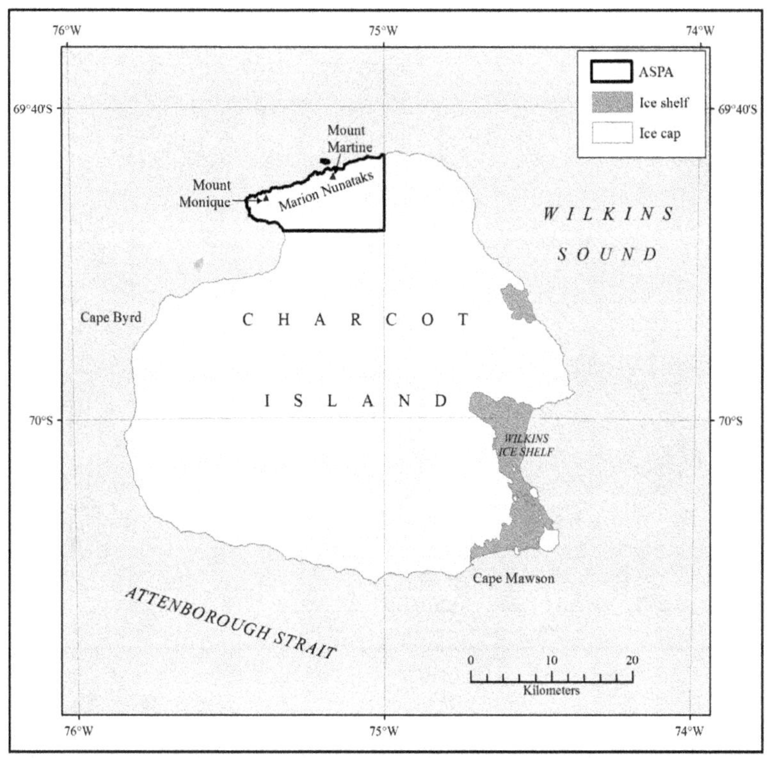

Map 3. ASPA 170 Marion Nunataks, Charcot Island, Antarctic Peninsula. Map specifications: WGS 1984 Antarctic Polar Stereographic. Central Meridian: -75°, Standard Parallel 1: -71.0°. Developed from USGS Landsat Image Mosaic of Antarctica, Scene ID: x-2250000y+0450000. Metadata available at http://lima.usgs.gov/.

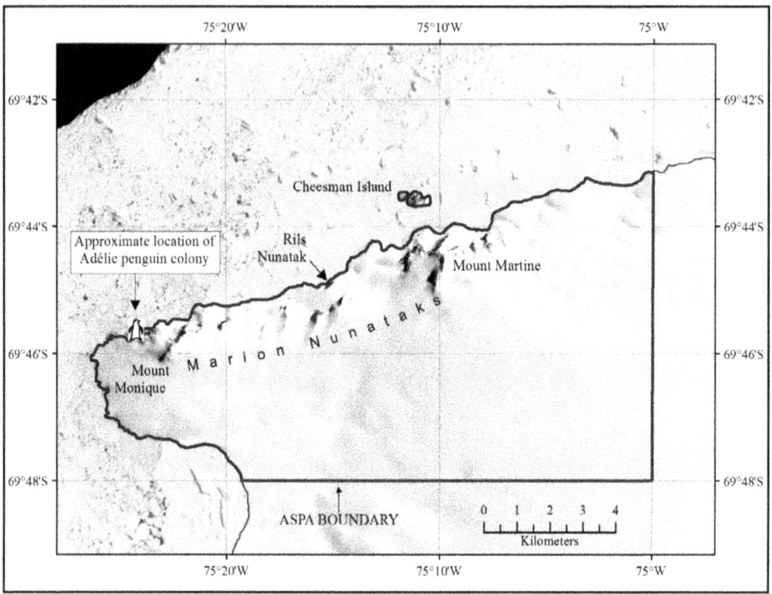

Management Plan for Antarctic Specially Protected Area (ASPA) No. 173 Cape Washington & Silverfish Bay Northern Terra Nova Bay Ross Sea

Introduction

Cape Washington and Silverfish Bay are located in northern Terra Nova Bay, Victoria Land, Ross Sea. Approximate area and coordinates: 286 km^2 (centered at 164° 57.6' E, 74° 37.1' S), of which 279.5 km^2 is marine (98 %) and 6.5 km^2 is terrestrial (2 %). The primary reasons for designation of the Area are the outstanding ecological and scientific values. One of the largest emperor penguin (*Aptenodytes forsteri*) colonies in Antarctica breeds on sea ice adjacent to Cape Washington, with around 20,000 breeding pairs comprising approximately eight percent of the global emperor population and ~21% of the population in the Ross Sea. Several factors, such as location, ice conditions, weather and accessibility provide relatively consistent and stable opportunities to observe emperor chick fledging reliably and the presence of a variety of other species make it an ideal place to study ecosystem interactions. The extended record of observations of the emperor colony at Cape Washington is of important scientific value. Approximately 20 km west of Cape Washington, the first documented 'nursery' and hatching area for Antarctic silverfish (*Pleuragramma antarcticum*) is located at Silverfish Bay. Recent research has shown that the concentration of spawning on occasions extends all the way across the embayment to Cape Washington. The first ground-breaking studies on the life-history of this species have been made at the site, and its relative accessibility to nearby research stations make the Area important for biological research. The Area also has important geoscientific values, as it features extensive volcanic rock exposures originating from the nearby active volcano Mount Melbourne.

The Area is situated in Environment U – North Victoria Land Geologic based on the Environmental Domains Analysis for Antarctica (Resolution 3 (2008)) and in Region 8 – Northern Victoria Land based on the Antarctic Conservation Biogeographic Regions.

1. Description of values to be protected

The Area at northern Terra Nova Bay comprising Cape Washington and Silverfish Bay (Map 1) was proposed by Italy and the United States on the grounds that it contains one of the largest emperor penguin (*Aptenodytes forsteri*) colonies known, and the colony and its associated ecosystem is the subject of on-going scientific studies that began in 1986. Recently, large quantities of eggs of the Antarctic silverfish (*Pleuragramma antarcticum*) were discovered under sea ice in northern Terra Nova Bay, making it the first documented 'nursery' and hatching area for this species. This discovery has greatly expanded understanding of the life-history of this species, and the proximity of the site to nearby scientific stations makes it of outstanding scientific value for continuing study. The site of the original Antarctic silverfish egg discovery was named Silverfish Bay (Map 2), and more recent research has revealed the rich concentration of *P. antarcticum* eggs found there extends in some years across the embayment towards Cape Washington. The total area is 286 km^2, of which the marine component is ~279.5 km^2 (98 %) and the terrestrial component is 6.5 km^2 (2 %).

The Cape Washington emperor colony, usually centered around one kilometer northwest of the cape (at 165°22' E, 74°38.8' S), was the largest known in Antarctica in the 1993 and 1994 seasons, with counts of around 24 000 chicks being slightly greater than that of nearby Coulman Island at the time. In other years for which counts are available the Coulman Island colony was the slightly larger of the two. The colony appears to maintain a reasonably stable population, with ~17 000 chicks being counted in 2010. This relative stability makes the colony particularly suited to scientific study and monitoring, since long-term trends may be more readily studied and detected. Moreover, a relatively long time-series of scientific data exists for the Cape Washington emperor colony. Because of the location, ice conditions, weather and accessibility, Cape Washington is one of only two Ross Sea colonies where October through December studies can be conducted and emperor chick fledging can be observed reliably. All of these qualities make the Cape Washington emperor colony of outstanding ecological and scientific value.

The Area at Cape Washington and Silverfish Bay is also of considerable scientific interest because of the variety of other species that frequent the Area, making it an ideal location to study ecosystem interactions and predator / prey relationships. Cape Washington itself is a nesting area for south polar skuas (*Catharacta maccormicki*) and snow petrels (*Pagodroma nivea*). Adélie penguins (*Pygoscelis adeliae*) are present in the emperor colony and on the sea-ice edge daily from November to mid-January. Large groups of killer whales (*Orcinus orca*) and other cetaceans such as Antarctic minke whales (*Balaenoptera bonaerensis*) are regularly observed foraging in this area, as well as Weddell (*Leptonychotes weddellii*) and leopard (*Hydrurga leptonyx*) seals. The embayment is an important haul-out and breeding area for Weddell seals, with several hundred typically congregating along sea ice leads and near Markham Island throughout the season. Crabeater seals (*Lobodon carcinophagus*) and Arnoux's beaked whales (*Berardius arnuxii*) are occasionally seen at the sea ice edge in the region. Cape Washington is the only place known where the interaction between leopard seals and emperor penguins can be so reliably observed.

The Area has exceptional value for observations of the interactions and predator / prey relationships between many different members of the marine ecosystem within a relatively compact area that is accessible to scientists supported by nearby research stations. The boundaries are defined taking an integrated approach to inclusion of all components of the local ecosystem.

The Area has considerable geoscientific value because it features extensive volcanic rock exposures related to the nearby active volcano Mount Melbourne. The Area serves as a key marker region for evaluating the young, neotectonic evolution of the western Ross Sea. It borders the deepest waters of the Ross Sea and includes Markham Island, a volcanic outcrop that is located over a negative magnetic anomaly, the origin of which is not yet known.

Cape Washington is relatively accessible by sea-ice, sea and air from nearby research stations in Terra Nova Bay. Aircraft activity in the region is frequent throughout the summer season, with fixed-wing aircraft operating from the sea ice runway in Gerlache Inlet (Map 2), and helicopter movements within the region around Mount Melbourne on a regular basis.

The Area requires long-term special protection because of the outstanding ecological and scientific values and the potential vulnerability of the Area to disturbance from scientific, logistic and tourist activities in the region.

2. Aims and objectives

Management at Cape Washington and Silverfish Bay aims to:

- avoid degradation of, or substantial risk to, the values of the Area by preventing unnecessary human disturbance to the Area;
- allow scientific research on the ecosystem, in particular on the emperor penguins and ecosystem interactions, while ensuring protection from oversampling or other possible scientific impacts;
- allow other scientific research, scientific support activities and visits for educational and outreach purposes (such as documentary reporting (visual, audio or written) or the

production of educational resources or services) provided that such activities are for compelling reasons that cannot be served elsewhere and that will not jeopardise the natural ecological system in that Area;

- prevent or minimize the introduction of alien plants, animals and microbes into the Area;
- minimise the possibility of the introduction of pathogens that may cause disease in faunal populations within the Area;
- allow visits for management purposes in support of the aims of the management plan.

3. Management activities

The following management activities shall be undertaken to protect the values of the Area:

- Signs showing the location of the Area (stating the special restrictions that apply) shall be displayed prominently, and a copy of this Management Plan shall be kept available, at all scientific stations located within 75 km of the Area;
- Copies of this Management Plan shall be made available to all vessels and aircraft visiting the Area and/or operating in the vicinity of the adjacent stations, and all pilots and ship captains operating in the region shall be informed of the location, boundaries and restrictions applying to entry and overflight within the Area;
- National programs shall take steps to ensure the boundaries of the Area and the restrictions that apply within are marked on relevant maps and nautical / aeronautical charts;
- Markers, signs or structures erected within the Area for scientific or management purposes shall be secured and maintained in good condition, and removed when no longer required;
- Any abandoned equipment or materials shall be removed to the maximum extent possible provided doing so does not adversely impact on the environment and the values of the Area;
- Visits shall be made as necessary (no less than once every five years) to assess whether the Area continues to serve the purposes for which it was designated and to ensure management and maintenance measures are adequate;
- National Antarctic Programs operating in the region shall consult together with a view to ensuring that the above provisions are implemented.

4. Period of designation

Designated for an indefinite period.

5. Maps and photographs

Map 1: ASPA No. 173: Cape Washington and Silverfish Bay – Regional map. Projection: Lambert Conformal Conic; Standard parallels: 1st 74° 20' S; 2nd 75° 20' S; Central Meridian: 164° 00' E; Latitude of Origin: 74° 00' S; Spheroid and horizontal datum: WGS84; Contour interval 200 m; Bathymetry 200 m at coast, then 500 m interval.

Inset: Location of Terra Nova Bay in the Ross Sea region.

Map 2: ASPA No. 173: Cape Washington and Silverfish Bay – topographic map. Projection: Lambert Conformal Conic; Standard parallels: 1st 74° 35' S; 2nd 74° 45' S; Central Meridian: 164° 42' E; Latitude of Origin: 74° 00' S; Spheroid and horizontal datum: WGS84; Contour interval 200 m; Bathymetry 100 m interval.

Map 3: ASPA No. 173: Cape Washington and Silverfish Bay – Access Guidance. Map details as per Map 2.

Map 4: ASPA No. 173: Cape Washington and Silverfish Bay – Restricted Zone. Map details as per Map 2 except Central Meridian: 165° 20' E. Satellite image Ikonos acquired 30 Dec 2011, © GeoEye (2011), courtesy of NGA Commercial Imagery Program.

6. Description of the Area

6(i) Geographical coordinates, boundary markers and natural features

General description

Cape Washington is situated in northern Terra Nova Bay, 40 km east of Mario Zucchelli Station (Italy) (Map 1). The Area is 286 km^2, of which the marine component is 279.5 km^2 (98 %) and the terrestrial component is 6.5 km^2 (2 %).

Sea ice persists in Silverfish Bay and across Closs Bay to Cape Washington from March until January, providing a stable and reliable platform on which the emperors can breed and suitable conditions for the silverfish 'nursery'. The Cape Washington peninsula provides shelter to the emperor colony, which is relatively protected from the strong katabatic winds that descend into other parts of Terra Nova Bay. The eastern coast of the Cape Washington peninsula comprises precipitous cliffs of several hundred meters in height, while the west side comprises more gentle mixed snow and ice-free slopes with some rocky outcrops extending down to sea level. Closs Bay extends uninterrupted across to the Campbell Glacier Tongue, punctuated by the solitary and small Markham Island close to Oscar Point (Map 2).

Boundaries and coordinates

The eastern boundary of the Area at the NE corner extends from the coordinates 165° 27' E, 74° 37' S on the eastern coast of the Cape Washington peninsula due south for ~5.6 km to 165° 27' E, 74° 40' S (Map 2). The boundary thence extends due west across Closs Bay on latitude 74° 40' S for ~26.8 km to the Campbell Glacier Tongue. It then follows the eastern margin of the Campbell Glacier Tongue for ~11.2 km northwards to the coast at Shield Nunatak. The boundary thence follows the coastline eastwards, around the Vacchi Piedmont Glacier, to the western coast of the Cape Washington peninsula, ~23 km in a straight-line from Shield Nunatak. The boundary thence follows the coastline southward ~7.5 km towards the first prominent rock outcrop at latitude 74° 37.03' S on the western coast of the Cape Washington peninsula. The boundary extends eastwards from this coast along the line of latitude 74° 37' S ~ 2.8 km to the NE corner boundary point located on the eastern coast of the Cape Washington peninsula.

Climate

Four meteorological stations are located in Terra Nova Bay, of which 'Eneide', located at Mario Zucchelli Station (164° 05.533' E, 74° 41.750' S) and ~ 25 km from the center of the Area, has the longest time series of data. The mean annual air temperature at Mario Zucchelli Station was -14.1° C during the period 1987 –2009, with the coldest month being July with an average minimum temperature of -28.2 °C and the warmest month is December with an average maximum temperature of 0° C. The mean annual wind speed at Mario Zucchelli Station was 6.56 m/s (23.6 km/h; 1987 –2009) with an average maximum of 11.6 m/s (41.8 km/h) in June and an average minimum of 2.6 m/s (9.4 km/h) in December.

The strongest mean annual wind speed in the Terra Nova Bay area has been recorded near Inexpressible Island, measured at 12.3 m/s (44.3 km/h) between Feb 1988 – 1989 (Bromwich *et al.* 1990). This is significantly stronger than ordinary katabatic winds (< 10 m/s), as local topographic features channel the air into the 'confluence zones' of the Reeves and the Priestley glaciers (Bromwich *et al.* 1990; Parish & Bromwich 1991). These offshore katabatic winds play a significant role in the formation of the Terra Nova Bay polynya.

Oceanography

Terra Nova Bay is a deep basin that reaches a maximum depth of ~1100 m, which is the deepest water in the Ross Sea (Buffoni *et al* 2002) (Map 1). Ocean circulation in the bay is characterized in summer by a prevailing northward movement in the upper layer, parallel to the coast, and a clockwise rotation with depth (Vacchi *et al.* 2012 in press). Warmer and more saline waters are observed near the coast, while cooler waters are found in the central part of the bay, and local eddies and upwelling processes are strongly influenced by katabatic winds (Budillon & Spezie 2000; Buffoni *et al.* 2002).

A perennial winter polynya forms in the bay through a combination of persistent katabatic winds driving newly formed ice offshore and the Drygalski Ice Tongue acting as a barrier to the northward drift of pack ice (Bromwich & Kurtz 1984; Van Woert 1999) (Map 1). The polynya generally forms with a maximum east-west extent that appears to be closely related to the length of the Drygalski Ice Tongue (Kurtz & Bromwich 1983). The polynya has been observed to cover a mean area of roughly 1300 km^2 (65 km N/S by 20 km E/W), although in some years it may not exist at all, while in others it can reach a maximum of ~ 5000 km^2 (65 km N/S by 75 km E/W) (Kurtz & Bromwich 1983).

This polynya plays an important role in the formation of High Salinity Shelf Waters (HSSW) in Terra Nova Bay (Buffoni *et al* 2002). The brine rejected during the ice formation process increases the salt content and density of the water, which consequently causes a thermohaline circulation and convective movements. The HSSW found in this area have the highest salinity content in Antarctica reaching up to 34.87 and a potential temperature near the sea surface freezing point of -1.9 °C.

Marine biology

The silverfish (*Pleuragramma antarcticum*) is the dominant pelagic fish in waters of the continental shelf in the Ross Sea and is considered a keystone species providing one of the major links between lower and higher trophic levels (Bottaro *et al.* 2009; La Mesa *et al.* 2010; Vacchi *et al.* 2012). Silverfish represent the primary food item for most marine vertebrates, such as marine mammals, birds, and other fishes (La Mesa *et al.* 2004), and are the primary fish prey for both emperor penguins and Weddell seals (Burns & Kooyman 2001).

Until recently little was known of the early life history of silverfish (Guglielmo *et al.* 1998; Vacchi *et al.* 2004). Marine surveys in Terra Nova Bay in the late 1980s yielded samples that suggested the northern part of the bay may represent a nursery ground for early stages of *P. antarcticum* (Guglielmo *et al.* 1998). From late October to early December 2002 large quantities of embryonated eggs of *P. antarcticum* were found floating among platelet ice under sea ice in northern Terra Nova Bay (Vacchi *et al.* 2004). This was the first documented nursery and hatching area of the Antarctic silverfish. Research conducted over subsequent years showed higher egg concentrations were consistently found within the embayment east of the Campbell Glacier Tongue (which led to naming this area Silverfish Bay), with greatest abundances in areas where the sea was at least 300 m in depth (Vacchi *et al.* 2012 in press) (Maps 1 & 2). Recent observations have revealed an abundance of *Pleuragramma* eggs beneath sea ice between Oscar Point and Cape Washington, indicating annual fluctuations in the abundance and spatial distribution of fish eggs in the Area (Vacchi pers. comm. 2012).

This and other research has indicated that habitats with particular combinations of geographic and oceanographic features and conditions (e.g. close ice shelf or glacier tongues, canyons, water mass stratification, polynyas, katabatic winds, and sea ice cover) are favorable for the early life history of the silverfish (Vacchi *et al.* 2012 in press, and references therein).

Birds

The emperor penguin colony at Cape Washington is one of the two largest known; the other is the Coulman Island colony 200 km to the north. While in some years the Cape Washington population has exceeded that at Coulman Island, available data suggests that usually the latter is the slightly larger of the two (Barber-Meyer *et al.* 2008). The population generally ranges between approximately 13,000 and 25,000 breeding pairs (Table 1; Barber-Meyer *et al.* 2008).

Data from earlier years indicate that live chick numbers have consistently remained around these levels since studies were initiated in 1986 (Kooyman *et al.* 1990).

Table 1. Cape Washington emperor penguin population 2000-05 and 2010.

Year	Live chick count [1]	Estimated breeding pairs (approx.)
2000	17397	20000
2001	18734	20000
2002	11093	13000
2003	13163	15000
2004	16700	20000
2005	23021	25000
2010	17000 [2]	20000

1. Barber-Meyer *et al.* 2008.
2. Kooyman pers. comm. 2012.

The emperor penguin colony breeds on sea ice that extends from Cape Washington to the Campbell Glacier Tongue in the northern part of Terra Nova Bay. Sea ice formation begins in March and the bay is generally covered by sea ice until ice break-up around mid-January. The Terra Nova Bay polynya generally offers the colony access to open sea throughout the breeding cycle.

The sea ice in the vicinity of the emperor breeding site may be covered with up to 25 cm of snow near the ice edge, with up to about 1 m of snow accumulating on the SW shoreline of the Cape Washington peninsula (Kooyman *et al.* 1990). This area is relatively sheltered from both SW and NW winds. The locality has been observed to enjoy relatively cloud-free conditions from October to January, resulting in elevated levels of direct solar irradiance. This causes the dirty guano-covered snow and ice to soften and melt, forming pools that are difficult or impossible for penguins, and humans, to walk through. As a result the birds need to shift their breeding sites regularly throughout the summer period. The incubating birds generally cluster adjacent to the SW coast of Cape Washington until September, before spreading away from the Cape in an expanding semi-circle.

The center of the incubation area in 1996 was approximately 165°22.0' E, 74°38.8' S. Observations in 1986-87 found the colony dispersed into several groups by the end of October, each containing 1000 to 2000 chicks with attendant adults (Kooyman *et al.* 1990). From the cape northward along the western coast of the peninsula, there was found to be a gradient in chick development, with the largest chicks in groups closest to the ice-edge near the cape. By the time of fledging some groups of chicks had moved 5 to 6 km away from the original breeding locality. In 1986-87 fledging occurred abruptly over a ten-day period at the end of December and the beginning of January.

There is evidence that the Cape Washington colony is comparatively stable in population and that it appears to enjoy relatively high levels of breeding success, averaging almost 95% of chicks successfully fledged over a six-year study period (Barber-Mayer *et al.* 2008). This compares with breeding successes of only around 60-70 % at the Point Geologie, Taylor Glacier and Auster colonies in the East Antarctic. The Cape Washington colony is particularly valuable for scientific study because of its comparative low variability in breeding success, which may be in part a function of its large size, with smaller colonies exhibiting greater population fluctuations (Barber-Mayer *et al.* 2008). Moreover, the colony is relatively accessible to nearby scientific stations, making research more practical.

A south polar skua (*Catharacta maccormicki*) colony comprising approximately 50 pairs is located on the ice-free slopes of Cape Washington, overlooking the emperor colony. Snow petrels (*Pagodroma nivea*) have been recorded as breeding in niches in the Cape Washington cliffs (Greenfield & Smellie 1992), feeding along the ice edge, and have been noted as the most abundant flying bird in the vicinity over the summer months (Kooyman *et al.* 1990). Adélie penguins (*Pygoscelis adeliae*) are observed along the ice edge and within the emperor colony during summer months, while Wilson's storm petrels (*Oceanites oceanicus*) are frequently observed along the ice edge from mid- to late-November. Southern giant petrels (*Macronectes giganteus*) have been observed overflying and landing within the Area (Kooyman *et al.* 1990).

Mammals (seals, whales)

Large groups of killer whales (*Orcinus orca*), with groups of up to 100 individuals, are regularly observed foraging in this area (Kooyman *et al.* 1990; Lauriano *et al.* 2010). Ecotype 'C' which typically forages on fish (e.g. Antarctic toothfish (*Dissostichus mawsoni*) and possibly Antarctic silverfish (*Pleuragramma antarcticum*) was the most common killer whale ecotype observed. A range of other cetaceans have also been observed, including minke whales (*Balaenoptera bonaerensis*), other *Balaenoptera* species, Arnoux's beaked whale (*Beradius arnuxii*) and other undetermined species (Lauriano *et al.* 2010). The Lauriano *et al.* (2010) study, carried out in January 2004, most frequently encountered killer whales, followed by minke whales. Significantly higher cetacean encounter rates were observed in the region between Edmonson Point and the Campbell Glacier Tongue than in the region further south from Mario Zucchelli Station to the Drygalski Ice Tongue, which emphasises the importance of northern Terra Nova Bay for these species.

Three species of seal – Weddell (*Leptonychotes weddellii*), leopard (*Hydrurga leptonyx*) and crabeater (*Lobodon carcinophagus*) – are common in the Area. The embayment is an important haul-out and breeding area for Weddell seals, which typically congregate along sea ice leads and openings that dynamically form throughout the season. At least 200 Weddell seals were recorded in the bay west of Cape Washington in 1986-87, with 31 pups counted near Markham Island (Kooyman *et al.* 1990), and a similar number of adults was counted in the same region from satellite imagery acquired in November 2011 (La Rue pers. comm. 2012).

Leopard seals (*Hydrurga leptonyx*) were recorded within the Area from mid-November through December in 1986-87, and were observed to prey on emperor penguins around the ice edge. Kooyman *et al.* (1990) estimated that the three individuals they monitored over this period would have taken approximately 150 – 200 adult birds, or about 0.5 % of breeding emperor adults at the colony. Crabeater seals were recorded on occasion at the ice edge or on nearby ice flows in the same season (Kooyman *et al.* 1990).

Human activities / impacts

Two permanent scientific stations and one under construction are located at nearby Gerlache Inlet. Mario Zucchelli (164° 06.917' E, 74° 41.650' S; Italy), established in 1987, operates summer only with a complement of up to 90 personnel, which may sometimes be expanded when the support ship *Italica* is present in the region. Gondwana (164° 13.317' E, 74° 38.133' S; Germany), established in 1983, operates on occasional summers with capacity for approximately 25 personnel. Jang Bogo (164° 11.950' E, 74° 37.250' S; Republic of Korea) will be a new permanent station, designed to operate year-round with a complement of 15 winter personnel in the and up to 60 in summer when construction is completed in 2014. China recently announced plans to establish a new station at approximately 163° 42' E, 74° 55' S on nearby Inexpressible Island (China Daily USA 2013).

The Cape Washington emperor colony has been of interest for tourism for around 20 years, with an average of ~200 tourists visiting C. Washington per annum over the last decade. The colony has also been of interest for recreational visits by station personnel from nearby Mario Zucchelli Station since it was established. An area frequented by emperor penguins lies immediately south of the southern boundary of the Area at 74° 40' S (Maps 3 & 4). This region lies within the approximate 6 km buffer from the nominal centroid of the breeding colony within which the birds have been consistently observed when sea ice is present. This region outside of the protected area allows continued opportunities for tourism or recreational visits to view emperor penguins in the Cape Washington vicinity, and other opportunities exist at colonies elsewhere in the Ross Sea and Antarctica more generally.

6(ii) Access to the Area

The Area may be accessed by traversing over land or sea ice, by sea or by air. Particular access routes have not been designated over land or sea ice or for vessels entering the Area by sea. Access to Cape Washington by helicopter should follow the designated access route over the northern part of the Cape Washington peninsula. Overflight, aircraft landing and ship access restrictions apply within the Area, the specific conditions for which are set out in Section 7(ii) below.

6(iii) Location of structures within and adjacent to the Area

There are no structures within the Area. Several geodetic reference markers have been established by the Italian Antarctic program at Markham Island and at Cape Washington on ice-free ground, and these are the only known permanent markers in the Area. Mario Zucchelli Station (164° 06.917' E, 74° 41.650' S; Italy) is situated ~13 km southwest of the western boundary of the Area on the southern shore of Gerlache Inlet (Map 2). Gondwana Station (164° 13.317' E, 74° 38.133' S; Germany) is located 8.7 km west of the western boundary of the Area, also in Gerlache Inlet and 7.2 km north of Mario Zucchelli Station. Jang Bogo Station (164° 11.95' E, 74° 37.25' S; South Korea, under construction) is planned to be located ~9 km west of the western boundary of the Area, ~1.8 km NW of Gondwana Station. A number of structures associated with national program operations are located nearby, such as a communications facility near the summit of Mount Melbourne, and several radar and non-directional beacons to assist summer air operations, although these are all outside of the Area.

6(iv) Location of other protected areas in the vicinity

The nearest protected areas to Cape Washington are Mount Melbourne (ASPA No.118) 23 km north of the northern boundary of the Area, Edmonson Point (ASPA No.165) 24 km north of the northern boundary of the Area, and Terra Nova Bay (ASPA No.161) 13 km from the western boundary of the Area.

6(v) Special zones within the Area

This Management Plan establishes a Restricted Zone within the Area which applies during the period from 01 April through to 01 January inclusive.

Restricted Zone

The Restricted Zone is designated east of the line of longitude 165° 10' E and south of the line of latitude 74° 35.5' S (Map 3), which encompasses the primary emperor breeding area and is considered the most ecologically sensitive part of the Area. The Restricted Zone has an area of 62.5 km^2. Access to the Restricted Zone should be for compelling reasons that cannot be served elsewhere within the Area and detailed conditions for access are described in Section 7(ii) below.

7. Permit conditions

7(i) General permit conditions

Entry into the Area is prohibited except in accordance with a permit issued by an appropriate national authority. Conditions for issuing a permit to enter the Area are that:

- it is issued only for scientific study of the ecosystem, or for compelling scientific or educational (such as documentary reporting or the production of educational resources or services) reasons that cannot be served elsewhere, or for reasons essential to the management of the Area;
- the actions permitted are in accordance with this Management Plan;
- the activities permitted will give due consideration via the environmental impact assessment process to the continued protection of the environmental, ecological and scientific values of the Area;

- access to the Restricted Zone is allowed only for compelling reasons that cannot be served elsewhere within the Area;
- the permit shall be issued for a finite period;
- the permit, or a copy, shall be carried when in the Area.

7(ii) Access to, and movement within or over, the Area

Access into the Area is permitted on foot or by vehicle, by ship or small boat, or by fixed-wing or rotor-wing aircraft.

Access on foot or by vehicle

No special access routes are designated for access to the Area on foot or by vehicle over sea ice or by land. Vehicles may be used over sea ice and glaciers although are prohibited from ice-free ground within the Area. Pedestrian and vehicular traffic should be kept to the minimum necessary consistent with the objectives of any permitted activities and every reasonable effort should be made to minimize disturbance. Vehicle use should be avoided within 100 m of concentrations of emperor penguins or Weddell seals, and permitted visitors should avoid entering penguin sub-groups or approaching seals except as required for essential scientific, educational or management purposes.

Access by aircraft

Resolution 2 (2004), the Guidelines for the Operation of Aircraft near Concentrations of Birds in Antarctica, should be followed at all times. Restrictions on aircraft operations apply during the period from 01 April through to 01 January inclusive, when aircraft shall operate and land within the Area according to strict observance of the following conditions:

- Aircraft landings within the Area are prohibited unless authorized by permit for purposes allowed for by the Management Plan;
- Overflight of the Restricted Zone below 2000 feet (~610 m) is prohibited, unless authorized by permit for purposes allowed for by the Management Plan;
- Aircraft landings on sea ice within ½ nautical mile (~930 m) of the emperor colony are prohibited. Pilots should note that the emperor colony may move throughout the breeding season up to six kilometers from the nominal center coordinate of the colony at 165°22' E, 74°38.8' S (Map 3), and the colony may break up into a number of smaller units within the Area;
- Aircraft landings on sea ice within ½ nautical mile (~930 m) of concentrations of Weddell seals are prohibited. Pilots should note that Weddell seals may be present throughout the Area, although tend to congregate along sea ice leads and around Markham Island (Map 3). In the context of management of the Area, a concentration is defined as five or more animals within 300 m of each other;
- Pilots shall ensure the aircraft maintains the minimum separation distance from any part of the emperor colony and / or any concentration of seals when operating over sea ice at all times, excepting when this is impractical because the animals have voluntarily moved closer to the aircraft after it has landed;
- Pilots making authorized landings beyond ½ nautical mile (~930 m) of the emperor colony and / or concentrations of seals may select landing sites according to visit needs, local conditions and safety considerations. Pilots should make a reconnaissance of suitable landing sites from above 2000 feet (~610 m) before descending to land;
- Landings by helicopter may be made on land within the Restricted Zone at Cape Washington. The preferred helicopter approach route to the cape is from the north over the Cape Washington peninsula, avoiding overflight of the emperor colony, breeding skua territories situated immediately west of the access route, and seabird breeding sites along the cliffs of the Cape Washington peninsula (Map 3). Pilots flying to the cape should follow the designated approach route to the maximum extent practicable and abort the

journey should it be likely that conditions would force a route that might lead to overflight of the emperor colony;

- Approaches by fixed wing aircraft to sea ice landing sites in Terra Nova Bay adjacent to Mario Zucchelli Station (Italy) (Map 2) should maintain designated approach paths and elevations as defined in the most recent edition of the Antarctic Flight Information Manual (AFIM). Should visibility or other conditions be prohibitive of maintaining these paths and / or elevations, pilots should ensure that alternative approaches adopted avoid exceeding the minimum overflight heights that apply within the Restricted Zone.

Access by ship or small boat

Restrictions on ship and / or small boat operations apply during the period from 01 April through to 01 January inclusive, when ships and / or small boats shall operate within the Area according to strict observance of the following conditions:

- Ships and / or small boats are prohibited from the Area, including entering sea ice within the Area, unless authorized by permit for purposes allowed for by this Management Plan;
- Ships are prohibited within the Restricted Zone;
- There are no special restrictions on where access can be gained to the Area by small boat, although small boat landings should avoid areas where penguins are accessing the sea unless this is necessary for purposes for which the permit was granted.

7(iii) Activities that may be conducted within the Area

- Scientific research that will not jeopardize the values of the Area;
- Essential management activities, including monitoring and inspection;
- Activities for educational or outreach purposes (such as documentary reporting (e.g. visual, audio or written) or the production of educational resources or services) that cannot be served elsewhere.

7(iv) Installation, modification or removal of structures / equipment

- No structures are to be erected within the Area except as specified in a permit and, with the exception of permanent survey markers and signs, permanent structures or installations are prohibited;
- All structures, scientific equipment or markers installed in the Area shall be authorized by permit and clearly identified by country, name of the principal investigator, year of installation and date of expected removal. All such items should be free of organisms, propagules (e.g. seeds, eggs) and non-sterile soil, and be made of materials that can withstand the environmental conditions and pose minimal risk of contamination of the Area;
- Installation (including site selection), maintenance, modification or removal of structures or equipment shall be undertaken in a manner that minimizes disturbance to the values of the Area;
- Removal of specific structures / equipment for which the permit has expired shall be the responsibility of the authority which granted the original permit, and shall be a condition of the permit.

7(v) Location of field camps

Permanent field camps are prohibited within the Area. Temporary camp sites are permitted within the Area. There are no specific restrictions on the precise locality for temporary camp sites within the Area, although it is recommended that initial sites selected should be more than 1000 m from concentrations of breeding emperor penguins. It is recognized that the birds move from their original breeding locations throughout the season. As the birds will subsequently set their own distance limits from any camp established, it is not considered necessary to keep moving the camp in response to the shifting positions of the emperor colony. It is recommended that camp sites be located approximately 500 m offshore from the western coast of the Cape Washington peninsula because the near-shore area is subject to snow overburden and subsequent meltwater flooding. Camping within the terrestrial part of the Area is not restricted to a particular location, but where possible camp sites should be located on snow covered ground.

7(vi) Restrictions on materials and organisms which may be brought into the Area

In addition to the requirements of the Protocol on Environmental Protection to the Antarctic Treaty, restrictions on materials and organisms which may be brought into the area are:

- deliberate introduction of animals, plant material, micro-organisms and non-sterile soil into the Area is prohibited. Precautions shall be taken to prevent the accidental introduction of animals, plant material, micro-organisms and non-sterile soil from other biologically distinct regions (within or beyond the Antarctic Treaty area).
- Visitors shall ensure that sampling equipment and markers brought into the Area are clean. To the maximum extent practicable, footwear and other equipment used or brought into the area (including backpacks, carry-bags and tents) shall be thoroughly cleaned before entering the Area. Visitors should also consult and follow as appropriate recommendations contained in the Committee for Environmental Protection *Non-native Species Manual* (CEP 2011), and in the *Environmental Code of Conduct for terrestrial scientific field research in Antarctica* (SCAR 2009);
- Dressed poultry should be free of disease or infection before shipment to the Area and, if introduced to the Area for food, all parts and wastes of poultry shall be completely removed from the Area or incinerated or boiled long enough to kill any potentially infective bacteria or viruses;
- No herbicides or pesticides shall be brought into the Area;
- Fuel, food, chemicals, and other materials shall not be stored in the Area, unless specifically authorized by permit and shall be stored and handled in a way that minimises the risk of their accidental introduction into the environment;
- All materials introduced shall be for a stated period only and shall be removed by the end of that stated period; and
- If release occurs which is likely to compromise the values of the Area, removal is encouraged only where the impact of removal is not likely to be greater than that of leaving the material *in situ*.

7(vii) Taking of, or harmful interference with, native flora or fauna

Taking of, or harmful interference with, native flora and fauna is prohibited, except in accordance with a permit issued in accordance with Annex II of the Protocol on Environmental Protection to the Antarctic Treaty.

Where animal taking or harmful interference is involved, this should, as a minimum standard, be in accordance with the SCAR Code of Conduct for the Use of Animals for Scientific Purposes in Antarctica.

7(viii) Collection or removal of anything not brought into the Area by the permit holder

- Material may be collected or removed from the Area only in accordance with a permit and should be limited to the minimum necessary to meet scientific or management needs.
- Material of human origin likely to compromise the values of the Area, and which was not brought into the Area by the permit holder or otherwise authorized, may be removed from the Area, unless the impact of removal is likely to be greater than leaving the material *in situ*: if this is the case the appropriate authority must be notified and approval obtained.

7(ix) Disposal of waste

All wastes, except human wastes, shall be removed from the Area. Small quantities of human wastes, such as arising from groups of no more than 10 people within a given season, may be disposed of onto annual sea ice or directly into the sea within the Area, or otherwise shall be removed from the Area.

7(x) Measures that may be necessary to continue to meet the aims of the Management Plan

Permits may be granted to enter the Area to:

- carry out monitoring and Area inspection activities, which may involve the collection of a small number of samples or data for analysis or review;
- install or maintain signposts, markers, structures or scientific equipment;
- carry out protective measures.

7(xi) Requirements for reports

- The principal permit holder for each visit to the Area shall submit a report to the appropriate national authority as soon as practicable, and no later than six months after the visit has been completed.
- Such reports should include, as appropriate, the information identified in the visit report form contained in the Guide to the Preparation of Management Plans for Antarctic Specially Protected Areas. If appropriate, the national authority should also forward a copy of the visit report to the Party that proposed the Management Plan, to assist in managing the Area and reviewing the Management Plan.
- Parties should, wherever possible, deposit originals or copies of such original visit reports in a publicly accessible archive to maintain a record of usage, for the purpose of any review of the Management Plan and in organising the scientific use of the Area.
- The appropriate authority should be notified of any activities / measures undertaken, and / or of any materials released and not removed, that were not included in the authorized permit.

8. Supporting documentation

Barber-Meyer, S.M., Kooyman, G.L. & Ponganis P. J. 2008. Trends in western Ross Sea emperor penguin chick abundances and their relationships to climate. *Antarctic Science* **20** (1): 3-11.

Bottaro, M., Oliveri, D., Ghigliotti, L., Pisano, E., Ferrando, S. & Vacchi, M. 2009. Born among the ice: first morphological observations on two developmental stages of the Antarctic silverfish *Pleuragramma antarcticum*, a key species of the Southern Ocean. *Reviews in Fish Biology & Fisheries* **19**: 249-59.

Bromwich, D.H. & Kurtz, D.D. 1984. Katabatic wind forcing of the Terra Nova Bay polynya. *Journal of Geophysical Research* **89** (C3): 3561–72. DOI:10.1029/JC089iC03p03561.

Bromwich, D.H., Parish, T.R., Pellegrini, A., Stearns, C.R & Weidner, G.A. 1993. Spatial and temporal characteristics of the intense katabatic winds at Terra Nova Bay, Antarctica. *Antarctic Research Series* **61**: 47-68. American Geophysical Union, Washington DC.

Budillon, G.& Spezie, G. 2000. Thermohaline structure and variability in Terra Nova Bay polynya, Ross Sea. *Antarctic Science* **12**: 493-508.

Buffoni, G., Cappelletti, A. & Picco, P. 2002. An investigation of thermohaline circulation in Terra Nova Bay polynya. *Antarctic Science* **14** (1): 83-92.

Burns, J.M. & Kooyman, G.L. 2001. Habitat use by Weddell seals and emperor penguins foraging in the Ross Sea, Antarctica. *American Zoologist* **41**: 90-98.

China Daily USA 2013. China selects 4th Antarctic station. Updated: 2013-01-08 14:36. http://usa.chinadaily.com.cn/china/2013-01/08/content_16095605.htm.

Committee for Environmental Protection (CEP) 2011. Non-native Species Manual – 1st Edition. Manual prepared by Intersessional Contact Group of the CEP and adopted by the Antarctic Treaty Consultative Meeting through Resolution 6 (2011). Buenos Aires: Secretariat of the Antarctic Treaty.

Greenfield, L.G. & Smellie, J.M. 1992. Known, new and probable Snow Petrel breeding locations in the Ross Dependency and Marie Byrd Land. *Notornis* 39: 119–124.

Guglielmo, L., Granata, A. & Greco, S. 1998. Distribution and abundance of postlarval and juvenile *Pleuragramma antarcticum* (Pisces, Nototheniidae) off Terra Nova Bay (Ross Sea, Antarctica). *Polar Biology* **19**:37-51.

Kooyman, G.L., Croll, D., Stone, S. & Smith S. 1990. Emperor penguin colony at Cape Washington, Antarctica. *Polar Record* **26** : 103-108.

Kurtz D.D. & Bromwich, D.H. 1983. Satellite observed behaviour of the Terra Nova Bay polynya. *Journal of Geophysical Research* **88**: 9717-22.

Kurtz, D.D. & Bromwich, D.H. 1985. A recurring, atmospherically forced polynya in Terra Nova Bay. In: Jacobs, S.S. (ed) Oceanology of the Antarctic continental shelf. *Antarctic Research Series* **43**: 177-201. American Geophysical Union, Washington DC.

La Mesa, M., Eastman, J.T., & Vacchi, M. 2004. The role of notothenioid fish in the food web of the Ross Sea shelf waters: a review. *Polar Biology* **27**: 321-338.

La Mesa M, Catalano B, Russo A, Greco S, Vacchi M & Azzali M. 2010. Influence of environmental conditions on spatial distribution and abundance of early life stages of Antarctic silverfish, *Pleuragramma antarcticum* (Nototheniidae), in the Ross Sea. *Antarctic Science* **22**: 243- 254.

Lauriano, G., Fortuna, C.M. & Vacchi, M. 2010. Occurrence of killer whales (*Orcinus orca*) and other cetaceans in Terra Nova Bay, Ross Sea, Antarctica. *Antarctic Science* **23**: 139-143. DOI:10.1017/S0954102010000908

Parish, T. & Bromwich, D. 1991. Automatic weather station observations of strong katabatic winds near Terra Nova Bay, Antarctica. *Antarctic Journal of the United States* **Review**: 265-67.

SCAR (Scientific Committee on Antarctic Research) 2009. *Environmental Code of Conduct for terrestrial scientific field research in Antarctica.* Cambridge, SCAR.

Vacchi, M., La Mesa, M. & Greco, S. 1999. Summer distribution and abundance of larval and juvenile fishes in the western Ross Sea. *Antarctic Science* **11**: 54-60.

Vacchi, M., La Mesa, M., Dalu, M. & MacDonald J. 2004. Early life stage in the life cycle of Antarctica silverfish, *Pleuragramma antarticum* in Terra Nova Bay, Ross Sea. *Antarctic Science* **16**: 299-305.

Vacchi, M., Koubbi, P., Ghigliotti, L. & Pisano, E. 2012a. Sea-ice interactions with polar fish – focus on the Antarctic Silverfish life history. In: Verde, C. & di Prisco, G. (eds.) *Adaptation and Evolution in Marine Environments*, From Pole to Pole Series Volume 1. Springer-Verlag, Berlin. DOI: 10.1007/978-3.

Vacchi, M., DeVries, A.L., Evans, C.W., Bottaro, M., Ghigliotti, L., Cutroneo, L. & Pisano, E. 2012b. A nursery area for the Antarctic silverfish *Pleuragramma antarcticum* at Terra Nova Bay (Ross Sea): first estimate of distribution and abundance of eggs and larvae under the seasonal sea ice. *Polar Biology* (in press).

Van Woert, M.L. 1999. Wintertime dynamics of the Terra Nova Bay polynya. *Journal of Geophysical Research* **104**: 1153-69.

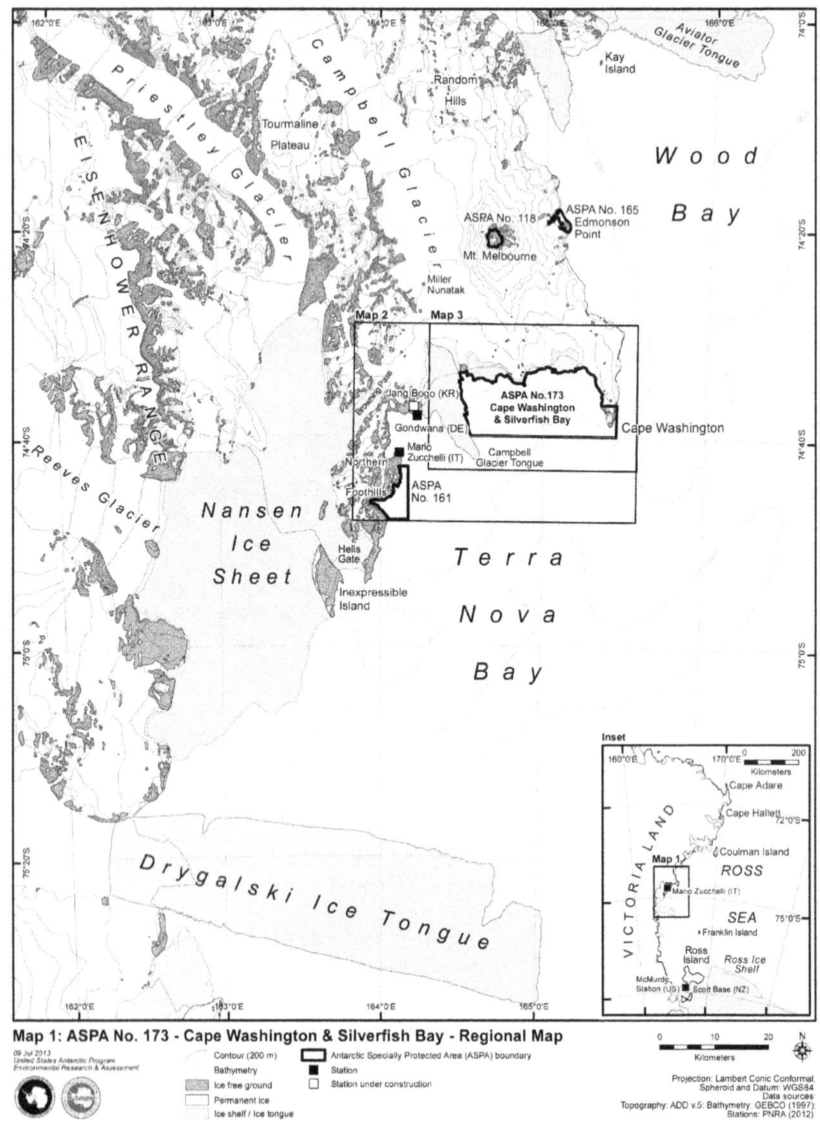

Map 1: ASPA No. 173 - Cape Washington & Silverfish Bay - Regional Map

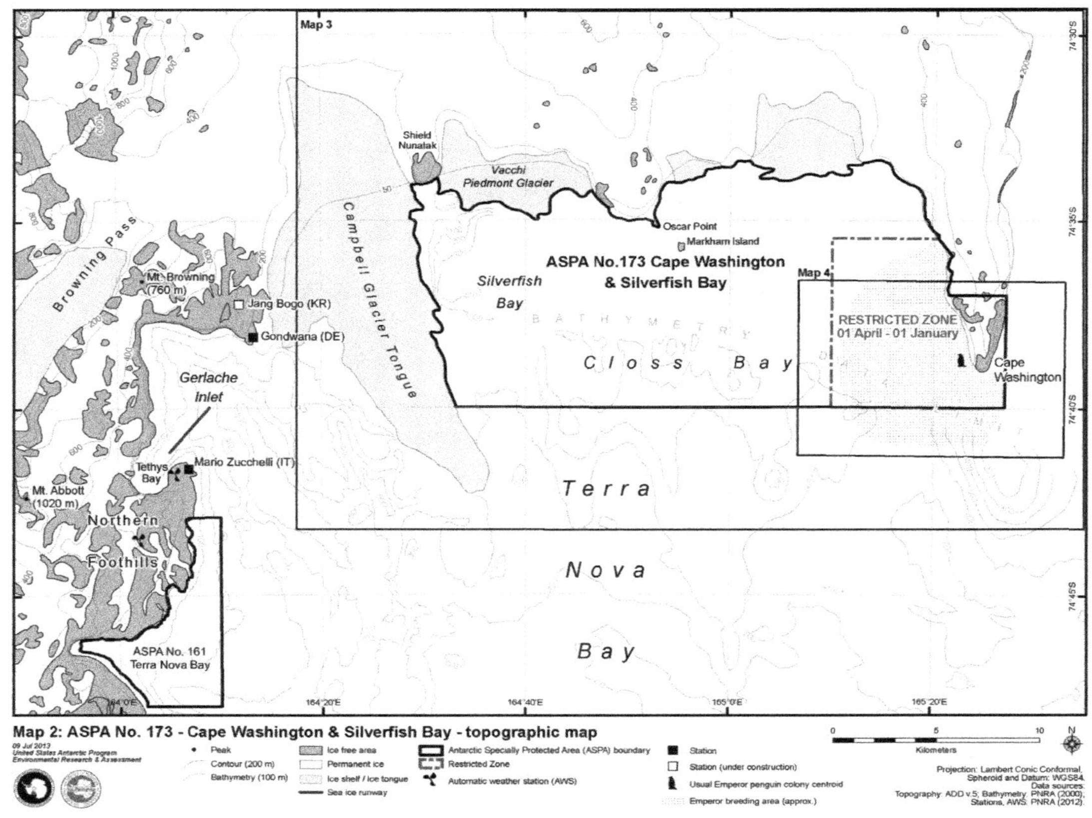

Map 3
Map 4
Shield Nunatak
Vacchi Piedmont Glacier
Oscar Point
Markham Island
ASPA No.173 Cape Washington & Silverfish Bay
Silverfish Bay
BATHYMETRY
Closs Bay
RESTRICTED ZONE
01 April - 01 January
Cape Washington
Campbell Glacier Tongue
Browning Pass
Mt. Browning (760 m)
Jang Bogo (KR)
Gondwana (DE)
Gerlache Inlet
Mario Zucchelli (IT)
Tethys Bay
Mt. Abbott (1020 m)
Northern Foothills
ASPA No. 161 Terra Nova Bay
Terra Nova Bay
74°30'S
74°35'S
74°40'S
74°45'S
164°0'E
164°20'E
164°40'E
165°0'E
165°20'E
Map 2: ASPA No. 173 - Cape Washington & Silverfish Bay - topographic map
09 Jul 2013
United States Antarctic Program
Environmental Research & Assessment
Peak
Contour (200 m)
Bathymetry (100 m)
Ice free area
Permanent ice
Ice shelf / ice tongue
Sea ice runway
Antarctic Specially Protected Area (ASPA) boundary
Restricted Zone
Automatic weather station (AWS)
Station
Station (under construction)
Usual Emperor penguin colony centroid
Emperor breeding area (approx.)
0 5 10
Kilometers
N
Projection: Lambert Conic Conformal,
Spheroid and Datum: WGS84.
Data sources:
Topography: ADD v.5; Bathymetry: PNRA (2000);
Stations, AWS: PNRA (2012).

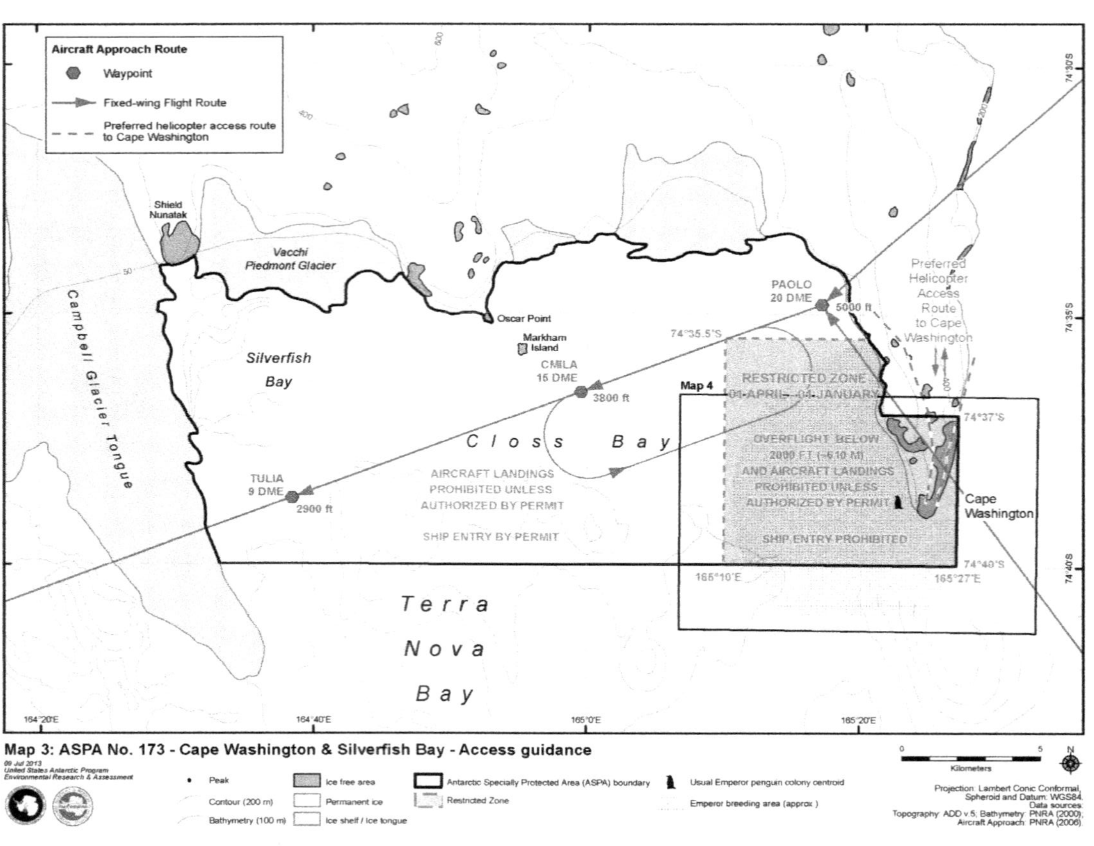

Map 3: ASPA No. 173 - Cape Washington & Silverfish Bay - Access guidance

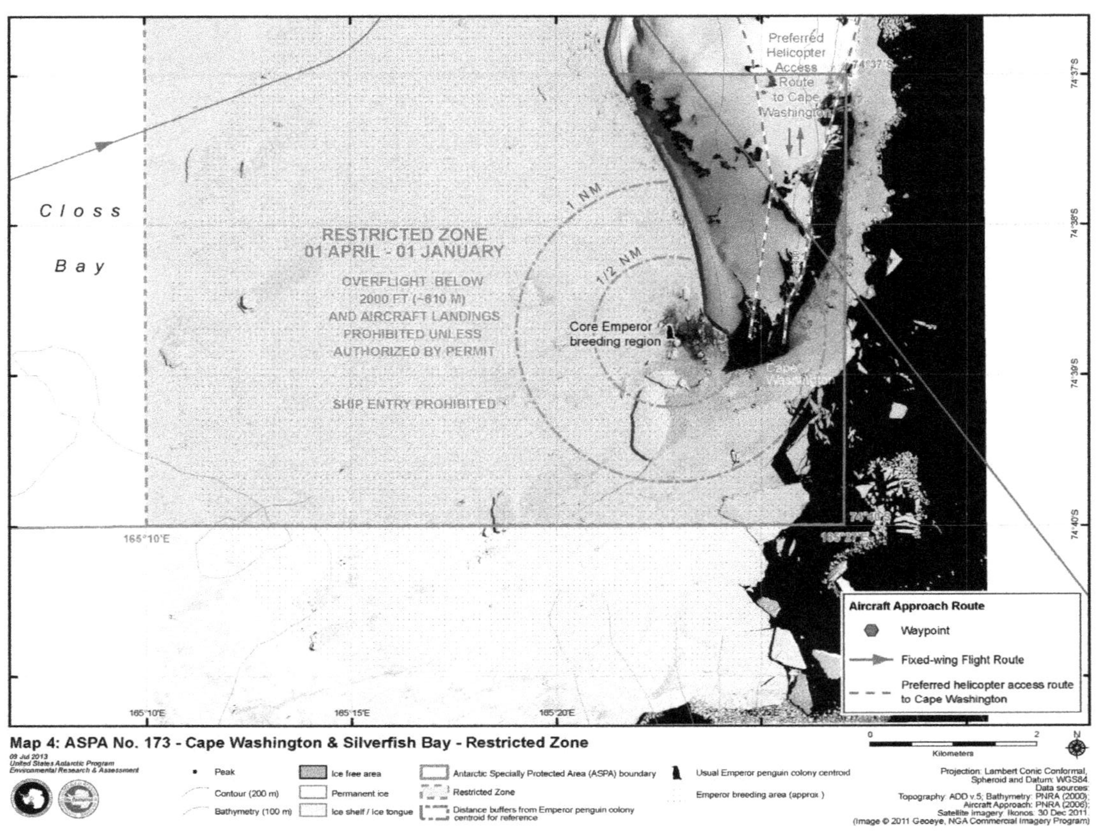

Closs Bay
RESTRICTED ZONE
01 APRIL - 01 JANUARY
OVERFLIGHT BELOW 2000 FT (~610 M) AND AIRCRAFT LANDINGS PROHIBITED UNLESS AUTHORIZED BY PERMIT
SHIP ENTRY PROHIBITED
1 NM
1/2 NM
Core Emperor breeding region
Preferred Helicopter Access Route to Cape Washington
74°37'S
74°38'S
74°39'S
74°40'S
165°10'E
165°15'E
165°20'E
Aircraft Approach Route
Waypoint
Fixed-wing Flight Route
Preferred helicopter access route to Cape Washington
Map 4: ASPA No. 173 - Cape Washington & Silverfish Bay - Restricted Zone
09 Jul 2013
United States Antarctic Program
Environmental Research & Assessment
Peak
Contour (200 m)
Bathymetry (100 m)
Ice free area
Permanent ice
Ice shelf / Ice tongue
Antarctic Specially Protected Area (ASPA) boundary
Restricted Zone
Distance buffers from Emperor penguin colony centroid for reference
Usual Emperor penguin colony centroid
Emperor breeding area (approx.)
0
2
Kilometers
Projection: Lambert Conic Conformal, Spheroid and Datum: WGS84
Data sources:
Topography: ADD v.5; Bathymetry: PNRA (2000);
Aircraft Approach: PNRA (2006);
Satellite imagery: Ikonos, 30 Dec 2011
(Image © 2011 Geoeye, NGA Commercial Imagery Program)

PART III

Opening and Closing Addresses and Reports

1. Reports by Depositaries and Observers

Report of the Depositary Government of the Antarctic Treaty and its Protocol in accordance with Recommendation XIII-2

Information Paper submitted by the United States

This report covers events with respect to the Antarctic Treaty and the Protocol on Environmental Protection to the Antarctic Treaty.

In the past year, there have been no accessions to the Treaty or the Protocol. There are fifty (50) Parties to the Treaty and thirty-five (35) Parties to the Protocol.

The following countries have provided notification that they have designated the persons so noted as Arbitrators in accordance with Article 2(1) of the Schedule to the Protocol:

Bulgaria	Mrs. Guenka Beleva	30 July 2004
Chile	Amb. María Teresa Infante	June 2005
	Amb. Jorge Berguño	June 2005
	Dr. Francisco Orrego	June 2005
Finland	Amb. Holger Bertil Rotkirch	14 June 2006
India	Prof. Upendra Baxi	6 October 2004
	Mr. Ajai Saxena	6 October 2004
	Dr. N. Khare	6 October 2004
Japan	Judge Shunji Yanai	18 July 2008
Rep. of Korea	Prof. Park Ki Gab	21 October 2008
United States	Prof. Daniel Bodansky	1 May 2008
	Mr. David Colson	1 May 2008

Lists of Parties to the Treaty, to the Protocol, and of Recommendations/Measures and their approvals are attached.

Date of most recent action: March 1, 2012

The Antarctic Treaty

Done: Washington; December 1, 1959

Entry into force: June 23, 1961
In accordance with Article XIII, the Treaty was subject to ratification by the signatory States and is open for accession by any State which is a Member of the United Nations, or by any other State which may be invited to accede to the Treaty with the consent of all the Contracting Parties whose representatives are entitled to participate in the meetings provided for under Article IX of the Treaty; instruments of ratification and instruments of accession shall be deposited with the Government of the United States of America. Upon the deposit of instruments of ratification by all the signatory States, the Treaty entered into force for those States and for States which had deposited instruments of accession to the Treaty. Thereafter, the Treaty enters into force for any acceding State upon deposit of its instrument of accession.

Legend: (no mark) = ratification; a = accession; d = succession; w = withdrawal or equivalent action

Participant	Signature	Consent to be bound		Other Action	Notes
Argentina	December 1, 1959	June 23, 1961			
Australia	December 1, 1959	June 23, 1961			
Austria		August 25, 1987	a		
Belarus		December 27, 2006	a		
Belgium	December 1, 1959	July 26, 1960			
Brazil		May 16, 1975	a		
Bulgaria		September 11, 1978	a		
Canada		May 4, 1988	a		
Chile	December 1, 1959	June 23, 1961			
China		June 8, 1983	a		
Colombia		January 31, 1989	a		
Cuba		August 16, 1984	a		
Czech Republic		January 1, 1993	d		1
Denmark		May 20, 1965	a		
Ecuador		September 15, 1987	a		
Estonia		May 17, 2001	a		
Finland		May 15, 1984	a		
France	December 1, 1959	September 16, 1960			
Germany		February 5, 1979	a		2
Greece		January 8, 1987	a		
Guatemala		July 31, 1991	a		
Hungary		January 27, 1984	a		
India		August 19, 1983	a		
Italy		March 18, 1981	a		
Japan	December 1, 1959	August 4, 1960			
Korea (DPRK)		January 21, 1987	a		
Korea (ROK)		November 28, 1986	a		
Malaysia		October 31, 2011	a		
Monaco		May 31, 2008	a		

Netherlands		March 30, 1967	a		3
New Zealand	December 1, 1959	November 1, 1960			
Norway	December 1, 1959	August 24, 1960			
Pakistan		March 1, 2012	a		
Papua New Guinea		March 16, 1981	d		4
Peru		April 10, 1981	a		
Poland		June 8, 1961	a		
Portugal		January 29, 2010	a		
Romania		September 15, 1971	a		5
Russian Federation	December 1, 1959	November 2, 1960			6
Slovak Republic		January 1, 1993	d		7
South Africa	December 1, 1959	June 21, 1960			
Spain		March 31, 1982	a		
Sweden		April 24, 1984	a		
Switzerland		November 15, 1990	a		
Turkey		January 24, 1996	a		
Ukraine		October 28, 1992	a		
United Kingdom	December 1, 1959	May 31, 1960			
United States	December 1, 1959	August 18, 1960			
Uruguay		January 11, 1980	a		8
Venezuela		March 24, 1999	a		

[1] Effective date of succession by the Czech Republic. Czechoslovakia deposited an instrument of accession to the Treaty on June 14, 1962. On December 31, 1992, at midnight, Czechoslovakia ceased to exist and was succeeded by two separate and independent states, the Czech Republic and the Slovak Republic.

[2] The Embassy of the Federal Republic of Germany in Washington transmitted to the Department of State a diplomatic note, dated October 2, 1990, which reads as follows:

"The Embassy of the Federal Republic of Germany presents its compliments to the Department of State and has the honor to inform the Government of the United States of America as the depositary Government of the Antarctic Treaty that, t[h]rough the accession of the German Democratic Republic to the Federal Republic of Germany with effect from October 3, 1990, the two German states will unite to form one sovereign state which, as a contracting party to the Antarctic Treaty, will remain bound by the provisions of the Treaty and subject to those recommendations adopted at the 15 consultative meetings which the Federal Republic of Germany has approved. From the date of German unity, the Federal Republic of Germany will act under the designation of "Germany" within the framework of the [A]ntarctic system.
"The Embassy would be grateful if the Government of the United States of America could inform all contracting parties to the Antarctic Treaty of the contents of this note.
"The Embassy of the Federal Republic of Germany avails itself of this opportunity to renew to the Department of State the assurances of its highest consideration."

Prior to unification, the German Democratic Republic deposited an instrument of accession to the Treaty, accompanied by a declaration, on November 19, 1974, and the Federal Republic of Germany deposited an instrument of accession to the Treaty, accompanied by a statement, on February 5, 1979.

[3] The instrument of accession to the Treaty by the Netherlands states that the accession is for the Kingdom in Europe, Suriname and the Netherlands Antilles.

Suriname became an independent state on November 25, 1975.

The Royal Netherlands Embassy in Washington transmitted to the Department of State a diplomatic note, dated January 9, 1986, which reads as follows:

"The Royal Netherlands Embassy presents its compliments to the Department of State and has the honor to request the Department's attention for the following with respect to the Department's capacity of depositary of [the Antarctic Treaty].
"Effective January 1, 1986 the island of Aruba – formerly part of the Netherlands Antilles – obtained internal autonomy as a country within the Kingdom of The Netherlands. Consequently the Kingdom of The Netherlands as of January 1, 1986 consists of three countries, to wit: the Netherlands proper, the Netherlands Antilles and Aruba.
"Since the abovementioned event concerns only a change in internal constitutional relations within the Kingdom of The Netherlands, and as the Kingdom as such, under international law, will remain the subject with which treaties are concluded, the aforementioned change will have no consequences in international law with regard to treaties concluded by the Kingdom, the application of which (treaties) were extended to the Netherlands Antilles, including Aruba.
"These treaties, thus, will remain applicable for Aruba in its new status as autonomous country within the Kingdom of The Netherlands effective January 1, 1986.
"Consequently the [Antarctic Treaty] to which the Kingdom of the Netherlands is a Party, and which [has] been extended to the Netherlands Antilles will as of January 1, 1986 apply to all three countries of the Kingdom of The Netherlands.
"The Embassy would appreciate if the other Parties concerned would be notified of the above.
"The Royal Netherlands Embassy avails itself of this opportunity to renew to the Department of State the assurance of its highest consideration."

The Royal Netherlands Embassy in Washington transmitted to the Department of State a diplomatic note, dated October 6, 2010, which reads in pertinent part as follows:

"The Kingdom of the Netherlands currently consists of three parts: the Netherlands, the Netherlands Antilles and Aruba. The Netherlands Antilles consists of the islands of Curaçao, Sint Maarten, Bonaire, Sint Eustatius and Saba.
"With effect from 10 October 2010, the Netherlands Antilles will cease to exist as a part of the Kingdom of the Netherlands. From that date onwards, the Kingdom will consist of four parts: the Netherlands, Aruba, Curaçao and Sint Maarten. Curaçao and Sint Maarten will enjoy internal self-government within the Kingdom, as Aruba and, up to 10 October 2010, the Netherlands Antilles do.
"These changes constitute a modification of the internal constitutional relations within the Kingdom of the Netherlands. The Kingdom of the Netherlands will accordingly remain the subject of international law with which agreements are concluded. The modification of the structure of the Kingdom will therefore not affect the validity of the international agreements ratified by the Kingdom for the Netherlands Antilles; these agreements will continue to apply to Curaçao and Sint Maarten.
"The other islands that have until now formed part of the Netherlands Antilles – Bonaire, Sint Eustatius and Saba – will become part of the Netherlands, thus constituting 'the Caribbean part of the Netherlands'. The agreements that now apply to the Netherlands Antilles will also continue to apply to these islands; however, the Government of the Netherlands will now be responsible for implementing these agreements."

[4] Date of deposit of notification of succession by Papua New Guinea; effective September 16, 1975, the date of its independence.

[5] The instrument of accession to the Treaty by Romania was accompanied by a note of the Ambassador of the Socialist Republic of Romania to the United States of America, dated September 15, 1971, which reads as follows:
"Dear Mr. Secretary:
"Submitting the instrument of adhesion of the Socialist Republic of Romania to the Antarctic Treaty, signed at Washington on December 1, 1959, I have the honor to inform you of the following:
'The Council of State of the Socialist Republic of Romania states that the provisions of the first paragraph of the article XIII of the Antarctic Treaty are not in accordance with the principle according to which the multilateral treaties whose object and purposes are concerning the international community, as a whole, should be opened for universal participation.'
"I am kindly requesting you, Mr. Secretary, to forward to all parties concerned the text of the Romanian instrument of adhesion to the Antarctic Treaty, as well as the text of this letter containing the above mentioned statement of the Romanian Government.
"I avail myself of this opportunity to renew to you, Mr. Secretary, the assurances of my highest consideration."

Copies of the Ambassador's letter and the Romanian instrument of accession to the Treaty were transmitted to the Antarctic Treaty parties by the Secretary of State's circular note dated October 1, 1971.

[6] The Treaty was signed and ratified by the former Union of Soviet Socialist Republics. By a note dated January 13, 1992, the Russian Federation informed the United States Government that it "continues to perform the rights and fulfil the obligations following from the international agreements signed by the Union of Soviet Socialist Republics."

[7] Effective date of succession by the Slovak Republic. Czechoslovakia deposited an instrument of accession to the Treaty on June 14, 1962. On December 31, 1992, at midnight, Czechoslovakia ceased to exist and was succeeded by two separate and independent states, the Czech Republic and the Slovak Republic.

[8] The instrument of accession to the Treaty by Uruguay was accompanied by a declaration, a Department of State English translation of which reads as follows:
"The Government of the Oriental Republic of Uruguay considers that, through its accession to the Antarctic Treaty signed at Washington (United States of America) on December 1, 1959, it helps to affirm the principles of using Antarctica exclusively for peaceful purposes, of prohibiting any nuclear explosion or radioactive waste disposal in this area, of freedom of scientific research in Antarctica in the service of mankind, and of international cooperation to achieve these objectives, which are established in said Treaty.
"Within the context of these principles Uruguay proposes, through a procedure based on the principle of legal equality, the establishment of a general and definitive statute on Antarctica in which, respecting the rights of States as recognized in international law, the interests of all States involved and of the international community as a whole would be considered equitably.
"The decision of the Uruguayan Government to accede to the Antarctic Treaty is based not only on the interest which, like all members of the international community, Uruguay has in Antarctica, but also on a special, direct, and substantial interest which arises from its geographic location, from the fact that its Atlantic coastline faces the continent of Antarctica, from the resultant influence upon its climate, ecology, and marine biology, from the historic bonds which date back to the first expeditions which ventured to explore that continent and its waters, and also from the obligations assumed in conformity with the Inter-American Treaty of Reciprocal Assistance which includes a portion of Antarctic territory in the zone described in Article 4, by virtue of which Uruguay shares the responsibility of defending the region.
"In communicating its decision to accede to the Antarctic Treaty, the Government of the Oriental Republic of Uruguay declares that it reserves its rights in Antarctica in accordance with international law."

PROTOCOL ON ENVIRONMENTAL PROTECTION TO THE ANTARCTIC TREATY

Signed at Madrid on October 4, 1991*

State	Date of Signature	Date deposit of Ratification, Acceptance (A) or Approval (AA)	Date deposit of Accession	Date of entry into force	Date Acceptance ANNEX V**	Date of entry into force of Annex V
CONSULTATIVE PARTIES						
Argentina	Oct. 4, 1991	Oct. 28, 1993 [3]		Jan. 14, 1998	Sept. 8, 2000 (A) Aug. 4, 1995 (B)	May 24, 2002
Australia	Oct. 4, 1991	Apr. 6, 1994		Jan. 14, 1998	Apr. 6, 1994 (A) June 7, 1995 (B)	May 24, 2002
Belgium	Oct. 4, 1991	Apr. 26, 1996		Jan. 14, 1998	Apr. 26, 1996 (A) Oct. 23, 2000 (B)	May 24, 2002
Brazil	Oct. 4, 1991	Aug. 15, 1995		Jan. 14, 1998	May 20, 1998 (B)	May 24, 2002
Bulgaria			April 21, 1998	May 21, 1998	May 5, 1999 (AB)	May 24, 2002
Chile	Oct. 4, 1991	Jan. 11, 1995		Jan. 14, 1998	Mar. 25, 1998 (B)	May 24, 2002
China	Oct. 4, 1991	Aug. 2, 1994		Jan. 14, 1998	Jan. 26, 1995 (AB)	May 24, 2002
Ecuador	Oct. 4, 1991	Jan. 4, 1993		Jan. 14, 1998	May 11, 2001 (A) Nov. 15, 2001 (B)	May 24, 2002
Finland	Oct. 4, 1991	Nov. 1, 1996 (A)		Jan. 14, 1998	Nov. 1, 1996 (A) Apr. 2, 1997 (B)	May 24, 2002
France	Oct. 4, 1991	Feb. 5, 1993 (AA)		Jan. 14, 1998	Apr. 26, 1995 (B) Nov. 18, 1998 (A)	May 24, 2002
Germany	Oct. 4, 1991	Nov. 25, 1994		Jan. 14, 1998	Nov. 25, 1994 (A) Sept. 1, 1998 (B)	May 24, 2002
India	July 2, 1992	Apr. 26, 1996		Jan. 14, 1998	May 24, 2002 (B)	May 24, 2002
Italy	Oct. 4, 1991	Mar. 31, 1995		Jan. 14, 1998	May 31, 1995 (A) Feb. 11, 1998 (B)	May 24, 2002
Japan	Sept. 29, 1992	Dec. 15, 1997 (A)		Jan. 14, 1998	Dec. 15, 1997 (AB)	May 24, 2002
Korea, Rep. of	July 2, 1992	Jan. 2, 1996		Jan. 14, 1998	June 5, 1996 (B)	May 24, 2002
Netherlands	Oct. 4, 1991	Apr. 14, 1994 (A) [6]		Jan. 14, 1998	Mar. 18, 1998 (B)	May 24, 2002
New Zealand	Oct. 4, 1991	Dec. 22, 1994		Jan. 14, 1998	Oct. 21, 1992 (B)	May 24, 2002
Norway	Oct. 4, 1991	June 16, 1993		Jan. 14, 1998	Oct. 13, 1993 (B)	May 24, 2002
Peru	Oct. 4, 1991	Mar. 8, 1993		Jan. 14, 1998	Mar. 8, 1993 (A) Mar. 17, 1999 (B)	May 24, 2002
Poland	Oct. 4, 1991	Nov. 1, 1995		Jan. 14, 1998	Sept. 20, 1995 (B)	May 24, 2002
Russian Federation	Oct. 4, 1991	Aug. 6, 1997		Jan. 14, 1998	June 19, 2001 (B)	May 24, 2002
South Africa	Oct. 4, 1991	Aug. 3, 1995		Jan. 14, 1998	June 14, 1995 (B)	May 24, 2002
Spain	Oct. 4, 1991	July 1, 1992		Jan. 14, 1998	Dec. 8, 1993 (A) Feb. 18, 2000 (B)	May 24, 2002
Sweden	Oct. 4, 1991	Mar. 30, 1994		Jan. 14, 1998	Mar. 30, 1994 (A) Apr. 7, 1994 (B)	May 24, 2002
Ukraine			May 25, 2001	June 24, 2001	May 25, 2001 (A)	May 24, 2002

United Kingdom	Oct. 4, 1991	Apr. 25, 1995 [5]		Jan. 14, 1998	May 21, 1996 (B)	May 24, 2002
United States	Oct. 4, 1991	Apr. 17, 1997		Jan. 14, 1998	Apr. 17, 1997 (A) May 6, 1998 (B)	May 24, 2002
Uruguay	Oct. 4, 1991	Jan. 11, 1995		Jan. 14, 1998	May 15, 1995 (B)	May 24, 2002

** The following denotes date relating either
to acceptance of Annex V or approval of Recommendation XVI-10
(A) Acceptance of Annex V (B) Approval of Recommendation XVI-10

State	Date of Signature	Ratification Acceptance or Approval	Date deposit of Accession	Date of entry into force	Date Acceptance ANNEX V**	Date of entry into force of Annex V
NON-CONSULTATIVE PARTIES						
Austria	Oct. 4, 1991					
Belarus			July 16, 2008	Aug. 15, 2008		
Canada	Oct. 4, 1991	Nov. 13, 2003		Dec. 13, 2003		
Colombia	Oct. 4, 1991					
Cuba						
Czech Rep.[1,2]	Jan. 1, 1993	Aug. 25, 2004 [4]		Sept. 24, 2004		
Denmark	July 2, 1992					
Estonia						
Greece	Oct. 4, 1991	May 23, 1995		Jan. 14, 1998		
Guatemala						
Hungary	Oct. 4, 1991					
Korea, DPR of	Oct. 4, 1991					
Malaysia						
Monaco			July 1, 2009	July 31, 2009		
Pakistan			Mar. 1, 2012	Mar. 31, 2012		
Papua New Guinea						
Portugal						
Romania	Oct. 4, 1991	Feb. 3, 2003		Mar. 5, 2003	Feb. 3, 2003	Mar. 5, 2003
Slovak Rep.[1,2]	Jan. 1, 1993					
Switzerland	Oct. 4, 1991					
Turkey						
Venezuela						

* Signed at Madrid on October 4, 1991; thereafter at Washington until October 3, 1992.
The Protocol will enter into force initially on the thirtieth day following the date of deposit of instruments of ratification, acceptance, approval or accession by all States which were Antarctic Treaty Consultative Parties at the date on which this Protocol was adopted. (Article 23)

**Adopted at Bonn on October 17, 1991 at XVIth Antarctic Consultative Meeting.

1. Signed for Czech & Slovak Federal Republic on Oct. 2, 1992 - Czechoslovakia accepts the jurisdiction of the International Court of Justice and Arbitral Tribunal for the settlement of disputes according to Article 19, paragraph 1. On December 31, 1992, at midnight, Czechoslovakia ceased to exist and was succeeded by two separate and independent states, the Czech Republic and the Slovak Republic.

2. Effective date of succession in respect of signature by Czechoslovakia which is subject to ratification by the Czech Republic and the Slovak Republic.

3. Accompanied by declaration, with informal translation provided by the Embassy of Argentina, which reads as follows: "The Argentine Republic declares that in as much as the Protocol to the Antarctic Treaty on the Protection of the Environment is a Complementary Agreement of the Antarctic Treaty and that its Article 4 fully respects what has been stated in Article IV, Subsection 1, Paragraph A) of said Treaty,

none of its stipulations should be interpreted or be applied as affecting its rights, based on legal titles, acts of possession, contiguity and geological continuity in the region South of parallel 60, in which it has proclaimed and maintained its sovereignty."

4. Accompanied by declaration, with informal translation provided by the Embassy of the Czech Republic, which reads as follows: "The Czech Republic accepts the jurisdiction of the International Court of Justice and of the Arbitral Tribunal under Article 19, paragraph 1, of the Protocol on Environmental Protection to the Antarctic Treaty, done at Madrid on October 4, 1991."

5. Ratification on behalf of the United Kingdom of Great Britain and Northern Ireland, the Bailiwick of Jersey, the Bailiwick of Guernsey, the Isle of Man, Anguilla, Bermuda, the British Antarctic Territory, Cayman Islands, Falkland Islands, Montserrat, St. Helena and Dependencies, South Georgia and the South Sandwich Islands, Turks and Caicos Islands and British Virgin Islands.

6. Acceptance is for the Kingdom in Europe. At the time of its acceptance, the Kingdom of the Netherlands stated that it chooses both means for the settlement of disputes mentioned in Article 19, paragraph 1 of the Protocol, i.e. the International Court of Justice and the Arbitral Tribunal.

   On October 27, 2004, the Kingdom of the Netherlands deposited a declaration accepting the Protocol for the Netherlands Antilles with a statement confirming that it chooses both means for the settlement of disputes mentioned in Article 19, paragraph 1 of the Protocol.

   The Royal Netherlands Embassy in Washington transmitted to the Department of State a diplomatic note, dated October 6, 2010, which reads in pertinent part as follows:

   "The Kingdom of the Netherlands currently consists of three parts: the Netherlands, the Netherlands Antilles and Aruba. The Netherlands Antilles consists of the islands of Curaçao, Sint Maarten, Bonaire, Sint Eustatius and Saba.
   "With effect from 10 October 2010, the Netherlands Antilles will cease to exist as a part of the Kingdom of the Netherlands. From that date onwards, the Kingdom will consist of four parts: the Netherlands, Aruba, Curaçao and Sint Maarten. Curaçao and Sint Maarten will enjoy internal self-government within the Kingdom, as Aruba and, up to 10 October 2010, the Netherlands Antilles do.
   "These changes constitute a modification of the internal constitutional relations within the Kingdom of the Netherlands. The Kingdom of the Netherlands will accordingly remain the subject of international law with which agreements are concluded. The modification of the structure of the Kingdom will therefore not affect the validity of the international agreements ratified by the Kingdom for the Netherlands Antilles; these agreements will continue to apply to Curaçao and Sint Maarten.
   "The other islands that have until now formed part of the Netherlands Antilles – Bonaire, Sint Eustatius and Saba – will become part of the Netherlands, thus constituting 'the Caribbean part of the Netherlands'. The agreements that now apply to the Netherlands Antilles will also continue to apply to these islands; however, the Government of the Netherlands will now be responsible for implementing these agreements."

Department of State,
Washington, April 18, 2013

Approval, as notified to the Government of the United States of America, of measures relating to the furtherance of the principles and objectives of the Antarctic Treaty

	16 Recommendations adopted at First Meeting (Canberra 1961) Approved	10 Recommendations adopted at Second Meeting (Buenos Aires 1962) Approved	11 Recommendations adopted at Third Meeting (Brussels 1964) Approved	28 Recommendations adopted at Fourth Meeting (Santiago 1966) Approved	9 Recommendations adopted at Fifth Meeting (Paris 1968) Approved	15 Recommendations adopted at Sixth Meeting (Tokyo 1970) Approved
Argentina	ALL	ALL	ALL	ALL	ALL	ALL
Australia	ALL	ALL	ALL	ALL	ALL	ALL
Belgium	ALL	ALL	ALL	ALL	ALL	ALL
Brazil (1983)+	ALL	ALL	ALL	ALL	ALL	ALL (except 10)
Bulgaria (1998)+						
Chile	ALL	ALL	ALL	ALL	ALL	ALL
China (1985)+	ALL	ALL	ALL	ALL	ALL	ALL (except 10)
Ecuador (1990)+						
Finland (1989)+						
France	ALL	ALL	ALL	ALL	ALL	ALL
Germany (1981)+	ALL	ALL	ALL (except 8)	ALL (except 16-19)	ALL (except 6)	ALL (except 9)
India (1983)+	ALL	ALL	ALL (except 8***)	ALL (except 18)	ALL	ALL (except 9 & 10)
Italy (1987)+	ALL	ALL	ALL	ALL	ALL	ALL
Japan	ALL	ALL	ALL	ALL	ALL	ALL
Korea, Rep. (1989)+	ALL	ALL	ALL	ALL	ALL	ALL
Netherlands (1990)+	ALL (except 11 & 15)	ALL (except 3, 5, 8 & 10)	ALL (except 3, 4, 6 & 9)	ALL (except 20, 25, 26 & 28)	ALL (except 1, 8 & 9)	ALL (except 15)
New Zealand	ALL	ALL	ALL	ALL	ALL	ALL
Norway	ALL	ALL	ALL	ALL	ALL	ALL
Peru (1989)+	ALL	ALL	ALL	ALL	ALL	ALL
Poland (1977)+	ALL	ALL	ALL	ALL	ALL	ALL
Russia	ALL	ALL	ALL	ALL	ALL	ALL
South Africa	ALL	ALL	ALL	ALL	ALL	ALL
Spain (1988)+	ALL	ALL	ALL	ALL	ALL	ALL
Sweden (1988)+						
U.K.	ALL	ALL	ALL	ALL	ALL	ALL
Uruguay (1985)+	ALL	ALL	ALL	ALL	ALL	ALL
U.S.A.	ALL	ALL	ALL	ALL	ALL	ALL

* IV-6, IV-10, IV-12, and V-5 terminated by VIII-2
*** Accepted as interim guideline
\+ Year attained Consultative Status. Acceptance by that State required to bring into force Recommendations or Measures of meetings from that year forward.

Approval, as notified to the Government of the United States of America, of measures relating to the furtherance of the principles and objectives of the Antarctic Treaty

	9 Recommendations adopted at Seventh Meeting (Wellington 1972)	**14 Recommendations adopted at Eighth Meeting (Oslo 1975)**	**6 Recommendations adopted at Ninth Meeting (London 1977)**	**9 Recommendations adopted at Tenth Meeting (Washington 1979)**	**3 Recommendations adopted at Eleventh Meeting (Buenos Aires 1981)**	**8 Recommendations adopted at Twelfth Meeting (Canberra 1983)**
	Approved	**Approved**	**Approved**	**Approved**	**Approved**	**Approved**
Argentina	ALL	ALL	ALL	ALL	ALL	ALL
Australia	ALL	ALL	ALL	ALL	ALL	ALL
Belgium	ALL	ALL	ALL	ALL	ALL	ALL
Brazil (1983)+	ALL (except 5)	ALL	ALL	ALL	ALL	ALL
Bulgaria (1998)+						
Chile	ALL	ALL	ALL	ALL	ALL	ALL
China (1985)+	ALL (except 5)	ALL	ALL	ALL	ALL	ALL
Ecuador (1990)+						
Finland (1989)+						
France	ALL	ALL	ALL	ALL	ALL	ALL
Germany (1981)+	ALL (except 5)	ALL (except 2 & 5)	ALL	ALL	ALL	ALL
India (1983)+	ALL	ALL	ALL	ALL (except 1 & 9)	ALL	ALL
Italy (1987)+	ALL (except 5)	ALL	ALL	ALL (except 1 & 9)		
Japan	ALL	ALL	ALL	ALL	ALL	ALL
Korea, Rep. (1989)+	ALL	ALL	ALL	ALL	ALL	ALL
Netherlands (1990)+	ALL	ALL	ALL (except 3)	ALL (except 9)	ALL (except 2)	ALL
New Zealand	ALL	ALL	ALL	ALL	ALL	ALL
Norway	ALL	ALL	ALL	ALL	ALL	ALL
Peru (1989)+	ALL	ALL	ALL	ALL	ALL	
Poland (1977)+	ALL	ALL	ALL	ALL	ALL	ALL
Russia	ALL	ALL	ALL	ALL	ALL	ALL
South Africa	ALL	ALL	ALL	ALL	ALL	ALL
Spain (1988)+	ALL	ALL	ALL	ALL (except 1 & 9)	ALL (except 1)	ALL
Sweden (1988)+						
U.K.	ALL	ALL	ALL	ALL	ALL	ALL
Uruguay (1985)+	ALL	ALL	ALL	ALL	ALL	ALL
U.S.A.	ALL	ALL	ALL	ALL	ALL	ALL

* IV-6, IV-10, IV-12, and V-5 terminated by VIII-2
*** Accepted as interim guideline
+ Year attained Consultative Status. Acceptance by that State required to bring into force Recommendations or Measures of meetings from that year forward.

Approval, as notified to the Government of the United States of America, of measures relating to the furtherance of the principles and objectives of the Antarctic Treaty

	16 Recommendations adopted at Thirteenth Meeting (Brussels 1985) **Approved**	10 Recommendations adopted at Fourteenth Meeting (Rio de Janeiro 1987) **Approved**	22 Recommendations adopted at Fifteenth Meeting (Paris 1989) **Approved**	13 Recommendations adopted at Sixteenth Meeting (Bonn 1991) **Approved**	4 Recommendations adopted at Seventeenth Meeting (Venice 1992) **Approved**	1 Recommendation adopted at Eighteenth Meeting (Kyoto 1994) **Approved**
Argentina	ALL	ALL	ALL	ALL	ALL	ALL
Australia	ALL	ALL	ALL	ALL	ALL	ALL
Belgium	ALL	ALL	ALL	ALL	ALL	ALL
Brazil (1983)+	ALL	ALL	ALL	ALL	ALL	ALL
Bulgaria (1998)+				XVI-10		
Chile	ALL	ALL	ALL	ALL	ALL	ALL
China (1985)+	ALL	ALL	ALL	ALL	ALL	ALL
Ecuador (1990)+				XVI-10		
Finland (1989)+			ALL	ALL	ALL	ALL
France	ALL	ALL	ALL	ALL	ALL	ALL
Germany (1981)+	ALL	ALL	ALL (except 3,8,10,11&22)	ALL	ALL	ALL
India (1983)+	ALL	ALL	ALL	ALL	ALL	ALL
Italy (1987)+		ALL	ALL	ALL	ALL	ALL
Japan	ALL	ALL	ALL	ALL (except 1, 3-9, 12&13)	ALL (except 1-2 & 4)	ALL
Korea, Rep. (1989)+	ALL	ALL	ALL (except 1-11, 16, 18, 19)	ALL (except 12)	ALL (except 1)	ALL
Netherlands (1990)+	ALL	ALL (except 9)	ALL (except 22)	ALL	ALL	ALL
New Zealand	ALL	ALL	ALL	ALL	ALL	ALL
Norway	ALL	ALL	ALL	ALL	ALL	ALL
Peru (1989)+			ALL (except 22)	ALL (except 13)	ALL	ALL
Poland (1977)+	ALL	ALL	ALL	ALL	ALL	ALL
Russia	ALL	ALL	ALL	ALL	ALL	ALL
South Africa	ALL	ALL	ALL	ALL	ALL	ALL
Spain (1988)+	ALL	ALL	ALL	ALL	ALL	ALL
Sweden (1988)+			ALL	ALL	ALL	ALL
U.K.	ALL	ALL (except 2)	ALL (except 3, 4, 8, 10, 11)	ALL (except 4, 6, 8, & 9)	ALL	ALL
Uruguay (1985)+	ALL	ALL	ALL	ALL	ALL	ALL
U.S.A.	ALL	ALL	ALL (except 1-4, 10, 11)	ALL	ALL	ALL

* IV-6, IV-10, IV-12, and V-5 terminated by VIII-2

*** Accepted as interim guideline

\+ Year attained Consultative Status. Acceptance by that State required to bring into force Recommendations or Measures of meetings from that year forward.

Approval, as notified to the Government of the United States of America, of measures relating to the furtherance of the principles and objectives of the Antarctic Treaty

	5 Measures adopted at Nineteenth Meeting (Seoul 1995)	2 Measures adopted at Twentieth Meeting (Utrecht 1996)	5 Measures adopted at Twenty-First Meeting (Christchurch 1997)	2 Measures adopted at Twenty-Second Meeting (Tromso 1998)	1 Measure adopted at Twenty-Third Meeting (Lima 1999)
	Approved	Approved	Approved	Approved	Approved
Argentina	ALL	ALL	ALL	ALL	ALL
Australia	ALL	ALL	ALL	ALL	ALL
Belgium	ALL	ALL	ALL	ALL	ALL
Brazil (1983)+	ALL	ALL	ALL	ALL	ALL
Bulgaria (1998)+					
Chile	ALL	ALL	ALL	ALL	ALL
China (1985)+	ALL	ALL	ALL	ALL	ALL
Ecuador (1990)+					
Finland (1989)+	ALL	ALL	ALL	ALL	ALL
France	ALL	ALL	ALL	ALL	ALL
Germany (1981)+	ALL	ALL	ALL	ALL	ALL
India (1983)+	ALL	ALL	ALL	ALL	ALL
Italy (1987)+	ALL	ALL			
Japan	ALL (except 2&5)	ALL (except 1)	All (except 1-2 & 5)		
Korea, Rep. (1989)+	ALL	ALL	ALL	ALL	ALL
Netherlands (1990)+	ALL	ALL	ALL	ALL	ALL
New Zealand	ALL	ALL	ALL	ALL	ALL
Norway	ALL	ALL	ALL		
Peru (1989)+	ALL	ALL	ALL	ALL	ALL
Poland (1977)+	ALL	ALL	ALL	ALL	ALL
Russia	ALL	ALL	ALL	ALL	ALL
South Africa	ALL	ALL	ALL	ALL	ALL
Spain (1988)+	ALL	ALL	ALL	ALL	ALL
Sweden (1988)+	ALL	ALL	ALL	ALL	ALL
U.K.	ALL	ALL	ALL	ALL	ALL
Uruguay (1985)+	ALL	ALL	ALL	ALL	ALL
U.S.A.	ALL	ALL	ALL	ALL	ALL

"+Year attained Consultative Status. Acceptance by that state required to bring into force Recommendations or Measures of meetings from that Year forward."

Approval, as notified to the Government of the United States of America, of measures relating to the furtherance of the principles and objectives of the Antarctic Treaty

	2 Measures adopted at Twelfth Special Meeting (The Hague 2000) Approved	3 Measures adopted at Twenty-Fourth Meeting (St. Petersburg 2001) Approved	1 Measure adopted at Twenty-Fifth Meeting (Warsaw 2002) Approved	3 Measures adopted at Twenty-Sixth Meeting (Madrid 2003) Approved	4 Measures adopted at Twenty-Seventh Meeting (Cape Town 2004) Approved
Argentina			*	XXVI-1, XXVI-2 *, XXVI-3 **	XXVII-1 *, XXVII-2 *, XXVII-3 **
Australia	ALL	ALL	ALL	XXVI-1, XXVI-2 *, XXVI-3 **	XXVII-1 *, XXVII-2 *, XXVII-3 **
Belgium	ALL	ALL	ALL	ALL	ALL
Brazil (1983)+	ALL	ALL	ALL	ALL	XXVII-1, XXVII-2, XXVII-3
Bulgaria (1998)+			*	XXVI-1, XXVI-2 *, XXVI-3 **	XXVII-1 *, XXVII-2 *, XXVII-3 **
Chile	ALL	ALL	ALL	ALL	ALL
China (1985)+	ALL	ALL	ALL	ALL	XXVII-1 *, XXVII-2 *, XXVII-3 **
Ecuador (1990)+			*	XXVI-1, XXVI-2 *, XXVI-3 **	XXVII-1 *, XXVII-2 *, XXVII-3 **
Finland (1989)+	ALL	ALL	*	XXVI-1, XXVI-2 *, XXVI-3 **	XXVII-1 *, XXVII-2 *, XXVII-3 **, XXVII-4
France	ALL (except SATCM XII-2)	ALL	*	XXVI-1, XXVI-2 *, XXVI-3 **	XXVII-1, XXVII-2 *, XXVII-3, XXVII-4
Germany (1981)+	ALL	ALL	ALL	ALL	XXVII-1 *, XXVII-2 *, XXVII-3 **
India (1983)+	ALL	ALL	ALL	ALL	XXVII-1 *, XXVII-2 *, XXVII-3 **
Italy (1987)+			*	XXVI-1, XXVI-2 *, XXVI-3 **	XXVII-1 *, XXVII-2 *, XXVII-3 **
Japan		ALL	*	ALL	XXVII-1 *, XXVII-2 *, XXVII-3 **, XXVII-4
Korea, Rep. (1989)+	ALL	ALL	*	XXVI-1, XXVI-2 *, XXVI-3 **	XXVII-1 *, XXVII-2 *, XXVII-3 **
Netherlands (1990)+	ALL	ALL	ALL	ALL	ALL
New Zealand	ALL	ALL	ALL	ALL	XXVII-1 *, XXVII-2 *, XXVII-3 **, XXVII-4
Norway		ALL	*	XXVI-1, XXVI-2 *, XXVI-3 **	XXVII-1 *, XXVII-2 *, XXVII-3 **
Peru (1989)+	ALL	ALL	ALL	XXVI-1, XXVI-2 *, XXVI-3 **	XXVII-1 *, XXVII-2 *, XXVII-3 **
Poland (1977)+		ALL	ALL	ALL	ALL
Russia	ALL	ALL	ALL	XXVI-1, XXVI-2, XXVI-3 **	XXVII-1 *, XXVII-2 *, XXVII-3 **
South Africa	ALL	ALL	ALL	ALL	ALL
Spain (1988)+			*	XXVI-1, XXVI-2 *, XXVI-3 **	XXVII-1 *, XXVII-2 *, XXVII-3 **
Sweden (1988)+	ALL	ALL	ALL	ALL	XXVII-1 *, XXVII-2 *, XXVII-3 **
Ukraine (2004)+					XXVII-1 *, XXVII-2 *, XXVII-3 **
U.K.	ALL (except SATCM XII-2)	ALL (except XXIV-3)	ALL	ALL	XXVII-1 *, XXVII-2 *, XXVII-3 **, XXVII-4
Uruguay (1985)+	ALL	ALL	*	XXVI-1, XXVI-2 *, XXVI-3	XXVII-1 *, XXVII-2 *, XXVII-3 **, XXVII-4
U.S.A.	ALL	ALL	*	XXVI-1, XXVI-2 *, XXVI-3 **	XXVII-1 *, XXVII-2 *, XXVII-3 **

"+Year attained Consultative Status. Acceptance by that state required to bring into force Recommendations or Measures of meetings from that Year forward."

* Management Plans annexed to this Measure were deemed to have been approved in accordance with Article 6(1) of Annex V to the Protocol on Environmental Protection to the Antarctic Treaty and the Measure not specifying a different approval method.

** Revised and updated List of Historic Sites and Monuments annexed to this Measure was deemed to have been approved in accordance with Article 8(2) of Annex V to the Protocol on Environmental Protection to the Antarctic Treaty and the Measure not specifying a different approval method.

Approval, as notified to the Government of the United States of America, of measures relating to the furtherance of the principles and objectives of the Antarctic Treaty

	5 Measures adopted at Twenty-Eighth Meeting (Stockholm 2005) Approved	4 Measures adopted at Twenty-Ninth Meeting (Edinburgh 2006) Approved	3 Measures adopted at Thirtieth Meeting (New Delhi 2007) Approved	14 Measures adopted at Thirty-first Meeting (Kyiv 2008) Approved	16 Measures adopted at Thirty-second Meeting (Baltimore 2009) Approved
Argentina	XXVIII-2 *, XXVIII-3 *, XXVIII-4 *, XXVIII-5 **	XXIX-1 *, XXIX-2 *, XXIX-3 **, XXIX-4 ***	XXX-1 *, XXX-2 *, XXX-3 **	XXXI-1*, XXXI-2*, . . . XXXI-14 *	XXXII-1*, XXXII-2*, . . . XXXII-14**
Australia	XXVIII-2 *, XXVIII-3 *, XXVIII-4 *, XXVIII-5 **	XXIX-1 *, XXIX-2 *, XXIX-3 **, XXIX-4 ***	XXX-1 *, XXX-2 *, XXX-3 **	XXXI-1*, XXXI-2*, . . . XXXI-14 *	XXXII-1*, XXXII-2*, . . . XXXII-14**
Belgium	ALL except Measure 1	ALL	ALL	XXXI-1*, XXXI-2*, . . . XXXI-14 *	XXXII-1*, XXXII-2*, . . . XXXII-14**
Brazil (1983)+	ALL except Measure 1	XXIX-1 *, XXIX-2 *, XXIX-3 **, XXIX-4 ***	XXX-1 *, XXX-2 *, XXX-3 **	XXXI-1*, XXXI-2*, . . . XXXI-14 *	XXXII-1*, XXXII-2*, . . . XXXII-14**
Bulgaria (1998)+	XXVIII-2 *, XXVIII-3 *, XXVIII-4 *, XXVIII-5 **	XXIX-1 *, XXIX-2 *, XXIX-3 **, XXIX-4 ***	XXX-1 *, XXX-2 *, XXX-3 **	XXXI-1*, XXXI-2*, . . . XXXI-14 *	XXXII-1*, XXXII-2*, . . . XXXII-14**
Chile	ALL except Measure 1	XXIX-1 *, XXIX-2 *, XXIX-3 **, XXIX-4 ***	XXX-1 *, XXX-2 *, XXX-3 **	XXXI-1*, XXXI-2*, . . . XXXI-14 *	XXXII-1*, XXXII-2*, . . . XXXII-14**
China (1985)+	XXVIII-2 *, XXVIII-3 *, XXVIII-4 *, XXVIII-5 **	XXIX-1 *, XXIX-2 *, XXIX-3 **, XXIX-4 ***	XXX-1 *, XXX-2 *, XXX-3 **	XXXI-1*, XXXI-2*, . . . XXXI-14 *	XXXII-1*, XXXII-2*, . . . XXXII-14**
Ecuador (1990)+	XXVIII-2 *, XXVIII-3 *, XXVIII-4 *, XXVIII-5 **	XXIX-1 *, XXIX-2 *, XXIX-3 **, XXIX-4 ***	XXX-1 *, XXX-2 *, XXX-3 **	XXXI-1*, XXXI-2*, . . . XXXI-14 *	XXXII-1*, XXXII-2*, . . . XXXII-14**
Finland (1989)+	XXVIII-1, XXVIII-2 *, XXVIII-3 *, XXVIII-4 *, XXVIII-5 **	XXIX-1 *, XXIX-2 *, XXIX-3 **, XXIX-4 ***	XXX-1 *, XXX-2 *, XXX-3 **	XXXI-1*, XXXI-2*, . . . XXXI-14 *	XXXII-1*, XXXII-2*, . . . XXXII-14**; XXXII-16
France	XXVIII-2 *, XXVIII-3 *, XXVIII-4 *, XXVIII-5 **	XXIX-1 *, XXIX-2 *, XXIX-3 **, XXIX-4 ***	XXX-1 *, XXX-2 *, XXX-3 **	XXXI-1*, XXXI-2*, . . . XXXI-14 *	XXXII-1*, XXXII-2*, . . . XXXII-14**, XXXII-15
Germany (1981)+	XXVIII-2 *, XXVIII-3 *, XXVIII-4 *, XXVIII-5 **	XXIX-1 *, XXIX-2 *, XXIX-3 **, XXIX-4 ***	XXX-1 *, XXX-2 *, XXX-3 **	XXXI-1*, XXXI-2*, . . . XXXI-14 *	XXXII-1*, XXXII-2*, . . . XXXII-14**
India (1983)+	XXVIII-2 *, XXVIII-3 *, XXVIII-4 *, XXVIII-5 **	XXIX-1 *, XXIX-2 *, XXIX-3 **, XXIX-4 ***	XXX-1 *, XXX-2 *, XXX-3 **	XXXI-1*, XXXI-2*, . . . XXXI-14 *	XXXII-1*, XXXII-2*, . . . XXXII-14**
Italy (1987)+	XXVIII-2 *, XXVIII-3 *, XXVIII-4 *, XXVIII-5 **	XXIX-1 *, XXIX-2 *, XXIX-3 **, XXIX-4 ***	XXX-1 *, XXX-2 *, XXX-3 **	XXXI-1*, XXXI-2*, . . . XXXI-14 *	XXXII-1*, XXXII-2*, . . . XXXII-14**
Japan	XXVIII-2 *, XXVIII-3 *, XXVIII-4 *, XXVIII-5 **	XXIX-1 *, XXIX-2 *, XXIX-3 **, XXIX-4 ***	XXX-1 *, XXX-2 *, XXX-3 **	XXXI-1*, XXXI-2*, . . . XXXI-14 *	XXXII-1*, XXXII-2*, . . . XXXII-14**, XXXII-15
Korea, Rep. (1989)+	XXVIII-2 *, XXVIII-3 *, XXVIII-4 *, XXVIII-5 **	XXIX-1 *, XXIX-2 *, XXIX-3 **, XXIX-4 ***	XXX-1 *, XXX-2 *, XXX-3 **	XXXI-1*, XXXI-2*, . . . XXXI-14 *	XXXII-1*, XXXII-2*, . . . XXXII-14**
Netherlands (1990)+	ALL except Measure 1	ALL	ALL	ALL	XXXII-1, XXXII-2, . . . XXXII-14
New Zealand	XXVIII-2 *, XXVIII-3 *, XXVIII-4 *, XXVIII-5 **	XXIX-1 *, XXIX-2 *, XXIX-3 **, XXIX-4 ***	XXX-1 *, XXX-2 *, XXX-3 **	XXXI-1*, XXXI-2*, . . . XXXI-14 *	XXXII-1*, XXXII-2*, . . . XXXII-14**
Norway	XXVIII-2 *, XXVIII-3 *, XXVIII-4 *, XXVIII-5 **	XXIX-1 *, XXIX-2 *, XXIX-3 **, XXIX-4 ***	XXX-1 *, XXX-2 *, XXX-3 **	XXXI-1*, XXXI-2*, . . . XXXI-14 *	XXXII-1*, XXXII-2*, . . . XXXII-14**
Peru (1989)+	XXVIII-1, XXVIII-2 *, XXVIII-3 *, XXVIII-4 *, XXVIII-5 **	XXIX-1 *, XXIX-2 *, XXIX-3 **, XXIX-4 ***	XXX-1 *, XXX-2 *, XXX-3 **	XXXI-1*, XXXI-2*, . . . XXXI-14 *	XXXII-1*, XXXII-2*, . . . XXXII-14**
Poland (1977)+	ALL	ALL	ALL	XXXI-1*, XXXI-2*, . . . XXXI-14 *	XXXII-1*, XXXII-2*, . . . XXXII-14**
Russia	XXVIII-2 *, XXVIII-3 *, XXVIII-4 *,	XXIX-1 *, XXIX-2 *, XXIX-3 **,	XXX-1 *, XXX-2 *, XXX-3 **	XXXI-1*, XXXI-2*, . . . XXXI-	XXXII-1*, XXXII-2*, . . . XXXII-

	XXVIII-5 **	XXIX-4 ***		14 *	14**
South Africa	XXVIII-2 *, XXVIII-3 *, XXVIII-4 *, XXVIII-5 **	ALL	XXX-1 *, XXX-2 *, XXX-3 **	XXXI-1*, XXXI-2*, . . . XXXI-14 *	XXXII-1*, XXXII-2*, . . . XXXII-14**
Spain (1988)+	XXVIII-1, XXVIII-2 *, XXVIII-3 *, XXVIII-4 *, XXVIII-5 **	XXIX-1 *, XXIX-2 *, XXIX-3 **, XXIX-4 ***	XXX-1 *, XXX-2 *, XXX-3 **	XXXI-1*, XXXI-2*, . . . XXXI-14 *	XXXII-1*, XXXII-2*, . . . XXXII-14**
Sweden (1988)+	XXVIII-1, XXVIII-2 *, XXVIII-3 *, XXVIII-4 *, XXVIII-5 **	XXIX-1 *, XXIX-2 *, XXIX-3 **, XXIX-4 ***	XXX-1 *, XXX-2 *, XXX-3 **	XXXI-1*, XXXI-2*, . . . XXXI-14 *	XXXII-1*, XXXII-2*, . . . XXXII-14**
Ukraine (2004)+	XXVIII-2 *, XXVIII-3 *, XXVIII-4 *, XXVIII-5 **	XXIX-1 *, XXIX-2 *, XXIX-3 **, XXIX-4 ***	XXX-1 *, XXX-2 *, XXX-3 **	XXXI-1*, XXXI-2*, . . . XXXI-14 *	XXXII-1*, XXXII-2*, . . . XXXII-14**
U.K.	XXVIII-2 *, XXVIII-3 *, XXVIII-4 *, XXVIII-5 **	XXIX-1 *, XXIX-2 *, XXIX-3 **, XXIX-4 ***	XXX-1 *, XXX-2 *, XXX-3 **	XXXI-1*, XXXI-2*, . . . XXXI-14 *	XXXII-1*, XXXII-2*, . . . XXXII-14**
Uruguay (1985)+	XXVIII-2 *, XXVIII-3 *, XXVIII-4 *, XXVIII-5 **	XXIX-1 *, XXIX-2 *, XXIX-3 **, XXIX-4 ***	XXX-1 *, XXX-2 *, XXX-3 **	XXXI-1*, XXXI-2*, . . . XXXI-14 *	XXXII-1*, XXXII-2*, . . . XXXII-14**, XXXII-15
U.S.A.	XXVIII-2 *, XXVIII-3 *, XXVIII-4 *, XXVIII-5 **	XXIX-1 *, XXIX-2 *, XXIX-3 **, XXIX-4 ***	XXX-1 *, XXX-2 *, XXX-3 **	XXXI-1*, XXXI-2*, . . . XXXI-14 *	XXXII-1*, XXXII-2*, . . . XXXII-14**

"+Year attained Consultative Status. Acceptance by that state required to bring into force Recommendations or Measures of meetings from that Year forward."

* Management Plans annexed to this Measure deemed to have been approved in accordance with Article 6(1) of Annex V to the Protocol on Environmental Protection to the Antarctic Treaty and the Measure not specifying a different approval method.

** Revised and updated List of Historic Sites and Monuments annexed to this Measure deemed to have been approved in accordance with Article 8(2) of Annex V to the Protocol on Environmental Protection to the Antarctic Treaty and the Measure not specifying a different approval method.

*** Modification of Appendix A to Annex II to the Protocol on Environmental Protection to the Antarctic Treaty deemed to have been approved in accordance with Article 9(1) of Annex II to the Protocol on Environmental Protection to the Antarctic Treaty and the Measure not specifying a different approval method.

Approval, as notified to the Government of the United States of America, of measures relating to the furtherance of the principles and objectives of the Antarctic Treaty

	15 Measures adopted at Thirty-third Meeting (Punta del Este 2010) Approved	12 Measures adopted at Thirty-fourth Meeting (Buenos Aires 2011) Approved	11 Measures adopted at Thirty-fifth Meeting (Hobart 2012) Approved
Argentina	XXXIII-1 - XXXIII-14* and XXXIII-15**	XXXIV-1 - XXXIV-10* and XXXIV-11 - XXXIV-12**	XXXV-1 - XXXV-10* and XXXV-11**
Australia	XXXIII-1 - XXXIII-14* and XXXIII-15**	XXXIV-1 - XXXIV-10* and XXXIV-11 - XXXIV-12**	XXXV-1 - XXXV-10* and XXXV-11**
Belgium	XXXIII-1 - XXXIII-14* and XXXIII-15**	XXXIV-1 - XXXIV-10* and XXXIV-11 - XXXIV-12**	XXXV-1 - XXXV-10* and XXXV-11**
Brazil (1983)+	XXXIII-1 - XXXIII-14* and XXXIII-15**	XXXIV-1 - XXXIV-10* and XXXIV-11 - XXXIV-12**	XXXV-1 - XXXV-10* and XXXV-11**
Bulgaria (1998)+	XXXIII-1 - XXXIII-14* and XXXIII-15**	XXXIV-1 - XXXIV-10* and XXXIV-11 - XXXIV-12**	XXXV-1 - XXXV-10* and XXXV-11**
Chile	XXXIII-1 - XXXIII-14* and XXXIII-15**	XXXIV-1 - XXXIV-10* and XXXIV-11 - XXXIV-12**	XXXV-1 - XXXV-10* and XXXV-11**
China (1985)+	XXXIII-1 - XXXIII-14* and XXXIII-15**	XXXIV-1 - XXXIV-10* and XXXIV-11 - XXXIV-12**	XXXV-1 - XXXV-10* and XXXV-11**
Ecuador (1990)+	XXXIII-1 - XXXIII-14* and XXXIII-15**	XXXIV-1 - XXXIV-10* and XXXIV-11 - XXXIV-12**	XXXV-1 - XXXV-10* and XXXV-11**
Finland (1989)+	XXXIII-1 - XXXIII-14* and XXXIII-15**	XXXIV-1 - XXXIV-10* and XXXIV-11 - XXXIV-12**	XXXV-1 - XXXV-10* and XXXV-11**
France	XXXIII-1 - XXXIII-14* and XXXIII-15**	XXXIV-1 - XXXIV-10* and XXXIV-11 - XXXIV-12**	XXXV-1 - XXXV-10* and XXXV-11**
Germany (1981)+	XXXIII-1 - XXXIII-14* and XXXIII-15**	XXXIV-1 - XXXIV-10* and XXXIV-11 - XXXIV-12**	XXXV-1 - XXXV-10* and XXXV-11**
India (1983)+	XXXIII-1 - XXXIII-14* and XXXIII-15**	XXXIV-1 - XXXIV-10* and XXXIV-11 - XXXIV-12**	XXXV-1 - XXXV-10* and XXXV-11**
Italy (1987)+	XXXIII-1 - XXXIII-14* and XXXIII-15**	XXXIV-1 - XXXIV-10* and XXXIV-11 - XXXIV-12**	XXXV-1 - XXXV-10* and XXXV-11**
Japan	XXXIII-1 - XXXIII-14* and XXXIII-15**	XXXIV-1 - XXXIV-10* and XXXIV-11 - XXXIV-12**	XXXV-1 - XXXV-10* and XXXV-11**
Korea, Rep. (1989)+	XXXIII-1 - XXXIII-14* and XXXIII-15**	XXXIV-1 - XXXIV-10* and XXXIV-11 - XXXIV-12**	XXXV-1 - XXXV-10* and XXXV-11**
Netherlands (1990)+	ALL	XXXIV-1 - XXXIV-10* and XXXIV-11 - XXXIV-12**	ALL
New Zealand	XXXIII-1 - XXXIII-14* and XXXIII-15**	XXXIV-1 - XXXIV-10* and XXXIV-11 - XXXIV-12**	XXXV-1 - XXXV-10* and XXXV-11**
Norway	XXXIII-1 - XXXIII-14* and XXXIII-15**	XXXIV-1 - XXXIV-10* and XXXIV-11 - XXXIV-12**	XXXV-1 - XXXV-10* and XXXV-11**
Peru (1989)+	XXXIII-1 - XXXIII-14* and XXXIII-15**	XXXIV-1 - XXXIV-10* and XXXIV-11 - XXXIV-12**	XXXV-1 - XXXV-10* and XXXV-11**
Poland (1977)+	XXXIII-1 - XXXIII-14* and XXXIII-15**	XXXIV-1 - XXXIV-10* and XXXIV-11 - XXXIV-12**	XXXV-1 - XXXV-10* and XXXV-11**
Russia	XXXIII-1 - XXXIII-14* and XXXIII-15**	XXXIV-1 - XXXIV-10* and XXXIV-11 - XXXIV-12**	XXXV-1 - XXXV-10* and XXXV-11**
South Africa	XXXIII-1 - XXXIII-14* and XXXIII-15**	XXXIV-1 - XXXIV-10* and XXXIV-11 - XXXIV-12**	XXXV-1 - XXXV-10* and XXXV-11**
Spain (1988)+	XXXIII-1 - XXXIII-14* and XXXIII-15**	XXXIV-1 - XXXIV-10* and XXXIV-11 - XXXIV-12**	XXXV-1 - XXXV-10* and XXXV-11**
Sweden (1988)+	XXXIII-1 - XXXIII-14* and XXXIII-15**	XXXIV-1 - XXXIV-10* and XXXIV-11 - XXXIV-12**	XXXV-1 - XXXV-10* and XXXV-11**
Ukraine (2004)+	XXXIII-1 - XXXIII-14* and XXXIII-15**	XXXIV-1 - XXXIV-10* and XXXIV-11 - XXXIV-12**	XXXV-1 - XXXV-10* and XXXV-11**
U.K.	XXXIII-1 - XXXIII-14* and XXXIII-15**	XXXIV-1 - XXXIV-10* and XXXIV-11 - XXXIV-12**	XXXV-1 - XXXV-10* and XXXV-11**
Uruguay (1985)+	XXXIII-1 - XXXIII-14* and XXXIII-15**	XXXIV-1 - XXXIV-10* and XXXIV-11 - XXXIV-12**	XXXV-1 - XXXV-10* and XXXV-11**
U.S.A.	XXXIII-1 - XXXIII-14* and XXXIII-15**	XXXIV-1 - XXXIV-10* and XXXIV-11 - XXXIV-12**	XXXV-1 - XXXV-10* and XXXV-11**

"+Year attained Consultative Status. Acceptance by that state required to bring into force Recommendations or Measures of meetings from that Year forward."

* Management Plans annexed to these Measures deemed to have been approved in accordance with Article 6(1) of Annex V to the Protocol on Environmental Protection to the Antarctic Treaty and the Measure not specifying a different approval method.

** Modifications and/or additions to List of Historic Sites and Monuments deemed to have been approved in accordance with Article 8(2) of Annex V to the Protocol on Environmental Protection to the Antarctic Treaty and the Measure not specifying a different approval method.

Office of the Assistant Legal Adviser for Treaty Affairs
Department of State
Washington, April 18, 2013.

Report of the Depositary Government for the Convention on the Conservation of Antarctic Marine Living Resources (CCAMLR)

Information paper submitted by Australia

Abstract

A report is provided by Australia as Depositary of the Convention on the Conservation of Antarctic Marine Living Resources 1980.

Background

Australia, as Depositary of the *Convention on the Conservation of Antarctic Marine Living Resources* 1980 (Convention) is pleased to report to the Thirty-sixth Antarctic Treaty Consultative Meeting on the status of the Convention.

Australia advises Antarctic Treaty Parties that, since the Thirty-fifth Antarctic Treaty Consultative Meeting, Panama acceded to the Convention on 20 March 2013. The Convention entered into force for Panama on 19 April 2013.

A copy of the status list for the Convention is available via the internet on the Australian Treaties Database at the following address:

http://www.austlii.edu.au/au/other/dfat/treaty_list/depository/CCAMLR.html

The status list is also available on request to the Treaties Secretariat of the Australian Government Department of Foreign Affairs and Trade. Requests can be conveyed through Australian diplomatic missions.

Report by the Depositary Government for the Convention for the Conservation of Antarctic Seals in Accordance with Recommendation XIII-2, Paragraph 2(D)

Report submitted by the United Kingdom

New Accessions to CCAS

During 2012, the United Kingdom received requests from both the Kingdom of Spain and the Islamic Republic of Pakistan to accede to CCAS. In accordance with the provisions of Article 12 of the Convention, the UK sought the consent of the Contracting Parties to invite both Spain and Pakistan to accede. The UK received notifications of consent from all Contracting Parties by 25th March 2013.

As Pakistan had already sent their instrument of accession to the UK on 17th January 2012, Pakistan will formally accede to CCAS on 24th April 2013 (being 30 days after the last notification of consent).

The UK sent an invitation to the Spanish Government to formally deposit their instrument of accession on 25th March 2012. Spain will formally accede 30 days after this is received by the UK.

The full list of countries which were original signatories to the Convention, and countries which have subsequently acceded is attached to this report (Annex A).

CCAS Annual Return 2011/2012

Annex B lists all capturing and killing of Antarctic seals by Contracting Parties to CCAS for the reporting year 1 March 2011 to 29 February 2012.

CCAS Annual Return 2010/2011

The United Kingdom regrets to inform Parties that two errors were identified with the Report submitted to ATCM XXXV (IP005):

a) The list of seals captured by the United States of America should have stated: 600 Antarctic fur seals, 50 Leopard seals, 50 Southern Elephant seals, 1380 Weddell seals. Total: 2080 seals; and
b) The number of seals captured by Australia should have stated 69 instead of 67.

A revised table for 2010/2011 is therefore included in this year's report at Annex C.

Next CCAS Annual Return

The United Kingdom would like to remind Contracting Parties to CCAS that the Exchange of Information, referred to in Paragraph 6(a) in the Annex to the Convention, for the reporting period of 1 March 2012 to 28 February 2013 is due by **30 June 2013**. CCAS Parties should submit their returns, including nil returns, to both the United Kingdom and to SCAR. The UK would like to encourage all Contracting Parties to CCAS to submit their returns on time.

The CCAS report for the reporting period 2012/2013 will be submitted to ATCM XXXVII, once the June 2013 deadline for exchange of information has passed.

ANNEX A

PARTIES TO THE CONVENTION FOR THE CONSERVATION OF ANTARCTIC SEALS (CCAS)

London, 1 June – 31 December 1972

(The Convention entered into force on 11 March 1978)

State	Date of Signature	Date of deposit (Ratification or Acceptance)
Argentina[1]	9 June 1972	7 March 1978
Australia	5 October 1972	1 July 1987
Belgium	9 June 1972	9 February 1978
Chile[1]	28 December 1972	7 February 1980
France[2]	19 December 1972	19 February 1975
Japan	28 December 1972	28 August 1980
Norway	9 June 1972	10 December 1973
Russia[1,2,4]	9 June 1972	8 February 1978
South Africa	9 June 1972	15 August 1972
United Kingdom[2]	9 June 1972	10 September 1974[3]
United States of America[2]	28 June 1972	19 January 1977

ACCESSIONS

State	Date of deposit of Instrument of Accession
Brazil	11 February 1991
Canada	4 October 1990
Germany	30 September 1987
Italy	2 April 1992
Poland	15 August 1980
Pakistan	25 March 2013

[1] Declaration or Reservation
[2] Objection
[3] The instrument of ratification included the Channel Islands and the Isle of Man
[4] Former USSR

ANNEX B

ANNUAL CCAS REPORT 2011/2012

Synopsis of reporting in accordance with Article 5 and the Annex of the Convention: Capturing and killing of seals during the period 1 March 2011 to 29 February 2012.

Contracting Party	Antarctic Seals Captured	Antarctic Seals Killed
Argentina	282 (a)	Nil
Australia	76 (b)	Nil
Belgium	Nil	Nil
Brazil	Nil	Nil
Canada	Nil	Nil
Chile	Nil	Nil
France	480(c)	2(e)
Germany	Nil	Nil
Italy	Nil	Nil
Japan	Nil	Nil
Norway	Nil	Nil
Poland	Nil	Nil
Russia	Nil	Nil
South Africa	Nil	Nil
United Kingdom	Nil	Nil
United States of America	1190(d)	1(f)

(a) 7 young Elephant seals, 200 adult Elephant seals, 31 young and re-captured Elephant seals, 40 Leopard seals and 4 recaptured Leopard seals.
(b) 26 Leopard seals, 50 Elephant seals.
(C) 170 Weddell seals, 65 adult Elephant seals, 125 juvenile Elephant seals, 50 adult Antarctic fur seals and 70 juvenile Antarctic fur seals
(d) 600 adult and juvenile Antarctic fur seals, 30 female Antarctic fur seals, 20 adult and juvenile Leopard seals, 50 juvenile Southern Elephant seals, 490 Weddell seals
(e) 2 Weddell seals
(f) 1 Weddell seal

All reported capturing was for scientific research.

ANNEX C

ANNUAL CCAS REPORT 2010/2011

Synopsis of reporting in accordance with Article 5 and the Annex of the Convention: Capturing and killing of seals during the period 1 March 20010 to 28 February 2011.

Contracting Party	Antarctic Seals Captured	Antarctic Seals Killed
Argentina	49 [a]	Nil
Australia	69 [b]	2 [c]
Belgium	Nil	Nil
Brazil	Nil	Nil
Canada	Nil	Nil
Chile	Nil	Nil
France	600 [d]	Nil
Germany	Nil	Nil
Italy	Nil	Nil
Japan	Nil	Nil
Norway	Nil	Nil
Poland	Nil	Nil
Russia	Nil	Nil
South Africa	Nil	Nil
United Kingdom	24 [e]	1 [f]
United States of America	2080 [g]	2 [h]

[a] 10 Elephant Seals, 20 Southern Elephant Seals, 19 Leopard seals
[b] 21 Elephant Seals, 28 Leopard Seals, 20 Weddell Seals
[c] 1 Weddell Seal and 1 Leopard Seal
[d] 160 Weddell Seals, 275 Elephant Seals, 165 Antarctic Fur seals
[e] 24 Weddell Seals
[f] 1 Weddell Seal
[g] 600 Antarctic fur seals, 50 Leopard seals, 50 southern elephant seals, 1380 Weddell Seals
[h] 2 Weddell Seals

All reported capturing was for scientific research.

Report of the Depositary Government for the Agreement on the Conservation of Albatrosses and Petrels (ACAP)

Information paper submitted by Australia

Abstract

A report is provided by Australia as Depositary of the *Agreement on Conservation of Albatrosses and Petrels* 2001.

Background

Australia, as Depositary of the *Agreement on the Conservation of Albatrosses and Petrels* 2001 (Agreement) is pleased to report to the Thirty-sixth Antarctic Treaty Consultative Meeting on the status of the Agreement.

Australia advises Antarctic Treaty Parties that, since the Thirty-fifth Antarctic Treaty Consultative Meeting, no States have acceded to the Agreement.

Australia further advises that the Fourth Session of the Meeting of the Parties, held at Lima from 23 to 27 April 2012, agreed to add the Balearic shearwater (*Puffinus mauretanicus*) to the list of petrel species in Annex 1 of the Agreement. This amendment entered into force on 26 July 2012.

A copy of the status list for the Agreement is available via the internet on the Australian Treaties Database at the following address:

http://www.austlii.edu.au/au/other/dfat/treaty_list/depository/consalbnpet.html

The status list is also available on request to the Treaties Secretariat of the Australian Government Department of Foreign Affairs and Trade. Requests can be conveyed through Australian diplomatic missions.

Report by the CCAMLR Observer to the Thirty-Sixth Antarctic Treaty Consultative Meeting

1. The Thirty-first Annual Meeting of the Commission for the Conservation of Antarctic Marine Living Resources (CCAMLR-XXXI) was chaired by Mr T. Løbach (Norway). Twenty-five Members, the Netherlands, Singapore, Viet Nam, and representatives of NGOs and industry participated. A copy of the Report of CCAMLR-XXXI is available in the public domain at www.ccamlr.org/node/72699.

Compliance

2. The Commission approved a Non-Contracting Party-IUU Vessel List (www.ccamlr.org/node/72732) noting at least seven vessels persistently engaged in IUU fishing activities in the Convention Area.

Finance and Administration

3. The Commission endorsed revised Staff Regulations, revised Financial Regulations including an investment policy, an implementation report for the Strategic Plan, a budget for 2014 and provisional budget for 2015 and the commencement of work on a sustainable financing policy.

Scientific Committee

Krill resources

4. In 2011/12, five Members harvested 161 143 tonnes of krill from Subareas 48.1 (75 495 tonnes), 48.2 (29 238 tonnes) and 48.3 (52 410 tonnes)[1]. In comparison, the total reported catch of krill in 2010/11 was 180 992 tonnes taken from Subareas 48.1 (9 215 tonnes), 48.2 (115 995 tonnes) and 48.3 (55 782 tonnes).

5. Notifications for krill fishing in 2012/13 were received from eight Members for 19 vessels with a total predicted catch of 597 700 tonnes.

6. The Commission endorsed the Scientific Committee's plan for the development of the feedback management strategy for the krill fishery in Area 48.

Finfish resources

7. In 2011/12, 11 Members fished for toothfish (Dissostichus eleginoides and/or D. mawsoni). The reported total catch was 11 329 tonnes2. In comparison, the total reported catch of toothfish in 2010/11 was 14 669 tonnes.

8. Two Members targeted icefish (Champsocephalus gunnari). The reported total catch of C. gunnari was 999 tonnes2.

9. The Commission noted possible signs of recovery for populations of C. gunnari and Notothenia rossii near the South Shetland Islands. The fishery targeting these species was closed in 1990 to allow the stocks to recover. The Commission agreed that this fishery remain closed until such time that research is undertaken to confirm the recovery of these populations and an assessment is provided.

Exploratory fisheries

10. Ten Members notified 26 vessels for exploratory longline fisheries for *Dissostichus* spp. for 2012/13. The Commission noted the increasing number of vessels notifying for exploratory fisheries and requested that further consideration be given to the issue of limiting capacity in exploratory fisheries. No new fisheries were notified for 2012/13.

---

1 CCAMLR-XXXI Report figures updated to end-of-season (30 November 2012) by the Secretariat.

Fish and invertebrate by-catch

11. The Scientific Committee's recommendations in relation to by-catch issues included the need to examine finfish by-catch across the krill fishing fleet for vessels using all trawl gears and the development of a risk-based sustainable management approach for the impact of toothfish fisheries on skates.

Assessment and avoidance of incidental mortality

12. The total extrapolated mortalities of seabirds within the French EEZs in 2011/12 were estimated to be 222 birds. A total of three seabird mortalities were recorded elsewhere in the Convention Area.

13. France stressed that some of the most important albatross and petrel breeding sites were located within its EEZs and that, despite France's efforts to protect them, it was regrettable that these populations remain at risk as a result of incidental mortality occurring north of the Convention Area.

Bottom fishing and vulnerable marine ecosystems

14. The Commission endorsed advice on the implementation of measures to avoid and mitigate significant adverse impacts on vulnerable marine ecosystems (VMEs) during bottom fishing, noting that 12 VMEs were added to the VME registry during 2012. There were 38 notifications of encounters with potential VMEs during exploratory bottom fisheries in 2011/12. A total of 150 VME risk-areas have been closed to fishing since the introduction of this conservation measure (CM 22-06) in 2008/09.

Marine Protected Areas

15. The Commission welcomed the Scientific Committee's progress towards establishing a representative system of MPAs arising from three technical workshops held during 2012 for Planning Domain 1 (Antarctic Peninsula), Domain 5 (Del Cano–Crozet), and Domains 3 (Weddell Sea), 4 (Bouvet and Maud Rise) and 9 (Amundsen and Bellingshausen Sea). It welcomed proposed collaboration between Sweden, the Republic of Korea and the USA to progress work on Domain 9.

16. The Commission noted the discussion of the Scientific Committee on the establishment of precautionary spatial protection to facilitate the scientific study of habitats and communities in case of the future collapse of ice shelves.

17. In accordance with ATCM Decision 9 (2005), the Commission endorsed the advice of the Scientific Committee in respect of:

(i) the revised management plans for ASPA No. 144, ASPA No. 145 and ASPA No. 146 noting the importance of these areas for scientific research that were unlikely to be subject to harvesting

(ii) the draft management plan for a new ASPA at Cape Washington and Silverfish Bay, Terra Nova Bay, Ross Sea

(iii) progress on a revised management plan for ASMA No. 1, Admiralty Bay, King George Island, South Shetland Archipelago, noting the proposal for a draft management plan to be submitted to CCAMLR in 2013.

18. The Commission agreed that no issues with respect to CCAMLR had been identified in these proposals and that this advice should be communicated to the ATCM.

19. The Commission noted that krill fishing had occurred in 2010 in ASPA No. 153, Eastern Dallmann Bay, and that the management plan for this ASPA does not allow for harvesting as a permitted activity.

20. The Commission agreed that fishing in ASPA No. 153 had occurred as a result of a lack of awareness of the requirements of the management plan and that there was a need for a mechanism to provide a direct link between CCAMLR conservation measures and the management plans for ASPAs and ASMAs as described in ATCM Decision 9 (2005) – see paragraph 26 below.

Climate change

21. The Commission noted the advice of the Scientific Committee with respect to climate change, including the discussion of the potential effects of climate change on krill.

Administrative matters

22. Progress was reported in addressing recommendations of the 2008 Performance Review Panel Report in respect of capacity building. In 2012 there were five applications from five Members for the CCAMLR Scholarship Scheme. Two candidates, one from Argentina and one from China, were selected. The contribution to the work of the Scientific Committee of the recipient of the 2011 Scholarship from Chile was warmly welcomed.

Scheme of International Scientific Observation

23. The Commission endorsed an external review of the CCAMLR Scheme of International Scientific Observation.

Conservation Measures

24. Conservation measures and resolutions adopted at CCAMLR-XXXI have been published in the *Schedule of Conservation Measures in Force 2012/13.*

Compliance Evaluation Procedure

25. The Commission endorsed a compliance evaluation procedure (CM 10-10 (2012)) to strengthen information available to the Commission in relation to compliance issues for Members.

ASPAs and ASMAs

26. The Commission agreed to a new conservation measure on the protection of the values of ASPAs and ASMAs (CM 91-02 (2012)) (Annex). This measure seeks to ensure that fishing vessels licensed in accordance with CCAMLR measures are aware of the location and relevant management plans of all ASPAs and ASMAs which include marine areas.

Revised Resolution

27. The Commission urged Members to consider ratifying the Cape Town Agreement of 2012 on the Implementation of the Provisions of Torremolinos Protocol of 1993 relating to the Torremolinos International Convention for the Safety of Fishing Vessels, 1977 ('Cape Town Agreement') in order to enhance the safety of fishing vessels in the Convention Area (revised Resolution 34/XXXI (Enhancing the safety of fishing vessels in the Convention Area).

Proposals for MPAs and special areas

28. The Commission considered proposals for MPAs in East Antarctica (one proposal), the Ross Sea region (two proposals – subsequently combined in a single proposal) and to establish Special Areas for Scientific Research (SASRs) in marine habitats and communities exposed following ice-shelf collapse (one proposal).

29. The Commission was unable to agree to the proposal in relation to protection of areas exposed as a result of ice-shelf collapse. In relation to the other two proposals the Commission agreed to convene an intersessional meeting of the Scientific Committee followed by a Special Meeting of the Commission to continue the Commission's work in relation to MPAs. The meetings will take place at Bremerhaven, Germany, 11 to 16 July 2013. The Special Meeting will consider MPA issues and make decisions, if possible, on the joint New Zealand and the USA MPA proposal for the Ross Sea region and the joint Australia, France and EU MPA proposal on East Antarctica.

Cooperation with the Antarctic Treaty System and International Organisations

Cooperation with SCAR

30. The Commission noted that a CCAMLR/SCAR Action Group will meet immediately prior to ATCM XXXVI in Brussels to discuss CCAMLR/SCAR strategic engagement.

Election of Chair

31. The Commission elected Poland as the Chair of the Commission.

Date and location of the next meeting

32. The Thirty-second Meeting will be held in Hobart from 23 October to 1 November 2013.

ANNEX

CONSERVATION MEASURE 91-02 (2012)
Protection of the values of Antarctic Specially Managed and Protected Areas

Species	all
Area	all
Season	all
Gear	all

The Commission,

Recognising that the protection of the Antarctic marine environment and of Antarctic marine living resources, including through Marine Protected Areas, has long been recognised as desirable and valuable within the agreements and bodies that make up the Antarctic Treaty System,

Recalling that the commitment towards the designation of spatial protection is clearly defined both within the 1991 Protocol of Environmental Protection to the Antarctic Treaty and the 1980 CAMLR Convention,

Recalling that in accordance with the Protocol, any Antarctic area, including any marine area, may be designated as an Antarctic Specially Protected Area (ASPA) or an Antarctic Specially Managed Area (ASMA),

Recognising that activities in ASPAs and ASMAs may be prohibited, restricted or managed, in accordance with management plans adopted under the provisions of Annex V of the Protocol,

Noting that the Convention (Articles V and VIII) provides for close cooperation between CCAMLR and the Antarctic Treaty,

Recalling that the competences of, and relationships between the ATCM and CCAMLR have been clarified and affirmed in the Protocol itself and subsequently by Decision 4 (1998) – *Marine Protected Areas*, and Decision 9 (2005) – *Marine Protected Areas and Other Areas of Interest to CCAMLR*, respectively,

Noting that the 2011 CCAMLR MPA Workshop noted that a harmonised approach in the Antarctic Treaty System to spatial protection may result in having ASPAs and ASMAs designated by the ATCM within CCAMLR MPAs,

Understanding that such a multi-level hierarchical approach to area management could harmonise decisions made at the ATCM and CCAMLR, allowing for detailed consideration of activities not normally considered by CCAMLR,

Concerned that potential harvesting in ASPAs and ASMAs could jeopardise the high scientific value of the long-term ecosystem studies being carried out in these areas, undermining the goals established in the management plans of these areas,

Noting that the presence of fishing vessels in ASPAs and ASMAs might have occurred due to a lack of awareness of the existence of these designated areas among those responsible for fishing vessels,

Recognising the need for more informative and timely communications between the ATCM and CCAMLR with regard to the publication and availability of management plans of ASPAs and ASMAs containing marine areas,

Recalling that the Commission has previously endorsed the harmonised approach in the Antarctic Treaty System to spatial protection,

adopts the following Conservation Measure in accordance with Article III of the Convention:

1. Each Contracting Party shall ensure that their fishing vessels licensed1 in accordance with Conservation Measure 10-02 are aware of the location and relevant management plan of all designated ASPAs and ASMAs which include marine areas listed in Annex 91-02/A.

[1] Includes permitted

ANNEX 91-02/A

LIST OF ASPAS AND ASMAS WHICH HAVE MARINE COMPONENTS AND ARE LOCATED WITHIN THE CONVENTION AREA[1]

The management plans for these areas can be found on the Antarctic Protected Areas (APA) database on the Antarctic Treaty Secretariat (ATS) website.

ASPAs which are marine or partly marine:

(1) ASPA 144, Chile Bay, Greenwich Island, South Shetland Islands (Subarea 48.1)
(2) ASPA 145, Port Foster, Deception Island, South Shetland Islands (Subarea 48.1)
(3) ASPA 146, South Bay, Doumer Island, Palmer Archipelago (Subarea 48.1)
(4) ASPA 152, Western Bransfield Strait, South Shetland Islands (Subarea 48.1)
(5) ASPA 153, Eastern Dallmann Bay, Palmer Archipelago (Subarea 48.1)
(6) ASPA 161, Terra Nova Bay, Ross Sea (Subarea 88.1)
(7) ASPA 121, Cape Royds, Ross Sea (Subarea 88.1)
(8) ASPA 149, Cape Shirreff, South Shetland Islands (Subarea 48.1)
(9) ASPA 151, Lions Rump, South Shetland Islands (Subarea 48.1)
(10) ASPA 165, Edmonson Point, Ross Sea (Subarea 88.1).

Partly marine ASMAs:

(11) ASMA 1, Admiralty Bay, South Shetland Islands (Subarea 48.1)
(12) ASMA 3, Deception Island, South Shetland Islands (Subarea 48.1)
(13) ASMA 7, Southwest Anvers Island, Palmer Archipelago (Subarea 48.1).

[1] The present list includes only those ASPAs and ASMAs for which management plans have previously been approved by CCAMLR in accordance with ATCM Decision 9 (2005). Additional ASPAs and ASMAs with small marine components are not included in this list, as they did not require CCAMLR approval under the ATCM Decision 9 'Criteria defining areas of interest to CCAMLR'.

The Scientific Committee on Antarctic Research (SCAR) Annual Report 2012/13

1. Background

The Scientific Committee on Antarctic Research (SCAR) is a non-governmental, Interdisciplinary Scientific Body of the International Council for Science (ICSU), and Observer to the Antarctic Treaty and the UNFCCC.

SCAR's Mission is (i) to be the leading, independent, non-governmental facilitator, coordinator, and advocate of excellence in Antarctic and Southern Ocean science and research and (ii) to provide independent, sound, scientifically-based advice to the Antarctic Treaty System and other policy makers including the use of science to identify emerging trends and bring these issues to the attention of policy makers.

2. Introduction

SCAR's scientific research adds value to national efforts by enabling national researchers to collaborate on large-scale scientific programmes to accomplish objectives not easily obtainable by any single country. SCAR's Members currently include 37 nations and 9 ICSU scientific Unions.

SCAR's success depends on the quality and timeliness of its scientific outputs. Descriptions of SCAR's research programmes and scientific outputs are available at: www.scar.org. This paper summarises SCAR highlights since the last annual report and future SCAR meetings we believe will be of interest to Treaty Parties. This should be read in conjunction with a separate Background paper that highlights recent science papers published since the last Treaty meeting.

SCAR produces an electronic quarterly Newsletter highlighting relevant science and other SCAR related issues (http://www.scar.org/news/newsletters/). Please email: info@scar.org if you wish to be added to the mailing list. As well as the web (www.scar.org), SCAR is also available on Facebook, LinkedIn, Google+ and Twitter.

3. SCAR Highlights (2012/13)

1. New SCAR Scientific Research Programmes

In July 2012, SCAR Delegates approved five new Scientific Research Programmes (SRPs). The new SRPs will continue the important scientific foci of SCAR, whilst expanding into newly identified high priority areas for research, including a stronger emphasis on scientific advice to the Treaty. For further details see http://www.scar.org/researchgroups/progplanning/. The new SRPs are:

- **State of the Antarctic Ecosystem (AntEco)**

  Biological diversity is the sum of all those organisms that are present in an ecosystem, that dictate how ecosystems function, and that underpin the life-support system of our planet. This programme has been designed to focus on patterns of biodiversity across terrestrial, limnological, glacial and marine environments within the Antarctic, sub-Antarctic and Southern Ocean regions, and to provide the scientific knowledge on biodiversity that can be also used for conservation and management. In essence, SCAR proposes to explain what biodiversity is there, how it got there, what it does there, and what threatens it. A primary product of this programme will be recommendations for its management and conservation.

- **Antarctic Thresholds - Ecosystem Resilience and Adaptation (AnT-ERA)**

  AnT-ERA will examine the current biological processes in Antarctic ecosystems, to define their thresholds and thereby determine resistance and resilience to change. The extreme environment and marked difference in community complexity between the polar regions and much of the rest of the planet may mean that consequences of stress for ecosystem function and services, and their resistance and resilience, will differ from elsewhere. Polar ecosystem processes are therefore key to informing wider ecological debate about the nature of stability and change in ecosystems. The programme will attempt to determine the likelihood of cataclysmic shifts or "tipping points" in Antarctic ecosystems.

- **Antarctic Climate Change in the 21st Century (AntClim^{21})**

  The goals of AntClim^{21} are to deliver improved regional predictions of key elements of the Antarctic atmosphere, ocean and cryosphere for the next 20 to 200 years and to understand the responses of the physical and biological systems to natural and anthropogenic forcing factors. A primary form of data that will be used by AntClim^{21} are the global coupled atmosphere-ocean model runs that form the basis of the Fifth Assessment Report (AR5) of the IPCC. Palaeo-reconstructions of selected time periods, recognised as past analogues for future climate predictions, will be used to validate model performances for the Antarctic region.

- **Past Antarctic Ice Sheet Dynamics (PAIS)**

  PAIS aims to improve our understanding of ice sheet dynamics during past warm world conditions by:

  - targeting the study of vulnerable areas around the continent;
  - linking ice-proximal records with coastal and offshore records including far field paleoceanographic and sea level records;
  - integrating data into the latest generation of coupled Glacial Isostatic Adjustment (GIA)-Ice Sheet-Climate models.

- **Solid Earth Response and Cryosphere Evolution (SERCE)**

  SERCE aims to improve understanding of the solid earth response to cryospheric and tectonic forcing. SERCE will:

  - Identify and develop key disciplinary and interdisciplinary science components of a science programme aimed at advancing understanding of the interactions between the solid earth and the cryosphere;
  - Coordinate with other groups investigating ice mass change, ice sheet contributions to global sea level rise, glacial isostatic adjustment models of ice caps, etc.;
  - Work with groups and research programmes to promote interdisciplinary science using POLENET project data;
  - Provide an international framework for maintaining, and potentially augmenting, the remote autonomous POLENET infrastructure.

2. The Southern Ocean Observing System (SOOS)

The Southern Ocean plays a key role in the climate and ecosystem functioning of the whole planet, but understanding has long been hampered by lack of data. A SOOS International Project Office, established in Australia and supported by the Institute for Marine and Antarctic Studies at the University of Tasmania in Hobart and Antarctica New Zealand, supports implementation of the SOOS. A new SOOS data portal has also been established: http://www.soos.aq/index.php/data/data-portal. See: www.soos.aq or the accompanying paper.

3. The Antarctic Climate Change and the Environment (ACCE) Report Update

SCAR has published a major update to the 'key points' from the Antarctic Climate Change and the Environment (ACCE) report. In this update we summarize subsequent advances in knowledge of how the climate of the Antarctic and Southern Ocean have changed in the past, how they might change in the future, and examine the associated impacts on the marine and terrestrial biota. See the accompanying paper.

4. The SCAR Science Horizon SCAN

The 1st SCAR Antarctic and Southern Ocean Science Horizon Scan will assemble some of the world's leading Antarctic scientists, policy makers, leaders, and visionaries to identify the most important scientific questions that will or should be addressed by research in and from the southern polar regions over the next two decades. The Scan outcomes will assist in aligning international programmes, projects and resources to effectively facilitate Antarctic and Southern Ocean science in the coming years. See the accompanying paper.

5. Antarctic Conservation in the 21st Century

SCAR, COMNAP, New Zealand and the IUCN, in collaboration with several partners, are developing a strategy entitled 'Antarctic Conservation for the 21st Century'. The activity will actively encourage participation from all stakeholders in the region. The approach will be structured to align with both the

Protocol on Environmental Protection to the Antarctic Treaty and the Five Year Work Plan of the Committee for Environmental Protection. The Antarctic Conservation Strategy links closely with the Environments Portal being developed by New Zealand, SCAR and Australia. See accompanying papers.

6. Fellowships and Prizes

In order to expand capacity in all its Members, SCAR runs several Fellowship and Prize Schemes, including:

- ***SCAR/COMNAP Fellowships*** (applications close 4 June 2013). The Fellowships are designed to encourage the active involvement of early career scientists and engineers in Antarctic scientific research, and to build new connections and further strengthen international capacity and cooperation in Antarctic research. This year they have been launched in tandem with the ***CCAMLR Scholarships***. For further details see: http://www.scar.org/awards/fellowships/information.html.
- ***Martha T Muse Prize for Science and Policy in Antarctica*** (nominations close 23 May 2013). Sponsored by the Tinker Foundation, this is a US$ 100,000 unrestricted award presented to an individual in the fields of Antarctic science or policy who has demonstrated potential for sustained and significant contributions that will enhance the understanding and/or preservation of Antarctica. See: www.museprize.org.
- ***SCAR Visiting Professor Scheme*** (nomination dates to be confirmed). The Visiting Professorships are for mid- to late-career stage scientists and academics. It provides them the opportunity to undertake short-term visits to a facility in or operated by SCAR Member countries, to provide training and mentoring. See: http://www.scar.org/awards/.

7. New SCAR Executive Committee

Jerónimo López-Martínez, from the Universidad Autónoma of Madrid, Spain, was elected the new SCAR President. SCAR also has two new Vice-Presidents: Karin Lochte from the AWI in Germany and Bryan Storey from the University of Canterbury, New Zealand. They will join Yeadong Kim (Korea) and Sergio Marenssi (Argentina) as well as Mahlon "Chuck" Kennicutt (USA), who will remain on the Executive Committee until July 2014 as Past President.

8. Venezuela joins SCAR

Venezuela is the latest country to join SCAR as an Associate Member in 2012.

4. Future SCAR Meetings

There are several major SCAR Meetings coming up (http://www.scar.org/events/), including:

- **SCAR Biology Symposium**. 15-19 July 2013, Barcelona, Spain. See: http://www.icm.csic.es/XIthSCARBiologySymposium.
- **SCAR Executive Committee Meeting and cross linkages meeting of the chief officers of SCAR Standing Scientific Groups, Committees and Research Projects.** 20-23th July 2013, Barcelona, Spain.
- **SCAR Astronomy and Astrophysics from Antarctica (AAA) Workshop.** 24 - 26 July 2013, Siena, Italy. See: http://www.astronomy.scar.org/AAA2013.
- **XXXIII SCAR Meetings and Open Science Conference.** 22 August - 3 September 2014, Auckland, New Zealand. The SCAR Open Science Conference will be held on 25-29 August. See: http://www.scar2014.com.

The Annual Report for 2012 of the Council of Managers of National Antarctic Programs (COMNAP)

COMNAP is the organisation of National Antarctic Programs which brings together, in particular, the managers of those programs, that is, the national officials responsible for planning, conducting and managing support to science in Antarctica on behalf of their respective governments, all Consultative Parties to the Antarctic Treaty.

COMNAP was established in September 1988, and so, 2013 marks the 25th anniversary of our association. The Council will mark the occasion with the publication of the book "A story of Antarctic Cooperation: 25 Years of the Council of Managers of National Antarctic Programs".

COMNAP has grown into an international association whose Members are the 28 National Antarctic Programs from Antarctic Treaty Consultative Parties from Argentina, Australia, Belgium, Brazil, Bulgaria, Chile, China, Ecuador, Finland, France, Germany, India, Italy, Japan, Republic of Korea, Netherlands, New Zealand, Norway, Peru, Poland, Russian Federation, South Africa, Spain, Sweden, United Kingdom, Ukraine, Uruguay and USA. Presently, the National Antarctic Program organisations of the Republic of Belarus and the Czech Republic are COMNAP observer organisations.

COMNAP's Constitution asserts its purpose: to develop and promote best practice in managing the support of scientific research in the Antarctic. As an organisation, COMNAP acts to add value to National Antarctic Program's efforts by serving as a forum to develop practices that improve effectiveness of activities in an environmentally responsible manner, by facilitating and promoting international partnerships, and by providing opportunities and systems for information exchange.

COMNAP also strives to provide the Antarctic Treaty System with objective, practical, technical and non-political advice drawn from the National Antarctic Programs' extensive pool of expertise and their first-hand knowledge of the Antarctic.

Increasingly complex science questions are being poised which can only be answered by multi-disciplinary and often multi-national science teams. This complexity, along with more demanding environmental measures and, in some cases, a reduced funding stream, contributes to added pressure on National Antarctic Programs and to an even greater need for international collaboration. COMNAP works in support of greater collaboration between National Antarctic Programs and recognises the need for robust partnerships with organisations with similar goals. COMNAP has also progressively assumed responsibility for the production of a number of practical tools related to safety, best practice and information exchange.

The COMNAP Annual General Meeting was held in August 2012 in Portland, Oregon, USA. Dr. Heinrich Miller (AWI) continues in his role as COMNAP Chair and Michelle Rogan-Finnemore continues in her role as Executive Secretary.

COMNAP Highlights and Achievements for 2012

COMNAP Symposium 2012: Sustainable Solutions to Antarctic Challenges

Lou Sanson (Antarctica New Zealand) convened the COMNAP Symposium which was themed "Sustainable Solutions to Antarctic Challenges" on Sunday 15 July, 2012, on the margins of the COMNAP AGM in Portland, Oregon, USA. This was the fifteenth symposium hosted by SCALOP or COMNAP. Invited keynote speakers included Professor Steven Chown and Dr. Gwynne Dyer. Sixteen presentations and eight posters were selected by the Symposium Review Committee for inclusion and each provided information on an innovative and sustainable product or process applied in, or being considered for, an Antarctic situation. The Symposium Proceedings have been published and distributed (ISBN 978-0-473-23259-7). Further copies are available from the COMNAP Secretariat by request.

Innovations in Antarctic Communications Workshop

COMNAP Energy & Technology Expert Group Leader, David Blake (BAS) convened the COMNAP Workshop "Innovations in Antarctic Communications" on Tuesday, July 2012. This open workshop provided an opportunity for National Antarctic Programs to discuss collective and regional communications needs and potential solutions that are likely to be required for the next decade or so. National Antarctic Programs recognise the need to work together to consider these issues in order to provide value and effective support to science. Representatives from commercial organisations were also in attendance.

Review of Recommendations on Operational Matters

COMNAP led a project to provide draft language for those recommendations identified by the ICG as requiring updating, and also to suggest draft report language for the XXXVI ATCM Final Report, in those cases where the general principles of the recommendations might still be valid, but the technical and practical aspects may be outdated and therefore no longer current. COMNAP invited IAATO, IHO, SCAR and WMO to participate and all are co-authors of a Working Paper as a result presented at this meeting.

COMNAP Antarctic Research Fellowship

Noting that education and capacity-building was an area of mutual interest to both SCAR and COMNAP, and in recognition of the depth and breadth of talent within National Antarctic Programs, COMNAP offered the COMNAP Antarctic Research Fellowship in May 2012. This year, COMNAP was able to offer a full Fellowship to Dr. Ursula Rack to undertake polar social history research at the Scott Polar Research Institute. In partnership with SCAR, COMNAP and SCAR each offered a half Fellowship to Mr. Jenson George to undertake biogeochemistry research at GEOMAR Helmholtz Centre for Ocean Research. COMNAP and SCAR have agreed to once again offer and jointly promote the Fellowships for 2013. The 2013 COMNAP Antarctic Research Fellow will be announced in July 2013 as part of the COMNAP AGM in Seoul, Republic of Korea.

COMNAP Products and Tools

Accident, Incident and Near-Miss Reporting (AINMR)

Information on problems encountered in Antarctica has always been exchanged. The very first ATCM agreed in Recommendation I-VII Exchange *of Information on Logistics Problems* that this should be so (effective 30 April 1962). COMNAP Annual General Meetings offer an opportunity for Members to exchange such information and also an on-line, comprehensive AINMR System is in place and is running on the members-only area of the COMNAP website. This on-line system allows COMNAP members to report accidents and incidents in a timely manner. The AINMR's primary objective is: to capture information about events that had, or could have had, serious consequences; and/or reveal lessons to be learned; and/or are novel, very unusual events. Full reports on accidents can also be posted on the site and can be discussed and reviewed. So that National Antarctic Programs can learn from each other to reduce the risk of serious consequences occurring in the course of their Antarctic activities.
www.comnap.aq/membersonly/AINMR/SitePages/Home.aspx.

COMNAP Ship Position Reporting System (SPRS)

The SPRS (www.comnap.aq/sprs) is an optional, voluntary system for exchange of information about National Antarctic Program ship operations. Its primary purpose is to facilitate collaboration between National Antarctic Programs. It can also, however, make a very useful contribution to safety with all SPRS information made available to the Rescue Coordination Centres (RCCs) which cover the Antarctic region, as an additional source of information complementing all other national and international systems in place. Position information is delivered via email and can be graphically displayed in Google Earth. There was a high level of usage of the SPRS this season with 23 vessels regularly reporting during their Antarctic voyages.

The Antarctic Flight Information Manual (AFIM)

AFIM is a handbook of aeronautical information published by COMNAP as a tool towards safe air operations in Antarctica as recommended by the ATCM Recommendation XV-20 *Air safety in Antarctica.* After an in-depth review of the current paper-based product, COMNAP is now developing an electronic version of AFIM, so that revisions can be made and distributed in a more efficient manner. The AFIM will continue to be updated via information from National Antarctic Programs. COMNAP has suggested language for an updated Measure for this ATCM to consider in order to recognise this change to the new format. The most recent AFIM revision set was produced and distributed to all AFIM holders on 15 February 2013.

Antarctic Telecommunications Operators Manual (ATOM)

ATOM is an evolution of the handbook of telecommunications practices to which ATCM Recommendation X-3 *Improvement of Telecommunications in Antarctica and the Collection and Distribution of Antarctic Meteorological Data* refers. COMNAP members and Search and Rescue authorities have access to the latest version (Feb 2013) via the COMNAP website. COMNAP has suggested draft Final Report language for this ATCM to consider in regards to ATCM Recommendation X-3.

For more information, please visit COMNAP's web site at www.comnap.aq or email us at info@comnap.aq. Also, see attachments to this Annual Report: Appendix 1 and Appendix 2.

Appendix 1. COMNAP officers, projects and expert groups

Executive Committee (EXCOM)
The COMNAP Chair and Vice-Chairs are elected officers of COMNAP. The elected officers plus the Executive Secretary, compose the COMNAP Executive Committee as follows:

Position	Officer	Term expires
Chair	Heinrich Miller (AWI) heinrich.miller@awi.de	AGM 2014
Vice-Chairs	Yuansheng Li (PRIC) lysh@pric.gov.cn	AGM 2013
	Mariano Memolli (DNA) mmemolli@dna.gov.ar	AGM 2013
	Juan Jose Dañobeitia (CSIC) jjdanobeitia@cmima.csic.es	AGM 2014
	Brian Stone (USAP/NSF) bstone@nsf.gov	AGM 2014
	Jose Olmedo (INAE) jolmedo@midena.gob.ec	AGM 2015
Executive Secretary	Michelle Rogan-Finnemore michelle.finnemore@comnap.aq	30 Sept 2015

Table 1 – COMNAP Executive Committee.

Projects

Project	Project Manager	EXCOM officer (oversight)
Antarctic Glossary	Valerie Lukin	Mariano Memolli
Antarctic Flight Information Manual (AFIM) – Implementation of new format	Paul Morin	Brian Stone
Tsunami Communications Brochure	Michelle Rogan-Finnemore	Heinz Miller
Antarctic Peninsula Advanced Science Information (APASI)	Jose Retamales	Heinz Miller
COMNAP 25th Anniversary Book	Christo Pimpirev	EXCOM All
Energy Management Guidelines and their application – Survey follow-up; Database of preferred suppliers	David Blake	Yuansheng Li & Juan Jose Dañobeitia
Oil Spill Contingency Planning & Response – Survey follow-up	Veronica Vlasich	Mariano Memolli
Southern Ocean Observing System (SOOS) Workshop	Rob Wooding	Heinz Miller

Table 2 – COMNAP Projects currently in progress.

Expert Groups

Expert Group (topic)	Expert Group leader	EXCOM officer (oversight)
Science	Jose Retamales	Heinz Miller
Outreach	Eva Gronlund	EXCOM All
Air	Giuseppe De Rossi	Brian Stone
Environment	Sandra Potter	Yuansheng Li
Training	Veronica Vlasich	Mariano Memolli
Medical	Jeff Ayton	Mariano Memolli
Shipping	Miki Ojeda	Juan Jose Dañobeitia
Safety	Robert Culshaw (until Sept 2012)	Jose Olmedo
Energy & Technology	David Blake	Yuansheng Li & Juan Jose Dañobeitia
Data Management	Michelle Rogan-Finnemore	Heinz Miller
External Relationships	Michelle Rogan-Finnemore	EXCOM All
Strategic Framework	Michelle Rogan-Finnemore	Heinz Miller

Table 3 – COMNAP Expert Groups.

Appendix 2. Meetings

Previous 12 months

14 July 2012, COMNAP/SCAR Joint Executive Meeting, Portland, Oregon, USA.

15 July, 2012, COMNAP Symposium "Sustainable Solutions to Antarctic Challenges: Supporting Polar Research in the 21st Century", Portland, Oregon, USA.

16–19 July, 2012, COMNAP Annual General Meeting (COMNAP XXIV), Portland, Oregon, USA.

17 July, 2012, COMNAP Workshop "Innovations in Antarctic Communications", Portland, Oregon, USA.

15–17 October 2012, COMNAP Executive Committee (EXCOM) Meeting, Alfred Wegener Institute (AWI), Bremerhaven, Germany.

Upcoming 12 months

7 July 2013, COMNAP SOOS Workshop (jointly convened with SCAR), Seoul, Republic of Korea.

8–10 July 2013, COMNAP Annual General Meeting (COMNAP XXV), hosted by KOPRI, Seoul, Republic of Korea.

September 2013 (date to be confirmed), COMNAP Antarctic Conservation Challenges Workshop (jointly convened with SCAR), Cambridge, UK.

September 2013 (date to be confirmed), COMNAP EXCOM Meeting.

2. Reports by Experts

Report of the Antarctic and Southern Ocean Coalition

1. *Introduction*

ASOC is pleased to be in Belgium for the XXXVI Antarctic Treaty Consultative Meeting. This report briefly describes ASOC's work over the past year, and outlines some key issues for this ATCM.

ASOC's Secretariat is in Washington DC, USA and its website is http://www.asoc.org). ASOC has 24 full member groups in 10 countries and supporting groups in those and several other countries. ASOC campaigns are carried out by teams of experts in Argentina, Australia, Chile, China, France, Germany, Japan, The Netherlands, New Zealand, Norway, South Africa, South Korea, Spain, Russia, Ukraine, UK and USA.

2. *Intersessional activities*

Since XXXV ATCM ASOC and its member groups' representatives participated actively in intersessional discussions in the ATCM and CEP fora.

In addition, ASOC and member group representatives attended a range of meetings relevant to Antarctic environmental protection including the XXXII SCAR Meeting, IUCN's World Conservation Congress and Assembly, XXX CCAMLR Meeting, two CCAMLR's Marine Protected Area Workshops, and all International Maritime Organization meetings relating to the Polar Code.

3. *Papers for XXXVI ATCM*

ASOC has introduced 11 Information Papers and one Background Paper. In addition, ASOC was involved in the development of Working Paper 046 reviewing site guidelines for Baily Head, Deception Island.

The various papers address key environmental issues, and contain recommendations for the ATCM and CEP that will help achieve more effective environmental protection and conservation of Antarctica.

Human impacts in the Arctic and Antarctic: Key findings relevant to the ATCM and CEP (IP 61) - At the IPY Oslo Science Conference in 2010, two writing projects were launched, involving 50 international experts exploring the subject of human impacts and future scenarios for the Antarctic environment. The vast majority of future scenarios concur that existing environmental management practices and the current system of governance are insufficient to meet the obligations of the Environmental Protocol to protect the Antarctic environment. If the Antarctic Treaty System is to satisfactorily address the challenges facing a warmer and busier Antarctic in the 21st century and beyond, significant improvements are required.

Update to vessel incidents in Antarctic waters (IP 59) updates ASOC's XXXV ATCM/IP53 and provides additional information and analysis of vessel incidents, including a map and case studies of several recent incidents. The case studies point to a number of inadequacies in the current draft Polar Code. ASOC recommends that Parties work toward addressing these inadequacies at the International Maritime Organization as a matter of priority if the final Polar Code is to be useful in the Antarctic.

SAR-WG: An Antarctic Vessel Traffic Monitoring and Information System (IP 63) – ASOC's XXXIV/IP082 called on the ATCM to adopt a Resolution or Decision on development of an Antarctic Vessel Traffic Monitoring and Information System (VTMIS). IP63 updates the information and includes a proposed Decision calling for all vessels operating in the Treaty Area to install and maintain constant operation of Automatic Identification Systems (AIS), to transmit long-range information and tracking (LRIT) data to an appropriate data centre, and to develop an Antarctic VTMIS, beginning with the Antarctic Peninsula area.

Discharge of sewage and grey water from vessels in Antarctic Treaty waters (IP 66) provides information on discharges of black (sewage) and grey water from vessels, expresses concerns that the current system for the management of water waste streams may not provide adequate protection for Antarctic ecosystems and wildlife, and summarises the current regulation. Concerns are not restricted to vessels carrying the greatest numbers of people i.e. cruise vessels that have the largest discharges. The paper proposes that ATCPs consider further the need for more stringent management of the disposal of water discharges from vessels.

Management implications of tourist behaviour (IP 67) - Many actual and potential impacts of tourism result from the behaviour of individuals, within the broader context of how tourism is conducted, regulated and managed. An understanding of basic tourist behaviour is relevant to inform management decisions. However, behaviour can be very diverse and cannot be regulated minutely, particularly in the context of tourism expansion and diversification. In this context, ASOC suggests that ATCPs tackle tourism regulation and management primarily from a strategic perspective, including through using ASPAs and ASMAs proactively as tourism management tools.

An Antarctic climate change report card (IP 62) - Climate change research has many implications for Antarctica's environment, and it is critical for the Antarctic Treaty System to understand the latest findings so that they can incorporate them into management decisions. IP62 summarizes these recent results regarding environmental and ecosystem changes, and finds that changes are occurring in a variety of areas, from the pH level of seawater to the stability of the West Antarctic Ice Sheet. Despite the complexities of global climate change, the ATS can take action in a number of areas to mitigate its impact on the Antarctic environment and on Antarctic species.

Black carbon and other short-lived climate pollutants: Impacts on Antarctica (IP 65) - Black carbon and other short-lived climate pollutants (SLCPs), especially from local and southern hemispheric sources, may be hastening warming and melting in Antarctica. Conversely, emission reductions from these sources could provide the possibility of slowing warming in the near-term, though only when combined with longer-lived greenhouse gas mitigation actions. Analysis of the extent of SLCP emissions and impacts on Antarctica, especially from local sources, should be a priority for ongoing research, and included in the Strategic Workplan.

Update: The future of the West Antarctic Ice Sheet (IP 69) - This paper updates from IP07 presented at the ATME on Climate Change in 2010 and concludes that:

1. WAIS is losing mass, and this loss is accelerating.
2. Widespread glacier retreat may already be set in motion.
3. Changes to WAIS are happening now and are related to anthropogenic climate change.
4. WAIS is likely to survive mostly intact for this century, but a "collapse," if and when it happens, will raise sea level at least 3 meters.
5. A West Antarctic Tipping Point threshold is likely to exist, though the science is not settled. The WAIS can disintegrate more quickly than the Greenland Ice Sheet.

Biological prospecting and the Antarctic environment (IP 64) - Biological prospecting is completely unregulated at present and there is limited response by Parties to the information requirements of Resolution 7 (2005). More information is needed to understand and regulate biological prospecting and to assess its environmental impacts. ASOC recommends greater use of the EIEs; EIAs; and environmental monitoring as they apply to biological prospecting activities. A mechanism should be established to identify harvesting of marine living resources in the Southern Ocean related to biological prospecting.

Reuse of a site after remediation. A case study from Cape Evans, Ross Island (IP 68) - The reuse of a remediated site may undo the effects of remediation. IP68 makes suggestions relevant to impact assessment and site management based on a case study of a small site that was remediated and is now being reused.

Mapping and modelling wilderness values in Antarctica: Contribution to CEP's work in guidance material on wilderness protection using Protocol tools (IP 60) summarizes the recommendations of the report "Mapping and modelling wilderness values in Antarctica" produced by the Wildland Research Institute. The report reviews existing literature on how wilderness quality is mapped and modelled worldwide, using Geographical Information Systems (GIS). IP 60 recommends that the CEP adopt the universal basic premise that wilderness conditions are seen to exist where a location is remote from settlement and mechanised access, and relatively free from human-induced changes to land cover.

Antarctic Ocean Legacy Update 1: Securing Enduring Protection for the Ross Sea Region (BP 17)
In October 2011, the Antarctic Ocean Alliance (AOA), of which ASOC is a member, proposed the creation of a network of marine protected areas (MPAs) and no-take marine reserves in 19 specific areas in the Southern Ocean. Subsequently, the AOA outlined a vision for marine protection in East Antarctica and the Ross Sea that in addition to the seven areas proposed by Australia, France and the EU, included four other areas to be considered for protection in the coming years, and proposed the creation of a fully protected

marine reserve of approximately 3.6 million square kilometers in the Ross Sea region. BP17 summarizes the AOA's Antarctic Ocean Legacy Update Report, "Securing Enduring Protection for the Ross Sea Region".

4. Other Important Issues for XXXVI ATCM

- **Annex VI on Liability Arising from Environmental Emergencies:** Bringing this important Annex into force should be a high priority for ATCPs. ASOC urges all Parties to redouble their efforts over the next year so that Annex VI can be ratified and enter into force as quickly as possible. ASOC congratulates Norway and the United Kingdom for passing Annex VI legislation.
- **Strategic planning:** ASOC supports the development of a multiyear strategic plan for the ATCM, which will help Parties in managing human activities sustainably over the longer term, and has been actively involved in the work so far.

5. Concluding Remarks

Antarctica is facing many pressures from global climate change and a wide range of human activities. ASOC looks forward to the ATCPs having the vision and political will in Brussels to take concrete actions that will help protect Antarctica's ecosystems and intrinsic values over the longer term.

Report by the International Hydrographic Organization

Status of Hydrographic Surveying and Charting in Antarctic Waters

Introduction

The International Hydrographic Organization (IHO) is an intergovernmental consultative and technical organization. It comprises 81 Member States. Each State is normally represented by its national Hydrographer.

The IHO coordinates on a worldwide basis the setting of standards for hydrographic data and the provision of hydrographic services in support of safety of navigation and the protection and sustainable use of the marine environment.

Importance of Hydrography in Antarctica

No human activity can take place in, on or under the sea in a safe, sustainable and cost effective way without hydrographic information.

Hydrography and hydrographic information is increasingly being recognised as a fundamental pre-requisite to the development of successful and environmentally sustainable human activities in the seas and oceans. Unfortunately, there is little or no hydrographic information for a number of parts of the world, but especially in Antarctica.

This should be a cause of particular concern to the ATCM.

Status of Hydrography and Charting in Antarctica

Over 90% of Antarctic waters are unsurveyed. Large areas are uncharted and where charts do exist, they have limited utility because of the lack of reliable information. The grounding of vessels operating outside previously navigated routes in Antarctica is not uncommon.

Hydrographic surveying in Antarctic waters is expensive and problematic. This is because of hostile and unpredictable sea conditions, short seasons for surveying and the very long logistic train involved in supporting ships and equipment. There is no indication of any significant improvement in the level of hydrographic surveying being conducted in Antarctica. Indeed, the national hydrographic authorities represented in the IHO report that government-sponsored surveying activity in Antarctica is decreasing because of financial pressures and competing priorities in home waters.

IHO Hydrographic Commission on Antarctica

The IHO Hydrographic Commission on Antarctica (HCA) is dedicated to improving the quality, coverage and availability of nautical charting and other hydrographic information and services covering the region. The HCA comprises 23 IHO Members States (Argentina, Australia, Brazil, Chile, China, Ecuador, France, Germany, Greece, India, Italy, Japan, Republic of Korea, New Zealand, Norway, Peru, Russian Federation, South Africa, Spain, United Kingdom, Uruguay, USA, Venezuela), all of which have acceded to the Antarctic Treaty and are therefore also directly represented in the ATCM.

The HCA works closely with stakeholder organizations to improve safety of navigation, ensure safety of life at sea, protect the marine environment and support other activities in Antarctica. The following participate in HCA and its activities: ATS, COMNAP, IAATO, SCAR, IMO, IOC.

The 12th meeting of the HCA took place in Uruguay in October 2012. The HCA reviewed the progress of charting and surveying and updated its plans for the coordinated production of nautical charts and associated publications. Notable conclusions from the meeting are described in the following paragraphs.

Hydrographic Data Collection

States represented in HCA report that the level of surveying in Antarctica is reducing because of financial constraints and priorities to survey in home waters. In 2012, a number of States that regularly operate surveying vessels in southern waters in the summer reported that those vessels were not available.

ATCM may wish to consider the serious shortfalls in hydrography and charting in Antarctica and its impact on all other activities being conducted there.

Hydrographic Data Collection Using Ships of Opportunity

The UK Hydrographic Office and several industry partners, have continued a demonstration programme to enable ships operating in Antarctic waters to collect hydrographic data automatically during their voyages. The data is transmitted to the software/hardware partners; processed, cleaned and forwarded to the UKHO for review and then used to improve existing charts.

This is described as "crowd-sourced bathymetry" and takes place predominantly around the Antarctic Peninsula where the majority of commercial vessels including cruise ships operate. It is possible that this automatic collection of hydrographic data could be extended to collect other environmental data at the same time. Issues of funding for the equipment required to be fitted to ships, data validation and reliability are still to be addressed.

There are other commercial initiatives, particularly in the fishing sector, that are engaged in similar "crowd-sourced" data gathering activities. Unfortunately, not all of the relevant data is being made available to improve nautical charts.

Satellite Derived Bathymetry

In clear water, it is possible to determine depth and other parameters in the water column down to about 20 metres by analysing imagery from multi-spectral satellite sensors. France has been using this technique to improve charts for many years. The IHO is encouraging further development of the technique which does not require significant ground infrastructure and is much less expensive than traditional surveying.

Lidar Surveying from Aircraft

In clear water, such as in Antarctica, it is possible to determine depth down to 70 metres or more using laser echo sounders mounted in light aircraft. The technique is used in many parts of the world but not yet in Antarctica.

Commercial Contract Support

An increasing number of the world's national Hydrographic Offices are using commercial contract support to supplement their own efforts. Reliable contractors are available to collect hydrographic data on behalf of governments using ships or LIDAR. Contractors are also available to assist in making the official charts issued under the authority of the relevant governments.

Contract support for hydrographic surveying or chart production is almost non-existent for Antarctica. A principal reason for this is that government priorities place charting of home waters first. In addition, unlike for home waters, the obligation placed on States by Regulation 9 of Chapter V of the Convention for the Safety of Life at Sea (SOLAS) to provide charting and hydrographic services for their waters does not apply to Antarctica where no territorial claims are currently recognised.

Continuing Requirement for Traditional Surveys

Crowd-sourced bathymetry and satellite derived bathymetry cannot replace systematic, fully regulated surveys, but they can provide rapid improvements to existing charts and help to identify and prioritise those areas that require more comprehensive surveys.

ATCM may wish to consider encouraging Member Governments to increase their level of support for surveying and charting in Antarctica including support for crowd-sourcing, the use of satellite derived bathymetry, and commercial contract support using ships and LIDAR.

Hydrography Priorities Working Group

The HCA Hydrography Priorities Working Group with input from COMNAP and IAATO maintains a long-term survey plan and a survey short list to reflect new survey requirements. The survey requirements plan is based on identified maritime shipping routes - it does not consider other areas of Antarctica, where there is also little or no survey data but shipping movements are less frequent.

The following paragraphs summarise key information available to the HCA.

Status of Surveys in Antarctica

Most Antarctic waters are unsurveyed. Few systematic surveys have been conducted. These are mostly centred on some of the Antarctic bases and around the Antarctic Peninsula.

Status of Nautical Charts of Antarctica

Paper Charts. According to the IHO INT chart schema, the following States have compiled paper charts covering Antarctica: Argentina (5), Australia (11), Brazil (1), Chile (6), Ecuador (1) France (4), Germany (2), Italy (2), Japan (3), New Zealand (9), Norway (1), Russian Federation (14), South Africa (1), Spain (1), UK (10), USA (2).

70 of an anticipated 108 charts in the schema have been published.

Electronic Navigational Charts. In accordance with recent revisions to the SOLAS Convention, passenger ships and many other ships engaged on international voyages are now being required to carry Electronic Chart Display and Information Systems (ECDIS) as their means for navigation. ECDIS is replacing paper charts for navigation in these vessels. Production of Electronic Navigational Charts (ENCs) for use in ECDIS is generally based on existing paper charts. The production of Antarctic ENCs is severely hampered by the poor state of the paper charts and the production and financial priorities of those States that have volunteered to make the ENCs. There is an urgent requirement for States to allocate sufficient resources to enable ENC production to be accelerated to provide at least the same level of coverage as for paper charts.

So far, 70 ENCs have been published, including ten created in 2012. A further 51 are planned for production in the next year. About 170 ENCs will be required to correspond to the IHO paper chart schema.

ATCM may wish to encourage States producing ENCs and paper charts to allocate appropriate resources to accelerate the production of paper charts and ENCs of Antarctica.

IMO Polar Code

The IHO is seeking to ensure that the shortcomings of hydrography and nautical charting services for Antarctica are properly highlighted in the Polar Code now in the latter stages of development and consideration by IMO.

Review and Consolidation of Extant ATCM Recommendations and Resolutions Relating to Hydrography and Nautical Charting

The HCA has reviewed the extant Recommendations and Resolutions relating to hydrography and nautical charting and concluded that the guidance contained in them would be clearer and better expressed in a single ATCM Recommendation. A proposed revised text has been forwarded to the ICG on the review of ATCM Recommendations on Operational Matters.

ATCM is invited to adopt the proposed Recommendation on hydrography and nautical charting developed by the HCA.

Summary

The state of hydrographic surveying and nautical charting of Antarctica is far from satisfactory. This poses serious risks for maritime incidents as well as impeding the conduct of most activities taking place in the seas and oceans surrounding Antarctica.

A number of IHO Member States, through their national Hydrographic Offices, are attempting to improve the situation. However, resources are limited and there does not appear to be much prospect of significant improvement in the near future unless new policy action is taken by governments.

The IHO, through its Hydrographic Commission on Antarctica, coordinates the work of States and organizations with interests in Antarctica in an attempt to maximize efforts and improve the situation. Increased level of support from governments, industry and organisations is required if significant further progress is to be made.

Recommendations

It is recommended that ATCM:

- Takes note of this Report.
- Considers the serious shortfalls in hydrography and charting in Antarctica and its impact on all other activities being conducted there.
- Considers encouraging Member Governments to increase their level of support for surveying and charting of Antarctica either directly or through contracted activities.
- Encourages States producing paper charts and ENCs to allocate appropriate resources to accelerate the production of paper charts and ENCs of Antarctica.
- Adopts the proposed ATCM Recommendation on hydrography and nautical charting developed by the HCA.

Report of the International Association of Antarctica Tour Operators 2012-13

Under Article III (2) of the Antarctic Treaty

Introduction

The International Association of Antarctica Tour Operators (IAATO) is pleased to report its activities to ATCM XXXVI, under Article III (2) of the Antarctic Treaty.

IAATO continues to focus activities in support of its mission statement to ensure:

- Effective day-to-day management of Member activities in Antarctica;
- Educational outreach, including scientific collaboration; and
- Development and promotion of Antarctic tourism best practices.

A detailed description of IAATO, its mission statement, primary activities and recent developments can be found in the *2013-14 Fact Sheet*, and on the IAATO website: www.iaato.org.

IAATO Membership and Visitor Levels during 2012-13

IAATO comprises 116 Members, Associates and Affiliates. Member offices are located worldwide, representing 61% of the Antarctic Treaty Consultative Party countries, and carrying nationals from nearly all Treaty Parties annually to Antarctica.

During the 2012-13 Antarctic tourism season, the overall number of visitors increased to 34,375, following a 22% decline the previous year (26,519). While this represented a 29% increase from the 2011-12 season, the total was not significantly different from 2009-10 and 2010-11, where totals were 36,881 and 33,824 respectively. Tourism continued well below the 2007-08 season, when IAATO operators transported 45,213 visitors to the continent.

These numbers reflect only those travelling with IAATO member companies. Details on tourism statistics can be found in ATCM XXXVI IP103 *IAATO Overview of Antarctic Tourism: 2012-13 Season and Preliminary Estimates for 2013-14*. The Membership Directory and additional statistics on IAATO member activities can be found at ***www.iaato.org***.

Recent Work and Activities

A number of initiatives were undertaken during the year, including:

- Adopting a new five-year Strategic Plan, which outlines a vision for the association: "Through self-regulation, Antarctic tourism is a sustainable, safe activity that causes no more than a minor or transitory impact on the environment and creates a corps of ambassadors for the continued protection of Antarctica."
- Instigating a Dockside Observer program for IAATO yachts, a new component in the association's enhanced observer scheme. The program will trial during the 2013-14 season and parallels an existing observer scheme that IAATO has had in place for many years for larger vessels operated by Members.
- Developing the Field Staff Online Assessment and Certification Program to include different activities, staff levels, and geographic areas. A total of 223 staff have passed at least one of the assessments, with more than 177 this past season alone. A new IAATO Field Staff Newsletter, with news and updates from around the Continent, was also initiated during the recently concluded season.
- Implementing a new IAATO Climate Change PowerPoint Presentation, for use by lecture staffs aboard IAATO vessels to assist visitors to understand the implications of climate change on the Antarctic environment. The presentation was reviewed by SCAR, and can be downloaded from the IAATO website at: http://iaato.org/climate-change-in-antarctica

- Collecting hydrographic data on a trial and opportunistic basis by a number of IAATO vessel operators. This includes the Crowd Sourcing Project with the involvement of the United Kingdom Hydrographic Office and other surveying initiatives. Captains of IAATO vessels also will contribute to a prioritization list for future surveys of Antarctic waters.

IAATO Meeting and Participation at Other Meetings during 2012-13

IAATO Secretariat staff and member representatives participated in internal and external meetings, liaising with National Antarctic Programs, governmental, scientific, environmental and industry organisations.

- The IAATO 24th Meeting (April 22-24, 2013, Punta Arenas, Chile) hosted over 130 participants. Representatives from Chile, Germany, UK, USA and COMNAP attended. In addition to the above-mentioned initiatives, notable meeting outcomes included:
  - Approval of three Associate Members as new (full) Members. IAATO now has 49 Member and six Associate operator/organizers among its Membership, and continues to represent 100% of SOLAS passenger vessels active in Antarctic tourism.
  - A report on the survey of IAATO operators relative to ATCM Visitor Site Guidelines and path use on Barrientos Island;
  - Adoption of guidelines for multi-night coastal camping, short overnight stays and emperor penguin colony visits;
  - Formal sharing IAATO vessel operators of carbon emission reduction actions and techniques currently being used.
- A full-day Search and Rescue Workshop followed the meeting, with more than 75 attendees including passenger ship captains, government rescue officials from Chile, Argentina and the USA, tour operators, logistics managers, expedition leaders and IAATO staff. The proceedings were chaired by David Edwards from the Office of Search and Rescue, US Coast Guard. The workshop included a morning of presentations on SAR from several different perspectives (MRCC's, COMNAP, IAATO and Operators), and included an interactive replay of a live February 8, 2013, SAR exercise conducted aboard Holland America Line's MV *Veendam*.
- The Association welcomed the opportunity to participate at COMNAP XXIV in Portland OR, USA (July 2013). IAATO places great merit in good cooperation and collaboration between its Membership and National Antarctic Programs.
- An IAATO representative attended the 12th International Hydrographic Organization / Hydrographic Commission on Antarctica (IHO/HCA) Meeting in Montevideo, Uruguay (October 2012). IAATO remains a strong supporter the ongoing work of the HCA, and will continue to work with HO's and HCA in the development of a crowd-sourcing hydrographic data collection scheme.
- As an advisor to Cruise Lines International Association (CLIA), IAATO continues to be active in the development of International Maritime Organization's (IMO) mandatory Polar Code. This included participation in a Polar Shipping Risk Assessment Workshop in Ottawa, Canada (June 2012); the 91st session of the IMO's Marine Safety Committee meeting; the 57th session of the IMO's Design and Equipment (DE) Subcommittee meeting; and intercessional correspondence group discussions.
- The IAATO 25th Annual Meeting will be held in Providence, Rhode Island, USA (dates TBA). Interested Treaty Parties are welcome to attend and should contact IAATO at iaato@iaato.org.

Environmental Monitoring

IAATO continues to provide ATCM and CEP with detailed information on member activities in Antarctica. For details see ATCM XXXVI/IP103 *IAATO Overview of Antarctic Tourism: 2012-13 Season and Preliminary Estimates for 2013-14 Antarctic Season* and ATCM XXXVI IP97 *Report on IAATO Operator Use of Antarctic Peninsula Landing Sites and ATCM Visitor Site Guidelines, 2012-13 Season.*

IAATO continues to work collaboratively with scientific institutions particularly on environmental monitoring and educational outreach. This includes working with Antarctic Site Inventory and the Zoological Society of London/Oxford University.

IAATO welcomes opportunities for collaboration with other organisations.

Tourism Incidents 2012-13

IAATO continues to follow a policy of disclosing incidents to ensure risks are understood and appropriate lessons are learned for all Antarctic operators. Incidents during the 2012-13 season included:

- On December 20, a chartered DC3 – operated by Antarctic Logistics Centre International (ALCI) and The Antarctic Company (TAC) and managed by Kenn Borek Air Ltd (KBAL) – struck a sastrugi on take off from a camp in the Holtanna Mountain Range in Dronning Maud Land. There were no major injuries and no environmental damage. A second plane was immediately deployed from Novo Runway to safely retrieve all the passengers and crew. The damaged DC3 will remain at the crash site until next season, with a full investigation underway by ALCI and KBAL.
- On January 18, MV *Orion* received a distress call while in the Southern Ocean regarding a solo sailor in a lifeboat. As closest vessel, MV *Orion* was tasked by MRCC to divert to assist. By the evening of January 20, the lifeboat had been spotted by MV *Orion*, a Zodiac was deployed despite rough weather, and the sailor – Frenchman Alain Delord – was rescued.
- On February 18, a group of six from the IAATO yacht *Santa Maria Australis* hiked up the ridge on the northern part of Hovgaard Island for a scenic view of Port Pléneau. IAATO yacht *Pelagic Australis* was also anchored in the same bay. One passenger separated from the group and left the prescribed route falling seven metres into a crevasse. The skipper of *Santa Maria Australis,* assisted by personnel onboard *Pelagic Australis,* proceeded with caution to the scene and successfully rescued the individual who had suffered a few non-life threatening injuries. Other IAATO operators were notified of the crevasse location on February 21.
- On March 12, the expedition leader of the *Plancius* notified Oceanwide Expeditions that a diver disappeared during a scheduled dive at Half Moon Island. A search found the diver unconscious at a depth of five meters. Following her recovery, extended CPR and attention by the ship's doctor, the passenger was pronounced dead. The passenger, 51 years old Japanese national, was an experienced diver with more than 1,500 hours dry suit experience. Oceanwide immediately notified all relevant authorities and IAATO. The Dutch government has requested Argentina, as the next port of call, to conduct a full investigation. The outcomes are pending.

Scientific and Conservation Support

During the 2012-13 season, IAATO Members cost-effectively or on *pro bono* basis transported approximately 100 scientific, support and conservation staff, and their equipment and supplies between stations, field sites and gateway ports.

IAATO Operators and their passengers also contributed more than US$440,000 to scientific and conservation organisations active in Antarctica and the sub-Antarctic (e.g. Save the Albatross, Antarctic Heritage Trust, Last Ocean, Mawson's Huts Foundation, Oceanites and World Wildlife Fund). Over the past nine years, these donations have totalled approximately US$3 million in cash donations.

With Thanks

IAATO appreciates the opportunity to work cooperatively with Antarctic Treaty Parties, COMNAP, SCAR, CCAMLR, IHO/HCA, ASOC and others toward the long-term protection of Antarctica.

PART IV

Additional Documents from ATCM XXXVI

1. Additional Documents

SCAR Lecture: "Probing for life at its limits: Technologies for the exploring Antarctic subglacial ecosystems"

Author: Professor Jemma Wadham is a low temperature biogeochemist at Bristol Glaciology Centre, School of Geographical Sciences, the University of Bristol, UK. She is co-chair of the SCAR ATHENA Expert Group (Advancing TecHnologies and ENvironmental stewardship in Antarctica).

Presenter and co-Author: Professor Mahlon "Chuck" Kennicutt II is a chemical oceanographer in the Department of Oceanography at Texas A&M University, College Station, Texas, U.S.A. He is Past President of SCAR and was Secretary of the SCAR Subglacial Antarctic Lake Environments (SALE) Scientific Research Program.

Background:

Antarctic Subglacial Aquatic Environments (SAEs) are recognized as central to many processes that have shaped the polar ice sheets both today and in the past. They include a range of features that differ in geologic setting, age, evolutionary history, hydrological conditions and size, and include subglacial lakes, ponds, swamps, intermittently flowing rivers and thick sediments. These environments are "natural" earth-bound macrocosms, which in some instances trace their origins to a time before Antarctica became encased in ice. Antarctic SAEs remain the least explored sector of the cold biosphere, yet are now known to be viable habitats for microbial life despite the harsh environmental conditions. Within these sub-surface aquatic environments microbial life drives chemical weathering, which in turn exports dissolved nutrients and carbon to downstream ecosystems and greenhouse gases to the atmosphere. The full spectrum of sub-ice environments present beneath the Antarctic continent provides an unparalleled opportunity to explore and study one of Earth's last frontiers and decipher fundamental clues to the planet's history, climate and biology.

The last 10 years has witnessed a dramatic increase in the profile of Antarctic SAEs and the impetus for their study. This raised profile was linked strongly to the activity of SCAR via SALE, AG-CCER-SAE and ATHENA. It culminated in the funding of four campaigns to access and directly sample SAEs (the Lake Vostok, WISSARD, Lake Ellsworth and BEAMISH programmes). The next phase of Antarctic SAE exploration is very likely to be shaped by the availability of technology for addressing core science goals. This lecture aims first, to identify the science questions driving technology development for the future exploration of subglacial aquatic ecosystems and second, to present the current status of available technologies for sub-Antarctic science.

For more information see the associated Information Paper IP82: *Advancing technologies for exploring subglacial Antarctic aquatic ecosystems (SAEs)*

2. List of Documents

2. List of Documents

Working Papers								
Number	**Ag. Items**	**Title**	**Submitted By**	**E**	**F**	**R**	**S**	**Attachments**
WP001	ATCM 5	Review of ATCM Recommendations on Operational Matters	COMNAP IAATO IHO SCAR WMO					Attachments A, B and C: Review of Recommendations
WP002	CEP 9a	Revised Management Plan for Antarctic Specially Protected Area No. 137 Northwest White Island, McMurdo Sound	United States					ASPA 137 Map 1 ASPA 137 Revised Management Plan
WP003	CEP 9a	Revised Management Plan for Antarctic Specially Protected Area No. 123 Barwick and Balham Valleys, Southern Victoria Land	United States					ASPA 123 Map 1 ASPA 123 Revised Management Plan
WP004	ATCM 12 CEP 12	Inspection by Germany and South Africa in accordance with Article VII of the Antarctic Treaty and Article 14 of the Protocol on Environmental Protection: January 2013	Germany South Africa					
WP005	CEP 9a	Revised Management Plan for Antarctic Specially Protected Area No. 138 Linnaeus Terrace, Asgard Range, Victoria Land	United States					ASPA 138 Map 1 ASPA 138 Map 2 ASPA 138 Revised Management Plan
WP006	CEP 9a	Revision of the Management Plan for Antarctic Specially Protected Area No.141 Yukidori Valley, Langhovde, Lützow-Holm Bay	Japan					ASPA 141 Revised Management Plan ASPA 141 Revised Map 4
WP007	CEP 3	CEP Five-Year Work Plan adopted at the XVth CEP Meeting at Hobart	France					Five Year Work Plan for CEP XVI
WP008	CEP 9a	Proposal for a new Antarctic Specially Managed Area at Chinese Antarctic Kunlun Station, Dome A	China					ASMA XXX Chinese Antarctic Kunlun Station Dome A Management Plan ASMA XXX Chinese Antarctic Kunlun Station Dome A Map 1 ASMA XXX Chinese Antarctic Kunlun Station Dome A Map 2 ASMA XXX Chinese Antarctic Kunlun Station Dome A Map 3 ASMA XXX Chinese Antarctic Kunlun Station Dome A Map 4
WP009	ATCM 12	General Recommendations from the Joint Inspections	United Kingdom					

Working Papers								
Number	Ag. Items	Title	Submitted By	E	F	R	S	Attachments
	CEP 12	undertaken by the United Kingdom, the Netherlands and Spain under Article VII of the Antarctic Treaty and Article 14 of the Environmental Protocol	Netherlands Spain					
WP010	CEP 10c CEP 9f	Identification of potential climate change refugia for emperor penguins: a science-based approach	United Kingdom					
WP011	CEP 9a	Revised Management Plan for Antarctic Specially Protected Area No. 108 Green Island, Berthelot Islands, Antarctic Peninsula	United Kingdom					ASPA 108 Revised Management Plan
WP012	CEP 9a	Revised Management Plan for Antarctic Specially Protected Area No. 117 Avian Island, Marguerite Bay, Antarctic Peninsula	United Kingdom					ASPA 117 Revised Management Plan
WP013	CEP 9a	Revised Management Plan for Antarctic Specially Protected Area No. 147 Ablation Valley and Ganymede Heights, Alexander Island	United Kingdom					ASPA 147 Revised Management Plan
WP014	CEP 9a	Revised Management Plan for Antarctic Specially Protected Area No. 170 Marion Nunataks, Charcot Island, Antarctic Peninsula	United Kingdom					ASPA 170 Revised Management Plan
WP015	CEP 9c	Policy Issues Arising from the 2013 On-Site Review of Guidelines for Visitor Sites in the Antarctic Peninsula	United Kingdom Argentina Australia United States					
WP016	CEP 9c	Site Guidelines for i) Orne Harbour and ii) Orne Islands	United Kingdom Argentina Australia United States					Site Guidelines for Orne Harbour Site Guidelines for Orne Islands
WP017 rev.1	ATCM 10	SAR-WG - Update on actions resulting from the two COMNAP SAR workshops, "Towards Improved Search and Rescue Coordination and Response in the Antarctic"	COMNAP					
WP018 rev.1	CEP 9b	Proposal to add the site commemorating the location of the former German Antarctic Research Station "Georg Forster" to the List of Historic Sites and	Germany					

Working Papers								
Number	Ag. Items	Title	Submitted By	E	F	R	S	Attachments
		Monuments						
WP019	CEP 10a	Report on the Research Project "The Impact of Human Activities on Soil Organisms of the Maritime Antarctic and the Introduction of Non-Native Species in Antarctica"	Germany					
WP020	CEP 9c	On-Site Review of Guidelines for Visitor Sites in the Antarctic Peninsula: summary of programme and suggested amendment of eleven Guidelines	United Kingdom Argentina Australia United States					Revised Site Guideline Brown Bluff Revised Site Guideline Cuverville Island Revised Site Guideline Damoy Point Revised Site Guideline Danco Island Revised Site Guideline Half Moon Island Revised Site Guideline Hannah Point Revised Site Guideline Jougla Point Revised Site Guideline Neko Harbour Revised Site Guideline Petermann Island Revised Site Guideline Pleneau Island Revised Site Guideline Yankee Harbour
WP021	CEP 9f	Analysis of the ASPA and ASMA wildlife values	Russian Federation					
WP022	CEP 9f	Russian Antarctic biogeographic regioning as compared with the New Zealand classification	Russian Federation					
WP023	CEP 9b	Proposed addition of the Professor Kudryashov's drilling complex building at the Russian Antarctic Vostok station to the List of Historic Sites and Monuments	Russian Federation					
WP024	CEP 8b	Approaches to study of the water layer of subglacial lakes in the Antarctic	Russian Federation					
WP025	ATCM 10	SAR-WG Proposed Agenda for Special Working Group Meeting on Search and Rescue (SAR)	United States					Draft Agenda for ATCM XXXVI Special Working Group on Search and Rescue
WP026	CEP 9c	Proposed Amendment for Antarctic Treaty Site Guidelines for Visitors Torgersen Island	United States					Revised Site Guideline Torgersen Island

Working Papers								
Number	**Ag. Items**	**Title**	**Submitted By**	**E**	**F**	**R**	**S**	**Attachments**
WP027	CEP 6	Repair or Remediation of Environmental Damage: Report of the CEP intersessional contact group	New Zealand					
WP028	CEP 3	Antarctic Environments Portal: Progress Report	New Zealand Australia Belgium Norway SCAR					
WP029	CEP 9a	Revision of Management Plan for Antarctic Specially Protected Area No.154 Botany Bay, Cape Geology, Victoria Land	New Zealand					ASPA 154 List of labels ASPA 154 Map A ASPA 154 Map B ASPA 154 Map C ASPA 154 Revised Management Plan
WP030	CEP 9a	Revision of Management Plan for Antarctic Specially Protected Area No. 156 Lewis Bay, Mount Erebus, Ross Island	New Zealand					ASPA 156 List of labels ASPA 156 Map A ASPA 156 Revised Management Plan
WP031	ATCM 7	Report of the open-ended intersessional contact group on further development of a multi-year strategic work plan	Australia Belgium					Report. Multi-Year Strategic Work Plan. Intersessional Contact Group on possible priority issues to be identified in the plan
WP032	CEP 6	An Antarctic Clean-Up Manual: report of informal intersessional discussion	Australia United Kingdom					Resolution 2 (2013) Annex: Clean-Up Manual
WP033	ATCM 11 ATCM 16	Report of the Intersessional Contact Group on Information Exchange and the Environmental Aspects and Impacts of Tourism	New Zealand					
WP034	ATCM 10	SAR-WG Lessons Learned from Search and Rescue Incidents in the Ross Sea Region	New Zealand					
WP035	CEP 9d	Possible guidance material to assist Parties to take account of wilderness values when undertaking environmental impact assessments	New Zealand					
WP036	CEP 9a	Review of Management Plans for Antarctic Specially Protected Areas (ASPAs) 135, 143 and 160	Australia					ASPA 135 Map A ASPA 135 Map B ASPA 135 Map C ASPA 135 Map D ASPA 135 Map E ASPA 135 Revised Management Plan ASPA 143 Map A ASPA 143 Map B ASPA 143 Map C ASPA 143 Revised

Working Papers								
Number	Ag. Items	Title	Submitted By	E	F	R	S	Attachments
								Management Plan ASPA 160 Map A ASPA 160 Map B ASPA 160 Revised Management Plan
WP037	CEP 11	www.biodiversity.aq The new Antarctic Biodiversity Information Network	Belgium SCAR					
WP038	ATCM 14 CEP 7	The Antarctic Climate Change and the Environment (ACCE) Report: A Key Update	SCAR					
WP039	CEP 9f	Human footprint in Antarctica and the long-term conservation of terrestrial microbial habitats	Belgium SCAR South Africa United Kingdom					
WP040	ATCM 6	Glossary of terms and expressions used by the ATCM	France Belgium Uruguay					French/English and English/French glossary of ATCM terminology
WP041	ATCM 13	Enhancing consultations in the use of logistical means to serve science in Antarctica	France Chile					
WP042	CEP 6	The need to take into account the dismantling costs of stations in Comprehensive Environmental Evaluations (CEE) relating to their construction	France Italy					
WP043 rev.1	ATCM 16	Importance of unique and common geo-referencing of toponymic data in the Electronic Information Exchange System	France					
WP043 rev.2	ATCM 16	Importance of common geo-referencing of toponymic data in the Electronic Information Exchange System	France					
WP044	ATCM 5	The exercise of jurisdiction in the Antarctic Treaty Area	France					
WP045	ATCM 6	Budgetary issues: proposal to ensure that the Secretariat of the Antarctic Treaty benefits from the expertise of the "Coordination Regime"	France					

Working Papers								
Number	Ag. Items	Title	Submitted By	E	F	R	S	Attachments
WP046	CEP 9c	Proposed Amendment for Antarctic Treaty Site Guidelines for Visitors Baily Head, Deception Island	United States Argentina ASOC Chile IAATO Norway Spain United Kingdom					Photo 1 Penguin Highway Revised Baily Head SGV Revised map for Baily Head SGV
WP047	ATCM 11	Report of the Informal Contact Group on the Increasing Diversity of Tourism and other Non-Governmental Activities in Antarctica	Netherlands					
WP048	ATCM 17	Biological prospecting in Antarctica – the need for improved information	Belgium Netherlands Sweden					
WP049	CEP 5	The Antarctic Treaty System role regarding the development of a comprehensive system of Marine Protected Areas	Belgium Germany Netherlands					
WP050	ATCM 1	Document withdrawn	ATS					
WP051 rev.1	ATCM 12 CEP 12	Additional availability of information on lists of Observers of the Consultative Parties through the Antarctic Treaty Secretariat	Uruguay Argentina					
WP052	ATCM 10	SAR-WG: Proposed Development of Regional SAR Standard Operating Procedures	United States					Action Card from IAMSAR Manual
WP053	ATCM 10	SAR-WG: Global Search and Rescue (SAR) System: Impacts of New Technologies	United States					Example Process Guide for distress alert from the Personal Locator Beacon (PLB)
WP054 rev.1	CEP 9a	Review of the Management Plan for ASMA No.1: Admiralty Bay, King George Island, South Shetland Islands	Brazil Ecuador Peru Poland					ASMA 1 Revised Management Plan
WP055	CEP 9f	Recovery of moss communities on the tracks of Barrientos island and tourism management proposal	Ecuador Spain					Comparative photos of the tracks in the 2012-2013 period
WP056	CEP 9a	Subsidiary Group on Management Plans – Report on 2012/13	Norway					ASPA 132 Revised Management Plan ASPA 151 Map 1

Working Papers								
Number	**Ag. Items**	**Title**	**Submitted By**	**E**	**F**	**R**	**S**	**Attachments**
		Intersessional Work						ASPA 151 Map 2 ASPA 151 Map 3 ASPA 151 Map 4 ASPA 151 Revised Management Plan ASPA 173 Cape Washington & Silverfish Bay Management Plan ASPA 173 Map 1 ASPA 173 Map 2 ASPA 173 Map 3
WP057	ATCM 15	International cooperation in cultural projects in Antarctica	Argentina					Actividades y Exposiciones Realizadas por el Programa de Arte y Cultura
WP058	CEP 3	Contributions to discussions on access to environment-related information and its management within the framework of the Antarctic Treaty System	Argentina					
WP059	CEP 9a	Revised Management Plan for Antarctic Specially Protected Area No. 134 Cierva Point and offshore islands, Danco Coast, Antarctic Peninsula	Argentina					ASPA 134 Revised Management Plan
WP060	CEP 9a	Revision of Management Plan for Antarctic Specially Protected Area N° 161 Terra Nova Bay, Ross Sea	Italy					ASPA 161 Revised Management Plan
WP061	ATCM 10	SAR-WG The Commission for the Conservation of Antarctic Marine Living Marine Resources' Vessel Monitoring System and Its Potential to Contribute to SAR Efforts in the Southern Ocean	CCAMLR					
WP062	CEP 9b	New Historic Sites and Monuments: Mount Erebus camp sites used by a contingent of the Terra Nova Expedition in December 1912	United Kingdom New Zealand United States					Terra Nova Expedition 1910-12 Campsites
WP063	CEP 9a	Draft Antarctic Specially Protected Area (ASPA) Management Plan for Stornes, Larsemann Hills, Princess Elizabeth Land	Australia China India Russian Federation					ASPA YYY Stornes, Larsemann Hills, Princess Elizabeth Land Management Plan ASPA YYY Stornes, Larsemann Hills, Princess Elizabeth Land Map A ASPA YYY Stornes, Larsemann Hills, Princess Elizabeth Land Map B
WP064	CEP 9c	Updated Map of Barrientos Island	Ecuador					Aitcho / Barrientos Este Aitcho / Barrientos Oeste Mapa Barrientos /Aitcho

Working Papers								
Number	**Ag. Items**	**Title**	**Submitted By**	**E**	**F**	**R**	**S**	**Attachments**
								Text tables for Barrientos (Aitcho Island) maps
WP065	ATCM 10	SAR-WG: Resources available on Antarctic bases for land support in emergency situations: inclusion in EIES	Argentina					
WP066	ATCM 5	Intersessional Contact Group Report on Cooperation in Antarctica	Chile					
WP067	ATCM 7	Co-chairs' Report of the Workshop on the Development of a Multi-Year Strategic Work Plan for the ATCM, Brussels, Belgium, 20-21 May 2013	Australia Belgium					

Information Papers								
Number	**Ag. Items**	**Title**	**Submitted By**	**E**	**F**	**R**	**S**	**Attachments**
IP001	ATCM 4	Report by the CCAMLR Observer to the Thirty-Sixth Antarctic Treaty Consultative Meeting	CCAMLR					
IP002	ATCM 4	Report by the International Hydrographic Organization	IHO					
IP003	ATCM 4 CEP 5	The Annual Report for 2012 of the Council of Managers of National Antarctic Programs (COMNAP)	COMNAP					
IP004	ATCM 4 CEP 5	The Scientific Committee on Antarctic Research (SCAR) Annual Report for 2012/13	SCAR					
IP005	ATCM 13 CEP 11	The Southern Ocean Observing System (SOOS) 2012 Report	SCAR					
IP006	CEP 5	Report by the SC-CAMLR Observer to the Sixteenth Meeting of the Committee for Environmental Protection	CCAMLR					
IP007	CEP 13	State of Japanese Environmental Management in Antarctica, with reference to the practices of other National Antarctic Programmes	Japan					
IP008	ATCM 9	Annex VI of the Protocol on Environmental Protection to the Antarctic Treaty: United Kingdom's Implementing Legislation	United Kingdom					UK Antarctic Act 2013 UK Antarctic Act 2013 Explanatory Notes
IP009	ATCM 13	Principales actividades realizadas en materia antártica por la República Bolivariana de Venezuela 2010-2013	Venezuela					
IP010	ATCM 15	Presentación del libro infantil: "la aventura de un osito polar perdido en la Antártida"	Venezuela					
IP011	ATCM 13	Video divulgativo de las relaciones de cooperación antárticas entre la República Bolivariana de Venezuela y la República de Ecuador	Venezuela					

Information Papers								
Number	**Ag. Items**	**Title**	**Submitted By**	**E**	**F**	**R**	**S**	**Attachments**
IP012	ATCM 4	Report Submitted to Antarctic Treaty Consultative Meeting XXXVI by the Depositary Government for the Convention for the Conservation of Antarctic Seals in Accordance with Recommendation XIII-2, Paragraph 2(D)	United Kingdom					
IP013	ATCM 11 ATCM 16	Antarctic Treaty System Information Exchange Requirements for Tourism and Non-Governmental Activities	New Zealand					
IP014	ATCM 10	SAR-WG Search and Rescue Incidents in the Ross Sea Region: 2004 - 2013	New Zealand					
IP015	CEP 5	CCAMLR MPA Technical Workshop	Belgium					
IP016	ATCM 12 CEP 12	Status of the fluid in the EPICA borehole at Concordia Station: an answer to the US / Russian Inspection in 2012	France Italy					
IP017	ATCM 15	El plan científico antártico argentino: una visión para el mediano plazo	Argentina					
IP018	ATCM 17	Reporte de las recientes actividades de bioprospección desarrolladas por Argentina durante el período 2011-2012	Argentina					
IP019	ATCM 13 CEP 11	1St SCAR Antarctic and Southern Ocean Science Horizon Scan	SCAR					
IP020	ATCM 11 CEP 9c	Antarctic Site Inventory: 1994-2013	United States					
IP021	CEP 8b	Initial Environmental Evaluation for the Construction of Inland Summer Camp, Princess Elizabeth Land, Antarctica	China					
IP022	ATCM 17	An Update on Status and Trends Biological Prospecting in Antarctica and Recent Policy Developments at the International Level	Belgium Netherlands					

Information Papers								
Number	**Ag. Items**	**Title**	**Submitted By**	**E**	**F**	**R**	**S**	**Attachments**
IP023	ATCM 10	SAR-WG: Summary of International Search and Rescue Activities Associated with an Aircraft Incident in the Queen Alexandra Range, Antarctica	United States Italy New Zealand					
IP024	CEP 8b	Progress of the Jang Bogo Station during the first construction season 2012/13	Korea (ROK)					
IP025	CEP 8b	Mitigation measures of environmental impacts caused by Jang Bogo construction during 2012/13 season	Korea (ROK)					
IP026 rev.1	CEP 9a	Management Report of Narębski Point (ASPA No. 171) during the 2012/2013 period	Korea (ROK)					
IP027	CEP 11	Korean/German Workshop about Environmental Monitoring on King George Island	Korea (ROK) Germany					
IP028	CEP 10a	Colonisation status of known non-native species in the Antarctic terrestrial environment (updated 2013)	United Kingdom					
IP029	CEP 11	Remote sensing for monitoring Antarctic Specially Protected Areas: Progress on use of multispectral and hyperspectral data for monitoring Antarctic vegetation	United Kingdom					
IP030	ATCM 13	Japan's Antarctic Research Highlights 2012–13	Japan					
IP031	CEP 10c	Use of hydroponics by national Antarctic programs	COMNAP					
IP032	ATCM 14 CEP 7	Cost/energy Analysis of National Antarctic Program Transportation	COMNAP					
IP033	ATCM 13 CEP 9d	Analysis of National Antarctic Program increased delivery of science	COMNAP					
IP034	ATCM 14 CEP 7	Best Practice for Energy Management – Guidance and Recommendations	COMNAP					

Information Papers								
Number	**Ag. Items**	**Title**	**Submitted By**	**E**	**F**	**R**	**S**	**Attachments**
IP035	CEP 10a CEP 9f	The non-native grass Poa pratensis at Cierva Point, Danco Coast, Antarctic Peninsula – on-going investigations and future eradication plans	Argentina Spain United Kingdom					
IP036	CEP 6	Clean-up of the construction site of unused airstrip "Piste du Lion", Terre Adélie, Antarctica	France					
IP037	ATCM 13	Opening of Halley VI Research Station	United Kingdom					
IP038	ATCM 12 CEP 12	Report of the Joint Inspections undertaken by the United Kingdom, the Netherlands and Spain under Article VII of the Antarctic Treaty and Article 14 of the Environmental Protocol	United Kingdom Netherlands Spain					Inspection Report
IP039	CEP 9d	Intersessional report on the provision of guidance material to assist Parties to take account of wilderness values when undertaking environmental impact assessments	New Zealand					
IP040	ATCM 4	Report of the Depositary Government for the Agreement on the Conservation of Albatrosses and Petrels (ACAP)	Australia					
IP041	ATCM 4	Report of the Depositary Government for the Convention on the Conservation of Antarctic Marine Living Resources (CCAMLR)	Australia					
IP042	CEP 8b	To discovery of unknown bacteria in Lake Vostok	Russian Federation					
IP043	ATCM 5	Implementation of the new Russian legislature "On regulation of activity of the Russian citizens and the Russian legal entities in the Antarctic"	Russian Federation					
IP044	ATCM 10	Joint Investigation Report of Breaking of ice barrier at Leningradsky Bay in April 2012 (Russian & Indian Antarctic Programmes)	Russian Federation India					

Information Papers								
Number	**Ag. Items**	**Title**	**Submitted By**	**E**	**F**	**R**	**S**	**Attachments**
IP045	ATCM 12 CEP 12	Report of Russia – US joint Antarctic Inspection, November 29 – December 6, 2012	Russian Federation United States					US/Russian Fed. Inspection Report
IP046	CEP 9f	Report of the Antarctic Specially Managed Area No. 6 Larsemann Hills Management Group	Australia China India Russian Federation					
IP047	ATCM 10	New infrastructure facilities of the Russian Antarctic Expedition	Russian Federation					
IP048	CEP 8b	Permit for the Activity of the Russian Antarctic Expedition in 2013-17	Russian Federation					
IP049	CEP 8b	Results of studies of subglacial lake Vostok and drilling operations in deep ice borehole of Vostok station in the season 2012-2013	Russian Federation					
IP050	ATCM 10	SAR-WG: Cooperation between Australia's search and rescue and Antarctic agencies on SAR coordination	Australia					
IP051	ATCM 10	SAR-WG: Overview of search and rescue conventions and international guidelines applicable to the Antarctic	Australia					
IP052	ATCM 14 CEP 5	Ocean Acidification: SCAR Future Plans	SCAR					
IP053	ATCM 12 CEP 12	Inspection by Germany and South Africa in accordance with Article VII of the Antarctic Treaty and Article 14 of the Protocol on Environmental Protection: January 2013	Germany South Africa					Inspection Report
IP054	ATCM 11	Data Collection and Reporting on Yachting Activity in Antarctica in 2012-13	IAATO United Kingdom					
IP055	CEP 10a	Final Report on the Research Project "The Impact of Human Activities on Soil Organisms of the Maritime Antarctic and the Introduction of Non-Native Species in Antarctica"	Germany					
IP056	ATCM	On planned activities of the Republic of Belarus in the	Belarus					

Information Papers								
Number	Ag. Items	Title	Submitted By	E	F	R	S	Attachments
	13	Antarctic						
IP057	ATCM 13	Foundation of Austrian Polar Research Institute (APRI) in April 2013	Austria					
IP058	CEP 8b	Terms of Reference of the Initial Environmental Evaluation (IEE): Reconstruction and Operation of Ferraz Station (Admiralty Bay, Antarctica)	Brazil					Terms of reference Ferraz Station
IP059	ATCM 10 CEP 11	Update to Vessel Incidents in Antarctic Waters	ASOC					Antarctic vessel incidents.kmz
IP060	CEP 9d	Mapping and modelling wilderness values in Antarctica: Contribution to CEP's work in developing guidance material on wilderness protection using Protocol tools	ASOC					Mapping and modelling wilderness values in Antarctica
IP061	ATCM 7 CEP 3	Human impacts in the Arctic and Antarctic: Key findings relevant to the ATCM and CEP	ASOC					Appendix to Human impacts in the Arctic and Antarctic
IP062	ATCM 14 CEP 7	An Antarctic Climate Change Report Card	ASOC					
IP063	ATCM 10	SAR-WG: An Antarctic Vessel Traffic Monitoring and Information System	ASOC					
IP064	ATCM 17	Biological prospecting and the Antarctic environment	ASOC					
IP065	ATCM 14 CEP 7	Black Carbon and other Short-lived Climate Pollutants: Impacts on Antarctica	ASOC					
IP066	ATCM 10 CEP 11	Discharge of sewage and grey water from vessels in Antarctic Treaty waters	ASOC					
IP067	ATCM 11 CEP 11	Management implications of tourist behaviour	ASOC					
IP068	CEP 6	Reuse of a site after remediation. A case study from Cape Evans, Ross Island	ASOC					
IP069	ATCM 14 CEP 7	Update: The Future of the West Antarctic Ice Sheet	ASOC					

Information Papers								
Number	**Ag. Items**	**Title**	**Submitted By**	**E**	**F**	**R**	**S**	**Attachments**
IP070	CEP 6	Environmental Damage Repair: Disassembling of Ferraz Station, Admiralty Bay, Antarctica	Brazil					
IP071 rev.1	ATCM 13	Romanian Scientific Activities proposed for Cooperation within Larsemann Hills ASMA 6 in East Antarctica – Plan for 2013-2014	Romania					
IP072	ATCM 4	Report of the Depositary Government of the Antarctic Treaty and its Protocol in accordance with Recommendation XIII-2	United States					Antarctic Treaty Status Table List of Recommendations/Measures and their approvals Protocol Status Table
IP073	CEP 9f	Antarctic trial of WWF's Rapid Assessment of Circum-Arctic Ecosystem Resilience (RACER) Conservation Planning Tool: initial findings	United Kingdom Norway					Map 1: Landform heterogeneity Map 2: Primary productivity
IP074	CEP 9a	Deception Island Specially Managed Area (ASMA) Management Group Report	Argentina Chile Norway Spain United Kingdom United States					
IP075	CEP 8b	Initial Environmental Evaluation for Establishment of the Ground Station for Earth Observation Satellites at the Indian Research Station Bharati at Larsemann Hills, East Antarctica	India					
IP076	CEP 11	Report on the accident occurred to an excavator vehicle at Mario Zucchelli Station, Ross Sea, Antarctica	Italy					
IP077	CEP 12	Italy answer to the US / Russian Inspection at Mario Zucchelli Station in 2012	Italy					
IP078	ATCM 10	31ª Operación Antártica (OPERANTAR XXXI)	Brazil					
IP079	ATCM 5	Strengthening Support for the Protocol on Environmental Protection to the Antarctic Treaty	Australia France Spain					

Information Papers								
Number	**Ag. Items**	**Title**	**Submitted By**	**E**	**F**	**R**	**S**	**Attachments**
IP080	CEP 8b	First steps towards the realization of a gravel runway near Mario Zucchelli Station: initial considerations and possible benefits for the Terra Nova Bay area	Italy					
IP081	ATCM 10	SAR-WG: SAR coordination case study – helicopter incident in Australia's search and rescue region, October 2010	Australia					
IP082	ATCM 13	Advancing technologies for exploring subglacial Antarctic aquatic ecosystems (SAEs)	SCAR					
IP083	ATCM 13 CEP 13	The International Bathymetric Chart of the Southern Ocean (IBCSO): First Release	SCAR					
IP084	ATCM 10	SAR-WG The Mandatory Code for Ships Operating in Polar Waters (Polar Code) – Update from the Perspective of Search and Rescue	United States					COMSAR 17 recommended text for Chapter 10 Communications
IP085	ATCM 9	Norway's Implementing Legislation: Annex VI of the Protocol on Environmental Protection to the Antarctic Treaty and Measure 4 (2004)	Norway					
IP086	ATCM 11	Report on Antarctic tourist flows and cruise ships operating in Ushuaia during the 2012/2013 Austral summer season	Argentina					
IP087	ATCM 11	Antarctic tourism through Ushuaia. Comparison of the last five Austral summer seasons	Argentina					
IP088	ATCM 11	Areas of tourist interest in the Antarctic Peninsula and Orcadas del Sur Islands (South Orkney Islands) region. 2012/2013 Austral summer season	Argentina					
IP089	ATCM 10	SAR-WG: Support provided by the Fildes Bay Maritime Station in Emergency Situations in the Antarctic Peninsula Year 2012	Chile					
IP090	ATCM 10	SAR-WG: Fire and Sinking of Fishing Vessel "Kai Xin"	Chile					

Information Papers								
Number	**Ag. Items**	**Title**	**Submitted By**	**E**	**F**	**R**	**S**	**Attachments**
IP091	ATCM 10	SAR-WG: International Regulations on Maritime Search and Rescue in the Antarctic Area	Chile					
IP092	ATCM 10	SAR-WG: Agreement between the Chilean Maritime Authorities and Maritime New Zealand for Maritime Search and Rescue Coordination Services	Chile New Zealand					
IP093	ATCM 10	SAR-WG: IAATO Information Submitted Annually to MRCC's with Antarctic Responsibilities	IAATO					
IP094	ATCM 10	Presentación de la nueva Base Antártica Brasileña	Brazil					
IP095	ATCM 10	Instalación de los Módulos Antárticos de Emergencia	Brazil					
IP096	ATCM 10	Demolición de la Base Antártica "Comandante Ferraz" (EACF)	Brazil					
IP097	ATCM 11 CEP 9c	Report on IAATO Operator Use of Antarctic Peninsula Landing Sites and ATCM Visitor Site Guidelines, 2012-13 Season	IAATO					
IP098	ATCM 11	IAATO Guidelines for Short Overnight Stays	IAATO					
IP099	ATCM 4	Report of the International Association of Antarctica Tour Operators 2012-13	IAATO					
IP100	ATCM 10	SAR-WG: Joint Search and Rescue Exercise in Antarctica	Chile IAATO					
IP101	CEP 7	IAATO Climate Change Working Group: Report of Progress	IAATO					
IP102	ATCM 11 CEP 9c	Barrientos Island Footpath Erosion	IAATO					

Information Papers								
Number	Ag. Items	Title	Submitted By	E	F	R	S	Attachments
IP103	ATCM 11	IAATO Overview of Antarctic Tourism: 2012-13 Season and Preliminary Estimates for 2013-14 Season	IAATO					
IP104	ATCM 5 CEP 13	Colombia in the Antarctic	Colombia					
IP105	CEP 5	Report of the CEP Observer to the XXXII SCAR Delegates' Meeting	Chile					
IP106	ATCM 4	Report of the Antarctic and Southern Ocean Coalition	ASOC					
IP107	CEP 11	Antarctic Center for Research and Environmental Monitoring, CIMAA: Advances in water quality monitoring and opportunities for cooperation	Chile					
IP108	ATCM 13	The Scientific Chilean Program and the international collaboration: Expedition 2012/13	Chile					
IP109	ATCM 10	SAR-WG: Decimoquinta Versión de la Patrulla Antártica Naval Combinada entre Chile y Argentina	Chile Argentina					
IP110	ATCM 13 ATCM 5	Development of Malaysia's Antarctic Research Programme since acceding to the ATS	Malaysia					
IP111	ATCM 16 CEP 9f	Management of Antarctic Specially Protected Areas: permitting, visitation and information exchange practices	Spain United Kingdom					

Secretariat Papers								
Number	**Ag. Items**	**Title**	**Submitted By**	**E**	**F**	**R**	**S**	**Attachments**
SP001 rev.2	ATCM 3 CEP 2	ATCM XXXVI and CEP XVI Agenda and Schedule	ATS					
SP002	ATCM 6	Secretariat Report 2012/13	ATS					Appendix 3: Contributions Received by the Antarctic Secretariat 2012/13 Decision 4 (2013) Annex 1: Audited Financial Report 2011/12 Decision 4 (2013) Annex 2: Provisional Financial Report 2012/13
SP003 rev.1	ATCM 6	Secretariat Programme 2013/14	ATS					Decision 4 (2013) - Appendix 1: Provisional Report for the Financial Year 2012/13, Budget for the Financial Year 2013/14, Forecast Budget for the Financial Year 2014/15 Decision 4 (2013) - Appendix 2: Contribution scale 2014/15 Decision 4 (2013) - Appendix 3: Salaries Scale 2013/14
SP004	ATCM 6	Five Years Forward Budget Profile 2013 - 2017	ATS					Five Years Forward Budget Profile 2013 - 2017
SP005	CEP 8b	Annual list of Initial Environmental Evaluations (IEE) and Comprehensive Environmental Evaluations (CEE) prepared between April 1st 2012 and March 31st 2013	ATS					
SP006	CEP 9a	Status of Antarctic Specially Protected Area and Antarctic Specially Managed Area Management Plans	ATS					
SP007	ATCM 14 CEP 7	Actions taken by the CEP and the ATCM on the ATME recommendations on climate change	ATS					Table with tracked changes
SP012	CEP 2	CEP XVI Summary of Papers	ATS					
SP013 rev.1	ATCM 1	Summary of papers Legal and Institutional WG	ATS					
SP014 rev.1	ATCM 3	Summary of papers WG Operational matters	ATS					

Secretariat Papers								
Number	**Ag. Items**	**Title**	**Submitted By**	**E**	**F**	**R**	**S**	**Attachments**
SP015 rev.2	ATCM 11	Summary of papers Tourism WG	ATS					
SP016	ATCM 10	Summary of papers SAR/WG	ATS					
SP017	ATCM 1	ATCM XXXVI Summary of Papers	ATS					
SP018	ATCM 1	List of Registered Delegates	ATS					

Background Papers								
Number	Ag. Items	Title	Submitted By	E	F	R	S	Attachments
BP001	CEP 9b	Antarctic Heritage Trust Conservation Update 2013	New Zealand					
BP002	CEP 8b	Assessing the vulnerability of Antarctic soils to trampling	New Zealand					
BP003	ATCM 10	The Third Antarctic Expedition of Araon (2012/2013)	Korea (ROK)					
BP004	ATCM 13	Scientific & Science-related Collaborations with Other Parties During 2012-2013	Korea (ROK)					
BP005	ATCM 13	CRIOSFERA 1 - A New Brazilian Initiative for the West Antarctic Ice Sheet	Brazil					
BP006	ATCM 13	The Importance of International Cooperation for Brazilian Scientific Research in Antarctica during summer 2012-2013	Brazil					
BP007	ATCM 13	Scientific Results of Brazilian Research in Admiralty Bay	Brazil					
BP008	ATCM 10	Enhancing Australia's Antarctic shipping and aviation systems	Australia					
BP009	ATCM 10 CEP 10a	Australia's new Antarctic cargo and biosecurity operations facility	Australia					
BP010	CEP 9f	Update on Developing Protection for a Geothermal Area: Volcanic Ice Caves at Mount Erebus, Ross Island	United States New Zealand					Mandatory Interim Code of Conduct for Mt Erebus Ice Caves
BP011	ATCM 10	Personal and social safety works at Vernadsky station during the season 2011/2012	Ukraine					
BP012	ATCM 13	Research at Vernadsky station in pursuance of the State Special-Purpose Research Program in Antarctica for 2011-2020	Ukraine					
BP013	ATCM 10	Operación Rescate del yate "Mar Sem Fim"	Brazil					

Background Papers								
Number	**Ag. Items**	**Title**	**Submitted By**	**E**	**F**	**R**	**S**	**Attachments**
BP014	ATCM 13	SCAR Lecture: "Probing for life at its limits: Technologies for the exploring Antarctic subglacial ecosystems"	SCAR					
BP017	CEP 9e	Antarctic Ocean Legacy Update 1: Securing Enduring Protection for the Ross Sea Region	ASOC					
BP018	ATCM 15	III Concurso Intercolegial sobre Temas Antárticos, CITA 2012	Ecuador					
BP019	ATCM 13	Programa de Cooperación Internacional en la Investigación Antártica Ecuatoriana (verano austral 2012-2013)	Ecuador					
BP020	ATCM 4 CEP 5	The Scientific Committee on Antarctic Research (SCAR) Selected Science Highlights for 2012/13	SCAR					
BP021	ATCM 4 CEP 5	Antarctic climate change and the environment: an update	SCAR					Antarctic climate change and the environment: an update
BP022	ATCM 15	Examples of educational and outreach activities of the Belgian scientists, school teachers and associations in 2009-2012	Belgium					
BP023	ATCM 13	Conmemoración del vigésimo quinto aniversario de la primera expedición científica del Perú a la Antártida y Realización de la XXI ANTAR (verano austral 2012-2013)	Peru					

3. List of Participants

3. List of Participants

PARTICIPANTS: CONSULTATIVE PARTIES				
PARTY	TITLE	CONTACT	POSITION	EMAIL
Argentina	Mr	Adad, Gabriel Carlos	Advisor	sism@ara.mil.ar
Argentina	Mr	Bunge, Carlos	Delegate	bng@mrecic.gov.ar
Argentina	Sr.	Conde Garrido, Rodrigo	Delegate	xgr@mrecic.gov.ar
Argentina	Mr	Figueroa, Victor Hugo	Advisor	vfexplorer@yahoo.com
Argentina	Min.	López Crozet, Fausto	Head of Delegation	digea@mrecic.gov.ar
Argentina	Dr	Marenssi, Sergio	Delegate	smarenssi@dna.gov.ar
Argentina	Dr	Memolli, Mariano A.	CEP Representative	drmemolli@gmail.com
Argentina	Mr	Monetto, Marcelo	Advisor	mjmonetto@hotmail.com
Argentina	Mrs	Ortúzar, Patricia	Delegate	portuzar@dna.gov.ar
Argentina	Min.	Pérez Gunella, Sergio	Delegate	sperezgunella@hotmail.com
Argentina	Mr	Rodríguez Lamas, Ezequiel	Delegate	rzq@mrecic.gov.ar
Argentina	Lic.	Vereda, Marisol	Advisor	marisol.vereda@speedy.com.ar
Argentina	Ms	Vlasich, Verónica	Delegate	vla@mrecic.gov.ar
Australia	Ms	Boyd, Denise	Advisor	deniseboyd2000@gmail.com
Australia	Dr	Fleming, Tony	Alternate	tony.fleming@aad.gov.au
Australia	Mr	Harper, Scott-Marshall	Delegate	scottmarshall.harper@dfat.gov.au
Australia	Dr	Jabour, Julia	Advisor	julia.jabour@utas.edu.au
Australia	HE Mr	Lewis, Duncan	Delegate	gaile.barnes@dfat.gov.au
Australia	Ms	Macmillian , Christine	Delegate	christine.macmillian@amsa.gov.au
Australia	Ms	McIntyre, Heather	Delegate	heather.mcintyre@dfat.gov.au
Australia	Mr	McIvor, Ewan	CEP Representative	ewan.mcivor@aad.gov.au
Australia	Dr	Miller, Denzil	Advisor	denzil.miller@development.tas.gov.au
Australia	Mr	Mundy, Jason	Delegate	Jason.Mundy@aad.gov.au
Australia	Dr	Riddle, Martin	Delegate	martin.riddle@aad.gov.au
Australia	Mr	Rowe, Richard	Head of Delegation	Richard.Rowe@dfat.gov.au
Australia	Dr	Tracey, Phillip	Delegate	phil.tracey@aad.gov.au
Belgium	Mr	André, François	CEP Representative	francois.andre@environnement.belgique.be
Belgium	Mr	Chemay, Frédéric	Delegate	frederic.chemay@environnement.belgique.be
Belgium	Mr	Hubert, Alain	Advisor	ah@polarfoundation.org
Belgium	Mr	Mayence, Jean-François	Delegate	maye@belspo.be
Belgium	Ms	Mirgaux, Sophie	Delegate	sophie.mirgaux@milieu.belgie.be
Belgium	Director general	Moreau, Roland	Head of Delegation	roland.moreau@environnement.belgique.be
Belgium	Ambassador	Otte, Marc	ATCM Chairman	marc.otte@diplobel.fed.be
Belgium	Director general	Régibeau, Jean-Arthur	Delegate	jean-arthur.regibeau@diplobel.fed.be
Belgium	Dr	Segers, Hendrik	Advisor	hsegers@naturalsciences.be
Belgium	Director	Touzani, Rachid	Delegate	touz@belspo.be
Belgium	Dr	Van de Putte, Anton	Advisor	antonarctica@gmail.com
Belgium	Ms	Vancauwenberghe, Maaike	Delegate	maaike.vancauwenberghe@belspo.be
Belgium	Mr	Verheyen, Koen	Delegate	koen.verheyen@diplobel.fed.be
Belgium	Ms	Wilmotte, Annick	Alternate	awilmotte@ulg.ac.be
Brazil	Mrs	Bassoi, Manuela	Delegate	manu.bassoi@gmail.com
Brazil	Ms	Boechat de Almeida, Barbara	Delegate	barbara.boechat@itamaraty.gov.br
Brazil	Mr	Catanzaro Guimarães, Hilton	Delegate	hilton.catanzaro@itamaraty.gov.br
Brazil	Commander	Corrêa Paes Filho, José	Delegate	josepaes@hotmail.com
Brazil	Dr	Gonçalves, Paulo Rogerio	Delegate	Paulo.goncalves@mna.gov.br
Brazil	Dr	Leal Madruga, Jaqueline	Delegate	jaqueline.madruga@mma.gov.br
Brazil	Commander	Leite, Márcio	Delegate	marcio.leite@secirm.mar.mil.br
Brazil	Ms	Schneider Costa, Erli	Delegate	erli_costa@hotmail.com
Brazil	Rear Admiral	Silva Rodrigues, Marcos	Delegate	silva.rodrigues@secirm.mar.mil.br

PARTICIPANTS: CONSULTATIVE PARTIES				
PARTY	**TITLE**	**CONTACT**	**POSITION**	**EMAIL**
Brazil	Comander	Teixeira, Antônio José	Delegate	ajvteixeira@hotmail.com
Brazil	Minister	Vaz Pitaluga, Fábio	Head of Delegation	dmae@itamaraty.gov.br
Bulgaria	Mr	Chipev, Nesho	CEP Representative	chipev@ecolab.bas.bg
Bulgaria	Mr	Ivanov, Tsvetko	Delegate	Tsvetko.Ivanov@bg-permrep.eu
Bulgaria	Mr	Mateev, Dragomir	Advisor	dragomir.mateev@gmail.com
Bulgaria	Prof.	Pimpirev, Christo	Alternate	polar@gea.uni-sofia.bg
Bulgaria	Mrs.	Popova, Anna	Delegate	anna.popova@mfa.bg
Bulgaria	Mr	Yordanov, Yordan	Advisor	agen_i@yahoo.com
Bulgaria	Ambassador	Zaimov, Branimir	Head of Delegation	bzaimov@mfa.government.bg
Chile	Mr	Cariceo Yutronic, Yanko Jesús	Delegate	ycariceo.12@mma.gob.cl
Chile	Ms	Carvallo, María Luisa	Delegate	mlcarvallo@minrel.gov.cl
Chile	Mr	Ferrada, Luis Valentín	Delegate	lferrada@ssdefensa.cl
Chile	Mr	Foxon, Javier	Delegate	jfoxon@minrel.gov.cl
Chile	Coronel	Guajardo, Claudio	Delegate	guajardo.antartica@gmail.com
Chile	Mr	Labra, Fernando	Delegate	cgamboa@minrel.gov.cl
Chile	Coronel	Madrid, Santiago	Delegate	smadrid@fach.cl
Chile	Ms	Navarrete, Gloria	Delegate	cgamboa@minrel.gov.cl
Chile	Dr	Retamales, José	Alternate	jretamales@inach.cl
Chile	Mr	Sainz, Manuel	Delegate	msainz@fach.cl
Chile	Coronel	San Martín, Guillermo	Delegate	gsanmartin@emco.mil.cl
Chile	Mr	Sanhueza, Camilo	Head of Delegation	csanhueza@minrel.gov.cl
Chile	Mr	Sepulveda, Victor	Delegate	vsepulveda@armada.cl
Chile	Ms	Vallejos, Verónica	CEP Representative	vvallejos@inach.cl
Chile	Mr	Velasquez, Ricardo	Delegate	rvelasquezo@dgtm.cl
China	Second Secretary	Kong , Xiangwen	Advisor	kong_xiangwen@mfa.gov.cn
China	Mr	Qu, Tanzhou	Advisor	chinare@263.net.cn
China	Mr	Qu, Wensheng	Head of Delegation	qu_wensheng@mfa.gov.cn
China	Mr	Wei, Long	Advisor	chinare@263.net.cn
China	Program Officer	Yang, Lei	Advisor	chinare@263.net.cn
China	Ms	Yu, Xinwei	Advisor	chinare@263.net.cn
China	Mr	Zhang, Tijun	Advisor	chinare@263.net.cn
China	Mr	Zhuo, Li	Advisor	zhuoli@msa.gov.cn
Ecuador	MSc	Cajiao, Daniela	Advisor	danicajiao@gmail.com
Ecuador	Mrs.	Jijon, Rosa	Advisor	rosajijon@gmail.com
Ecuador	Mr	Maldonado, Jorge	Delegate	jmaldonado@mmrree.gob.ec
Ecuador	Captain	Olmedo Morán, José	Head of Delegation	pinguino.olmedo@yahoo.com
Ecuador	Commander	Pazmiño, Pablo	Advisor	pipm467@hotmail.com
Ecuador	Mrs	Serrano, Mariana	Delegate	mserrano@mmrree.gov.ec
Finland	Mr	Kalakoski, Mika	Advisor	mika.kalakoski@fimr.fi
Finland		Leisti, Hanna	Advisor	hanna.leisti@fmi.fi
Finland	Ms	Mähönen, Outi	CEP Representative	outi.mahonen@ely-keskus.fi
Finland	Ms	Naskila, Annika	Alternate	annika.naskila@formin.fi
Finland	Ms	Valjento, Liisa	Head of Delegation	liisa.valjento@formin.fi
France	Mr	Babkine, Michel	Delegate	michel.babkine@pm.gouv.fr
France	Mrs	Belna, Stéphanie	CEP Representative	stephanie.belna@developpement-durable.gouv.fr
France	Dr	Choquet, Anne	Delegate	annechoquet@orange.fr
France		Dalmas, Dominique	CEP Representative	dominique.dalmas@interieur.gouv.fr
France	Dr	Frenot, Yves	CEP Representative	yves.frenot@ipev.fr
France	Dr	Guyomard, Ann-Isabelle	Delegate	ann-isabelle.guyomard@taaf.fr
France	Mr	Guyonvarch, Olivier	Head of Delegation	olivier.guyonvarch@diplomatie.gouv.fr
France	Mr	Lebouvier, Marc	CEP Representative	marc.lebouvier@univ-rennes1.fr

PARTICIPANTS: CONSULTATIVE PARTIES				
PARTY	**TITLE**	**CONTACT**	**POSITION**	**EMAIL**
France	Mr	Mayet, Laurent	Delegate	laurent.mayet@diplomatie.gouv.fr
France	Mr	Reuillard, Emmanuel	Delegate	emmanuel.reuillard@taaf.fr
France	Ambassador	Rocard, Michel	Delegate	laurent.mayet@diplomatie.gouv.fr
Germany	Ms	Boecker, Frauke	Advisor	frauke.boecker@diplo.de
Germany	Mr	Brink, Josef	Delegate	brink-jo@bmj.bund.de
Germany	Mr	Crocker, Brian	Advisor	bcrocker@borekair.com
Germany	Ms	Fabris, Rita	Advisor	rita.fabris@uba.de
Germany	Dr	Gaedicke, Christoph	Advisor	christoph.gaedicke@bgr.de
Germany		Guessow, Kerstin	Advisor	kersin.guesow@bmbf.buud.de
Germany	Dr	Hain, Stefan	Advisor	Stefan.Hain@awi.de
Germany	Dr	Herata, Heike	CEP Representative	heike.herata@uba.de
Germany	Mr	Hertel, Fritz	Advisor	fritz.hertel@uba.de
Germany	Ms	Heyn, Andrea	Delegate	Andrea.Heyn@bmbf.bund.de
Germany	Dr	Holfort, Jürgen	Delegate	juergen.holfort@bsh.de
Germany	Dr	Kohlberg, Eberhard	Advisor	eberhard.kohlberg@awi.de
Germany	Dr	Lassig, Rainer	Alternate	504-RL@diplo.de
Germany	Dr	Läufer, Andreas	Advisor	andreas.laeufer@bgr.de
Germany	Mr	Liebschner, Alexander	Delegate	alexander.liebschner@bfn-vilm.de
Germany	Mr	Lindemann, Christian	Delegate	christian.lindemann@bmu.bund.de
Germany	Mr	Lorenz, Sönke	Head of Delegation	504-0@diplo.de
Germany	Mr	Mengedoht, Dirk	Advisor	dirk.mengedoht@awi.de
Germany	Prof. Dr	Miller, Heinrich	Delegate	heinrich.miller@awi.de
Germany	Dr	Ney, Martin	Head of Delegation	Martin.Ney@diplo.de
Germany	Dr	Nixdorf, Uwe	Delegate	Uwe.Nixdorf@awi.de
Germany	Dr	Vöneky, Silja	Advisor	silja.voeneky@jura.uni-freiburg.de
India	Dr	Bhat, Kajal	Delegate	bhatkajal@yahoo.com
India	Dr	Mohan, Rahul	Delegate	rahulmohangupta@gmail.com
India	Dr	Rajan, Sivaramakrishnan	Head of Delegation	rajan.ncaor@gmail.com
India	Dr	Sharma, R K	Delegate	rks@nic.in
India	Dr	Tiwari, Anoop	Delegate	anooptiwari@ncaor.org
Italy	Amb.	Fornara, Arduino	Head of Delegation	arduino.fornara@esteri.it
Italy	Mr	Frezzotti, Massimo	Delegate	massimo.frezzotti@enea.it
Italy	Ing.	Mecozzi, Roberta	Delegate	roberta.mecozzi@enea.it
Italy	Dr	Tamburelli, Gianfranco	Delegate	gtamburelli@pelagus.it
Italy	Ms	Tomaselli, Maria Stefania	Delegate	tomaselli.stefania@minambiente.it
Italy	Dr	Torcini, Sandro	Delegate	sandro.torcini@enea.it
Japan	Mr	Hasegawa, Shuichi	Delegate	SHUICHI_HASEGAWA@env.go.jp
Japan	Prof	Motoyoshi, Yoichi	Delegate	motoyoshi@nirp.ac.jp
Japan	Dr	Suginaka, Atsushi	Head of Delegation	atsushi.suginaka@mofa.go.jp
Japan	Ms	Takeda, Sayako	Delegate	sayako_takeda@nm.maff.go.jp
Japan	Mr	Teramura, Satoshi	Delegate	satoshi_teramura@env.go.jp
Japan	Prof.	Watanabe, Kentaro	Delegate	kentaro@nipr.ac.jp
Japan	Prof	Yamonouchi, Takashi	Delegate	yamanou@nipr.ac.jp
Korea (ROK)	Dr	Ahn, In-Young	CEP Representative	iahn@kopri.re.kr
Korea (ROK)	Dr	Choi, Chang-yong	Advisor	subbuteo@hanmail.net
Korea (ROK)	Director	Chung, Kee-young	Head of Delegation	weltgeist@gmail.com
Korea (ROK)	Dr	Kim, Yeadong	Delegate	ydkim@kopri.re.kr
Korea (ROK)	Dr	Kim, Ji Hee	Advisor	jhalgae@kopri.re.kr
Korea (ROK)	Ms	Kim, Yunok	Advisor	kimyunok@gmail.com
Korea (ROK)	Prof.	Lee, Dr. Woo-shin	Advisor	krane@snu.ac.kr
Korea (ROK)	Mr	Lee, Seung-wook	Advisor	SWLEE2006@Korea.kr
Korea (ROK)	Mr	Seo, Young-min	Delegate	ymseo05@mofa.go.kr
Korea (ROK)	Dr	Seo, Hyun kyo	Delegate	shkshk@kopri.re.kr
Korea (ROK)	Dr	Shin, Hyoung Chul	Delegate	hcshin@kopri.re.kr
Korea (ROK)	Mr	Yang, Seoung-jo	Delegate	ysj102msw@korea.kr

PARTICIPANTS: CONSULTATIVE PARTIES				
PARTY	TITLE	CONTACT	POSITION	EMAIL
Netherlands	Prof. Dr	Bastmeijer, Kees	Advisor	c.j.bastmeijer@uvt.nl
Netherlands	Mr	Brandt, Patrick	Advisor	Patrick.Brandt@minbuza.nl
Netherlands	Ms	Elstgeest, Marlynda	Advisor	marlynda@waterproof-expeditions.com
Netherlands	Mr	Hernaus, Reginald	Advisor	Reggie.hernaus@minienm.nl
Netherlands	Ms	Kock, Hetty	Delegate	hetty.kock@minienm.nl
Netherlands	Prof. Dr	Lefeber, René J.M.	Head of Delegation	rene.lefeber@minbuza.nl
Netherlands	drs. ir.	Martijn, Peijs	Advisor	m.w.f.peijs@mineleni.nl
Netherlands	Ms	Nachtegaal, Anja	Delegate	anja.nachtegaal@kustwacht.nl
Netherlands	Ms	Noor, Liesbeth	Advisor	l.noor@nwo.nl
Netherlands	Mr	Pieter, VAN BAREN	Advisor	xxx@xxx.nl
Netherlands	Drs	van der Kroef, Dick A.	Advisor	d.vanderkroef@nwo.nl
New Zealand	Mrs.	Dempster, Jillian	Head of Delegation	Jillian.Dempster@mfat.govt.nz
New Zealand	Dr	Gilbert, Neil	Alternate	n.gilbert@antarcticanz.govt.nz
New Zealand	Miss	Kendall, Rachel	Delegate	rachel.kendall@mfat.govt.nz
New Zealand	Mr	MacKay, Don	Delegate	don_maria_mackay@msn.com
New Zealand	Ms	Newman, Jana	Delegate	j.newman@antarcticanz.govt.nz
New Zealand	Mr	Sanson, Lou	Delegate	l.sanson@antarcticanz.govt.nz
New Zealand	Ms	Stent, Danica	Delegate	dstent@doc.govt.nz
New Zealand	Mr	Williams, Andrew	Delegate	andrew.williams@mfat.govt.nz
New Zealand	Mr	Wilson, Dave	Delegate	david.wilson@martimenz.govt.nz
Norway	Ms	Askjer, Angela Lahelle-Ekholdt	Delegate	angela.askjer@jd.dep.no
Norway	Mrs	Eikeland, Else Berit	Head of Delegation	ebe@mfa.no
Norway	Ms	Gaalaas, Siv Christin	Delegate	scg@nhd.dep.no
Norway	Mr	Guldahl, John E.	Advisor	john.guldahl@npolar.no
Norway	Mr	Halvorsen, Svein Tore	Delegate	sth@md.dep.no
Norway	Ms	Ingebrigtsen, Hanne Margrethe	Delegate	hanne.margrethe.ingebrigtsen@jd.dep.no
Norway	Ms	Johansen, Therese	Delegate	therese.johansen@mfa.no
Norway	Mrs.	Korsvoll, Marie Helene	Delegate	mhk@md.dep.no
Norway	Ms	Njaastad, Birgit	CEP Representative	njaastad@npolar.no
Norway	Mr	Solberg, Stein	Advisor	stein.solberg@jrcc-stavanger.no
Norway	Ms	Strengehagen, Mette	Delegate	mette.strengehagen@mfa.no
Norway	Mr	Svanes, Tønnes	Advisor	tonnes.svanes@mfa.no
Norway	Mr	Winther, Jan-Gunnar	Delegate	winther@npolar.no
Peru	Ms	Bello, Cinthya	Delegate	cinthyabch@gmail.com
Peru	Mr	Del Aguila, Oswaldo	Advisor	odelaguila@embaperu.be
Peru	Amb.	Isasi-Cayo, Fortunato	Advisor	fisasi@rree.gob.pe
Peru	Ambassador	Velasquez, María Elvira	Head of Delegation	evelasquez@rree.gob.pe
Poland	Mr	Dybiec, Leszek	Delegate	Leszek.Dybiec@minrol.gov.pl
Poland	Dr	Kidawa, Anna	Delegate	akidawa@arctowski.pl
Poland	Mr	Kułaga, Łukasz	Delegate	lukasz.kulaga@msz.gov.pl
Poland	Mr	Marciniak, Konrad	Delegate	konrad.marciniak@msz.gov.pl
Poland	Ambassador	Misztal, Andrzej	Head of Delegation	Andrzej.Misztal@msz.gov.pl
Poland	Professor	Symonides, Janusz	Delegate	januszsymonides@poczta.onet.pl
Poland	Dr	Tatur, Andrzej	Delegate	tatura@interia.pl
Poland	Ms	Wieczorek, Renata	Delegate	Renata.Wieczorek@minrol.gov.pl
Russian Federation	Ms	Antonova, Anna	Delegate	avant71@yandex.ru
Russian Federation	Mrs.	Bystramovich, Anna	Delegate	antarc@mcc.mecom.ru
Russian Federation	Mr	Gonchar, Dmitry	Head of Delegation	dp@mid.ru
Russian Federation	Mr	Kremenyuk, Dmitry	Delegate	d.kremenyuk@fishcom.ru
Russian Federation	Mr	Lukin, Valery	Alternate	lukin@aari.ru
Russian	Mr	Masolov, Valerii	Delegate	pom@aari.ru

PARTICIPANTS: CONSULTATIVE PARTIES				
PARTY	TITLE	CONTACT	POSITION	EMAIL
Federation				
Russian Federation	Ms	Molyakova, Marina	Delegate	dp@mid.ru
Russian Federation	Mr	Pomelov, Victor	Delegate	pom@aari.ru
Russian Federation	Mr	Tsaturov, Yuri	Delegate	tsaturov@mecom.ru
Russian Federation	Mr	Voevodin, Andrey	Delegate	pom@aari.ru
South Africa	Mr	Blows, Jared	Delegate	jblows@samsa.org.za
South Africa	ADv	Dwarika, Yolande	Delegate	DwarikaY@dirco.gov.za
South Africa	Mr	Gordon, Mark	CEP Representative	mgordon@environment.gov.za
South Africa	Ms	Jacobs, Carol	CEP Representative	cjacobs@environment.gov.za
South Africa	Mr	Janse Van Noordwyk, Christo	Delegate	JanseVanNoordwykC@dirco.gov.za
South Africa	Ms	Malefane, Nthabiseng	Alternate	malefanen@dirco.gov.za
South Africa	Mr	Modiba, Patrick	Delegate	modibap@dot.gov.za
South Africa	Dr	Mphepya, Jonas	Delegate	jmphepya@environment.gov.za
South Africa	Ambassador	Nkosi, Mxolisi	Head of Delegation	nkosin@dirco.gov.za
South Africa	Dr	Siko, Gilbert	Delegate	Gilbert.Siko@dst.gov.za
South Africa	Mr	Skinner, Richard	Delegate	Rskinner@environment.gov.za
South Africa	Mr	Smit, Johnny	Delegate	johnnys@atns.co.za
South Africa	Mr	Valentine, Henry	Delegate	hvalentine@environment.gov.za
Spain	Mr	Catalan, Manuel	CEP Representative	cpe@mineco.es
Spain	Mr	Muñoz de Laborde Bardin, Juan Luis	Head of Delegation	juanluis.munoz@maec.es
Spain	Mr	Ojeda, Miguel Angel	Delegate	maojeda@cmima.csic.es
Spain	Ms	Puig Marco, Roser	Advisor	pruigmar@gmail.com
Spain	Mrs	Ramos, Sonia	Delegate	sonia.ramos@mineco.es
Sweden	Ambassador	Ödmark, Helena	Head of Delegation	helena.odmark@foreign.ministry.se
Sweden	Mrs.	Selberg, Cecilia	CEP Representative	cecilia.selberg@polar.se
Sweden	Mr	Tornberg, Henrik	Delegate	henrik.tornberg@polar.se
Sweden	Mr	Widell, Lars	Delegate	lars.widell@sjofartsverket.se
Ukraine	Mr	Fedchuk, Andrii	Delegate	andriyf@gmail.com
Ukraine	Dr	Lytvynov, Valerii	Head of Delegation	uac@uac.gov.ua
Ukraine	Mr	Tereshchenko, Artur	Advisor	uac@uac.gov.ua
Ukraine	Ms	Tereshchenko, Zoia	Advisor	uac@uac.gov.ua
United Kingdom	Mr	Burgess, Henry	CEP Representative	henry.burgess@fco.gov.uk
United Kingdom	Ms	Clarke, Rachel	Delegate	racl@bas.ac.uk
United Kingdom	Mr	Dinn, Michael	Delegate	medi@bas.ac.uk
United Kingdom	Mr	Downie, Rod	Delegate	rhd@bas.ac.uk
United Kingdom	Ms	Fawkner-Corbett, Isabelle	Delegate	Isabelle.Fawkner-Corbett@fco.gov.uk
United Kingdom	Ms	Fothergill, Clare	Delegate	Clathe@bas.ac.uk
United Kingdom	Mr	Hall, John	Delegate	jhal@bas.ac.uk
United Kingdom	Dr	Hughes, Kevin	Delegate	kehu@bas.ac.uk
United Kingdom	Mr	Khan, Akbar	Delegate	akbar.khan@fco.gov.uk
United Kingdom	Mr	McKie, Roland	Delegate	Roly.McKie@mcga.gov.uk
United Kingdom	Ms	Rumble, Jane	Head of Delegation	Jane.Rumble@fco.gov.uk
United Kingdom	Dr	Shears, John	Delegate	jrs@bas.ac.uk

PARTICIPANTS: CONSULTATIVE PARTIES				
PARTY	TITLE	CONTACT	POSITION	EMAIL
United Kingdom	Miss	Taylor, Victoria	Delegate	victoria.taylor@fco.gov.uk
United States	AMB	Balton, David	Delegate	baltonda@state.gov
United States	Mr	Bloom, Evan T.	Head of Delegation	bloomet@state.gov
United States	RDML	Brown, Peter	Advisor	peter.j.brown@uscg.mil
United States	Ms	Cooper, Susannah	Alternate	cooperse@state.gov
United States	Ms	Dahood-Fritz, Adrian	Delegate	adahood@nsf.gov
United States	Mr	Edwards, David	Delegate	david.l.edwards@uscg.mil
United States	Ms	Engelke-Ros, Meggan	Delegate	meggan.engelke-ros@noaa.gov
United States	Dr	Falkner, Kelly	Delegate	kfalkner@nsf.gov
United States	Ms	Hessert, Aimee	Delegate	hessert.aimee@epamail.epa.gov
United States	Mr	Israel, Brian	Delegate	israelbr@state.gov
United States	Dr	Karentz, Deneb	Advisor	karentzd@usfca.edu
United States	Ms	Landry, Mary	Delegate	mary.e.landry@uscg.mil
United States	CAPT	Martin, Peter	Delegate	peter.f.martin@uscg.mil
United States	Mr	Naveen, Ron	Advisor	oceanites.mail@verizon.net
United States	Dr	O'Reilly, Jessica	Advisor	jessyo@gmail.com
United States	Dr	Penhale, Polly A.	CEP Representative	ppenhale@nsf.gov
United States	Mr	Rudolph, Lawrence	Delegate	lrudolph@nsf.gov
United States	Mr	Stone, Brian	Delegate	bstone@nsf.gov
United States	Ms	Trice, Jessica	Delegate	trice.jessica@epamail.epa.gov
United States	Mr	Watters, George	Delegate	George.Watters@noaa.gov
United States	Ms	Wheatley, Victoria	Advisor	vewheatley@gmail.com
Uruguay	Lic.	Abdala, Juan	CEP Representative	jabdala@iau.gub.uy
Uruguay	Min. Dr	González Otero, Alvaro	Head of Delegation	alvaro.gonzalez@mrree.gub.uy
Uruguay	Mr	Lluberas, Albert	Alternate	alexllub@iau.gub.uy
Uruguay	Dr	Vignali, Daniel	Advisor	dvignal@adinet.com.uy

PARTICIPANTS: NON-CONSULTATIVE PARTIES				
Party	Title	Contact	Position	Email
Austria	Minister plenipot.	Hack, Norbert	Alternate	BRUESSEL-OB@bmeia.gv.at
Austria	Dr.	Sattler, Birgit	Alternate	birgit.sattler@uibk.ac.at
Austria	Ambassa dor	Schramek, Karl	Head of Delegation	BRUESSEL-OB@bmeia.gv.at
Belarus	Mr	Filimonau, Uladzimir	Delegate	vladivaf2010@mail.ru
Belarus	Mr	Gaidashov, Alexey	Delegate	alexis_33@inbox.ru
Belarus	Prof. Dr.	Loginov, Vladimir F.	Delegate	nature@ecology.basnet.by
Belarus	Mr	Rahozin, Ihar	Head of Delegation	depzam@pogoda.by
Canada		Sadar, Kamuran	Head of Delegation	kamuran.sadar@ec.gc.ca
Colombia	Mrs	Barrios, Lina María	Delegate	linambarrios@dimar.mil.co
Colombia	Brigadier General	Forero Montealegre, José Francisco	Delegate	gordoforero@hotmail.com
Colombia	Mr	Higuera, Javier	Delegate	javier.higuera@cancilleria.gov.co
Colombia	Ms	Mikan, Sandra Lucía	Delegate	sandra.mikan@cancilleria.gov.co
Colombia	Mr	Molano, Mauricio	Delegate	mmolano@minambiente.gov.co
Colombia	Capitán de Navío	Molares Babra, Ricardo	Delegate	ricardomolares@yahoo.com
Colombia	Ms	Pelaez, Carolina	Delegate	carolina.pelaez@cancilleria.gov.co
Colombia	Mr	PONGUTA, Nestor	Advisor	nestor.ponguta@cancilleria.gov.co
Colombia	Capitán de Navio	Reyna, Julian Augusto	Delegate	oceano@cco.gov.co
Colombia	Ambassa dor	Rivera Salazar, Rodrigo	Head of Delegation	rodrigo.rivera@cancilleria.gov.co
Colombia	Mrs	Alba Marina, Lancheros	Staff	albamla@hotmail.com
Cuba	Ms	Viera Gallardo, Yudith	Delegate	oficome4@embacuba.be
Czech Republic	Mr	Bartak, Milos	Advisor	mbartak@sci.muni.cz

PARTICIPANTS: NON-CONSULTATIVE PARTIES				
Party	**Title**	**Contact**	**Position**	**Email**
Czech Republic	Mr	Galuška, Vladimír	Head of Delegation	nmgv@mzv.cz
Czech Republic	Dr.	Kapler, Pavel	Advisor	kapler@sci.muni.cz
Czech Republic	Mr	Prošek, Pavel	Advisor	prosek@sci.muni.cz
Czech Republic	Dr.	Smuclerova, Martina	Alternate	Martina_Smuclerova@mzv.cz
Czech Republic	Mr	Venera, Zdenek	CEP Representative	zdenek.venera@geology.cz
Greece	Dr.	Gounaris, Emmanuel	Head of Delegation	d01@mfa.gr
Hungary	Ministre	Andras, BALOGH	Advisor	albalogh@MPA.GOV.HU
Hungary	Mr	Gergely, Balazs	Advisor	balazs.gergely@mfa.gov.hu
Malaysia	Prof.	Abu Samah, Azizan	Alternate	azizans@um.edu.my
Malaysia	Dr	Hamzah, B.Ahmad	Advisor	bahamzah@pd.jaring.my
Malaysia	Mr	Ho, Koon Seng	Delegate	ksho@mosti.gov.my
Malaysia	Ms	Jayaseelan, Sumitra	Delegate	sumitra@mosti.gov.my
Malaysia	Dr	Mohd Nor, Salleh	Advisor	salleh.mohdnor@gmail.com
Malaysia	Prof.	Mohd Shah, Rohani	Advisor	rohanimohdshah@yahoo.com
Malaysia	Dato' Dr	Yahaya, Mohd Azhar	Head of Delegation	drazhary@mosti.gov.my
Monaco	S.E.M.	Fautrier, Bernard	Advisor	bfautrier@gouv.mc
Monaco	S.E.M.	TONELLI, Gilles	Advisor	gtonelli@gouv.mc
Monaco	Del.	Van Klaveren, Céline	Alternate	cevanklaveren@gouv.mc
Monaco	Mr	Van Klaveren, Patrick	Head of Delegation	pvanklaveren@gouv.mc
Portugal	Dr	Xavier, José	Advisor	jxavier@zoo.uc.pt
Romania	Ms	Badescu, Adina	Delegate	adina.badescu@roumanieamb.be
Romania	Dr.	Cotta, Mihaela	Delegate	mihaelacotta@yahoo.com
Romania	Mr	Puie, David	Advisor	david.puie@coleeurope.eu
Romania	Ambassador	Tinca, Stefan	Head of Delegation	olivia.toderean@roumanieamb.be
Romania	Ms	Toderean, Olivia	Alternate	olivia.toderean@roumanieamb.be
Romania	Dr.	Toparceanu, Florica	Delegate	florisci@hotmail.com
Slovak Republic	Dr	Hana, Kovacova	Delegate	hana.kovacova@mzv.sk
Switzerland	Counsellor	Beltrametti, Siro	Alternate	siro.beltrametti@eda.admin.ch
Switzerland	Attaché	Charlet, François	Delegate	francois.charlet@eda.admin.ch
Switzerland	Ambassador	de Cerjat, Bénédict	Delegate	benedict.decerjat@eda.admin.ch
Switzerland	Dr.	Dürler, Reto	Head of Delegation	reto.duerler@eda.admin.ch
Switzerland	Prof. em.	Schlüchter, Christian	Advisor	schluechter@eo.unibe.ch
Turkey	Mr	Tabak, Haluk	Delegate	takbam@takbam.org
Turkey	Mr	Türkel, Mehmet Ali	Head of Delegation	takbam@takbam.org
Turkey	Mr	Türkel, Ebuzer	Delegate	takbam@takbam.org
Venezuela	Dr	Barreto, Guillermo	Head of Delegation	despacho.barreto@gmail.com
Venezuela	Capitan de Corbetas	Carlos, Castellanos	Delegate	luispibernat@gmail.com
Venezuela	Mr	Francesco, FERNANDEZ	Advisor	frangollen@gmail.com
Venezuela	Lic.	Gilberto, Jaimes	Delegate	gilbertojaimes@gmail.com
Venezuela	Capitan de Fragata	Javier, Méndez Guerrero	Delegate	luispibernat@gmail.com
Venezuela	Capitan de Navío	Luis, Pibernart	Delegate	luispibernat@gmail.com
Venezuela	Dr	Sira, Eloy	Delegate	esira@ivic.gob.ve

PARTICIPANTS: OBSERVERS				
Party	**Title**	**Contact**	**Position**	**Email**

CCAMLR	Dr	Jones, Christopher	CEP Representative	chris.d.jones@noaa.gov
CCAMLR	Dr	Reid, Keith	Advisor	keith.reid@ccamlr.org
CCAMLR	Mr	Wright, Andrew	Head of Delegation	andrew.wright@ccamlr.org
COMNAP	Ms.	Rogan-Finnemore, Michelle	Head of Delegation	michelle.finnemore@comnap.aq
SCAR	Dr.	Badhe, Renuka	Delegate	rb302@cam.ac.uk
SCAR	Prof.	Chown, Steven L.	CEP Representative	steven.chown@monash.edu
SCAR	Prof	Kennicutt, Mahlon (Chuck)	Delegate	m-kennicutt@tamu.edu
SCAR	Prof	López-Martínez, Jerónimo	Delegate	jeronimo.lopez@uam.es
SCAR	Dr.	Sparrow, Mike	Head of Delegation	mds68@cam.ac.uk
SCAR	Prof.	Wadham, Jemma	Delegate	j.l.wadham@bristol.ac.uk

PARTICIPANTS: EXPERTS				
Party	**Title**	**Contact**	**Position**	**Email**
ASOC	Mr.	Barnes, James	Head of Delegation	james.barnes@asoc.org
ASOC	Ms	Barrett, Jill	Advisor	j.barrett@biicl.org
ASOC	mr	Bauman, Mark	Advisor	mbauman@ngs.org
ASOC	Ms.	Benn, Joanna	Advisor	jbenn@pewtrusts.org
ASOC	Mr.	Bodin, Svante	Advisor	svante@iccinet.org
ASOC	Mr	Campbell, Steve	Advisor	steve@antarcticocean.org
ASOC	Mr.	Chen, Jiliang	Advisor	julian@antarcticocean.org
ASOC	Ms.	Christian, Claire	Advisor	Claire.Christian@asoc.org
ASOC	Mr	Hajost, Scott	Advisor	scotthajost@yahoo.com
ASOC	Ms.	Kavanagh, Andrea	Advisor	akavanagh@pewtrusts.org
ASOC	Mr	Keey, Geoff	Advisor	geoff.keey@gmail.com
ASOC	Mr.	Leape, Gerry	Advisor	gleape@pewtrusts.org
ASOC	Ms.	Mattfield, Donna	Advisor	donna@antarcticocean.org
ASOC	Mr.	Nicoll, Rob	Advisor	robertanicoll@yahoo.com
ASOC	Mr	Page, Richard	Delegate	richard.page@greenpeace.org
ASOC	Ms.	Pearson, Pam	Advisor	pampearson44@gmail.com
ASOC	Dr	Roura, Ricardo	CEP Representative	ricardo.roura@worldonline.nl
ASOC	Mr.	Tak, Paulus	Advisor	ptak@pewtrusts.org
ASOC	Dr.	Tin, Tina	Advisor	tinatintk@gmail.com
ASOC	Mr.	Tsidulko, Grigory	Advisor	grigory@antarcticocean.org
ASOC	Mr	Werner Kinkelin, Rodolfo	Advisor	rodolfo.antarctica@gmail.com
IAATO	Dr.	Crosbie, Kim	Head of Delegation	kimcrosbie@iaato.org
IAATO	Mr	de Keyser, Marc	Advisor	marc.achiel@gmail.com
IAATO	Ms	Haase, Janeen	Delegate	jhaase@iaato.org
IAATO	Ms.	Hohn-Bowen, Ute	Delegate	ute@antarpply.com
IAATO	Ms	Holgate, Claudia	CEP Representative	cholgate@iaato.org
IAATO	Mr	Inman, Michael	Advisor	MInman@HollandAmerica.com
IAATO	Mr.	Rootes, David	Alternate	david.rootes@antarctic-logistics.com
IAATO	Ms.	Schillat, Monika	Delegate	Monika@antarpply.com
IAATO	Ms	Vareille, Isabelle	Delegate	ivareille@ponant.com
IHO	Mr	Ward, Robert	Head of Delegation	robert.ward@iho.int
IUCN	Ms	McConnell, Martha	Head of Delegation	martha.mcconnell@iucn.org
WMO	Mr	Ondras, Miroslav	Head of Delegation	mondras@wmo.int
WMO	Mr	Pendlebury, Steve	Alternate	stevefp@bigpond.com

PARTICIPANTS: SECRETARIATS				
Party	**Title**	**Contact**	**Position**	**Email**
HCS	Mr	Marsia, Luc	HC Secretary	luc.marsia@diplobel.fed.be
ATS	Mr	Acero, José Maria	Alternate	tito.acero@antarctictreaty.org
ATS	Mr	Agraz, José Luis	Staff	pepe.agraz@antarctictreaty.org
ATS	Ms	Balok, Anna	Staff	anna.balok@antarctictreaty.org
ATS	Mr	Davies, Paul	Staff	littlewest2@googlemail.com
ATS	Ms	Guretskaya, Anastasia	Staff	a.guretskaya@googlemail.com

PARTICIPANTS: SECRETARIATS				
Party	**Title**	**Contact**	**Position**	**Email**
ATS	Dr	Reinke, Manfred	Head of Delegation	manfred.reinke@antarctictreaty.org
ATS	Mr	Wainschenker, Pablo	Staff	pablo.wainschenker@antarctictreaty.org
ATS	Prof.	Walton, David W H	Staff	dwhw@bas.ac.uk
ATS	Mr	Wydler, Diego	Staff	diego.wydler@antarctictreaty.org
Trans. & Interp.	Mr	Barchenkov, Alexander	Staff	project@itamalta.com
Trans. & Interp.	Ms	Beauvez, Ingrid	Staff	project@itamalta.com
Trans. & Interp.	Ms	Bocharova, Elena	Staff	project@itamalta.com
Trans. & Interp.	Ms	Castell, Monica	Staff	project@itamalta.com
Trans. & Interp.	Ms	Daletchina, Dina	Staff	project@itamalta.com
Trans. & Interp.	Mr	Dodon, Oleg	Staff	project@itamalta.com
Trans. & Interp.	Ms	Dusaussoy, Chloe	Staff	project@itamalta.com
Trans. & Interp.	Mr	Fermin, Marc	Staff	project@itamalta.com
Trans. & Interp.	Ms	Hamdini, Nadia	Staff	project@itamalta.com
Trans. & Interp.	Ms	Henkinet, Laurence	Staff	project@itamalta.com
Trans. & Interp.	Ms	Hourmatallah, Hind	Staff	accounts@itamalta.com
Trans. & Interp.	Ms	Ignatova, Evgenia	Staff	project@itamalta.com
Trans. & Interp.	Ms	Janybek Kyzy, Elmira	Staff	intergov@itamalta.com
Trans. & Interp.	Mr	Klevansky, Anton	Staff	project@itamalta.com
Trans. & Interp.	Ms	Koreneva, Julia	Staff	project@itamalta.com
Trans. & Interp.	Ms	Lantsuta-Davis, Ludmila	Staff	project@itamalta.com
Trans. & Interp.	Ms	Leyden, Gabrielle	Staff	project@itamalta.com
Trans. & Interp.	Ms	Niang, Anna	Staff	project@itamalta.com
Trans. & Interp.	Ms	Ooms, Anita	Staff	project@itamalta.com
Trans. & Interp.	Mr	Titouah, Rachid	Staff	corporate@itamalta.com
Trans. & Interp.	Ms	Tomkins, Marion	Staff	project@itamalta.com
Trans. & Interp.	Mr	Van Delft, Jozef	Staff	project@itamalta.com
Trans. & Interp.	Mr	Zingale, Ricardo	Staff	project@itamalta.com

www.ingramcontent.com/pod-product-compliance
Lightning Source LLC
Chambersburg PA
CBHW051341200326
41521CB00015B/2582

* 9 7 8 9 8 7 1 5 1 5 5 8 5 *